# How
# to Live
# on
# Your
# Income

READER'S DIGEST

# HOW TO LIVE ON YOUR INCOME

The Reader's Digest Association, Inc.
Pleasantville, New York

The acknowledgments which appear on pages 630-632
are hereby made a part of this copyright page.

Library of Congress Catalog Card No. 72–97902

Printed in the United States of America

# CONTENTS

**PART I: MONEY IS A FAMILY AFFAIR**
1. You're Richer Than You Think .................... 8
2. Where Do the Dollars Go? .................... 12
3. How to Appraise Your Family's Security .................... 21
4. The Fine Art of Family Budgeting .................... 47
5. When Mother Brings Home the Bacon .................... 63
6. Keeping Those Vital Family Records .................... 69
7. Six Basic Rules for Staying Solvent .................... 83

**PART II: A ROOF OVER YOUR HEAD**
8. Choosing the House That's Right for You .................... 88
9. You Can Buy *and* Build .................... 102
10. How Much House Can You Afford? .................... 109
11. When You Buy a House .................... 117
12. Taking the Mystery Out of Mortgages .................... 137
13. Moving Without Tears .................... 148
14. How to Get More When You Sell Your Home .................... 156

**PART III: KEEPING UP WITH UPKEEP**
15. Your Home: A Haven or a Headache? .................... 168
16. What You Should Know About Contractors .................... 179
17. You Really Can Save on Utilities .................... 191
18. Home Improvement: A Good Investment or a Poor One? .... 202
19. Seven Tips on Insuring Your Home .................... 206

**PART IV: INSIDE THE HOME—YOUR SECOND BIGGEST INVESTMENT**
20. Furnishings That Are Right for Your Family .................... 214
21. How to Buy Appliances .................... 229
22. You *Can* Get Your Money Back .................... 235
23. New Isn't Always Best .................... 242

**PART V: 1095 MEALS EVERY YEAR**
24. How Much Do *You* Spend for Groceries? .................... 246
25. Planning Your Food Dollar .................... 252
26. When a Woman Goes to Market .................... 263
27. Keeping Foods Fresh .................... 280
28. How to Avoid Being Cheated by the Pound .................... 288
29. Big Supermarket Is Watching You .................... 292

**PART VI: CLOTHING FOR THE FAMILY**
30. Ten Cents Out of Every Dollar .................... 298
31. What You Should Know About Sizes .................... 304
32. Smart-Money Clothes Shopping .................... 312
33. Fabrics—Facts and Fallacies .................... 326
34. Saving on Wear and Tear .................... 330

## PART VII: THE FAMILY CAR

35. How to Save Money Buying a Car ............................ 340
36. The Real Cost of Running Your Car ........................ 348
37. Facts You Should Know About Auto Insurance ............. 352
38. Good Driving Habits That Put Dollars in Your Pocket ...... 358
39. Taking the Sting Out of Garage Bills ...................... 366

## PART VIII: COLLEGE WITHOUT BANKRUPTCY

40. The High Cost of Higher Education ....................... 372
41. How to Go to College on Almost Nothing a Year ......... 379
42. Study Now, Pay Later ................................... 386
43. You Can Still Work Your Way Through College ........... 391

## PART IX: HOW TO HAVE MORE FUN FOR YOUR MONEY

44. Timing Your Vacation to Cut Costs ...................... 400
45. Go Farther on Your Travel Dollar ....................... 414
46. The Nation's Best Vacation Buy ......................... 433

## PART X: WHEN SICKNESS OR ACCIDENT STRIKES

47. What You Should Know About Life Insurance ............. 442
48. You Can Afford the Best Care ........................... 459
49. Ten Ways to Cut Your Medical Bills ..................... 468

## PART XI: WHAT YOU SHOULD KNOW ABOUT CREDIT

50. Money When You Need It ................................ 476
51. How's Your Credit? ..................................... 487
52. Watch Those Interest Rates! ............................ 493
53. When You Borrow on Your Assets ....................... 505
54. The Credit Card Revolution ............................. 509

## PART XII: MAKING YOUR MONEY WORK FOR YOU

55. Watching Your Savings Grow ............................ 516
56. The ABCs of Stocks and Bonds ......................... 525
57. Mutual Funds and Your Family .......................... 542
58. What You Can Do About Inflation ....................... 549

## PART XIII: PLANNING TO ENJOY YOUR RETIREMENT YEARS

59. What You Can Expect from Social Security ............... 560
60. Pension Plans and Programs ............................ 568
61. All About Annuities .................................... 574
62. Pros and Cons of Joint Ownership ...................... 579
63. Can Your Wife Afford to Be a Widow? .................. 584

## HOW TO SAVE MONEY UNDER THE NEW TAX LAW

The New Tax Law — And What It Means to You ............. 590
How to Save Money Under the New Tax Law ............... 594

## INDEX ......................................................... 633

# 1
## MONEY IS A FAMILY AFFAIR

*Get the whole family involved in planning what to spend and how to spend it. The savings may surprise you*

CHAPTER 1

## You're Richer Than You Think

*Your family can have more buying power and greater financial security on what you make now—if you plan and spend wisely*

Money is important to everyone. How much money we have and how we use it affect our feelings of success or failure, our relationships with others both within the family and outside it, and—to some extent—the things we will be able to achieve in our lifetimes.

But money is complicated, and almost everyone has financial problems. Even great wealth does not necessarily bring its possessor a sense of happiness and satisfaction unless he knows what he wants to do with it and how to handle it. Money is really a tool, and to derive the most useful and satisfying results from whatever income you have you must know what results you can expect from it and how to handle it to your best advantage. This requires hard thinking, because today the pitfalls and opportunities you encounter in managing your family's money are more numerous and more diversified than ever before.

Since the beginning of the century the income and the standard of living of most Americans have risen steadily, until in the 1950s economist John Kenneth Galbraith felt justified in calling us the affluent society. Today this is more true than ever. Comparatively few Ameri-

8

cans find it necessary to spend all of their salaries on supplying the basic day-to-day necessities of life; most of us find that there is money left over after the rent and grocery bills have been paid to spend as we choose. It is how we use this money—economists call it discretionary income—that determines our families' long-term financial security.

Just as we, as a people, are bringing in more money, so our opportunities for using it wisely (or unwisely) have greatly increased. Most of us invest in the Social Security program, and many of us put money in private pension plans or annuities. In most families the breadwinner is covered by life insurance. Various forms of health insurance for both major and minor medical expenses are available, and the cost is frequently shared by an employer. Investment programs for the small investor are mushrooming, and more of us own some variety of stocks or bonds than ever before. More companies every year invite employes to join profit-sharing plans. Savings accounts are at an all-time high. Credit is more readily available than ever and can be a boon if you use it wisely. A greater variety of low-cost, quality, time-saving products are found in our stores than grandmother could have dreamed of. In addition to this, most of us have an increasing amount of leisure time in which to enjoy the fruits of this active and diversified economy. Truly, you are—or can be—richer than you think.

Taking advantage of these opportunities, however, requires careful planning, cooperation, self-discipline and a realistic attitude toward your family's income. Few of us are expecting a windfall, and although salaries do rise, a sudden spurt in your earning power can't be counted on. The best way a family can increase its income and capital is by wise spending and planning. And as the growing demand for financial counseling shows, it's sometimes easier to earn money than it is to spend it prudently. So the first step toward achieving your new riches is to become an intelligent consumer.

The intelligent consumer is a smart shopper. Remember:

Every dollar you spend wisely buys you greater value and leaves you more money for long-term financial growth.

Every dollar you spend on impulse for merchandise you don't want or need, or on shoddy merchandise that will wear out quickly, cuts down on your spending power now and in the future.

9

These rules apply to the minor purchases you make on a day-to-day basis just as much as to larger expenditures. Smart shopping helps the family stretch its dollar income.

HOW TO LIVE ON YOUR INCOME will help you to become an intelligent consumer. You will learn the advantages of dealing with reliable merchants and manufacturers, the art of comparison shopping, the dangers of misleading advertising, when to watch out for unexpected "extra" costs, how to judge quality, when you can afford to make do with less than the best—and how to get the most vacation for the least money. By learning and practicing these methods you will increase the amount of extra money—or discretionary income—that your family can devote to the building of a richer, more relaxed life with financial security for the future.

The second step toward making the most of your money is to become a sensible planner. Remember:

To save money successfully and build financial security you need agreed-upon goals and consistent management.

To manage money effectively you need to know where it goes now, so you can see which expenses can be cut, which cannot and where you should be spending more.

*Failure* to allocate money for such items as insurance, savings, routine medical and dental checkups, home maintenance and repairs and the like can be far more disastrous than indiscriminate impulse buying.

In HOW TO LIVE ON YOUR INCOME you will find many chapters devoted to sensible and efficient financial planning for your family, plus advice on analyzing your expenses and setting up basic budgets.

Include the whole family in your financial planning. The decisions you make and the goals you set affect all of you. If everyone participates there will be fewer misunderstandings and more joint effort in reaching your goals smoothly. Discussing and sharing the solutions to your family's money management problems with your wife and children can lead to a harmony and cooperation within your home far different from the divisive squabbling and bitterness that so often arise within a family as a result of poor financial planning or from a warped view of the role and function of money.

So learn—as a family—to avoid financial pitfalls and seize opportunities, and you will indeed find that you are richer than you think.

10

## WORDS YOU SHOULD KNOW

Books about finance often use special words whose meanings are not clear to the layman. Even a seemingly simple word like *wealth* can be hard to define. Understanding expressions like this is important to your understanding of good money management. Here, for example, are explanations of some key terms that appear in this and other chapters.

**Money.** Coin or paper bills issued by a government or a bank as a means of payment and as a measure of value. *Cash* is money in hand. *Currency* is money in circulation. *Legal tender* is money a creditor must accept as lawful payment for goods or services.

**Wealth.** The total of your possessions which have a money value—hence, your purchasing, spending and borrowing power. Also called your *capital*.

**Gross annual income.** Your total yearly receipts from your work, business and property before any deductions have been made for taxes or expenses.

**Net income.** The money available to you to spend after your taxes, Social Security payments and other mandatory deductions, such as health insurance and union dues, have been subtracted from your gross income. This is known as disposable income.

**Discretionary income.** The money that you can spend as you please after you have paid for such necessities of life as food, housing, clothing, transportation, utilities and taxes and set aside amounts to meet your fixed commitments and your debts.

**Standard of living.** The level at which you and your family consume goods and services. This can also be expressed as the amount of money that you need to support yourselves in the manner and style to which you are accustomed. American families today enjoy the highest standard of living in the world.

**Asset.** Anything you own that has a money value. A financial asset of one person is the debt or obligation of another. Your financial assets may include, besides cash on hand, accounts receivable, loans and securities owned and any other claims that are debts of other parties. A careful totaling of your financial assets is essential to a sensible family money plan. (For details, see Chapter 3, "How to Appraise Your Family's Security," page 21.)

**Investment.** The money you put into some form of property for income or profit or into some form of security, as a home or pension plan.

**Credit.** Your power to borrow money, based on your reputation for repayment, your net income and your assets.

11

## CHAPTER 2

## Where Do the Dollars Go?

*If your money just seems to melt away, it's time to find out how you really spend it. You may be surprised!*

True or false? On the average, families spend about $2500 a year on food. Out of every $10 of a family's spending, $1 generally goes for clothing.

If you answer true to both statements, you're right. You are also more knowledgeable about where the money is going than most people.

Ironically, the hardest-working family may not know what is happening to its own money, much less understand how other people spend theirs. This is a common, understandable failing, for most spending is done in dribs and drabs. You can probably remember what your television set cost because it was a big one-time expenditure. The odds are, though, that you can't recall precisely how much you spent last month for food. That money was doled out.

So for some insights into where your money may be going—and to compare your expenses with other people's—come take this conducted tour of family spending. The figures are estimates based on spending patterns revealed by government surveys of families of various incomes, sizes and ages.

### The Roof over Your Head

Your largest single expense probably is the cost of running your house or apartment. It's most families' biggest bill.

Try listing all the costs involved. There are, as starters, rent or payments on your homeowner's mortgage, utilities, repairs and maintenance; purchase and upkeep of home furnishings and equipment such as washing machines and driers; real estate taxes and property insurance; gardening supplies.

Together, they add up to a staggering sum. And the more you earn, the larger the total is likely to be. Higher-income people tend to buy fancier houses, more expensive home furnishings, costlier equip-

| HOUSING | | |
| --- | --- | --- |
| AFTER-TAX INCOME | HOUSING COSTS | HOUSING AS A PERCENTAGE OF LIVING COST |
| $ 5,000–$6,000 | $1,843 | 29.7 |
| 6,000–7,500 | 2,154 | 29.1 |
| 7,500–10,000 | 2,470 | 27.6 |
| 10,000–15,000 | 3,119 | 27.0 |
| 15,000 and over | 5,184 | 29.6 |

ment. Look at the average expenditures above for five income groups. The figures do not include payments on the mortgage principal because that money is considered money saved.

The figures may well keep on increasing if recent trends continue. Building costs have gone up 15 percent in the past three years. Land costs have also been rising. So, too, have family incomes. People want bigger homes and are willing to pay for them.

The average price of new homes bought with conventional mortgages (those not insured, or guaranteed, by the Federal Housing Administration or Veterans Administration) rose from $22,700 in 1965 to $29,900 in 1969. The average resale price on existing homes rose from $21,300 to $24,900.

For every $1000 increase in the price of a new house, you can expect to spend about $10 more a month for mortgage payments, insurance, real estate taxes, heating and utilities. The difference is usually larger on older homes.

And that additional $10 a month is only part of the extra cost of a larger home. You will need more furniture, carpets and curtains. You may want another phone extension. Little by little, your costs mount to a permanently higher level.

To some extent, housing costs weigh more lightly on the home-owner than on the renter, for the owner can take an income tax deduction for the interest on the mortgage and for his real estate taxes. When he sells the house, he may be able to defer paying income tax on the profit. On the other hand, the renter gets interest on money he might otherwise tie up in a house and he can often enjoy the scenery without having to take care of it.

13

## The Cost of the Cupboard

After housing, your most important expense is food. The way food prices have risen over the past years, you may feel that every spare cent is going to the supermarket. Actually, your food bills probably are nearly as great as your housing bill.

How much you spend on food depends, of course, on what you eat. If you insist on steaks and chops, you will spend more than if you dine occasionally on fowl, fish or eggs.

Food costs also move up with income, but not at the same rate. A family making $10,000 a year normally will not spend twice as much as a $5000-a-year family. The table here shows how the percentage of living expenses devoted to food declines at the higher income levels.

Whatever your income, your food costs naturally reflect the size of your family. On the average, food accounts for about 26 percent of the living expenses of a family of five, compared with 23 percent for a family of two. And if some of those five happen to be teen-age boys, the sky's the limit.

| FOOD | | |
|---|---|---|
| AFTER-TAX INCOME | FOOD COSTS | FOOD AS A PERCENTAGE OF LIVING COST |
| $ 5,000–$6,000 | $1,568 | 25.0 |
| 6,000–7,500 | 1,805 | 24.2 |
| 7,500–10,000 | 2,166 | 24.0 |
| 10,000–15,000 | 2,591 | 22.2 |
| 15,000 and over | 3,375 | 19.1 |

## Getting Around—Your Next Biggest Expense

The next largest living expense is the cost of getting from one place to another, accounting for about $15 of every $100 spent by the average family. For many people, most of that $15 goes for the purchase and upkeep of cars.

There are more than 80 million cars on the road, and 80 out of every 100 families own at least one. About 25 out of 100 own two or more.

Over the past few years, car buyers have been paying roughly

$3250 on the average for new cars and about $930 for used cars. A majority of the new cars are bought on credit. Of course, you don't normally buy a new car every year; the average family trades every four years.

The cost of maintaining your car depends in part on how much it is used. City dwellers drive approximately 9000 miles a year, suburbanites 10,500 miles. About 44 percent of that mileage is commuting to work and other business travel.

As a rule high-income families spend more on transportation than lower-income families, as the table below reveals. Nevertheless, you tend to spend a smaller share of your income on transportation as you move into the upper income brackets. Notice that the $15,000-and-over family typically devotes 14.2 percent of its money to these expenses, compared with 15.4 percent for the $5000 to $6000 family. In all income groups, though, cars are the major transportation cost.

| TRANSPORTATION AFTER-TAX INCOME | TRANSPORTATION COSTS | TRANSPORTATION AS A PERCENTAGE OF LIVING COST |
|---|---|---|
| $ 5,000–$6,000 | $ 937 | 15.4 |
| 6,000–7,500 | 1,103 | 15.3 |
| 7,500–10,000 | 1,398 | 16.0 |
| 10,000–15,000 | 1,848 | 16.4 |
| 15,000 and over | 2,433 | 14.2 |

## What You Spend on What You Wear

Fashion trends come and go, hemlines rise and fall, but most average families still use about $10 out of every $100 they spend to keep themselves clothed in style, as the chart on page 16 shows.

Larger families obviously need more clothing than smaller ones; but what you need often has little to do with what you want. You can buy a good suit for $100 or spend $250. One woman buys two pairs of shoes a year; another "needs" ten.

Nothing seems to stimulate the appetite for clothes like having the money to buy them. People spend more money and a larger share of their budget on clothing as income improves.

Women ordinarily spend more for clothing than men. In the $5000 to $7500 income group, women outspend men by about 26 percent. Among $15,000-and-over families, women are 58 percent ahead.

These costs—housing, food, transportation, clothing—account for 78.8 percent of the average family's expenses. The proportion is somewhat higher, 80 percent, for families in the $5000 to $6000 income group, and lower, 75.2 percent, in the $15,000-and-over income group.

CLOTHING

| AFTER-TAX INCOME | CLOTHING COSTS | CLOTHING AS A PERCENTAGE OF LIVING COST |
|---|---|---|
| $ 5,000–$6,000 | $ 627 | 9.9 |
| 6,000–7,500 | 779 | 10.3 |
| 7,500–10,000 | 1,019 | 11.1 |
| 10,000–15,000 | 1,403 | 11.9 |
| 15,000 and over | 2,199 | 12.3 |

## Where the Other Dollars Go

What happens to all the rest of your income? The table below gives the general pattern.

The figures are national averages for families of all income groups. Some of those expenses vary with income or age; others don't. Higher-income families, for example, tend to devote a larger share of their money to recreation and education, a lesser share to tobacco. Most families, whatever their income brackets, spend the same percentage for alcoholic beverages.

Keep in mind that any one of many factors—a severe illness, per-

OTHER EXPENDITURES

| ITEM | AMOUNT SPENT YEARLY | PERCENTAGE OF LIVING COST |
|---|---|---|
| Tobacco | $115 | 1.8 |
| Alcoholic beverages | 109 | 1.7 |
| Personal care | 184 | 2.9 |
| Medical care | 490 | 6.6 |
| Recreation | 265 | 4.0 |
| Education | 72 | 1.1 |
| Miscellaneous | 202 | 3.1 |

haps, or financing a child's college education—can force a family's spending away from the norm.

Another point to remember is that spending figures used here generally represent the full price paid for an item, whether it was bought for cash or on credit. (Car purchases are calculated at the net trade-in price.) If you have done a lot of credit buying recently, your current cash outlays may understate your expenses.

## Debts and Savings—Items in Your Budget

The University of Michigan Survey Research Center estimates that just over half of the nation's families have some installment debts outstanding. For many people, buying on credit is safe and convenient. Families often buy on time because they do not want to disturb their savings accounts. All too frequently, however, the disadvantages are overlooked.

Credit is expensive. The service charge on an ordinary department store account works out to an annual interest rate of about 18 percent. The usual 6 percent bank installment loan really costs you about 12 percent, because the bank charges 6 percent of the face amount although by the middle of the loan period you have repaid half the principal. Similarly, the $5\frac{1}{2}$ to 7 percent car loan really costs 11 to 14 percent.

Each time you assume a debt, you commit some future income to debt repayments. There's nothing particularly risky about this if you don't mortgage so much future income that you leave no margin for emergencies. Unfortunately, many people have passed the danger line. According to the Michigan survey, one out of ten families has committed 20 percent or more of its annual income to debt repayment (not counting mortgage payments). And as more of a family's present income goes toward the repayment of old debts, the greater becomes the pressure to seek more credit to meet current needs. Moreover, most debtors either have more debts than liquid assets—bank accounts and government Savings Bonds—or have no liquid assets at all.

Despite all the heavy expenses of day-to-day living, you probably are saving some of your income, even though it may not look like it. The monthly payments on the principal of the mortgage, your contribution to the company pension plan, the cash values of your life insurance policies—all constitute an accumulation of assets. True, those assets are not usable cash until they are converted in some way. For example, usually you can't touch your pension money until you leave the job or retire. Most families try to build a fund of liquid assets, that is, assets they can cash in easily.

A survey made a few years ago showed that people in the $5000 to $10,000 income group generally had about $1200 in savings. The average may be much higher now. In one recent year, personal savings accounts increased by more than $28 billion. Obviously many people are managing to put something aside. If you aren't among them, it is time to take stock.

The only way to manage your spending so that there will be something left over for saving is, of course, to budget. Knowing how other people spend their money can help you size up your own spending habits. But to construct your own workable budget, you'll have to know the truth about your own spending.

So get out the check stubs and the bills, estimate expenses where you must and find out as accurately as you can just where *your* dollars are going. Start building a budget from there. (For details on budgeting, see Chapter 4, page 47.) Then, instead of spending as others do, you can begin spending the way you want to.

## WORDS YOU SHOULD KNOW

**Expenses.** Any spending that uses up your money rather than saves it.

**Liquid assets.** Cash or savings easily converted into cash, such as stocks, bonds, bank savings.

**Homeowner's mortgage.** A special form of long-term loan in which your home is pledged as security for payment of the difference between your down payment and the total cost of the property. The interest is not included in the face amount of the loan. (See Chapter 12, page 137.)

**Guaranteed mortgage.** A loan on which the Veterans Administration, the Federal Housing Authority or some other guarantor insures the lender against loss if you do not pay.

**Conventional mortgage.** A loan on your house that you arrange directly with a bank or some other lender without an outside agency guaranteeing the lender against loss if you do not repay.

## HOW DO THOSE JONESES DO IT?

Nearly everyone knows how much his neighbor makes, approximately. Although people don't go around reporting their incomes out loud, money still has its ways of sounding off. It talks, as they say, and you don't need especially sharp ears to hear its message.

Take your neighbor Jim Jones. Nice fellow, Jim. Good neighbor. Your two families enjoy a casual, easy, back-fence relationship. Yet you're quite capable of discussing the Joneses' financial affairs—in the privacy of the kitchen, with the kids in bed.

A husband might speculate, "Oh, I don't know, but Jim must make around fifteen thousand dollars." Or $10,000. Or $20,000. Whatever the going rate is on your block for gross annual incomes of envied neighbors.

A wife puts her comments differently: "They've had three new cars since we got our first one. . . . They plan to send Martha to camp this summer—for two whole months! . . . They're ripping out every last bit and doing it all over in avocado. . . . Some mob scene they had last night. It must have been at least four in the morning before those patio lights went off."

A certain brittleness underneath suggests, "How come we can't do all those nice things they do?"

If you live in a highly diversified neighborhood where high-income people rub shoulders and share interests with those of more modest means,

there may be less of this green-eyed concern about the Joneses. But most people don't live in such places. They tend to get sorted out by age, family size and income into neighborhoods of look-alikes. And then, being merely human with human doubts, everyone is quick to take note when a similarly situated neighbor seems to get dissimilar results for his money.

Let's take a look at Dogwood Garden Estates, a superficially homogeneous suburban community. It is comparatively small and expensive and populated by junior executives and young professionals who earn a bit more than is the norm in the average suburban community. Here are reports on five families whose fiscal behavior in one way or another tended to disturb the neighborly peace.

Family No. 1 always seemed to have money left over, a condition rare elsewhere in the vicinity. The source of the surplus was a mystery. But the fact of its existence was not, for the head of the household had an active, often-expressed interest in investments and was capable of dropping such depth charges as, "I don't have a dime's worth of oil stock right now."

Family No. 2 were the lively ones, always on the go—theater, night spots, the best restaurants, football games, weekend trips, frequent vacations.

Family No. 3 were outstanding in only one way, but a way that had wives reeling for blocks around. Imagine, a maid five days a week! How in the world did they manage to afford an expensive luxury like that?

Family No. 4 won attention not for anything it did but for what it possessed, mainly an elegant car—this year's, every year—and a houseful of furniture that looked just like the pictures in a home and garden magazine.

Family No. 5's conspicuous distinction was owning a summer home at the seashore. The minute school closed in summer, the wife and kids vanished until Labor Day.

How did these families come by their exceptional arrangements? Had they found some magic? Did they simply manage better, more expertly? Or did each hold some secret his neighbors had yet to unlock?

Through circumspect inquiry it was learned that there were indeed some special reasons behind these special circumstances. And the inside stories were scarcely miraculous. On the contrary, they were prosaic, disillusioning and anticlimactic.

The facts were these:

The secret of the family that had the inexplicable surplus available for saving simply was split-level economics. They earned at one income level and lived at a slightly lower one. Result: surplus. Their economies were not drastic ones but little ones, spread widely and evenly, so that they never pinched and didn't show to onlookers. Because the family had been living this way for some years, they were beginning to enjoy the fruits of their prudence. Their investments' earnings were paying for occasional small splurges, the kind that other families had to carve out of their regular budgets.

The facts behind the family whose endless round of entertainment caused such consternation proved to be equally mundane. He had a good sales job. Most things the family did had business connections for him, thus bringing his generous expense account into play. Others in the community had various fringe benefits from their jobs too; this family just happened to have unusual ones about which they were unusually closemouthed.

There was a sad irony in the story of the family with the full-time maid. Instead of being better off than most, they were below par for the community. They had a bigger family, a bigger house, a bigger mortgage and bigger monthly payments. They had to economize heavily on clothes, food and recreation. And that full-time maid didn't figure in their budget at all. A concerned in-law paid for her—an arrangement that began "just to help out temporarily" when the youngest boy was born, six years ago.

The family with the elegant car and elegant furniture had nothing special at all to reveal. They just preferred to use their money for car payments and furniture rather than for fancy food or lots of clothes or away-from-home entertainment. So cars and furniture were what they spent it for.

As for the family with the seaside summer home, their affluence traced back to financial help from well-heeled relatives and from inheritances that had come to them at the time they bought in Dogwood Garden Estates. That financial advantage enabled them to pay mostly cash, so they had a small mortgage. They could budget a lot more for recreation than any other family in the community—and a lot less for mortgage payments.

Like the citizens of Dogwood Garden Estates, today's Joneses appear to owe the little material successes that set them apart from their neighbors to such humdrum, practical factors as previous savings; money-managing skill; hidden financial help; job-related benefits; choice of priorities.

One could draw a couple of lessons from the Joneses and their neighbors: (1) Never conclude that because someone else affords something, you should be able to afford it too. (2) Never conclude that because some people spend in ways that you cannot, you aren't managing right.

Maybe you aren't managing right, but maybe the Joneses aren't either. All you know for sure is that you and the Joneses manage differently. The judgments on what's right and wrong—for you—are yours alone. Make them. Leave the Joneses out of it.

CHAPTER 3

# How to Appraise Your Family's Security

*You should check your financial health regularly. This chapter provides the facts and forms you need, so grab a pencil and see how you're doing*

You and your family have regular physical checkups, even when you're feeling well. It's smart—a sane and systematic way to prevent many problems that might otherwise come your way.

Do you handle your financial affairs that sensibly?

Too many of us simply lurch from paycheck to paycheck, never quite sure whether we will come out ahead or behind. Big expenses like a new car, a vacation, house repairs or college bills take us by surprise—although each could have been foreseen and provided for.

There is a better way. You apply the lesson learned in health care to your financial affairs: You have regular financial checkups.

This chapter is designed to tell you how it's done. The procedure can be adjusted to fit individual needs and circumstances. And when you finish, you will be able to diagnose any financial ills and prescribe appropriate remedies.

## What You Spend

How much did you spend last year?

If you can estimate the total within a few hundred dollars, you are exceptional. So many people simply spend when they have the money, with little more than a glance into the checkbook to make sure that this check won't bounce.

Take an easier question: How much did you make last year?

You think you know, of course. If you are salaried, your base pay is the figure that comes to mind. If you are a self-employed professional or in business for yourself, you may be less certain. But even those on straight salary forget that they may have income from interest on savings, perhaps from stock dividends, maybe even from gifts or moonlighting pay.

Pinning down income and outgo is the obvious first step in sizing up your financial position. What could be more basic? And yet how long has it been since you troubled to do it?

Worksheet No. 1 on page 39 will enable you to take that first important step easily. If you haven't been keeping track of income and outgo all along, your calculations are going to be rough. You can recall big expenditures but not what goes out in dribs and drabs. Reconstruct the figures as best you can, though, preferably for one year. Then examine the results:

1. If income and outgo are equal, allowing some give and take for errors, you can credit yourself with living within your means—which is hardly cause for celebration. That close correspondence between what you make and what you spend shows that you live on the brink of trouble, with no margin for savings or investment, no slack for emergencies.

2. If outgo runs ahead of income, the message is clear. You have been financing spending by tapping savings, selling off assets, borrowing money or buying on credit—all ways of depleting past or future savings. It can't go on forever.

3. If income exceeds outgo, you may indeed have cause to cheer provided the surplus goes into savings or investment. More likely, though, the figures show surplus but your pockets show empty. If that's the problem, you simply have not put down all your spending. Yet there is hope. If your figures for major expenditures are at all

realistic, they suggest that there is room for investment and saving—once you have managed to plug the leaks.

So go over your spending record and decide whether it is completely satisfactory. You may find too much expenditure on things that don't much matter, too little on some things that are important to your family's future happiness and security.

Two essentials for getting more mileage from your income are planning and control. You have to decide how to spend before you

▭▭▭▭▭▭

## SEE HOW YOUR FAMILY COMPARES

You can use this table to match your spending patterns against the national averages for families with after-tax incomes of $5000 and up.

Begin with your income after taxes for last year and deduct life insurance premiums, gifts and contributions, loan payments, payments on the principal of your mortgage, pension-plan contributions, savings, investments. The remainder—which represents spending for current consumption—is the base on which to calculate the percentage spent for each category. For example, if your current consumption total is $7500 and your housing expenses are $1500, the housing share is 20 percent.

Include in the transportation category all fares and the cost of using your own car during vacations. Housing takes in everything spent on the home except payments on the mortgage principal.

Special expenditures, such as tuition for a child at school or the purchase

| ITEM | NATIONAL AVERAGE | WHAT YOU SPEND |
|---|---|---|
| Housing | 27%–30% | % |
| Food | 19%–25% | % |
| Transportation | 14%–17% | % |
| Clothing | 9%–13% | % |
| Medical care | 6%– 7% | % |
| Recreation | 4%– 5% | % |
| Personal care | 2%– 3% | % |
| Tobacco, alcoholic beverages | 3%– 4% | % |
| Education | 1%– 3% | % |
| Miscellaneous | 3%– 6% | % |

of an automobile last year, may cause your expenses to vary markedly from the averages. Or, you may be spending either more or less than what other families consider reasonable in the same categories.

▭▭▭▭▭▭

spend; then you must make sure that what you spend conforms to your plan.

These two concepts—planning and control—are combined in the idea of budgeting. If you have never lived on a budget, don't let the term frighten you. You took the first step toward budgeting when you itemized your spending and income. The next step is to decide how you want to split up your income among the various spending categories. When you make that decision, you have made a budget. (For a detailed discussion of budgeting, see Chapter 4, "The Fine Art of Family Budgeting," page 47.)

## What You Owe

While most families borrow with sensible restraint, some tend to forget that loans have to be repaid eventually and that the payments will come from their future earnings.

They also fail to realize how much they pay for credit. The average 6 percent bank loan costs about 12 percent a year simple interest because of the way the payments are arranged. A charge account fee of $1\frac{1}{2}$ percent on the unpaid balance works out to 18 percent a year. Small-loan companies charge as much as 30 or 40 percent a year.

Credit is so freely available nowadays that almost one out of every two families is usually paying installments. Ironically, the big problem for the family with a fair-to-good credit rating is not how to get credit; it's how to resist accepting too much.

| TOTAL FAMILY INCOME | AVERAGE INSTALLMENT DEBT PER FAMILY |
|---|---|
| $ 5,000–$7,500 | $1,230 |
| 7,500–10,000 | 1,220 |
| 10,000–15,000 | 1,470 |
| 15,000 and over | 2,120 |

To gauge your credit position, tabulate your debts (excluding mortgages) on Worksheet No. 2 on page 40. Then compare your total with these averages from a report from the Survey Research Center of the University of Michigan.

Of course, other people's averages can't be hard-and-fast standards for your family. Each family has its own set of needs. These change over the years too. Generally you borrow most when you and your children are young and you're still acquiring all the things that make a home but you haven't yet hit your earnings stride.

How do you know, then, when you have passed the safe debt limit for your family? Here are the main danger signals:

1. You have to skip payments occasionally to leave enough money for regular living expenses.

2. You have to take out new loans to pay off old ones.

3. Your debts add up to more than you have in bank accounts, government Savings Bonds and readily salable securities.

4. Loan payments amount to 20 percent or more of your net pay.

If any of those conditions fit, you are highly vulnerable. Try to get your debts down.

Another trouble point to watch for—not as serious as the others— is borrowing for overlong periods. Stretching out payments cuts the size of installments but also runs up interest costs and prolongs the strain on your income.

If you find it difficult to curb your appetite for credit, try setting aside a fixed amount each week or month in a separate savings account for the expensive things you normally buy with loans. Say you plan to trade in your car in two years for a new model that will cost about $3000. You expect to get about $1000 for the old car, leaving a $2000 balance. To accumulate that amount in two years, put aside $85 a month. You will end up with both your new car and money to spare, for the savings will have earned interest. At 5 percent interest, the account will earn $85 or more, depending on how the interest is calculated.

If you can't afford $85, settle for the largest amount you can regularly set aside. You may have to wait a bit longer for your new car, or you may have to borrow just a little. But at least you won't have to finance the whole $2000. (The subject of credit is covered more fully in Part 11, "What You Should Know About Credit," which begins on page 475.)

## Your Taxes

Income taxes are the first charge against your income—and a big one. Every tax dollar, moreover, is a dollar that you can neither spend nor save. Are you sure you are doing all possible to minimize those tax bills—to pay what you owe but no more?

Use this checklist to decide. Give a yes or no answer to each statement that applies to you:

1. You use the many sources of information on taxes, both government and private, that are available.

2. You keep good records throughout the year of taxable and non-taxable income and of deductible or potentially deductible expenses.

3. You are as careful with state and local tax returns as you are with federal ones.

4. You go over your tax records toward the end of the year to see whether there are steps you might take before December 31 to save on taxes.

5. You have a good general working knowledge of the tax structure and regulations.

If you can say yes to all those statements, you're probably doing a good job of holding down your tax bill. But if you had to answer no to any of them, you may be missing out on legitimate tax economies.

With a particularly large income or a complicated return—many investment transactions, for instance, or a home business—you should have help from an accountant or tax attorney. In the usual case, however, you don't have to master all the intricacies of tax law to manage your own taxes. Patience and effort will do the trick.

You have three main sources of information: (1) the tax instructions for income tax form 1040; (2) *Your Federal Income Tax*, a big booklet published annually by the Treasury Department and available from local Internal Revenue Service offices; (3) privately published tax guides as well as articles in magazines and newspapers. The special tax-saving section that begins on page 589 of this book contains up-to-date information and advice.

As a backstop, you can call the local IRS office for advice. You are not required to divulge your name to the agent, so you need not hesitate on that account.

Generally, there are three avenues that can lead a family to achieve substantial savings on its federal income tax:

*Owning a home*. The tax laws favor the family that buys rather than rents its home. An owner, for example, can deduct the interest on the mortgage and local property taxes. He can often defer paying tax on any profit made on the sale of the house by buying another house. And he may be able to avoid the tax completely by waiting until he is sixty-five or older before selling his last house. If he rents out his home, the house is considered a business and he can offset his expenses, including depreciation, against the rent.

*Investing.* The tax on long-term capital gains is generally only half that on regular income. The rate doesn't exceed 25 percent on gains of $50,000 or less, and never exceeds 35 percent. That's one reason why it is usually advisable to invest part of your savings and funds for college and retirement. No tax is due on the gain in value until the investments are sold, and then you pay at bargain rates. Meanwhile, certain dividends can be excluded from taxable income. In contrast, the interest earned on a savings account is taxed as it is earned, and at the full rate.

*Taking advantage of deductions and exemptions.* There are dozens of them in the tax regulations. Read through that government booklet, *Your Federal Income Tax*, for instance, and you are almost sure to spot one you've been bypassing. (For more detailed information on taxes, read "How to Save Money Under the New Tax Law," page 589.)

## Your Job and Its Future

Your financial health depends primarily on your source of income —your job. Have a look, then, at your earning power. Are you doing as well on the job as you ought to be for your experience and training? See how you compare on the table on page 29. These are rough estimates, so don't take the figures literally. If you're somewhere near the income given for your occupation, you're in the middle: Half in your age group make more, half less than you do.

Your salary, though, is probably not all your income from your job. For a full evaluation of what you are earning, add in the fringe benefits. If they come to about 25 percent of your salary, that's average. Use the form on the following page to evaluate your total compensation.

Now, what about your job future? First, for your line of work. Here are fields where there will be an increase in demand for workers, good opportunities for advancement: construction, furniture manu-

Payments by your employer for Social Security, disability
insurance, workmen's compensation, etc.............. $ _____

Company services provided you: value of free parking, _____
free medical services, discounts, recreation facilities, etc. _____

Bonuses................................................ _____

Pension: what employer pays........................... _____

Health insurance: what employer pays.................. _____

Life insurance: what employer pays.................... _____

Profit sharing......................................... _____

Stock options......................................... _____

*Total*.... $ _____

facturing, rubber and plastics, fabricated metal products, machinery (nonelectrical), services (business, health, personal). Other fields with a growing job demand include computer technology, electronics, oceanography, space, antipollution and urban rehabilitation. Here are the lines in which job demand will lag: agriculture; mining; ordnance; food, tobacco, lumber and wood products; oil refining; leather.

Next, what about your own prospects for advancement on the job? Use Worksheet No. 3 on page 40 to make this personal evaluation. A perfect score in the top section, as you can see, is 30. In the bottom section it's 25. Obviously, your performance on the job is more important than other things that influence promotions.

If you score 20 or more points in the first section and 17 or more in the second, then your prospects for promotion are probably OK. But note weak spots, and see what you can do about them.

## Your Home

A home is a place to live in and enjoy. But it also is the family's largest single investment, and the family may spend more on it each month than it does on food.

Of course, mistakes made in this sector of family money management can be whoppers. Yet often they are made innocently and unknowingly; a family merely finds its finances out of whack without knowing why.

## WHAT OTHERS MAKE

| OCCUPATION | AGE AND MEDIAN INCOME | | | |
|---|---|---|---|---|
| | 25–34 | 35–44 | 45–54 | 55–64 |
| Accountants, auditors.................. | $ 7,500 | $ 9,375 | $10,140 | $ 8,750 |
| Artists, art teachers.................... | 7,250 | 8,875 | 9,490 | 8,250 |
| Clergymen............................ | 4,875 | 5,625 | 5,590 | 5,000 |
| College professors, instructors.......... | 6,875 | 10,250 | 11,570 | 11,600 |
| Elementary school teachers............. | 6,125 | 7,250 | 7,670 | 7,000 |
| Secondary school teachers.............. | 6,375 | 8,125 | 9,100 | 8,625 |
| Dentists.............................. | 13,125 | 18,750 | 17,420 | 12,250 |
| Designers, draftsmen................... | 7,500 | 8,875 | 9,360 | 8,750 |
| Editors, reporters..................... | 7,750 | 10,000 | 10,790 | 10,850 |
| Aeronautical engineers................. | 10,375 | 13,250 | 13,200 | 11,875 |
| Civil engineers........................ | 8,750 | 10,375 | 11,050 | 10,750 |
| Electrical engineers................... | 10,000 | 11,750 | 12,220 | 11,750 |
| Mechanical engineers.................. | 9,875 | 11,375 | 11,830 | 10,500 |
| Lawyers, judges...................... | 9,000 | 15,000 | 17,940 | 15,125 |
| Musicians, music teachers............. | 6,125 | 7,500 | 7,800 | 6,125 |
| Chemists............................. | 8,250 | 10,250 | 10,790 | 10,125 |
| Physicians, surgeons................... | 6,000 | 24,375 | 27,040 | 21,125 |
| Economists........................... | 8,625 | 12,375 | 12,870 | 14,125 |
| Electrical, electronic technicians........ | 7,500 | 8,125 | 8,100 | 8,500 |
| Store buyers, department heads......... | 7,500 | 9,875 | 9,600 | 8,500 |
| Public officials, administrators.......... | 7,000 | 8,500 | 9,100 | 8,125 |
| Bank tellers.......................... | 5,500 | 6,200 | 6,850 | 6,500 |
| Clerical workers...................... | 6,125 | 6,750 | 6,500 | 6,375 |
| Bookkeepers......................... | 5,750 | 6,500 | 6,400 | 5,875 |
| Office machine operators.............. | 6,625 | 7,375 | 7,020 | 5,875 |
| Salesmen, salesclerks................. | 6,750 | 7,625 | 7,410 | 6,125 |

Here are three prevalent errors. Does any one apply to you:

1. *Underestimating expenses.* As a rule, people estimate housing expenses at less than what they really are. Try it yourself. Guess what your housing expenses are each month, then use Worksheet No. 4 on page 41 to calculate your actual outlay. Notice that only interest counts in your mortgage expense; the part that's repayment of principal counts as savings because it increases your equity. Also, note that mortgage interest and real estate taxes are to be adjusted because they are federal income tax deductibles.

Underestimating housing expenses can not only play havoc with a budget but also mislead you into buying a more expensive house than you can afford. Before you buy, make a survey of expenses.

2. *Falling behind on upkeep.* Some people act as though nothing will ever go wrong with their houses. So when the roof starts to leak,

29

the furnace gives up or the washing machine quits, there's simply no money set aside to take care of it. Your housing budget should have a savings allowance built into it for those inevitable eventualities. (For complete information on upkeep, see Chapter 15, "Your Home: A Haven or a Headache?" page 168.)

3. *Overinvesting in improvement.* Adding extras to your home seldom means adding to its value by the amount you spend. When you sell, you usually get back only part of what you put in for the improvements.

This does not mean that substantial remodeling never makes sense. Sometimes it does, if it cures a basic defect in the house, provides an essential addition (such as a bedroom), repairs the ravages of wear and tear or corrects some detrimental obsolescence. And improvements that have no function except to keep you contented are fine too. Just don't make the mistake of thinking that the next owner will necessarily pay for them.

Perhaps to your surprise, your improvements will net even less if they result in making your property conspicuously more expensive than surrounding places. It's something to think about before you set out to become the envy of your neighbors. (For more on home improvement, see Chapter 18, "Home Improvement: A Good Investment or a Poor One?" page 202.)

## Your Life Insurance

The average amount of life insurance carried by a family today is about $20,000. That may be too little or a lot for you, depending on your requirements.

Life insurance can serve many functions. For example, endowment policies are used as a means of saving a specific sum by a fixed date. Retirement income policies are designed to provide a steady income beginning at some time in the future. However, the primary—and most important—purpose of life insurance is to leave your family money to live on if you die while others are dependent on you.

Generally, you can separate your family's needs into three distinct categories: (1) money to pay burial expenses, outstanding bills and the cost of settling the estate; (2) a dependable income to support the family while the children are young and a somewhat smaller income for your wife after the children are on their own; (3) a fund for education for the children.

For an idea of how much your present insurance, combined with your other financial resources, will provide for those purposes, use Worksheet No. 5 on page 42.

As a rule, a family's insurance requirements can be covered through some combination of straight life and term insurance. A straight, or ordinary, life policy is the type that accumulates a cash value and stays in force at the same annual premium until you die or cash the policy. Term insurance policies generally build no cash fund to borrow against or to use for paying premiums in emergencies; they are in force for a specific period only, and if a policy is renewed, the premium goes up for the next period. Term policies cost considerably less than straight life when first bought, however; so a young man trying to buy maximum protection for his family does better by buying a heavier proportion of term insurance.

Most companies sell a special combination of straight life and term, known as family income insurance, specifically for younger families. When the husband dies, the wife receives a stipulated monthly income for a certain period—presumably while the children are growing up—from the proceeds of the term policy. The straight life policy may be paid off in a lump sum, either immediately or when the monthly payments end.

Unless you are counting on insurance for part of your retirement income, you should be able to do with less coverage once your children are out in the world. Many older people continue paying premiums for superfluous protection.

You can get a complete analysis of your insurance position through the free "programming" services offered by many life insurance companies. They will show you in detail how far your present coverage will go and what additional insurance, if any, is required to fulfill your objectives.

Remember that insurance is not the only resource you can draw on to provide for your family's security. Your wife will be able to use savings, investments and other assets. She may also be entitled to Social Security and veterans' benefits and payments from your company pension plan. Make sure that all those factors are con-

31

sidered in your insurance program. (This subject is covered in detail in Chapter 47, "What You Should Know About Life Insurance," page 442.)

## Savings and Investments

If all goes well, a family sooner or later begins to accumulate "extra" money. It has adequate emergency money and life insurance; now it can start thinking about putting some funds to work through investments that will not only earn interest or dividends but also appreciate in value over the years.

The first problem for such a family is to decide how much it can afford to invest and how to allocate its money among the various kinds of investments. The following four basic principles can be used to formulate an investment plan to fit almost any family's needs. (For more detail on investing, see Chapter 56, "The ABCs of Stocks and Bonds," page 525.)

1. Invest only your spare cash—money that you can afford to do without for a number of years.

2. Put 50 percent to 75 percent of that money into equities, such as stock and real estate, and the remainder into additional "fixed-dollar" funds, such as high-grade corporate bonds, government bonds, certificates of deposit and savings accounts. People under fifty might well divide their investments into 75 percent equities, 25 percent fixed-dollar funds. After fifty, when a person is building a steady income for retirement, it could be divided half and half.

3. Think about investing a fixed amount on a regular schedule. This evens out the price at which you acquire any particular security. As prices rise, your dollars buy fewer shares; as prices decline, your dollars buy more shares. Dollar cost averaging, as this practice is known, is a method of operation that the smaller investor might well consider rather than trying to outguess the market.

4. If you can't resist speculating, do it only occasionally and then just with money you can afford to *lose*.

Of course, there is no formula that will assure you of making money on your investments. The best strategy is the simplest: Buy good stocks and hold them for the future. In the five-year period 1962 through 1966, there were two major declines in stock market prices. Yet stock values, as measured by the Standard and Poor and Dow-Jones indexes, made a net gain of about 17 percent for the five-year span. In addition, the same stocks paid about 3 percent a year in dividends.

To achieve even an average performance, though, requires alert management. Here's a list of questions designed to test your investment practices. If you can answer yes to all of them, you are doing an outstanding job:

1. Are you concentrating on securities of well-established companies? New, untried firms are always risky, no matter how bright their prospects.

2. Are you concentrating on securities of companies in fast-growing industries? There are prosperous companies in all fields, but a company has more opportunity to make good when it's in a business with expanding markets.

3. Are you diversifying your investments into different companies and industries? Diversification gives you a better chance to cash in on market upswings and ride out downswings.

4. Do you check out a company's record before buying a recommended stock? Playing tips and hunches is a bad business.

5. Do you regularly review your stockholdings and weed out the losers? One of the most common errors is to hang on grimly to a company that has lost its momentum. Better to take your loss quickly and put the money to work in a company with a more promising future.

If you haven't appraised your investment results lately, perform this little exercise with each company or mutual fund that you have owned shares in for at least five years:

1. Present market value of what you own.............. $ ⎯⎯⎯⎯⎯⎯
Less the price you paid......................... ⎯⎯⎯⎯⎯⎯
*Capital gain....* $ ⎯⎯⎯⎯⎯⎯
Plus total dividends and capital gains distributions
received in cash................................. ⎯⎯⎯⎯⎯⎯
*Total gain....* $ ⎯⎯⎯⎯⎯⎯

2. Divide the total gain by the number of years you have
owned the shares, to get an average annual gain...... $ ⎯⎯⎯⎯⎯⎯

3. Divide the average annual gain by the price you paid,

    to get an average annual percentage gain..............   _____

This is only a rough measure, not mathematically precise, but it will give you a fair evaluation of your results. How does your figure compare with the average scored by the Dow-Jones index stocks over the past five years?

## Your Will and Estate

One of the tasks of life is to provide for the distribution of your property when your life ends. How you go about that can make a tremendous difference to your wife, children or others who survive you. Here are three steps you should have already taken:

*Have you made out a will?* Without one, your assets will be disposed of according to a formula fixed by state law. Your widow may receive a smaller share than you intended. She might have difficulty, too, in tapping funds set aside for the children's needs.

In some instances, a sizable share might go to parents who are too old or too ill for the burdens of handling money. Your estate will be managed not by someone you choose but by someone the court appoints.

Maybe you have heard that you really don't need a will if you and your wife own everything jointly. Don't believe it. Joint ownership is no substitute for a will. Putting every asset in both names can create estate problems rather than solve them.

Consider what can happen without a will when a husband and wife are both involved in a fatal accident but she survives him by a day. All their jointly owned property becomes hers even though no actual distribution is made. When she dies, the state law takes over, and all their joint assets may go to her side of the family, none to his. Moreover, the court will have to appoint a guardian for any minor children, again perhaps not the person the parents would have selected. (For more on this subject, see Chapter 62, "Pros and Cons of Joint Ownership," page 579.)

To spare your survivors many problems, have an attorney draw up wills for both you and your wife. He can also advise you on the beneficiary arrangements to use for pension and profit-sharing plans and life insurance.

*Have you kept your will up to date?* Many families have wills drawn long ago and now all but forgotten. Wills have to be updated occasionally to take account of such changes as these:

1. You move to another state. Although one state will recognize a will validly drawn in another state, some terms of the will may become inoperative because they contravene the second state's statutes.

2. Someone named in your will dies.

3. You sell property once designated for distribution to an heir.

4. You acquire new assets and want to earmark them for heirs.

5. An executor of your will dies or becomes so seriously ill that he can't serve.

6. A child, now grown, no longer needs as much help as when the will was written.

*Have you kept track of your assets?* You should be maintaining up-to-date records for your family and your executor showing your assets (bank accounts, stock, and so on) and where the relevant documents (bank books, stock certificates) are kept. This will greatly simplify the executor's work. (See Chapter 6, "Keeping Those Vital Family Records," page 69.)

One further step, often wise although not usually as essential as the other three, is consultation with an estate-planning specialist. Any attorney can write a simple will. A lawyer who concentrates on estate planning, however, may be more versed in ways in which you can better accomplish your aims and also save on estate taxes. Say you have been helping support an older sister and want to make sure she continues to receive assistance when you are gone. You could leave her a lump sum in your will. But can you be sure now that she will be able to handle the money properly then? And what will happen to any money left over when she dies?

Estate planners often deal with that problem by creating a trust to be activated on your death. The fund provided for your sister is transferred to the trust. The trustee pays out the income and capital to your sister during her lifetime, and at her death the remaining capital goes to whomever you have named. Similar arrangements can be made for a wife or children. Your bank probably can suggest names of estate-planning specialists.

Trusts also are frequently employed to reduce estate taxes. Through the use of one common trust plan, for example, it's possible to save as much as $26,000 in federal taxes on the passage of a $200,000 estate from husband to wife and then, upon her death, to their children.

Of course, $200,000 is a good-sized estate. But in these days of pension and profit-sharing plans and company-provided insurance, many men can expect to leave that much. Use Worksheet No. 6 on page 43 to make a quick estimate of your own estate. You may be closer to $200,000 than you think.

## Money for Retirement

When should you begin serious thinking about your retirement income? The sooner the better, but certainly do not put it off later than your early forties. By that time, you have reached a crucial financial stage. Many pension plans require 15 to 20 years of participation in order to qualify for the highest benefits. The man of forty, then, should be thinking of the pension plan and other fringe benefits his job offers.

Also, he is near his last chance to start building retirement savings without a great strain. For example, a man of forty who sets out to accumulate $20,000 by the time he is sixty can do it by saving about $49 a month if his account pays 5 percent compounded semiannually. If he waits until he is fifty to begin, he will have to put away approximately $130 a month.

So if you're forty or over and haven't yet begun planning for retirement you are shortchanging your future.

You can estimate how much retirement income your present resources will produce by filling in Worksheet No. 7, pages 44–45. Then consider whether that amount will be enough to live on when you retire. Don't forget that the cost of living probably will go up. You may believe, for example, that $400 a month is adequate on the basis of today's living costs. But if prices rise as fast as they have over the past decade, you will need $462 to live as well ten years from now.

To fill in the first part of the form, check your local Social Security office for an estimate of your Social Security benefits, or see Chapter 59, "What You Can Expect from Social Security," page 560. Ask your insurance company for the annuity value of your life policies.

If there is any possibility that you may leave your present company for another job, what you would get from your pension plan would depend on the extent to which you are "vested."

"Vesting" refers to an employe's rights to pension benefits financed by his employer's contributions. In some plans the employe doesn't have any claim on the company's contributions unless he works there until retirement. If he leaves earlier, he usually gets back only his own contributions, plus some interest. Most plans, though, provide for some vesting before retirement. In those cases, the employe who leaves early can take with him part or all of the employer's contributions, either in the form of a life insurance policy (which can be cashed in) or a right to a future pension if the money is left in the company fund.

Usually, an employe has to participate in a plan for a number of years and reach a certain age before any vesting takes place. It's fairly common, too, for vesting to be scheduled over several years before an employe acquires rights to 100 percent of his employer's contributions.

The best way to determine your pension status is to consult with the company representative responsible for pensions.

## Progress and Goals

Here is where all the bits and pieces of your financial checkup come together: Finish up with an assessment of the progress you have made and of the progress you expect and plan for in the future.

If you're like the majority of people, you do manage to save. It's quite possible, in fact, that you are saving more than you realize, for you may not be looking at the right figures. Instead of thinking of savings as cash in the bank, look at them in terms of an accountant's phrase: net worth. Look at the value of what you own (your assets) less the amount you owe (your liabilities).

Start with the conventional kind of savings—cash savings accounts and government Savings Bonds. Both have a fixed value. They don't fluctuate as stocks or corporate bonds do. And they can be mobilized almost instantly. For those reasons, cash and Savings Bonds are your first line of defense for emergencies.

How much emergency savings should you have? One commonsense

rule is to maintain a fund equal to at least half of your annual take-home pay. If that seems excessive, consider how much you would need if you were laid up in the hospital for several months.

The cash value of your ordinary life insurance policies rises each year according to a prescribed schedule (see the table in your policy), and this adds to your assets. Some people include these cash values in emergency funds because the money can be utilized quickly by either cashing in the policy or borrowing against it. You buy life insurance for long-term protection of your family, however, so you don't want to tamper with it if you can possibly help it.

Your other savings are spread out. Part of each mortgage payment, for example, goes to build your equity. You may have some securities and a stake in a pension or profit-sharing plan. You may have an interest in a business. Paying off a debt is also a form of saving, for it increases your net worth.

Even some of what you think of as spending adds to your net worth: Your car, furniture and other personal property, jewelry, paintings, collections and antiques represent assets you could liquidate for cash if you had to. Be very conservative in valuing these "major personal property" items, however. Some, like the car, decline in value from year to year; and you would be unlikely to get a top price for any of them in a quick liquidation.

## Adding It All Up

For a full accounting of your overall worth, and an estimate of where you're heading, use Worksheet No. 8 on page 45. Don't forget to fill in the line on outstanding debts. They are deducted from assets because to the extent that you owe money you actually own less. The balance due on your mortgage is excluded, however, because the mortgage has already been subtracted from the value of the house to calculate your equity.

Value stocks at their current market value. (But remember that 75 percent of market value is the most you could count on if you were to use the shares as collateral for a bank loan.) Ask your employer for the figures on your equity in retirement and profit-sharing plans.

The extra columns in the table are for future years. They serve a very important function. A family that is managing successfully

MONEY IS A FAMILY AFFAIR

should be growing financially over the years, not standing still. It is not going to be content with merely accumulating an emergency fund—it has its sights on many things: a college education for the children, a larger home, a more comfortable retirement income or perhaps some luxury such as a summer place.

So after you've figured how you stand now, estimate the changes taking place in your assets and liabilities and see how you'll stand a year from now at the present pace. Then look farther ahead and see where you want to be, realistically, at some future date; put these figures in the column for "your goal." Next time you calculate your net worth—and you should do this every year or two—you will be able to see what progress you are making toward that goal.

---

## WORKSHEET No. 1: INCOME AND OUTGO

### *Expenses*

**FIXED**

| | |
|---|---|
| Mortgage or rent............................. | $ *3660.* |
| Life insurance................................. | *297.* |
| House insurance............................... | *INCL. IN MORT.* |
| Auto insurance................................ | *100.* |
| Local taxes.................................... | *INCL. IN MORT.* |
| Payments on loans............................. | *INCL. IN MORT.* |
| Other......................................... | |

**VARIABLE**

| | |
|---|---|
| Utilities...................................... | $ *660.* |
| Medical (including health insurance)............. | *250. + 400* |
| Food.......................................... | *1200.* |
| Clothing...................................... | *700* |
| Recreation.................................... | *500* |
| Home furnishings, other household expenses....... | *300* |
| Other......................................... | |
| Total expenses.... | $ *8100* |

### *Receipts*

| | |
|---|---|
| Net pay....................................... | $ *13,400* |
| Other income.................................. | *200* |
| Total income.... | $ *13,600* |

39

---

## WORKSHEET NO. 2: YOUR DEBTS

| PURPOSE OF LOAN | AMOUNT LEFT TO PAY | MONTHLY OR WEEKLY INSTALLMENTS | DATE LAST PAYMENT IS DUE |
|---|---|---|---|
| Car................... | $ — | $ | |
| Household equipment... | ⌐ | | |
| Charge accounts....... | — | | |
| Other................. | 4250 | | |
| *Total*.... | $ 4250 | $ 50⁰⁰ | 1980 |

---

## WORKSHEET NO. 3: YOUR JOB PERFORMANCE

1.  Rate your performance on the job. How do you stack up in the following categories? Be realistic. Make comparisons.

|  | WEAK | MEDIUM | STRONG |
|---|---|---|---|
| *Quantity:* Compare the amount of acceptable work done by you, or the group you supervise, with what others turn out................................ | 2 | 4 | (8) |
| *Quality:* How do you or your group compare with others in overall caliber? In absence of errors?..... | 2 | (4) | 8 |
| *Judgment:* Are you among the few who need little supervision? Does the boss think highly enough of you to toss you most of the "tough ones"? ....... | 1 | (2) | 6 |
| *Originality:* Do you have more than your normal share of suggestions accepted?.................... | 1 | (2) | 4 |
| *Cooperation:* How well do you get along with your co-workers at all levels?........................ | 0 | 2 | (4) |
| *Score....* | | 20 | |

2.  Rate the other factors.

|  | WEAK | MEDIUM | STRONG |
|---|---|---|---|
| *Company's outlook:* Is business booming? Is management in good shape? Or has the firm had some setbacks? Is it in one of the fast-growing lines listed in this chapter?................................ | 0 | (6) | 12 |
| *Company's pay policy:* Is there a regular salary review plan? Does the company promote from within? Or are personnel policies lax and turnover high? | 1 | 3 | (5) |
| *The people upstairs:* Do they know your work, and will they go to bat for you? Or is your light hidden under a bushel?........................ | 0 | (3) | 5 |
| *Your bargaining position:* Is there a shortage of people with your skills? Do other companies pay them more? Or would it be tough to find another job if you left this one?........................ | 1 | (2) | 3 |
| *Score....* | | 16 | |

## WORKSHEET NO. 4: YOUR HOUSING COSTS

| | TOTAL FOR YEAR | MONTHLY AVERAGE (DIVIDE TOTAL BY 12) |
|---|---|---|
| **Utilities** | | |
| Electricity...................... | $ | $ |
| Gas.......................... | 250, | 20, |
| Oil........................... | | |
| Telephone..................... | 60 | 5 |
| Water........................ | | |
| Refuse collection.............. | R2160 | 13. |
| Sewage charges............... | | |
| **Maintenance** | | |
| Lawn and garden.............. | 80 | 7, |
| Painting...................... | 60 | 5, |
| Replacement of equipment (washing machine, drier, etc.)... | 2 300. | 25, |
| **Repairs** | 60 | 5, |

**Tax-deductible costs**

Interest on
   mortgage.... $ 200,      per mo

Real estate
   taxes........ 74,      per mo

   *Total*.... $ 274.      per mo.

Tax deduction
(multiply
total by per-
centage rate
for your
income tax
bracket)..... $ 58.      per mo

| | | |
|---|---|---|
| Subtract deduction from total for interest and taxes....... $ | | $ 216, |
| *Total*.... $ | | $ 296. |

41

## WORKSHEET NO. 5: DEATH PROTECTION

To figure out approximately how much monthly income your life insurance policies and other resources would provide for your family, follow these four steps:

Step 1. Add the face amount of all your policies.

Military service insurance.......................... $ _10,000_

Company plans.................................... _20,000_

Others:

_S. F._ ......................................... _5000_

_____

_____

Total.... $ _35,000_

Step 2. Deduct from the total the amount your family would need to take from insurance in a lump sum for final expenses, education funds, etc. Remember that savings and investments may also be available for these lump-sum expenses.

Total face amount of policies........................ $ _35,000_

Amount needed in lump sum from insurance........... _5000_

Amount of insurance available for monthly income..... $ _30,000_

Step 3. If your insurance has already been programmed by your insurance agent—as it should have been—you know the monthly income planned for your wife. Enter the amount on the "insurance income" line in Step 4. If no definite plan has been set up, you can get an approximate idea by using the table below. Enter the number of thousands of dollars available for monthly income (for example, 21 if the total is $21,000) on the line closest to your wife's present age. Multiply the number of thousands by the corresponding "income per thousand" figure. The result is the guaranteed income your wife would start receiving now from the insurance company under a "ten-year certain" settlement option. (Many companies will pay somewhat more than the guarantee.) That plan pays her a life-time income, but if she dies before the end of ten years, the remaining payments for the ten-year period go to another beneficiary. There are many other ways to schedule payments that would produce higher or lower monthly incomes. Ask the insurance company for details.

| WIFE'S AGE | INCOME PER THOUSAND | | AMOUNT AVAIL-ABLE FOR MONTHLY INCOME | | LIFETIME MONTHLY INCOME |
|---|---|---|---|---|---|
| 35 | $3.22 | × | $ 30 | = | $ 97. 00 |
| 40 | 3.43 | × | | = | |
| 45 | 3.67 | × | | = | |
| 50 | 3.99 | × | | = | |
| 55 | 4.38 | × | | = | |
| 60 | 4.86 | × | | = | |
| 65 | 5.47 | × | | = | |

**Step 4.** Add the income available from insurance to other resources to determine the total monthly income your family would have.

Insurance income............................................$_____

Social Security............................................_____

Job or business interest...................................._____

Investment income........................................._____

Other...................................................._____

Total monthly income....$_____

## WORKSHEET NO. 6: YOUR ESTATE

How much will you leave behind? Use this form to estimate your estate.

Savings.................................................$ ²850

Investment (market value)..................................5600.  incl Fis. Trend

Insurance policies (face value)..............................35,000,

Equity in house...........................................3500,

Major personal effects (cars, boat, antiques, etc.)............500,

Pension plan death benefits.................................—

Profit-sharing fund........................................1100

Loans owed you...........................................—

Total....$ 46550

Minus your outstanding loans (do not include loans covered by credit life insurance policies that will pay off the debt if you die)..............................................35,000

Total estate....$ 11,550

43

## WORSHEET NO. 7: YOUR RETIREMENT FUNDS

For a summary of the approximate monthly retirement income you can expect from your present assets, follow these five steps:

Step 1.  Add the monthly benefits expected from:

Social Security......................................$_____

Pension.............................................  _____

Life insurance converted into an annuity................  _____

*Total*....$_____

Step 2.  Add your cash holdings and those that can be converted into cash.

Bank accounts......................................$_____

Securities..........................................  _____

Business interests....................................  _____

Others..............................................  _____

*Total*....$_____

Step 3.  The following longevity table (used in calculating annuities) shows the number of years people can expect to live on the average after a designated age. Select the age at which you would like to retire and take the corresponding longevity figure. As a safety factor (to avoid running out of money), add another ten years to your life expectancy.

| AGE | | LIFE | AGE | | LIFE |
| MALE | FEMALE | EXPECTANCY | MALE | FEMALE | EXPECTANCY |
| --- | --- | --- | --- | --- | --- |
| 51 | 55 | 28 | 64 | 68 | 17 |
| 52 | 56 | 27 | 65 | 69 | 16 |
| 53 | 57 | 26 | 66 | 70 | 16 |
| 54 | 58 | 25 | 67 | 71 | 15 |
| 55 | 59 | 24 | 68 | 72 | 14 |
| 56 | 60 | 23 | 69 | 73 | 13 |
| 57 | 61 | 23 | 70 | 74 | 13 |
| 58 | 62 | 22 | 71 | 75 | 12 |
| 59 | 63 | 21 | 72 | 76 | 11 |
| 60 | 64 | 20 | 73 | 77 | 11 |
| 61 | 65 | 19 | 74 | 78 | 10 |
| 62 | 66 | 19 | 75 | 79 | 10 |
| 63 | 67 | 18 | | | |

Step 4. Divide the Step 2 total by the adjusted life expectancy you looked up in Step 3. The result is an approximation of the annual amount provided by regularly withdrawing your assets over that number of years. (Note that it's only an approximation, for it does not take into account interest your assets may earn or increases in their value that may occur during the withdrawal period.)

Step 5. Divide the annual amount by 12 for the monthly income provided. Add that monthly income to the income from Step 1 to get your total monthly retirement income.

Monthly benefits (from Step 1) . . . . . . . . . . . . . . . . . . . . . . . . . . $_____

Monthly income (from Step 5) . . . . . . . . . . . . . . . . . . . . . . . . . _____

*Total monthly retirement income* . . . . $_____

---

## WORKSHEET NO. 8: WHAT YOU'RE WORTH

Fill out this form for a full accounting of your overall worth. Don't neglect to enter your estimate for next year and your long-range goals. The financially healthy family should be increasing its assets over the years, not standing still.

| | NOW | NEXT YEAR | YOUR GOAL FOR 19____ |
|---|---|---|---|
| Bank accounts . . . . . . . . . . . . . . . . | $ 3 850 | $_____ | $_____ |
| Savings Bonds . . . . . . . . . . . . . . . | — | _____ | _____ |
| Insurance policy cash values . . . . | 1500 | _____ | _____ |
| Major personal property . . . . . . . | 500 car | _____ | _____ |
| Stocks and corporate bonds . . . . | 5600 | _____ | _____ |
| Interest in business . . . . . . . . . . . | — | _____ | _____ |
| Equity in home . . . . . . . . . . . . . . | 3800 | _____ | _____ |
| Equity in pension plan . . . . . . . . . | — | _____ | _____ |
| Equity in profit-sharing plan . . . . | 1100 | _____ | _____ |
| Loans owed you . . . . . . . . . . . . . . | — | _____ | _____ |
| *Total assets* . . . . | $13350 | $_____ | $_____ |
| Minus your outstanding loans . . . | $_____ | $_____ | $_____ |
| *Net worth* . . . . | $_____ | $_____ | $_____ |

TO LIVE ON YOUR INCOME

## WORDS YOU
## SHOULD KNOW

**Retirement income.**  Money you receive regularly for life after you retire from your job, your reward for an investment program you bought or earned during your working years. Today this usually includes Social Security benefits and business or labor union pension plans, as well as insurance or other annuities you may have bought.

**Equity.**  The value to you of a property after all mortgages, liens and other claims against it are paid off. Example: You own a home mortgaged for $15,000; you owe the bank $3200 for a home improvement loan, and you also owe a carpenter $182 for which he has filed a lien. Thus $18,382 in debts stand against the house. If you sell the property for $26,000, your equity is $7618 minus the sales expenses.

**Vested right.**  Your claim to a share of some future benefit, such as a business pension program toward which you have paid or earned credits. This claim can be the basis for a settlement before the future benefit falls due. A simple example of vested right, or interest, is the surrender value of your life insurance: If you give up the policy, you get something back starting in the second year. If you change jobs, your vested interest is your former employer's obligation to pay you your equity in the fringe benefit

programs of the company. (See Chapter 60, "Pension Plans and Programs," page 568.)

**Anticipated income.**  Money you know you will receive in the future.

**Long-term gain.**  Your profit from the sale of property which you have owned more than six months.

**Stock dividend.**  Additional stock distributed by a corporation to its shareholders in proportion to shares already owned. Example: You own 100 shares of XYZ Corporation, common stock, on which is declared a 10 percent stock dividend. You receive 10 additional shares.

**Mutual fund.**  A pool of money from many investors used to buy securities under the supervision of professional managers. (See Chapter 57, "Mutual Funds and Your Family," page 542.)

**Life Expectancy.**  A statistical estimate of how long a person of a certain age and sex will normally live. Life insurance companies and public health authorities keep these figures up to date. Your life expectancy at a given age—which is only an average—can be used as a basis for figuring the minimum number of years during which you will need retirement income.

**Estate taxes.**  Taxes levied by the state and federal government on property you own that passes to others after your death according to the terms of your will or the law of your state. Consulting a lawyer can help cut down on these taxes.

## CHAPTER 4

## The Fine Art of Family Budgeting

*Don't let the word* budget *scare you off. It's shorthand for a sensible spending plan that can do away with your money worries*

To many people the word *budgeting* has an unpleasant ring. It has come to mean time-consuming bookkeeping, penny-pinching and frustrating attempts to live according to some financial expert's rules. But budgeting does not have to be so restrictive. As this chapter will show you, a family budget is simply a way of getting more happiness and less worry out of your money.

### Setting Your Family Goals

Step 1 in making a budget is to set your goals. What does your family really need and want? You must know this before you can work out the details of a budget.

Let the entire family in on the discussion of goals, if the children are old enough to take part. Consider all suggestions so everyone will be satisfied with the results. Try to keep aims realistic in relation to present and estimated future income. Decide which goals are most important, giving priority to those that will benefit the whole family.

You may find it helpful to think first about your long-term targets —those you hope to reach in 10 or 20 years, perhaps, or even longer. Next decide your aims for the more immediate future—the next 5 years, for example. Then list your goals for the coming year. This way, your budget will include some savings toward long-term and intermediate aims, and you won't let immediate goals push others aside.

Be as specific as possible in setting goals. Your family may decide its long-term goals are a debt-free home, education for children and savings for retirement. For the coming five-year period, objectives might be buying a car, making a down payment on a home and buying an automatic washer-and-drier. Goals for this year might be reducing debts, starting a reserve fund and buying a vacuum cleaner.

47

Goals change, of course, as the size, age and income of the family change. For example, a young couple works to establish and furnish its home. The family with growing children tries to provide adequate food, clothing and housing, and to plan for education costs. After children leave home, the parents concentrate on arrangements for retirement years.

When you have decided on your goals, write them in your record book or some other convenient place. (See Chapter 6, page 69, for information on family record keeping.) List separately your long-term goals, those for the next five years and those for this year. You will want to refer to them as you plan your budget.

## Estimating Your Income

The next step in making a budget is estimating your family's income. Before you can plan wisely, you need to know how much money you will have during the planning period.

A family budget may cover any convenient period. Most budgets are for 12 months; they may coincide with the calendar year, school year or a special period.

If this is your first budget, you may want to set up a three-month trial plan. After you see how your plan works, you can revise it to cover a longer period.

Use the form on page 49 as a guide to figuring your total family income. Write down all funds that you expect to receive during the planning period. Start with fixed amounts that your family gets regularly—wages, salaries, Social Security benefits, pensions, allowances and any other payments.

Then put down the variable income that you anticipate—interest from savings accounts and bonds, dividends from stocks, rents, gifts and money from other sources.

When your earnings are irregular, base your estimate on your past income and current prospects. If your income fluctuates sharply —as it may for seasonal workers, salesmen on commission, farmers and other self-employed people—play it safe by making two estimates. Work out the smallest and largest figures you can reasonably expect. Plan first on the basis of the low income figure. Then consider how you will use additional amounts.

STEP 2: ESTIMATED INCOME FOR _____

| ITEM | AMOUNT |
|---|---|
| Wage or salary of | |
| Husband........................................ | $_____ |
| Wife.......................................... | _____ |
| Net profit from business, farm or profession ........... | _____ |
| Interest, dividends................................ | _____ |
| Other income..................................... | _____ |
| Total.... | $_____ |

After you have figured how much your income will be for the planning period, it's time to estimate your expenses.

## Finding Out Where Your Money Goes

If you have records of family spending, they can serve as a basis for your budget. List all the expenses that your family had, with the amount you spent for each item. If you haven't been keeping records, checkbook stubs, receipts and old bills can serve as reminders.

If you are new at budgeting, you may want to start by finding out where your money goes. Keep a record of current spending for two or three months. The sample form, Step 3, on pages 50 and 51, can help you set up a record of your spending.

Use your records to help you decide whether to continue your present spending pattern or to make changes. If you are satisfied with what your dollars have bought in the past, continue to use similar amounts in your estimates for the spending plan. If you are not satisfied with what you got for your money last year or last month, look at your spending critically. Until you study your records, you may not be aware of overspending and poor buying habits.

Be realistic in revising your allowances for expenses. Resolve to cut out shopping sprees, bargains you don't need and overuse of credit. (Find out all you should know about credit in Part 11, page 475.)

Of course, you will need to plan for new situations and changing conditions. For example, a child entering a new school may cause increased expenses, or your property tax rate may go up.

## Step 3:  Record of Your Expenses

| DATE | ITEM (OR SERVICE) BOUGHT | FOOD AND BEVERAGES | HOUSEHOLD OPERATION & MAINTENANCE | FURNISHINGS AND EQUIPMENT |
|---|---|---|---|---|
| | | $ | $ | $ |
| | | | | |
| | | | | |
| | | | | |
| | | | | |
| | | | | |
| | | | | |
| | | | | |
| | | | | |
| | | | | |
| | | | | |
| | | | | |
| | | | | |
| | **TOTAL** | $ | $ | $ |

50

| CLOTHING | PERSONAL | TRANSPOR-TATION | MEDICAL CARE | RECREATION AND EDUCATION | GIFTS AND CONTRI-BUTIONS |
|---|---|---|---|---|---|
| $ | $ | $ | $ | $ | $ |
| | | | | | |
| | | | | | |
| | | | | | |
| | | | | | |
| | | | | | |
| | | | | | |
| | | | | | |
| | | | | | |
| | | | | | |
| | | | | | |
| | | | | | |
| $ | $ | $ | $ | $ | $ |

Space your large expenses at intervals over several years. If your son gets a bicycle this year, your daughter may have to wait until next year for a record player. New curtains may take turns with baby needs, weekend trips or a TV set.

Keep your record of expenses handy so that you can refer to it whenever necessary. You will find that the figures you put down not only will help you plan future spending but will come in handy when you list your income tax deductions each year.

The best way to have money available for major expenses and future goals is to set it aside regularly. The secret is to earmark the money *before* you spend your income. If you wait until the end of the week or month, you may have nothing to save. By putting away a planned amount every pay period, you have greater flexibility in managing your money.

Keep these funds separate from your other funds so you won't be tempted to spend them impulsively. If possible, put them in a savings account where they will earn interest.

## Emergencies and Future Goals

When you start to budget you should designate a small amount of money for emergencies. Of course, one way to protect your family against major disasters is to take out insurance. But every family has frequent minor crises—too small to be covered by insurance, but too large to be absorbed into a day-to-day budget—a blown-out tire, for example, or an appliance that needs replacing.

Decide how large a cushion you want for meeting emergencies. Work out the amount you need to set aside each year and each month and enter this on the form for Step 4 on page 53.

When your fund reaches the first figure—the one you have allowed for emergencies—you can start saving for something else.

Consider your future goals. Give each one a dollar cost and set the date you hope to achieve it. Next, determine the amount that must be saved each month. Remember that interest on your savings will help them grow.

Now put the figures you have allowed for emergencies and future goals in the space provided on your "Monthly Plan for Family Spending," on page 55.

STEP 4: DETAILED PLAN FOR SET-ASIDES
FOR EMERGENCIES AND FUTURE GOALS

| TYPE OF FUND | PROBABLE TOTAL COST | DATE DESIRED | AMOUNT TO SET ASIDE THIS YEAR | AMOUNT TO SET ASIDE EACH MONTH |
|---|---|---|---|---|
| Emergency.......... $____ | | ____ | $____ | $____ |
| Education.......... | ____ | ____ | ____ | ____ |
| Home or business*... | ____ | ____ | ____ | ____ |
| Home improvement.. | ____ | ____ | ____ | ____ |
| Major equipment.... | ____ | ____ | ____ | ____ |
| Retirement.......... | ____ | ____ | ____ | ____ |
| Other goals (list below) | | | | |
| ____ | ____ | ____ | ____ | ____ |
| ____ | ____ | ____ | ____ | ____ |
| Total.... $____ | | ____ | $____ | $____ |

*This fund might include money you set aside to make a down payment or money (in addition to fixed mortgage payments) you reserve to reduce remaining interest and principal cost.

## Seasonal Expenses

Some large expenses occur seasonally. These include taxes on real estate, personal property and income; school books and supplies; life, household and car insurance; fuel; and travel. Other expenses might be car license plates, medical checkups or Christmas gifts. You may want a season ticket to baseball games or a concert series. Try to anticipate these expenses far ahead and include them in your budget.

By setting aside a definite amount each month, you spread the cost and have money to meet such expenses when they are due. For example, if you put aside $15 each month earmarked for real estate taxes, at the end of the year you will have accumulated $180 to pay your tax assessment. You might set aside money for a large annual insurance premium in the same way.

To determine how much you need to take care of these seasonal expenses this year, use the form for Step 5, or one like it that you have tailored to your finances.

STEP 5: DETAILED PLAN FOR SEASONAL EXPENSES THIS YEAR

| EXPENSE | DATE NEEDED | AMOUNT PER YEAR | AMOUNT PER MONTH |
|---|---|---|---|
| Taxes...................... | _____ | $_____ | $_____ |
| Insurance.................. | _____ | _____ | _____ |
| School expenses............. | _____ | _____ | _____ |
| Fuel....................... | _____ | _____ | _____ |
| Vacation................... | _____ | _____ | _____ |
| Other...................... | _____ | _____ | _____ |
| | _____ | _____ | _____ |
| Total.... | | $_____ | $_____ |

## Taking Care of Debts

If you have debts or past-due bills, you will want to plan your budget so you can clear them up in a reasonable amount of time. Here is how to go about it.

First, carefully review the way you manage your money. If your family has heavy debts, find the reason. Were they caused by sickness or other emergencies that probably won't be repeated soon? Or are they part of a consistent pattern of buying too much on credit? If buying too much is the reason, get your whole family together and work out a plan to avoid credit buying until your outstanding debts are paid.

Work out a practical, systematic plan to repay your debts. Begin immediately to earmark at least a small amount for debt payment every payday, and enter the debt payment on your "Monthly Plan for Family Spending," on page 55.

## Your Monthly Spending Plan—Or Budget

On your plan, enter the expenses usually expected each month. You can estimate quite accurately your family's regular, or fixed, monthly expenses. These may include rent or mortgage payments, installment payments, hospital or health insurance, support or regular payments to relatives. There are utility bills for electricity, gas, water, telephone and garbage collection. Other regular expenses might be board and room for a child away at school, music or danc-

STEP 6: MONTHLY PLAN FOR FAMILY SPENDING

Total monthly income.............................. $_____

Set-asides:
    Emergencies and future goals...................... $_____
    Seasonal expenses................................ _____
Debt payments................................... _____
Regular monthly expenses:
    Rent or mortgage payment............ $_____
    Utilities............................. _____
    Installment payments................. _____
    Other................................ _____
                                 *Total....* $_____

Day-to-day expenses:
    Food and beverages.................. $_____
    Household operation and maintenance.. _____
    Furnishings and equipment........... _____
    Clothing............................ _____
    Personal allowances................. _____
    Transportation...................... _____
    Medical care........................ _____
    Recreation and education............ _____
    Gifts and contributions............. _____
                                  *Total....* $_____
          *Total set-asides and expenses....* $_____

ing lessons, nursery school, or a practical nurse's salary to care for an invalid member of the family.

You are now ready to plan your day-to-day expenses—those that vary from week to week or month to month. Because these are the most flexible entries in your budget, they are the easiest to cut when you need to economize.

Use your records to estimate how much you spend on food, clothing, transportation and other budget categories. You may decide to spend more in some areas and adjust your plan accordingly.

Try to fit some of your immediate goals into the category of day-to-day expenses. For instance, school shoes and a blouse for your daughter can go under clothing; a kitchen stool and a scatter rug go under furnishings and equipment.

Give each member of the family a small allowance that does not have to be accounted for.

Now you're ready to set up your spending plan, Step 6, the basis of every budget. The sample form shown on page 55 can be changed by adding or deleting categories to suit your family's needs.

Work on one section of your expense record (Step 3) at a time. When you are satisfied with your figures, put them in your monthly spending plan.

Add the figures in your spending plan. Now compare the total

▱ ▱ ▱ ▱ ▱

## THESE BONERS WRECK BUDGETS

Where did that new budget go wrong? Your intentions were the best, your resolution was firm. Yet here you are at the end of the month with a stringy bank balance that doesn't come close to covering that fat bunch of bills on your desk.

Well, you could have been snared by one or more of half a dozen budget boners. Go over the list to find the problem (or problems) that tripped you up and see how it can be avoided next time.

• You forgot the "little" expenses. Over the course of several weeks, you can spend a fair amount on gifts, newspapers, shoeshines, afternoon snacks and the like. Expenses such as those are hard to plan for in neat budget categories. But you should allow for them in some way. Try padding one of your regular accounts or setting up a bigger miscellaneous account. If

you still fall short, increase your estimate again and examine your casual spending habits.

• You tried to cut costs too much. You may have started by vowing to cut expenses to the bone so you could bank a certain amount each month. And you might have left yourself so little leeway that you dip into savings for small additional expenses. Actually, you are probably in better shape than you think. Just give yourself a more realistic allowance for living expenses and reduce your savings goal to conform to it.

• You neglected the contingencies. Normally, big unexpected expenses are paid for out of savings. But it's the day-to-day budget that bears the brunt of the minor ones—a school trip, a new tire, repairs for the washing machine, entertainment for unanticipated out-of-town guests, and so on. Set a contingency fund for those out-of-pocket surprises. If you don't need it during any particular month, let the

▱ ▱ ▱ ▱ ▱

with your estimated income for the matching budget period. If the two figures balance—fine.

If your income is more than your estimated expenses, so much the better. You may decide to buy something you want immediately or to set the surplus aside and increase your family's savings account for future goals.

If your outlay exceeds your income, go over your plan. Adjust the budget. Can you reduce expenses? Can you postpone or drop some items you have included?

Consider ways you can trim expenses. This can be challenging if your family agrees to cut the budget as a family project. Ask members to suggest economies they are willing to accept. You may decide

☐☐☐☐☐☐

money accumulate in the checking account. With luck, you may have a big enough surplus left at the end of the year to transfer some to your savings account.

• You tailored your budget to fit some ideal standard rather than your own needs. Averages showing what other people spend are interesting and instructive. Just don't try to squeeze your family into that mold. Each family has its special spending patterns and its own ways of economizing. One family may be able to afford expensive vacations because the wife makes many of her own clothes and the husband copes with the household repairs. Another family with the same income may have to limit vacation spending because the wife and husband have other interests or responsibilities.

• You made things too complicated. The novice budgeter tends to separate expenses into narrow, rigid categories and wrap them in a lot of paper work. Before long, he and his wife are so

overwhelmed by the complexity of the system that they are happy to forget the whole business. You may be able to simplify your budget in several places to make it more workable. For instance, why bother to have a separate account for gardening when it can be lumped in with housing? Meals out can be included with your overall food expenses; cleaning bills can be put in with clothing costs.

• You failed to keep track of the amounts spent. Basically, a budget is nothing more than a guide for allocating your funds. To make it effective, you must keep an eye on your actual spending to make sure you stay within the limits of your plan. If you're on a monthly budget, it's best to check at least a week before the end of the month to find out where you stand and cut back, if necessary. (See Chapter 6, page 69, for more details on record keeping.) Keep in mind that unless you periodically review your spending, you really don't have a budget.

☐☐☐☐☐☐

to make clothing for the children in order to save enough money to give them music lessons. Or you may drive a smaller car in order to live in a neighborhood you enjoy.

Take a good look at your day-to-day expenses. To cut them down to a more manageable level you might:

1. Substitute articles that cost less, but serve the same purpose (buy a new slipcover instead of a new sofa).

2. Use your own family's skills (refinish furniture; grow vegetables and fruits; wash and set your own hair; make curtains).

3. Shop for specials and buy in quantities that fit your family's need (take advantage of seasonal sales, such as household linen "white" sales).

4. Make use of free or inexpensive educational and recreational services (enroll in sewing or craft classes, attend free concerts, patronize a public library, camp at public camping sites).

Scan your regular expenses critically. If you do not have enough money for your family's day-to-day needs, you may want to reduce or eliminate installment payments and other fixed obligations. You might exchange a large car for a smaller one that costs less to operate —or, if you live in a large city, you might even go without a car until you "catch up."

If you find you just can't balance your budget by cutting expenses, you may have to increase your family's income. If the wife is not working, she could take a full- or part-time job. However, it's a good idea to compare the added costs of working outside the home— clothing, lunches, transportation, child care—with the added income. (See Chapter 5, "When Mother Brings Home the Bacon," page 63.) Children can baby-sit, deliver newspapers or do odd jobs.

You may plan to draw on your reserves when you know your income will be particularly low or expenses particularly high. Or you may intentionally spend more than your income when you use the money you have set aside for a special purpose—a new roof, college expenses, a vacation trip. But you may need to review your goals.

At the end of your budget period, compare what you spent with what you planned to spend. If your spending was quite different from your plan, find out why. The answer to the question "Why?" will help you find ways to improve your next plan.

If your plan did not provide for your family's needs, you'll want to revise it. If the plan fitted your needs, but you had trouble sticking to it, you'll have to use more self-discipline and better management next time. Enlist greater cooperation from your family.

A budget is something you keep working and reworking until it "fits" your family and satisfies individual members. Don't expect to have a perfect budget the first time you set one up. But with each succeeding one you can expect improvements.

Although you may be satisfied with your present plan, you will need to alter it from time to time. As circumstances change, you will have to reorganize your budget around your new goals, needs and wants.

## WORDS YOU SHOULD KNOW

**Budget.** A systematic plan for spending your income over a definite period of time, based on your expected revenues and expenses.

**Contingencies.** Unexpected expenses which cannot be budgeted but must be met. Examples: a son's eyeglasses, a daughter's dental braces; a wedding present for a friend; entertainment of an unexpected guest; a funeral.

**Reserve.** Money set aside for a special foreseeable need, such as a vacation trip, a new roof or college tuition. A "contingency reserve" is a fund set up to pay unexpected expenses, such as a bridesmaid's dress or repair of hurricane damage. A "depreciation reserve" is a fund set up over the life of a property like a washing machine, furnace or automobile, to replace it when it wears out.

**Fixed Expenses.** Sums that you must pay every month and that constitute the basic part of your expense budget. They include housing costs (rent, mortgage payments, property tax, school tax); utilities (gas, oil, electricity, telephone, water); installment payments (automobile loans, personal loans, revolving charge accounts); taxes—both federal and local; regular set-asides for your savings account or investment plan; dues; insurance premiums; automobile fees and maintenance fund; regular contributions to church or charities; set-asides for education.

**Deferred pleasure (or gratification).** The key principle of budgeting—the idea that you deny yourself something today in order to save for something better in the future.

**Variable income.** Money you make that does not bring in regular amounts at regular intervals. This could be fees for free-lance work or unexpected dividends.

59

## TEACHING CHILDREN
## TO MANAGE MONEY

When and how do you get children started on learning how to manage money? Virtually all authorities agree that training should start whenever a child begins to receive money from the parents at regular intervals—an allowance, nickels for milk, Sunday school money, or whatever. Children can and should begin to learn at this time the two basic components of money management.

The first is learning how to make money last over a given period of time, and the second is learning how to have something left over. In more familiar terms, the two components are budgeting and saving.

Making money last means learning not to spend it all at once—looking ahead to tomorrow, next week and next month, when there will be things a child will want or need more than he needs, right now, that piece of candy in the shop window.

It means control of impulse buying. Systematic methods of making money last are planned spending, or budgeting. Children can begin at a very early age to acquire the habits that are basic to all this.

If it's milk money, for example, don't hand your child the nickel or dime each morning with the daily injunction, "Be sure not to lose it, now." Instead, turn over the whole week's supply of nickels or dimes some time before Monday morning, and make Junior the custodian of the cache, with the responsibility for taking out the daily nickel or dime each morning as part of the routine of getting ready for school.

Later, when the children start getting spending money, make it a regular allowance right from the beginning, instead of doling out a coin or two whenever the ice cream man passes by.

Let your child receive his allowance along with his milk money or carfare—always with a clear distinction of which is which, even though it's all in one handful. This requires him to begin learning to think in terms of this money for that purpose, and that much for something else. That is the beginning of learning to budget.

Of course, children need some supervision—though the less the better—and of course they'll overdraw and overspend at times, splurge on that piece of candy, or spend the Sunday school money for ice cream. The system should work so that when such a thing happens, they learn they have to do without.

The earlier children begin to acquire a sense of future needs, and the habit of making money last, the better your chances of making good money managers of them later on.

The second fundamental—learning to save—is frequently mishandled by parents. The piggy bank, for example, can help children to learn saving habits, but usually doesn't.

What generally happens is that when Daddy is in an expansive mood he'll give Junior the pennies out of his change, and Junior in turn will put the pennies in piggy. Or when Uncle Henry is visiting, he'll add a nickel, dime or maybe a whole quarter to piggy. Then Junior gets to shake piggy while everybody exclaims, "My! Just listen to how much money you're getting in piggy!"

All of this doesn't teach Junior a thing about saving. On the contrary, it may only convey the idea that if he is cute and charming, and runs to get piggy when Uncle Henry is visiting or when Daddy has change jingling in his pocket, money will be visited upon him like manna from heaven.

Children who learn about "saving" in this way frequently carry over into adult life a notion that somebody, somewhere, is always going to be around to hand out money, or the other good things in life.

The saving habit is acquired only when Junior learns not to spend money that's in hand, and could be spent, but instead puts it aside for some good and compelling reason. The reason, of course, is to take care of some future need or want. It's the principle of deferred pleasure at work.

Remember that the carrot has to be close and appealing enough to provoke a response—to make the donkey move. What motivation is there for Junior in watching a piggy bank fill up with coins he will never get his hands on—at least, not to spend? Where's the carrot if he finally sees piggy's contents counted out and deposited in "his" savings account in the bank? It may give his parents a feeling of satisfaction to see $10.58 added to the passbook

balance, but it does little for Junior's training in money management.

Children can be encouraged to begin saving only if they have a more or less immediate and reachable goal—one that they can see, and want, and expect to get.

If Junior saves 20 cents a week for ten weeks, and is then able to buy the $2 bike horn that he's had his heart set on, he's made an important discovery about saving. He now knows that it really is worth denying himself something this week, and next, in order to gratify some important desire in the future. He's sold on the idea of saving, because his self-denial for ten weeks paid off.

Children have to achieve short-term goals, over and over, until they develop enough maturity and foresight to understand the importance of goals that are well in the future. A child's earliest savings plans are really spending plans, and he must be allowed to spend what he saved, so that he can personally experience the gratification of reaching a future goal through present self-denial. As he develops enough maturity to understand the value of permanent savings, it's time enough to get him started on putting money into long-range savings.

Until the age of about ten, if you succeed in getting a child to develop the two basic habits of "budgeting" and saving for short-term goals, you've accomplished most of what a child can really learn about money management at this age—and you've accomplished a great deal. From ten on—or perhaps earlier—you can begin training him in systematic methods of making his money last and of accumulating savings.

A Memphis father made a success, for example, of setting up a family bank for this purpose. He reproduced a simple check form and provided each child with a book of "checks." On allowance day, the children received their allowances not in coin of the realm, but in the form of a credit to the checkbook balance. Expenses during the month were covered by drawing checks against the account and cashing them with Daddy, the teller. At the end of the month, each child got his canceled checks and a bank statement against which he could reconcile his account.

The experience of seeing where the money had gone during the month proved to be highly educational—as it is, indeed, to adults in the family if they'll sit down periodically with the year's canceled checks, to see where the money went, and how many pieces of candy they've bought during the year.

In addition, teaching children how to keep a checkbook in order is probably one of the more valuable money management skills you can impart to them. It's one in which many adults are woefully inadequate, in fact.

Some such device as this will probably succeed, in most families, much better than trying to teach children the habit of using a conventional budget. In any case, if the adults in a family don't operate on a formal budget, it should hardly be expected that the children could be trained to devise a budget and stick to it.

In fact, in all likelihood you'll succeed in teaching the children to manage money just about exactly the way you do it, and as well as you do it. But understanding the basic principles and basic good habits of successful money management can improve the skill with which both Dad and Mother, and hence the kids, take care of their personal finances.

## TWELVE KEYS TO BUDGETING

- Set your family's goals.
- Make them realistic.
- Know what you make now and where it comes from.
- Find out what you spend now and where it goes.
- Set up a spending plan that will help you achieve your goals.
- Include regular savings.
- Provide an adequate "cushion" for emergencies.
- Include a personal allowance for each member of the family.
- Plan to clear up your debts.
- Keep a record of expenses.
- Let the whole family take part in the planning.
- Keep the budget flexible—it's supposed to serve you, not the other way around!

## CHAPTER 5

# When Mother
# Brings Home the Bacon

*A job for the lady of
the house? Most families
find the extra expenses
and minor inconveniences
well worth it*

The day is coming when little girls will talk about getting married and going to work when they grow up as naturally as they now talk about getting married and keeping house. Right now more than a third of all women in the labor force are working wives, either full or part time. And with the average American woman packing her youngest child off to school when she is still in her mid-thirties, with her family's cost and standard of living rising and with her education better than ever before, this is a trend that's not likely to slow down.

Working wives today make a sizable contribution to family income. In 1966 (the last year for which figures are available from the Department of Labor), the majority of employed wives contributed more than 20 percent of their family's total income. If the wife was on the job full time all year, her contribution went up to 38.6 percent. And it was among families in the $10,000 to $15,000 income bracket that she most consistently brought home a substantial share of the total. Thus her addition to the weekly paychecks was probably helping to pay for things that middle-income families take for granted: a college education for the children, a home in a good community, modern appliances, family vacations, maybe even a vacation hideaway.

Before World War II single working women outnumbered their married co-workers by about 1½ to 1. Since then the number of working women has more than doubled, and now married women, including those with young children, outnumber singles 2½ to 1.

And along with this growth in sheer numbers has come a surprising acceptance of working wives and mothers. Whether more women are taking jobs because attitudes have changed or attitudes have changed because more women are working is something like the chicken-or-the-egg controversy. But there is much less feeling that a woman is taking away a man's job, undermining her husband's status or damaging her children's personalities if she chooses to exchange her broom for a steno pad, a salesbook or a classroom.

## The Pros and Cons

These days the major question is, Does it really pay a wife to work? This is particularly pertinent if she has young children who will require some care while she is away. Consider the fairly typical case of Nancy Farrell, who decided to return to the business world as a secretary when the younger of her two children became of school age. From her gross salary of $95 a week, her employer deducted about $23 a week for taxes, Social Security and group life and health insurance. From the remaining $72, she found she was paying out $33 for her extra expenses, including transportation, lunches, additional clothes, a baby-sitter for the children after school, trips to the hairdresser, more convenience foods and dinners out and more household help. This left her with a profit of about $39 weekly, or an hourly wage—figuring a 35-hour week—of just a fraction more than $1—scarcely a staggering rate of pay.

Is it worth it? That depends on your viewpoint. A woman who is planning to work full time only long enough to pay for something special, such as new furniture for the living room, might be better off if she worked part time. She would have lower expenses for household help and child care, less need to use convenience foods or eat out and, if she worked in a more modest suburban office or store, fewer demands on her wardrobe. On the other hand, if she plans to continue working full time the situation is different.

For one thing, her household expenses will remain relatively stable for several years, while her prospects of earning more money will increase as she either brushes up on old skills or acquires new ones. As time goes by, her children will require less outside care and may even take over some of the household chores that now have to be paid for.

There are several other aspects of the working wife situation worth pointing out. One has to do with the ability of a one-paycheck family to keep up with a two-paycheck society. As those Department of Labor figures show, more wives than ever are back in the commercial arena trying to supplement the family income, prodded on by others who pay for otherwise impossible-to-obtain luxuries and conveniences. (Entire industries are now based on the two-paycheck system; among them are convenience foods, automatic dishwashers and "instant" everything.) Today the husband who puts his foot down and says, "I'm simply not going to allow my wife to leave home to work; she should be minding the house and children as women always have done," needs to be an exceptionally good provider and manager. Otherwise his family's standard of living will differ noticeably from those of his friends and business associates.

There is another important point to bear in mind. Considering all the automation and technological change, no man's job is completely secure. A young man just emerging from college must face the fact that he may have to change not only his job but his actual line of work several times before he retires. And during that span of time, the odds are heavy that he'll be almost without income more than once. Isn't it wise to have another source of income, just in case?

Consider, too, the matter of life insurance protection. The husband who insists his wife remain at home assumes an enormous security burden. What if something happens to him? Just thinking about that possibility often leads him to buy more insurance than he can comfortably afford. He may subscribe to the full, and expensive, treatment: guaranteed monthly income, disability insurance, double indemnity, options to buy additional protection without a medical examination and huge face-value coverage. So he channels a great deal of his salary into the expense of hazard insurance, rather than into estate building or better living.

But the husband with a wife already working doesn't panic so easily. He knows his wife definitely has some earning power. If something happens to him, there will be shock and emotional upheaval, but the economic disruption will be manageable. Instead of having to spend so much guarding against the unthinkable, a husband with a wage-earning wife can begin to build a security estate.

A near-perfect situation could result if the wife were able to earn extra money without leaving home. But work like this is hard to find, and unreliable at best. Now and then such opportunities present themselves, but they are rare indeed. Enjoy the best of both worlds if you can, but you may not have a chance.

Here's another point that is important to a family's health and security. A working wife is usually a better answer to supplementing the family income than is the practice of moonlighting, where the husband has two jobs. While it is true that a working wife is in effect holding down two jobs, the moonlighting husband, then, has to work at three. There is not enough left of a man who is holding down two paying positions to act as head of the household when he arrives home for a brief rest.

## Extra Costs to Consider

If you are debating whether or not to become a two-income family, here are the things you will want to keep in mind. How will the two-salary income affect your tax bracket? The new tax bracket may mean a considerable outlay of cash when the tax deadline comes around each April. Both of you might want to check your deductions and find out if they will cover the federal taxes on a joint return. If they do not, it is often possible to have one employer (usually the wife's) take off an extra deduction so there won't be a big bite just about the time when the family car needs tuning up after a long difficult winter or the children have outgrown all of last year's lighter-weight clothes.

In figuring the extra costs of a wife's working, remember, in addition to the federal taxes, there are often state and sometimes city taxes, as well as deductions for Social Security, probably for group health insurance and perhaps for union or employe club dues.

If you are planning to hire someone to help look after your children or your house, there are expenses besides her salary that must be considered. You will probably be expected to pay for carfare and you will have to provide some extra food for breakfasts or lunches. You may have to supply uniforms or, at the very least, aprons. And as an employer you are expected to pay half of the Social Security tax (the 1970 rate is 9.6 percent for anyone who works for you and earns more than $50 during a three-month period). There may be some additions to your phone bill (it pays to set ground rules on these from the very beginning when hiring someone) and there may be more breakage or less careful use of food than if you were home. All of these items are the "overhead" of the working wife, and they have to be allowed for in figuring net "profit" on the job.

Even if the whole family pitches in and helps, a working mother has extra burdens, and if she attempts to keep up both jobs she may end up paying out her whole salary in extra doctor bills. Some of the work she formerly did when she was home can easily be farmed out, including laundry, dry-cleaning at self-operated dry-cleaning centers, rug shampooing and perhaps some gardening. These extras also have to be deducted.

Adding up all these items over the period of a year will give you an idea of your true costs for that extra income. Against these costs, however, you'll want to chalk up some benefits that don't appear in the paycheck, such as added health insurance, life insurance that many companies offer to wives (though often not on as generous terms as that offered to husbands), deposits in the wife's Social Security account and company contributions to profit-sharing and pension plans. These, plus the less tangible but nevertheless real contributions to what might be called the wife's "skills and experience bank," must also be considered in estimating the value of a working wife's addition to the family income.

## Deciding Where the Money Will Go

Regardless of the amount there is always the question, Where will the money go? This, of course, depends on where you are in the marriage merry-go-round at the moment. (Marriage counselors agree, however, that no matter what your plans are for the extra income you should start from the premise that the two paychecks should be joined in financial matrimony just as *you* are. One partner holding out "my" money is inviting trouble.)

If you are in the just-the-two-of-us stage but planning to make it three, four or more someday, the wife's income should be looked on as "diaper pin" money, and not counted on in the family's budget since it is going to stop. If you commit yourself to long-range, sizable installment payments that are dependent on the wife's income, you are committing yourself to economic hardship when a baby comes along, which is not a very relaxed way to start parenthood. So in this newlywed period it's a good idea to plan your basic budget around one income only, and set aside the wife's earnings for the specials— expensive pieces of furniture, appliances and, ultimately, the baby.

When the children are very young, whether or not a wife chooses to work is a very complicated and personal decision. The psychological factors involved carry as much, if not more, weight than the economic ones, since most women will find that their take-home pay is not much more than their pay-out pay. The exception is the highly skilled or professional woman whose earnings more than cover her extra household and child care expenses. Income tax deductions for child care are not allowed for a joint gross income of more than $6600 per year for one dependent or $6900 per year for two or more dependents, unless the husband is incapacitated, so the deductions are of little help to any middle-income family.

It is during these years that wives may want to "invest" in their future, by taking courses that will prepare them for a career when their children are older, or by doing volunteer work that can someday be useful as experience for paid employment.

It is when the youngest child buys his first schoolbag and sets off for his school career that most women decide that they are going to join the nine-to-five club. So it's at this point the decision is made as to whether or not the money is really going to make a difference in the family's standard of living. And the difference is going to be based on how the money is handled from the very beginning.

The first step is to go over all the possible expenses listed before, so that you have a realistic appraisal of how much cash will actually land in the bank account. On the basis of this *net amount* decide how and where the money is to be allocated. If it is for a specific purpose, such as a fund for the children's college education, see that it goes into a bank account earmarked for the purpose, that very month.

If the money is for a more immediate purpose, such as paying off the dentist's bill for Billy's braces or buying new dining room furniture, use the money as soon as you get it to make the payment to Dr. Smith or the furniture store. Then, if there is any left over and you want to indulge in golf clubs or a weekend away, you can go ahead, feeling secure because you have taken care of your obligations.

## The Importance of Being Realistic

What it comes down to is what all family finances come down to, namely, the importance of being realistic, setting goals, planning carefully and then sticking to your plan. Being realistic means knowing how much the second paycheck will really add to the family coffers. It means recognizing that some of the family's living and spending patterns must change to accommodate the extra burden placed on the lady of the house. (If the children learn to be more helpful and self-reliant, consider it an extra bonus.) Being realistic means planning specific uses for the money so that it isn't carelessly leaked through the budget with very little to show for the extra effort. Above all, it means not taking on any long-term obligations that can be met only with the extra income, as long as family responsibilities may cause mother to stop working.

To look at the bright side, however, the extra income can contribute substantially not only to a family's standard of living but also to its peace of mind. It is very reassuring to know that most bills are paid, that there is some money put aside for future college expenses, that the man in the family has some leeway in refusing bad working conditions or accepting new jobs that may not, for instance, offer more immediate income but do offer chances for future advancement. When mother helps bring home the bacon she's also helping to bring home a nice fat slice of family security.

CHAPTER 6

## Keeping Those Vital Family Records

*A lost sales contract or canceled check can cost you plenty. Here are valuable tips on what records to keep and where to keep them*

What records should be kept? For how long? Where? If you're like most families you don't know the answers. You're afraid to throw out something that you might need in the future, and so you accumulate piles of unnecessary receipts, old bills and outdated statements along with the papers you do need. Then comes that frustrating day when you have to find Jimmy's birth certificate in a hurry—and you spend hours going through your own "paper work explosion," looking for the certificate which is, inevitably, on the bottom of the pile. When this happens you promise yourself that, this time, you're really going to get organized.

Getting organized is not as difficult as you might think. It takes some planning, the knowledge of what you have to keep and what you can safely discard and a certain amount of "maintenance" along the way. Moreover, though it's a one-time job, it can serve a dual purpose—while keeping your records you can keep a running check on where the family income is going, and use it as the basis for planning a realistic budget.

## The Family Checkbook

One of your most valuable record-keeping tools is the family checkbook; the canceled checks are both proof of payment and a record in themselves. In addition, when you write a check you can add some specifics to your stub entry that will prove useful later on. For instance, you might note for what purpose the money was used: for example, "winter coat for Jane," "sheets and towels," "kitchen cannisters." If you don't want to be that explicit, just add a note: "clothes" or "household." At the end of the year, by flipping through the checkbook and adding the totals under such categories as clothing, household items, groceries, you can get a general idea of where your income has gone. If your entries have been detailed, and you have kept a record of clothing expenditures for each member of the family, you are in good shape for estimating next year's clothes allowances. If you have itemized expenditures for gifts you can discover one of the "leaks" in your budget.

You can keep track of your magazine subscriptions in a similar way. When you pay the bill, write on the stub: "Expires June 1972," for example. Then, should the magazine bill you early, you have a record to refer to. The same method works for membership fees in organizations, pledges to charitable organizations, payments on installment loans—in short, for any expenditure that can be recorded for future reference. If the checkbook you are using doesn't allow room for detailed entries, ask your bank for a bigger one. Most banks have a variety of sizes and are happy to supply them, either at no cost or for a nominal charge.

Since you will have other records besides canceled checks and used checkbooks, you also need some kind of simple filing system in which to keep various receipts. Some families like file folders, properly labeled and kept in one desk drawer, or a set of small manila envelopes. Paper portfolios, available at variety and stationery stores, are inexpensive, sturdy and expansible. They can be placed upright on a shelf, out of the reach of children, if need be.

Since most expenses are paid by check, used checkbooks should be retired to a safe place for about a year, as a ready reference source. If each book is identified on the outside by month and year, with the numbers of the checks it covers, the old books are easier to use. And it's also easier to look up a payment record in a checkbook than to have to go thumbing through a pile of loose checks. Most of the canceled checks can be discarded after about six months. If there is a question about one of them at some later date your bank can supply you with a microfilm copy.

## Keeping Tax Records

Keeping accurate income tax records is very important. As a general guide the Treasury Department says, "All receipts, canceled checks and other evidence to prove amounts claimed as deductions must be retained as part of your records. Records that support an item of income or a deduction appearing on a return must be kept until the statute of limitations for the return expires. Usually this is three years from the date the return was due or filed, or two years from the date the tax was paid, whichever occurs later." In other words, if you claim a deduction for a charitable donation and the Internal Revenue Service calls some months after you've filed your return and questions the deduction, you should be able to show canceled checks or receipts. If you cannot, even though your conscience is clear, the IRS will question and undoubtedly triumph over your claim to virtue.

Despite the three-year statute of limitations, there are some property and stock records that you should keep longer. If you sell your house, buy another within a year and make a profit on the house that you sold, you can defer the capital gains tax on that profit until you sell the new house. But to prove this you need to keep complete records on *both* houses for three years after the due date of the tax return for the year in which you sell the new, or second, house. And "complete" means the original purchase price of each house, legal fees, title insurance and any other charges incurred. It also means a record of the date that each house was first acquired and then sold, the selling prices, costs of making the sales and records of any major improvements or additions you have made.

You should also keep complete records of any stocks you buy until three years after the due date for the tax return for the year in which you *sell* the stock. "Complete" in this case means purchase price, date of purchase, commissions, number of shares, records of any stock splits, swaps and dividends. And when you sell one company's stock, if you have bought the shares in more than one batch, know which lot you are selling and be sure that your broker makes a note of this on the statement of sale. If not, the IRS will assume that you sold the first batch. If it was bought at a lower price than the later one, which was the one you actually sold, you will be charged for income that you didn't receive.

Tax records of assets such as property deeds and stocks are not the only records that a family needs. Proof of ownership of all assets —car, insurance policies, bank accounts—is very important for the time when the asset may be sold or passed on through inheritance.

## Your Safe-Deposit Box—When to Use It

Where should these records be kept? Which ones are valuable? How long should they be kept, and who should have access to them? (For a useful record-keeping form, see pages 78–80.)

Most of us would answer the first question by saying a "safe-deposit box," the traditional storage place of all family papers. But it's not always the best place. Take life insurance policies, for example. Most people think they are a *must* for a safe-deposit box. But this is not necessarily true. According to Blake T. Newton, Jr., president of the Institute of Life Insurance, "Policies are of no use to a thief and can be replaced without cost if stolen, lost or destroyed. They can be kept in any reasonably secure place in the home. . . .

"In fact," he adds, "a safe-deposit box presents certain difficulties. If the husband dies the wife would probably have to get permission from the tax authorities to open the box. This could seriously delay payment of the insurance. In general we recommend that a record of the policies be kept in a different location from the policies themselves, to facilitate replacement, if necessary." (See page 457, in

Chapter 47, for a sample form you can use for your insurance records.)

The same rule applies to fire, accident and theft policies—duplicates of them are also free. The simple rule is this: If it's going to cost you money, time or trouble to replace a document, keep it in the box. This would include marriage, adoption and divorce papers, change-of-name legalization and naturalization papers and any other court- or government-recorded document. You should also keep installment sales contracts in your safe-deposit box, so that you have proof of just what the terms were. In some 40 states in which auto titles and registration cards are issued separately, keep the titles in the vault; they're vital for transferring ownership.

What about wills? The original should be kept in the safe of the lawyer who drew it up for you, a carbon copy in your vault and another at home. Leaving the original will in the vault can mean needless complications and delay.

Stock and bond certificates are a special case. They are expensive to replace. Generally, you have to post a bond, costing about 4 percent of the stock's or bond's market value, and wait several months for the replacement. You don't have to post a bond on U.S. Savings Bonds, but you do have to wait six months before they can be replaced. Many people prefer to leave their stock and bond certificates in the safekeeping of their brokers. The dividends and annual statements come to them just the same, and they don't have to worry about the physical safety of the papers. If they are burned or stolen the firm will replace them. Note, however, that some brokers charge for the safekeeping service.

You'll also want to keep a record of the inoculations you and your children have had, so that you know when booster shots are needed. These shots, too, should be recorded but can be stored at home.

At $6 to $8 a year for a small box, the safe-deposit box is the best security bargain available today, and should be the foundation of a family's safekeeping plan. But it cannot, and should not, hold everything—which means that most of your papers and records have to be kept at home. Where? And for how long?

The "Family Record Guide" on the next two pages will tell you at a glance the 12 most important kinds of documents to keep, which are the most difficult to replace and where you should keep them.

# FAMILY RECORD GUIDE

| DOCUMENTS | IMPORTANCE | WHERE TO KEEP |
|---|---|---|
| Auto titles | Issued in 40 states and District of Columbia as evidence of ownership. Essential for transfer to new owner when car is sold. | Safe-deposit box. |
| Auto bills of sale | Submitted to state on new car to obtain title or to register. May be required as evidence of car ownership should you move from a nontitle to a title state. | Safe-deposit box. |
| Notes and debts | Promissory notes, installment sales contracts, etc., serve as evidence of what you owe or what people owe you. Checks and receipts of payments are important for interest deductions on tax returns and to indicate fulfillment of contract terms. | Notes, contracts in safe-deposit box; others in home file. |
| Real estate ownership | Usually a deed fulfills its legal function when recorded with the proper county office, but it is worthwhile retaining for description of property. | Home file. |
| | In some areas real estate transfers involve summation of legal actions affecting property. Difficult to prepare in many instances and expensive. | Safe-deposit box. |
| Insurance policies | Easily replaced by insurance company if lost. | Policies in home file; list of policy numbers, amounts, companies, in safe-deposit box. |
| Marriage and birth records | May take time and small fee to replace by writing to county or state bureau of vital statistics. If original birth record is lost from state or county files, substitutes such as U.S. Bureau of Census record, baptismal certificate or affidavit from doctor or hospital must be used. | Safe-deposit box. |
| Military discharge | Cannot be replaced, but services will issue "certificate in lieu of discharge" at no cost. | Safe-deposit box. |
| School records | Transcripts of courses and grades available from schools at modest fee. | Home file. |

| DOCUMENTS | IMPORTANCE | WHERE TO KEEP |
| --- | --- | --- |
| Social Security card | Social Security Administration provides replacements free and furnishes temporary certificates when employer insists employe have card before starting work. | Home file. |
| Stocks and bonds | Company securities and bonds are difficult and expensive to replace. | Safe-deposit box or with your broker; list in home file. |
| | Savings Bonds are replaced by government at no cost, but it normally takes six months to get the new ones. | Safe-deposit box, but can be held in home file if you put in safe-deposit box a list of bonds with year of issue, name and address of owner, serial number and letter. |
| Tax records | Federal government can question tax return within three years of filing, and six years if you omit from gross income an amount exceeding 25% of the total. Keep checks, receipts, supporting evidence, copy of tax withholding statement for at least three years. Keep copies of returns. | Home file. |
| | Home improvement records should be handled differently. Tax on profit made on sale of a house is calculated on difference between price received and cost plus sums spent to improve property. Thus, these sums act to reduce taxable profit. Retain receipts, bills of sale, checks, etc. evidencing money spent for three years after you've reported sale of the house in your tax return. | Safe-deposit box. |
| Wills | Vital. Make several copies. | Original with lawyer or corporate executor; copy in safe-deposit box. If executor is individual, give him copy, put another copy in home file and store original in lawyer's vault, not in your safe-deposit box. |

In considering a home file, the protection it offers against fire and theft is of primary importance. An executive of the Safe Manufacturers National Association doesn't offer much comfort about the possibility of obtaining real protection against burglary, unless you are ready to invest about $1000 in the type of safe that can withstand a competent safecracker. However, the important protection for home valuables and papers, the experts believe, should be against fire—67 American homes are destroyed or damaged by fire every hour!

Some of the most telling lessons about which parts of the home are most fire-resistant came from "Operation Teapot," which in 1955 tested the effects of nuclear bomb explosions in Nevada on various buildings and on records and storage equipment. The president of the National Records Management Council (Naremco), a nonprofit research and advisory service whose prime purpose is to assist industry, government and individuals in improving management of paper work, participated in the tests.

"We learned that the two most vulnerable parts of the average home are the attic and the kitchen—and many valuable records are kept in just those places," he reported. "Next most dangerous is the room with the most windows, usually the living room, which often has the family desk, a traditional repository of important papers. In the average home the safest place against fire is that part of the basement farthest from the oil burner or furnace. In apartments or in homes without basements the safest place is a closet in or near a bathroom: There are fewer flammables there, the wall tiles provide extra protection and there are several water outlets."

In what should you keep home records?

"Most of us keep these records in a 'little tin box' or a thin steel file," the representative of the Safe Manufacturers National Association states. "They are dangerous receptacles in case of fire. Paper burns at 350 degrees. In seven minutes every paper in such a box would be charred beyond use. Worse, many of these family boxes are kept in a bedroom dresser drawer, which simply acts as a furnace in a fire. Ordinary steel files are no better. Papers will last perhaps ten minutes in them during a real fire."

In seeking effective protection against fire some people ask themselves: What is the most insulated spot in the house? As a result, in a surprising number of homes valuable papers are kept in a plastic envelope in the back of the refrigerator. There is a lot of insulation in a refrigerator, but most boxes cannot withstand high temperatures —and the average fire reaches 1000 degrees in five minutes.

Seeking other solutions, many people buy small asbestos-lined steel boxes which sell for $8 to $12. "We've tested hundreds of these," a safe manufacturer says. "Not one of them will protect the contents for more than ten minutes."

The only portable safes and chests that the Safe Manufacturers National Association recommends for the average home are insulated steel boxes that will provide one hour's protection against fire for your papers. They sell for $70 to $80 and have a capacity of about one cubic foot, generally more than sufficient. These insulated boxes are not waterproof, and water from fire hoses could render documents illegible. So oiled silk or polyethylene pouches are also advisable for the best home protection.

## Throwing Away Selectively

Which papers can you do without?

Says Naremco's president, "The trouble with most of us is that, when in doubt, we keep everything. In millions of homes you find canceled checks from 1951 and payroll check stubs or itemized tax deductions going back even further. Nearly all of them are totally unnecessary."

Every state has a time limit within which the courts will entertain a suit. In 21 states, shopkeepers have six years to sue you for an unpaid bill. Many others have three years, and Texas is the tidiest, with a two-year limit.

Naremco's president advises families to destroy all canceled checks of a small or routine amount and save only those involving large purchases or tax-deductible items (to justify income tax deductions).

Payroll check stubs are also kept without reason, he believes. The yearly withholding statement has all the necessary information on it. Routine bills, such as utility and telephone bills, are also collected pointlessly: The latest one lists the balance owed, thus giving you proof of previous payments.

Worthy of safekeeping in the home storage box are the following: savings bankbooks; all insurance policies; important canceled checks; educational records; equipment and appliance records; appraisals of furs and jewelry pieces; medical immunization records; mortgage amortization records; copies of tax returns and withholding tax forms; and a list of all credit cards and numbers. Both the safe-deposit box and the home record box should have a duplicate list of what papers are to be found in each.

## Your Personal Affairs

In addition to this list of records and documents, you should prepare a summary of pertinent information about all your personal affairs and leave copies in the home record box, in your safe-deposit box, with your wife, your lawyer and the executor of your will. This can prove invaluable in an emergency. A suggested form for such a list appears below:

*Basic information:*

Location of your will...................................................

Date of your will and lawyer's name....................................

.......................................................................

Executor's name and address............................................

.......................................................................

.......................................................................

Your Social Security number............................................

Wife's Social Security number..........................................

Military service number................................................

Veterans Administration number.........................................

List employers, dates and positions held...............................

.......................................................................

.......................................................................

.......................................................................

List on insurance form your insurance policies by type, and list here where they are located..........................................................

.......................................................................

.......................................................................

Name of your insurance adviser................................................

.............................................................................

Are there any unpaid loans against these policies?........................

.............................................................................

Location of your securities.................................................

.............................................................................

.............................................................................

Your investment adviser or broker..........................................

.............................................................................

Do you have hospitalization insurance?............ Surgical?............

Medical?....................................................................

Contract numbers...........................................................

Where are your copies of income tax returns? (These may be needed for

settling your estate.).......................................................

## Bank accounts:

Checking (bank name, branch, location and account number)............

.............................................................................

.............................................................................

Savings (bank name, branch, location and book number)................

.............................................................................

.............................................................................

## Safe-deposit box:

Bank....................... Number........................

If a joint box, with whom?..................................................

Keys are kept where?.......................................................

## Certificates:

Location of birth certificates for each member of the family..............

.............................................................................

.............................................................................

Citizenship papers.........................................................

Marriage certificate........................................................

Military discharge papers...................................................

Other......................................................................

.............................................................................

*Business connections:*

Do you have partnership agreements?...............................

........................................................................

Employment contract?...............................................

........................................................................

Pension or profit-sharing agreements?............................

Union papers?........................................................

Explain and give location of these.................................

........................................................................

*Real estate:*

Residence located at.................................................

........................................................................

Ownership in joint names, or yours alone?.......................

If mortgaged, who is mortgagor?...................................

........................................................................

The following documents should be located in one place: deed, insurance policies, title insurance, closing statement, title abstract, surveys and maps, tax receipts, mortgage, improvement costs. Where are they? (Preferably in your safe-deposit box.)...........................................

Other real estate......................................................

........................................................................

Give same information as above...................................

........................................................................

........................................................................

Cemetery plot location..............................................

Deed location.........................................................

*Other personal property:*

Automobile (bills of sale, engine numbers, locations)..................

........................................................................

........................................................................

Boat (bill of sale, name, number, location)...........................

........................................................................

*Other records:*

Loans...................................................................

Other debts............................................................

Other contracts.......................................................

Date this form was completed.......................................

80

## WHAT RECORDS TO CHANGE AT MARRIAGE

When a bride changes her name at marriage, a number of records should be corrected to conform to her married name. Many changes are not required by law, but making them will be convenient for the new couple. Some of these take several weeks and can be started in advance of the wedding; others can be made only after marriage. Many organizations to which the new name and address are to be sent have special forms available on request, or a note can be written requesting the change. The bride should:

• Send each publisher a mailing label from the magazine to which she subscribes, along with a note giving her new name and address. Follow the same procedure with record clubs, book clubs and alumnae associations. Since this will take a few weeks, it is advisable to give a change-of-address form to the local post office so that mail arriving before the change is effected will be forwarded to her at her new home.

• Make a new will—as should her husband—after the ceremony. In many states, marriage voids an existing will.

• Have the name changed on life insurance policies. Beneficiaries can also be changed at the same time. Do the same with any property and liability insurance. Changes can be made through either the insurance company or the agent who sold the policy. When you make the request for a change, be sure to give the policy numbers.

• Change hospitalization insurance (hers or her husband's) to a family plan with maternity benefits. Some plans require ten months of coverage before maternity benefits are available. If a bride has a separate policy, it may be wise to keep it in effect until benefits are available under a family policy. Check group insurance.

• Get a new Social Security card. Application forms for this usually are available through company payroll departments. The card will bear the applicant's new name but the same number she had before. The Social Security Administration advises that this change be made so that credit will include earnings both before and after marriage.

• Change payroll records. This is especially important if changing the number of exemptions.

• Fill out new bank signature cards. If opening a joint account, both husband and wife should apply.

• Close charge accounts and reopen them in her married name. If any of a husband's credit cards are to be used by both, he can arrange new ones for his wife.

• Apply for a new driver's license and change the car registration, if it has been in her single name. Check automobile club registrations. Some clubs offer reduced registration fees to married couples.

• Have school records, church and club memberships brought up to date. Change voter registration records.

## WORDS YOU
## SHOULD KNOW

**Statute of limitations.** A law that sets a definite period of time beyond which you may not be sued by an individual for recovery of damages or prosecuted by the government for certain offenses. Examples: Normally, a federal tax return may not be reviewed after three years from date of filing, unless cheating is suspected. If you sell a property, you may not be sued for misrepresenting its condition after a time limit that varies with each state. Both crimes and civil wrongs are governed by statutes of limitations in various states.

**Capital gains tax.** A tax levied on the profit you make from the sale or exchange of some kind of property. (See Chapter 56, "The ABCs of Stocks and Bonds," page 525.)

**Stock split.** The exchange, by a corporation, of its shares for a greater number, without increase in nominal value. Example: You own 100 shares of XYZ Corporation common stock, valued at $5 each by the company. These shares are recalled and you are issued 200 shares of a new stock valued by the company at $2.50 each. The stock has been split in half but your holdings have the same total face value as before.

**Unearned income.** Money you get from investments instead of from work at your job. Examples: rent from a building you own; interest paid on savings accounts or bonds; dividends declared on stocks or insurance policies.

**Swap.** An exchange of one capital asset for another, usually without money changing hands. Example: You trade a $1000 industrial bond for 100 shares of XYZ Corporation common stock.

**Property deed.** Written certification proving a legal right to ownership of a property, signed by the seller and delivered to the buyer, explaining exactly what property has been transferred. In most states this deed must be recorded with a local public official as proof of ownership of real estate, but a specific title must be given by the seller to the buyer of such articles as automobiles, stating all the facts of the sale which entitle the new owner to exclusive possession.

**Bill of sale.** The legal written evidence of transfer of ownership of any property. Examples: a department store sales slip; a list of purchased merchandise marked "Paid" by an auctioneer or antique dealer, which transfers ownership from seller to buyer.

**Promissory note.** A written promise to pay at some exact date or series of dates, certain sums of money to a specified person or someone named by him. Examples: a simple IOU, a contract with a bank or loan company on a personal loan or even a pawn ticket.

CHAPTER 7

## Six Basic Rules
## for Staying Solvent

*A handful of*
*simple suggestions*
*that can help*
*end your*
*money worries*

Today you may have the highest income you've ever earned. Yet, if you're like millions of others, never before have you fretted so much about making your income match your outgo, nor so eagerly sought financial peace of mind.

You won't attain these goals by trying to live according to a rigid plan, nor by trying to fit yourself into a ready-to-wear budget worked out for the "average family." You will be on your way to financing your bread and your dreams only when you work out your own plan, designed to make your money buy things you want and need.

From the studies of experts on money management, a half-dozen basic guides emerge. They can help anyone, whether he is earning $7000 a year or $27,000:

1. Make your program a family project. Call the family together and discuss what you're trying to do. Let the children become part of the team.

This really is the only way to make any program work, for if each member knows the family's aim, each will try to reach it. Early in one couple's married life they sat down to discover why they were so persistently close to zero in their joint bank account: Each of them, they found, was keeping a separate, "secret" budget, each buying and paying for things without the knowledge of the other. Right then they made their money management a family project—one of their soundest decisions.

2. Whatever records you keep, keep them simple. Never try to keep detailed records of where every penny goes—these only consume time and produce pain.

Buy an inexpensive notebook. On one page jot down your monthly income; if you don't have an income 12 months a year, spread what you have into 12 "spending periods." On a second page jot down what you must put aside for major, unavoidable expenses—rent, taxes, debts, savings—and prorate them on a monthly basis. On a third page put down what you have left after you have subtracted these unavoidable expenses from your gross income; this is the total you have with which to meet day-to-day expenses. On a fourth page juggle your day-to-day expenses until you come out better than even and are satisfied that you're getting the maximum benefit and comfort from what you're spending.

If you have no past records, collect what receipts you can find and call on the family to supply what figures they can remember. Work along with trial records first and soon you'll adjust them so they fit your life.

3. Deduct the money for your savings as an "unavoidable expense" *before* you start spending for the pleasant but unessential things of life. That's the secret of solvency and saving.

You should have a rainy-day fund to take care of the unexpected bills that come up in every family's life. This fund should hold two months' income at least—six months' if you can manage it. If it doesn't, agree in your family conference on how much can be put aside each month until your nest egg is assured.

4. Provide personal allowances for each member of the family, including the children. Then let each one decide what he wants to do with the amount allotted.

No one should have to account for his allowance. If a husband wants to blow the entire sum on one evening with the boys, that's his affair. If a wife wants to spend it on what appears nonsense to everybody but her, it's her business. Children learn to handle money surprisingly fast when they are given the chance.

5. Don't be too arbitrary about your figures or set limits that are impossible to meet.

You cannot anticipate an illness or accident and its cost. If you set limits that are too tough for your family, your search for financial peace of mind will end in discouragement. If, after you've tried a plan for a few months, you find your limits are too stiff—change them. It's your budget and it's up to you to make it fit.

6. Finally, if after all your efforts you still cannot make your income match your outgo, cut your spending or raise your income.

That's the most fundamental rule of all. For if you cannot make ends meet even after the most careful budgeting, you are living beyond your means and you might as well face it. But there are still ways out.

You may think it impossible to increase your income now, yet many resourceful people have found ways of making their time produce more. One young mother takes care of small children along with her own when their mothers are at work or shopping. A man whose hobby is puttering in the workshop brings in respectable extra amounts by repairing furniture.

You may suppose it is impossible to cut your spending; but when you think it over, changes sweeping enough to reduce expenses all along the line may seem not only possible but desirable. You would not be lowering your fundamental standards, but maintaining your integrity and independence.

There they are—six guides that may seem deceptively simple but actually are basic for financial peace of mind. Apply them and you'll discover how much they help you live on what you make.

▭▭▭▭▭▭

## TRICKS TO HELP YOU SAVE

"I couldn't save a dollar bill even if it were tattooed to my hide." "The more I earn, the more I spend, so when the end of the month rolls around, I'm right where I was the month before. What can I do?" How often have you said things like this?

The solution is obvious: Spend less than you earn. But the fact that it's obvious doesn't mean it's easy.

Fortunately, the human animal is a creature of boundless ingenuity. People who have a tough time saving money have devised dozens of tricks and gimmicks to prod themselves into thrift. A few of the most popular stratagems are listed below. Some are quick and easy, others more elaborate and time-consuming. Among them perhaps you'll find one that can help you.

*The Golden Goal.* This system is patterned after the well-known Christmas savings account. It requires some willpower. Set up a reasonable but very specific savings goal for the year. At the beginning of each pay period deposit a proportionate amount of the total into a savings account. Treat this savings just as you would any other important bill.

*Cash on the Barrelhead.* In this era of credit cards, it's easy to get carried away and forget that real money is still required sooner or later. If you are a victim of the credit card syndrome, your best bet is to burn the cards and pay cash for the things you buy. This will cut down on impulse spending and will also save you the interest that

▭▭▭▭▭▭

most stores charge on so-called revolving and installment accounts.

*The Shrunken Wallet.* This is an adjunct to the "cash payment only" plan and is designed particularly for impulse buyers. It consists of planning ahead and carrying only as much money as you'll reasonably need during any given day. After a few tries, you may find this a challenge well worth rising to meet. And if you do see something enticing, you can plan to buy it the following day—if by then you still feel you need it.

*Let George Do It.* If you can't save money yourself, maybe someone else can do it for you. In this case "George" can be any one of a number of people or institutions: your wife, if she's good at saving; your boss, if he offers payroll savings or U.S. Savings Bond purchase plans; a mutual fund with a periodic-purchase plan that allows you to make small, regular purchases; a life insurance company, which will demand payment of premiums; or even the U.S. Treasury, which will refund anything you've had over-withheld on your income tax.

This system takes less willpower because either the savings are deducted automatically before you have a chance to squander them or you are penalized for failure to live up to the terms of a contract.

*Marked Money.* This is one of the oldest and simplest money-saving methods known to man. All you have to do is decide ahead of time that you won't spend any coins of a particular denomination. At the end of each day,

put all such coins into a piggy bank or other container where they can't be got at easily. Even the nickels and dimes can add up surprisingly fast. And if you feel flush right after payday and wish to sweeten the pot with a bill or two, so much the better.

A variation of the marked money method that brings faster results is to put all the coins you don't absolutely need into the bank at the end of each day.

*The Windfall Approach.* Has the cleaning lady quit? Are you due for a raise? Have you just made the last payment on the car? Have you stopped smoking?

If so, look upon these events as a golden opportunity to save. Put the raise in the bank. Keep up the auto payments—only from now on put each month's payment into your savings account. The same goes for any other windfalls that may come along. Don't let them disappear into routine living expenses without a fight.

*Automatic Savings.* In this new twist to the "Let George Do It" approach, you simply authorize your bank to take a certain amount from your checking account each month and transfer it to a savings account. But don't forget to enter each withdrawal in your checkbook on the agreed date!

As you see, there are no magic tricks to this business of saving. What it takes, in most cases, is a desire to save and the ingenuity to come up with the method that'll get you into the habit of doing what may not come naturally.

# 2
# A ROOF OVER YOUR HEAD

*The house you live in is your biggest investment. Here's how you can cut costs whether you buy, build or rent*

## CHAPTER 8

## Choosing the House That's Right for You

*You should ask these questions to find a home that suits your family's special needs*

One of life's most exciting adventures is choosing a home. It is both a rewarding and a perilous adventure, since the decision you make fundamentally affects your life—both your finances and your whole way of living. The decision is crucial financially, because whatever you spend for your home in rent, mortgage and taxes is more or less *fixed,* and the higher these costs, the less you will have to spend on everything else, from education to clothing. Remember, you really won't be happy living in a home you can't afford. And where you live can also mean the difference between happiness and misery.

When you look for your first home, your job is apt to determine where you live. If you work in the city you can probably choose between an apartment in town and, if you are willing to commute, the suburbs or country nearby. Newlyweds often have not amassed sufficient capital to meet the down payment that is required to buy a home, and they may be forced to rent. There are many possible choices you and your spouse should discuss, and some general rules it would be wise to apply, to avoid the kind of disaster that befell Bill and Deborah Thaxter.

The Thaxters are an example of a well-intentioned, idealistic young couple who acted too impulsively. They were fortunate in having a small inheritance, which they both wanted to invest in a house of their own in the country. They fell in love with an old farmhouse, located 55 miles away from Bill's job in the city. Deborah's inheritance just covered the down payment, and the mortgage payments would take a little over one third of Bill's salary. The taxes, at least, were relatively low, since their farm was definitely not a part of a thriving community.

A few weeks after they moved in, the oil burner quit with a mournful wheeze. The repairman told them he had been working on the contraption for 20 years and this time it couldn't be fixed because it was no longer possible to get parts. After a new oil burner had been installed on a monthly payment plan, with the added expense of bringing the outmoded wiring system up to date, the plumbing gave out. The plumber sighed and told the Thaxters the pump never had been much good and the previous owner was a man who economized by using secondhand appliances whenever possible.

By this time, Deborah, who was pregnant, was thoroughly fed up and lonely, having no one to talk to during the day except the cat. She longed for her friends and for the ready conveniences of a city apartment. Bill, disconcerted at having a money-eating monster on his hands, was no longer willing to endure the two-hour commuting. Selling and moving seemed the only answer. But the Thaxters found their property was too isolated for most prospective buyers and almost out of the question for couples with children, since the local school had a poor reputation. Finally, they sold the place at a loss.

The Thaxters' experience is more extreme than most people's, but it could have been avoided if they had borne in mind that usually it is economically unwise to spend more than one quarter of your income on rent or mortgage payments, and that it is advisable to call in an expert to check such features as electricity, plumbing and heating before buying a house. (See Chapter 11, "When You Buy a House," page 117, for specific details.)

## Basic Decisions to Make

Before you begin to look for a new home you should make a few basic decisions. For instance:

Given the choice, would you prefer to live in the city or the country? It's easier to decide first on a specific area where you would like to live and then to look for a home within those confines.

Are you going to rent or buy—a house, an apartment, a condominium? If you have not had any previous experience with the neighborhood, particularly if you choose a suburb or town, it is a good idea to consider renting before buying, to try out the location and your neighbors.

If you are contemplating moving to a suburb, is the community you are thinking about appealing from an economic, educational and cultural point of view? Do you have something in common with the other inhabitants?

Will you be close enough to, or far enough away from, friends and relatives?

If you have children, is the school system a superior one?

Is the house or apartment convenient to your work, to shopping centers, to entertainment? How far are you willing to commute?

If you have decided to live where it is necessary to commute, what will be the cost of your commutation ticket? Will it be necessary to add the cost of a car to your home?

Are the taxes within your economic range?

Are the price and the cost-of-living range right? These vary greatly from community to community and tend to be higher in the city. Generally, the farther removed the community, the cheaper living is apt to be. Find out which communities you can afford.

If this is your first home, is it big enough to accommodate a child for at least a little while, or would you have to move when the first baby comes?

Does the *fixed* cost exceed one fourth of your income? Fixed cost includes rent and/or mortgage and taxes. (See Chapter 10, "How Much House Can You Afford?" page 109, for more details.)

Above and beyond fixed costs, there are other monthly expenses you should try to estimate. How much per month will electricity, gas, telephone, fuel and insurance cost?

What is the cost of any basic improvements you may want to make immediately? (Is it necessary to buy a new refrigerator or stove, put in a bathroom, move a wall, build on an addition?)

If you buy a house, what about its resale value? Are you buying in a desirable, stable neighborhood?

Have you thought seriously about what you want in your house or apartment? It's a good idea to list your minimum needs. You may find that even your minimum requirements won't be within your reach financially.

## Questions to Answer Before You Rent

There are differing financial considerations when you rent and when you buy. When you rent, find out specifically what the limitations of your lease are. Some of the questions about renting you should be able to answer include:

1. Who is responsible for payment of utilities (gas, electricity, heat)? Usually the tenant is responsible for gas and electricity, although some landlords supply these. Most apartment buildings supply heat, but a renter of a house generally pays the fuel bills.

2. To what degree is the tenant responsible for damages? He is asked to maintain the apartment or house in the condition in which he found it. He is liable for any damage he causes beyond "normal wear and tear," and can be sued by the landlord for repair or replacement. A month's rent is usually asked for security and returned to the renter at the end of his lease, provided no damage has been done to the property. Fire insurance is usually carried by the landlord, but if a fire is the result of negligence on the part of the tenant, either the landlord or the insurance company can sue the tenant for damages.

3. How often must the landlord paint or redecorate a rented house or apartment? This depends upon the provisions in the lease and is agreed upon between the landlord and the tenant. In some cities, especially where rent control laws exist, the housing board specifies that the landlord must redecorate or paint within a certain number of years. The term "redecorating" generally includes repainting the walls, ceilings and windows, but often does not include wallpapering or refinishing floors.

4. Who is responsible for upkeep of the grounds? Most often the tenant, and the lease should specify exactly what the tenant is responsible for (mowing the lawn, clipping the hedges, maintaining the garden). Sometimes the landlord will make an arrangement for these services and pay for them himself or charge the tenant.

5. Is the landlord responsible for replacing kitchen or bathroom equipment? An agreement is usually reached between the tenant and the landlord at the time the lease is signed. If, as a prospective tenant, you feel a new stove, refrigerator, sink or bathtub is needed, you should come to an agreement with your landlord before the lease is signed. When these facilities break down through no fault of the tenant, it is the responsibility of the landlord to replace or repair them. Naturally, if the tenant damages the equipment, it is his responsibility to have it fixed.

6. What structural or wiring changes is the tenant allowed to make? None, unless you have specific approval from the landlord. If

you want to put a light fixture on the wall or ceiling or install a mirror or wall unit, you are obligated to remove such objects and leave the walls in the same condition as you found them when you move.

7. What about raises in rent? Under some state and local laws, increases that result directly from an increase in service (new elevator, additional maintenance help in the building) or from increased real estate taxes are proper and can be imposed by the landlord. In most cases, however, raises in rent can be negotiated only with a new lease.

8. Is the tenant allowed to sublease? There is usually a specific clause in the lease specifying whether or not this is allowed. Generally, if it is permitted, it is subject to approval by the landlord, and the original renter is responsible for collecting the rent and liable for any property damage.

## Investigating the Surroundings

If you are looking for an apartment either to rent or buy, it's a good idea to check out the services and facilities as well as the building and the grounds.

Find out if there is additional storage space (sometimes in the basement), laundry equipment (also sometimes in the basement), parking space, trash disposal and collection, package delivery (is there someone to receive packages for you when you are not at home?), a fire escape, adequate elevator service, a repairman available at most times (if a toilet overflows or a fuse blows). What kind of service does the building provide, such as doormen, elevator men or even maid service?

Look carefully at the building to see if it appears to be well maintained, well constructed and noiseproof; has good protection from outsiders either through good locks or men on duty; has an attractive lobby and clean, well-lit halls and staircases. Notice whether the grounds are attractively landscaped and well kept.

Inside the apartment you should make sure that the room sizes and wall spaces are right for your furniture; that the decorating and fixtures appeal to you; that the windows work well and have the necessary screens, storm windows, blinds or shades; that the apartment is easy to clean and maintain; that the appliances are in good condition; that the heating is controllable; that there are sufficient outlets and sufficient closets, cabinets and space for bookshelves. Make sure your kitchen equipment is adequate—do you need a dishwasher, disposal, freezer? Do you want extras such as air conditioning or a fireplace?

Each time you move, most of the same considerations apply, but if you are making your second move because you have children and are faced with problems of space and schooling, the question of where to live becomes more complex. Because by this time in their lives most couples are surer of their tastes and ideals and because the second move is presumably a longer lasting one, the alternatives have to be considered more carefully.

Anxiety about schools and fresh air often forces many couples with young children to move to the country too precipitously. The Bradfords, proud parents of two little girls, aged two and three, did not really want to live in the suburbs but felt they must for the sake of the children. They settled on a suburb 35 miles away from the city in which they both worked, and bought a solidly built 60-year-old house that Jill admired for its generous, traditional lines. They were told that the school system in their community was good, but that a proposed new highway might radically change their zoning and, in fact, the whole neighborhood. The old house may have been a joy to look at, but Jill soon found it monstrously inconvenient to work with. Unfortunately, her combined cleaning woman and baby-sitter—a vital element in the household because Jill worked—felt the same way. Replacing her was next to impossible, since local help was extremely scarce. Jill struggled along with the aid of erratic neighborhood girls, often leaving the office early to relieve the sitter and more often than not coming home to face a workload of dirty children's clothes and dishes.

Alex Bradford was equally miserable. He worried about the costs of the structural changes the house required to make it livable, about the expense of their commutation added to the expense of the sitters. These financial burdens—plus the fact that neither of them had seen their city friends in months and that they badly missed their occasional nights at the theater—made it all seem hardly worthwhile. The suburban air really didn't seem that much fresher than the air in the city, and it probably would be better for them in the long run to send the children to a private city school while living comfortably in a rented apartment where the burdens of ownership didn't occupy every waking moment. In the end, the Bradfords sold their house at a loss because the proposed highway became a fact and their property was much less desirable.

The Goodhues, on the other hand, couldn't wait to move from their cramped city apartment to a broken-down old frame house in what was, nonetheless, a good section of a suburban area. Tom was talented at home repairs and Betty loved painting, tiling, wallpapering and the like. Between them they wrought a small miracle on the house they had bought for very little money, and loved every moment of it. They also quickly became an integral part of their community—something the Bradfords had never achieved, because to them homeownership meant a nightmare of unforeseen expenses and responsibilities.

## Advantages and Disadvantages of Homeownership

Obviously, there are both pros and cons to owning your own home. But more than 50 percent of American families do live in their own homes, and this percentage has been increasing over the past ten years. The following advantages help explain why:

*More adequate housing.* Most homeowners have better housing and living conditions than apartment dwellers have. More living space, greater privacy, recreation room (such as gardens and back-yards) and independence from landlords are among the benefits homeowners enjoy.

*Better surroundings and neighborhood.* Fewer people live on each block, creating less congestion, traffic, noise and dirt. Owning your home gives you more freedom to choose a community with the kind of neighbors and atmosphere you prefer.

*Sound investment.* Each monthly mortgage payment is a form of enforced savings; this is particularly advantageous in periods of inflation when the homeowner is repaying dollars that are declining in value while inflation increases the value of the investment they have made in their house.

*Tax benefits.* Real estate taxes and interest on mortgages are deductible; the homeowner can also deduct some uninsured casualty losses from fire, flood, hurricanes and other natural disasters. If the house is sold at a profit, tax payment on the profit can be deferred under certain circumstances.

*Status.* Homeownership is a sign of prestige and establishes the owner as a solid citizen. Regular repayment of mortgage loans ensures credit rating.

*Security.* Owning a house and land tends to make people feel secure. Homeowners take pride in the community and find satisfaction in maintaining and preserving their property.

The disadvantages of owning your own home are:

*Depletion of savings.* The down payment on a house usually involves a substantial outlay of cash, to which must be added the amount you have to spend for improvements, closing costs, legal fees and many other expenses. If you anticipate high expenses beyond these in the future, it may not be practical to buy a house.

*High running costs.* Fuel, taxes, repairs and commutation are among the recurrent expenses that do not generally occur when you are living in a rented apartment. These costs may consume money that you previously used for savings, vacations and recreation.

*Commutation.* A majority of homeowners are also commuters. Time spent, crowded conditions and the inconvenience of living by a timetable are deterrents to some.

*Chores.* Most homeowners are faced with do-it-yourself repairs, mowing the lawn, shoveling snow, raking leaves, gardening, painting and similar tasks. While some persons take pride and satisfaction in accomplishing these chores, others loathe them.

*Limitations of living in suburbia.* Some people are natural cliff dwellers and enjoy the cultural and entertainment benefits the city offers. They dislike the self-imposed limitations of a suburban community and prefer to be free to travel or change their residence when they feel like it.

## Planning for Present and Future Needs

You should approach the matter of house or apartment hunting with an awareness that your needs and those of your family will change over the years. Since families expand and shrink, the ideal house or apartment for a lifetime is difficult to obtain. Find out how easy the house you are contemplating buying would be to sell or the apartment you want to rent would be to sublease. Don't feel you have to live in one home forever. Chances are, you won't. On the other hand, remember it's not economical to outgrow your home every year or so.

You and your family should outline your space needs quite carefully. Call a family conclave and let the children have a voice in the matter. Try to consider how long you think you might want to stay in the home you are choosing. If this move is planned to last through the years when the children are grown up, will you eventually need a room where they can entertain their friends? Is there space to add such a room, or could a part of the basement be turned into a children's recreation room?

This is all part of carefully mapping out your practical needs. It's a good idea to list and categorize them. What are your needs in these general areas?

1. Housekeeping: appliances and equipment; kitchen cabinet space and counters; breakfast nook or room in kitchen for a dining table; dining room; place for children to play near enough for supervision and far enough away for privacy; space for laundry equipment.

2. Entertainment and recreation: living room and dining room big enough to entertain; space for visiting children to play; teen-age recreation room; place for outdoor entertaining and sports; space for piano, records, hi-fi set; room for workshop, hobbies and games; library or space for books.

3. Number of rooms: bedrooms; bathrooms; den, library or guest room; maid's room.

4. Storage: garage (room for one or two cars); clothes closets (remember out-of-season clothes), linen closet; tool shed (for lawn mowers, wheelbarrows, other big outdoor equipment); place for sports equipment (skis, bicycles, sleds, wagons, fishing tackle).

The age or stage of development of a community or neighborhood often influences local economic conditions. If a town is fairly new, for example, property prices are relatively low and the chances of doubling or tripling your initial investment are often good. However, there may be possible problems, particularly if schools, libraries, roads and other facilities have not been developed. As they are built, taxes will increase to pay for them. There is the additional danger that an undeveloped piece of land near your property might be used for a shopping center, gas station or factory unless there are zoning laws to prevent it. If commerce invades your immediate neighborhood, the resale value and desirability of your property will plummet.

An older community generally offers a more established way of life. Public facilities, shops, roads, restaurants, and so on, have been built. The houses have had a chance to acquire lovely lawns and other landscaping. But naturally you pay more for property in such towns, and taxes as well as other living costs may be higher. Unfortunately, deterioration and decline of property values can take place anywhere. Always try to find out as much as you can about the future of your prospective neighborhood or community.

## What Kind of Neighborhood?

There are specific neighborhood considerations it is important for you to think about. Use the following checklist to guide you:

1. Observe nearby houses and look for similarity of price, age, architecture. Watch for neatness, good landscaping, cleanliness. Be sure of zoning laws to protect your property against multifamily structures, business and commercial buildings.

2. Is there a vacant lot nearby? Even if zoning laws prevent commercial use, it could be used for a school, church or firehouse that you might not want too close to your home.

3. Be sure the general area is free of structures—such as a firehouse, factory or gravel pit—that might cause danger, odor, smoke, dust or noise. A swampy area nearby could breed mosquitos.

4. Check transportation thoroughly: cost, reliability of public transport systems, adequate parking facilities, length of time to get to work, amount of traffic if you plan to drive to work.

5. Be sure that public service and utilities provide adequate fire and police protection; sewage; garbage collection; snow removal from streets; gas, electricity and telephone facilities; water supply.

6. Find out how convenient shopping areas are to you.

7. Try to be reasonably certain that your neighbors will be comfortable to live with. They don't have to become your best friends,

but you don't want to be saddled with a nearby chronic complainer or a loudly argumentative couple.

8. Look into recreation possibilities. Are there nearby facilities for golf, tennis, swimming? Are playgrounds for children, movies, theaters, restaurants conveniently located?

9. Find out if the established organization of your religious preference is conveniently located.

## What Type of House?

There are three basic types of houses you can invest in—a new house, a resale house and a custom-built house. You should understand the basic differences between them.

"New house" is a term often used to describe a house in a development of five or more houses built to conform to model specifications. If you move into a new house you will have an initial period of adjustment, and there probably will be some defects in workmanship which may take a little while to iron out. After that, though, you shouldn't have to worry about repair or replacements for several years. You are usually allowed to arrange some structural changes while the house is being built; afterwards, such changes are apt to be impossible or prohibitively expensive. You can probably select colors, tiles, countertop materials, picture windows, and so on, or, if you want, go to the expense of an extra bathroom or a fireplace. Since the builder usually negotiates the preliminary mortgage arrangements, mortgage applications and approvals are relatively simple. Balanced against these advantages is the fact that yearly real estate taxes can only be estimated and taxes in a new community are likely to increase. It is difficult to time your move because completion dates are rarely definite. Houses in a new development usually look pretty barren until the planting has had a chance to grow.

A resale house is one that has been previously occupied. In this case you know or can find out what you are getting through hiring a professional house inspector. The costs are more certain than those of a new house, since the present taxes are known and are not likely to increase sharply, and the previous owner can give you figures on maintenance costs. You are buying into an established community and can presumably acquire some knowledge about your neighbors.

The landscaping and surrounding assets or liabilities are apparent. (For more information on how to evaluate a resale house, see Chapter 11, "When You Buy a House," page 117.)

The custom-built house is one that you have built to your specifications—always with the help of a qualified architect. This is obviously a more expensive and time-consuming procedure, and you must be prepared to take into consideration the cost of establishing facilities for water and sewage, as well as connections for electricity, gas and telephone service. Either you or your architect would make arrangements for a contractor; in any case, always consult your lawyer and follow his advice to protect your interests.

Homeownership is not limited to houses. You can buy an apartment as a cooperative or as a condominium. When you buy a cooperative apartment you become part owner in an owner corporation, made up of your co-tenants and generally managed by the firm the tenants have chosen. Certain tenants are selected as directors by other tenants to represent them in the management of the building. Usually directors meet several times a year and there is a general tenants' meeting at least once a year. As a tenant, you own a proportion of stock in the building corresponding to the size of your apartment. Each month, on the basis of the number of shares of stock you own or the size of your apartment, you pay your share of the cost of maintaining the building, the taxes, amortization of, and interest on, the mortgage. This is usually called the monthly maintenance charge. The tax and mortgage-interest portions of your maintenance are tax-deductible items.

Cooperative living tends to ensure a regularity of expenditure. You are not subject to rent increases at the landlord's whim, though you are subject to raises in maintenance if the cost of running the building or the taxes or assessments go up. There is also the strong possibility of appreciation on your investment. If you wish to sell, however, the board of directors must approve of the buyer.

When you buy a condominium, you buy an individual title to the apartment you occupy rather than a share in a corporation. You also have your own individual mortgage, which can be an advantage because it permits you to refinance if necessary. While you are not personally liable for the mortgage debt in a cooperative apartment,

99

your investment could be jeopardized if the corporation fails to meet its mortgage payments. You pay individual taxes in a condominium based on an assessment of your apartment. Closing costs are higher for a condominium than for a cooperative since the purchase of shares of stock in a cooperative is a relatively simple legal transaction. As in a cooperative, a board of managers or directors is elected to supervise the property, and if you want to sell your condominium you must have their approval of the buyer. However, condominiums are usually more readily salable than cooperatives because the purchaser may obtain a new mortgage if needed. Condominium owners also share a proportionate part of the expense of maintaining the building and, as in a cooperative, if any of the owners defaults and no replacement is found, the other owners have to absorb those maintenance costs. This is not very likely in times of general prosperity but could become a real threat during a recession. It is relatively easy to dispossess a defaulting owner of a cooperative, but if a condominium owner defaults, complicated foreclosure proceedings are necessary to remove him from his premises.

You may have moved once or twice during the course of your married life, but when your children are grown, you may want to live in a smaller home. Perhaps your financial picture has changed, or maybe you are ready for retirement. Again, the same rules previously discussed apply as you search for what you want.

It isn't likely that you will make the same kind of mistakes the Tuttles did, but they are a fine example of what not to do. Mr. Tuttle's hobby was collecting books and Mrs. Tuttle loved antiques. They had lived for 20 years in a large, sprawling town house and had raised three children, all of whom were now married. When Mr. Tuttle retired, both he and Mrs. Tuttle felt the house was too big and too much to care for. Besides, they wanted to move to a warmer climate. They found a modern cooperative apartment in a state 600 miles away. Mrs. Tuttle gave the children as much of her furniture and beloved objects as she could bear to part with, and Mr. Tuttle spent days and days going over his books. In the end, feeling too sheepish to tell Mrs. Tuttle, he arranged to have almost all of them shipped to their new home. When they arrived, after their belongings, they found the new apartment so cramped that it was literally impossible to unearth a bed to sleep on. They spent that night (and several following) at a hotel. After some weeks the Tuttles settled in, to find they were really quite miserable. Mrs. Tuttle liked neither the climate nor her neighbors. Mr. Tuttle, who suffered from a bad back, couldn't find a doctor he liked and was profoundly bored with doing nothing. After a year the Tuttles sold their new home, happily at a profit, and moved back to the town where they had lived for so long. Mr. Tuttle is now the busy head of the town library committee.

Probably the home you choose at any stage in your life won't be perfect, and certainly compromise is something to be prepared for. Consider thoughtfully what things you would be prepared to give up and what things mean the most to you. It's conceivable that you might have to choose between a modern kitchen and a swimming pool: Which, in the end, would give you more pleasure? Choose your home with as much foresight as you can muster, and remember it's not just your money, it's your future.

▭▭▭▭▭▭

## WORDS YOU SHOULD KNOW

**Fixed cost.** Expenses over which you have little or no control once you have obligated yourself, such as monthly mortgage payments, property taxes and rent.

**Sublease.** A lease by a tenant to another person for part or all of the premises. Example: You have a two-year lease on an apartment, but after 12 months your employer transfers you to Helsinki. You sublease your apartment to someone else for the second year of your lease. If he does not pay the rent, you are usually liable for it.

**Zoning.** A local law that specifies what uses may or may not be made of property situated within certain areas of a city or county. Examples: A residential zone may be used only for private homes and sometimes for apartment buildings; an industrial zone permits factories; a commercial zone allows businesses, gas stations, and the like.

**Cooperative apartment.** An apartment unit in a building owned jointly by all its tenants, each of whom pays his proportion of upkeep and taxes. The tenant owns a share of the entire building.

**Condominium.** An apartment unit owned by a tenant who has no other equity in the building as a whole; the owner pays a proportion of the building's maintenance expenses and may mortgage his apartment, which a co-op dweller may not do.

▭▭▭▭▭▭

## CHAPTER 9

## You Can Buy **and** Build

*How to get a
"custom-built" house
at a development price
by taking some standard options*

Assume you're looking for a new home. You have definite ideas about what your family wants and needs, but you have no intention of going to the very considerable trouble and expense of buying land and hiring your own architect and contractor to design and erect a truly custom-built house. You have, however, found a likely sub-division and a model house in it that appeals to you very much. But you want your house to be a little different. First, you want indoor-outdoor carpeting in the kitchen in place of tile; second, instead of the model's standard concrete patio, you'd like the builder to construct a sun-room; and, third, you need five bedrooms and three baths instead of the three bedrooms and two baths planned for the model.

Provided you pay the difference in cost, your chances for getting the first are excellent; the second, good; and the third, fair.

Most builders—over 90 percent in a recent survey—are willing to alter the decor of a model when they build your house. A great many will make minor structural changes, provided you ask them during the blueprint stage, and a few of the more accommodating builders are so flexible they'll change whatever you want. Said one Texas man: "If the buyer pays for it, we'll build him a ladder to the moon."

Not every builder, however, will make changes for you. Some won't move a single partition or replace a window. But such con-tractors are in the minority now—a sharp contrast to the late 1940s and early 1950s. It was a seller's market then. Today, despite strong demand, it's a buyer's market, and this partially explains the grow-ing flexibility on changes among home builders.

Whatever the cause, the results for you are quite favorable. If you're seeking a house, this, in detail, is what you'll find.

Every builder will offer you some opportunity for free choice. Selection of decorative lighting fixtures is generally up to you. The not-so-ordinary kitchen appliances (a built-in toaster) are often added or deleted, as you dictate. Much more usual is a choice of colors—for painted walls, bathroom tile, kitchen counters.

Others go further. Here are some of the options offered by a southern California builder. They are taken directly from a printed sheet given to each prospective buyer. Prices refer to installed materials and equipment, or, where one product substitutes for another, the difference in price. (This is the way most builders present you with optional possibilities: item, clearly described, and price.)

| OPTION | PRICE |
|---|---|
| Central air conditioning............................................... | $1225 |
| Cedar shakes in lieu of cedar shingles............................... | 270 |
| Plastic counter tops in lieu of ceramic tile........................... | no charge |
| Parquet wood tile in lieu of vinyl-asbestos tile in family room.......... | 270 |
| Travertine marble in entry.......................................... | 230 |
| Mirrored wardrobe doors on all bedroom closets (4)................... | 520 |
| Clothes washer..................................................... | 200 |
| Clothes drier...................................................... | 175 |
| Each additional wall outlet.......................................... | 15 |
| Television outlet................................................... | 20 |

Standard options aren't restricted to products. One builder offers to add a fourth bedroom. Another allows a choice of three baths in place of two and a half. A third will build a one-, two- or three-car garage. Optional decks or patios, fireplaces, extra landscaping and finished basement rooms are typical of extras offered by perhaps one builder out of three.

Because each buyer is free to select from a normally substantial list of options, he has a good opportunity to individualize his home— just as he would a car. If the plan is one that suits your family's needs, and the house is built in a style that appeals to you, adding the extras can provide you with what no doubt would be very close to the custom house you might have had designed and built.

Why does a builder offer standard options? To make his model more salable. That's obvious. But there's a more subtle reason, one that may help you understand why some builders resist special changes you suggest. Says a Virginia builder: "At a point around 1960 we were probably the world's champion customizers. Move a partition, put in a hobby room, enlarge a bath. Buyers asked for it.

103

We did it. But the further we went, the gloomier our profit picture became.

"We were spending enormous amounts of time redrawing plans, calling back subcontractors, tearing out and replacing walls. The catch: If we charged the buyer what it really cost us, we'd price ourselves out of the market. Finally we were forced to make a decision: Either become a custom builder or deliver the extra value of a development house by building a development house. Period. As it turned out, we found the perfect compromise by offering standardized extras—a set list of changes we carefully worked out, on which we had costs figured to the penny. Now our buyers are happy. And we're making a fair profit again."

Applying a rule of thumb that is dependable most of the time, multihouse builders (say, 100 houses per year and up) will offer some standard options and be most resistant to unlisted changes you request. A builder who erects from 10 to 30 houses a year is most likely to go along with the customizing you want. Contractors who fall in the 30 to 100 category are sometimes yes and sometimes no on the subject of special alterations.

These rules fly out the window when there's a unique need. For example, if you have an invalid in the family and are anxious to buy a subdivision house, many of the big builders will relent enough to put in ramps for short runs of stairs.

## Where and How Builders Make Changes

It would be a rare builder who didn't offer you some choice of colors and patterns in tile, paint, wallpaper, counter topping and flooring. Some present you with a choice of three or four standard alternatives. Others turn over the name of the subcontractor or dealer and suggest you visit the showroom to pick out whatever pleases you, provided it's in the same price range as the original.

More flexible builders permit practically unlimited substitutions of interior-finish materials. If your choice is an item less expensive than the original, you'll probably get a credit refund. Should you want rosewood wall paneling in place of white-painted gypsum board, you'll be asked to pay the difference.

A cash allowance for decorative lighting fixtures is standard. You visit the lighting showroom and, based on the allowance, pick out the fixtures you want. In many cases, you'll find the allowance discouragingly low. Provided, once again, you pay the difference, builders will have no objection to installing more expensive fixtures. However, only the most cooperative builders will permit you to specify additional built-in lighting—a move that would call for a new wiring diagram and, perhaps, additional construction.

Even an amenable builder would stiffen, though, if you asked for such changes after construction begins. Here's what happened to a Maryland builder. When a buyer signed up for a house based on the model, a hardwood floor was specified for the sun-room. Nothing was said during the closing, so construction began, and eventually a hardwood floor was laid in the sun-room.

"But," says the builder, "the buyer's wife wandered in one day and exclaimed to my superintendent, 'Oh, no! I said that I wanted a stone floor in the sun-room.'

"Well, we had to call back the carpentry crew not only to tear out the wood floor but to rebuild the understructure—strengthening it to receive the much heavier flagstone. The total cost, for what could have been an insignificant change during the blueprint stage, was $1500. The buyer practically had apoplexy, but he paid."

Appliances are now so much a part of model home interiors that they bear mentioning. For at least ten years, a built-in range and oven have been standard equipment in model home kitchens. Gradually the range hood and exhaust fan have worked their way into the basic house price.

Additional appliances—washer, drier, dishwasher, refrigerator, freezer, garbage disposer, electric can opener, incinerator, mixing center, intercom and central vacuum systems—are sometimes included, sometimes not. When they are not, you generally have the option to have them put in. As long as the item is built in, you can assume its cost will blend into the total house price; you can then include the financing in your mortgage.

## Exterior Changes

You want a house that expresses your taste for styling and color. Little does this so quickly as the exterior appearance of a house. In fact, what probably attracts you to a particular model in the first place is the way it looks from the street. Once you've selected the model, what further choices do you have: Can you pick your colors? Will the builder replace asbestos-cement siding with brick? Are you permitted a voice in selecting the style of window?

Answer: Not very often. Here's why. Most responsible builders today plan an entire subdivision before the first house goes up. Aiming at harmony with variety, they coordinate adjacent homes and studiously avoid placing the same model side by side on a street.

For example, an Indiana builder offered six models in a subdivision planned for 55 houses. Before he opened the models, his architect sited the houses on all 55 lots. He placed Model A—a traditional house with white clapboard siding and dark green shutters—on Lots 1, 6, 11, 16, 21, and so on, doing this, of course, on the site plan. Thus, a buyer who was among the first to select Model A could study the plan and have several choices as to where in the subdivision he would like his house built. On the other hand, a buyer who demanded Model A for lot No. 2 would be out of luck.

If you run into the same builder resistance, pause a moment and consider that this policy does have value. The builder mixes models because he knows he can't sell a subdivision in which every house is white with dark green shutters. Those days are over. But the builder is also acting in your interest. Just as he won't let you duplicate the house next door, so he won't let the next buyer duplicate your house.

What changes are open to you? A limited choice of siding and roofing colors may be offered occasionally. Some builders will permit switching materials. For example, you might be able to select brick in place of vertical board siding, or specify a premium-weight asphalt shingle for the minimum product. And you may be able to alter the way your house sits on the lot, at least to the extent of reversing the plan. Thus you might have the north-south axis flipped, or the east-west axis, or both. The builder would veto the idea if a reversed plan meant the glass doors of your family room looked directly into the neighbor's bedroom windows, or if the change brought about a less-than-attractive view of the house from the street.

A strict rule of economics applies for all structural changes, whether on a development house or a one-of-a-kind custom-built residence. Move partitions, knock out walls, alter the plumbing— make any changes you wish before construction begins and the cost, if any, will be nominal. But walk into a three-quarter finished structure and demand the same changes and you'll wind up paying double or triple the cost of material and labor for the new work. Why? Because you pay for tearing out, repairing and building up.

For example, a Nebraska builder moved an interior wall two feet. "If the buyer had asked me to do it while we were talking over the blueprints, when all it would have taken is a notation on the floor plan, I wouldn't have charged him a penny," said the builder. "But because we had to rip out a finished partition, move it, rebuild it and repair the openings in the floor and ceiling, I had to charge him $500."

Although it's probably difficult to appreciate, since you would be paying the bill, builders who accede to your request for changes after the house is nearly complete seldom do more than break even on the alteration. The reason: They may cover the cost of materials and labor on the change, but they lose time moving ahead on other houses.

Extravagant additions, even when mentioned before construction begins, get a negative response from the great majority of builders interviewed. A Dayton, Ohio, builder explains: "One couple wanted us to add an indoor swimming pool off the family room. I turned them down because in the time it would have taken our crew to put it in, we could have built and sold three other houses."

Sometimes it isn't time or money that kills the request. Reports a San Mateo, California, builder: "One man wanted us to build a special room to house his calliope. It would have violated the lot restrictions, but even if it hadn't, we would have scotched the deal. Can you imagine what the neighbors would say about that big steampipe organ blasting away? And those neighbors happen to be my customers too."

## Making Structural Changes

Who will make structural changes? As mentioned earlier, the large-volume builder is less likely to carry out your requests no matter what stage of construction your house is in. On the other hand, a man who builds fewer than 50 houses a year in a price range that starts around $30,000 is much more inclined to sit down with you and plan alterations that will make you a buyer instead of a looker.

Of course, there are exceptions to every generalization. A Greensboro, North Carolina, builder who starts on the average of 350 houses every year says he will completely redesign a model if necessary. "In most cases," he explains, "customizing is more troublesome than selling a stock model, but we've found that in a competitive market the extra trouble is well worth the effort."

And on the other side of the coin, a 20-house-a-year builder from New London, Connecticut, says flatly, "Absolutely no changes beyond the half-dozen options we offer. Too much bother and worry at any reasonable price."

Most of the advantages of buying a development house add up, in the end, to dollar savings. Buy an exact duplicate of the builder's model and you reap the maximum savings over having the identical house constructed by a custom builder on your own lot.

Even adding optional extras won't close the gap between custom-built and development-built. But the more custom changes you

▭▭▭▭▭▭

## WORDS YOU SHOULD KNOW

**Custom-built house.** A home built to the owner's specifications on land he has acquired. Like a tailor-made suit, it answers its owner's needs exclusively and is considerably more expensive than a standard model.

**Development house.** One of a series of dwellings built on a mass production basis for resale by a promoter or contractor on land subdivided by him. Houses in the same development are usually similar or identical in design.

**Subdivision.** A tract of land that a developer cuts up into smaller plots on which to build a community of houses.

**Standard options.** Changes the builder routinely agrees to make for the buyer of a development house. These are much like the "extras" that are available when you buy an automobile.

**Structural changes.** Alterations that change the basic plan or shape of the house. Example: moving a wall, which may involve such expensive changes as rerouting electric wires, plumbing, and heating conduits.

▭▭▭▭▭▭

request, the narrower this margin of savings grows. Therefore, if it is terribly important to you to have a house that is uniquely yours inside and like no other house nearby in appearance, avoid the development house and pay a custom price for your persistence. But if your family needs are relatively uncomplicated, and if there are at least a dozen merchant builders in your area, then you have an excellent chance of finding the model you want in the price range you want to pay, and of making the minor changes that will give you an "almost custom-built" development house at a cost that is realistic for your family.

CHAPTER 10

# How Much House Can You Afford?

*Down-to-earth advice
to help you determine
what part of your family
income can comfortably
be spent on housing*

Shopping for a house is a little like buying at an auction. You generally start bidding low and find yourself going higher and higher. The crucial problem is knowing when to stop.

How can you tell when a house costs more than you can afford? For example, can a man making $12,000 a year afford a $20,000 house? Can he go as high as $25,000? Actually, some people with $12,000 a year can prudently go to $35,000 while others would be foolhardy if they spent a dollar more than $18,000.

And you've heard those rules of thumb, such as, "You can afford to pay two-and-a-half times your annual salary." Forget them. They're catchalls. They can't be applied to any particular family without such elaborate qualifications that they become useless.

You can determine your buying maximum fairly accurately, but not by plucking figures out of the air or applying handy-dandy rules. Instead, you make a careful evaluation of your financial situation and then match it against the price of the house and its running costs. The worksheet on pages 115–116 tells you how to do it step by step. But finish reading this chapter first to learn the principles involved.

Keep in mind that the object is to figure out your top limit—the highest price and operating-expense total you can afford to pay. You may not have to spend that much. You may find a suitable home for far less.

When you buy a home, you commit yourself to certain fixed monthly expenses. You can hold down costs temporarily by deferring repairs and such maintenance projects as repainting. But you can't delay these expenses indefinitely, and an irreducible outlay remains that must be paid month after month and year after year.

When you add up the income you have available to cover these expenses, be careful to include only the money you can regularly depend on. For most people, the mainstay is their base salary. Other sources of income have to be adjusted to even out the variations from one year to the next or perhaps must be eliminated entirely. For example:

*Commissions.* You may have had a flush sales record last year. But one or two years' commissions are not a particularly reliable guide to future earnings. To be on the safe side, average the commissions you have earned over the past three or four years.

*Overtime pay.* Again, an average might be better than last year's total or this year's estimate. However, overtime opportunities can change so suddenly that you may want to arbitrarily reduce the figure to what you consider the absolute minimum. When considering mortgage loan applications, one national insurance company doesn't even count overtime pay for work over 48 hours a week.

*Bonuses.* If the company you work for is firmly committed to paying bonuses whenever profits warrant, average the amounts for several back years (include at least one bad year) and add the result to your income. But if the company passes out bonuses only once in a while, it may be prudent to ignore them in your calculations.

*Wife's pay.* The critical question here is: How long will your wife work? An older couple with grown children can generally rely on the wife's income, especially if she is in a profession, such as teaching or nursing. But a young couple who haven't yet begun building a family would be foolish to base their housing budget on a continuing income from the mother-to-be. On the other hand, if they can bank enough of her income to make a bigger down payment on the house and thereby reduce the monthly mortgage installments, her earnings can help them to have a more comfortable home.

## How Much Money for a Home?

Use the worksheet (pages 115–116) to add up all your steady income. Subtract from the total all your nonhousing expenses—food, transportation, clothing—to find how much you have regularly available every month for running a house and for savings.

Now, how much of the total that you have available can you—or do you want to—put into a house?

To bring your circumstances into sharper focus, compare the average available income with what you spend right now on housing expenses. If you are already spending all that's available, you obviously cannot consider spending more. Indeed, you are spending too much on housing because you are using some money that should be going into savings.

Maybe there are items in the budget that you can trim down to free more money for housing. If so, fine. Just don't expect living in your own home to reduce your other living expenses materially. It seldom works out that way.

Be realistic, too, about the contention that a homeowner needn't save as much as other people because the part of his mortgage payments that increases his equity in the property is a form of savings. Remember that your equity is frozen into the house. You can't cash it in until you sell the house, use the increased equity to obtain a second mortgage or refinance entirely. Moreover, there is no natural law that prevents the resale value of a house from declining, a misfortune that could wipe out part of the accumulated equity.

As a homeowner, you will get an income tax break because both the interest on the mortgage and the real estate taxes can be deducted. But you won't know how much the tax saving will be until you fill in your return.

If your figures show that your present housing costs are materially less than the amount that could be made available for housing and savings, in effect you have been managing to save. Perhaps the money did go into a savings account or investments, or perhaps you bought expensive items for cash instead of financing them. At any rate, your savings margin gives you some freedom of choice. Should you use some of it for housing? If so, how much?

Estimates based on Federal Housing Administration data indicate that homeowners spend about 24 percent of their after-tax monthly income on the basic housing expenses—the mortgage payment, house insurance, maintenance, repairs, heating, utilities and real estate taxes. As you might expect, people with larger incomes buy larger homes and have larger monthly expenses. Nevertheless, higher-income families spend a smaller percentage of their earnings on housing, as these figures, based on thousands of home purchases made in a recent year, show:

BASIC MONTHLY HOUSING EXPENSES

| MONTHLY BEFORE-TAX INCOME | AVERAGE AMOUNT | PERCENTAGE OF AFTER-TAX INCOME |
|---|---|---|
| $ 400–$499 | $120 | 28.8% |
| 500–599 | 135 | 27.0 |
| 600–699 | 148 | 25.5 |
| 700–799 | 160 | 23.9 |
| 800–899 | 169 | 22.5 |
| 900–999 | 179 | 21.3 |
| 1000–1099 | 190 | 20.6 |
| 1100–1199 | 195 | 19.3 |
| 1200 and over | 210 | 16.9 |

Interesting as they are, these indications of what other people do can't solve your personal problem. Ultimately, your budget has to be tailored to your particular situation.

Consider a few factors that could lead you to adopt a higher housing budget than another family with precisely the same income:

You plan to have more children and want to avoid having to move to a larger house later on.

Your position or profession makes a steady, long-term increase in income fairly certain.

You entertain a great deal or frequently bring business associates home.

You intend to use part of the house for an office.

One or more of your parents probably will come to live with you.

You must live in a certain section so your children can attend a school with special facilities.

You can't commute, or don't want to, so you live in a relatively close-in, more expensive neighborhood than you might.

Both of you work.

Similarly, there are many reasons why a family might choose a lower-cost house than others of equal income:

Your children will soon be grown and going off to work or to college.

You are near the income peak for your type of work and can't expect any sizable pay increases.

There's a possibility your company will transfer you to another city within the next year or two.

Whatever figure you finally select for your maximum housing budget, try to retain some margin for savings. Don't let that dream house wipe out your other plans. It shouldn't interfere with building a college fund or investing for retirement.

## The Down Payment

The next problem is deciding how much down payment you are prepared to make. You'll get plenty of conflicting advice on this point. Some people say put in as much as you can to reduce mortgage payments and save interest charges. Others advocate the smallest down payment you can get away with, arguing that a house with a big mortgage is easier to sell and that you don't save as much interest as you think you do anyhow because the money that would go into a higher down payment can be invested or earn interest in a bank.

Many home buyers don't have much choice in this matter. They have trouble enough scraping together the minimum down payment. If you're in that fix, be sure to leave money at the bottom of the barrel for moving expenses and settlement charges. And don't dip too deeply into your reserves. Every family needs a rainy day fund— and because boilers burst and roofs leak and other catastrophes befall them, homeowners need one most of all.

You would be surprised how many families do all the right things in shopping for a home except check on how much it will cost to run the place. It's an understandable failing. The real estate agent may have only sketchy facts to go on and the owner himself may be unable to provide hard figures on any expenses other than the mortgage payment and real estate taxes.

If you have trouble pinning down actual expense figures, here's a method you can use as an expedient: Take the cost of the house, subtract 5 percent from it and then take 1 percent of the remainder. The result is the approximate amount you should expect to spend each month on the mortgage payment, insurance, taxes, maintenance, repairs, heating and utilities. This 1 percent figure is based on FHA-insured homes bought on average 5 percent down payments and 30-year mortgages. (For mortgage information, see Chapter 12, page 137.) If the house costs $30,000, for example, the 5 percent down payment would be $1500, leaving a mortgage of $28,500. One percent of this is $285, the monthly estimate for all housing-expense items.

If you pay more than 5 percent down, or have a shorter mortgage, you can adjust the total monthly housing expense by subtracting or adding the amount by which the monthly mortgage payment would be changed. More money down leaves a smaller mortgage and lower monthly payments, while a shorter term naturally increases the payments. Your bank can tell you how much the payments on a particular mortgage would differ from those you would have with a 30-year mortgage and 5 percent down payment.

Remember that this formula produces only a rough estimate of expenses, not precise figures. If actual figures are available to you, by all means use them.

One more expense remains to reckon with—commuting. If transportation costs will be higher in your new neighborhood, add the difference to the monthly costs.

## Work Out Your Own Buying Limit

You have finally arrived at the point where you can work out a buying limit, using the following form. This procedure has been designed to establish a conservative, safe maximum. No doubt some families will press beyond that limit, banking on future pay increases to keep them afloat. In an inflationary period that policy can succeed —if you don't have any financial bad luck. On the other hand, it's hard to put a value on the peace of mind that comes from living in a house that you can prove you can afford—with real figures.

---

**HOUSING BUDGET WORKSHEET**

---

**I.** *Family income:*

Salaries.......................................... $_____

Bonus, commissions, etc............................ _____

Interest, dividends................................ _____

Other............................................. _____

*Total....* $_____

Annual tax, Social Security, pension deductions.......... _____

*Subtract to get net annual income....* $_____

Monthly income (divide annual income by 12)........ $_____

**II.** *Family expenses, other than rent or housing costs enumerated in Section III:*

Food............................................. $_____

Church and charities.............................. _____

Clothing.......................................... _____

Debt payments.................................... _____

Education......................................... _____

Home furnishings................................. _____

Life, health, auto insurance........................ _____

Recreation........................................ _____

Transportation.................................... _____

Medical care...................................... _____

Other............................................. _____

*Total annual expenses....* $_____

Monthly expenses (divide annual total by 12)......... $_____

**III.** *Housing budget:*

Monthly income, from Section I..................... $_____

Monthly expenses, from Section II.................. _____

*Subtract to get amount available for savings and basic housing expenses: mortgage payment, heating, utilities, repairs, maintenance, home insurance, taxes.........* $_____

Amount you want to save........................... _____

*Subtract to get your maximum monthly housing budget..* $_____

115

**IV.** *Shopping guide:*

| | HOUSE 1 | HOUSE 2 |
|---|---|---|
| Price.............................. | $_____ | $_____ |
| Subtract maximum down payment you are prepared to make.............. | _____ | _____ |
| *Mortgage needed....* | $_____ | $_____ |
| Monthly housing expenses (if figures are unavailable, use 1% method explained in article)................ | $_____ | $_____ |
| Mortgage payment................. | _____ | _____ |
| Maintenance, repairs.............. | _____ | _____ |
| Heating, utilities.................. | _____ | _____ |
| Home insurance.................. | _____ | _____ |
| Real estate taxes................. | _____ | _____ |
| Additional commuting cost, if any... | _____ | _____ |
| *Total expenses....* | $_____ | $_____ |
| Your maximum monthly housing budget, from Section III............ | $_____ | $_____ |
| Is the house within your budget?...... | _____ | _____ |

Filling out this worksheet will do two things for you. In the first three sections, you will calculate just how much you can afford to earmark for buying and running a house. The last section applies that information to your house shopping and will enable you to make direct cost comparisons of the houses you consider buying.

Note that in the first two sections about family income and family expenses, you enter annual figures for each item first, then divide the totals by 12 to get monthly figures. Thus you also take into account income and expenses that come along quarterly, annually or on any basis other than once a month.

Remember as you make these calculations that it's important to be honest with yourself. The temptation to stretch a point so that you seem able to afford the somewhat larger house or the house in a slightly more convenient neighborhood is a strong one. But committing yourself to larger payments than you can really afford over a long term can cause your family serious financial distress in return for benefits that will then seem small by comparison.

116

## CHAPTER 11

# When You Buy a House

*A step-by-step guide to help you avoid the most common pitfalls in choosing and buying a house*

Buying a house is a tricky business. Countless snares await the unwary buyer, and it's easy to make a mistake. A house that seems just perfect to you may be full of hidden traps: It may be infested with termites, the plumbing cracked and corroded, the foundation weak. You could be saddled with a stack of bills for unforeseen expenses or discover with horror that a new highway will be built through your backyard.

Once you make a mistake you're stuck. If you decide to bail out you stand to lose money, and if you stick with it you lose anyway. So beware. Find out as much as you can *before* you buy, not afterward. If you don't have enough experience, hire an expert. Don't let the real estate agent or owner pressure you into a hasty decision. After all, this is one of the biggest investments you'll ever make. Take your time, and compare and evaluate the alternatives.

You can avoid the most common pitfalls of house buying and be sure to get your money's worth if you follow these guidelines. First, know what you want, need and can afford before you start looking. Second, make a thorough check of the entire house, lot and neighborhood. Find out what it will be like to live there and how much it will cost. Be particularly wary of hidden flaws that could spell years of discomfort or financial strain. Third, be prepared to spend a few hundred dollars extra for expert advice. Hire a structural expert to be sure there are no major defects, and consult a lawyer before you sign anything. Together they may save you hundreds or thousands of dollars.

Let's assume you already know what type of house you want, where you want to live and how much you can spend. You're ready to start shopping for the right house. How do you begin? Unless you are familiar with the section, your best bet is to consult a real estate agent. He knows the housing market in the area and will probably be able to show you several houses within your price range. Tell him as much as you can about the style, number of rooms, price, location and other requirements. It will be easier for him to decide which of the houses fit your needs. But if some of his suggestions don't interest you, don't bother visiting them.

A good real estate agent can help you in other ways too. If you find a suitable house, he can advise you about a fair offering price and will handle the delicate price negotiations between you and the owner. He will also know where you can get a mortgage, the policies of the local lending institutions and how much money you will be able to borrow.

On the other hand, don't be taken in by the agent's sales pitch or rely on his unsupported assurances. He represents the seller and is answerable to him, not to the buyer. Remember, too, that he has a stake in selling the house. If he doesn't make a sale he gets no commission. So he will tend to emphasize the good points about the house and play down any shortcomings.

To be sure you see all the houses in the area, consult several real estate agents, and do some shopping on your own as well. Check the local newspaper for houses being sold directly by the owner. You will get a better idea of property value in the area.

So far your job has been easy. The agent has done most of the work. But once you start visiting houses the real work begins. Keep your eyes open as you tour each house. Find out yourself about local real estate values, zoning rules, taxes, public utilities, schools and stores. It is you, finally, who will have to decide whether any of the houses are worth your money.

It's a tough job because there is so much to consider: the neighborhood, the yard, exterior, interior, heating, plumbing, construction, wiring, lighting, stairways, insulation—every aspect of the house. And the most crucial parts are hard to get at. You can't pull out the walls to see whether the insulation and wiring are good. You can't tear down the facade to check for sagging floors. You can't actually live there to see what it would be like.

It takes a first-rate detective to size up a house. You have to be observant, thorough, critical and shrewd. You must look beyond the gloss and frills for the true signs of value and quality. Be as realistic and hardheaded as possible. Don't be swayed by emotion. If you are bothered by a detail, ask yourself why. Is it an insignificant point or a major one? Do other features of the house compensate for its drawbacks? If the kitchen is really smaller than you want, for example, are there other aspects of the house that make up for it?

A house that is worth your money should satisfy three basic criteria. First, it should be a sound financial investment. This means it should have good resale prospects and be situated where property values will increase. Second, it should be comfortable and convenient to live in. Third, it should be in satisfactory condition, with a sound structure and no major defects.

## Location—A Key Factor

The location of a house is the real key to its value. An expensive house in a neighborhood of more modest houses will be worth less than the same house in a neighborhood of similar houses. A well-kept home in a run-down neighborhood will lose value nevertheless, because of its poor surroundings. Houses in places that are considered "desirable" are more valuable than houses in less prestigious areas. Other factors, such as distance from the city, convenience to shops and schools, zoning laws and traffic conditions, also influence property values. A house in a district where property values are on the upswing could be a profitable investment.

As you drive through the neighborhood, look for indications of the general trend of property values. Is the area well kept up? Do the owners seem to take pride in the appearance of their homes? Are there any large, undeveloped areas of land that could be used—zoning laws permitting, as explained below—for commercial or industrial buildings? If the neighborhood is old, look for signs of deterioration, such as run-down houses or abandoned buildings. Check on the location of stores, schools and transportation. Find out about local utilities, taxes and other services and expenses.

Be sure to check the local zoning regulations. These laws specify the type of buildings that can be constructed in an area, and have a direct influence on property values. Unless the zone is protected against commercial construction, stores and businesses may invade the area and lower the value and desirability of houses. Zoning laws also specify the minimum size for house lots and the ratio of house to land. If you plan to build a garage or enlarge a house, to add a bedroom for example, be sure the zoning rules will permit you to do so.

The general appearance of a house and lot will also affect its resale value. Think twice before you sink your money into a highly unusual house. You may love those towers and gabled roof and gargoyles, but will anyone else? The chances of reselling a more conventional house are better. A house will command a higher price if it blends in with the others in the neighborhood. People tend to shy away from a building that sticks out like a sore thumb.

## Exterior Versus Interior Design

The design of a house is the key to its livability. While a well-planned one is a pleasure to live in, a badly designed one can be a constant source of discomfort and inconvenience. Little annoyances such as inadequate closet space, a single bathroom in a two-story

▭▭▭▭▭▭

### TWENTY–TWO
### COMMON LITTLE TRAPS

Here is a list of common design flaws found in houses. Watch out for them when you are looking for a home.

1. No separate entranceway or foyer to receive visitors.

2. No opening in the front door, or no window or glass outlook alongside, to let you see who's ringing the bell.

3. No roof overhang or similar protection over the front door to provide shelter in bad weather while you are fumbling for your key and to protect guests waiting to enter.

4. No direct access route from the driveway to the kitchen.

5. No direct route from outdoors to bathroom so children can come in and out with minimum of bother and mud tracking.

6. Gas, electric and water meters inside the house or in the garage or basement, rather than outside. Outside meters do away with the need to let meter men in.

7. Fishbowl picture window in the front of the house, exposing you to every passerby.

8. Driveway that opens out on a blind curve so you cannot see oncoming traffic when backing out. A driveway that slopes up to the street is almost as bad, especially for trapping you hopelessly on an icy winter morning.

9. Isolated garage or carport with no direct or protected access from car to house.

10. Accident-inviting doors that open toward the basement stairs.

11. Cut-up rooms with windows haphazardly located. Sometimes too

▭▭▭▭▭▭

house or a bedroom that can only be reached by walking through another bedroom can add up to a lot of misery.

The exterior of a house is often a clue to the inner design. Has the builder planned for visual beauty as well as practicality? A well-designed exterior should look uncluttered and harmonious. Or does the house seem hastily thrown together with frills and doodads to cover up the absence of planning? Do the house and lot form an attractive unit, or does the house look awkward and out of place? Is there a private backyard shielded from public view? Is there a convenient place to park your car? Be sure the front and back doors are easily accessible from the driveway or garage so that you and your guests can enter the house easily.

Consider how the sun will hit the house. Rooms that face south are the sunniest because they get the sun's rays throughout the year. Rooms that face north receive very little sunlight. Try to picture the

▭▭▭▭▭▭

many doors make it impossible to arrange furniture.

12. In children's rooms, windows that are too low for safety, too high to see out of, too small or difficult to get out of in case of fire.

13. A hard-to-open window over the kitchen sink, usually the double-hung type. An easily cranked casement window is usually best here, a sliding window second best.

14. A window over the bathtub. This generally causes cold drafts, and the condensation will ultimately cause rotted windowsills.

15. Stage-front bathrooms placed squarely in view of a space like the living room, or right at the top of a stairway. Ideally, you should be able to go from any bedroom to the bathroom without being seen from another part of the house.

16. Only one bathroom, especially in a two-story or split-level house.

17. No light switch at every room entrance and exit.

18. No light or electrical outlet on a porch, patio or terrace.

19. No outside light to illuminate the path to the street or to a separate garage, and the front and back porches, if any.

20. Noisy light switches that go on and off like a pistol shot. Silently operating switches cost only a little more.

21. Child-trap closets that can't be opened from inside.

22. Small closets that are hardly big enough for half of your wardrobe; narrow closet doors that keep half the closet out of reach; shelves too high for persons of normal height; and horizontal closet poles so low that dresses and trousers hit the floor.

▭▭▭▭▭▭

house in different seasons. If it is spring or summer, ask yourself how it will look in winter. Maybe the lovely trees and bushes keep you from seeing the true character of the exterior.

Inside the house, look for indications of careful planning and functional and convenient use of space. The rooms should be arranged in a logical order: The kitchen and dining room should be close together. The living room should be near the front entrance, and there should be a hall or foyer with a coat closet directly inside the front door. Bedrooms should be set off from the rest of the house for privacy, with bathrooms located near them and possibly one near the living room. You should be able to reach one room without walking through another room.

Try to imagine living in the house. Have the woman of the house map out her daily routine. Decide whether she would be able to carry it out conveniently or would she be constantly racing from one part of the house to another. Is there a place for laundry and ironing? Are the closets large enough? If family members have a special hobby or interest, is there space to pursue it? Will it be easy to entertain guests? Is there a place for the children to play on rainy days? Can their mother keep an eye on them from the kitchen when they play in the yard?

Since the woman of the house spends much of her time in the kitchen, she will want to be sure it has been planned well. She should be able to prepare meals and clean up after them with a minimum of effort. To save steps, the sink, stove and refrigerator should be near one another. There should be plenty of counter space, shelves and cabinets and a broom closet. Are there enough outlets for plugging in all your kitchen appliances? Be sure lighting and ventilation are good. It should be easy to reach other rooms from the kitchen, and there should be a back door leading to the kitchen from the garage or driveway for carrying groceries from the car.

There should be enough bathrooms to accommodate your family comfortably. If the house has only one bathroom, it should be located near the bedrooms and within easy reach from other parts of the house. Check for storage space for medicine and toiletries. Be sure there is an outlet for an electric shaver and electric toothbrush. For safety, the lighting should be bright.

The bedrooms and living room should be large enough to hold essential furniture, with enough unbroken wall area for arranging it properly. Look for several electrical outlets for lamps, television, record player, and so on. Bedrooms need generous closets to hold all your clothes and provide some easily accessible storage space as well. Look for a linen closet.

## Checking for Structural Defects

If a house you like has passed the first two tests—it's a good investment and comfortable to live in—you must still look further. Find out how it has been put together and be sure you can afford to correct any defects.

Be especially wary in older houses. Pipes, wiring, heating and roofing are often inadequate or in need of repair. Kitchens and bathrooms may need remodeling; walls, ceilings and floors, refinishing. The structure may be sagging or infested with termites. The furnace and water heater may be obsolete. An ambitious couple may relish the thought of buying an old relic and restoring it. The price may be temptingly low, but making such a house livable can be very expensive and time-consuming.

Even brand-new houses can have serious defects. Unless they have been built carefully, you may discover problems such as poor drainage, weak foundations, ill-fitting windows and doors, inadequate cesspool. If cheap materials and fixtures were used, they will have to be replaced before long.

Only an expert can advise you on correcting structural defects, but you can detect signs of flaws or sloppy workmanship if you keep your eyes open. Take a critical look at the exterior first.

Is the paint in good repair? Blisters and peeling may simply indicate a hasty, poorly prepared paint job. On the other hand, they may signify a moisture problem within the walls that could plague you indoors and out, no matter how often you repaint. Are there any bulges on the walls? These could mean the structure is sagging.

Notice the state of the siding too. Are any pieces broken, warped or loose? Is the trim around doors and windows whole and well painted? Are gutters and downspouts free of rust and rot, firmly fastened with no sections dangling, drooping or bent?

And what can you see of the roof? Are there any shingles missing? If the roofing is composition covered with mineral granules, do you see any spots where the asphalt has dried and cracked? If possible, find out from the owner or agent when the present roof was put on and what kind of roofing material was employed. You can check later with a roofing contractor to find out the normal

## HOW MANY OUTLETS?

This chart gives the minimum requirements for the number and placement of outlets, lights and switches in each room.

| AREA | CONVENIENCE OUTLETS | SPECIAL OUTLETS | PERMANENT LIGHTING | SWITCHES |
|---|---|---|---|---|
| **Indoors** | | | | |
| Living rooms, recreation room, general living areas | Placed so that no point along floor line of usable wall space is more than 6 feet from an outlet. | FM radio, television, room air-conditioner. | From ceiling, wall, cove or valance lights. Switched convenience outlets may be substituted in living rooms. | Near doorways. |
| Dining areas | Placed near hostess's chair, so that no point along floor line of usable wall space is more than 6 feet from an outlet. One above counter or table next to wall. | | Ceiling light over table. | Near entrance. |
| Bedrooms | Placed on each side and within 6 feet of each bed location. Apply living room rule to remaining space. | Room air-conditioner. | From ceiling, wall, cove or valance lights. | On latch side of each doorway. |
| Kitchen | For each 4 feet of work counter, for refrigerator, for planning desk, at table space. | Electric range, dish-washer, dis-posal, home freezer, clock, fan. | General light and light over sink, others over work counters as needed. | Multiple control switches for rooms with entrances more than 10 feet apart. |
| Laundry | | Washer, drier, iron, fan. | At washing and ironing areas. | Near working areas. |

124

life expectancy of the roof and what it will cost to replace it.

Next, examine the interior. As you go through the door, observe whether it swings without binding and whether it has a good, sturdy lock. Make sure that the weather stripping forms a tight seal all around the door. You can check this by spreading a sheet of newspaper over the threshold and closing the door. The paper should be

| AREA | CONVENIENCE OUTLETS | SPECIAL OUTLETS | PERMANENT LIGHTING | SWITCHES |
|---|---|---|---|---|
| Bathrooms | Adjacent to mirror. | Built-in heater, ventilating fan. | Light both sides of face at mirror; 1 light enclosed in shower. | Near doorway. |
| Hallways | For each 15 feet of hallway. | | At least 2 in long halls. | |
| Utility room or basement | 1 at workbench; 1 near furnace. | Fuel-fired heating equipment, electric water heater. | For each enclosed space; at workbench; near furnace; at foot of basement stairs. | At head of stairs or at entrance. |
| Attic | 1 for general use. | Summer cooling fan. | 1 for each separate space. | At bottom of stairs. |

## Outdoors

| AREA | CONVENIENCE OUTLETS | SPECIAL OUTLETS | PERMANENT LIGHTING | SWITCHES |
|---|---|---|---|---|
| Entrances | Near front entrance; weatherproof. | | At front entrance and tradesmen's entrance. | Inside front and trade entrances. |
| Closets | | | For each closet. | |
| Porches, terraces, patios | For each 15 feet of usable outside wall; weatherproof. | | For each 150 square feet of porch. | Inside door to porch. |
| Garage or carport | 1 for general use. | For food freezer, workbench, door opener. | Interior light, exterior light if detached garage. | At door, multiple switches at garage and house. |

held so tightly that you can't pull it out. Interior doors between rooms, on the other hand, should not fit snugly. You ought to be able to see light underneath. And if the doors are hung properly, the gap between door and floor will be even, not high at one end and narrow at the other.

Then head straight for the basement. There you should search for signs of moisture, that bane of all basements. Look for dampness in corners, water stains on walls, water streaks from window wells. If the house is too new to show these tattle marks, ask for a dry-basement guarantee. And in both old and new houses, look for floor drains. It's not a bad idea to empty a pail of water onto the drain to see what happens. Some basements are so low in relation to sewer lines in the street that water runs off very slowly or not at all.

The basement is also the place to look for foundation cracks and signs of termite infestation. For either a brick or a frame house, you should be furnished a certificate of recent termite inspection. And if any damage is discovered, the seller should correct it at his own expense and give you a guarantee against recurrence.

## Plumbing, Heating and Wiring

Belowstairs also is the ideal place to check on three other important components—plumbing, heating and wiring.

Plumbing pipes may be of iron, steel, brass or copper. Plastic pipe, which gives good service, is being introduced in some areas but still is not common. Older houses frequently have iron or steel pipes, which may corrode over long years of use, reducing water pressure in the system. The usual test for low pressure is to open all faucets and then flush a toilet. If the pressure does not get noticeably less as a result, the system is in good order. Copper piping is more common in newer houses and is regarded as a durable, high-quality material.

While water is on your mind, check the age and size of the water heater. A good new one will last ten years, a cheap one with a few years of service to its credit may soon fail and require replacement. With automatic dishwashers, automatic washing machines and multiple bathrooms, any heater of less than 40 gallons capacity is undersized, especially for a family with several growing children.

It's not easy for a layman to judge the design and capacity of a heating system, although its faults and virtues will become plain enough over a winter or two. Forced warm-air systems are the most common—the kind in which air warmed in a gas or oil furnace is blown through ducts to all parts of the house. These systems can be both economical and effective, if well designed and correctly sized. Other types, such as the various hot water systems and electric systems, offer more selective controls and even heat but often are substantially more expensive to install and operate.

A heating contractor probably can give you an off-the-cuff opinion of a system's adequacy just by looking at the data on the furnace nameplate. You would be wise to seek some such knowledgeable judgment. At the least, ask the people who lived in the house before or those who live in similarly equipped houses what their heating experience has been.

If the system uses any fuel other than the customary one in the locality, be cautious. Find out how much the fuel will cost—before the bills start coming. And switch on the furnace, set the thermostat high and listen. A rumbling, rattling system will be a constant irritant and may be an indication that the equipment is in bad repair.

If there is air conditioning, be sure it is adequate. (Ask an air-conditioning contractor.) Check that it is in good condition. If there is no air conditioning, find out the cost of installing it.

As for wiring, remember that no home today is likely to be seriously oversupplied with electric service. Standards are rising all the time. Less than 20 years ago, 60-amp, 115-volt service was the norm. Now it is a rare house that can run on anything less than 100-amp, 220-volt service. And if there is central air conditioning or any other heavy power user, 150-amp or 200-amp service may be required.

Look at the service-entrance equipment—the box housing the fuses or circuit breakers—for information on the capacity provided. If you find a low-amp service entrance, you'll have to think about adding to its capacity.

## Walls, Ceilings and Floors

Go back upstairs to examine the walls, ceilings and floors. A few houses are wood-paneled throughout. In most, the walls and ceilings are what the building trades call either wet wall or dry wall. Dry wall is built by gluing and nailing large sheets of gypsum board to the framing, then covering with a tape the joints where sheets meet. Wet wall is the traditional finish for walls—plaster, applied wet as a mortar.

If you look at a wall and see tape lines or nailheads, it's dry wall, poorly done. If you see a wavy, rippling surface (try shining a flashlight beam along the wall), you are looking at imperfect plaster. If you detect hairline cracks, don't worry; most plaster walls develop these inconspicuous cracks and they can be repaired easily when you

## THE VANISHING BUILDER

There is no surer way to get stuck with a new house than to buy it from a "vanishing" builder. The builder may seem completely trustworthy, and the house may be spanking new and look as solidly constructed as any other. It may even have been approved by the Federal Housing Administration or the Veterans Administration.

But if something goes wrong with it, the builder is no longer around. It may be a small thing—a warped door, sticky windows or a busted faucet; or it may be something really serious, such as chronic flooding of the basement, a defective furnace or a bad septic tank. Your calls for help go unanswered. Or you may find, to your surprise and distress, there's no phone listing for him. He may have gone out of business or left town quietly. Whatever has happened, he has vanished as far as you are concerned. And you are left high and dry.

Take the case of the Johnsons and ten other families who bought $30,000 to $35,000 houses in a new develop-

ment called Paradise Knolls. After they had moved in, the Johnsons' house developed a series of troubles due to poor drainage. The septic tank system constantly overflowed. "The sewage smell is awful," Mrs. Johnson reported. "Water has seriously damaged our floor tiling, and the wallboard is mildewing. We brought in 32 truckloads of earth to divert the water—it only comes in slower. The State Supreme Court granted us a $3000 judgment against the builder, but we can't collect."

Other families in Paradise Knolls must cope with similar problems. They have tried for months to get the builder who constructed and sold the houses to remedy the situation—but to no avail. He is from another part of the state and won't make the repairs. In effect, he has "vanished." It is said, however, that he is building elsewhere under a different company name.

How do such builders get away with it? One widespread method used by unscrupulous builders (who often don't know anything about house construction) is to form a corporation to paint. Wide, yawning cracks are another matter. They may result from excessive settling or from the use of green framing lumber that has warped.

Next take a look at the floor. What is it made of? Oak strips? Good, provided that they are long pieces and not short scrap. There should be no wide gaps, no high edges. If the floor is made of cork, asphalt or vinyl tiles, there should be no chipped or dented squares, no adhesive oozing up through joints. And the blocks should fit together snugly, right to the walls.

build the houses and then dissolve it as soon as the houses are sold. This way, the company cannot be prosecuted when the houses start to collapse. Another scheme is to drain the corporation of all its assets, so that when the homeowners try to collect, the builder can plead that the corporation is bankrupt and unable to pay for damages. In most cases, there is little law enforcement agencies are able to do for the defrauded homeowners.

For these reasons, you should be extremely careful when buying a new house. Make sure you are dealing with a good builder. One sign of a quality builder is that he uses his name as part of the firm name. Here are a few additional pointers for avoiding the vanishing builder and getting a good house:

• Deal only with an established builder. A builder with an established reputation for quality is unlikely to gyp you. Ask him for credit references to find out how long he has been in business and how reliable he is.

• Check the quality of other houses he has built. A good builder should tell you where you can see houses he

has built and give you names of past buyers.

• Ask the local material suppliers (lumber, plumbing, and so on) and subcontractors what they think of the builder. Also ask the local building department about him.

• Is he a member of the Registered Builder program of the National Association of Home Builders? If so, he will display the Registered Builder emblem of the NAHB, showing he has passed certain professional and financial requirements set up by the local builders' board.

• Call the local Better Business Bureau and ask if they have received any complaints about the builder.

• Check whether he has a listed telephone number under his own name or that of his firm. The number should not be a new number under the name of the development, such as "Sunset-by-the-Sea."

Remember, if the builder is good, chances are the quality of the house will be high. Conversely, if he is disreputable, his houses will be shoddy, and he will probably "vanish."

Now pace the floor slowly. Feel any spring, any bounce? You shouldn't. If you do, suspect either inadequate joists or too thin sub-flooring. Listen for squeaks too. If you are on a tile floor, expect a good solid thud from each square. A hollow sound reveals that the block is loose and only partly bonded to the subfloor.

Kitchens and bathrooms are special cases because they are specialized rooms. In the baths look for ceramic tile on floors and walls. Other materials are finding favor, including various plastic tiles, and synthetic fibers have made carpeted bathrooms practical. Nevertheless, ceramic tile is still the traditional material, looked on as standard in older homes.

In the kitchen note whether counters are topped with serviceable plastic laminate, whether cutoff valves are present and accessible for every faucet and water-using appliance, whether there is adequate toe space under base cabinets and if the toe space is finished with a curved coving to leave no corner for dirt.

In both kitchen and baths check the ventilation and lighting. Exhaust fans should work smoothly and quietly but have a noticeable effect. The most common lighting fault is fixtures placed so that you can't avoid working in your own shadow. In both rooms, look for enamel or semigloss painted surfaces that can be wiped clean and withstand water.

Go up to the attic to check on the condition of the roof. Look for signs of leakage, such as water stains on the beams. If you can, climb out on the roof and look for missing tiles or holes that you might not have noticed during your outside inspection.

As you roam the house seeking specific signs of quality, try to bear in mind one general query: What kind of workmanship put this house together? The finest materials are wasted, you know, if some haphazard craftsman slaps them around and butchers them.

## A Close Look at Details

So take the trouble to look closely at some picky details, say the places where two pieces of molding meet or where the molding has been cut and fitted to go around a corner. If those pieces don't fit together as though made for each other or if there is a gaping joint crammed with a glob of calking, the workmanship has not been good.

A small point? Yes, perhaps. And it is not a certain index to the quality of work beneath, for the men who did the finish carpentry probably were not the ones who put together the framing. Still . . . can you believe a builder would permit sloppy workmanship where it shows but demand fine workmanship underneath?

Before you leave the house, ask the owner a few questions: How long has he lived there? Has he made any improvements? When was the house last painted? How old are the furnace and boiler? What are his annual maintenance costs, such as heating and electricity? If he is unable to answer some of your questions, find out from other sources.

Let's say you have found an acceptable house. You've looked it over from top to bottom, and you're satisfied that it will be a good investment, that it will be right for your family and that you will enjoy living there. Don't be in a rush to buy it. Before you make an offer, visit the house one or two more times. You'll be surprised how many things you notice on the second and third visits. Then hire a professional contractor to go over the house thoroughly and make a report on its condition and the cost of repairs.

If you are still interested, consult your own lawyer or a local real estate lawyer. Don't sign anything or deposit any money without his approval. No matter how shrewd you may be, an experienced lawyer is more qualified to handle such a complicated transaction.

## Negotiating a Price

The first step in the buying transaction is to agree on the price. The seller will have placed an "asking price" on the house. This is not necessarily the only price he will accept. It is just the starting point for bargaining. In most cases the asking price is the most the owner feels he can get for the house.

To get the bargaining off to a start, you make the owner an offer based on what you feel the house is worth. If you are not certain of its value, hire an appraiser. He may charge anywhere between $25 and $100, but a professional appraisal may save you from paying hundreds or thousands of dollars more than the house is worth.

Once you know roughly the value of the house, make a bid. To give you bargaining leverage, the amount you first offer should be

▭▭▭▭▭▭

# CHECKLIST FOR SIZING UP A HOUSE

### THE NEIGHBORHOOD

_____Quiet, residential street—no noisy traffic

_____Attractive, well-kept houses

_____Price comparable to prices of other houses in the area

_____Zoning laws that protect against commercial or industrial buildings

_____Will it be expensive to get to work, stores, schools, and so on?

_____Does the house have good resale potential?

_____Is there a public water supply or do you need a well?

_____Adequate fire and police protection

_____Neighbors of similar age and interests

_____Who is responsible for garbage removal?

_____Is there public provision for plowing snow and sanding icy streets?

_____Will you need a car? Two cars?

_____Can you walk to schools, church, playgrounds, stores?

_____Are there sidewalks for children to walk to school?

_____Can you foresee any possibility of increased taxes for new schools, sewers, libraries, roads or other facilities?

_____Is the local government good?

_____Any public nuisances nearby such as smoke, noxious odors, unpleasant noises?

### THE HOUSE AND YARD

_____House similar in age, size and design to other houses on the street

_____Is the exterior attractive and well-designed?

_____Is there room for expansion and will zoning laws permit it?

_____Does the yard need landscaping?

_____Will the yard be difficult and expensive to keep up?

_____Good drainage

_____Yard large enough for privacy—space for children to play

_____Driveway adequate in size and conveniently located

_____Path from driveway to front and back doors

_____Convenient place to park the car

_____Does the house seem suited to its natural surroundings?

_____Trees for shade and privacy

_____Front and back entrances sheltered from bad weather

_____Will the house need to be painted or repaired?

### OUTSIDE CONSTRUCTION

_____Roofing of good-quality material

_____Weather stripping on doors and windows

▭▭▭▭▭▭

━ ━ ━ ━ ━ ━

_____Flashing around eaves and chimney to protect against freezing weather, heavy storms

_____Adequate gutters and downspouts, in good condition

_____Solid brick and masonry—no cracks

_____Screens, storm windows and doors

_____Water taps for garden hose

_____Outside electrical outlet

_____Solid foundation walls extending 6 inches above ground and 5 inches thick

## INTERIOR CONSTRUCTION

_____Well-fitted doors and windows

_____Level floors with no splinters, cracks or wide spaces between floorboards

_____Carefully installed tile floors—no cracks, holes or visible adhesive

_____Straight, sturdy walls—no holes, cracks, visible nails or seams

_____Clean, dry basement

_____Adequate furnace and water heater

_____Leakproof roof

_____Would it be expensive to install air conditioning?

_____Good drain in basement

_____Dry, ventilated attic

_____Good-quality carpentry work—carefully fitted joints and moldings

_____Smoothly working windows, doors, drawers, cabinets

_____Adequate electrical outlets and sufficient amperage for your appliances and electrical equipment

_____Adequate water pressure for kitchen and bathroom

_____Good insulation

_____Well-lit stairways with railings—solidly built, not too steep

_____Ceilings in good repair—no cracks, holes, peeling plaster

## INTERIOR LIVING SPACE

_____Well-laid-out floor plan, with separate living, working and sleeping areas

_____Hall or foyer with coat closet at front entrance

_____Sufficient wall space in rooms for arranging furniture

_____Rooms large enough to hold your furniture

_____Sufficient number of bathrooms, conveniently placed

_____Laundry room or space for washer

_____Adequate closet space

_____Convenient storage space

_____Adequate, well-lit counter space in kitchen

_____Sufficient storage space in kitchen

_____Bedrooms located for maximum privacy and quiet

_____Spacing and location of windows for light, ventilation

_____Broom closet and linen closet

━ ━ ━ ━ ━ ━

lower than what you are prepared to pay eventually—but not so low as to be insulting. If the owner turns it down, make a slightly higher offer. He may then begin to come down on his price. Then you may raise your offer a little, and so on until you finally arrive at an acceptable price.

Timing can be a crucial factor in the final price of a house. If a house has been for sale several months, the owner may be willing to sell it for a low price to get rid of it. If, on the other hand, it has just come on the market, the owner will be more hopeful of getting his full price for the house and will probably be willing to wait.

The most important rule in price negotiation is to keep cool. Don't let the agent pressure you into paying too high a price. Take your time, and if the owner doesn't accept your highest offer, go on to other houses.

After you agree on the matter of price, the agent will probably ask you to sign a binder and make a deposit on the house. Consult your lawyer first. Unwitting buyers have signed what they thought was a harmless piece of paper and later discovered they have actually contracted to buy the house.

---

### GET A LAWYER BEFORE YOU SIGN ANYTHING

It pays to get a lawyer before you take any steps toward buying a house. If you don't, you may find yourself in trouble. Here's what happened to some unsuspecting buyers:

• A purchase agreement described the property only as 1335 South Oak Street. No boundaries were mentioned, and it turned out that they were not where the salesman said they were. A group of fine fruit trees belonged to the man next door.

• A house on a narrow lot had no garage, but the agent pointed out a spot where one could be built. Too late, the buyer discovered that zoning laws forbade building so close to the property line.

• An agent said the owner would pay the cost of a well if the spring went dry. It did, but the stipulation wasn't in the contract, so he didn't pay.

• The buyer understood that the electric kitchen stove, about a ton of coal and the screens and storm windows went with the property. They didn't.

• No date was set for giving possession, and the seller refused to move out until he found another place.

---

Several days after you agree on a price for the house, you will be asked to sign a conditional sales contract and make a cash down payment on the house, usually 5 to 10 percent of the purchase price. Have your lawyer look over the contract carefully before you agree to sign it. He will want to add certain conditions to the contract: He will probably make the contract conditional on your obtaining a satisfactory mortgage. He will see that it specifies a date by which the owner must vacate the property and provides for any unforeseen developments, such as the death or disability of either party. Be sure to have him include any promises the owner may have made to you, such as the items he included in the price of the house. If you are planning to use the home for business, or rent a floor to a tenant, make the contract conditional on your being allowed to do so.

## The Closing

The actual buying transaction (the closing) will take place a month or two later. In the meantime you will obtain a satisfactory mortgage. (For more information on mortgages, see Chapter 12, page 137.) At the closing you will have to pay, in addition to the price

• A man bought a two-family house and the contract mentioned that the tenant on the upper floor had a lease. It didn't mention, however, that the tenant had paid three months' rent in advance. The new owner couldn't collect that money.

• A buyer accepted a quit-claim deed, under which the seller delivered only whatever rights he had in the property. A search of the title showed that the seller's brother, who was in a mental hospital, held an interest in the property. The buyer had to spend a lot of money to clear the title in court.

In some states, if the buyer has merely signed a simple binder his lawyer usually is helpless in bargaining about whether buyer or seller will pay back taxes; unpaid interest on the mortgage; overdue telephone, electricity, gas and water bills; and taxes for special assessments. He may find that he must raise considerably more money for a down payment than he had expected.

The average buyer employs a lawyer to close the deal, yet for an additional fee of probably not more than $25 or $50 he could have had legal advice before he took his first risky step. It is cheap insurance not only for making a good deal but also for keeping out of a bad one.

of the house, a number of miscellaneous fees known as closing costs. Prepare yourself for these "costs of buying" by making out a list like the one that is shown on page 140. They could run as high as $800.

You have to be on your toes when you tackle the intricacies of house buying. You must know exactly what you want and how to spot the house that will fill the bill. With so much money involved, you want to be sure to make a good investment in money and comfort. No one can make such a crucial decision on the spur of the moment or on the basis of some vague intuition. So take your time and explore all the angles. Be sure you are completely satisfied with your choice before you agree to buy it.

Remember, however, that no house will be absolutely perfect. Unless you are prepared to accept a few shortcomings you will never find the right house. The inside may be lovely and the outside unappealing. Or the house may be warm and cozy, but the kitchen archaic. Be prepared to compromise. If you feel that the good features outweigh the bad in terms of cost, convenience and livability, then it's a wise choice, and you'll be happy in the new home you have so carefully selected.

---

## WORDS YOU SHOULD KNOW

**Binder.** A receipt for a sum of money—or the sum of money itself—paid by the buyer to the seller or agent to secure the right to buy a property on agreed terms. This is usually the first step in purchase of a property.

**Conditional sales contract.** A written agreement to buy a property provided certain conditions are met, such as the ability of the agent to arrange mortgage financing or an inspection proving the absence of termites. Most often, this contract requires the seller to deliver a deed showing the property free of all claims, mortgages, liens, delinquent taxes or other restrictions that might qualify the buyer's rights.

**Septic tank.** A concrete receptacle to which waste is carried from the house and in which chemical action breaks down the solids; an underground network of tiles disperses the liquids. Septic tanks are used in rural areas without central sewage systems. In older houses a cesspool (a simple hole in the ground covered by a cement slab) may be found.

## CHAPTER 12

## Taking the Mystery Out of Mortgages

*How large a mortgage will you need? Where can you get the best mortgage at the lowest cost? Here's what you need to know*

"Owning your own home." It's an appealing phrase—but most of us know that the ownership is, for a long time, really a partnership between a mortgage company and ourselves. It's the terms of the mortgage that are the key to successful homeownership, and the better the terms the happier the homeowning. So, before you buy a home, it's important to know as much as possible about mortgages. The knowledge will pay off in dollars and cents, not only at the time the house is bought, but also for the duration of the mortgage—frequently as long as 30 years.

A mortgage is a specialized form of long-term loan to make up the difference between the price of your dream house and the cold reality of the amount of down payment you can make on that dream. The loan has two major components: the principal, which is the amount of money actually lent you, and the interest on that principal, which is figured at an annual rate for the length of the mortgage. In addition, there are smaller payments for both taxes and hazard insurance (fire, storms, and so on), also computed at an annual rate for the length of the mortgage. Many families add a life insurance policy that pays off the mortgage in full should something happen to the family's breadwinner before the end of the mortgage. All these figures are totaled for the length of the mortgage, say 30 years, and divided into 360 equal payments for which you will have to write a check every month.

In the first year of your mortgage the bulk of the money will be interest, but as the number of your payments mount, more and more of each payment will be principal and less and less will be interest. It's the principal that represents your ownership, or equity, and as you build up this equity you own more and more of those bricks and pipes and roofing. At the end of the mortgage period the partnership between you and the mortgage company dissolves, and you will own your home "free and clear." (This doesn't mean the end of payments—you still have taxes, insurance, utility bills and upkeep—but you will be paying out much less every month.)

The total that you pay *in the long run* depends on the size of the initial down payment, the interest rate, the insurance premium and the duration of the mortgage. A $20,000 mortgage for 20 years at $7\frac{1}{2}$ percent will end up costing $38,668.80. For a 30-year mortgage at the same interest rate the cost will be $50,346.00; the interest of $30,346.00 is more than the principal and, depending on the down payment, may even be more than the price of the house itself! So the decisions you make on large versus small down payment, shorter mortgage versus long one or conventional versus FHA mortgage are dollars and cents decisions.

## How Large a Down Payment?

Let's consider the down payment first. Assuming you have the choice, is it better to make a larger down payment and assume a smaller mortgage, or vice versa? There is one very good argument for the larger down payment—the smaller the mortgage, the less interest you will pay in the long run and the less your house will cost. Furthermore, with a larger down payment you are more likely to be able to get a mortgage with a lower interest rate, whether it's for 15, 20 or 25 years, and that too will save you money.

However, there are arguments for a smaller down payment and a longer mortgage. For one thing, you have less cash "frozen" in the house, and the money that would be out of circulation can be invested in stocks or bonds or simply left in the bank to earn interest. Furthermore, the interest you pay on the principal amount of the mortgage is deductible for tax purposes and so doesn't cost as much as it may appear to.

Inflation is another consideration. We've had a long-run inflationary trend that doesn't show much sign of halting, though it may slow down. So the dollars that go into your monthly mortgage payments buy more goods today than they will 5, 10 or 20 years from now. Why not, the argument goes, hold on to your cash and put it to work earning interest or dividends, since you will be paying off a long-term mortgage in dollars that will buy less and less.

The question of resale value is still another factor. You may assume, when you buy your first house, that it's forever—or at least for a very long time. You may think you never again want to go through the anxiety of worrying about a mortgage, or unpacking all those cartons, or getting a house livable. But, like many American families, as more children come along, or you change jobs, or you decide you want to live in a particular school district, you will probably sell your house before you make that last mortgage payment. And the kind of mortgage you have may influence the ease with which you sell your house.

Let's assume that you bought your house when mortage rates were lower and you have a 20-year mortgage at 5 percent, with 15 years to go. Obviously, if the present mortgage rate is 8 percent, a prospective buyer would be delighted if he could take over your mortgage—provided he could swing the down payment. And though the 20-year mortgage means higher monthly payments, it is still less total money paid out because there is less interest. Some real estate men say the shorter mortgage (and of course the lower interest rate) makes your house more attractive.

On the other hand, suppose your mortgage had been for 5 percent but for 30 years. A prospective buyer would have to make smaller monthly payments, but the total amount of interest would be more. Some real estate men say this would make your house easier to sell because there are more buyers when monthly payments are lower, even if the total cost is higher.

Of course, when you take over someone else's mortgage on a house then *you* will be the one to save, if the interest rate on the mortgage is below the current market. This is a good deal for you since, in addition to your long-run savings, you will probably save several hundred dollars in closing costs.

## Sources for Mortgages

With all these factors in mind (and a bit of a scared feeling at the thought of such a long-term commitment) you've decided on the down payment, the terms you prefer (if you can get them) and the length of the mortgage your budget can absorb. Now you are ready to look into the sources for mortgages and the kinds of mortgages available.

Since mortgages are loans, it isn't surprising that commercial and mutual savings banks do a big mortgage business. So do life insurance companies, savings and loan associations and mortgage companies. All of them arrange all three kinds of mortgages, distinguished by who insures, or guarantees, the loan: conventional, that is, not backed by any government agencies; FHA, that is, granted by a private lender, such as a bank, insurance company or other source, but guaranteed by the Federal Housing Administration; and VA, again granted by a private lender but guaranteed by the Veterans Administration. There are differences among these five sources as to down payment, interest rates, prepayment rules, length of mortgage, plus individual differences depending on the area of the country, the state within the area, state regulations, individual operating pro-

▭▭▭▭▭▭

## THE COST OF BUYING A HOUSE

All too many people forget that when they acquire a new home there is more to pay for than the house itself. In planning to buy a home you should take into account these additional expenses, which may occur before or at the time of "closing"—the actual transfer of title. Estimate how much they will be and have a cash reserve ready to cover them.

| *Expenses* | *Estimated Cost* |
|---|---|
| Inspection and appraisal | $ |
| Property survey | |
| Title search and insurance | |
| Tax stamps | |
| Recording fees | |
| Notary fee | |
| Lawyers' fees | |
| Mortgage-processing charge | |
| Credit report | |
| Deposit on annual taxes, insurance and special assessments | |
| Premiums on transferable insurance | |
| Other | |
| *Total cash needs* | $ |

▭▭▭▭▭▭

cedures and practices. Mortgage interest rates are often cheaper in the Northeast, and more expensive in the Southwest and West.

In the past decade a new kind of mortgage insurance, sponsored by private insurance companies, has developed—somewhat similar in principle to FHA and VA insurance except that it is underwritten by private, not government, funds. These commercial mortgage insurance companies, by guaranteeing the top 20 percent of conventional mortgage loans (the FHA guarantees 100 percent) take some of the risk from these mortgages and enable savings and loan associations, banks and insurance companies to offer more generous terms. With this kind of insurance, for instance, families who qualify because they have a good income, good credit rating, good prospects and a minimum of other debts can get a mortgage with a down payment of only 10 percent. There are other advantages too, including lower mortgage insurance rates, faster processing of applications and the possibility of ending the mortgage insurance payments when a good payment record proves that the insurance is no longer needed.

Though it is difficult to state precise differences among the kinds of mortgages, since the exact terms vary, it is possible to state some general differences. Usually conventional loans require a larger down payment (about 20 to 25 percent), have a high upper limit on the size of the mortgage available, charge a higher rate of interest, are for a shorter length of time and permit prepayment only with restrictions. The FHA mortgages require a smaller down payment (3 to 13 percent), have a middle limit on the amount of mortgage offered, charge a lower rate of interest, are for a longer length of time and permit prepayment without penalty of up to 15 percent of the loan in any one year. The VA loans are the most generous of all, but of course are restricted to veterans. They require a minimum down payment or none at all, depending on the value of the property, charge a rate of interest lower than the FHA and permit prepayment with no penalties. (The FHA also insures loans to veterans on somewhat more liberal terms than to other borrowers.) When evaluating which kind of loan you want, you'll naturally choose the one that offers the best terms for you, taking into account your long-range plans.

You will note that only the VA permits "prepayment without penalty." What does this mean? The banks and other private financial institutions who lend you money do so because they earn income when you repay the loan with interest. If you pay back the loan faster than anticipated they not only lose this income but have to go to the time and expense of finding new borrowers. Because they don't want to do this they charge you for paying your loan in advance and thereby costing them money; the amount of this charge is the "penalty." The VA, however, which was set up specifically to make it easier for veterans to own their homes after their time in the service, doesn't have this penalty. No penalty on prepayment is always a benefit, but it can be a real money saver if you sell your house before your mortgage has been paid off. You can settle the old mortgage without penalty before undertaking a new one.

## Varieties of Mortgages

There are other differences in mortgages that are worth knowing about. The *open-end mortgage* permits you, after you have paid off part of your loan, to borrow more, up to the amount of the original mortgage. You then have cash on hand to pay for repairs, remodeling or expansion. An open-end mortgage usually has three possible reborrowing rates: the original rate (this is good, since it's usually lower than the prevailing rate, but it is rarely granted); a split rate with the old rate applied to the unpaid balance of the original mortgage and a new (higher) rate applied to the amount being reborrowed; and a new and customarily higher rate for the entire mortgage. Clearly the last choice is the least desirable of the three and should be avoided in times of high mortgage rates.

A *package mortgage* allows the borrower to include the cost of extra appliances and equipment—washers or carpeting, for instance—as part of the mortgage. Typically, package mortgages are offered by builders who include these extras as part of the "package" for financing a new house in their development. While it is an advantage for you as a buyer if you have little or no reserves to pay for these extras, it does have a drawback. It means that, with a 20-year mortgage, you might find yourself near the end of your mortgage paying for carpeting that had once been the pride of your living room but has been lining the doghouse for the past ten years.

Finally, there are *second mortgages*. What happens if you fall in

## WORDS YOU SHOULD KNOW

**Mortgage.** A long-term loan in which your home itself is pledged as security for eventual payment of the difference between your down payment and the total cost of the property. The "principal" is the amount of money loaned to you, which diminishes as you pay off the installments; the "interest" is the price you pay, usually by the month, for the use of the lender's money until the mortgage is liquidated (paid off), at which time you own the property "free and clear," without debt.

**Conventional mortgage.** A mortgage negotiated between you and the lender without an insurer like the Federal Housing Administration (FHA) or the Veterans Administration (VA).

**Insured mortgage.** A mortgage in which the lender is insured against loss by an agency such as the FHA or VA.

**Open-end mortgage.** A loan that permits a borrower who has paid off part of his mortgage to borrow again without putting up further security.

**Package mortgage.** A mortgage that includes financing for items such as kitchen equipment and wall-to-wall carpeting.

**Second mortgage.** An additional loan beyond the first mortgage. The lender in a second mortgage cannot enforce his claim against the property until the first mortgagor has been satisfied. Since the risk is high, so is the interest rate. The VA and FHA will not insure a property on which there is a second mortgage.

**Prepayment of mortgage.** Repayment of part of the loan ahead of schedule. This usually involves a penalty, except on VA-guaranteed loans. If you agree to a 30-year mortgage, then sell your house after only five years, paying off the mortgage, the lender will charge you a special additional fee to compensate for his loss of interest.

**Points.** A charge made by the lender to sidestep the low interest ceiling permitted on government-insured mortgages. Each point is 1 percent of the mortgage loan. Example: As a buyer with a VA-insured mortgage, you need $8000 to swing the deal. Each point is therefore $80. The lender asks for five points, or $400. You accept and pay interest on a mortgage of $8000, but the lender gives you only $7600.

**Warranty.** A written pledge by the seller that the property is all he has represented it to be. This guarantee usually is extracted by a buyer when he buys in a subdivision from a speculative builder. Usually such a warrant expires one year after date of purchase.

**Quiet possession.** A provision in a warranty deed conveying title to a property, guaranteeing the buyer that no one will pop up to dispute his untroubled ownership and occupation of the premises.

love with a house that costs $25,000 but can afford only a $5000 down payment and can get a mortgage of only $15,000? Unless you suddenly make a killing in the stock market or win a "name-this-detergent" contest you may be tempted to take a second mortgage to make up the missing $5000. Such mortgages are sometimes available from the seller, private sources and some commercial lenders. As with a first mortgage the house is the security, and you make monthly payments consisting of principal, interest and other charges.

Since the holder of the first mortgage gets paid first, the second mortgagee's claim is riskier and he naturally charges a higher interest rate and a higher service fee. But his claim is a solid one. Even if a borrower pays off his first mortgage, should he default on his second, the holder of the second mortgage has the right to foreclose—the kind of situation that might arise, for example, if the husband dies and the first mortgage is paid off by the mortgage insurance.

Aside from this risk, a second mortgage means paying out two substantial installments every month, for a long period of time. Most families who are in a position to pay out such a large total sum every month would probably qualify for a greater mortgage in the first place. If they do not, they are probably taking on more debt than they can handle easily, and they run the risk of losing their home even if they manage to keep up the first mortgage. The FHA and the VA require borrowers to certify that they hold no secondary mortgages or promissory notes before they can be approved for a mortgage.

## Shopping for a Mortgage

Where should you shop for your mortgage, to be sure you get the best possible deal? Since the terms are going to depend not only on the market value of your house but also on your credit rating, your best bet is someone who already knows you, such as your own bank, a credit union at your job or your life insurance company. Some lenders charge an application fee and ask for this fee if they *offer* you a mortgage, even if you decide not to accept it. Others absorb the fee as part of doing business, and still others include the fee in the cost of servicing your loan. It's a good idea to check on this fee before applying to too many sources.

▭▭▭▭▭▭

## WHAT KIND OF DEED WILL YOU GET?

There are four possible kinds of deed that you can get when you buy a house, depending on the history of the house, local lawyers and how often the house has changed hands. The best deed is the "full covenant and warranty" deed, in which the seller gives you a number of permanent commitments on such things as: the title is free and clear and the owner has full rights to it; there will be quiet possession; the property is free of encumbrances of any kind; the seller will execute any papers needed to prove his title to the property. Next best is the "bargain and sale with covenants against the grantor's act," in which the seller says that he has not done anything to affect the title. Next is "bargain and sale without covenant," where the seller makes no such claim. And finally there is the "quit-claim" deed, in which the seller gives you all his rights, title and interest but offers no assurance as to what these rights are. Though the risks vary with the kind of deed, it's clear that *all* deeds involve some risks—and title insurance is a good investment if it is available in your area.

▭▭▭▭▭▭

When you do apply be prepared to give all the information the lender will need to determine your credit standing, including where you work, how long you've been there, your salary, the number of dependents you have, your assets and liabilities, whether or not you are planning to borrow money in addition to your mortgage.

The actual process of getting the mortgage works like this: You make your application, and before processing it the lender sends an appraiser to look at the house and evaluate its worth. After the amount of the mortgage is decided upon, there is a check on your credit rating to determine how good a risk you are. If the property is worthwhile and you are considered financially solid, you will be notified both of the lender's approval and of the amount of the mortgage that can be granted. The process can take anywhere from a week to a month or more, so be prepared to wait.

Be ready also for some "one time only" costs in addition to the mortgage, including what are called points and the various closing fees you may be expected to pay.

Points are a feature of tight money periods, and very much a part of the mortgage scene at present. FHA and VA maximum interest rates are set, by law, on a national basis. Many states also have banking commissions that set their own statewide limits on the maximum that can be charged for conventional mortgages. Both the state rates and the FHA and VA rates are below the interest rates on nonmortgage loans, and since money is tight, lenders who can get higher rates for nonmortgage loans are understandably reluctant to place mortgages unless they can make up the difference between the two interest rates. This is done by charging the buyer or the seller, or sometimes both, a one-time charge of a percentage of the loan, called a point. One point is 1 percent of the loan, two points is 2 percent, and so on. The charge is a legally accepted way for a lender to get a better return on his money without violating the law regarding charges for interest rates.

---

## UNDERSTANDING YOUR BUILDER'S WARRANTY

On a home approved by the FHA for mortgage insurance before building is started, the builder must warrant that the house will conform substantially to the plans and specifications on which the FHA based its appraisal.

The warranty is in effect for one year. The year begins on the date the first buyer takes title to the home or on the date the home is first lived in—whichever comes first.

If during that year the owner sees defects that he believes the builder should correct, he should ask the builder, in writing, to do so.

If the builder fails to correct them the owner can write to the FHA insuring office. He should give his FHA case number and state the problem.

If the FHA finds that the defect is one the builder should correct, it will try to persuade him to do so. Usually the FHA is successful.

## GOOD IDEA: MORTGAGE INSURANCE

What happens if the head of the household dies and there is a sudden drop in income, with the possibility of not being able to meet mortgage payments? To guard against loss of your home, it's a good idea to buy an insurance policy especially designed to pay off the unpaid balance of the mortgage in just such an emergency. This means that your family still has a home at a time when they may need it most. If they do decide to sell, it can be when the time is best—not when a sale is forced because of mortgage pressure and they have to take whatever price they can get. If or when a family does decide to sell after the mortgage has been paid, all the proceeds belong to them.

This kind of insurance should not be confused with mortgage title insurance which is required by the lender and protects him, not you.

When you are asked for points you are actually being asked to accept a smaller total loan than the one you've requested, but to pay interest on the full amount for the full length of your mortgage. For instance, if you want to get a $20,000 mortgage on a house, and you are asked for five points, you are being asked to take 5 percent less than $20,000, or $19,000. But the interest portion of your monthly mortgage payments will be a percentage of $20,000, not $19,000—so in effect you are paying a higher interest rate than the one that appears on the note.

## Closing Costs

Closing costs include title insurance, to assure the lender but *not you*, the borrower, of the validity of the deed to the property being transferred; lawyer's fees for preparing the documents and other services he may have given during the prepurchase period; a processing fee, also called the origination fee, which is a percentage of the borrowed amount and is given to the lender for arranging the loan, including the cost of the appraisal, of the check made on your credit and of copies of your schedule of payments; and miscellaneous fees, such as notary charges and recording fees. The inclusion of these costs is just about standard at every closing. The costs themselves vary, however, depending on where you live, since different states have different fees; the kind of mortgage you have; and lawyers' rates in your area. Prepayment of taxes and various fees are often added to the closing costs and the total can well be around $600 to $800 for a $15,000 to $20,000 mortgage. (For help in figuring closing costs, see the form on page 140.)

Note that the title insurance included in the closing costs protects the lender for the amount of the mortgage only, and offers *you* no protection at all. Since you will, someday, be the sole owner of the house, and since, with your down payments, you already have some equity in it, it's very important that you too have title insurance. It gives you protection against mistakes that may have been made in recording and searching the title of your house and against the carelessness or possible dishonesty of previous owners. They may, for instance, neglect to report mechanics' liens (money owed craftsmen such as plumbers or carpenters) for work done but not paid for, or they may have given away some rights, such as access to private roads or beaches, without entering these facts into the deed of the house. Title insurance is a guarantee that if there is a future question about the title, the insurance company will fight for your rights, and if they lose, will compensate you for any losses you may incur. Some states require owner title insurance as part of the mortgage transaction, but others do not, so check with your lawyer before you incur this expense. The cost is usually about $3.50 to $5 per $1000 of coverage but it may save you much more than this if the title is questioned.

One final word of caution. No matter how carefully you have examined the house and how firmly you have resolved to "make do" with the house as is, until you can afford improvements, there are always going to be unforeseen expenses. Curtains don't fit the windows they were planned for; pipes burst; the town governing board votes a special assessment to repair road damage from an unusually snowy winter. So put aside an emergency fund to take care of the unforeseen, and then settle into your new home, planning to enjoy it with a minimum of financial worries.

CHAPTER 13

## Moving Without Tears

*How to minimize
the expense and headache of
moving into a new house*

People on the move often find, to their sorrow, that the moving industry is in the driver's seat as far as the consumer is concerned. Though the industry operates under the regulation of the Interstate Commerce Commission there have been few controls and, in the past, consumer complaints have frequently gone unanswered. The ICC recently proposed a group of new rules that would put the consumer in a better position to understand his rights and to insist on certain guarantees from the mover. But it may be some time before these rules assume the force of law, and in the meantime moving is still a time of toil and trouble. The process can be made easier, however, through careful planning. Here's how to go about it.

As soon as you know you're moving, begin looking for a good mover. The 13 largest movers that operate throughout the country are: Allied Van Lines, American Red Ball Van Lines, Atlas Van Lines, Bekins Van Lines, Dean Van Lines, Global Van Lines, Greyhound Van Lines, John F. Ivory, Mayflower, North American Van Lines, Republic Van Lines, United Van Lines and Wheaton Van Lines. Many of these moving companies have one or more agents in your city, whose advertisements appear in the Yellow Pages of the telephone directory with the name of the national affiliate, for example, "Ryan Moving and Storage, Agent of Allied Van Lines." Pick the mover whose reputation is best in your area. Ask friends who moved recently for their recommendations.

Before you make any decision, call two or three recommended movers and make an appointment with a representative of each to come to your house and give you an estimate. If you are unable to communicate with a company's representative, or you are not impressed by his interest in your move, eliminate his company. Four points should be discussed with the mover's representative: Will he give you an accurate cost estimate (not one designed to win your business)? Can the mover meet your timing requirements? What insurance coverage does the mover offer and will it pay legitimate claims? What special preparations can be made for antiques, valuables and appliances?

Ask your moving company representative whom you should call on moving day if problems arise. Look over the written agreement and note whether departure date and destination date are specified. Choose the company that best meets your requirements. (If you have any doubts, ask the Better Business Bureau about the company.)

To obtain an estimate that is as accurate as possible, show the representative everything that is to be moved. Don't neglect to show him certain closets, for example, because they are disorganized! He must see the contents of every closet, the basement, attic, garage and workshop. Only then can he give you an idea of the cost of your move. The actual cost is determined when your van is loaded and weighed. At that time, if the cost of the move is 10 percent or $25 more than the estimate, the van line is required to notify you of this difference by telephone so that you will be prepared to pay the right amount. Moving companies usually insist that payment be made by certified check, cash or money order before your possessions are unloaded at the new house. If there is any difficulty about payment, your goods will be put in storage until the company has your money.

Each moving company determines its own cost for extra services, such as packing, providing boxes and barrels, moving pianos, picking up goods in more than one place, unpacking and servicing appliances. These special services are usually priced competitively. Look carefully at the detailed costs that are listed in your written estimate. Be sure that only the services you want and need are included.

## Long-Distance Moves

Since timing is a frequent cause of annoyance to families moving for a long distance, determine your time requirements before you talk with a mover, then let him know how important your time schedule is. If you are counting on being able to move out on a certain day and on getting into your new house as soon as possible, choose a mover who can accommodate your wishes. Every day that you must wait for the van in the new area will mean the expense of meals and lodging.

A long-distance move is often complicated by the fact that a family does not have enough furniture to fill the usual large long-distance van. By coordinating with other agents of the same nationwide company, your agent will plan to load the remainder of the van with another family's possessions and then deliver one load en route to the other destination. Even the most reputable mover has his own problems: He cannot afford to transport a half-full van, nor can he unload your goods first if the other family's house is located on the way to your new home.

Your first question, then, is whether the estimated weight of your belongings is enough to fill a van. If it is, you can probably count on a prearranged time schedule based on the distance and the season. If not, you can pay an additional fee and request exclusive use of the van in order to meet your time requirement. If your belongings fill only part of a van and another family's possessions will be loaded with yours, inquire where else the van is going and how long it will take to reach your house.

The dates should be specified in writing on the mover's contract, but since moving companies must cope with "other people" and the weather, timing cannot be guaranteed. (Ask your mover whether he will pay for your lodging and food for the days he keeps you waiting beyond the agreement.) The following questions may help you avoid an unexpected delay: (1) On moving day ask the driver where he is going next and when he expects to reach your new house. (2) Give the driver your interim address and the telephone number where you can be reached after you arrive in the new city so that he can notify you in case of delay. (3) Get the name and address of the agent in your new city so that you can contact him for information when you arrive.

Moving companies are most in demand between June 1 and September 1 and on the 15th and 30th of each month. Try to avoid the busiest days in order to get the best service. Call a moving company as far ahead of time as possible and try to reserve the dates you want.

Your moving company is responsible for all goods at the rate of 60 cents per pound. (If a $50 Steuben bowl weighing two pounds were to be broken, you would be reimbursed $1.20.) However, if you have a number of antiques and other valuable possessions and wish to cover your shipment in excess of this rate, the company will provide full-value protection insurance at the cost of 50 cents per $100 value. For contents valued at $10,000, for example, $50 will fully protect all your possessions. This may seem costly, but with this coverage you should receive full payment on lost or broken articles. The additional protection can also apply to goods you packed, provided the mover declares your packing adequate; ask beforehand how difficult it is to obtain this approval. The paper declaring the amount of your full-value protection must be in your possession before the van leaves. Despite the amount of coverage you have discussed previously with the mover, the figure listed on that paper is the one that counts.

You can ask your local insurance broker if he can provide coverage for your move, but many local brokers prefer not to insure you for a long-distance move because it is difficult for them to inspect any damage that may occur en route or during the unloading.

## Loading and Unloading

When the unloading process begins at the new house, make sure all cartons are still sealed. Check each piece of furniture for damage or loss. Make a written note of any damage when you sign the inventory, or indicate that the contents of boxes have not yet been checked. Final complaints in writing must be made within a specified period. If you can't get satisfaction from your moving company, notify the Interstate Commerce Commission of your complaint. The ICC is listed in your directory under "U.S. Government."

The driver of the van is in charge of your move; he will be assisted by one or two other movers who are employes of the local moving company. The driver has two additional responsibilities besides driving—preparing the inventory and presenting the bill of lading.

Before the van is loaded on moving day, the driver will inspect every item of furniture throughout the house and put an identifying number on it. Accompany him while he writes down the condition of each piece. You may be appalled if every piece of furniture is listed as "s & m" (scratched and marred). The driver must protect himself against unjust claims by an owner who hadn't noticed an old scratch, but you must, at the same time, watch out for your own interests. It's your job to see that the inventory is accurate, particularly in the description of relatively new furniture and of the extent of defects on old pieces. The inventory will also include the number and size of boxes, barrels and wardrobes that you are moving. You will be asked to sign a statement that the driver's inventory is correct.

When your shipment has been loaded, the driver will give you a bill of lading, which is your contract. It should show the mover's name, address and telephone number, and the address and telephone number where you can be reached, the address where the goods are going, the date of loading, the preferred date of delivery and the declared valuation of the contents. This bill of lading must be signed by you and by the driver.

If you have to store your furniture before settling, you should inquire into the cost ahead of time. Unless the mover is able to grant you several days of "in transit" storage (meaning your van will remain intact), you will have to pay for the second unloading and loading. Everything should be cleaned thoroughly if you anticipate storing. Check the storage facilities and make sure your full-value protection insurance will remain in effect.

The movers who unload the van will unpack for you too. It may be necessary for them to come back the following day to finish unloading. They may agree to return a day or two later to unpack if you request this service in advance. If you have a large load, you may find it helpful to arrange to have some items unpacked on moving day so you can put these away before other boxes and barrels are unpacked.

The same driver who loaded your possessions will appear at your new house with one or two movers who are employes of the destination agent. Someone must be at the house to pay the driver, to open the house and to indicate where furniture should be placed. If it is impossible for you to be there, make careful arrangements with your realtor or a friend in the new area to be present. Provide that person with a key and a general floor plan to indicate placement of furniture.

It's the mover's responsibility to place rugs and furniture where you want them, and to set up beds. Appliances will not be connected unless previous arrangements have been made. The movers may appear hurried if the driver has to unload another shipment after yours. Nevertheless, see that they place each carton and barrel where you want it and unpack the containers you want unpacked; this is part of your contract. Don't let the movers leave until they have completed all the services to which you are entitled.

## Local Moves

So far we've been talking about long-distance moves, regulated by the Interstate Commerce Commission; a local move is almost entirely unregulated. Individual states have rules governing a move within that state, but these rules vary considerably and are not nearly so extensive as the interstate rules. A local move presents fewer hazards to your belongings than a long-distance move. You can supervise the movers closely at both ends of the move without the immediate concerns of departing on a long trip; you can also follow the van to its destination and thus prevent loss of possessions. But don't be too casual in choosing a moving company just because you feel safer about a local move. Knowing something about local companies and how they operate can help you to save money and eliminate frustration in these short-haul operations.

Many of the 13 companies listed at the beginning of this chapter have agents in each city who make local moves as well as long-distance moves. Other moving companies are not affiliated with a national company; they make only local moves. A reputable local mover need not be nationally affiliated to be responsible and efficient. The most important guideline for you in choosing a local mover is word-of-mouth recommendation. If you cannot obtain a good recommendation, then choose a local agent whose affiliate is well-known, rather than an unknown local mover. You can also check the reputation of local movers with the nearest Better Business Bureau.

Local moving charges are based on the length of time it takes to make your complete move. Although some local movers may give you a flat rate, they usually quote you an hourly rate for the truck and two or three men. Your charge is then based on the amount of time spent on your move. The cost of your local move can therefore vary greatly, depending on your mover.

A flat rate per hour might vary by as much as $10, but don't make the mistake of choosing the mover with the cheapest hourly charge. Choose the best mover, even though his rates may be higher. His efficient workers will complete the move quickly, and your total cost will be less.

Another factor to consider is the charge for the van's traveling time between the warehouse and your house. Some state regulations call for a flat travel-time fee of approximately $25, regardless of the distance. Other states allow the moving company to charge you from the time the van leaves the warehouse. Know which system of charges is applicable. If you are being charged for the exact amount of travel time, then it is important to choose the most reputable mover nearest to you.

To further decrease the cost of a local move, ask whether the mover charges for new boxes or whether he can make used boxes available. If used boxes are not supplied by the moving company, gather your own.

To compare charges for a local move, obtain estimates by telephone. The dispatcher will discuss with you his company's cost per hour and give you a general estimate based on the number of rooms in your house and the approximate distance between the two houses. Remember, however, that estimates can be misleading. As with a long-distance move, if you call a reputable mover, his estimate will be more reliable than the one given by an unknown mover who may underestimate purposely in order to win your business.

In a local move the agreement between you and the moving company may be a verbal telephone agreement. But you should, if possible, have someone from the moving company come and look at your furnishings. If you have an odd-size couch, for instance, that won't fit into a standard apartment-house elevator, he may have to make arrangements to have it moved on top of the elevator. Or if you have antiques he may send a man who has had experience handling such valuable possessions. Call the moving company you have chosen at least two or three weeks ahead of time; be specific about the day you want to be moved. Ask for the first move of the day in order to avoid having to wait for a delayed van. Don't plan to move on the very day that the house to which you are moving is being vacated. If your van were to reach the new house before the other van departed, the delay would be costly.

The following steps will ensure a successful local move:

1. Call the moving company the day before you move to be sure of your schedule.

2. Request that the movers cover floors in well-traveled areas.

3. Stay with the movers the entire time they are moving your belongings. They will be more careful if you are present.

4. Tell the movers which outside door in your new house is the widest. Encourage them to bring the truck as close to that door as possible.

5. Provide coffee or soft drinks and be tactful in making requests.

6. Take down or prepare everything you can in readiness for the movers. Save yourself money by not using their time.

7. If the movers arrive at your house much later than you had expected, ask them to sign their time of arrival so that you will have an accurate record in case of a disagreement later.

In dealing with a moving company for either a local or a long-distance move, know what to expect and what you can insist on; at the same time, be tactful with the men who are moving you. If you are organized, informed and specific in your requirements, and if you have chosen a reliable company, your move will be a success.

CHAPTER 14

## How to Get More
## When You Sell Your Home

*A few tips that can
add hundreds or thousands
of dollars to the resale
value of your home*

A growing family needs more space. A company transfer requires a move to another state. Retirement time means a smaller house. What's the common denominator here? The people involved will be selling their homes. When the time comes for *you* to sell *your* house your primary consideration will be to get the best price possible.

To determine the right price for your house, first compare it with the houses for sale in your immediate area. Then ask two well-recommended realtors to see your house separately. After a brief tour they will give you a verbal estimate of its present market value. Usually no cost is involved, and you don't have to commit yourself to selling your house through a realtor to get an estimate from him. But if you are considering selling your house by yourself, without using a real estate salesman, make this clear when you ask a realtor to make an estimate.

An appraisal from two different realtors gives you a better idea of price and with whom to list. Some may give you a low estimate knowing that they can sell the house faster; others may quote you the highest possible price hoping you will want the top dollar. Try to obtain from each one an accurate idea of a fair asking price as well as an expected selling price. Choose the realtor you consider to be the best salesman, not merely the one who quotes the highest market price.

If you want a detailed written appraisal of your house, call a professional real estate appraiser. This service usually costs $2 to $3 per $1000 value of your house.

A Federal Housing Authority appraisal of your house will eventually be necessary if you sell to a buyer who obtains an FHA-insured loan, so you will save time in the process of selling if you obtain an FHA appraisal ahead of time. Besides, it will be an additional help in pricing your house. Any bank can tell you how to obtain an FHA appraisal in your area. The fee is about $35.

If you already know a well-qualified salesman you may want him to sell your house. If several people in your area have successfully sold a house "by owner" you may be tempted to try selling your house directly. In either case, you will need a lawyer. His assistance is always essential, but probably more extensive if you are selling your house yourself.

## Selling by Owner

The basic decision between selling through a realtor or by owner depends on whether you can cope with the responsibility of selling your own house or prefer to pay a professional salesman part of your selling price to take that responsibility. Don't decide to sell by owner because you want to save money unless the conditions and your situation are favorable. Try selling by owner if: (1) you are not in a hurry; (2) houses in your area are in demand; (3) mortgage money is generally obtainable; (4) your house is appealing and has standard features; (5) you have a particularly attractive asset, such as a big family room or a modernized kitchen; (6) it is spring or early fall, the most likely time for buyers; (7) the local school district is good; (8) the surrounding neighborhood is appealing; (9) your house is where a For Sale sign can be seen by Sunday drivers; (10) your price is right and you know that selling by owner has been successful in your area.

The advantage of selling by owner is that you save the percentage of the price that would otherwise go to a realtor. However, there is no guarantee that you will get the price for your house that a realtor may get. His experience and position enable him to bargain more objectively. Moreover, many buyers make a lower offer on a house being sold by an owner because they know the owner is saving the commission.

In exchange for the money you might save, the entire responsibility

157

for marketing your house is yours. You have to write the ads, place them, pay for them, answer the inquiring calls, receive the Sunday-lookers, conduct tours for all interested, stay home to answer the telephone and negotiate the contract of sale with your lawyer's help. The responsibility is time-consuming and demanding. Decide whether you can give the necessary time to selling your house. If you are determined to try, the following suggestions will be helpful:

Set a time limit of two to four weeks. After this time, you will have exhausted the local supply of potential buyers as well as your own enthusiasm!

Obtain two verbal price estimates from realtors.

Pick the salesman who has impressed you most favorably and tell him you plan to list your house with his agency if you are not successful in two to four weeks. Or, plan to list your house with several local agents.

Write a newspaper ad stating the basic assets of your house, the asking price and address. Here is an example:

> 6-room split-level, 3 bedrooms, $1\frac{1}{2}$ baths, family room with fireplace. 2-car garage. Modern kitchen, wall oven, dishwasher. On landscaped $\frac{1}{2}$ acre near schools. $30,000. 55 Maple Gardens. 443-9111.

Gather the following information about your house: taxes, cost of heating, room sizes, size of lot, square footage of house and age of house.

Prepare three-by-five-inch cards or a sheet of paper with your name and address and all pertinent information about your house. Place these on bulletin boards of apartment buildings nearby and give them to local industrial personnel offices. State your price and the possession date.

Consider whether you will allow a buyer to assume your mortgage. If your interest rate is low, it may provide additional incentive for a buyer. (For more detail on mortgages, see Chapter 12, page 137.) Stipulate that mortgage assumption is possible only if you can be released from responsibility by the bank.

Prepare a professional-looking For Sale by Owner sign that includes your telephone number. Add By Appointment Only if you want to have time to prepare for each visitor.

Make available pictures of the outside of your house in the best seasons of the year if you are selling in winter.

Don't be overenthusiastic when you are showing your house. On the other hand, don't let visitors wander about on their own—take them around yourself, making minimum explanations. Most people know what they're looking for.

Obtain several copies of the local real estate contract form to have on hand. Make decisions concerning terms you prefer before an offer is made, and be familiar with the amount of earnest money, or deposit, you want from the buyer, the date of closing and possession you prefer and the items you plan to sell with the house.

Contact a good attorney who is familiar with real estate transactions when an offer is made. Discuss the attorney's fee with him before you engage him.

If an offer doesn't come and you decide to list with a realtor, give the realtor the names of any potential buyers who are still showing interest, and ask that he waive his right to a commission if your house is sold to any of these parties.

When an offer comes discuss with the buyer the most important terms—the price, your mutual timing needs and his plans for financing. If these terms are satisfactory to both parties, the buyer and his lawyer should immediately draw up a contract using a standard form. You should supply a legal description of the property from your deed or former purchase contract. When the contract is presented the buyer should give you 5 to 10 percent of the purchase price as a deposit. Have your lawyer check the contract before you sign it.

## Selling Through an Agent

In contrast to selling by owner, it's wise to list with a realtor when: (1) there are a lot of houses for sale in your area; (2) you are in a hurry to move or to sell your house; (3) mortgage money is hard to borrow; (4) it's midwinter and few people are house hunting; (5) your house is in an out-of-way place; (6) your house has drawbacks (lack of a downstairs lavatory, garage or center hall); (7) it is difficult for you to handle telephone calls or show the house.

Listing your house with a realtor always saves you work and often brings a quicker and more profitable sale than trying to sell by owner.

"Listing" a house means signing an agreement to pay a salesman or broker part of your selling price to find a buyer for you. In some areas, each agency maintains exclusive listings; a salesman can only show and sell houses listed by his own agency. The local real estate board dictates whether you can list with more than one agency. You may not even have to sign a contract when you list with several agencies; thus, if you find your own buyer, you do not have to pay a real estate commission. In some areas, real estate companies have a cooperative service called multiple listing; they agree to share their own listings with other nearby agencies. If the agency which lists a house also finds a buyer, that agency retains the full commission (6 percent in many areas). If one agency has listed the house and another agency finds the buyer, the commission is divided by those two agencies. Real estate listing procedure differs widely from one place to another. Find out what policy is followed in your area.

The real estate commission is always paid by the owner of the house to the agent who has listed his house. Selling through a realtor eliminates the seller's expense in advertising and may decrease his attorney fees, but the closing costs are not affected.

Listing with a realtor is advantageous, especially if you are moving out of town, because your realtor will: (1) inspect your house and help you arrive at a good price; (2) arrange for all realtors in the area to tour your house; (3) make appointments with you for all potential buyers; (4) expose your house to out-of-town buyers; (5) keep in touch with potential buyers and encourage them to buy your house; (6) handle all aspects of presenting offers to you and discuss them with you; (7) arrange the closing between you, the buyer and the lender providing the mortgage. While someone else handles the buyers you can leave your house anytime, knowing that buyers are still able to see it, and devote yourself to the enormous job of getting your family and your possessions ready for the move.

Your salesman has the main responsibility of selling your house, but you can help by giving him full, accurate information about your house from taxes to heating bill. (Check his listing ticket to be sure it is correct and complete.) Make it clear to the agent that your mortgage cannot be assumed unless the bank agrees to release you from liability.

## Showing the House

Get the house ready quickly when an appointment is made. Raise shades, open draperies and turn on necessary lights before potential buyers come through. Put your dog in the yard or the garage. Leave the house or keep away from the room the visitors are in. Don't volunteer information to visitors unless you are asked; the selling job belongs to the realtor. Provide pictures of the house taken in summer if you are selling in winter.

Keep off the telephone. Salesmen will come to the house if you are not there, but if you are talking on the telephone, they must wait to make an appointment.

Indicate to your salesman whether draperies, rugs, appliances and other movables are to be included in the price of the house. Some-

---

### WORDS YOU SHOULD KNOW

**Appraisal.** An expert opinion, either oral or in writing, of the cash value of a property. For FHA-insured loans, a written appraisal is always required.

**Listing.** The offering to real estate agents of a property for sale by the owner. The listing is *exclusive* if limited to a single realtor, a *multiple listing* if open to more than one agent.

**Asking price.** The price the owner puts on the property when it is listed.

**Selling price.** The amount the owner will accept.

**Firm price.** An asking price that is not subject to bargaining.

**Offer.** The bid of a prospective buyer to the owner.

**Counteroffer.** Revised terms submitted by the owner in response to an offer—usually lower than the original asking price but higher than the prospective buyer's first bid.

**Assumption of mortgage.** When the buyer, rather than negotiating a new mortgage from a lender, takes on the existing mortgage of the seller.

**Closing.** The formal meeting at which the seller conveys to the buyer the deed to the property and receives his money. A representative of the mortgagor is also present to protect his interest.

**Adjusted sales price.** The actual amount the seller receives for his property at the closing after deduction of agent's commission, legal and transfer fees, federal tax stamps, prepayment penalty to mortgagor and discharge of any liens against the property.

**Date of possession.** The date on which the seller surrenders the property to the buyer, also called the date of access.

times you can use these extras for bargaining when a bid comes in.

Keep the house in good order inside and out. As soon as you know that you are moving, give all the time you can to preparing your house for prospective buyers. They will inspect it in every detail. The first few weeks of showing your house are the most crucial. A house that stays on the market tends to be forgotten. Salesmen are trying to keep in touch with new listings, and potential buyers wonder, "Why hasn't this house sold? What's wrong with it?" Prevent the discouragement that comes from not selling your house. Give up everything else to get your house in good shape. Show each room to best advantage by removing extra furniture and knick-knacks. House hunters are impressed by large, light rooms. They don't always realize that your extra furniture is making the room appear smaller. Every closet in your house will look more spacious if you throw away or donate ruthlessly before you put your house on sale. The basement, workbench, garage, and attic should be thoroughly clean too.

Decide whether a paint touch-up is necessary inside the house on woodwork and walls. If your back porch or garage is in need of paint, or you want a small dark-green bedroom to look larger, hire a teen-ager for a one-day painting session under your supervision. The result could mean a quicker sale and a higher price. The advice of your realtor will help you decide what projects are necessary to improve your house quickly.

If your house remains on the market for more than a month without selling, and the number of people looking at the house diminishes to just one or two each week, you will naturally be disappointed, especially if your realtor and your friends have assured you that your house will sell quickly. You may wonder with despair over how much you will have to lower your price and how long you will have to wait for the house to sell. The thought of having to finance your new house without a down payment will weigh on you. There isn't any magic formula for selling a house or for enduring the days of waiting for a buyer, but when you begin to feel desperate, you can do these things:

1. Call a conference with your salesman to see what additional projects might help. Discuss the possibility of lowering the price.

2. Get busy with any useful project related to moving that will get your mind off the For Sale sign outside.

3. Refrain from telling your woes to all your friends. You will only be advertising your problem in selling.

4. Wax, trim, edge, polish and sort once more!

An offer from an interested buyer is usually presented to you by your own salesman. Many realtors say that the first offer is the best one, so consider it carefully. Sometimes a realtor's policy is to continue showing a house when an offer has been made until the buyer has obtained his mortgage. More often, realtors will take your house off the market as soon as an offer comes in.

Three courses are open to you when you receive an offer: (1) If the price and the terms satisfy you, have your attorney approve it, then sign the offer and return it, completing a legal contract. (2) If the offer is not satisfactory to you, return it unsigned and indicate that you are not interested. (3) If the terms of the offer are partly acceptable to you, change the contract by making a counteroffer. If the prospective buyer agrees to your terms, he will sign your counteroffer. The process of making a counteroffer can continue back and forth until an agreement is reached, or until the buyer or seller decides not to sign and returns the contract.

## Making a Counteroffer

When you receive an offer request your realtor's advice, but keep in mind that because he wants to make a sale he may advise against a counteroffer, asking you to accept the offer as it stands. If you suspect that the buyer would pay more, don't let your realtor discourage you from making a reasonable counteroffer. To prevent any misunderstanding, let your realtor know from the beginning that you must stand firm on price. Discourage him from indicating to the buyer, "They're asking $28,500 but I think they'll take less." If you won't negotiate, say so from the beginning; make your realtor bargain for *you*.

If your house has been on the market a short time and other people still seem interested in it, a counteroffer that comes closer to your asking price is justified. On the other hand, if you have had trouble selling your house and a low bid comes in, weigh the fact that a counteroffer may discourage the buyer completely. Between these two extremes are the many variables which affect a counteroffer, and if you're a novice at house selling, your realtor's advice will be particularly helpful to you. As you work out the contract, be sure to write down all specific agreements to avoid confusion. Insist on

▭▭▭▭▭▭

## HOW TO TURN DISCARDS INTO DOLLARS

One Saturday an Evanston, Illinois, family gathered gleefully around their kitchen table to count up the contents of a battered cardboard box crammed with change, bills and checks. It totaled over $1000—not bad for the three-day chore of selling excess household and personal belongings before moving to California.

In Wichita, Kansas, recently three young wives pooled their children's outgrown clothing, plus a miscellany of bric-a-brac, put a classified ad in the local paper and held a sale in the garage. At the end of the day they divided up $50.

Such on-premises sales are increasing all across the country as more families discover that what is trash to one—old Ping-Pong paddles, costume jewelry, phonograph records, ashtrays, paperback books—may be treasure to another.

There are no statistics available on the size of this business, but suburban publications run hundreds of classified house-sale ads each week. And the treasure-hunt appeal is not limited to any one economic group. Often, owners of secondhand stores and antique shops are among the most avid buyers.

There are now professionals who will take over house sales for a fee of 20 to 25 percent of the gross. They will price (with the owner's approval), mark and arrange; supply a sales force; handle all publicity, which usually includes fliers to a regular mailing list as well as advertising in the local want ads. The moving months, September and April, are the busiest times.

Here are a few tips about how to run a successful sale. Price realistically—remember, the buyer is looking for a bargain. Set the scene and consolidate all sale items in one place—the basement, garage, patio, front or back porch, backyard or barn. Buy marking pencil, price tags and labels and have a stack of old newspapers for wrapping purchases. For small items arrange 10-, 25- and 50-cent and $1 tables.

What accounts for the growing popularity of house sales? Mobility is one factor. As families are transferred or move to retirement homes, many find it simpler to sell excess chattels when they sell their house, rather than to store or transport them. But the real reason goes deeper. House sales represent a return to the spirit of the bazaar.

And always, of course, there are those ancient and irresistible appeals: the lure of a bargain for the buyer, a windfall for the seller.

▭▭▭▭▭▭

$1000 to $3000 as earnest money, or deposit. If the buyer reneges on the contract, you've lost time in selling the house, but the earnest money will be yours.

You'll have an additional cost if you sign a contract with a buyer who is obtaining an FHA loan. By law, you may have to pay "points" —which means more money—to sell to an FHA buyer. Find out the exact amount of money involved in paying the necessary "points." (See Chapter 12, page 137, for a complete explanation of points.)

When the offer is made, the closing date and date of possession must be established and included in the contract. The closing, or settlement, date that you and the buyer agree on is the day the financial transaction will take place. At that time the buyer will become the legal owner of your house. On the day of possession the new owner must have access. In many cases the day of possession will be the same day as the closing; however, in some cases possession can be delayed from several days to several weeks after the financial transaction. The closing and possession dates must be clearly specified in the contract.

After the closing you will no longer make mortgage payments on your house, but until you officially give possession to the new owner you will probably have to pay prorated taxes and utility bills. At closing the new owner will assume the insurance coverage for the house, but you should continue your own insurance to cover possible loss of your possessions. Local real estate practices may dictate that you pay the buyer an established amount of rent for the period between closing and possession. These financial terms must be specified if possession date is after the closing; ask your attorney to check the complicated proration of funds.

Avoid the pressure of having to move before you wish to by establishing a closing date as early as possible for the buyer and by setting the date of possession as far ahead as you reasonably can. The objectives in setting an early closing date and a later possession date are: (1) to receive your money from the old house before you must close on the new house; and (2) to avoid having to move out of your old house before you have gained possession of your new one. Timing in making a move is important. Think of all the factors involved before you sign the contract.

On the agreed-upon closing day you must meet with the buyer and his lender. You will be responsible for turning over the title and the keys to the house, in return for a certified check.

Closing costs that you do not anticipate may arise. Selling costs vary. Besides the realtor's commission, if you used an agent, and the attorney's fee, selling costs may include certification of title to date; federal revenue stamps; prepayment penalty and state real estate transfer tax, if applicable.

If you are figuring your financial obligations closely, get the exact list of closing costs well before closing day. Also determine whether you are entitled to a refund for prepaid taxes or funds held in escrow by your present lender.

As you begin to think of leaving your house, it's hard to imagine that another family is getting excited about moving into it. After the contract is signed, mention to your realtor that the buyers are welcome to see the house again. You'll discover yourself how important that second visit to a new house can be after you buy your new house.

⊏⊐⊏⊐⊏⊐⊏⊐⊏⊐⊏⊐

## TAX ASPECTS OF SELLING YOUR HOME

When you sell your home for more than you paid for it plus improvements, as is usually the case today, the difference is a taxable capital gain. When you sell your home at a loss, you get no deduction for that loss.

If, however, you buy a new residence within one year before or after the sale of your old residence and move into the new residence within one year after the sale of the old one, you may not be taxed on the gain on the old one. If you build a new home and the construction begins within a year after you sell your old home, you have 18 months after the sale of the old home to move into the new one.

If you meet these requirements, compare the "adjusted sales price" of the old residence with the cost of the new residence. The adjusted sales price was introduced into the law to allow you to deduct from the sales price of the old residence—for purposes of comparing it to the cost of the new one—so-called fix-up costs you incur in order to be able to sell your old residence.

If the cost of the new residence is at least equal to the adjusted sales price of the old, no part of the gain on the sale of the old property is taxable. If the cost of the new residence is less than the adjusted sales price of the old, the difference between the two figures is the most that can be taxed on the sale of the old residence.

⊏⊐⊏⊐⊏⊐⊏⊐⊏⊐⊏⊐

# 3
# KEEPING UP
# WITH UPKEEP

*Periodic maintenance and sensible*
*home improvements can keep down monthly*
*bills and actually make you money*

## CHAPTER 15

## Your Home:
## A Haven or a Headache?

*Are you a slave to home maintenance? Learn the causes of most household headaches and what to do about them before they make trouble*

Human nature being what it is, we naturally tend to put off until tomorrow what should be done today, particularly the chores about a house. Actually, the few periodic checks and repairs required take little time and can pay off in handsome dividends.

Here is a summary of common causes of damage and repair bills in houses and what to do about them before they make trouble. Many are simple jobs that almost anyone can do with a screwdriver, pliers or swab of paint. Others may require an expert, but by being familiar with them you will know what to request and will also know if the work is done properly.

*Heating systems.* If you have warm-air heating, inspect the air filter of the furnace at least once a month, since dirt-clogged filters are the biggest single cause of constricted heat supply and false-alarm service calls. If the filter looks dirty, remove it from the furnace and shake it outdoors or vacuum it. It is clean if you can see clearly through it when you hold it up to the sun or a bright light.

Some types of filters should be hosed with water. Follow the instructions in the furnace manufacturer's service booklet for this and other maintenance requirements.

Oil the blower motor and its pulley once a year, but don't overdo it—too much oil is as bad as none at all. Not all motors, however, require oil. Some have sealed bearings, lubricated for life. This should be noted either on the blower or in the manufacturer's instructions.

The blower pulley belt, like an automobile fan belt, should be checked for proper tension. It normally should have about an inch of slack. If it is badly worn, have it replaced.

Remove the air-outlet registers and return-air grilles in your rooms about once a month and clean out the dust and dirt inside the duct throats, preferably with a vacuum cleaner nozzle.

With hot-water and steam heating systems, "bleed" the convectors or radiators every fall, especially balky ones that do not heat up well.

Open the water valve at the end of the radiator and drain off a bucket or two of water. This releases trapped air which prevents hot-water or steam circulation inside the radiator. If a radiator still does not heat properly, drain off more water. Don't be afraid of releasing too much water, since it is automatically made up by a water-supply valve at the boiler.

There are three kinds of bleed vents for radiators: manual, disk and automatic float. Most radiators have the manual vent, which sticks out near the top of one end of the radiator, is circular in shape and about a half inch long. It has a slot that you open with a radiator key (sold in hardware stores) or merely with a dime. Turn it open until water comes out, then close it.

The disk vent looks like the manual kind but contains a series of fiber disks. It operates by automatically letting out air when necessary. The disks swell up when wet, that is, when there is water in the radiator, as there should be, and not air. If air gets in, the disks contract, opening the vent to let out the air. Sometimes the disks get worn or dirty and drip water on the floor. Replacements for worn or dirty disks are sold in hardware stores and by heating dealers.

The automatic float vent, which is highest in price, is a small tank and float device much like a toilet tank float but on a smaller scale. Water in the radiator keeps the float up and the vent closed. Air instead of water in the radiator will lower the float and open the vent, which lets the air escape. The automatic vent seldom needs attention and does away with the periodic need to bleed radiators.

It is also a good idea to drain and flush all the water in a hot-water or steam system every two or three years, particularly if you have hard water. This will prevent rust and corrosion from building up in the pipes and heating unit.

The water-circulating pump may require a drop of oil occasionally, unless it is a sealed, permanently lubricated pump. Refer to the manufacturer's manual about this.

With oil-fired furnaces, the burner should be checked, cleaned and readjusted every fall before cold weather sets in. The service charge will come back with interest. While the serviceman is there, have him drop an anticorrosion capsule into your oil tank. Oil-heat men report more and more cases of tank leaks caused by corrosion.

With gas heat, cleaning and adjustment by a serviceman is recommended every three or four years.

*Hot-water heater.* Once every month or two open the valve at the bottom of the water-heater tank and drain out a bucketful of hot water. This will get rid of accumulated scale and sediment.

## Regular Inspections

*Termites.* Have a semiannual termite inspection (or at least one every year). It's best to employ an expert, though any moderately conscientious person can learn to do it once he sees how it is done. A step-by-step check should be made all around the interior and exterior walls of the house, including the foundation, the cellar, under porches and steps and inside crawl spaces. Look for suspicious veins of dirt and termite "mud tunnels," which may be anywhere from a quarter inch to as much as a foot wide in places. Wood at or near ground level should be jabbed with a knife to detect infested sections under the surface. Wood window frames near the ground, floor beams and posts also should get the knife test.

Don't leave wood piled up near the house, since dead wood is a magnet for termites. Fireplace logs should not be stored in the basement or near the house. Keep at least four to eight inches of clearance between the ground level and the lowest exposed wood of the house.

Cracks and crevices in foundation walls should be plastered with cement. If your house has a concrete floor directly on the ground, inspect the plumbing access hole regularly. This is the floor opening for pipes, usually located behind a panel in the bathroom. It is a point of entry for termites from the ground.

*Wood rot.* Infected wood can be searched out during a termite inspection. Rotted wood is soft and decayed and breaks easily when knifed. If caught in time, replacement may not be necessary, providing the cause of the rot—moisture—is eliminated.

A certain amount of moisture is usually inevitable in a house. It can be controlled by providing constant ventilation where it occurs. This means plenty of natural air flow through crawl spaces, under porches and steps and in attics. If necessary, install large vents in such spaces for air flow in and out. Inspect the spaces periodically to be sure they are not damp.

170

*Drainage.* Two of the biggest causes of wood rot and wet basements are clogged roof drains and poor water drainage away from the house. The vertical downspout pipes from the roof should be inspected to make sure that they are not leaking and are dumping their water away from the house or into a dry well. If downspouts drain into ground pipes or a dry well, disconnect them periodically where they are joined to make sure the ground drainpipe is not clogged. Squirt water from a hose into each ground pipe to be sure the water is carried away. If it backs up, the drainage system is clogged and must be freed. It also means that the water from the roof is probably backing up in the ground and very likely into the house substructure, causing a wet basement.

Keep roof gutters free of leaves and other debris. Gutters require checking and cleaning quite frequently, especially with trees around. You can save yourself this periodic chore by putting screening across the top of all roof gutters. Special gutter screening, usually in six-inch widths, can be bought at hardware stores.

---

## HOME MAINTENANCE TIPS

1. Know your own house. Try to get a complete set of blueprints and a plot plan, which is a map of your lot, showing placement of house and garage, location of driveway, water pipes, utility lines, septic tank and drain lines. Find out where the main shutoff water valve, the main electric switch and the fuse or circuit-breaker box are.

2. If fire or smoke breaks out in the house or in an appliance, shut off the main electric switch immediately. Make sure when you pull the switch, or remove the master-fuse plate, that you are standing on a dry floor and your hands are dry. Have a chemical fire extinguisher available. Not all fires can be extinguished with water.

3. Tag the main water valve so you'll know which one it is. Turn it off once or twice, to make sure that you actually *can* shut off the water in an emergency.

4. Get yourself a good reference book that will tell you simply and clearly what you should know about minor repair work. It is also wise to find a hardware dealer you can trust.

5. Here are the tools you're most likely to find use for: claw hammer, large and small screwdrivers, crosscut saw, block plane or larger bench plane, half-inch and one-inch wood chisels, a quarter-inch electric drill and bits, a square and a jackknife. Dull and neglected tools can cause accidents. So keep them sharp, oiled to prevent rust and all stored in the same place.

Don't allow water to pool up next to the house. The earth around your walls should slope gently away to shed rainwater. Look for depressions and fill them in with dirt, and regrade where necessary. Incidentally, it is best not to put flower beds against the house, because when you water them the water may seep into the basement.

*Plumbing.* Check faucets and water outlets for drips and leaks. A hidden cause of leakage and high water bills is the toilet flush tank. To test for a leak here, deposit a dye—obtainable in a hardware store—in the tank. If the dye appears in the toilet bowl without the water being flushed, you have a leak. Often it can be corrected by a new rubber flush ball. If not, call a plumber.

Other periodic plumbing checks: Remove bathroom shower heads and flush them out in the sink; remove and clean kitchen sink drains, especially the pop-up kind; and every fall make sure that outside water faucets and pipes are drained and shut off from the inside to prevent freezing and broken pipes.

*Septic tanks.* A properly sized tank normally does not require cleaning more often than every two or three years, but it is a good idea to have the tank inspected every year. An inspection will determine if the tank is filling up to the point where it should be cleaned out.

The cleaning should be done by a professional septic-tank cleaner. He checks the level of the three layers of waste in the tank: a surface layer of scum, then several feet of liquid effluent and the settled sludge on the bottom. In general, a tank should be cleaned when the distance between the sludge surface at the bottom and the scum on the top is one half, or less, the total depth of the tank. This is determined with a special stick.

Have the tank cleaned in spring or summer. If it is done during cold weather, the essential decomposition action of the bacteria within the tank is slowed down, and there may be trouble getting the tank to function properly again.

A variety of septic-tank-cleaning chemicals are on the market, but experts say that none do any real good. They may help a bit but decidedly do not take the place of regular cleaning and proper care. Don't drain foreign matter into a tank, such as paper towels, wrapping paper, old rags, coffee grounds, cooking oils and fats, cigarette and cigar butts, or anything other than regular food and waste.

To avoid damage to the septic tank and its tile-pipe network just under the ground, don't allow trucks or other heavy equipment in this area. Don't plant shrubs and trees here either, as their roots can damage or clog the pipes. Check the area once in a while to see that it remains well drained, since storm water can flood the system and make it inoperative.

*Outside walls, windows, doors.* It's a good idea to inspect the outside of your house every spring and fall, and after bad storms. Worn and damaged spots should be repaired or painted. Cracks around windows and doors should be caulked. Don't put off exterior painting too long or it may cost twice as much, because badly worn or peeled paint has to be burned off and a new prime coat applied. Most houses require a fresh paint job every three to five years.

Brick, stone or masonry walls should be checked for cracks, breaks and holes. If they are not repaired immediately, rain can get inside the house, damaging walls and ceilings. Oil the hinges and roto-operators of metal casement windows at least once a year. The channels of sliding windows and wood windows should be cleaned periodically with steel wool.

*Roof and attic.* The roof should be inspected at the same time that the walls and windows are checked, and broken or loose shingles should be repaired.

Check the attic for good ventilation all year round. Keep attic vents open in the winter too, because year-round ventilation is needed to prevent condensation of moisture. If the attic floor is properly insulated, you need not worry about excessive heat leakage from the house. Repair holes in attic vent screens to keep out birds and bees.

## More Routine Economy Checks

*Chimney.* Cleaning is needed every three or four years, normally, particularly if you have oil heat. Once a chimney becomes clogged with soot, blow-back is a dangerous possibility; so much soot accumulates that sometimes it may be blown back into the house.

A chimney also should be checked for cracks and loose or broken masonry. Repair immediately holes or breaks in the protective screen on top; otherwise birds and small animals can nest inside and even enter the house.

# Home Maintenance Calendar

Periodic checkups around your house can keep a minor defect from turning into a major repair job. You can keep bills down by practicing preventive maintenance. Use this calendar as a handy reminder of what needs looking into, and when.

| | JANUARY | FEBRUARY | MARCH | APRIL | MAY | JUNE | JULY | AUGUST | SEPTEMBER | OCTOBER | NOVEMBER | DECEMBER |
|---|---|---|---|---|---|---|---|---|---|---|---|---|
| | Inspect air filter in heating system. | Inspect air filter. | Inspect air filter. | Inspect air filter. | Inspect air filter. | Inspect air filter. | Inspect air filter. | Inspect air filter. | Inspect air filter. | Inspect air filter. | Inspect air filter. | Inspect air filter. |
| | Drain bucketful of hot water from water heater. | Remove and clean bathroom shower heads. | Have termite inspection. | | Remove and clean bathroom shower heads. | Clean air-conditioning filters. | Lubricate exterior door locks (every 4 or 5 years). | Plan now to have oil burner checked in September or October. | Bleed radiators. | Have oil burners checked and cleaned. | Remove and clean bathroom shower heads. | Clean kitchen sink drains. |
| | Check for exposed wiring and frayed electrical cords. | | Check attic for ventilation. | | Clean air-conditioning units. | Clean kitchen sink drains. | Have chimney cleaned every 3 years. | Remove and clean bathroom shower heads. | Have termite inspection. | Clean air-conditioning filters. | Drain bucketful of hot water from water heater. | |

| | | | |
|---|---|---|---|
| Drain outside water pipes and faucets. | | | |
| Inspect outside of house for cracks and peeling paint. | Inspect roof. | | |
| Clean air-conditioning filters. | Clean oil burners or furnaces. | Drain bucketful of hot water from water heater. | Clean kitchen sink drains. |
| Clean air-conditioning filters. | Check attic for ventilation. | Oil the blower motor in the heating system. | Check for exposed wiring and frayed electrical cords. |
| Clean air-conditioning filters. | Drain bucketful of hot water from water heater. | | |
| Have septic tank inspection and cleaning if necessary. | Drain bucketful of hot water from water heater. | Inspect outside of house for cracks and peeling paint. | Inspect roof. |
| Drain bucketful of hot water from water heater. | Clean kitchen sink drains. | | |

*Wiring.* Since faulty wiring is a major cause of household fires, check all exposed wiring regularly, including appliance and lamp cords. Replace worn or frayed cords. If possible, check the wiring cables leading from your main electric switch box (usually located near the meter). If they are hot to the touch, call an electrician at once. *Be careful.* Use gloves and don't touch exposed wires, and allow no one but an electrician to touch anything inside the box.

*Door locks.* Exterior door locks need to be lubricated every four or five years to prevent sticking. The best lubricant is powdered graphite, available at hardware stores. Squirt it into the lock opening. A little graphite is also good for balky inside locks—especially the bathroom door lock, which has a way of getting stuck when children are in the bathroom.

*Air conditioning.* As with furnaces, dirt-clogged air-conditioner filters often cause inadequate cooling and unnecessary service calls. Filters should be cleaned at least once a month, more often if you live in a smoggy city. If you have a central air-conditioner, an annual check and adjustment is recommended.

*Appliances.* Run-down appliances are the most frequent cause of service calls. Since the maintenance required varies according to type and brand of appliance, you should consult the manufacturer's instruction booklet and carry out the checks recommended. If you have lost your copy, write for another. (For details on service contracts, see Chapter 22, "You *Can* Get Your Money Back," page 235.)

A few specific tips on appliances: Neglecting to clean out the clothes-drier lint trap is a widespread cause of operating trouble and fires. It should be emptied at least once a week, but preferably after each load. Don't overload washers and driers. If the hot- and cold-water pipe valves on some washers should be shut when the machine is not in use, the manufacturer's instructions will mention this.

## Saving Money When You Buy Maintenance

Despite all the potential savings from preventive maintenance, you will need help for some jobs. How and where you buy professional maintenance greatly affect the cost.

Find local tradesmen for your home maintenance. The town jack-of-all-trades, who could fix anything with little more than a screwdriver and paintbrush, has disappeared. But there are many hardworking journeymen painters, plumbers, carpenters, concrete finishers, masons and gardeners dependent on repeat business.

Nearly every community has these home maintenance specialists— your problem is to find them! They don't advertise. They are like good dentists or doctors; they already have so much business they have difficulty finding time to handle all the jobs offered by satisfied customers, so they may not be taking on any new clients. The reason they are so busy is that they work hard, know their business, make good on any unsatisfactory work, use reliable materials and charge a fair price—not a low price, but a fair one. You'll probably pay them in cash. How do you find these paragons of home maintenance service? Try one or all of these ideas:

Ask a longtime resident of your community. The man you're looking for has probably been around for years, so a native or longtime resident is likely to know of him.

Ask friends, neighbors or business associates for leads. Maybe they have been over the route of looking for help and can recommend someone. Also, you can check on the man's or company's record. If the man did a good job for your friend, he is likely to do a good job for you.

Ask another tradesman you respect for a reference. If you have found a good car mechanic or gardener, ask him for a lead to a plumber or painter. Tradesmen get to know other professionals—and can also warn you of those who are merely out to make a fast dollar.

Join one of the local homeowners' associations. These locally organized associations act as your agents when you have an emergency or a maintenance problem. They check out self-employed tradesmen and home maintenance companies for their skill, fair dealing and prices. Your membership fee covers a number of services, including referral to reputable professionals for doing your home repair and maintenance. You're not likely to get any price bargains through a homeowners' association, but you should get good work at a fair price. If you don't, you have a place to bring your complaint.

Many of your maintenance tasks may not need the practiced hand of a pro. In that case, consider hiring willing hands that you may find through a variety of sources listed in the following section.

## Amateur and Part-time Helpers

High school students vary widely in skills and attitude, but if you find a good one, you can get your house painted, lawn and garden cared for, and other heavy work done for less money than you would spend hiring a tradesman. Students have little overhead and seldom earn enough to pay income taxes, so they work for less. However, they may not be worth as much, either, unless they have learned basic skills.and know how to work. Before hiring students, check their references by calling others they have worked for. If you find a student through some agency, such as a Kiwanis Student Job Service project or some other plan for helping students find work, ask for comments from others who have hired that boy. Observe and rate a boy's performance during the first few hours or days he is working for you. You can tell, for example, after watching him handle paintbrushes, ladders and drop cloths whether he will do the kind of paint job you require. You're likely to get more work for your money if you have the student work along with you on a project than if you turn him loose by himself.

Moonlighters may help you when specific skills are needed, such as plumbing, laying tile, painting or carpentry. These skilled workers have a regular job during the day, but they also work for themselves during the evening or on weekends. Union regulations vary in different communities, and enforcement is not uniform. Usually, union members are forbidden to work at their own skill, but they may work at some other related skill. You can locate moonlighters through stores that sell supplies—paint shops, lumberyards, floor-covering stores, hardware stores.

Other part-timers may be looking for extra work outside of their own skills. Teachers, firemen or factory workers often work after hours to earn extra money. These part-timers, like students, may not be as skilled as professionals, so check references and watch their progress at the beginning. Some part-timers sell skills learned in their own do-it-yourself activities; you can find them through ads in the classified section of local and weekly newspapers, through inquiries posted on community bulletin boards, through local employment agencies or by word of mouth and recommendations from friends and neighbors.

## CHAPTER 16

# What You Should Know About Contractors

*Planning to add an extra room or remodel an existing one? Read how you can maximize results and minimize problems*

One day it happens. You get tired of sharing the living room with neighborhood children every evening—a playroom has become indispensable. Or you decide that the kitchen must have more cabinet space. Or you realize that a single bathroom will no longer suffice for a growing family.

You know that remodeling requires experience, skills and compliance with building codes—so it's not a do-it-yourself proposition. You check the bank balance, estimate that the family budget will allow for some expenditure on home improvement and decide to have the job done.

Should you get on the phone right away and start calling local contractors? Absolutely not. Instead, you should call a family conference and discuss or even debate all the details of the proposed remodeling. It's not enough, for instance, just to know that you want to remodel a kitchen or add a family room. You also have to know, among other things, how much you are willing to spend, what style addition you would like, how much equipment you want to replace and what purposes the new space or new arrangement should serve.

Let's say you need more living space. Should it be another room added to the side of the house? Or should it be carved out of the basement or attic? Should it have built-in furniture or ready-made? Will it be reserved for recreation or include a work bench, serving equipment, storage space? These are the kinds of questions that ought to be tentatively answered by family consensus before calling a contractor. They affect not only what you will require from him but also how much you'll spend.

No matter what kind of a remodeling job you are planning, however, visits to local appliance stores, home equipment showrooms, home decorating centers and lumberyards will give you some background on the kind of equipment and materials available, their cost and what installation problems may arise. This information will also help you to estimate what your budget will bear and to appraise the expertness of the contractors you deal with.

Let's say that you have held the family conference, agreed on your basic needs and estimated how much you can reasonably afford to spend. Your next, and most important, step is to find a *reliable* contractor. Even though the need seems urgent, this is not the time to settle for any contractor who promises instant dream kitchens, playrooms and bathrooms. You're about to make a big investment in money, time and household disruption—and if you make mistakes you will probably have to live with them for a long, long time.

What makes a contractor reliable? Many things. He has been in business long enough to have established himself as responsible and trustworthy. He has a crew of subcontractors and workmen whose work and dependability he is sure of. (Most contractors are small-business men, who subcontract parts of the job, such as the carpentry, the painting or the electrical work.) He knows the state, county and local laws that regulate rebuilding and remodeling and will make sure that your job, when finished, conforms with all these regulations. He carries insurance covering workmen's compensation, property damage and personal liability and can provide you with a certificate of insurance to show his coverage. He will maintain a maximum of cleanliness and order on the job.

There is one thing a reliable contractor will *not* do, however. He will not give you a firm date on which the job will be finished—and with good reason. He knows that it is almost impossible to estimate exactly how long a job will take, and what unforeseen problems may be encountered along the way. He is dealing with independent craftsmen who are in diminishing supply, and he can't be sure that they will always adhere precisely to his schedule. And he must allow for factors beyond his control, such as delays in delivery, bad weather and illness. So he will probably be able to give you only a tentative completion date. But he will try to keep to it, not only because he wants to please you as his customer, but also because it is to his advantage to finish as quickly as possible so he can collect his money and start on a new job. If he is experienced and reliable, moreover, he will not take on more work than he can reasonably handle.

How do you check the reputation of a contractor? William P. Youngclaus, Jr., managing director of NERSICA, Inc. (National Established Repair Service Improvement Contractor Association), a national association of home improvement contractors, suggests asking if the contractor is a member of NERSICA or a similar trade organization; such organizations have codes of ethics that contractors are expected to adhere to. (NERSICA doesn't accept members until they've been in business three or more years—and 70 percent of new contractors go out of business during their first three years!)

You can also check with your local bank, Better Business Bureau or Chamber of Commerce. Don't hesitate to ask them about the contractor's reputation for financial stability, quality of workmanship and his follow-up when there have been complaints about his work. You can also form an opinion on your own by visiting the contractor's headquarters to see if he appears to be firmly established.

## Working Out the Specifics

Once you have satisfied yourself about the reputability of several local contractors, you're ready to call one or more to visit your home and discuss the job that you're planning. This first appointment is always on the contractor's time—it's an investment he makes in the hope that he will get the job. Though he expects to invest this time, the more businesslike and informed you are, the more satisfactory the meeting will be. This is the moment when the "homework" you've done—on plans, materials and appliances—will begin to pay off.

Though you are wise to start with some of your own ideas, don't ignore suggestions and advice from the contractor. He has had experience with remodeling problems, with various materials, with different appliances, and is in a position to give you good advice. Sometimes he may be quite right in saying a material or an appliance is not suitable for the purpose you have in mind, or has not held up as well as it should, or is more expensive than another brand that will serve exactly the same purpose. But he may also suggest an alternative simply because he gets a better discount on it or because it's easier to work with. You will have to use your own judgment.

Take the Blakes, for instance. When they decided to add a deck to their house they specified redwood with aluminum nails. They knew the redwood was more expensive but felt it would save them money in the long run, because it didn't require upkeep. And they asked for aluminum nails because they knew they were rustproof. Their contractor tried to discourage them, partly because the wastage on an expensive material like redwood would be costlier to him and partly because aluminum nails require a more experienced carpenter than steel nails, which don't bend as easily. In this case, the Blakes stood firm and got what they wanted. If you are in doubt about a material, however, and the contractor is reliable, it will probably pay you to go along with his suggestion.

When it comes to appliances, be sure to specify the year and the model that you want, especially if there is a choice between a regular and a deluxe model. When the Allens were remodeling their kitchen they asked for a particular brand of dishwasher that had been well rated by several consumer organizations, but neglected to specify the deluxe model. The contractor supplied a standard model with a much smaller capacity than the deluxe model, and the Allens were stuck with it.

For a major remodeling job a good contractor will give you plans and insist that you approve them before he begins working. Study them carefully—it's easier and much, much cheaper to make changes in a plan than to wait until work is in progress and then decide you really wanted the door to be in the middle of the wall, not off to the side. If you do change your mind midway, there may be wiring or plumbing to be undone in addition to changes in the working drawings and the schedules of the workmen involved. All these things are time-consuming, and the contractor is perfectly within his rights in adding the costs of the extra time as well as additional materials onto your original bill.

You'll want to check with the contractor to be sure that he is adequately insured and that he will provide all the permits required by your local building laws. Be sure, too, that your agreement has a written provision freeing you from liability if the contractor goes bankrupt before the job is finished. Under existing mechanic's lien laws, you can be held liable for payments on materials and labor on your remodeling job—even though the material or the workmen

## WATCH OUT FOR
## PHONY HOUSEHOLD
## REPAIRMEN

Do you plan to order a new roof, siding, carport or patio for your home? Have you visions of a house rewired to power the latest appliances, of combination storm windows, an enclosed porch or dazzling modern kitchen like the one you saw in the latest magazine?

If so, beware the "fix-up phonies" who infest this lush market. They are cheating American homeowners of an estimated $1 billion a year through bad workmanship and broken promises.

"They and their shoddy work and fraudulent deals currently cause more complaints than any other source," says the president of the National Better Business Bureau. And from the avalanche of 275,000 indignant letters and personal complaints on the problem that pour in annually to the Better Business Bureaus, authorities have been able to classify the most flagrant and widespread swindles.

1. *The "model home" swindle.* In one of the most common fakeries, the victim is led to believe that he will receive commissions from similar sales to persons impressed with the improvement on his property, thus enabling him to recoup his investment. A young Philadelphia couple, for example, are now in danger of losing their home because of this scheme. The wife told a salesman who came to the door last February that they could not afford an aluminum re-siding job because her husband was out of work. The salesman claimed that they could have the work done "without cost." All they had to do was sign a contract for the job at $1600. The house would be used as a "model," and they would receive a $100 check for every person within a radius of ten miles who placed a similar order after seeing the improvement in their home's appearance.

The couple signed, and to date they have received no $100 checks. The salesman's company disclaims all knowledge of the promise. The husband is still not back at work, and the finance company is pressing for payment.

Because his victim is hypnotized by the mirage of future rebates, the "model home" swindler usually is able to put an inflated price tag on the job he offers to do. In Waco, Texas, for instance, an out-of-town operator quoted $2305 as the price of a re-siding job, and this was supposedly already reduced 40 percent because the home would be "shown." A local contractor gave an estimate of $976.

A popular variation of the model home gyp is referral selling. This scheme is used to sell almost anything, but, as just one example, a salesman tells you that you can get a carpet "for free" if you simply show it to your friends and refer them to the same outfit. You are promised a hefty commission for each new customer you find—at least enough to cover the total cost of the rug. But it's almost impossible to find enough other customers to cover your own bill. Let's say 6 new customers would cover that cost. Each of them will be approached with the same referral pitch. The geometric progression goes like this: 1... 6.... 36 . . . 216 . . . 1296 . . . 7776 . . . 46,656 . . . 279,936 . . . 1,679,616. . . . The price you pay, moreover, is grossly inflated, and you'll be lucky if the promoter doesn't skip before he credits you with even the few customers you may find.

2. *"Bait and switch" advertising.* The Federal Trade Commission defines this racket as follows: "Bait advertising is an alluring but insincere offer to sell a product the advertiser does not intend to sell. Its purpose is to switch consumers from buying the advertised merchandise, in order to sell something else, usually at a higher price."

A typical "bait" ad cited by Buffalo, New York, investigators features a drawing of an "aluminum patio" for $79.50. It depicts a happy couple relaxing under a gleaming metal awning over a flagstone terrace. Most persons who answered this ad were switched to awnings costing $300 to $1900, it is reported. Out of 67 cases investigated, only 1 person had had the stamina to insist on the $79.50 job. He got a plain sheet of metal held up by slanting two-by-fours.

The "easy contest" type of bait also lures many potential victims. The Fort Wayne, Indiana, BBB tells of a couple who were notified that the wife's entry had won a "Match the Stars" contest.

Because she could tell the difference between Bob Hope and Rudy Vallee, they had won free siding for their home.

"Congratulations!" boomed the sponsoring "contractor." "Naturally, there'll be a lot of publicity about this—photographs and so forth—so we'll install the free siding for you. That will be three hundred dollars!" When the winner's husband insisted that he would install the free siding himself, the entry was suddenly ruled ineligible.

A potent variation of the bait approach is used by itinerant repairmen who state, "We can give you a good price because we have some material left over from another job and want to get rid of it."

Another scheme adapts this lure to "sealing" driveways. These operators apply a thin coat of asphalt sprayed from an aerosol container, collecting up to $125 for ten minutes' work. The material weathers away in a few weeks. "It should take two men several hours to seal the average driveway, using a coal-tar pitch emulsion with silica sand added, and spreading the mixture with squeegees," says the president of a reliable company that specializes in such work. "And the surface should last from five to ten years."

A close relative of the bait-and-switch ploy is "crew switching." A team of high-pressure salesmen divides into two crews. Crew A fans out into one part of town, selling products ranging from awnings to wall-to-wall carpeting. Crew B, under a different

□□□□□□

company name, but selling the same products, heads for another part of town. Both quote fantastically inflated prices, almost never make a sale—and now comes the catch. The crews switch. Crew A approaches the same houses Crew B already has visited and this time quotes much lower prices. Crew B goes into A's territory and ridicules the "other company" for its high prices. What the homeowner doesn't know is that the two outfits are working together, that all prices quoted are inflated and that he is being softened up for the kill.

3. *Fake chimney, roof, furnace and termite "inspectors."* These operators prey largely on widows and elderly couples, using fear as their chief weapon. A Chicago homeowner tells of his experience last February: "The chimney was working fine, but these 'free inspectors' insisted they'd check it for me, so I finally said they could. Right away they smashed at it with crowbars. Bricks came tumbling down, sealing the chimney. I asked the crew boss what he was doing. He handed me a contract for two hundred and thirty dollars, and said I would have to sign or they wouldn't fix the chimney. It was winter, I had to have the heat, so I signed."

A woman who allowed a "furnace inspector" into the basement was shocked to discover later that the oil burner had been taken apart and was spread over the floor. "Put it together," she demanded. "It would be against the law, lady," was the reply. "It's in

bad shape. You'd be asphyxiated." Solution: She should buy new parts costing $300.

Sharpsters claiming to be termite inspectors have victimized many unsuspecting homeowners. Here's how they operate:

A truck pulls into your driveway and a man, introducing himself as a termite inspector, informs you that a termite problem has cropped up in your neighborhood. He offers to "inspect" your home—free—to see whether termites have reached its underpinnings. He disappears into your basement, and later emerges with the frightening news that your own house has become infested. As proof, he displays a jar of live termites he says he has found downstairs.

The "inspector" may tell you that you are lucky because your termite problem has been discovered "in the nick of time" and he urges you to act immediately, "before your house collapses." He then summons a couple of men from his truck, and tells them to bring a tank full of insecticide. You will pay only for the number of gallons actually sprayed in your cellar, and there will be a ten-year guarantee on the job. A little later, the men return to inform you that the complete spraying required 85 gallons at $4 a gallon—or $340.

But here are the key points. There is no such occupation as "termite inspector" (or, in some cases, "government termite inspector"). Despite the living display of termites, there may

□□□□□□

not be a single termite in your home to begin with. Even if there are, the chemical spray used by the termite gypsters is probably worthless because termites live as far as ten or more feet underground. Moreover, reputable exterminators normally do not guarantee a single termite control job for as long as ten years.

4. *The signed completion certificate.* This swindle enables the crooked contractor to collect his money from the bank or loan agency financing the work and leave the victim with repairs that are not completed or with a job partly done. In a classic case, the contractor pleaded, "Just sign so I can give the boys their money before Christmas." "The boys" never returned to finish the work.

5. *Debt consolidation.* Only quick work by the Cleveland BBB saved homeowners there $350,000 after they had entered "debt consolidation" arrangements. Under such an agreement, if you owe $7000, for example, and want $5000 worth of work done on your house, you may sign a new mortgage to pay the builder $12,000. The builder supposedly pays off the $7000 for you, and your subsequent monthly payments to him—over a longer period of time than the original mortgage called for—are no larger than your previous payments. Only this builder does not pay the debts. Instead he sells the mortgages to a finance company and skips town with a pocketful of cash. You end up with no repairs and a higher mortgage then ever.

How can the average homeowner protect himself against these tricksters? Here are the combined recommendations of the Federal Housing Administration, the Home Improvement Council and the BBB:

Get several written bids from local, well-established dealers. Check on the firms with your BBB, Chamber of Commerce and lending institutions. Get names of persons in your area for whom the firms have done work, and ask these homeowners if they were satisfied or if they had any difficulty in having complaints adjusted.

Place no reliance on verbal promises. Insist that any contract contain a complete description of the improvements and total cost of the job, including financing charges. Before you sign, look out for fine-print exclusion clauses. Have a lawyer check the contract if the job is at all sizable. Obtain a signed copy of the contract and keep it handy until all its terms have been satisfied.

Never sign a completion certificate until the work is actually completed, and to your satisfaction.

Don't deal with itinerants. Beware of all gimmicks such as "model home" offers and low bait-advertising prices. Close the door on anyone who attempts to frighten you into giving an order.

Your best defense against phony home repairmen is knowing how they operate and how to spot them when they descend on you—and to say no firmly.

were to have been paid by the contractor—unless your agreement specifically protects you against such liens.

Another important part of your agreement is how and when you pay. The contract should state specifically the scope of the work to be done and how much it will cost. It is customary for the contractor to get a down payment, about 10 to 15 percent of the finished price, before he begins. The remainder is paid when the job is completed. On a very large job the contractor may specify progress payments, but this is less customary. If there is such a clause in your contract, be sure it provides for some relationship between the progress of the work and the amount of payment to be made.

You will also want to give some thought to the guarantees on the materials and appliances you are getting. Usually they are given not by the contractor but by the suppliers or manufacturers. In any case it pays to find out what you can expect of the materials being used, and where you can complain if something proves defective. The Fair Trade Commission has set up guidelines on some materials that the contractor should know and tell you about. Roofing and siding materials, for instance, can only be guaranteed for 15 years, and anyone who guarantees them for longer is either misinformed or trying to mislead you.

For appliances such as dishwashers, air-conditioners, washers and driers, find out if there are local service offices so that you can get repairs or replacement parts quickly if needed, and ask the contractor what experience he has had with the service organization. (For more on "How to Buy Appliances," see Chapter 21, page 229.)

When it comes to the installation of plumbing, heating systems and water heaters, find out whether the contractor or the subcontractor is going to be responsible if something goes wrong after the job is completed. Get written guarantees.

You might also ask the contractor for the name of the supply house that will provide the material for the job. Then you can check to be sure that he has ordered what is specified in the agreement. If you find out that the supplier will deal with the contractor only on a cash-on-delivery basis, proceed with caution—a man with a poor credit rating may not be a good risk.

Find out also about cleaning up and removing debris. A good

contractor will clean up as he goes along, but there are bound to be some materials left over when the job is finished. Most contractors offer a clause in their contract that guarantees they will leave your house and premises "broom clean." There may be a charge for this (NERSICA estimates about $35 to $40 as average), but it could be well worth it to be spared the annoyance and expense of getting rid of the debris yourself. (If there is scrap lumber, and you have a fireplace, ask the contractor to leave the scraps. They make fine kindling wood for a roaring midwinter fire.)

## Making the Right Choice

When you have satisfactory proposals from several (if you are fortunate) reputable contractors you will have to choose among them. How should you make the choice? Though it may *seem* thrifty, the lowest bid is not necessarily the best. The contractor may have underestimated the time and work involved, and may cut corners later trying to make up for his mistake. Moreover, if he is losing money on your contract, he may give a higher priority to more profitable jobs, and your work will drag on and on. Mr. Young-claus puts it this way: "Many times what you are paying for in a bid is experience. Most remodeling jobs are done on older houses, and the experienced contractor knows that he is almost sure to run into problems that cannot be foreseen, but must be allowed for. In older homes it is not unusual to find walls several feet thick, gas pipes left over from the days of gas lights, rotting timbers and other unexpected difficulties."

This does not mean, however, that the contractor who submits the highest bid is necessarily the best—he may simply be the most expensive. There are no firm rules on how to make this decision; you will have to rely on the contractor's reputation, your own judgment based on your dealing with him and a little bit of luck. One word of caution: Don't tell one contractor what another one has bid or you may unwittingly cause the second bidder to ask a higher price than he had intended.

After you've chosen the contractor and an agreement has been put in writing, have it checked by a lawyer who has experience with such agreements, by your mortgage company or, if you have arranged for bank financing, by the home improvement loan department of the bank. When none of these checks is possible, read the contract carefully yourself. Be sure, if you have been dealing with a representative of the contractor, that the name of the contractor, not the name of the salesman or the representative, is on the contract. Otherwise, you may find that the salesman has made promises that the contractor can disavow.

## How to Make Sure the Work Is Satisfactory

Hopefully, after the work has been started, all will go well. But since you and the contractor are dealing with human beings who are going to make mistakes, it's a good idea to know what to do when you have complaints while work is in progress. Let's say, for instance, that a painter is using a wrong color. Insist that he stop immediately, even if he assures you that the deep blue you see on the wall will dry to exactly the blue you chose. He may be right—but don't take a chance on it. *Don't* deal with him directly and permit him to make changes on the spot. If you do, *you* become responsible. Instead, even though it means a delay (remember, you'll be looking at that wall for a long time), ask the workman to wait for further instructions from the contractor and in the meantime work on something else in the house, or, if need be, to leave and return another day. Then call the contractor, make your complaint and let him decide what to do. In this way the contractor becomes responsible for the change and for guaranteeing satisfaction.

There is always the possibility, too, that you are very pleased with one of the workmen—the carpenter, for instance—and you decide that instead of hanging the bookcases yourself, you will ask Mr. Smith, the carpenter, to come on the weekend and do the work. You are then setting up what contractors call the S-and-S job, that is, Saturday and Sunday work. You expect to save through this direct hiring, of course; the workman looks forward to picking up some extra money; and the contractor is not involved at all. No one can prevent this fairly common arrangement, but you should be aware of the risks involved. Suppose the bookcases topple after they have been up a month? What guarantee do you have that the carpenter will make good on his work? If you are lucky he will make good, but you may end up paying for the S-and-S job and hanging the bookcases yourself.

Even more serious, suppose the carpenter falls off a ladder while hanging a high shelf and has to be hospitalized. You could be sued for his hospitalization, since the accident occurred on your property. Homeowners have been caught in just such situations and have ended up with expensive court judgments against them.

This is not to say that such an arrangement cannot work out well sometimes, saving you money. But, at the very least, you should not enter into this arrangement without checking with your insurance agent.

Suppose you are not satisfied when the work is near completion or even finished. Don't just sit there—complain! Call the contractor right away and tell him what's wrong. If there seems to be the slightest hesitation on his part, send him a letter detailing the trouble. Keep a carbon as a record of what went wrong and the date you complained. If you have chosen your contractor carefully, he values his reputation and will do his best to be sure that everything is all right. If he doesn't make good within a reasonable amount of time— allowing for other commitments he has and getting replacement parts—then you write (again with a carbon for your file) to let him know that you intend to pass on your complaint to the bank where he gets financing or to the Better Business Bureau, the Chamber of Commerce or a local trade association.

Your best assurance for getting a satisfactory finished job, of course, is the rule of the purse string. Pay only when you are pleased. The generally accepted rule is that if a contract doesn't specify time of payment, the work must be virtually completed before payment can be demanded. As long as you haven't paid in full, you are in control. You can insist on completion to your satisfaction, or if you think the contractor just can't do any better you can insist on a price adjustment.

Another approach, if you cannot reach agreement on what is an equitable settlement, is to try sending a check for the amount that you feel is justified. Mark the check "payment in full." If the contractor accepts—by cashing the check, depositing it or using it to pay someone else—you have legally reached an "accord and satisfaction" and the question is closed. Your very last resort is a court of law, but this can be time-consuming, frustrating and, worst of all, expensive. In the meantime you have to live with the leaky pipes or the peeling plaster or the uneven flooring, so look to the courts only when all else has failed. However, the contractor should understand that you are prepared to take even this last step in order to get satisfaction.

But chances are, if you allow ample time for discussion and planning, follow the precautions suggested and keep close check on the progress being made, you'll end up with a family room or new kitchen or bathroom that will make your house more valuable and your daily living more agreeable.

CHAPTER 17

## You Really Can Save on Utilities

*Simple cost-saving tips can help you trim hundreds of dollars from your annual utility bills— without pain*

Utilities are the nitty-gritties of running your house. You'd like to spend less, but the oil or gas bills and the water bills just keep coming in—higher all the time, you feel. Maybe you believe the amount of money spent for heating, cooling, water, electricity, sewer service, garbage removal and telephone is fixed. It just isn't so. There are many ways you can cut these costs. Here are some sensible tips to help you save money every month on fuel, heating, air-conditioning, electricity, water and telephone bills.

Selecting the least expensive fuel is probably the best way to trim your heating costs. Unfortunately, most of us are saddled with the heating plant that came with the house. If you are building a new house or installing a new heating system, remember that oil and gas are the most economical fuels. Electric heat is several times more expensive in most areas.

Insulation also cuts heating expenses, reduces air-conditioning costs and increases the comfort level inside your house. How much insulation do you need? How cold are the winters? How hot and muggy the summers? You need lots of insulation where winters are frigid or where summers are steamy. On the basis of a 1000-square-foot home, six-inch-thick attic insulation for a house in an extreme temperature zone might cost as much as $150 but would save $80 to $95 worth of heat in one season. You'll save most with ceiling insulation because of heat's natural tendency to rise. But don't overlook the savings possible from insulating outside walls, installing storm windows and doors and weather-stripping doors and windows.

Good insulation also saves money in another, basic way. A smaller heating plant can be installed in a house with full insulation. With less heat escaping, less heating capacity is needed. You pay less initially by installing the small furnace and then cut fuel costs with more efficient operation.

Insulating exterior walls also brings greater room comfort. Heat loss by radiation to a cool surface can make you feel chilly even though the air temperature is above 70° F., since the inside surface of a frame wall without insulation will register only 59 degrees. Sitting near a cool wall, you feel uncomfortably chilly, so you raise the thermostat for higher air temperature. You lose two ways: by greater heat loss through the wall and by operation at a higher air temperature to compensate for the cold wall. But with wall insulation the inner wall temperature is 67 degrees, and you feel warm at a lower room temperature, which costs you less to maintain.

Simply installing wall and ceiling insulation isn't enough, however. When the difference between outside and inside temperatures increases to 50 degrees or more (72 degrees inside and 22 degrees outside, for example), your house needs two layers of glass at windows and doors to prevent heat loss and to protect against wind. In one extensive research program, adding storm doors and windows to a large uninsulated two-story house saved 22 percent of the fuel normally burned. When the same house was fully insulated, the saving was about 15 percent.

## Keeping in the Heat

Here are other heat-saving insulation tricks that can save you real money over the years:

*Don't overlook the door to your attic.* Cover a lift-up attic door with blanket insulation and seal the edges with weather stripping, just as you would with an outside door. If you have a walk-in door at the top of a staircase to the attic, tack blanket insulation or thick insulating siding onto the attic side and weather-strip the door.

*Insulate the underside of floors.* If your house is built over a crawl space, install insulation with vapor protection from two sides—the warm floor side and the damp ground side. If the ground under the floor is continually damp, cover it completely with a plastic vapor barrier to prevent water from evaporating into the crawl space.

*Cover the hot-water pipes and hot-air ducts.* Pipes and ducts that run through unheated areas, such as a crawl space or attic, lose significant amounts of heat before the hot water, steam or air reaches the room distribution point. Builders frequently omit these niceties because few buyers notice. But the increased operating expense costs the homeowner every year. Cover pipes with asbestos-fiber cellular coating and seal joints with wrapped asbestos-fiber tape. Cover the outside of hot-air ducts with slabs of semirigid fiber glass and tape the joints.

Any central heating system, whether steam, hot water or hot air, works best only when properly adjusted. Between calls by a professional furnace repairman, you can adjust your heating system to generate more heat for your home for fewer dollars by using some or all of these tactics:

1. Check the chimney of the furnace for draft. Chimneys should be free of soot and not obstructed by any foreign matter. Check the draft damper. It will be in the smoke pipe between the furnace and chimney. Open the lightly weighted valve and blow talcum powder a foot or two from the entrance. The powder should be drawn into the valve and up the chimney. If not, some plugging may be present. A heavily sooted furnace chimney is the clue to a problem in combustion, for a flame burning efficiently will not generate enough soot to clog a chimney. If the furnace has much soot, hire a professional to clean it with the proper tools.

2. Keep filters clean. In a hot-air system return air is filtered on the inlet side of the furnace. Loosely packed glass-fiber filters strain big particles of dirt and lint from the air; a sticky film on the fibers attracts fine particles. But if these filters get clogged they slow airflow. With less air flowing more heat escapes up the chimney. During the

winter open the access door and remove the filter packs. Vacuum the incoming air surface and then blow through from the back side. At least once each heating season, replace the filter packs.

3. Remove loose soot from the firebox. Even the best oil or gas furnace deposits small amounts of soot when starting or stopping. Soot is an insulator that slows the flow of heat from the firebox to the air being circulated. An additive can be mixed with burner oil to remove soot by combustion. Check with your supplier. If his oil does not contain the additive, ask him to supply enough for an injection once or twice a season.

4. Adjust the furnace flame-and-air mixture valves regularly. Oil furnaces work themselves out of adjustment more easily than do gas furnaces. Unless you are fairly expert, hire a burner serviceman to adjust your furnace to peak efficiency, preferably at the beginning of really cold weather. You then will be assured of getting the most heat from every drop of oil when you need the heat the most. Gas flames can usually be adjusted once a year (without regard to season) by simple adjustments of the air intake. If these don't keep the gas burning with a clear blue flame, the burner jets may need cleaning.

5. Check steam and hot-water systems. Single-pipe steam systems operate effectively only if the inlet valve to each radiator is fully open to permit water to flow back to the boiler.

6. Adjust the fan control on a hot-air system. With a hot-air system the fan that forces hot air through the duct system operates on a different cycle from the burner. The fan comes on after the burner has warmed the air in the furnace to a comfortable level. Frequently, the control turns the fan on when the furnace air temperature reaches between 130 and 150 degrees and shuts it off again when the air temperature drops to between 115 and 120 degrees. These temperatures are unnecessarily high when you realize that room temperatures average 72 degrees. Adjust the thermostatic switch to turn the fan on when the furnace air temperature reaches 110 degrees, instead of the average setting of 135 degrees, and to shut the fan off when the air temperature falls to 95 degrees. (You'll find the fan switch on a control box near the firebox end of the furnace.) Such a setting will keep the fan on for longer periods, but you'll be getting a larger share of the heat generated in the furnace.

7. Check steam vents and radiator valves. Leaky vents or valves that permit air to enter radiators can cause inefficient heating. Extract both water and air from radiators at the beginning of each heating season. Also check the valve to the water system that adds make-up water; a leak here could flood the system.

Should you turn down the thermostat at night to cut fuel costs? Tests conducted at the University of Illinois determined that turning back the thermostat by 11 degrees with a *hot-air system* reduced fuel costs by about 9 percent. Tests on a *hot-water system*, however, indicated no savings in fuel cost without producing an unacceptable amount of discomfort in the morning hours. The reason: Hot-air systems respond quickly to changes in temperature; hot-water systems do not. With the hot-air system, air temperature quickly built up each morning after the house had cooled down during the night. With the hot-water system the house stayed warm longer at night and took longer to build back heat the following morning. So with a hot-air system you can expect to save 6 to 10 percent of a season's fuel by turning back the thermostat 10 to 12 degrees.

## How to Trim Fuel Costs

Regardless of the kind of heating system installed in your house, you can cut fuel costs by following these heat-saving practices:

*Close off rooms not used.* Sun-rooms, unused bedrooms and storage rooms should be closed off and the heat to those rooms shut off. When closing off a room, pad the air gap at the bottom of the doors and weather-strip around doors to keep cold air from escaping into the rest of the house.

*Keep doors and windows closed.* Don't try to heat the outdoors by leaving a window open when the heat is on. If you prefer to sleep in a cool bedroom, shut off the heat at the register or radiator, then open the window a crack. Train your children to close doors quickly and tightly.

*Check the accuracy of room thermostats.* Sometimes the thermostat controls temperature to a different degree than indicated. For example, you may set a thermostat at 72 degrees, but the room temperature may actually hover close to 74 degrees.

*Keep temperatures as low as comfortable.* Tests have indicated that for each degree the house temperature is set below 70 degrees, the furnace burns 3 percent less fuel. While temperatures much below 70 degrees can be uncomfortable, similar *additional* costs are incurred for each degree above that temperature. If the thermostat is set for 72 degrees, your furnace may burn 6 percent more fuel than if the thermostat is set for 70 degrees.

*Pull draperies across windows to reduce the effect of cold glass surfaces.* Your body loses heat to such cold surfaces by radiation. In really cold climates insulating drapes over large windows save a remarkable amount of fuel. Lining curtains with reflective, insulating cloth or foam will reduce heat loss to windows.

*Keep humidity levels up by adding moisture to heated air.* An automatic humidifier in a hot-air furnace or a mechanical atomizer replaces the moisture frozen out of air as it cools outside. When such dry air is heated, relative humidity drops even lower. Dry air contacting your skin dries surface moisture and cools you. More humid air feels warmer.

*Install a reflective insulation barrier between radiators and outside walls.* An aluminum-foil layer over a one-inch thickness of insulation prevents as much as 35 percent of the radiator heat from escaping through the wall. Reflective foil radiates the heat out into the room.

*On warm, sunny days open curtains and turn on a circulating fan* to distribute the solar heat that streams into south-facing rooms. Distributing this heat saves on fuel. As soon as the sun disappears, draw the curtains or drapes to prevent a reverse flow of heat.

*Close the damper when the fireplace is not in use.* Cold air flows down the chimney and spreads out over the floor as a cool draft if the damper is open.

*Add a radiant panel or heat lamp to the bathroom.* Since we all wear fewer clothes in a bathroom, temperatures must be higher to maintain comfort levels. Instead of supplying extra heat to the bathroom 24 hours a day, install a supplementary heat lamp in a strategic position to maintain warmth only when needed.

*Keep hot-air registers and radiators free of obstructions.* Don't place furniture directly over ducts or in front of radiators and expect them to work effectively. Magazines stacked on ducts or on top of radiators will interfere with hot-air flow.

*Turn down the thermostat to 55 degrees* any time you will be away from the house for a full day or more.

Prices of electricity and gas are controlled by public utility commissions. But if you burn oil, shop around for a supplier who will sell oil at 10 to 15 percent less than the so-called standard price. As a starter try these leads:

Ask your friends, neighbors and co-workers where they buy oil. Someone will have a line on a discount oil dealer. Watch for ads to locate a low-cost supplier. Work through your union or neighborhood association, or combine your orders with those of others to get a group rate. Ask for a volume discount if your oil tank holds more than 300 gallons. Negotiate with several dealers for a lower price. Just for the asking, one or more dealers may break the price barrier. The standard price isn't fixed. If your present supplier believes he may lose you as a customer, he may reduce the price; or a new supplier may cut his price to gain a customer.

## Air-Conditioning Economies

Everything said about insulation and weather stripping earlier in this chapter applies even more strongly to air conditioning. The cost of keeping the inside of a whole house cooled to 75 degrees when the outside temperature is 95 degrees is several times more expensive than keeping the same house warmed to 70 degrees when the temperature outside is only 50 degrees. Several factors account for this difference: Air-conditioning systems use electricity for fuel; the cooling cycle is a complex mechanical-chemical process; and much of the energy goes for condensing water vapor out of the air to maintain comfort. Normally, centrally air-conditioned houses in warm climates have insulation twice as thick as homes to be heated in moderately cold areas. The extra insulation definitely pays off.

When you buy air conditioning you are buying comfort: cooler temperatures and reduced humidity. How much comfort you buy affects the cost of air conditioning. If you buy only a single-room unit for sleeping comfort, you will obviously spend less than if you keep your whole house cool with a central unit. Anything that keeps heat outside the house permits you to get the same cooling inside with a smaller unit and less electricity. These tips will save you money:

197

1. Leave storm windows and doors installed for the summer. Any kind of double glazing increases insulation value by keeping hot air out in summer as well as cold air out in winter.

2. Paint a reflective aluminum coating on your roof. Special paints (many available in color) contain millions of tiny aluminum flakes that reflect the sun's radiant heat. You can make temperatures inside your house 10 degrees lower by simply using your roof as a reflector, rather than an absorber, of heat.

3. Install an attic fan. Preventing heat buildup under the roof reduces the heat load on any air-conditioning unit. Where temperatures are not extreme, an attic fan may be all that's needed to keep your home reasonably comfortable.

4. Spray your roof with water to reduce the heat load and provide enough cooling to avoid the need for air conditioning. Roof spraying works best if the attic is uninsulated or if the roof is flat or has a low slope. Roof water cools a house in two ways: by absorbing heat and carrying it away in the runoff, and by evaporative cooling. As much as 250 gallons of water per hour may be needed for effective roof-spray cooling. If water is expensive in your area, added insulation and a bigger air-conditioner may be less costly.

5. Shades, awnings and trees keep the sun's direct light and heat off the house. Windows, particularly, need to be shaded to keep the sun's heat from streaming through the glass. Remember, once the sun's radiant heat gets into the house, it stays there. Roll shades on the outside of the house, for example, are much more effective in keeping the interior cool than curtains or drapes inside the house.

6. Plantings and walls are needed along western exposures to block the sun's heat. By the time the sun gets around to the west during the hottest part of the day, its rays are almost horizontal. Only a vertical wall placed some distance away from the house or a thick hedge of plants can keep out the low-angle rays. A wide overhang is effective along south-facing windows because of the high angle of the sun during the middle of the day.

7. Reflecting insect screens effectively block the sun from entering windows. Reflecting screens are built with many tiny strips of metal canted to reflect the sun without blocking vision.

8. Use a range-top exhaust fan to carry both cooking heat and

moisture out of the house. If your bathroom is not ventilated by an exhaust fan, set up a portable fan to blow hot air and steam out through an open window.

9. Schedule for early morning housecleaning chores that release lots of moisture into the air, such as floor mopping, washing windows and laundry—or postpone them to a cooler day. Don't leave wet clothes to dry in a kitchen, laundry or bathroom, as this moisture must be removed by the dehumidifying section of the air-conditioning unit or system. Ironing clothes also releases considerable moisture into the air, particularly if you use a steam iron. Moisture, once it gets into the house air, must then be extracted or the cooled air feels clammy.

10. Begin air conditioning early in the day. A small unit will keep a house cooler if you anticipate the heat load and keep the house cool from morning on. Otherwise, you may need a big unit to handle the heat load after it builds up.

11. Set indoor temperatures at about 15 degrees cooler than outside or at about 76 to 78 degrees. Greater temperature differentials increase operating costs.

12. Close hot-air registers in any room where a window air-conditioning unit is operating, to prevent cooled air from draining into the duct system. Also, close the door to the room unless you wish cooled air to circulate through the rest of the house.

13. Clean unit fans and radiators frequently to keep them free of dust and lint. Efficient heat transfer depends on air movement, so make sure the air passages and the filters are not plugged. Also, blow out or vacuum the metal areas; accumulated lint and dust act as insulators.

## Saving on Water and Electricity

Two other utilities, water and electricity, regularly drain a variable amount of cash from your money pool. Wasteful or unknowing habits in using both can increase your costs. You may feel there is little you can do to save on either water or electricity usage. Not so— and the repetitive savings each month add up to a sizable sum by the end of the year. These power-saving ideas will help you cut your electricity bills:

Hot-water tanks heated electrically use large quantities of power. In areas where electric rates are high, it pays to use some alternate fuel, such as natural gas, or a heating coil, in an oil-burning furnace.

Insulate hot-water pipes that run considerable distances from the heater. You probably allow the hot-water tap in a distant bathroom to run for several minutes before the water warms up. Electricity used to heat this water that has cooled in the pipe is wasted. Insulation keeps the water from cooling between uses.

Keep the lint filter on a clothes drier cleaned regularly. A plugged lint trap prevents a free flow of air, so the drier must operate for longer periods to dry clothes.

Turn lights off when they are not needed, and eliminate unnecessary lights. Despite the obvious fact that a single light bulb burns little "juice," the electricity burned by all the light bulbs in a house forms a sizable part of the monthly bill. A light left on in a closet or furnace room may burn for days before it is discovered. Use low-cost fluorescent lamps where light is needed for long periods. Fluorescents generate more light per watt than incandescents. Use only as big a bulb as needed. In hallways and closets or for general exterior lighting, use bulbs of the size for the minimum light required.

The only way to cut water costs is to reduce the amount of water you use. Here are some painless, effective ways to cut down on water consumption:

Install a half-flush toilet bowl mechanism. According to one estimate, about 43 percent of the water used in a house is flushed down the toilet. Most of these flushes require considerably less than the usual six to ten gallons used. So install a mechanism that flushes only half of the bowl water when a full flush isn't necessary.

Use a control valve in the shower head to slow the rush of water while soaping or while washing your hair. Then, when a rush of water is needed, simply open the valve for a full flow. Reducing the flow when it is not necessary saves water and also saves the electricity or gas needed to heat the water.

Prepare lawn beds with an idea to saving water. A deep seedbed encourages deep root growth and access to the water contained naturally in a large volume of soil. Properly prepared seedbeds for lawns can almost eliminate watering.

Soak lawns when watering is required. Deep watering pays off, because enough water is laid on to soak deep below the surface and grass roots are encouraged to grow deeper when the surface layers of soil dry up between waterings. Deep watering every week or ten days builds a better lawn than shallow watering every two or three days. Frequent watering simply allows much of the sprinkled water to evaporate.

Don't attempt to keep your lawn green all summer. When soil temperatures get too hot, perennial grasses turn dormant in order to survive—much as they do when soil temperatures become too cold to allow continued growth throughout the winter. Later, when cool weather and moisture are present, the grass begins growing again and turns green.

## Cutting the Phone Bill

Your monthly telephone bill is probably one of your biggest items, particularly if you have teen-age daughters or sons. Cutting the number and length of calls will reduce the cost considerably. Timing your calls to take advantage of reduced rates also helps keep phone bills down. The highest rates are in effect on weekdays between 7 a.m. and 5 p.m. Rates are lower between 5 and 7 p.m. and still lower after 7 p.m. and on weekends and holidays. The lowest rates are for calls placed between midnight and 7 a.m. to cities more than 354 miles away.

Here are other ways to save money on phone bills:

Station-to-station calls are always less than person-to-person calls.

A private line costs as much as $1.60 more a month than a party line. Decorator phones cost up to $1 or so more a month than a plain black phone. A touch-tone phone runs around $1.50 extra. Depending on where you live, a colored phone can cost from $2 to $7.50 extra to install. Extension phones and extralong cords also cost more to install. You pay more, too, for an unlisted number.

Have all your telephones installed at the same time, since you will be charged for each visit by the phone installer.

In many large metropolitan areas, where local calls are billed as units, people who make less than 50 calls a month may qualify for lower rates. Special plans are available to provide a specified number

of units at a flat monthly rate. People who make many local calls
may be able to buy unlimited local calls for a specified rate.

In most parts of the country special extended-area service rates
are available for residents outside metropolitan areas. For a flat
monthly charge a caller's toll-free area may be extended to include a
larger area. The Wisconsin Telephone Company, for instance, offers
"Tel-a-Visit" service to private-line customers; during certain hours
they may call anywhere in the state at no extra charge. Consult your
local phone directory or company to find out about special rates
available in your community.

Saving on utility bills is a matter of good planning and careful
habits. If you follow the suggestions in this chapter you can trim
valuable dollars from your utility costs.

CHAPTER 18

## Home Improvement: A Good Investment or a Poor One?

*Not all "improvements"
pay off when you sell.
Before you add that extra
room, be sure your money
will be well spent*

Stan Fulton and his wife were being transferred back to his home
office. With only a week left till moving day, Stan had just reluctantly
accepted a bid for their house that he thought was far too low. Not
ruinously low. It was about $2000 less than he'd expected to get.

The sore point was that the difference was almost exactly the
amount he'd invested in what his wife could sometimes get away with
calling Fulton's Folly. A year before, with heavy assistance from a
home improvement loan, Stan had built a small greenhouse on to
a back corner of the house. Like Nero Wolfe, Stan was an amateur
orchid grower, and he'd wanted that greenhouse with a passion.
It was equipped for precise control of temperature and humidity,
and Stan had once admitted, "It cost almost as much as a new car.
But it's worth it, to me. I get more pleasure from it than I would
from having a Rolls-Royce."

Unfortunately, when the house had to be put on the market the greenhouse proved to have somewhat less sales appeal than a Rolls. A stream of prospective buyers trooped through the house, but Fulton's Folly didn't draw a single glimmer of interest. They couldn't get even a nibble at the price Stan had set, which included the cost of his "home improvement." One prospect was even heard to mutter to his wife that "it would probably cost five hundred to get it torn down."

When Stan finally understood that he'd have to write off the cost of his beloved greenhouse and absorb a loss, he'd learned rule No. 1 in home improvement: You don't always get your money back.

You shouldn't always expect to, of course. The primary reason for any home improvement is the comfort, beauty or convenience it adds to your home while you're occupying it. But Americans move frequently these days, so frequently that it's been estimated the typical house is resold about every seven years. As a result, families sometimes don't have the opportunity to get their value out of an improvement in personal pleasure alone.

It's wise, therefore, to know your chances of recovering your investment if you have to put your place up for sale. That's the test of whether you're adding salable value to your home or only buying personal satisfaction.

The key to any home improvement's actual value is its popularity with home buyers in general. If you add something everybody wants, your chances of getting your investment back are excellent. If you create something only 1 buyer in 100 will want, watch out. Your chances of finding that buyer in the hurry and scurry of home selling are slim indeed.

The worst home improvements—from an investment standpoint—are the highly specialized ones. As Stan Fulton discovered, few people want a home greenhouse, and fewer still are willing to lay down hard-earned money for one. Some even regard it as a detriment. Fortunately, the list of poor-investment improvements of the greenhouse type is small. It includes lily ponds, especially those with fountains, elaborate barbecue pits and even swimming pools.

Obviously, these are the exceptions. What about the more common improvements—bedrooms, baths, recreation rooms, garages, porches and remodeled kitchens? Here you are on firmer ground. None of these can possibly be regarded as a drawback at selling time. They are all positive additions to any dwelling, but they don't all pay off equally well.

## Determining the Value of an Improvement

Two basic elements affect the investment value of the improvement. The first is the nature of the improvement itself. For example, a bedroom added to a two-bedroom house is almost certain to repay a good percentage of its cost when the house is sold, since the three-bedroom house is much more in demand. But adding a fifth bedroom will be viewed by most buyers as something they'll accept if it's there, but they'll be darned if they'll pay extra for it.

The second consideration is the home that's being improved. The value of the other homes in the neighborhood should be taken into account when adding to or fixing up your own. To be on the safe side, don't improve your home so that its value is more than 15 percent higher than the general run of the neighborhood.

Keeping in mind that it's possible to overimprove, let's take a look at some of the more common home improvements to see what percentage you can expect to recover if you have to sell. Here are the estimates of the National Home Improvement Council:

*Added bedroom.* This is one of the soundest investments. Adding a third bedroom is particularly wise, since two-bedroom homes sell poorly. You stand to get almost all of your money back from a third bedroom, and you'll do almost as well if you're adding a fourth. On a fifth, however, you can't count on much more than a 50 percent recovery.

*Added bath.* A second bath is now considered a necessity by most home buyers, so again you're adding sound value and should be able to recover most of your expense when selling. Another full bath is still a good bet even if your home boasts a lavatory. In this case, however, you may have to be satisfied with a return of two thirds of your investment.

*Remodeled kitchen.* If your kitchen needs remodeling, do it. An up-to-date kitchen is one of the best possible investments in your home. Chances of recovering your investment are excellent, and the kitchen may prove the home's prime selling point when you move.

*Family room.* The pertinent question here is, Where? If you're planning a reasonably priced family room added at ground level, you can confidently expect to get back three quarters of what you put into it. But the basement "rumpus room" has lost popularity in some parts of the country. Don't hope for a return of more than half of what you put into a basement room.

All of the above situations assume that you're having a contractor do the work. However, the age of do-it-yourself isn't yet dead, or even dying, so this can be an alternative. If you and your family can really do all the work yourselves, you can expect to cut 40 to 50 percent from the cost of most of these jobs. This means you stand to get at least your money back on most improvements, and a premium on some.

If your inclination is toward do-it-yourself, take a long, hard look at what you're proposing: Have you done this kind of work before? How did it come out? Do you have the necessary tools? How long will it take? What disruptions will it cause in family life while the work is under way?

For many people, do-it-yourself is too frequently a delusion. Uncertain as to how to proceed, unused to heavy demand on marginal skills and weary from a regular job, many husbands find the task too much. The result is unfinished jobs that drag on for months, poor workmanship or contractors called in to salvage the operation.

---

## WORDS YOU SHOULD KNOW

**Contractor.** A professional builder who "contracts" to complete a construction or renovation job expertly. He usually maintains a crew that does part of the work, but farms out to a subcontractor such specialties as electric wiring, plumbing and plastering.

**Workman's compensation.** A kind of insurance required of employers by all states to cover workers who may be injured, maimed or killed in on-the-job accidents.

**Progress payment.** A partial payment on the contract price of a job while the work is in progress.

**Mechanic's lien.** A legal claim by the contractor or workman against the property if the owner fails to pay for improvements. The property may not be sold or title transferred until the time when the lien is discharged.

But there is a middle ground between contracting and do-it-yourself, which for many people offers an economical yet sensible alternative. This is to have part of the job done by a contractor. The toughest parts of any improvement are those requiring special skills—plumbing, wiring and structural framing. Yet a good portion of the cost of any improvement is accounted for by such reasonably easy tasks as insulating, tile laying, shingling, painting and installing hardware.

Not all contractors are willing to accept less than the complete job, but many are. When you've located one, discuss thoroughly which parts of the job each of you will undertake. It is wise to get this division down in writing to prevent misunderstandings. (For complete information on contractors, see Chapter 16, "What You Should Know About Contractors," page 179.)

CHAPTER 19

## Seven Tips on Insuring Your Home

*Do you have enough coverage? Are you spending too much on household insurance? Find out how to get the best deal*

If your house is one of the 400,000 that will catch fire in the United States this year, odds are you'll end up taking a considerable financial licking—even if you're insured.

"You're lucky you had insurance," your friends will say, assuming that everything will be taken care of. The facts, however, are often quite to the contrary. Although 90 percent of homes are covered by some form of fire insurance, most householders do not have sufficient coverage, nor do they know how to figure losses and settle claims. Here are some tips on how to avoid the financial grief that can follow fire and other calamities:

1. *Don't be underinsured.* One survey of some 9000 insured dwellings in one midwestern state disclosed that more than one out of five were seriously underinsured. Typical was a homeowner with $8000 insurance on a house that would cost $15,000 to rebuild. Another home was insured for $20,000, though replacing it would

cost $35,000. Insurance executives say similar conditions exist all across the nation.

Inflation makes frequent review of your coverage particularly advisable. A national appraisal firm estimates that a $20,000 dwelling built in 1950 would cost more than $34,000 to construct today. And *Business Week* reports that building costs went up 17 percent from 1962 to 1969. Conclusion: If the amount of your insurance wasn't increased during that period, a big fire would probably cost you several thousand extra dollars.

There is an additional advantage to being adequately insured. Some policies stipulate that you can recover full replacement value (up to the amount of the policy) for losses only if your coverage is 80 percent or more of the market value of your house. If your coverage is less, the settlement will be based on replacement cost minus depreciation. For example, suppose you have less than 80 percent coverage on your home, and fire ruins some eight-year-old wallpaper that has a normal life of ten years. If comparable new wallpaper costs $1000, you will collect only $200 from your insurance—that is, $1000 minus $800 for eight years' depreciation.

Insurance experts report that thousands of homeowners carry enough insurance to cover the mortgage—but not their own equity. Thus, many houses burn down with just enough insurance to protect the lending institution. Another widespread error is using "tax value" as a measure of the amount of insurance to carry. Since tax valuations in many communities are deliberately set at only 40, 50 or 60 percent of actual value, reliance on these figures can result in disastrous consequences.

If you are in doubt about your house's market value, ask your agent to look it up. He has insurance publications designed to give this information. You may double-check his figures with a local builder.

2. *Get the right kind of policy.* There is no one type of home insurance that fits everyone. The standard policy protects against loss from fire, lightning, smoke and the water or chemicals used to fight the fire. For an extra premium you can get extended coverage, which will protect you against explosion, riot, aircraft, vehicles, windstorm and hail. In most states you can get additional extended

coverage, for another extra premium, against such hazards as van-dalism; glass breakage; ice, snow and freezing; falling of trees; bursting pipes.

The recently developed package policy combines theft and liabil-ity coverage with fire protection. Also called a homeowner's package, or, if you are renting a house, a tenant's package policy, its savings are often considerable. Of course, before you choose such a plan, you must decide whether you need all the theft and liability pro-tection it provides. (For more details, see page 210.)

3. *Know what losses you can claim.* Many people fail to recover certain losses because they don't know that these losses are covered by their policies. For example, most policies automatically provide coverage—up to 10 percent of your insurance on your household furnishings—on personal effects away from home.

Most homeowner's policies also protect against extra living ex-penses incurred by fire or other damage to a home. In June 1966, when a tornado swept through Topeka, Kansas, nearly 2000 tem-porarily homeless families collected some $145 million in claims for motel bills, meals and other essentials.

An inventory of your household furnishings and personal property can be invaluable, since it is virtually impossible to remember every-thing that a fire has destroyed. Your insurance agent can give you a room-by-room form which makes inventory-taking easier. Some families make their inventories with a camera, photographing each room, then storing the pictures in a safe-deposit box.

4. *Avoid costly mistakes.* If you pay your premiums on a three-year basis rather than annually, you may save 10 percent. You can also cut your insurance bill by agreeing to a deductible clause—where you pay the first $50 of any property loss. The real purpose of insurance, after all, is not minor reimbursement but protection against major losses.

Make sure that your home is accurately described in the policy and its ownership correctly stated. Notify your agent or broker whenever there is a change. If you add a room, air-condition your house or install wall-to-wall carpeting, you may need more insurance.

A top executive of a large insurance company warns of two typical mistakes. One is the purchase of residential insurance by letter or phone. Instead, you should meet with the agent or broker and discuss in detail all aspects of your situation, so that he can tailor coverage to fit your particular needs. Some people in modest homes, for instance, own antique furniture, jewelry or art objects of great value. Without detailed discussion, such people might end up with the homeowner's policy which limits coverage on contents to 40 percent of the coverage on the house itself.

The other error is failure to tell your agent about personal property which you occasionally take away from home. There's coverage under the 10 percent off-premises clause, of course, but many vacationing families take along possessions worth far more than that.

5. *Know what to do after fire strikes.* Phone your agent. Then take all reasonable steps to hold down the damage; for instance, wipe water off furniture, close windows against rain, see that roof holes are temporarily covered. Start cleaning up—your policy probably requires you to separate damaged from undamaged personal property—but don't throw away the debris.

Above all, don't sign anything until you have discussed it with

▭▭▭▭▭▭

## WHEN YOU RECEIVE YOUR POLICY

As soon as your fire or homeowner's insurance policy arrives in the mail you should read it carefully. Misunderstandings about the terms or mistakes in the policy should be corrected at once. If allowed to stand, they may limit your chances of recovery later on.

As you read, ask yourself these questions:
• Does it give your name and address and the location of the insured property?
• Is it the kind of coverage you agreed on?
• Is it for the amount of insurance you agreed on?
• Are the amounts and the due dates of the premium payments correctly stated?
• Is the policy for the length of time you agreed on?
• What is the starting date of the policy and what is its expiration date?
• To whom are you supposed to report a loss?
• How soon are you supposed to report a loss?

If you cannot answer any of these questions, contact your agent at once for clarification and a correction of your policy.

▭▭▭▭▭▭

your agent. An insurance authority once said, "If anyone asks a homeowner to sign anything immediately after a fire, that's proof he's up to no good."

In many metropolitan areas there are some unscrupulous public adjusters—often confused with insurance company adjusters—who rush to fires and try to get the excited homeowner to sign a document authorizing the stranger to act on the owner's behalf. Actually, that little piece of paper gives this stranger 10 percent or more of everything the insurance company pays. One man whose house burned to the ground refused the blandishments of such a flame-chasing operator. He had $50,000 insurance on the dwelling, and $20,000 on contents, all of which was paid in full. Had he yielded to the public adjuster, it would have cost him $7000.

6. *Check with outside experts.* Before you talk to your insurance

---

## SAVING ON HOMEOWNER'S INSURANCE

If you are now on the verge of buying, and insuring, a new home for the first time, this is the time to weigh the comparative costs of traditional coverages against the booming homeowner's, or multiple perils, insurance.

Check your fire insurance policy now to see whether you are missing out on big savings. If your property is presently covered by separate insurance policies for fire, burglary and theft, and comprehensive personal liability, you may be paying as much as one third more than is necessary.

What is a homeowner's insurance policy? It is a policy combining a host of major and minor disasters in a single package, including fire, lightning, wind, hail, burglary and theft. It pro-

vides comprehensive personal liability insurance. It is a policy which, above and beyond the traditional fire, theft and liability coverages, also insures you against loss or theft of property away from home and pays living expenses for you and your family in the event your home is destroyed by fire.

Moreover, instead of paying only an amount equal to the depreciated value of destroyed property, homeowner's insurance pays the full replacement cost. Let's say the front porch you built ten years ago is ripped off by a hurricane. It will cost you $400 to replace the porch. Under the traditional arrangement, you would be paid only half the replacement cost, or $200 based on a 20-year life of the porch. But under the homeowner's policy the full $400 cost would be paid.

And most significantly, coverage under homeowner's insurance today costs adjuster, remember that you are involved in a business matter; in a few days you can lose as much money as you could save in several years. Arm yourself with facts and evidence concerning your losses. Don't throw yourself trustingly into the hands of the adjuster. He's there to represent the company, not you. Before you meet with him, obtain professional opinion as to what is your fair due.

A good contractor can estimate the cost of putting your house back in prefire condition. Get him to help you figure depreciation, a subject that should never be left to the adjuster. Have experts evaluate your losses in furniture and other major household articles. Insurance policies reimburse you for what a new item will cost, less depreciation—which varies widely. For example, clothing depreciates rapidly, furniture more slowly. A good specialty or department store can help you arrive at accurate figures.

□□□□□□

you a full 20 to 30 percent less than separate coverages would cost you. To illustrate the savings, here is a breakdown of the $237 cost of three separate policies insuring a $25,000 frame house: fire and extended coverage (including $8000 on house contents), $167; burglary and theft, $38; comprehensive personal liability, $32.

This $237 is 26 percent more than the $175 total you would pay for the identical coverage plus certain extras in a homeowner's policy.

Cost obviously is the key reason why millions of American families are now buying package insurance for their homes. From 1957 to 1969 premiums written for homeowner's insurance soared from $179 million to $2.5 billion. Today more premiums are being written for homeowner's insurance than for straight fire insurance.

To help forestall rate rises on home-owner's insurance policies, the insurance industry has in a growing number of states been writing policies with $50 deductible provisions. But most of these policies have what is called a "disappearing deductible" under which the amount paid by you, the insured, drops as your loss rises above the $50 line. For example, if the loss amounts to just $50, you pay the entire amount; if the loss is $500 or more, the insurance company pays the entire amount.

Will the time come when all the separate insurance policies we buy today are bundled into a single package? Not soon, says the industry, primarily because most of today's insurance writers specialize in just one or two fields. But at least a single, economical insurance package for the homeowner is readily available, and you should be fully aware of its advantages.

□□□□□□

Don't settle for an unsatisfactory sum because you are in a hurry to get your check. If you and the adjuster are completely at loggerheads, take the matter to your agent. If he agrees with your figures, he can intercede in your behalf, if necessary asking the insurance company for a special investigation, which sometimes results in greatly increased settlements. In cases involving really unfair handling, you can ask for a review by your state insurance department.

7. *Get a good agent.* Next to a fire, nothing can be more costly than a careless agent. A good one, on the other hand, will see that you get the right insurance in the right amount at the right price. Also, he will help you get the proper settlement in case of a loss. Your lawyer, banker or perhaps the firm you work for can help you locate him.

If you have doubts about the agent or broker now handling your insurance, ask yourself whether, in the past five years, he has: (1) advised you of savings through deductible clauses; (2) recommended that your coverage be brought up to date; (3) advised switching from separate policies to a homeowner's package.

If the answer to these questions is no—and you haven't been brushing off your agent's attempts to help you—then you have reason to question whether your insurance is being properly handled.

---

## WORDS YOU SHOULD KNOW

**Depreciation.** The reduction in value of property due to wear, use, age and obsolescence. A depreciation charge is a percentage of the original cost set aside each year to replace the property at the end of its useful life; such a hoard is a depreciation fund. The book value of a property is its original cost less the existing depreciation fund that covers it.

**Tax value.** The value of your house on the books of the local tax collector, on the basis of which your real estate tax is figured. This is usually not more than half the real, or market, value, which is the price the property would bring if sold.

**Extended coverage.** Greater insurance protection for the homeowner than is provided in the standard policy, which covers only damage from fire, lightning, smoke and firefighting. Extended coverage is tailor-made and can include liability against damage suits, protection of furniture from theft and vandalism, and coverage of plumbing damage.

---

# 4

# INSIDE
# THE HOME—
# Your Second
# Biggest Investment

*Knowing how to pick furniture,
fabrics and appliances can give you
more satisfaction at a lower cost*

CHAPTER 20

# Furnishings That Are Right for Your Family

*Picking and choosing for your home can be fun—and rewarding—if you know how to get the most for your decorating dollar*

You can have a genuinely satisfying experience furnishing and decorating your home and save money while you're at it. Few projects are as much fun, have that much excitement and, in the long run, provide as much reward for everyone concerned. Use your imagination, learn all you can and, above all, plan.

Don't even begin until you are sure of your general goals. For ideas read magazines, consult your library for books on decorating, take advantage of free consultant services offered by department and home furnishing stores. When you are ready to buy, try to appraise the quality of the salespersons with whom you deal; if they are well informed, you can gain from their superior information on the items they sell. Remember, though, that everyone is prey to impulse buying, and use all your willpower to avoid it. In the end your satisfaction will be far greater if you have taken exact measurements, if you have carefully considered what functions you want each room to perform and if you have thought about the furniture you have on hand and how it might be used.

Before you start furnishing your home, look at yourself and where you are going. Needs and interests change over the years; when you can, try to include the future in your planning.

Are you newly married? Think about what usable furnishings either of you may have; what you need that must be purchased immediately and what can be postponed; which purchases are temporary and which, such as rugs and beds, should last for years; how much you can afford; perhaps even how soon you think you'd like to start a family.

Are you a beginning family? The first baby will bring a drastic change to your life. The furniture needs just for that little baby can seem overwhelming. Look at them realistically and note that a great many expensive and appealing items on the market are useful for only the first few months or first year of the baby's life. Stay away

214

from the temptation to buy short-term equipment such as Bathinettes, bassinets, baby bureaus, expensive carriages, unless you can really afford them.

Are you a family with growing children? Think about bookcases for the children's books, desks for studying, shelving room for hobby equipment like records, paints, building materials. In view of the punishment even the best of children inevitably give to furnishings and walls, consider durability.

Does your family have adolescent children? You will need space for entertaining the children's friends, reading, enjoying hobbies, and so on. You can turn a child's bedroom into a bed-sitting room by using a daybed or convertible sofa, by adding additional shelving or cabinets that would substitute as bureaus.

Have your children grown and moved away? Furniture needs are reduced when the children leave home, but you will probably want to plan for visits from sons, daughters, grandchildren. You may want to turn a former children's bedroom into a library, den, workroom or bed-sitting room, or even to move to a smaller home that requires less care and buy modern furnishings and equipment.

## Function First

Where, logically, do you begin if you need to decorate or furnish one or several rooms? It is important to consider exactly how each room is to be used. Is the den also going to double as a guest room? If you have a good-sized dining room and not so large a living room, would it make sense to use part of the dining room as a sitting room or as a television headquarters? Is there room for a desk and bookcases in your child's room? Have you thought about storage space for fishing tackle, tennis rackets, records, other hobby equipment? Is the living room also going to be used as a dining room, a TV room, a library, an activity room for the children? Look carefully at each room you are decorating and try to think of all the functions you could conceivably—now or later—want it to perform.

The next step is to take an inventory of your existing furniture, your basic furniture needs, the available space and the money you can afford for furnishing and decorating expenses.

You may find it advisable to list first-year needs, second-year needs, and so on through the next five years, and then divide the yearly costs by the number of your paychecks, to get some indication of how much you should set aside each payday for furnishings. If you feel that some furniture needs are immediately essential, even though you do not have the cash on hand to pay for them, perhaps you'll want to consider borrowing money for home furnishings. (See Chapter 50, "Money When You Need It," page 476, for information on how to shop around for the best credit terms.)

Before you actually start to invest in home furnishings, here are some tips that will help you become a thrifty and skillful shopper:

1. Before making a purchase final, you should discuss it with your family and, if possible, take your husband along so that you both agree on the choice.

2. Go shopping equipped with information on items you intend to buy—possibly pictures or descriptions of the items. Take along fabric swatches, measurements, color samples to coordinate your shopping.

3. Buy from reliable stores. Check on written guarantees, adjustments for unsatisfactory equipment, delivery, installation, servicing.

4. Read labels, seals and tags, and keep tags specifying use and care.

5. Examine merchandise. Lie down on beds, sit in chairs and sofas, check colors in different lights, check joint construction, pull out drawers, open doors, switch lamps on and off.

6. Compare prices in several stores.

7. Consider secondhand furniture. You may find good furniture in secondhand shops and auctions a better value than low-quality new furniture. (For more on secondhand furniture shopping, see Chapter 23, "New Isn't Always Best," page 242.)

8. Consider unfinished furniture that may save you money if you have the time and skill to finish it yourself.

9. Be on the lookout for seconds or slightly damaged furniture. Such a purchase can be economical if the damage is not great or the cost of repair nominal. This can apply to carpeting, rugs and floor and wall tiles as well. Often the slight flaw or imperfection that makes the product a second can't be discovered by anyone except a professional, and in no way detracts from the use of the object or the material.

10. Watch for furniture sales.

11. Think in terms of "doing it yourself." If you sew, upholster, apply paint, finish furniture, hang paper, lay tile or build furniture, your costs will be far less. These days one can find remnant or bargain fabric stores in almost any town. They are worth looking into because the stocks are made up of odd-width goods, remnant yardages, slightly damaged stock or out-of-stock printings that sell for considerably less than fabrics in a regular fabric store.

A word of caution here about buying inexpensive furniture. As a rule of thumb it often doesn't pay, because shoddy construction and poor materials mean a short life. But there are exceptions: Some unpainted furniture (modestly priced) is of very good design, and if treated with paint, lacquer or one of the various "antiquing" kits sold in many paint and department stores, can add to the appearance of a room. Covering these unpainted pieces with wallpaper, fabric or good-looking vinyl gives an unexpected custom touch. But remember always to watch out for quality of construction.

## How to Judge the Quality of Construction

Use the following tips to determine quality construction: Tables, chests, buffets, desks and other pieces of furniture should stand firm. They should have movable parts (drawers, doors, drop leaves) that operate smoothly and fit properly; joints that are tight fitting; hard, smooth and evenly applied finishes; and knobs, pulls and handles that are attached firmly, evenly placed and easy to grasp.

When you are buying upholstered furniture, try to check the following points: Ask the salesman about the things that you cannot see, but that should be there. In the construction, for instance, are the joints reinforced and glued? Are the legs supported within the overall frame so they will remain rigid, particularly on chairs that will get much hard wear? Is the webbing on the underside of chairs, sofas and sofa beds wide and closely interlaced for firm support? Are the springs firmly anchored? If not, the piece will develop lumps or the upholstery may shift and get ripples in it.

If the fabric is patterned, check to see that it is carefully matched and centered from the top and sides. The pattern on loose cushions should also be carefully matched. The seams and welts should be straight at such stress points as the arms of chairs and sofas and on skirts and cushions. Ask whether the fabric has been protected with a spot-resistant finish.

The purchase of well-made unfinished furniture can save you money, since finishing costs determine a large portion of the final price. Look for the same qualities of construction that you look for in finished furniture. Remember to add the cost of finishing materials to the purchase price.

There are many fabrics to consider for upholstery, draperies and slipcovers. Tight weaves mean more strength and better wear, particularly for those pieces that are in daily use. Loosely woven fabrics tend to sag and stretch. (Hold the sample up to the light to see how dense or how loose the weave is.) Plastics which look like leather and vinyls are also practical, especially for casual pieces that will take hard wear. Heavy draperies require material that will not sag. The chart on the next page gives you an idea of fabrics, their uses and characteristics. Remember that the quality of whatever material you choose will, in the end, determine its excellence. As noted in Chapter 33, "Fabrics—Facts and Fallacies," page 326, finishes are important. Excellent ratings on the chart presuppose that the quality of the particular material is good and that the correct finish has been applied. Buying poor-quality or improperly finished material is uneconomical.

## The Importance of Color

Color is the first thing you notice in a room, and it is largely responsible for the general atmosphere you create. It is also about the cheapest decorating tool you can use. Pale tints make objects seem to recede, bold hues advance them. If you keep this in mind when you're considering the size or the architectural elements of the room you are decorating, you won't draw attention to an inferior piece of furniture or an architectural defect with bold color. On the other hand, to emphasize your most attractive pieces or an unusual architectural detail, by all means give them all the color you can comfortably live with.

Don't get carried away! Too many colors can badly damage an entire room. Let your accent colors come in small doses for the most effect. Successful combinations of color can mean the difference

# Durability of Fabrics

| MATERIAL OR FIBER | WHEN USED FOR UPHOLSTERY | WHEN USED FOR SLIPCOVERS | WHEN USED FOR DRAPERIES | WHEN USED FOR WINDOW CURTAINS | QUALITIES |
|---|---|---|---|---|---|
| Cotton | Good | Good | Good | Excellent | Washable. Needs ironing. If properly finished (preshrunk) will not shrink. Has good abrasion resistance. |
| Cotton blended with polyester | Excellent | Excellent | Excellent | Excellent | Washable. Available in permanent press for washing with no ironing. Has excellent abrasion resistance. |
| Wool | Excellent | Excellent | Not generally used | Not used | Should be dry-cleaned and mothproofed. |
| Acetate | Good when used with other fibers | Good when used with other fibers | Excellent when used with other fibers | Fair to poor | Poor sunlight resistance. Has silklike appearance when combined with other fibers. |
| Nylon | Good | Good | Good when used with other fibers | Good when used with other fibers | Has undesirable static qualities unless treated with antistatic finish. Has excessive stretch. A strong fiber that adds strength to fibers with which it is blended. Washable, needs no ironing. |
| Polyester | Excellent when used with other fibers | Excellent when used with other fibers | Excellent | Excellent | Washable; needs no ironing. Good resistance to sunlight and good abrasion resistance. Imparts these qualities to fibers with which it is blended. |
| Rayon | Good when used with other fibers | Good when used with other fibers | Good when used with other fibers | Not used | Has a silklike look. Usually combined with other fibers. By itself, not washable. Best when combined with other fibers and used as decorative addition. |
| Fiber glass | Not used | Not used | Excellent | Excellent | Easily machine- or hand-washed. Will not fade in sunlight. No ironing needed. |

219

between harmony and hysteria. And remember the temperature value of color. Bright red for a hot southern exposure would be a hard choice to live with, whereas light green or blue would bring pleasant relief.

Here are some points for you to consider when selecting colors:

*Personal preferences.* If someone in the family hates purple, don't use it in large doses; treat personal rooms, like bedrooms, according to individual preferences.

*Furnishings on hand.* Pick colors that will harmonize with what you already have.

*Durability.* Light colors show dirt easily and dark colors reveal dust and lint. Use spot-resistant fabrics and washable paint or wallpaper for lighter colors. Use fade-proof colors in places exposed to sunlight.

*Textures.* Shiny surfaces reflect light and tend to make a color seem lighter and brighter, just as rough surfaces have the opposite effect. Polished materials like chintz have more light and verve.

## Wall Coverings

Paint, vinyl and paneling are the most commonly used wall coverings. Paint, relatively inexpensive, is available in three finishes: gloss, semigloss and flat. Paints on the market today include: (1) latex (for ceilings and walls), which has little or no odor, is easy to apply, touches up without showing, but is limited to flat finishes; (2) alkyd (for walls, ceilings and woodwork), which can be applied to all surfaces and is durable and washable, but from which it is difficult to remove smudges and stains; (3) gloss (for woodwork and walls), which is durable, washable and dries to a high gloss finish, but shows touch-ups and has a strong odor when wet; and (4) casein and resin emulsion (for ceilings and walls), which are inexpensive and quick-drying, but are the least practical, since they wash poorly and chip and crack easily.

Wallpaper can add pattern and texture to make a fascinating room background. Even if you prefer solid color, wallpaper is sometimes a better choice than paint, especially when your walls are in bad condition. And wallpaper can be a good investment. Initially, it may cost more than paint, but it tends to look better longer.

Most present-day papers are washable; the plastic-coated ones are even scrubbable. You can remove spots in one area of washable wallpaper without having to wash an entire wall. This makes for easy care and longer-lasting beauty.

Wallpapers are made by various methods. Screen prints, or hand prints, are colored manually by using a separate silk screen for each color in the final coloration of a design. Since this is a hand process, the screen-printed papers are the most expensive.

Roller prints are machine-made prints. Colors are applied simultaneously from 1, 2 or as many as 12 rollers. Prices of roller prints can vary greatly, depending on the quality and weight of the paper used, the complexity of the design and the number of yards manufactured. Both hand and machine prints are made on washable grounds as well as on those that have been plastic-coated for scrubbability. In most cases a plastic coating is not noticeable to the eye, and it does not change the finish.

Vinyl papers are in another category. There are paper-backed and fabric-backed vinyls. The design is printed on the vinyl surface. These wallpapers are considerably heavier than the others mentioned. Most of them can be scrubbed, and they are almost impervious to most soiling and staining. They are ideally suited, therefore, to kitchens, utility rooms and baths. When you want to replace them, vinyl fabrics will pull off the wall in strips, an advantage not to be overlooked by the do-it-yourselfer.

In addition to patterned, solid-color and textured papers, you will find scenics, murals and border prints.

Wood paneling is also more expensive than paint, but it is easy to maintain and more durable than any other type of wall covering. It is appropriate for almost any area that is free of excessive moisture. A wide range of woods is used, including ash, birch, cherry, pine, gum, mahogany, maple, oak, redwood and walnut. Pine is the least expensive, and walnut and cherry the most expensive. Panels are available in a variety of finishes, including varnish and lacquer, or can be bought unfinished, allowing you to paint, wax or stain to the finish you prefer.

If you feel you want to change the existing surface of your floor, there are a number of floor coverings on the market. (It is also possible to refurbish a damaged wood floor by sanding it down and refinishing it; ask your local paint dealer or department store for advice about this.) When you are purchasing new flooring, remember to shop different dealers for price estimates and comparisons, including the price of installation if you are not doing it yourself. These are some of the characteristics of different kinds of flooring that may help you make your selection: *Wood* is durable and resilient, but not washable. *Vinyl* is stain-resistant, resilient and durable, but fairly expensive. *Linoleum* is inexpensive, grease- and stain-resistant, durable and resilient. (All three of these are sound-absorbent.) *Asphalt* is inexpensive, but has low resilience and reflects noise. *Ceramic tile* is durable, stain-resistant, but expensive and "noisy"; the individual tiles may break if things are dropped on them, though they are replaceable.

## Choosing Carpeting

Carpeting is one of the most important purchases you will ever make for your home. A carpet can transform a barren, cold room into a rich, warm one. It sets the scene for your entire decorating theme. So when you shop for carpeting and rugs, you'll want to know

### HOW TO BUY WALLPAPER

Wallpapers are made in varying widths, that is, 18 inches, 20½ inches and 27 inches. The length of a single roll will vary proportionally. There are 36 square feet in a single roll of 18-inch or 20½-inch wallpaper and 33 square feet in a single roll of 27-inch paper. Allowing for repeats in a pattern that will have to be matched from one strip to the other when the paper is hung, estimate that a single roll of paper will cover 30 square feet of wall space. If the repeat is very large, check the square feet of usable paper in the roll before you buy.

To estimate how much paper you will need for a given room, measure the distance around the room in feet and multiply this by the height of the walls. Divide this figure by 30, rather than 36, to arrive at the number of single rolls needed. Deduct one single roll for every two doors or windows of average size. This will give you the number of rolls of wallpaper to order. It's usually a wise investment, however, to order an extra roll of paper for insurance. This paper can be kept for repairing damage or lining a closet.

as much about them as possible. Here are some rules to help make your shopping easier and your selections right for your home, your needs and your budget.

Because your carpet is the second largest area of color in your room (only your walls are larger), selecting its color is all-important. When choosing color, remember that medium shades are the most practical. Very dark and very light colors show the most soil. If you must have a light color, be prepared to clean it often or put it in a light traffic area, such as a bedroom. Multicolored carpets—such as tweeds, floral designs and stripes—usually wear better and disguise soil more effectively than do solid-color carpets. Texture and pattern give your carpet style. Both help your room achieve its final character.

Velvet-weave carpets are often the most elegant, but remember that if a velvet carpet is thin and of a color susceptible to dirt, it will require a lot of care. Velvet carpets look best in formal surroundings —in traditional living rooms, for example. (Incidentally, there is some confusion about the word *broadloom:* It does not define any particular quality or type of construction, but simply indicates that the carpet or rug is made in widths of six feet or more.)

When estimating how much of a border pattern to order, measure the running yards you wish this pattern to cover, rather than square feet. Border patterns can be found in widths up to 18 inches, and many of the widest ones are designed so that they can be cut to make borders of varying widths, adapting easily to your needs. Borders are purchased by the yard.

When shopping for mural or scenic wallpapers, consider three important factors: (1) the number of strips needed for a specific area; (2) the placement of the whole design horizontally; (3) how high you want the design from the floor and whether there will be a dado or chair rail. Additional ground paper to match the background of the mural is usually included with the set to help you fill out space.

Most wallpapers are pretrimmed at the factory. If yours is not, and you plan to hang the paper yourself, ask your dealer to trim it for you. Many papers are even pasted at the factory and only need dipping in water to activate the paste. New developments have now made it possible to peel paper off walls in sheets, and some of the new papers can even be reapplied in another location.

Twists and shag carpets require less care and are more casual. Their surface is difficult to "mess up." Twists are at their best in heavy traffic areas such as foyers or entrances. Shag carpets, even more tousled than twists, add welcome warmth to modern rooms. Both wear well and don't show dirt.

Textured designs are achieved through embossing, sculpturing, carving, random shearing or by combining cut and uncut yarns or high and low yarns. Depending on their design, they can be used in any type of room. Because they do not have a plain surface, soiling and shading are less apparent. Their many levels form natural shadows which disguise footprints.

Tweeds that depend for their final effect on the colors blended are excellent soil disguisers.

Patterned carpets are excellent for reinforcing your decorating scheme and require a minimum of maintenance.

When you start looking for your carpet you will find there are six major carpet fibers: wool, acrylic, nylon, polypropylene, polyester, and modacrylic. Cotton and rayon are used in a very small percentage of carpet production; they are found more frequently in small area rugs. Identifying the fibers by their generic names is important, and it's also helpful to know their respective brand names. For example, acrylic fibers may be known as Acrilan, Creslan, Orlon or Zefran. Trade names of nylon are Caprolan, Cumuloft, Enkaloft, Nyloft, Tycora and Du Pont 501 carpet. An example of polypropylene is Herculon.

Your requirements will most likely determine what fiber you should choose. When you decide on the appearance and the performance qualities you want, then stop to consider the price you can afford, there are usually only one or two fibers that will fill the bill. Each fiber lends itself in different ways to styling, construction and quality. For example, if you are looking for a bright color in a budget-price carpet, you probably won't find it in wool or acrylic. You will, however, find it in nylon and may soon find it in polypropylene. Keep in mind also that each fiber can be made into carpets of many different qualities. The fiber alone does not guarantee quality or performance. Fiber should be considered in relation to general quality of construction. Density, discussed below, is the most important factor in determining the performance and the durability of carpeting.

Wool is the standard with which all other carpet fibers are compared, because it has a balance of all the desirable qualities a carpet should have: resilience, or the ability to bounce back; abrasion and soil resistance; luxury, warmth and the ability to clean well.

All man-made fibers resist rapid water absorption. Man-mades also are nonallergenic, moth- and mildew-proof and resistant to insects. Natural fibers can be treated to perform in the same ways. The following fibers are man-made:

Acrylic fibers have the most similarities to wool, according to some experts. They have clear, even colors and resemble wool in feeling, abrasion resistance, resiliency and warmth. Although acrylics in light colors do not hide dirt as well as wool, they are easier to clean. Modacrylics are used mostly in combination with acrylics.

Nylon rates highest of all carpet fibers in wearability. It offers outstanding value in medium-priced carpets for heavy traffic areas. There are two types of nylon fiber: staple and continuous filament. Continuous filament nylon was designed to eliminate the tendency to fuzzing and pilling associated with staple nylon. Nylon cleans well, but has a tendency to show soil quickly. Antron nylon, however, manages to keep its pristine look longer.

Polypropylene is another addition to the economically priced carpet range. Like continuous filament nylon, it is noted for its toughness and durability. It resists soil and cleans well. Because it is solution-dyed, or has the color "built in," color will not fade or wear out. It is said to be almost static-free.

The density of carpeting is determined by the number or mass of fibers in a given area of carpet. When buying, consider two factors: the height of the pile and the weight per square yard. Neither means anything without the other. If a salesman tells you a carpet weighs 23 ounces per square yard it matters little unless you know the height of the pile. For example, if this 23-ounce carpet has half-inch pile, it is denser than a carpet of the same weight with a two-inch pile, because in the latter there are obviously fewer fibers per square yard. Just say to yourself: "The deeper and denser, the better." Density has more to do with the strength of a carpet than the fiber has.

Judge carpet quality with your eyes and fingers. Press your fingers into the surface pile to determine resiliency. Thickness and closeness of pile indicate good quality. Sparse pile and gaps indicate poor quality. It is usually best to buy top-quality carpeting, but look for the quality that best suits your needs. If the carpet is for short-term use or for an area of light traffic an inexpensive carpet may be practical. However, skimping on quality in a heavy-duty area can be much more expensive in the long run.

Your carpet should have proper padding to add depth and to prolong wear by absorbing shocks. There are two types of padding: (1) Felted padding is made from all jute, all hair or a combination of the two. A 40-ounce per square yard pad is a good weight for home use. (2) There is also rubber cushioning that ranges in thickness from an eighth to a half inch. Rubber padding of one quarter or three eighths of an inch is usually sufficient for home installation. Carpet backing on most carpets is coated with latex for security of surface yarns. An extra layer of backing is added to most good-quality tufted carpets for greater strength.

Before you buy, be sure that you are dealing with a reliable store and salesman. If you are not sure, check with the Better Business Bureau. Know the store's service details and delivery dates. Read carpet labels carefully for manufacturer's name, exact fiber content and name of the fiber supplier. Also look for important information such as on mothproofing. Get a notation made on the bill of sale stating the brand name and manufacturer. Be sure that guarantees are in writing. Do not rely on the salesman's word, such as: "This carpet will not shrink." If the carpet, pad and installation are offered in a package, find out exactly how much you are paying for each item.

Discuss installation of wall-to-wall carpeting with your retailer to determine what he offers and what it will cost. Modern tackless methods permit inconspicuous seaming and keep yardage requirements at a minimum. It is not advisable to have low-grade rugs installed wall-to-wall. The labor may cost almost as much as the rug, and the short life of the rug makes the added expense impractical.

## Draperies

Windows are considered the "eyes" of a room, and the way you treat them can dramatically alter the entire appearance of your room. Often, for very little money, a well-thought-out window treatment can add a totally new dimension to your room and draw attention away from bad features. Before you invest in curtains or draperies, check the following points for quality construction:

1. Hems: at least one inch on sides and headings, four inches on bottom hems; all hems blindstitched with no indication of puckering.

2. Pleats: generous in order to give proper fullness—at least four inches allowed for each pleat—spaced no more than five inches apart.

3. Seams (in draperies using more than one width of fabric): no puckering at seams.

4. Width: nearly twice the width of window area to create full, billowy look; sheer curtains even fuller.

5. Lining: for a richer, custom look; helpful in cutting out sound and protecting draperies from soil and grime. Insulated linings shut

## CARING FOR YOUR CARPET

The amount of care your carpet will need depends on color, texture, traffic and the area of the country in which you live. Here are some good general rules to follow:

• In heavy traffic areas go over the carpet with a carpet sweeper once a day. This removes surface dirt before it has a chance to penetrate.

• Vacuum thoroughly once a week, especially the dark surfaces under and around furniture.

• Have the carpet cleaned professionally once a year.

• When spots occur take immediate action. Blot excess liquid at once, working from the outside in. Do not rub or brush. Then place absorbent material over the damp area and weigh it down with books for at least six

hours. The longer the spill remains on the carpet, the more difficult it will be to remove.

• Never use soap to clean your carpet—this will only cause it to resoil faster. A soapless powder detergent of low alkalinity is usually satisfactory. For more detailed cleaning information, write to: National Institute of Rug Cleaning, 1815 North Fort Meyer Drive, Arlington, Virginia 22209.

• To equalize wear, rotate rugs once or twice a year. On wall-to-wall carpets, try to rearrange your furniture occasionally.

• A good point to keep in mind when carpeting stairs: Tight-textured rather than shaggy carpeting is recommended, since it's easy to catch your heel in shaggy carpets. Double thickness of rug cushion is also an excellent idea because it tends to prolong the life of the carpet.

out cold and heat, but for most draperies, noninsulated linings such as sateen or muslin are sufficient.

For picture windows which let in a lot of sunlight, use fiber-glass draperies. Other fabrics will fade or disintegrate.

## Buying Mattresses and Springs

When it comes to buying beds, quality always pays off. Most manufacturers feel that the more expensive the mattress and springs, the better the bargain. In any case mattresses and springs should be bought for comfort, not for looks. Save your esthetic feelings for bed casings.

What is a good mattress? It should be firm or soft strictly according to individual preference. But the vital test is how it supports you— it should keep the spine straight and not allow the hips to sink. Most double beds last longer if the mattress is on the firm side. Before buying, *lie down* on your prospective purchase.

A good mattress should be 10 inches longer than the tallest occupant and allow each sleeper 38 inches of width. The standard double-bed size (54 inches by 75 inches) is giving way to "queen" (60 by 80) and "king" (from 72 by 80 and 72 by 84 inches up to 78 by 80 and 79 by 84 inches) as Americans grow bigger and bigger. Twin beds come in sizes ranging from 39 by 75 inches to 39 by 80 inches. Allow enough room, but remember, if you go overboard, your bedroom may consist of nothing but bed. Also, the bigger the bed, the more expensive the sheets and other bedding materials.

If the bed has an innerspring mattress, coils or springs should range roughly from 200 to 320 coils, although the range can be as high as 1000. If the mattress is the type in which each spring has its own cloth pocket, it should have at least 800 innersprings.

Inner materials (insulation, filling of cotton felt, foam latex, urethane foam or hair) should be securely fixed by either under tufting, precompression or quilting. Ask your salesman if all inner materials that could shift are secured by one of these methods.

A good mattress should be covered with at least 26-ounce ticking. It should have strong borders, preferably double-stitched and pre-built. If the mattress has innersprings, be sure the box spring fits underneath perfectly. Check the bedding-law label attached to the mattress for information about interior construction; it will identify mattresses and box springs made of reused material.

If you buy a foam mattress, it should be made of foam latex (rubber) or urethane foam (plastic or synthetic). Urethane is lighter than foam latex and both are lighter than an innerspring mattress. Foam mattresses are designed to give a floating feeling; they must be supported by an excellent box spring, since the box spring takes most of the stress.

As important as a good mattress is a good box spring: It absorbs shock and supports weight. Mattresses and box springs usually wear out at the same time and may need to be replaced simultaneously.

When you buy a box spring, lie down on it. If you can feel the coils, reject it. Feel the underside; there should be a horizontal wood slat to support each row of springs. Think about firmness. If you want a very firm foundation, the box spring should contain 72 to 80 coils. This is essential if you use a foam mattress.

CHAPTER 21

## How to Buy Appliances

*In the market for a new stove or refrigerator? Knowing what to look for and when to buy can save you time and money*

Buying a major appliance is no snap, haphazard action. You should think seriously before the purchase, because large appliances represent a considerable investment. If they are chosen carefully, they will be a source of great convenience and service over many years. But if they are not, the mistake will be costly and difficult to live with. Here are some guidelines.

Even before you start shopping around, analyze your situation. What size is your family? What size is it likely to be in ten years? What conveniences do you find useful on the equipment you now have? You might have to weigh the desired conveniences against the practicality of your budget. If you plan to buy with time payments, how much can you afford to commit? And for what period of time?

Pay special attention to articles about appliances and to advertisements. You'll probably seek recommendations from, and compare notes with, neighbors, relatives and friends. After you've listened to their likes and dislikes, think again in terms of your own family.

When you're ready to begin shopping for the appliance, go to several stores, ask questions and make comparisons among the many brands and different models within each brand. By doing this, you'll become familiar with all the features and can arrive at a realistic choice. Comparison shopping can be confusing if you try to hurry, so take your time before making the final decision. While looking, keep these points in mind:

Remember that brand-name appliances are backed by manu-facturers who are concerned with the design, construction, function, service and safety of their products. Their objective is to satisfy you in all these areas.

Find reliable dealers, who are more likely to have competent personnel for the three important areas of sales, installation and servicing. Their salesmen should be willing to give you complete information, courteously. A dealer close to your home may offer the advantage of prompt service. If you think you may move away from your present neighborhood or area, it's advisable to buy appliances that have assured service throughout the country.

Read the warranty or guarantee carefully and be sure you under-stand it. Many of them are now simple and easy to understand. Also, read all available descriptive material, to help you in choosing style, capacity and other pertinent features. If your particular choice of model isn't immediately available, the dealer usually can order it for you from the manufacturer. It is probably worth waiting for the right appliance for you.

Look for the UL (Underwriters Laboratories) seal on electrical appliances and the AGA (American Gas Association) seal on gas appliances. These assure you that the product has met national safety standards.

Double-check the capacity and dimensions of the appliance. Is it large enough for your present and future needs? Do you have adequate space for proper installation and operation? Know the exact dimensions of your available space before you go shopping.

Ask about the construction of the appliance. What materials were used? Are the finishes durable? Are there safety signal lights that indicate when the equipment is in operation? Where necessary, as with clothes washers and driers, for example, are there switches that stop all action if doors or lids are opened? Are the doors flush and handles located where clothing will not catch? Are the controls clearly marked, easily adjustable and accessible? Are they safely out of children's reach? And if shelves and racks pull out, do they have a locked position that prevents them from slipping out and dropping?

Consider the care of the appliance. Is any special care required? Are the removable parts, such as oven doors, oven liners, heating units, burners, racks and shelves, really easy to take apart for cleaning? Check the appliance for crevices or cracks that would be catchalls for dirt.

Are the styling, design and color new and exciting? Color plays an important part in today's appliances. And many manufacturers are offering changeable panels, for a new face whenever you tire of the old one.

Check over the year-end models. If available, they might be a good buy. Make sure, however, that the guarantee still applies and that the value is worth your invested dollars.

Expect to pay a reasonable price for a good product. The cheapest is not always the best buy. But remember that most stores occasionally have sales, when comparison shopping and planned shopping mean savings. The most expensive equipment might not fit your needs, either. As a gauge of the appliance's value to you, consider what features would save you time and work or add to its flexibility. Convenience features will increase the cost, so balance their usefulness against the price.

Go over the wiring, gas and plumbing situation. Most new electrical appliances come with a three-prong plug (grounded for your safety), which means you may need new outlets. You can save yourself the cost of installing new outlets by using inexpensive adapters, but these tend to work loose and will prove less satisfactory in the long run. Include the cost of such changes in your plans for new equipment. Special wiring and plumbing work should be handled by a qualified person.

Time- and labor-saving features are common to all equipment, but their usefulness varies according to the job to be done. In the different categories of equipment, there are certain basic functions for you to consider. The rest you'll find out when you do your shopping research. Just remember to judge the value by your own needs and what you can afford.

## Buying a Range

When purchasing a range, consider these features: Automatic temperature controls on the surface units or burners and infinite-heat control switches on electric stoves let you adjust the heat to any degree of temperature needed for the food you are cooking. Meal preparation becomes more efficient when you don't have to watch the pot continually.

Automatic time controls of the oven and of outlets on the range (for operating small appliances) free you from the kitchen. You just set the timer and walk away.

Two ovens may be the answer if you need room for multiple baking. They're available in various styles of ranges: (1) freestanding wall ovens with ovens side by side; (2) freestanding with one oven above the surface unit and one below; (3) built-in wall ovens.

Warming shelves and compartments are useful when your family or guests are late and the entire meal must be delayed.

Eye-level panels and warming shelves and high ovens can be beneficial for working at the range, but shorter-than-average women may find them beyond comfortable reach.

Broilers have been improved considerably. Heat control is better and more even. Selection for degree of doneness is easier with ad-justable racks and control knobs. And several gas ranges now have the broiler at waist height.

Ease-in-cleaning features are important. Both gas and electric ovens that clean themselves are available. On some models, even the drip bowls from the surface units can be cleaned in the oven. With ranges that aren't self-cleaning, look for oven liners coated with a nonstick material and removable liners and oven doors.

Electronic ovens can be separate units or incorporated within a range. They offer high-speed thawing of frozen foods and a whole new world of quick cooking.

## Selecting a Dishwasher

Dishwashers come in three types—portable, convertible (a heavier portable, which can later be permanently installed) and built-in. The convertible unit, being the most expensive, may not be the best investment unless you're fairly certain of future installation. Top-loading portables are the least expensive and take up the least room. But they are difficult to load and have less usable counter-top space. Front-loading portables are easier to load because of the roll-out racks, but they take up more space when open. The initial cost of installing a built-in dishwasher should be considered.

When selecting a dishwasher, remember that flexibility in the type of cycles means more convenience. Cycles can go from a light touch for fine crystal to the heavy-duty cycle for pots and pans. Temperature control of the water is important for the best cleaning and sanitizing. Some models have a control that makes sure the water is at the correct temperature before the cycle proceeds. Racks can now be positioned for loading different-sized items.

## What Type of Refrigerator?

The type of refrigerator or refrigerator-freezer you buy should be determined by your food-shopping habits, freezer needs and budget. The least expensive model is a one-door refrigerator. Its frozen-food compartment, with a temperature range between 10° F. and 20° F., is adequate only for short-term storage. The two-door refrigerator-freezer (side by side or with the freezer above or below the refrigerator) maintains an average temperature of 0° F. in the freezing section.

Top freezers usually have smaller capacity, but many women find them more convenient. Of course, the unit's size depends on the size of your family and the space you have available. For the fresh-food section, count on eight cubic feet for a family of two; add one cubic foot for each additional person and two more if you do much entertaining. For the freezer, figure on two cubic feet for each family member.

Separate compartments, such as meat drawers and vegetable crispers, are helpful for extending the storage times of particular foods. The storage baskets and shelves should slide out, for easy access to food. Adjustable shelves let you vary storage space.

Nonfrosting equipment saves hours by eliminating the defrosting job, but it will add a slight amount to your electricity bill. A refrigerator larger than your present one will also increase your bill slightly.

Automatic ice makers, ice-cube ejectors and storage bins are very handy, especially if you have thirsty, hasty teen-agers. Models with automatic ice makers need a separate water supply, so figure the cost of plumbing in the purchase price.

## Shopping for Washers and Driers

When you shop for a washing machine, keep in mind that the abundance of new fabrics demands adaptability in machine cycles, agitation and spin speeds, water temperature and level.

Machines vary a great deal in the amount of water they use per cycle. If your water supply is limited, compare machine water-consumption ratings. If your water pressure is low, consider a washer with a device to assure a full fill.

Automatic dispensers for detergent, bleach and fabric softener can cut down on trips to the washer for a single load.

Clothes driers with automatic dry cycles, which have dryness-sensing devices, do away with the guesswork of timing. Most driers have a special cycle for durable-press clothes, so there's a proper cooling down before the tumbling stops. Many also have an end-of-cycle buzzer that goes off when the clothes are ready to be removed. Two added conveniences for properly treating various synthetic fabrics are no-tumble drying and a no-heat cycle that tumbles clothes with room-temperature air.

These are suggested guidelines for important appliance purchases; becoming an informed consumer will take an effort on your part. After you have made your selection and purchase and are ready to use your new appliance at home, reread the instruction booklet, to check on installation, use, cleaning and upkeep. File the booklet and guarantee or warranty in a handy place. And remember that you must plan for the eventual replacement of any appliance. Even the best machine has only a certain "life expectancy" you can count on.

The following figures show the average number of years that new household appliances are kept in service by one owner, as estimated by the U.S. Department of Agriculture.

| APPLIANCE | YEARS OF SERVICE | APPLIANCE | YEARS OF SERVICE |
|---|---|---|---|
| Clothes drier | 14 | Television set | 11 |
| Freezer | 15 | Vacuum cleaner | |
| Range | 16 |   Tank type | 15 |
| Refrigerator | 16 |   Upright | 15 |
| Sewing machine | 24 | Washing machine, automatic | 11 |

Say your drier is eight years old now and you want to be able to replace it instantly and easily the moment its days are done. As the figures show, an eight-year-old drier has only six years left. So you take the going price for a drier, divide by six and put that sum aside every year. When the drier cashes in its chips, you're ready to cash in yours and buy a new one.

CHAPTER 22

## You Can Get Your Money Back

*If you have been bilked by a seller of goods or services, here is a way of getting fair treatment*

In Illinois recently, a widow bought a glossy 1965 sedan from a used-car dealer. Its odometer read 23,000 miles. She had barely driven the car into her driveway when the transmission rasped and died. A garage reported that the odometer had been rolled back many thousands of miles, and estimated the cost of repairs at $350. The car dealer's reaction: "Tough luck, lady!"

In Montreal, a Canadian discovered that a camera light meter he had purchased while visiting the United States was defective. His letters to the store asking for a refund were ignored.

In Connecticut, a housewife ordered, and paid for, 205 pounds of meat, but the frozen-food firm delivered only 111 pounds. The manager, leaning on a weasel-worded contract, refused to yield an ounce or a dollar.

The U.S. Department of Justice estimates that through such frauds hundreds of millions of dollars are sucked out of the pockets of American families every year. Getting a refund or a credit on an unsatisfactory product is often painful, sometimes impossible. Many people feel that the results—getting back $2.98 or even $29.98— frequently do not justify the time and effort involved in battling tired clerks, impatient assistant managers or uninterested vice-presidents. Now, through a growing development in state government, thousands of formerly losing battles are being won.

The Illinois used-car dealer not only was made to pay for the $350 repair job but had to add $250 to compensate the widow for the

ⵣⵣⵣⵣⵣⵣ

## HOW TO COMPLAIN AND GET ACTION

You buy an expensive new toaster and a month later it doesn't toast. You take it back to the store and yell at the clerk who sold it to you, demand a new toaster—and are told no replacement can be made because there is no warranty.

You spend $75 to have your TV set repaired and one day later the set conks out again. You phone the repairman and insist he return at once to fix your set at no charge—and are told he won't come now or ever.

You may have been "done wrong" in both these cases, but if this is "you," you've done plenty wrong too. How, then, should you complain—to a retailer, a serviceman, a manufacturer— to get results?

The National Retail Merchants Association and the Better Business Bureau concur on these basic rules:

• Put together all the facts and records supporting your complaint. Facts should include the date and identification of your purchase, name of the store or branch from which the purchase was made, the department involved, model numbers. Records might include warranties, price tags, sales slips, instruction booklets.

• State the key facts—by letter, telephone or personally. If you have made previous complaints, give the dates of these. If you complain in person, bring copies of sales slips and warranties, but *don't* send these with a letter of complaint. Instead, keep all these records in a single file at home until they are no longer needed, and quote from them in your letter.

• State what you think went wrong. Don't fly off the handle and don't generalize about what a crook the seller is or how shoddy his products

ⵣⵣⵣⵣⵣⵣ

42,000 miles of driving depreciation he had concealed. The Canadian got his money back for the defective light meter. And the Connecticut housewife jubilantly deposited a check from the frozen-food firm for the undelivered 94 pounds of meat, at 57 cents a pound.

In each instance restitution was obtained through a state bureau of consumer fraud. The first of these fast-sprouting agencies was set up 13 years ago, and the attorneys general of more than a dozen states have already won back millions of dollars in cash or services for consumers. In New York State alone, in one year, some 9200 complaints were processed, and $1.2 million in cash and services was refunded.

The consumer fraud bureaus are state agencies with legal enforcement powers, while the 135 Better Business Bureaus are voluntary,

are. Let the facts speak for themselves.

• Be businesslike but *don't* try to be an amateur lawyer, insisting on your "rights." The businessman probably knows a lot more about your rights than you do. If he's reputable and if your complaint is valid, he'll make an adjustment.

• Propose a specific remedy. Do you want a refund? Repairs? Replacement? An apology? Be fair and realistic here.

• Address your complaint to the person most likely to be able to help you. Don't accost an innocent salesgirl when decisions of this type are up to her supervisor. Many businesses have customer-relations departments to handle complaints.

• If you don't get satisfaction at this level, write directly to the president of the company. His office usually will act quickly on your complaint. Restate all the key facts—including a summary of your previous correspondence with other employes in the organization.

• If you still don't get results, write to your local Better Business Bureau. (Note: Better Business Bureaus won't handle complaints which have not first been referred to the company that is involved.)

• If merchandise you have bought on your charge account is unsatisfactory or is not delivered, tell the store you don't intend to pay for it until an adjustment has been made.

• Don't fail to complain if you feel you have a valid gripe—not only about a money loss but also about rude salespeople, deceptive advertising, late deliveries, confusing warranties or outright gyps. It may be embarrassing to admit you've been had, but your complaints—if you make them fairly and coolly—will win better products and better service not only for yourself but also for other shoppers.

business-supported agencies. Attorneys general can force a company to cease malpractices. They can also dissolve a corporation for persistent violation and fraud. As New York State Attorney General Louis J. Lefkowitz has said in addressing BBB meetings, "You make voluntary self-regulation work. We can step in when it doesn't."

## Most Common Frauds

Here are the areas of most frequent and flagrant abuse where the bureaus are helping consumers:

*Worthless guarantees.* Guarantees and warranties, bureaus find, are often so vaguely worded that they cover little besides the paper they are printed on. One upholsterer had a way of parrying complaints with, "Ah, but our guarantee doesn't cover that!"—until the consumer fraud bureau called on him. He then clarified the wording of his guarantee and has been backing it ever since.

*Bait advertising.* The Federal Trade Commission aims to protect consumers from abuses in interstate advertising, but locally the shopper is frequently easy prey for misleading advertising assertions. An item is sometimes advertised at "an unbelievably low price," then is reported "sold out" no matter how early a shopper reaches the store. One couple read an ad for an $83 television set and arrived ten minutes before the store opened. "Sorry, none left," they were told, "but we have a beauty here for only . . ." When the bureau of consumer fraud phoned, the manager suddenly found an $83 set in stock and delivered it to the couple's home.

*High-pressure doorbell pushers.* A housewife is often harassed into buying products of unknown quality by a salesman who never expects to see her again. During the early 1960s a rash of complaints alerted an eastern bureau to a new gimmick. Door-to-door salesmen were leaving vacuum cleaners with housewives "on approval, to show your husband." Next day, a bill for the full price of the machine—usually an outrageous price—would arrive, and a call to the company's office would yield the information that the "approval slip" the housewife had signed was actually a sales contract. The consumer fraud bureau summoned company executives, warned them that further complaints would mean legal action, persuaded them to void the high-pressured contracts.

*Dishonest repairmen.* Unscrupulous repairmen take advantage of the fact that much of our way of life depends upon complex machines most of us know little about. A single staff member at one bureau has settled more than 150 complaints against TV repairmen—most of whom removed sets from homes and then refused to return them until exorbitant charges were paid, using the threat of daily "storage fees." Bureau intervention aided a man whose car broke down one evening and was towed to a nearby garage for an "overnight check." The mechanic told the car owner next day that a new motor had been installed for $400, and that, if he didn't pay, his car would be sold on an artisan's lien. Under threat of investigation the mechanic admitted that he had not put in a new motor, and reduced the price accordingly.

*Misrepresentation.* "You get what you pay for" is a familiar theme. Consumer fraud bureaus find that you often don't. An appliance salesman pointed to the floor model of an air-conditioner a couple wanted to buy and said, "You want that one?" A week later, "that one"—the scratched floor model—was delivered at the same price as brand-new equipment. A consumer fraud bureau got the couple a new air-conditioner.

*Industry-wide malpractice.* When hundreds of complaints are lodged against dealers in one industry in a short period, bureaus take massive action. In California, for instance, dance-studio contracts for sums as high as $30,000—sold mostly to elderly persons—brought about legislative action against the studios. The result: California dance-studio contracts are now limited to $500.

Though the list of cases successfully handled by bureaus is impressive, assistance isn't possible in every case. Says New York bureau chief Barnett Levy: "We can help about 90 percent of the time. In the other 10 percent, the firm involved may have gone bankrupt or the claim may be unreasonable. When we feel that a consumer's claim is unjustified we tell him so. We won't knuckle under to a firm, but neither will we browbeat it."

The New York State Consumer Frauds and Protection Bureau (part of the state's Department of Law) was conceived by Attorney General Louis Lefkowitz, and is the oldest in the nation. It was established in 1957 as a two-desk division where the power and prestige of state government could be placed at the service of the consumer. Today it has nine regional offices throughout the state; in New York City, the largest office, the staff numbers 18 assistant attorneys general, plus investigators and clerks who work full time helping consumers in need. Consumer fraud units are also in operation in Alaska, California, Connecticut, Illinois, Kansas, Massachusetts, Michigan, Minnesota, Missouri, New Jersey, Ohio, Pennsylvania and Washington.

"The most effective protection against fraud and deception, of course," says Attorney General Lefkowitz, "is an alert and wary consumer." An official of the Illinois bureau adds: "The consumer brings a lot of unnecessary trouble on himself. Many buy on the spur of the moment, fail to read a contract or even may sign a blank one. This is like signing a blank check!"

## Six Rules for Safe Buying

For safer buying, the following rules, based on thousands of experiences related to consumer fraud bureaus, are recommended:

*Get it in writing.* Whether it's a guarantee or a receipt, be certain that the terms are spelled out in detail. (Are installation and delivery charges included? Are length and extent of warranty stated? Will the

---

### BEWARE OF THE TOO-GOOD-TO-BE-TRUE BARGAIN

The most common type of sales fraud is known as bait-and-switch selling. Bait advertising capitalizes on the consumer's inability to resist a "bargain." A store or company will advertise a nationally known product at an unbelievably low price to lure the unwary shopper into the store. When the shopper arrives to buy the product, he is told that it is out of stock or defective. Then a slick salesman will persuade

him to buy another product, often at a grossly inflated price. Sometimes a free home demonstration or free gift is thrown in to make the offer even more alluring. According to the National Better Business Bureau, the most common bait-and-switch routines involve household appliances, sewing machines, meat and home siding.

Here is an example of how such schemes work. In Illinois Fred Boyle heard a wonderful TV bargain offered over the air: "No money down . . . Take as long as you want to pay . . . Free home demonstration . . . All

---

seller pick up the article for servicing or must you bring it in?)

*Know your dealer.* If you have any doubts about the seller's reliability or honesty, check with your local Better Business Bureau or attorney general's office. The company's record will speak for itself.

*Get advance estimates on repairs.* On TV sets, auto, furnaces, and so on, the repairman has the upper hand if you don't obtain an advance estimate in writing. Without such an understanding, the repairman may leave your furnace in pieces on the cellar floor or sell your repaired auto on an artisan's lien, if you refuse to pay his price.

*Watch out for extras.* Don't permit a household appliance or television set to be taken from your home for repairs without getting written assurance that no additional charges will be made without your consent. And the assurance should include a guarantee that the appliance or set will be returned to you promptly if you don't want the extra repairs.

*Beware of too-good-to-be-true bargains and promises.* Be particularly skeptical of sucker signals like "last chance," "you have been selected," "at no cost to you, if . . . ," "made to sell for . . ."

*Beware of switch selling.* If the item delivered is not the one you ordered, notify the dealer immediately and do not use it.

types of nationally known brands . . . If you act at once, you can buy a set for 50 percent off!" Boyle phoned immediately for a home demonstration. The salesman brought pictures showing several sets and prices—but no demonstration model. He explained that the big name brands were all sold out. He then persuaded Boyle to pay full price for an off-brand set, which he claimed was really produced by a nationally known manufacturer. The set proved to be defective, but Boyle could not get his money back.

Despite attempts by reputable newspapers and magazines to eliminate obvious bait ads, such misleading advertising often finds its way into the classified sections. A large number of television and radio stations also carry bait ads. Your best protection against fraudulent advertising is awareness. Ask yourself whether the advertised price could possibly be true. Compare it to the prices asked for the same merchandise in reputable stores. A ridiculously low price is nearly always a sign of bait advertising. If you do answer the ad, insist on buying only the advertised merchandise.

## CHAPTER 23

# New Isn't Always Best

*Secondhand furniture may be the answer to your decorating dilemma. With a little know-how, you can achieve surprising results for next to nothing*

Budget-minded furniture hunters can achieve individualized, decorative results at surprisingly low cost. The secret: bargain sources like secondhand stores, thrift shops, auctions, low-priced importers, even junkyards—and loads of energy, enthusiasm and ingenuity.

Decorating on a "mini" budget calls for basic, down-to-earth purchases. For best results, keep in mind that you will probably have several more homes over a lifetime. Buy with an eye toward the future. Avoid permanent purchases like wall-to-wall carpeting, built-in bookshelves, custom draperies and odd-shaped or oversize furniture. Select versatile and adaptable colors, combinations and styles. Think of studio couches that could serve as twin beds in a future guest room, an area rug instead of wall-to-wall carpeting, a drop-leaf dining table that goes against the wall now and can be opened up when you have a dining room. Look for solid construction, good materials and simple, timeless design. Spend your money on the basics—quality rugs, chairs and sofa—and improvise on accessories. Experiment with do-it-yourself lamps, $2 posters, eye-catching mobiles, brick-and-board bookshelves, plastic throw pillows.

## Where to Look for Furniture Bargains

For the best secondhand buys, check the ads in your local paper. Some communities even have weekly or monthly newspapers devoted entirely to advertising secondhand items. Here you will find ads placed by people who are moving or redecorating and who will often sell good items for a fraction of their retail value. Look for ads for "garage" or "yard" sales—a popular way other people use to get rid of unwanted pieces and often a source of great finds. Many local radio stations have "swap shop" bargain programs.

Secondhand stores are another good source. Check the classified telephone directory under secondhand stores for the addresses of

Salvation Army, Goodwill Industries and other welfare-operated stores, as well as thrift shops and flea markets.

The knowledgeable bargain hunter can sometimes find fabulous buys at local auctions too. But it pays to know the ropes. Be sure to examine each article carefully before the bidding starts, keep a level head during the bidding and don't buy anything that will be costly to move.

In the last few years another source of inexpensive furnishings has appeared: the import shops. These colorful stores—often with exotic or whimsical names like The Pink Balloon, Azuma, The Noisy Oyster or Zagazig Bazaar—are treasure troves of unusual and inexpensive items that can give your home a unique decorator look. Among them: "mod" plastic pillows and chairs; wicker baskets, headboards and chairs; beaded curtains; birdcages; giant pop and op art posters; colorful bedspreads, kitchenware, pottery and paper flowers; and plastic hanging lamps.

Other, more offbeat sources include wrecking companies, where you may unearth newel posts or banisters you could use as table legs, old mantelpieces, footed bathtubs, mirror frames, fireplace tiles, old-fashioned doors. Print shops can sometimes give you large-size broken type or worn-out wood blocks, which, with a little imagination, can become attractive and unusual bookends, wall plaques or other decoration. Restaurant and hotel suppliers often have carts, stainless steel pots, platters and beautiful French chef equipment. At boat suppliers you can find large pieces of canvas with grommets to hang as a room divider or window shade. Hobby shops and junkshops can also be gold mines for the adventurous bargain seeker.

Patience is the bargain hunter's best friend. It may take days or weeks of browsing to track down a particular item. You may see something one day, come back to buy it the next and find it has been sold. You may answer an advertisement only to discover that someone else has bought the chair you wanted. Or you may have trouble finding exactly what you're looking for. Take a tip from experienced bargain hunters: Visit secondhand and import stores regularly every two or three weeks. The stock is constantly changing. You might find rattan chests and chairs this week; bentwood chairs next week; straw mats, lacquered trays, pillows, copper ornaments or something else to jog your creativity next month.

## Choose with Care

The key to saving money on secondhand furniture is careful selection. A $10 chair that needs $90 worth of upholstering is clearly no bargain. On the other hand, a $25 table that's slightly marred by scratches and dents is a real find. It pays to consider how much time and effort will be needed to fix up an old relic before you buy it.

Flaws that may be difficult or impossible to repair include serious breaks, warped or cracked finish, cracked or peeling paint or varnish and ripped, worn-out upholstery. Less serious damages—like dents, scratches, loose hinges, missing hardware or wobbly arms and legs—are relatively simple to fix. Unless you want to, you needn't make extra work for yourself by trying to restore the original finish on a $25 bureau. Paint it instead. Sand away dents and scratches before painting. Glue or nail together loose joints and other parts. Add new hardware or trim for the finishing touch.

The best money-saving ideas are the ones you dream up yourself. With a little ingenuity you can improvise attractive furnishings for next to nothing. For example, you can make a lamp from a piece of driftwood, an old wine bottle or a vase. Just buy the socket and cord at a local hardware store, add a bulb and shade—and presto, you have a distinctive lamp. You can decorate a wall or table top with used fireplace tiles, fashion billowing nylon curtains from a parachute found in an Army-Navy store, add colorful pillows to a wooden bench for extra seating.

The real secret is being able to see the possibilities. An old coffee tin, for instance, is a potential object of beauty to the seasoned bargain hunter. It could be covered with paint or paper for a canister. Painted silver, punched with holes and strung up with a light bulb, it becomes an unusual Spanish-style hanging lamp. Painted and glued together, several coffee tins are transformed into an abstract sculpture. Just think of what you have lying around that could be pressed into service. Maybe the Sunday paper could be turned into wallpaper with the aid of some varnish and glue. That oval letter holder could live a second life as a lampshade. All it takes is a little inventiveness.

# 5

# 1095 MEALS
# EVERY YEAR

*Even with prices going up, the
smart shopper can control her food bill
by intelligent planning and selection*

## CHAPTER 24

## How Much Do You Spend for Groceries?

*Is your spending high or low? Check it against the averages. See where you stand . . . and why*

Eavesdrop on three wives chatting about food bills and you're likely to hear a conversation like this:

First wife: "John gives me thirty dollars a week for food. I can just about feed the four of us on that."

Second wife: "Goodness, you must starve them. I couldn't feed ours for less than forty dollars."

Third wife: "Why, thirty dollars is positively exorbitant. Anyone who can't feed four on twenty-five dollars is—well, I just don't know."

This little dialogue points up what's wrong with that man-made creation, the average. In this particular case, the three families concerned spend an average of about $32 each for groceries in a week. Yet no one of them spends exactly that much. And two of them lay out considerably different amounts.

Averages, in short, tell you nothing about the differences among the people involved—their tastes, eating habits or skill as shoppers. For all their pitfalls, however, averages can be helpful if properly used. True, there's no set amount you "ought" to spend for food. But everyone wants yardsticks to guide them. And looking at what others pay at the grocery counter gives you some idea how close to the line you fall.

First, let's define "food." Some statisticians include in that category the cost of alcoholic beverages and meals eaten in restaurants. Most families, however, do not. So "food" here means all food eaten or prepared at home. This includes packed lunches and snacks, but not things that are bought and eaten out or any liquor or beer.

Of all the things that influence your grocery bill, your earnings and the size of your family count most. As you would expect, the more money you make or the greater the number of mouths you must feed, the higher your food outlays tend to run. But what you choose to buy will also affect your food expenses.

| AVERAGE FAMILY FOOD EXPENDITURES IN NORTHERN URBAN AREAS | | | | |
|---|---|---|---|---|
| | WEEKLY EXPENDITURE FOR FAMILY OF: | | | |
| WEEKLY INCOME AFTER TAXES | 2 | 3 | 4 | 5 |
| $115 | $25.68 | $30.89 | $34.90 | $38.11 |
| $155 | 28.89 | 36.91 | 40.12 | 46.14 |
| $250 | 32.10 | 40.36 | 47.34 | 52.56 |

Above are estimates of what families spend each week on the average in urban areas of the North. These figures are based on 1970 data.

*Family Size.* See what happens, at the same income level, as the family grows larger. Dollar outlays for food go up, certainly, but less money is spent on each individual member of the bigger household.

Take the $155-a-week bracket. It costs the average family of three about $12 a week to feed each member. Yet it would cost less than a total of $10 to feed two additions to the family, because a family of five can be nourished for an average of $9.20 a person.

Why this drop in per capita cost? Three reasons, in the main:

1. There is economy in buying larger quantities of food. There's less waste, too, in preparing meals for more mouths.

2. Most larger families include younger children, who generally consume less food than grown-ups do.

3. There are budget limitations as family size increases while weekly income remains the same. A family can afford to spend so much on food and that's all.

*Income.* Study the figures closely and you will discover an interesting fact. Although people spend more as they earn more, the share of earnings that is literally eaten up declines as income rises.

Consider, for example, the family of four. With a weekly take-home pay of $115, the average household spends a bit more than $1 of every $3 on groceries. At $155 a week, $1 of every $4 goes for food. And at $250 a week, just $1 of every $5.30.

What about families outside these income brackets? At the bottom of the scale, families might spend as much as 45 percent for food. At the top, grocery bills would shrink to 10 percent or less of income.

247

Translate these averages into personal terms. Say you get a raise. Are you in the lower brackets? Then, out of $10 of additional weekly income, after taxes, expect to spend $1.50 to $2 for food. At a higher income level, you might eat up 50 cents to $1 of the extra $10 in your paycheck.

Just why food outlays go up so slowly as you earn more is plain enough. Assuming you get enough to eat now, there's really not much need to eat more. So why spend more at all? Because people do want to eat more, whether they need to or not. And more important, because they buy costlier foods—both higher-quality items and convenience foods.

Where you live and the kind of work you do also have an effect on your food bill.

*Geography.* Food prices vary from one city to another. Even more significant are regional eating patterns. Differences between the North and Far West are generally small, but city dwellers in the South tend to spend less for groceries than those outside Dixie.

Here's how the table on food expenditure according to income and family size looks when computed for average families in southern urban areas:

| AVERAGE FAMILY FOOD EXPENDITURES IN SOUTHERN URBAN AREAS | | | | |
|---|---|---|---|---|
| | WEEKLY EXPENDITURE FOR FAMILY OF: | | | |
| WEEKLY INCOME AFTER TAXES | 2 | 3 | 4 | 5 |
| $115 | $23.33 | $27.38 | $29.94 | $34.05 |
| $155 | 25.19 | 31.40 | 36.51 | 44.18 |
| $250 | 28.48 | 35.41 | 40.53 | 50.75 |

Why do people spend less on food in Dixie? Measured by sheer bulk, there's little appreciable difference in the amount of food consumed by families of comparable income and size in the North and South. The difference lies in what is eaten.

A glance at the shopping lists of a northern and of a southern urban family would show these differences: The northern housewife tends to buy better cuts of meat than her southern counterpart. More butter and salad oil and less margarine and lard too. The southern family consumes more fresh fruits and vegetables, while the northern family eats produce out of costlier cans and frozen packages.

Why the difference in eating patterns? Tradition, mixed with lagging incomes in the South. Hot breads, grits, rice and sweets have long been popular in Dixie. Such low-cost foods became favorites to a large extent because the average southerner usually had less money to spend. And regional eating habits tend to change slowly even as incomes rise.

*Urban versus rural living.* Is your home in a city or suburb, or on or near a farm? If you live in a rural area, you're almost sure to spend less in the grocery store than an urban family of the same size and earnings.

The Department of Agriculture recently surveyed spending patterns among families in cities, on farms and in small towns. Look at the findings for families of four in the $7000 to $8000 bracket (after taxes):

The average city family spent $38.32 for food used at home each week.

The average small-town family spent $35.68, or 7 percent less.

The average farm family spent only $24.90, or 35 percent below the city family.

Farm households, of course, raise right on their land a sizable chunk—roughly one third—of the food they eat. Families in rural towns produce 5 percent of their own food and make further savings by purchasing food from nearby farms at prices below what city folks pay.

*Job.* The heavier the work you do, the more food you need to keep going. Families headed by factory workers, mechanics or unskilled laborers pay out more for groceries than the average for their particular income group and family size. Conversely, households headed by professional people or white-collar workers tend to spend less than the average.

Average family spending is one kind of yardstick you can use. But your household, after all, is really a collection of individuals of different ages, each with dietary requirements of his or her own.

Generally, individual food costs increase with age until a person turns twenty. Then costs start going down. Until the age of nine, girls eat as much as boys. But after that, the male of the species gradually asserts his natural superiority at the dinner table.

The Agriculture Department recently figured out how much you may reasonably expect to spend each week to feed adequately people of various ages, male and female, in a family of four or more. Here are the results. Work out your own family requirements.

WEEKLY FOOD COSTS PER PERSON
ACCORDING TO AGE, SEX AND INCOME

| | WEEKLY INCOME AFTER TAXES | | |
|---|---|---|---|
| AGE AND SEX | $115 | $155 | $250 |
| Children | | | |
| Under 1 year | $ 3.60 | $ 4.50 | $ 5.00 |
| 1–3 years | 4.50 | 5.70 | 6.80 |
| 3–6 years | 5.40 | 6.90 | 8.30 |
| 6–9 years | 6.50 | 8.40 | 10.40 |
| Girls | | | |
| 9–12 years | 7.40 | 9.60 | 11.20 |
| 12–15 years | 8.20 | 10.60 | 12.80 |
| 15–20 years | 8.40 | 10.50 | 12.50 |
| Boys | | | |
| 9–12 years | 7.60 | 9.80 | 11.80 |
| 12–15 years | 8.90 | 11.70 | 13.90 |
| 15–20 years | 10.20 | 13.00 | 15.60 |
| Women | | | |
| 20–35 years | 7.70 | 9.80 | 11.70 |
| 35–55 years | 7.40 | 9.40 | 11.30 |
| 55–75 years | 6.20 | 8.10 | 9.60 |
| 75 years and over | 5.70 | 7.20 | 8.80 |
| Pregnant | 9.10 | 11.40 | 13.50 |
| Nursing | 10.50 | 13.10 | 15.30 |
| Men | | | |
| 20–35 years | 8.80 | 11.20 | 14.00 |
| 35–55 years | 8.20 | 10.50 | 12.80 |
| 55–75 years | 7.30 | 9.50 | 11.40 |
| 75 years and over | 6.80 | 9.10 | 11.00 |

Are there fewer than four in your family? Then to the total cost for the individual members in your household add 20 percent if you are single, 10 percent for a household of two and 5 percent for three. Subtract 5 percent if there are five or six persons in the household.

The Agriculture Department's estimates are based on specific grocery lists and menus that meet basic nutritional standards. Thus they are more in the nature of suggested costs rather than actual amounts people spend. But they do reflect average eating habits, so the totals you work up probably won't be too much off the family spending averages shown above.

However you approach your own food budget, remember the point made at the start. There's no need to feel you should follow the averages or suggestions. Use them as guides, but keep in mind all the things that averages don't divulge.

▭▭▭▭▭▭

## MEAT COSTS PER SERVING

To help select the most economical cuts of meat for family meals, consult the chart below, which lists servings per pound and cost per serving for common retail cuts.

| RETAIL CUT | SERVINGS PER POUND | PRICE PER POUND (in cents) | | | | | | | | | | | |
|---|---|---|---|---|---|---|---|---|---|---|---|---|---|
| | | 69 | 79 | 89 | 99 | 109 | 119 | 129 | 139 | 149 | 159 | 169 | 179 |
| | | COST PER SERVING (in cents) | | | | | | | | | | | |
| **Beef** | | | | | | | | | | | | | |
| Sirloin steak | 2½ | 28 | 32 | 36 | 40 | 44 | 48 | 52 | 56 | 60 | 64 | 68 | 72 |
| Porterhouse, T-bone steak | 2 | 35 | 40 | 45 | 50 | 55 | 60 | 65 | 70 | 75 | 80 | 85 | 90 |
| Round steak | 3½ | 20 | 23 | 25 | 28 | 31 | 34 | 37 | 40 | 43 | 46 | 49 | 52 |
| Chuck roast, bone-in | 2 | 35 | 40 | 45 | 50 | 55 | 60 | 65 | 70 | 75 | 80 | 85 | 90 |
| Rib roast, boneless | 2½ | 28 | 32 | 36 | 40 | 44 | 48 | 52 | 56 | 60 | 64 | 68 | 72 |
| Rib roast, bone-in | 2 | 35 | 40 | 45 | 50 | 55 | 60 | 65 | 70 | 75 | 80 | 85 | 90 |
| Rump, sirloin roast | 3 | 23 | 26 | 30 | 33 | 36 | 40 | 43 | 46 | 50 | 53 | 56 | 60 |
| Ground beef | 4 | 17 | 20 | 22 | 25 | 27 | 30 | 32 | 35 | 37 | 40 | 42 | 45 |
| Short ribs | 2 | 35 | 40 | 45 | 50 | 55 | 60 | 65 | 70 | 75 | 80 | 85 | 90 |
| Heart, liver, kidney | 5 | 14 | 16 | 18 | 20 | 22 | 24 | 26 | 28 | 30 | 32 | 34 | 36 |
| Frankfurters | 4 | 17 | 20 | 22 | 25 | 27 | 30 | 32 | 35 | 37 | 40 | 42 | 45 |
| Stew meat, boneless | 5 | 14 | 16 | 18 | 20 | 22 | 24 | 26 | 28 | 30 | 32 | 34 | 36 |
| **Lamb** | | | | | | | | | | | | | |
| Loin, rib, shoulder chops | 3 | 23 | 26 | 30 | 33 | 36 | 40 | 43 | 46 | 50 | 53 | 56 | 60 |
| Breast, shank | 2 | 35 | 40 | 45 | 50 | 55 | 60 | 65 | 70 | 75 | 80 | 85 | 90 |
| Shoulder roast | 2½ | 28 | 32 | 36 | 40 | 44 | 48 | 52 | 56 | 60 | 64 | 68 | 72 |
| Leg of lamb | 3 | 23 | 26 | 30 | 33 | 36 | 40 | 43 | 46 | 50 | 53 | 56 | 60 |
| **Pork—Fresh** | | | | | | | | | | | | | |
| Center cut or rib chops | 4 | 17 | 20 | 22 | 25 | 27 | 30 | 32 | 35 | 37 | 40 | 42 | 45 |
| Loin or rib roast | 2½ | 28 | 32 | 36 | 40 | 44 | 48 | 52 | 56 | 60 | 64 | 68 | 72 |
| Boston butt, bone-in | 3 | 23 | 26 | 30 | 33 | 36 | 40 | 43 | 46 | 50 | 53 | 56 | 60 |
| Blade steak | 3 | 23 | 26 | 30 | 33 | 36 | 40 | 43 | 46 | 50 | 53 | 56 | 60 |
| Spare ribs | 1⅓ | 52 | 59 | 67 | 74 | 82 | 89 | 97 | 104 | 112 | 119 | 127 | 134 |
| **Pork—Cured** | | | | | | | | | | | | | |
| Picnic, bone-in | 2 | 35 | 40 | 45 | 50 | 55 | 60 | 65 | 70 | 75 | 80 | 85 | 90 |
| Ham, fully cooked | | | | | | | | | | | | | |
| Bone-in | 3½ | 20 | 23 | 25 | 28 | 31 | 34 | 37 | 40 | 43 | 46 | 49 | 52 |
| Boneless and canned | 5 | 14 | 16 | 18 | 20 | 22 | 24 | 26 | 28 | 30 | 32 | 34 | 36 |
| Shankless | 4¼ | 16 | 19 | 21 | 23 | 26 | 28 | 30 | 33 | 35 | 37 | 40 | 42 |
| Center slice | 5 | 14 | 16 | 18 | 20 | 22 | 24 | 26 | 28 | 30 | 32 | 34 | 36 |

▭▭▭▭▭▭

## CHAPTER 25

# Planning Your Food Dollar

*If grocery bills are burning a hole in your budget, these tips can help you cut food costs without skimping on quality*

Planning on a moderate budget imaginative meals that please your family is pure pleasure to many—and to others, a ghastly chore. The variety of choices is endless and the price of food ranges from exorbitant to fairly reasonable. You can, nevertheless, save a great deal of money on food, provided you learn how to shop warily and with latitude.

Presumably your object is to feed your family (and your guests) as tasty meals as possible with a well-balanced diet on a reasonable amount of money—reasonable in the sense that it's pointless to spend so much money on food that there is very little left for other pleasures. With this in mind, there are some general rules you should follow:

1. Know nutrition.

2. Avoid impulse buying and, if possible, shop alone. Husbands and children are notorious cart fillers. While a child is having a good time in the candy and cookie section, a husband might have a heyday in the exotic food department.

3. Plan the week's menu, allowing for substitutes, and, if possible, shop only once or twice a week. Inevitably the more times you shop, the more money you spend.

4. Watch for specials and sales. Buy fresh vegetables and fruits at the peak of their season. Buy in quantity when it means a saving, you have storage room and you know that the item won't spoil before you use it.

5. Be aware of brand and nonbrand names and the savings that can be had by using private labels.

6. Read labels describing contents.

7. Know how to store foods properly.

8. Learn to think in terms of portions, instead of merely pounds and ounces, and be aware of how much waste is involved in the product you are buying.

9. Learn how to stretch food with good use of leftovers.

10. Don't buy items that cost more just because they have "extra" qualities you may not need.

11. Watch out for "the games people play"—know what stamps and premiums cost.

12. Don't avoid unfamiliar, unusual food items, especially meats that are on sale, because you don't know how to cook them. Invest in a comprehensive cookbook that tells you how to prepare the lesser-known cuts of meats or the unusual vegetables you may find, which are often less expensive.

13. If you find that you can't always remember what you had planned to buy, by all means take a shopping list with you. (But see Chapter 29, "Big Supermarket Is Watching You," page 292, for surprising news about the shopping list.)

14. Think in terms of "double duty" foods, especially meats. Remember that the expensive cuts of meats, the steaks and chops, are usually good for one meal only, while leftovers from all kinds of roasts can be used for another meal.

Always try to make your weekly menu flexible. If you had planned a ham steak dinner and you find there is a special on lamb, switch to the cheaper meat. If you have space for extra supplies of canned foods, keep a good supply of canned meat, poultry and fish products (tuna fish, chicken à la king, hash, salmon). Buy these items when they are on sale to have on hand for emergencies and to avoid last-minute shopping trips. If you have a freezer or enough room in your freezing compartment, buy meats on sale and freeze them.

## Taking Advantage of Specials

Specials, or sales, occur when the supply exceeds the demand, when the harvest is abundant or at its peak and when grocers make their end-of-the-year inventory. (At that time canned and frozen foods are often bargains; January sales on odd lots of canned goods, discontinued lines or items that are moving slowly are good for stocking the cupboard.) Beware of going overboard, however. You can lose money by buying foods that are subject to spoilage if not used quickly enough, or by thoughtlessly grabbing a dozen cans of split pea soup when the family hates it.

To watch for specials, read supermarket advertisements in the newspapers, especially on Wednesday and Thursday. These advertisements offer food at prices often 6 to 34 percent below regular prices. Don't be put off by the unfamiliar, especially at the meat counter where you are apt to find the greatest bargains. If one of the specials is breast of lamb and you haven't a clue what to do with it, consult a cookbook. Experimentation with foods can mean savings.

The specials frequently offer savings on staples: fruit, juices, vegetables, jellies, coffee, catsup, soups. When you find a good special on items you use daily, stock up and save. But do remember to watch quantity. For instance, two No. 303 cans of pears (total weight, 1 lb.) for 78 cents (nearly $2\frac{1}{2}$ cents per ounce) are not a bargain if you can buy one No. $2\frac{1}{2}$ can (weight, 1 lb. 13 oz.) for 49 cents (well under 2 cents per ounce).

## Other Money-Saving Tips

Both frozen and fresh vegetable prices fluctuate. Frozen foods, especially vegetables and fruits, are affected by the crop year just as fresh vegetables and fruits are, and are priced economically only when they are in season and in abundance. Don't buy strawberries flown in from out of state in January when you know native ones will probably be plentiful in your area in June.

It can be a mistake to rely on a particular market solely because you are attracted by its specials. Be sure that the prices of the rest of the items that you buy are competitive with those in other stores. Specials in one store can be attractive enough to make you overlook the fact that the prices of butter and milk, for example, are considerably higher than in the store across the street.

Buying staples in large quantities is usually economical. Items such as sugar, flour, baby food, cereals, rice, potato flakes, spaghetti products, and so on, are better buys in quantity, provided the food won't go to waste. Even purchasing a product such as milk in a two-quart container is often less expensive than buying two separate quarts.

Buying only familiar brand names can be costly. Because brand names tend to guarantee consistency, are generally high in quality and are advertised heavily, they cost more. In fact, a survey by the

National Commission on Food Marketing indicates they cost about 16 percent more than lesser-known private or store brands. Many supermarkets put out their own brands at a considerable saving to the consumer, and often these products are packaged by the same companies that process the name brand. The commission study indicated that a number of top lines of private labels deliver "equivalent products at lower prices." The only way you can find out whether you can save by buying nonbrand names is by trying them. If you find you like the product the saving may be considerable.

By law the net contents of a package must be stated on the principal display panel of the label. For all packages under four pounds, the net contents must be expressed both in total number of ounces and in pounds and ounces. The label on a bottle, can or jar containing fluids must state the contents in both fluid ounces and in quarts, pints and ounces. The object of this law is to enable you to compare prices more easily. Always read these labels so that you know what you are getting, though it is still not always simple to compare prices.

Proper food storage is important, both for retarding spoilage and for saving food value. (See Chapter 27, "Keeping Foods Fresh," page 280, for a complete guide to storage, and the chart on page 285 for the maximum storage time for frozen foods.)

You will certainly raise your shopping IQ if you remember that many meat, fruit and vegetable products are subject to a great deal of waste—and so the only way to judge an economical food buy is to think in terms of portions.

A popular rule of thumb for gauging the amount of meat to buy is to allow one-quarter pound per person if there is little fat and no bone; one-third pound per person if there is some fat and a small amount of bone; one-half to three-quarters pound per person if there is a substantial amount of fat and bone; and one pound per person if there is a great deal of fat and bone. Never forget that you are paying for inedible parts of meat. For instance, a canned ham which is boneless and has little fat but whose initial cost is higher than one with the bone and fat may still prove to be the better buy. Meats shrink in cooking: Hamburger meat with a great deal of fat can dwindle alarmingly, as can steak or domestic duck, a very fatty bird.

Fresh vegetables must be judged by the portions they yield too. Remember that you have to buy fresh spinach practically by the barrel (one pound for two persons in generous measure) to come out with enough. Vegetables and fruits that have to be pared or shelled contain waste too. Canned peas are more economical than fresh ones.

The thrifty housewife should always think in terms of leftovers. For that reason, she will, very likely, buy more roasts than meats that will do for only one meal. Leftover broccoli or asparagus isn't very pleasing to look at, but it can be fairly sensational if put on some leftover slices of turkey, chicken, duck or ham, covered with cream sauce (if you're not calorie-conscious), sprinkled with grated cheese and placed in the oven until brown and bubbly. Cold lamb may not stir appetites the second time around, but if you combine it with some leftover mashed potatoes, onion juice and lamb gravy, you have created shepherd's pie. You can grind up leftover meats for hash, cut up leftover poultry, meats and vegetables for pies, stews and salads. Using leftovers cleverly is a part of creative cooking; throwing them out or allowing them to spoil is wasteful.

## Buying Meat

Since meat is a very important part of the American family's diet, it's at the meat counter that you can make some basic choices that will affect your food budget. When you buy meat, the thing to remember is that all meat has about the same nutritional value. The difference you pay for when buying well-marbled beef or the more costly cuts of veal or lamb chops is not in the nutrition but in the flavor and tenderness.

By law all meats are inspected before being shipped across state lines and stamped with a harmless vegetable dye (usually purple). Some meats, at the request of the processor, are graded by government inspectors. Federal grading standards for meat are: *prime* (for beef, veal and lamb), highest quality and premium priced; *choice* (for beef, veal and lamb), very good but in the case of beef less marbled than prime; *good* (beef and veal), less tender with less fat but good flavor; *standard* (beef and veal), not as much flavor and usually best prepared with liquid cooking methods; *commercial*

256

(beef), meat produced from older cattle, tougher and requiring long, slow cooking with moist heat.

The higher grades of beef are expensive, but a great many lower grades are completely suitable and tasty if cooked with liquids, as in stews and casseroles. Remember that it is wasteful to buy very high grade beef for hamburger. Good chuck is about right because it contains enough fat; expensive ground top round can be too dry.

The best veal comes from milk-fed calves between six to ten weeks of age. It has much less fat than beef and little or no marbling. Top-grade veal is grayish-pink; if the meat is reddish, it means the animal has had feed other than milk. Because veal lacks fat and has connective tissue, it needs long, slow cooking.

Veal is expensive but if you should want to splurge, you can buy veal cutlets or veal scallops, where there is very little waste. A veal cutlet is similar in cut to a beef round steak; veal scallops are generally cut from the leg and pounded very thin. Less expensive cuts of veal are breast of veal and those from the shoulder (chops, steaks and blade roast).

Lamb, not as popular a meat as beef, has a very wide price range. Lamb chops (from the loin) are inordinately expensive, as are rack and crown roasts of lamb. A leg of lamb is medium in price and provides a great deal of meat which can be used to great advantage in leftovers (lamb curry, shepherd's pie, hash). Take advantage of leg of lamb on sale (it is often a supermarket special). Instead of loin or rib chops, try shoulder lamb chops, which are much less expensive and have quite good flavor. Look into neglected, inexpensive cuts like lamb shanks and breast of lamb which, prepared properly, can be delicious. As with other meats, the shoulder cuts are less expensive. You can buy a cut called cushion shoulder from which the bones have been removed, and stretch it with two or three cups of stuffing (using sausage meat, bread crumbs and herbs).

Pork products offer the consumer a bewildering multitude of choices, ranging from various loin and rib cuts of pork to ham and bacon. Depending upon supply, prices fluctuate widely, more so than for any other meat. Fatty cuts shrink more in cooking. So for economy look for leanness and watch those changing prices.

Hams come fresh or cured or canned; whole, boneless or cut up in portions such as ham steak. Some hams (those that are smoked and fully cooked) have water added; the label should state this if a ham contains as much as 10 percent added moisture. A ham either cured and smoked or tinned may have a great deal of meat on it and, depending on the price, can be an economical buy. Picnic "hams," considered by some to be economical, are from the pork shoulder and have been smoked and cured to enhance flavor. While they are less expensive than ham, they often contain a large amount of fat.

Pork is one of the most common ingredients of luncheon meats—though they may often include other meats in combination with the pork. The variety of luncheon meats is astounding—well over 200. The cheapest way to buy them is in bulk, which is not only cheaper per pound than sliced luncheon meat but keeps longer since you can slice it as needed. If you prefer luncheon meats already sliced, the prepacked ones are usually cheaper than those you have cut to order at the delicatessen counter.

## Poultry and Fish

A "chicken in every pot" is much more easily accomplished today than it used to be, for chicken is one of the most reasonable buys on the market. And happily there are endless ways to prepare it. Think of chicken when you are thinking of economizing, and remember that it can be used equally as well for a formal as for a family meal. Stun your guests by producing chicken Kiev (deep-fried rolled chicken breasts), *suprême de volaille archiduc* (stuffed breasts with Gruyère cheese) or *coq au vin* (chicken with wine). *Coq au vin*, using the whole chicken, not just the breasts, is less extravagant than the first two dishes.

Generally whole chickens cost less per pound than the same size chicken cut into parts. Sometimes two or three chickens are sold in a single bag at a saving to the consumer. You can economize by buying two or three at a time and freezing the ones you don't use immediately. Young chickens, ranging in age from 6 to 20 weeks, are used as broilers and fryers. Older chickens (over 20 weeks) are used mainly for soups and stews.

In the poultry class, turkey, available all year (either fresh or frozen), is a good buy for large-group entertaining. Leftover turkey, like chicken, can be used in many dishes. Big turkeys are better buys than small ones since there is proportionately more meat and less bone. If you don't want to roast the whole bird, ask your butcher to saw a large turkey into halves or quarters and freeze what you don't use immediately. Turkey is also processed, and sometimes turkey rolls are economical.

Under recent legislation all poultry is subject to inspection. Surveys in various states around the country have shown that meats prepared and packed locally, and therefore not coming under the inspection laws of the U.S. Department of Agriculture, were often processed in shockingly bad sanitary conditions. These surveys led to the Wholesome Meat Act of 1967 and the Wholesome Poultry Products Act of 1968. The acts were passed, according to the USDA, to "assure consumers that the poultry and red meats they buy and eat are safe, wholesome, unadulterated and truthfully labeled."

The earlier Poultry Products Inspection Act of 1957 provided for federal inspection of poultry and poultry products sold in interstate or foreign commerce. Under the 1968 act all poultry and poultry products—including those sold within the state of origin—are in-

▭▭▭▭▭▭

## THE HIGH COST OF DIETING

Canned fruits and vegetables, packed either in water or with a sugar substitute, and known as dietetic, usually cost more than the regular cans. The difference ranges from a penny up to five cents or more, depending on the brand, or the fruit or vegetable in it. Generally, the price difference is smallest for the water-packed cans and greatest for the deluxe brands of canned fruits. If you are weight watching you may count these extra pennies spent as another reason to take off the pounds.

But there's another aspect to this—be sure that your sacrifice is not in vain. Although the difference in calories between regular and diet pack is considerable in canned fruits, there is not a very significant difference between such naturally low calorie items as ginger snaps or angel food cake and the more expensive cookies and cakes made with special flours and artificial sweeteners. And since everyone in the family can enjoy the regular foods, they are less likely to be thrown out. Be sure to check the calorie count on the label before you put out the extra money for a low calorie food.

▭▭▭▭▭▭

spected under a uniform standard for wholesomeness, by either the USDA or the state.

Fish is often neglected on family menus, but it is high in protein and comparatively low in cost, and should be a part of your meal planning. Supply and demand set the prices, and these of course vary seasonally from region to region. Here, too, your willingness to experiment and be adaptable will pay off—get the less popular fish and you'll probably save money while still having meals that are just as tasty.

Waste is a price factor in buying fish too. One pound of whole fish will feed only one person, a pound of dressed fish will feed two, and a pound of canned or frozen fish will feed three. So when you are deciding which is the best buy, judge price per portion, not price per pound, and you'll be sure to get your money's worth. As with the less expensive cuts of meat, the less choice kinds of fish—pink salmon, for instance, as compared to red—are just as good if they are going to be combined with other ingredients in casseroles, and you may be admired for your tasty dishes while saving money.

## Dairy Products and Produce

Milk is a big item on the budget of any family with children. If you find it necessary to have the convenience of delivery to your door you pay for the service. You will pay less if you pick it up yourself at the supermarket, and still less if you buy it in bulk—half gallons or gallons—rather than in quarts. If your family is diet-conscious, you will save money by buying skim milk to drink and using powdered skim milk as a substitute for whole milk in recipes. If you don't worry about weight, canned milk is another money-saving substitute for whole milk in recipes. Some people who don't like the taste of skim milk alone find a half-whole, half-skim milk mixture a perfectly acceptable drink.

Butter, another dairy product, is more expensive than oleomargarine and differs from the margarine in both price and taste. Margarine is as nutritious as butter though it costs only one third to one half as much. If you don't want to serve it with meals, where taste may make a difference to your family, then consider it for cooking, where the difference in taste is just about nonexistent and the saving is considerable. When you buy butter, check the grade that you want; the three U.S. Department of Agriculture grades—AA, A and B—differ in taste and in price. If your family can't distinguish between the grades you might as well save the pennies in price.

The more expensive ice creams are also the richest in butterfat and sometimes eggs. You can save money and calories by substituting sherbets or milk ices for the creamier ice creams.

When it comes to eggs there are few better buys for protein and versatility. Egg protein is so near perfection that it is often used as a standard to measure protein values. But you don't have to get the best eggs to get the best value. The USDA grades eggs according to freshness; you can do your own grading depending on use. The top grade eggs (AA, Fresh Fancy or A) are fine for all purposes, but are best used where appearance counts—for fried and poached eggs. Grade B eggs are fine where appearance is secondary or doesn't count at all—for scrambled eggs, egg salad, general cooking and baking. Size and color don't influence the nutritive value of eggs, so buy the size that suits your family and the color that is cheapest in your markets. In general, if there is less than a seven-cent price differential between two sizes of eggs in the same grade, the large egg is the better buy.

Fresh fruits and vegetables are priced according to the season. The better buys, of course, are those in season. Keep up with prices by following the ads in the newspapers and consumer reports on your local radio station.

Canners also take advantage of seasonal variations to buy large quantities of fruits and vegetables. Stock up on canned fruits and vegetables when the prices are particularly right. (See Chapter 27, page 280, for tips on buying and storing canned goods.) If you can use large quantities you are often able to save by buying case lots.

## Cereals and Breads

Variety seems to be the spice of the cereal department—cereals come plain, sugared, puffed, with fruit added, coated with honey; in packages ranging from enough for one breakfast to enough to feed a family for practically a week. You pay for the packaging and you pay for the extras. Though it's only pennies you will undoubtedly save money if you put in your own raisins or syrups. Estimate your family's consumption to find out whether you can use up the giant box before it becomes stale, and see if you can add enough variety to keep your family happy with the plainer cereals rather than the higher priced novelty brands.

If you are looking for real budget stretchers that are also rich in nutrition, find some recipes that make good use of dried beans and peas and enriched macaroni. They are also good additions to leftover meats and poultry.

Your daily bread can be either plain or fancy, a nationally advertised brand or a private-label brand packed by a local chain. Generally the private-label brands are cheaper than the better-known brands but equally nutritious. Here you will probably be influenced by family preference. Don't overlook the shelves set aside in some markets for day-old bread: If you toast the bread freshness is really not a consideration anyway. Pastries, pies and cakes can be bought fresh, frozen or off the shelf—your family's tastes are the guide. But you can educate your family to prefer the simpler sweets, which are not only better for them but also less expensive. You can also take advantage of specials to economize. (For the costs of using cake mixes and baking "from scratch," see "The Cost of Convenience Foods," page 274, in Chapter 26.)

Part of the game of food buying is to know exactly what you are buying and for what purpose. Don't buy uniformly packed canned tuna if you're going to flake it for a sandwich filling. In other words, don't pay more for an item that has qualities you don't need.

## Games and Stamps—At Your Expense

Speaking of games, the grocery stores themselves invite you to play—sometimes in the form of a game of chance and more often as trading stamps. This practice has caused considerable furor. Two cents of the dollar you spend at some grocery stores and supermarkets is handed back to you in the form of premium stamps (which may or may not be an economical boon), and legislation has been considered to allow the customer to have the choice between accepting the stamps or the cash. Sometimes grocery stores offer a game of chance; in effect, the customer bets a small portion of his food dollar on winning a cash prize. Supporters of the stamp system include women who feel stamps are a part of enforced savings that allow them to buy new and needed home furnishings. Some store owners claim that the use of stamps or games of chance has become so attractive to customers that the increased volume in store business has made it possible to pass a savings equal to the two cents out of the dollar along to the customer. If you deal at a store that offers such premiums you should deduct their cost from your food bill— that is, if you want to keep a totally honest account of what you are spending on food.

Finally, remember that while you're out stocking up on foods you are also often picking up many nonfood items: household soaps and detergents, paper goods, light bulbs, drugs, magazines, food for the bird and the dog, and sometimes even stockings, slippers or aprons. You may also pay a sales tax on these goods and on certain nonessential items like carbonated beverages and synthetic food products. So when you're estimating how much you spend for food, deduct these nonfood items to get the true picture.

CHAPTER 26

# When a Woman Goes to Market

*Knowing what to look for when you are at the supermarket will save you pennies that add up fast*

"To market, to market, to buy a fat pig"—that's the way the old nursery rhyme goes. These days it's to supermarket, chain store or corner grocery to buy everything from lean bacon and exotic teas to TV dinners. It's no consolation to you, as the family's purchasing agent, to know that the cost of foods has risen less than the cost of other items in the family budget. You still leave a good portion of your budget in the food market's cash register, and you like to be sure that every dollar left behind has bought its full quota of value.

Because you've planned your shopping stratagems beforehand, you know in general how your food budget will be apportioned. But when you arrive at the store you also want to know how to tell the freshness of the meats and produce, and what's the meaning of

263

the different labels, grades and cuts of meat and the varieties of cheese. You know that your food has been inspected for wholesomeness while packing, but you also want to be able to judge the safety of storage in the market itself. And you want to be sure, when you choose a particular cut of meat, or a can of string beans, or a package of frozen vegetables, that you've made the best choice for your budget. Here are some suggestions to make your shopping easier on your budget, your time schedule and your feet.

## Learning the Different Cuts of Meat

Let's start with the meat section, since your choice here is often the keystone of the rest of the menu. Some cuts of beef are naturally more tender than others, depending on what part of the cow they come from. Since veal, lamb and pork all come from younger animals than beef, they don't have as many varieties of cuts or degrees of tenderness. Cuts from the less-used muscles along the back, rib and loin sections of an animal will always be more tender than those from the active muscles such as those of the shoulder. In beef the less tender cuts come from the so-called chuck (shoulder), flank and round sections of the cow. The chart opposite, prepared by the U.S. Department of Agriculture, shows the sources of the various cuts of beef.

You may know these facts, but when you're out shopping it's not always easy to identify a particular cut of meat, since names of beef cuts vary from store to store and from region to region. To complicate the problem even further, the same name doesn't always mean the same thing. When you see a package labeled "crosscut rib roast," for instance, it could come from either the blade or the shoulder of the chuck, depending on what city you're in. But the one place it hasn't come from is the more tender rib, as the name implies. So when you are buying meat and are not sure which part of the cow it's from and therefore how tender it is and how you should cook it, don't hesitate to ask the butcher. In a short time you will know the terminology of the store you shop in and then you'll be an expert at the meat counter. (You may even persuade the butcher to change the labeling, so you don't have to translate the butcher's jargon.)

# Beef Chart

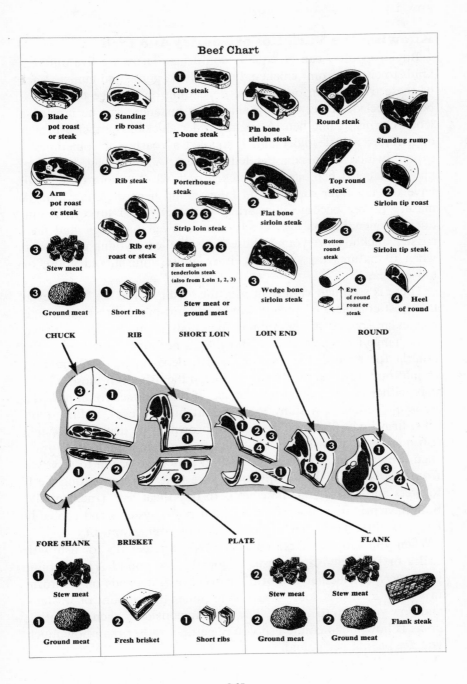

**CHUCK**

1. Blade pot roast or steak
2. Arm pot roast or steak
3. Stew meat
3. Ground meat

**RIB**

2. Standing rib roast
2. Rib steak
2. Rib eye roast or steak
1. Short ribs

**SHORT LOIN**

1. Club steak
2. T-bone steak
3. Porterhouse steak
1 2 3 Strip loin steak
2 3 Filet mignon tenderloin steak (also from Loin 1, 2, 3)
4. Stew meat or ground meat

**LOIN END**

1. Pin bone sirloin steak
2. Flat bone sirloin steak
3. Wedge bone sirloin steak

**ROUND**

3. Round steak
1. Standing rump
3. Top round steak
2. Sirloin tip roast
3. Bottom round steak
2. Sirloin tip steak
3. Eye of round roast or steak
4. Heel of round

**FORE SHANK**

1. Stew meat
1. Ground meat

**BRISKET**

2. Fresh brisket

**PLATE**

1. Short ribs
2. Stew meat
2. Ground meat

**FLANK**

2. Stew meat
2. Ground meat
1. Flank steak

265

## Knowing the Varieties of Poultry and Fish

Buying poultry can be equally confusing. There are five different kinds to choose from: chicken, turkey, duck, goose and guinea. Each of these five has various names, depending on the age of the bird being labeled. A very young chick, for instance, can be labeled a Rock Cornish game hen. A slightly older chicken is either a broiler or a fryer; a little older and it's called a roaster or sometimes a capon (which is an emasculated rooster). A middle-aged chicken may be labeled hen, stewing chicken or fowl. A young turkey will have the tag fryer-roaster, and later young hen or young tom. A mature turkey becomes a yearling or, simply, old turkey. Young ducks, depending on age, are broiler or fryer ducklings, and later roaster ducklings. A young goose is also called a young guinea and when it matures may become either goose, guinea, old goose or old guinea.

There is so much variety in fish, the "fruit of the sea," that even the most complete of anglers would be hard-pressed to recommend particular species of the animal that man might be happy to eat as a change from a meat diet. But there's not much variation in the criteria for a good fish market or fish department. Your market should buy fresh supplies daily and keep the fish, even those on display, either in a refrigerator or on ice. If this is done, you'll note the signs of freshness: a shiny look, bright bulging eyes, reddish-pink gills, firm body flesh and no sign of browning or drying out. Stale fish may have pinkish eyes, gills that turn a lighter pink, then gray, then brownish or reddish; and its flesh may have begun to separate from the bones. If you want to be sure that you are getting fresh lobsters and crabs, your best bet is to buy them live. (Incidentally, both have primitive, poorly developed nervous systems and probably feel very little when they are plunged into boiling water.)

When you shop for fresh or frozen fish, whether it's for fish with scales or for shellfish, it's usually sold by the pound. The amount you buy, and whether or not it's a good buy, depends on the form in which the fish is sold—which determines the amount of waste— and how you plan to serve it. The thing to consider, when estimating price, is how much edible fish you're getting, rather than how much you are paying per pound.

Here's how you'll find fish described in the ads and at the market, according to the U.S. Fish and Wildlife Service of the Department of the Interior.

*Whole or round fish:* fish as it comes from the water. Before cooking it must be scaled, and the innards removed. You may also want to cut off the head, tail and fins. The edible portion averages about 45 percent of the total weight, but this varies with the size and kind of fish.

*Drawn fish:* the whole fish with the innards removed, leaving an edible portion of about 48 percent.

*Dressed or pan-dressed fish:* a whole fish with scales and innards removed, and usually also the head, tail and fins. It is ready to cook and about 67 percent is edible.

*Steaks:* cross-section slices from large dressed fish, usually about three quarters of an inch thick and ready to cook. About 84 percent or more is edible.

*Fillets:* sides of a fish cut lengthwise from the backbone. Fillets are practically boneless, have little or no waste and are ready for cooking. A fillet cut from one side of a fish is called (not surprisingly) a single fillet. It's the type you're most apt to find at your market. Butterfly fillets are the two sides of a fish, corresponding to two single fillets, which are held together by the uncut flesh and skin of the belly.

*Sticks:* elongated pieces of fish cut from blocks of frozen fillets. Each stick usually weighs not less than three quarters of an ounce and not more than one and one quarter ounces.

*Portions:* uniformly shaped pieces of boneless fish cut from blocks of frozen fillets. A portion has a thickness of three eighths of an inch or more and is much larger than a fish stick.

If the fillets or steaks you buy are wrapped, be sure that wrapping is of some moistureproof material, with little or no air space between the fish and the wrapping. (For information on selecting frozen fish, see page 276 in this chapter.)

If you're buying shellfish like lobsters, shrimp, crabs, clams and oysters, you'll find them labeled "live"—that is, still living in their shells—or "shucked"—which means either out of the shell or still in the shell but no longer living, as with clams and oysters. Shrimp labeled "headless" are still in their shells, and some spiny-lobster tails are labeled like this too.

Add to these the variety of smoked, pickled and canned fish and you have many answers to what's for lunch or dinner.

## Looking for Signs of Freshness

When you reach the vegetable counter you know you want freshness, not only because the freshest vegetables have the most vitamins, but also because they keep longest. But how can you tell what's fresh and what isn't? This varies, of course, from vegetable to vegetable, but there are some telltale signs. Watch out for asparagus or broccoli tips that are open and spread out. In selecting beans and peas, beware of pods that are blemished, flabby-looking or thick and tough-looking. Avoid artichokes and beets with scaly areas or surfaces. Mold, of course, is always a sign of decay, and so usually are yellow leaves or brown edges. With potatoes it's a greenish color that's not good—since this means sunburn or too much exposure to light in the store. It doesn't pay to buy vegetables with a slightly decayed area, even if they are marked down. Despite the fact that you trim away the decayed portion, the decay will spread quickly to what's left.

In the cabbage family, watch out for leaves that are separated from the central stem at the base, or are badly discolored. Small holes or ragged leaves in cabbages and other leafy vegetables may show that the worms got to the vegetable before the farmer did.

Among salad greens such as chicory, endive and escarole don't buy those with leaves that have a brownish or yellowish discoloration, leaves with coarse fibrous stems, or flabby leaves or stems, a sign of decay. Among the lettuces—Bibb, iceberg and romaine—check for tipburn, a tan or brown area which is dead tissue, around the edge of the leaves. Avoid iceberg lettuce heads with irregular shapes and hard bumps on top, since these have overgrown central stems and may be tough.

Tomatoes for your salad should be firm and free of sunburn (green and yellow areas near the stem scar) and of deep cracks around the stem scar.

When vegetables have hard outer skins, such as some squashes,

beware of cuts, punctures and sunken or moldy spots on the skin—
all are signs of decay. The neck area is the place to look when buying
onions; onions with wet or very soft necks are usually either immature or already decaying. Also avoid onions with thick, hollow woody
centers in the neck and those that have begun sprouting.

When vegetables are fresh they can be safely stored for from two
to five days, except for root vegetables like carrots and turnips that
will keep from one to several weeks. (For complete details on proper
storage of all foods, see Chapter 27, "Keeping Foods Fresh," page
280.) When you're tempted by bargains in the market, stop a minute
before you load your basket and consider how soon you'll be able to
use up your purchases. If it's not within their storage limits, don't
buy, even at a bargain price, for you'll end up throwing away in
spoiled vegetables more than you saved at the cut price.

## Basics About Cheeses

Who hasn't stood in front of the cheese counter, mouth watering,
and debated which of the many delights to indulge in, knowing that
all of them are good sources of nutrition as well as good eating. And
who hasn't, at the same time, been confused by the phrases "pasteurized process cheese" as opposed to "pasteurized process cheese
food," or "farmer style," "pot" or "cup" cottage cheese. Since there
are 400 types of cheeses described by the Department of Agriculture, only a real connoisseur could possibly know all. But there are
some basics that will help you make a good choice for your money.

The two main categories of cheese are the so-called natural
cheeses, made from milk processed in a particular way to get a particular variety; and the cheese foods and spreads that are made from a
natural cheese base plus a variety of flavorings and such additives
as nonfat dry milk, whey solids or water. Most of the cheese foods
and spreads have less butterfat content than the natural cheese
(the range of butterfat content is controlled by the Department of
Agriculture). They may or may not have the same nutritional value
as the natural cheese on which they are based, depending on the
kind.

When you are buying cheese, look for the labels that say whether
it is a process cheese, a spread or a cheese food. In that way you'll

know whether the type is suitable for your purposes and whether you are getting the butterfat content that you want or whether you are buying a product with more moisture and nonfat milk solids.

Here are the varieties of cheeses and cheese foods and their contents and characteristics:

*Pasteurized process cheese:* a blend of fresh and aged natural cheeses that have been shredded, mixed and heated (pasteurized). The blend may consist of one or two or more varieties of natural cheese plus flavorings such as pimentos, fruits, vegetables or meats. It melts easily when reheated.

*Pasteurized process cheese food:* a blend prepared in just about the same way as the pasteurized cheese except that nonfat dry milk, whey (the liquid that separates from the curd during the cheese-making process) and water have been added. This means that it has a lower butterfat content and more moisture than the process cheese. It is also milder, softer, spreads more easily and melts quicker than the process cheese.

*Pasteurized process cheese spread:* a blend prepared very much like the process cheese food except that it has even less butterfat content and even more moisture. A stabilizer is usually added to prevent the separation of the ingredients.

*Club, or cold-pack, cheese:* a blend of the same or two or more varieties of fresh and aged natural cheese. The cheeses are mixed into a uniform product without heating. The main varieties are American and Swiss; the flavor is the same as that of the natural cheese but the cheese may be aged longer and therefore sharper. It is softer, spreads more easily and may be packed in jars or in rolls.

*Club, or cold-pack, cheese food:* made in the same way as club or cold-pack cheese, except that it includes some nonfat dry milk or whey solids or water, and may also have sugar or corn syrup in it. It spreads more easily. It is frequently sold in a pottery crock or a round package.

## Selecting Fresh Fruits

A good accompaniment to cheese, and an essential to any family's nutrition, is fresh fruit. Shopping rules for buying fresh fruit are often helpful, but can only supplement the knowledge you will acquire as you shop. Don't be bashful about asking the clerks or even the manager in your local market how to judge individual fruits.

Here are some general rules; your clerk or store manager may advise you of them when you get to know him:

Don't buy just because of low prices if you are going to throw away fruits that spoil before you get a chance to use them. Of course, if the price is low because the fruit is seasonal, you do have a bargain, provided you plan its use sensibly to avoid waste.

Don't buy on account of size alone. Large-sized fruits are not necessarily the best, nor the most economical. One of your criteria has to be what you want to use the fruit for. Take apples, for instance: Rome Beauty, Northern Spy or Winesap apples, all of which are good for baking, are often larger than the Delicious, Mc-Intosh and Stayman apples meant for eating.

Don't judge solely by appearance, either, because the best-looking fruit is not necessarily the most economical or best-tasting. Although appearance and quality frequently do go together, sometimes a particular variety of fruit has a characteristic appearance that is deceptive and has nothing to do with its freshness, palatability or nutritive value. Oranges, for instance, are strictly regulated by all of the states that grow them and must be matured before being harvested and shipped. But if oranges have a greenish cast or green spots, it doesn't mean that the fruit is immature; often fully matured oranges will turn greenish (the process, not surprisingly, is called regreening) late in the season. To offset this, since people do associate green color with either immaturity or mold, some growers give their fruit artificial color, which has no effect on eating quality. This fruit must be labeled "color added."

### How to Avoid Confusion by Labels

Much as we all like fresh fruit and vegetables, none of us could or would want to get along without canned and frozen goods. How do you know what size can to buy? On the following page is the chart that the canning industry uses. Familiarize yourself with the various sizes, their contents and serving portions, and you'll be able to determine which size to pick off the shelf, depending on the use you have in mind.

271

## COMMON CONTAINER SIZES

| INDUSTRY TERM | APPROXIMATE NET WEIGHT OR FLUID MEASURE | APPROXIMATE NUMBER OF CUPS | PRINCIPAL PRODUCTS |
|---|---|---|---|
| 8 oz. | 8 oz. | 1 | Fruits, vegetables, specialties* for small families. 2 servings. |
| Picnic | 10½ to 12 oz. | 1¼ | Mainly condensed soups; some fruits, vegetables, meat, fish, specialties.* 2 to 3 servings. |
| 12 oz. (vac.) | 12 oz. | 1½ | Principally for vacuum-packed corn. 3 to 4 servings. |
| No. 300 | 14 to 16 oz. (14 oz. to 1 lb.) | 1¾ | Pork and beans, baked beans, meat products, cranberry sauce, blueberries, specialties.* 3 to 4 servings. |
| No. 303 | 16 to 17 oz. (1 lb. to 1 lb. 1 oz.) | 2 | Principal size for fruits and vegetables; some meat products, ready-to-serve soups, specialties.* 4 servings. |
| No. 2 | 20 oz. (1 lb. 4 oz.) or 18 fl. oz. (1 pt. 2 fl. oz.) | 2½ | Juices,** ready-to-serve soups, some specialties,* pineapple, apple slices. No longer in popular use for most fruits and vegetables. 5 servings. |
| No. 2½ | 27 to 29 oz. (1 lb. 11 oz. to 1 lb. 13 oz.) | 3½ | Fruits, some vegetables (pumpkin, sauerkraut, spinach and other greens, tomatoes). 5 to 7 servings. |
| No. 3 cylinder or 46 fl. oz. | 51 oz. (3 lb. 3 oz.) or 46 fl. oz. (1 qt. 14 fl. oz.) | 5¾ | Fruit and vegetable juices,** pork and beans; institutional size for condensed soups, some vegetables. 10 to 12 servings. |
| No. 10 | 6½ lb. to 7 lb. 5 oz. | 12–13 | Institutional size for fruits, vegetables and some other foods. 25 servings. |

*Specialties: usually food combinations such as macaroni or spaghetti with sauces, Spanish style rice, Mexican type foods, Chinese foods, tomato aspic, etc.
**Juices are now being packed in a number of can sizes.

The label on the can is the source of other detailed information. The U.S. Department of Agriculture has developed grades which may appear on the label. Canners are not required to use or display the grade, but if they do it means that they have paid to have a U.S. inspector on their premises during the canning process to certify that the grades are accurate. The usual grade names are U.S. Grade A or U.S. Fancy; U.S. Grade B, also called Choice or Extra Standard; U.S. Grade C, also called Standard.

Grade A means a properly matured, excellent quality of fruit or vegetable, of uniform size and color, virtually free from defects. It's suited for special uses, such as in desserts or salads, where appearance and texture are important.

Grade B indicates good quality, but somewhat less uniform in size and color and not quite as free from blemishes. The fruit may be a little less tender. Most processed fruits and vegetables are Grade B; they are just as nutritious as Grade A.

Grade C means fairly good quality, the same nutrition as the other two grades, but even further down the scale on appearance, lack of blemishes and tenderness.

When you reach for a can to put in your shopping cart, the grade you decide on will depend on the purpose you have in mind. If you plan to decorate a scrumptious cake with some peach slices, you'll want a Grade A can, but if you're going to add some peaches to a cooked compote of fruit you'll be just as happy, and a few pennies richer, if you buy Grade C.

## Buying Quality Frozen Foods

Unlike canned foods, the quality of frozen foods is in large part dependent on the conditions in which the foods are delivered to the store, and handled and stored after they arrive. Be sure that your store buys frozen fruits or vegetables from refrigerated trucks and unpacks them promptly on arrival. If you notice cases of frozen foods standing in the aisle, the store is not handling these packages properly. If they are allowed to defrost even partially before being stored, they will inevitably lose flavor and nutrition and you will not get your money's worth. You should occasionally check the thermometer in the market's frozen-food case, to be sure that it is 0° F., or lower, for

273

proper storage. Never select foods that are stocked above the load-line, the line painted inside the freezer to indicate the upper limits of the cold area.

Some foods, such as breads, can be safely refrozen at least once. In general, however, food that has thawed has to be considered highly perishable, and possibly even harmful, since bacteria could have formed. So not only should frozen food be properly shipped and stored, but you should also take it home promptly, preferably in a double-insulated bag, and store it quickly.

Be wary of unusual "bargains" in frozen foods. If your store has made a good deal with a distributor it may really be able to offer you an excellent buy, but there is also the possibility that a whole shipment of frozen foods wasn't stored properly and the market is

▭▭▭▭▭▭

## THE COST OF CONVENIENCE FOODS

Convenience foods have become a part of our way of life. The variety of semi-prepared and fully prepared food products you can find in your local supermarket ranges from dehydrated foods in foil containers to completely cooked dishes in boilable plastic bags.

Not all convenience foods cost more. A surprising number of them cost less than their homemade counterparts.

A U.S. Department of Agriculture study reported that, of the 158 foods surveyed, 42 actually cost less in their convenience form than they do when they are prepared at home. A canned beef stew that saves you 28 minutes of preparation time also saves you 6 cents on four servings. The tab for your from-scratch version is 99 cents; for the ready-to-heat stew, 93 cents. However, the factory-prepared, ready-

to-heat stew usually provides less meat than its homemade counterpart.

Among fruits and vegetables, four servings of frozen whole-kernel corn cost less than an equal amount cut fresh from the cob. Fresh peas are more than twice as expensive as frozen peas, and the margin of difference is even greater with canned peas. Four servings of squeezed orange juice from the store cost 25 cents; of frozen juice concentrate, 18 cents; and of home-squeezed juice, 30 cents. Fresh pineapple costs more than canned pineapple, fresh grapefruit more than canned.

When it comes to baked goods, the story is much the same. A devil's food cake mix, with one egg added, produces four servings for less money than it costs to bake four homemade slices. And as for coffee—depending on how strong you make it—the instant version is one third to two thirds

▭▭▭▭▭▭

trying to recoup a loss by unloading the goods in a hurry. If you have doubts, ask the clerk.

## What Grades Mean

The U.S. Department of Agriculture has developed standards for frozen fruits and vegetables comparable to those for canned goods. As with canned goods there is no law that says these standards have to be on the labels. They are really standards that the packers and distributors use for quality control. But since they often do appear on labels, it's worthwhile knowing what they represent.

U.S. Grade A or Fancy means that the fruit or vegetable has good color for its variety, is practically free from defects and nearly uniform in size and symmetry. With fruits, the consistency should be

□□□□□□□

cheaper than the home-brewed kind.

Many convenience foods are more expensive than home-prepared foods, however. Canned carrots, ready-to-serve rolls, frozen blueberry pie, frozen french fries and puff potatoes, canned brussels sprouts, frozen cleaned and peeled shrimp and frozen chicken dinners, for example, all cost more than it would cost to make the same dish at home. Frozen waffles and pancakes are two to three times as expensive as homemade ones; frozen pizza costs twice as much as the pizza you make yourself. White frosting mix is double the price of frosting made at home.

When you buy specially prepared foods like frozen spinach soufflé or beef bourguignon you are paying for the cost of a cook in addition to the cost of the food. You also pay more for little extras like frozen peas with mushrooms added.

Many forms of packaging increase the convenience of foods, but they may also increase the price. Potato chips, for example, cost 39 cents if sold in a large six-ounce bag, but the same amount costs 52 cents in individual one-serving bags. Individually wrapped quarters of butter are a few cents more expensive than the one-pound brick form.

Other more expensive convenience forms include boilable bags of frozen vegetables; tea bags; picnic-size salt shakers; and disposable cans and bottles of beer and soft drinks.

Compare prices and be selective. Ask yourself whether the extra cost is worth it to you in terms of time and effort saved. But don't feel guilty about spending an extra few cents for the added efficiency, variety and pleasure of convenience foods—especially if it means more time to spend with your family or on a relaxing hobby or course of study.

□□□□□□□

right for the type of fruit; if the category of peaches, for instance, is "soft ripe" or "firm ripe" all the pieces should be like that.

Grade B or Choice indicates that each of these specifications applies at a somewhat lower level of quality. Fruits should be reasonably free of blemishes, for example, but not totally free.

Grade C or Standard is further down the line on all counts but still perfectly wholesome. As with the canned goods, what you buy will be determined by the purpose you have in mind.

Frozen citrus fruit juices have only two grades, A and B. The standards are good flavor, good color and the absence of portions of seeds, particles of skin and membrane.

Good quality frozen fish is solidly frozen when bought. It has no discoloration or brownish tinge on the flesh and little or no odor. The wrapping of frozen fish steaks or fillets, like the wrapping of fresh fish steaks and fillets, should be moistureproof and vaporproof, and there should be little or no air space between the fish and the wrapping.

It's difficult for shoppers to judge tenderness in frozen beef products because the label usually doesn't tell the grade or the cut of meat from which the meat was taken. When a shopper from the Extension Service of the U.S. Department of Agriculture checked New York City markets, she reported that there was no way of telling whether the ground beef used in a package of frozen Salisbury steak, for instance, was hamburger (which contains the highest proportion of fat), ground chuck or ground round. Frozen minute beefsteaks in another market were described as "wafer-sliced beef," again without saying what cut of beef was used.

She suggested that trying different brands might be the only satisfactory way of judging, since there were price ranges of about 30 cents among various brands, with no indication of the difference in quality. However, the labels of frozen meat products are supposed to list ingredients in order of the amount of each ingredient in the package, so you can tell whether you are buying more beef or more water. In the frozen-food department it's *essential* that you read the label if you want to get your money's worth. A picture may be worth a thousand words in some cases, but this isn't one of them. Pictures on the outside of packages look very much the same and can't be relied on to represent the contents; only the labels tell which comes first—and most—the gravy or the meat.

The frozen-food counter is the place, above all, where you will find many of the newest and most tempting convenience foods. Here is where you'll have to put your arithmetic to work to evaluate whether that vegetable in butter sauce is what you want or whether it may turn out to be a very expensive pat of butter.

Consider another report from the U.S. Department of Agriculture on frozen vegetable shopping in a big city supermarket. Ten-ounce boxes of frozen peas that yielded three servings varied in cost from 17 cents for the store's own brand to 31 cents for a nationally advertised brand and 33 cents for a national brand in a boilable pouch with butter sauce. The department estimated that adding the butter at home would have meant about 2 cents per tablespoon. Peas combined with celery or pearl onions cost no more than plain peas in one brand, but 5 cents more in some other brands.

Unfortunately, the department has no guidelines to offer, so your only defense is taking the time to compare the prices, noting the brand names and the contents of the packages. If you see that the store's own brand of frozen foods is always cheaper or that one nationally advertised brand is usually a better buy than another, you will have some guidelines for that market. If no pattern seems to emerge, ask the store clerks or the manager of the frozen-food department what are the best buys.

## Some Final Tips

Finally, just to be sure that you are squeezing that last penny's worth of value out of your food-buying budget, consider these dos and don'ts as a guide:

1. *Do* carry a copy of advertised specials, clipped from your paper, while shopping. You'll be reminded what to look for, and you'll be sure of the new, lower price if you happen to pick a can not properly marked or if the checkout clerk isn't aware of the special.

2. *Do* watch for unadvertised specials that may have been made available to the market by a wholesaler or a grocery manufacturer, but not in large enough quantity to make it worthwhile for the store to run an ad.

3. *Do* ask your grocer for a rain check if he happens to run short of advertised specials before you get to the store. If he advertises, unless the ad specifies "limited quantity," he should have enough stock to fill the demand or get more at the special price for the smart customer who asks for it.

4. *Do* check the date stamps on packages, which tell the store manager the latest date that a product can be sold, so that you are sure you are getting the freshest of the batch.

5. *Do* try to plan your schedule to allow you to shop early in the morning (but not so early that shelves haven't been stocked or produce unloaded) so that you get the pick of the crop before it's been handled.

6. *Do* keep a careful watch at the checkout counter to be sure that items are rung up properly. You can assume that the clerks are honest but you can also assume that they are human and will make errors. If your children are with you, keep a toy or a book handy for this moment so they will be occupied and keep *you* from being distracted.

1. *Don't* let quantity specials tempt you to buy more than you need. Five pounds of potatoes are no bargain, even if you save three cents a pound, if you can use only half of them before the others spoil.

2. *Don't* be misled by prices that only seem to be bargains. Five bottles of clam juice for $1, for instance, is still 20 cents a bottle, and all your recipe may call for is two bottles.

3. *Don't* automatically assume that a special table of items is a bargain table. They may be regular-price items put on the table just to tempt you to buy on impulse, without noticing the price.

4. *Don't* overlook the possibility of finding fruit and vegetable bargains in the frozen-food section when fresh fruits and vegetables are at their peak. It is often a good time to stock up for the less plentiful months ahead.

5. *Don't* neglect the chance of picking up bargains if you shop late in the day or just before a weekend, especially a long holiday weekend, when the store manager is anxious to clear his shelves. If you are having company, if you have room to store things that will keep, if you can change your menu plans to take advantage of these bargains, you may end up with considerable savings.

6. *Don't* insist on freshness when it's not important and the not-as-fresh is cheaper. Day-old bread and cake, if you only shop once a week and keep these things in your refrigerator anyway, make sense and savings. If your family likes nothing but toast, why pay for fresh bread?

7. *Don't* undo all your careful planning and money saving by failing to unpack your groceries promptly and to store them properly so that they will keep. The storage charts and hints on keeping your food fresh, in the next chapter, will give you the proper follow-up to your careful buying.

## ANSWERS TO SOME QUESTIONS ABOUT CANNED FOODS

• **Where should canned foods be stored?** Almost any place. The best is a dry place with a moderately cool temperature, such as a cool, dry cellar. In kitchen storage, avoid placing the food near steam pipes, radiators, furnaces or kitchen ranges.

• **How long will canned foods keep?** Indefinitely, if nothing happens to the container to cause a leak. Extremely long periods of storage at high temperatures may result in some loss in color, flavor, appearance and nutritive value, although the food will remain wholesome. It is probably best and safest to have a regular turnover, say once a year.

• **Does damage to the outside of a can indicate damage to the food?** Rust and dents do not affect the contents of a can, as long as the can does not leak. Don't buy a container that leaks or bulges. If any that you are storing do this, discard them—the food could be badly spoiled.

• **What effect has freezing on canned foods?** Except for a slight breakdown of texture in a few products, a single freezing and thawing does not usually affect canned foods adversely. Some foods of creamy consistency may curdle or separate upon freezing. Heating the product in preparing it usually restores the original consistency.

• **Is it safe to leave unused portions of canned foods in the can after it is opened?** It is perfectly safe to leave opened food in the can. The U.S. Department of Agriculture states in its Home and Garden Bulletin No. 105 (1965): "Food may be left in tin cans after opening. Put a cover on the can and store in refrigerator." The important thing to remember is any unused portion should therefore be stored refrigerated. Plan to use it within a few days.

• **Why does the same product in the same size can sometimes vary in weight?** Because of the way it's packed. Tuna is a good example. The same size can of solid-pack tuna will weigh more than one of chunk, flaked or grated tuna.

279

## CHAPTER 27

## Keeping Foods Fresh

*Spoiled food is money
in the garbage can.
Learn how to cut down
on waste and maximize
flavor and freshness*

Waste through spoilage can be a constant drain on your food budget unless your meats, fruits, vegetables and groceries are properly stored once you get them home. Here are the basic rules for keeping your foodstuffs fresh and nutritious.

Remember that a properly functioning refrigerator is your most important aid in keeping perishable foods fresh (see the diagram on page 283). The temperature in the general storage area of your refrigerator should be between 38° and 42° F. when the control knob is set for normal operation.

### BREADS AND CEREALS

*Breads:* Store in original wrapper in breadbox or refrigerator. Bread keeps its freshness longer at room temperature than in the refrigerator. In hot, humid weather, however, bread is better protected against mold in the refrigerator. Breads will retain their good quality for two to three months if frozen in their original wrappers and stored in the home freezer.

*Cereals, flours, spices and sugar:* Store at room temperatures in tightly closed containers that keep out dust, moisture and insects. During summer, buy flours and cereals in small quantities. Inspect often for weevils.

*Dry mixes:* Cake, pancake, cooky, muffin and roll mixes may be held at room temperatures.

### EGGS

*Shell eggs:* Store promptly in refrigerator. Eggs retain quality well in the refrigerator; they lose their mild flavor quickly at room temperature. To ensure best quality and flavor, use eggs within a week. If eggs are held too long, the white may grow thin and the yolk membrane may weaken and break when the shell is opened.

Cover leftover yolks with cold water and store in the refrigerator in a covered container. Egg whites should be refrigerated in a covered container. Use leftover yolks and whites within a day or two.

*Dried egg:* Keep in refrigerator. After a package has been opened, store unused portion in an airtight container. Dried egg will keep its good flavor for about a year if it is stored properly.

## FATS AND OILS

Most fats and oils need protection from air, heat and light. Fats and oils in partially filled containers keep longer if they are transferred to smaller containers in which there is little or no air space.

*Butter, fat drippings and margarine:* Store, tightly wrapped or covered, in the refrigerator. These products are best used within two weeks. Keep only as much butter or margarine in the butter compartment of the refrigerator as needed for immediate use. Don't let butter or margarine stand for long periods at room temperature; exposure to heat and light hastens rancidity.

*Cooking and salad oils:* Keep small quantities at room temperature and use before flavor changes. For long storage, keep oils in the refrigerator. Some oils may cloud and solidify in the refrigerator, but this is not harmful. If warmed to room temperature, they will become clear and liquid.

*Hydrogenated shortenings and lard:* Most of the firm vegetable shortenings and lard have been stabilized by hydrogenation or antioxidants. These shortenings can be held at room temperature without damage to flavor. Lard that is not stabilized should be refrigerated. Keep these products covered.

*Mayonnaise and other salad dressings:* Keep all homemade salad dressings in the refrigerator. Ready-made mayonnaise and other salad dressings should be refrigerated after jars have been opened.

## FRUITS

Sort fruits before storing. Discard any bruised or decayed fruit to keep it from contaminating sound, firm fruit.

*Apples:* Store mellow apples uncovered in the refrigerator. Unripe or hard apples are best held at cool room temperature (60° F. to 70° F.) until ready to eat. Use ripe apples within a week.

*Apricots, avocados, grapes, nectarines, pears, peaches and plums:* When these fruits are ripe, store them uncovered in the refrigerator

281

and use within three to five days. When unripe, allow to ripen in the open air at room temperature. Do not place in the sun.

*Bananas:* Store bananas at room temperature.

*Berries and cherries:* Keep whole and uncovered in the refrigerator until ready to use. Washing and stemming these fruits before refrigerating results in loss of food value and increased spoilage. Use within one or two days.

*Citrus fruits and melons:* These fruits are best stored at a cool room temperature (60° F. to 70° F.). But short-time holding in the refrigerator is not harmful to their quality. If citrus fruits are kept too long at low temperature, the skin becomes pitted and the flesh discolors. Use these fruits within a week.

*Pineapples:* If fully ripe, these may be refrigerated for a day or two. Wrap them tightly to prevent other foods from taking up the odor of the pineapple. If pineapples are not ripe, keep them above refrigerator temperature.

*Canned fruits, canned fruit juices:* After canned fruits and canned fruit juices have been opened, cover and store in the refrigerator. They can be safely stored in their original containers.

*Dried fruits:* Keep in tightly closed containers. Store at room temperature, except in warm, humid weather; then refrigerate.

*Frozen fruit juices:* Cover reconstituted fruit juice concentrates and keep in the refrigerator. For best flavor, keep in glass or plastic containers.

*Jellies, jams and preserves:* After these fruit products have been opened, store them, covered, in the refrigerator.

## MEAT, POULTRY, FISH

*Cold cuts:* Store in the refrigerator. Use within three to five days.

*Cured and smoked meats:* Store ham, frankfurters, bacon, bologna and smoked sausage in the refrigerator in their original packagings. Uncooked cured pork may be stored longer than fresh pork, but the fat will become rancid if held too long.

Bacon should be eaten within a week for best quality. Use a half ham in three to five days, a whole ham within a week; wrap ham slices tightly and use within a few days.

*Fresh fish, poultry, meat roasts, chops and steaks:* Store all fresh

# A Guide to Refrigerator Storage

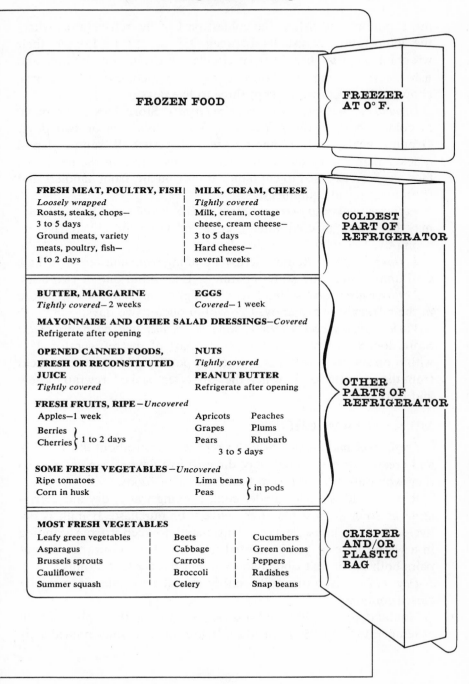

**FROZEN FOOD**

**FREEZER AT 0° F.**

**FRESH MEAT, POULTRY, FISH**
*Loosely wrapped*
Roasts, steaks, chops—
3 to 5 days
Ground meats, variety
meats, poultry, fish—
1 to 2 days

**MILK, CREAM, CHEESE**
*Tightly covered*
Milk, cream, cottage
cheese, cream cheese—
3 to 5 days
Hard cheese—
several weeks

**COLDEST PART OF REFRIGERATOR**

**BUTTER, MARGARINE**
*Tightly covered*— 2 weeks

**EGGS**
*Covered*— 1 week

**MAYONNAISE AND OTHER SALAD DRESSINGS**—*Covered*
Refrigerate after opening

**OPENED CANNED FOODS,
FRESH OR RECONSTITUTED
JUICE**
*Tightly covered*

**NUTS**
*Tightly covered*

**PEANUT BUTTER**
Refrigerate after opening

**FRESH FRUITS, RIPE**—*Uncovered*
Apples—1 week

Berries 〉
Cherries 〈 1 to 2 days

Apricots    Peaches
Grapes      Plums
Pears       Rhubarb
    3 to 5 days

**SOME FRESH VEGETABLES**—*Uncovered*
Ripe tomatoes
Corn in husk

Lima beans 〉
Peas 〈 in pods

**OTHER PARTS OF REFRIGERATOR**

**MOST FRESH VEGETABLES**
Leafy green vegetables
Asparagus
Brussels sprouts
Cauliflower
Summer squash

Beets
Cabbage
Carrots
Broccoli
Celery

Cucumbers
Green onions
Peppers
Radishes
Snap beans

**CRISPER AND/OR PLASTIC BAG**

meat, poultry and fish in the coldest part of the refrigerator, where the temperature is usually between 35° to 38° F. Loosen their wrappings as they benefit from circulation of air. For poultry and fish, short holding—one or two days—is recommended. Roasts, chops and steaks may be kept three to five days.

*Ground and mechanically tenderized meats:* Store, loosely wrapped, in coldest part of the refrigerator. Use within one or two days. Ground meats, such as hamburger and fresh bulk sausage, spoil quicker than roasts, chops or steaks because more of the meat surface has been exposed to contamination from air, from handlers and from mechanical equipment.

*Leftover cooked meats and meat dishes:* Cool quickly (container may be placed in cold water), cover or wrap loosely, refrigerate promptly. Use with one or two days.

*Leftover stuffing:* Remove leftover stuffing from chicken or turkey, cool immediately and store separately. Use within one or two days.

*Leftover gravy and broth:* These are highly perishable. Cover, store in the refrigerator promptly. Use within one or two days.

*Variety meats such as liver, kidneys, brains and poultry giblets:* Store, loosely wrapped, in the coldest part of the refrigerator. Use within one or two days. Before storing poultry giblets remove them from the separate bag in which they are often packed, rewrap loosely and refrigerate.

## MILK, CREAM, CHEESE

*Fresh milk and cream:* Store in refrigerator at about 40° F. Milk and cream are best stored only three to five days. Keep covered so they won't absorb odors and flavors of other foods.

Rinse bottle or carton under cold, running water, dry and refrigerate as soon as possible after delivery or purchase. If milk is delivered to your house, make arrangements to keep it from standing in a warm place or being exposed to sunlight. Exposure to sun impairs both flavor and riboflavin (Vitamin $B_2$) content of milk.

*Dry milks:* Keep dry milk—either nonfat or whole—in a tightly closed container.

Nonfat dry milk will keep for several months on the cupboard shelf at temperatures of 75° F. or lower. Close the container immediately

## TIPS ON STORAGE OF FROZEN FOODS

1. Use frozen foods as quickly as possible, and replace them often. Long storage doesn't add to food value or to eating quality.

2. Keep a record, so you know what kinds of food, in what quantities, are being stored in your freezer or freezing compartment.

3. Rotate the food, with new packages at the bottom or back of the storage area and the old ones on top or up front. Keep unfrozen packages from touching those already in storage.

4. For best eating quality use frozen food before its suggested maximum storage time has expired. If you don't know how long a certain food can be safely stored, consult the chart on this page.

| FROZEN FOOD | MAXIMUM NUMBER OF MONTHS OF STORAGE |
| --- | --- |
| **FRUITS** | |
| Cherries, peaches, raspberries, strawberries | 12 |
| Fruit juice concentrates: | |
| Apple, grape, orange | 12 |
| **VEGETABLES** | |
| Asparagus, beans, cauliflower, corn, peas, spinach | 8 |
| **MEAT** | |
| Beef: | |
| Roasts, steaks | 12 |
| Ground beef | 3 |
| Lamb: | |
| Roasts | 12 |
| Patties | 4 |
| Pork (fresh): | |
| Roasts | 8 |
| Sausage | 2 |
| Pork (cured) | 2 |
| Veal: | |
| Roasts | 8 |
| Chops, cutlets | 6 |
| Cooked meats: | |
| Meat dinners, meat pies, Swiss steak | 3 |

| FROZEN FOOD | MAXIMUM NUMBER OF MONTHS OF STORAGE |
| --- | --- |
| **POULTRY** | |
| Chicken: | |
| Whole | 12 |
| Cut-up | 9 |
| Livers | 3 |
| Turkey: | |
| Whole | 12 |
| Cut-up | 6 |
| Duck, goose (whole) | 6 |
| Cooked chicken and turkey: | |
| Sliced meat and gravy | 6 |
| Pies | 12 |
| Fried chicken | 4 |
| **BAKERY PRODUCTS** | |
| White bread, plain rolls | 3 |
| Cakes: | |
| Angel, chiffon | 2 |
| Chocolate layer | 4 |
| Pound, yellow | 6 |
| Fruit | 12 |
| Doughnuts | 3 |
| Pies (unbaked): | |
| Apple, boysenberry, cherry, peach | 8 |
| **ICE CREAM, SHERBET** | 1 |

after using. If long exposed to air, dry milk takes up moisture and becomes lumpy, making reconstitution difficult.

Dry whole milk is marketed only on a small scale, chiefly for infant feeding. Because of its fat content, it does not keep as well as nonfat dry milk. After opening the container store dry whole milk, tightly covered, in the refrigerator.

Refrigerate reconstituted dry milk like fresh milk.

*Evaporated milk and condensed milk:* Store at room temperature until opened, then cover tightly and refrigerate like fresh milk.

*Cheese spreads and cheese foods:* After containers have been opened, store, covered, in the refrigerator.

*Hard cheeses such as cheddar, Parmesan and Swiss:* Keep in the refrigerator, wrapped tightly to keep out air. The original packaging may be used. Stored this way, hard cheeses will keep for several months unless mold develops.

*Soft cheeses such as cottage, cream, Camembert:* Store, tightly covered, in the coldest part of the refrigerator. Use cottage cheese within three to five days, others within two weeks.

## VEGETABLES

The fresher vegetables are when eaten, the better.

With only a few exceptions vegetables keep best in the refrigerator, The exceptions—potatoes, sweet potatoes, dry onions, hard-rind squashes, eggplant and rutabagas—keep well in cool rather than cold storage.

Sort vegetables before storing them. Discard any that are bruised or soft, or show evidence of decay or worm injury.

The vegetable crisper in your refrigerator performs better if it is at least two thirds full. If crisper is less full than this, vegetables will keep better if they are first put in plastic bags and then in the crisper.

*Asparagus:* Discard tough parts of stalks. Store in the refrigerator in crisper or in plastic bag. Use within one or two days.

*Broccoli and brussels sprouts:* Store in refrigerator crisper or in plastic bag. Use within one or two days.

*Cabbage and cauliflower:* Store in the refrigerator in crisper or in plastic bags. Use cabbage within one or two weeks, cauliflower in three to five days.

*Carrots, beets and radishes:* Remove root tips and tops. Store covered in refrigerator. Use within one or two weeks.

*Cucumbers.* See *Peppers* below.

*Green peas and lima beans:* Leave in pods and store in refrigerator. Use within a day or two.

*Lettuce and other salad greens:* Store in crisper or in plastic bags to hold down loss of moisture. Use within one or two days.

*Onions:* Store dry onions at room temperature, or slightly cooler, in loosely woven or open-mesh containers. Stored this way, they keep several months. At high temperatures and humidity they sprout and decay.

Keep green onions cold and moist in the refrigerator. Store in plastic bags. Use within one or two days.

*Peppers and cucumbers:* Wash and dry. Store in crisper or in plastic bags in the refrigerator. Use within three to five days.

*Potatoes:* Store in a dark, dry place with good ventilation and a temperature of 45° F. to 50° F. Light causes greening, which lowers eating quality. High temperatures hasten sprouting and shriveling. If necessary to store at room temperature, use within a week.

*Spinach, kale, collards, chard, and beet, turnip and mustard greens:* Wash thoroughly in cold water. Lift these leafy green vegetables out of the water as grit settles to the bottom of the pan. Drain. Store in refrigerator in crisper or plastic bags. Use within one or two days.

*Sweet corn:* Store, unhusked and uncovered, in the refrigerator. Use within one or two days.

*Sweet potatoes, hard-rind squashes, eggplant and rutabagas:* Store at cool temperature around 60° F. Temperatures below 50° F. may cause chilling injury. These vegetables will keep several months at 60° F., but only a week at room temperature.

*Tomatoes:* Store ripe tomatoes uncovered in the refrigerator. Keep unripe tomatoes at room temperature away from direct sunlight until they ripen.

## MISCELLANEOUS FOODS

*Honeys and syrups:* Store at room temperature until opened, then refrigerate to protect from mold. If crystals form, dissolve them by placing container of honey or syrup in hot water.

287

*Nuts:* Store in airtight containers in the refrigerator. Because of their high fat content, nuts require refrigeration to delay development of rancidity. Unshelled nuts keep better than shelled. Unsalted nuts keep better than salted because salt speeds rancidity.

*Peanut butter:* After a jar of peanut butter has been opened it should be kept in the refrigerator. Remove it from the refrigerator a short time before using to allow it to soften.

CHAPTER 28

## How to Avoid Being Cheated by the Pound

*Are you being shortchanged by misleading packaging or phony labels? Here's how you can protect yourself against costly flimflammery*

In days of yore you bought mostly by the pound, peck and gallon. If the storekeeper included the weight of his thumb or left out a couple of potatoes, at least you had a sporting chance of spotting the oversight.

No longer. Stroll the aisles of the supermarket today. More and more of the 8000 or so products on display are in opaque containers that ask you to accept the veracity of the sparse data that is on their labels.

Despite the passage of the Fair Packaging and Labeling Act (known to most of us as the truth-in-packaging law) in 1966, most housewives still find it difficult to spot the best bargains by comparing costs and quantities in the store. One consumer service tested a group of college graduate women on shopping trips before and after the introduction of the new law and found that they came up with *fewer* correct choices after the law was passed than they had before.

You pay with a minimum of fuss and a maximum of faith. Yet have you ever wondered whether you really get all you pay for? How do you know there are 5 pounds of apples in a bag labeled 5 pounds? You have to rely on the honesty of those from whom you buy to give you full weight and measure. Probably 95 percent of them do. To deal with the other 5 percent, we have laws, regulations and ordinances empowering federal, state or local officials to make sure a pound's a pound and a pint's a pint.

The U.S. government's inspection and enforcement powers in this field mainly concern canned and packaged foods, meat and poultry. The authority of federal agents applies only to products in interstate commerce and imported products, but it includes such activities as these:

Since 1938 Food and Drug Administration inspectors have had power to deal with labels that lie about contents. Recently, at the FDA's request, authorities seized 800 cases of apple juice in a Santa Fe Springs, California, supermarket. Measurement showed the half-gallon bottles to be 1.1 fluid ounces, or 1.69 percent, short and the gallon bottles to be 3.8 fluid ounces, or 2.97 percent, short.

In San Francisco 83 cases of instant coffee were seized after it was found that the 6-ounce jars contained, on the average, a quarter of an ounce, or 4.2 percent, less than labeled. In Minneapolis a shipment of 49 jars of imitation strawberry preserves turned up as 3.08 percent short, and in Philadelphia bags of lollipops were about one-half ounce, or 9.33 percent, underweight.

The FDA itself doesn't seize goods. After its inspectors have found short-weight items, they ask the court to hold up sale or shipment of the contested goods. At this point the owner has three choices: He can do nothing and the court will give the goods to charity or see that they are destroyed; he can admit in writing that the goods were misrepresented and relabel them under the FDA's supervision; or he can protest the charge in court. Most sellers relabel or surrender contested products, rather than bother with formal court procedures.

Is short weight relatively rare? Probably. But it's hard to pin down the frequency, since weighing and measuring are secondary to the FDA's main job of checking for health violations, and the agency has no figures on its batting average.

The Department of Agriculture inspects meat and meat products. Four thousand inspectors in 1500 federally inspected plants check not only for unwholesome conditions but for short weight, like that detected recently in a 30,000-pound shipment of bacon, which was held up until it was repackaged and labeled properly.

The problem is not always a matter of a missing ounce or two. Occasionally something is added, perhaps a nonedible packing or preserving material, which could go into the weight you pay for. For example, in hams rapidly cured by injecting a curing solution it is legal for the product to have up to 10 percent moisture if the label says "ham, water added." In canned hams the fluid can be 8 percent of the precooked weight.

Certain meat products, such as moist sausage, may shrink in transit from packer to store, so many responsible processors add an ounce or so more than the labeled net weight. Those who don't do this risk being tripped up by state or county inspectors when the products reach their destination.

About 87 percent of the poultry sold off farms undergoes federal

▭▭▭▭▭▭

## A BIT MORE TRUTH PER PACKAGE

Here are some shopping benefits you gain from the 1966 Fair Packaging and Labeling Act. These rules are enforced by the Federal Trade Commission and the Food and Drug Administration.

*Contents.* Labels must show what is in a package and where it came from. The name of the product ("beets," "peaches," and so on) must appear in bold type on the main display panel, as must the name and address of the manufacturer, packer or distributor. Ingredients must be shown in descending order of importance.

*Quantities.* Net weight must be stated in the lower third of the panel in type you can actually read. In packages over 1 pound but under 4 pounds, expect a double statement, as: "Net weight: 50 oz. (3 lb. 2 oz.)" or "Net contents: 46 fluid oz. (1 qt. 14 oz.)."

The idea is to make it easier to compare pounds with pounds, ounces with ounces, when you shop for the best value. If "servings" are mentioned, the number and description of the size of each must appear on the label. Puffs that exaggerate contents—"giant quart," "jumbo pound"—are out.

*Empty space.* Slack fill for some products that require space around the contents for protection is still allowed, as well as space caused by limitations of filling machines. But packages obviously too big for their contents or otherwise deceiving are outlawed.

The object is to prevent such deceptions as the California case in which a national manufacturer of instant mashed potatoes concealed a price increase of 36.6 percent per pound over four years by keeping the package price roughly the same and cutting down on contents, even though each package was labeled "8 servings."

▭▭▭▭▭▭

inspection in 450 slaughtering plants and more than 580 processing and packaging plants. The Poultry Products Inspection Act of 1957 provides some 2000 inspectors to see that packages have accurate labels that include net weight. Violators can be fined up to $3000 on a first conviction.

Poultry that is quick-chilled and packed in ice usually oozes fluid and hence weighs less when it gets to market. To keep this loss to "unavoidable" levels, inspectors limit the amount of water the birds are allowed to soak up in the first place to 4 percent to 8 percent, depending on the type of fowl.

Until recently you paid the meat rate on the total weight of turkeys and chickens that come stuffed with dressing, although the dressing is mostly bread. Now labels must include a "minimum weight" of the bird, too. So if you buy a turkey marked "net weight 10 lb., minimum weight of poultry 8 lb.," you know you are paying for not more than two pounds of dressing.

Nonfederal officials—city, county or state—also police weights and measures, but keep in mind that your own community may not be nearly as vigilant as it should be. The instances that follow show why local enforcement is needed.

Pennsylvania recently checked 600,000 packages, including meat, pastries, soft drinks and tobacco. Sale of 25,100 of these was forbidden because of short weights or misleading labels. Of more than 13 million packages examined in 18,000 lots during one year, 7.8 percent were found to be short weight and were ordered off sale or returned for reweighing and relabeling. Warnings were issued to nine big food chains because of shortages.

In 1966 California county inspectors tested more than 29 million packages and found 6 percent below the net-weight labeling claims. Most of the packages checked, however, held a bit more than the label said.

In 1966–1967 Virginia rejected 11 percent of 371,170 "random weight" packages, that is, goods such as cuts of meat wrapped at the counter. Of regularly packed items, inspectors turned back 1 percent of 25,690,782 packages. Michigan's checkers have found short weights or short measures in prepackaged meats, potato chips, butter, cottage cheese, potatoes, strawberries, cherries.

There are conflicts, cross-purposes and great gaps in the protection offered consumers from place to place. Before the labeling act, for example, nine states didn't even require a packer to show his name on the label. The 1966 Fair Packaging and Labeling Act prevails in states whose labeling laws are weaker than the federal standards. And although all states have passed rules requiring the inspection of packages to determine net weight, budgetary limitations prevent many from doing a thorough job. The extent of inspections varies, too.

If our nonfederal governments cared to do so, they could end this confusion. A model law providing uniformity in weights and measures has been available since 1911. It was devised by the National Conference on Weights and Measures, which is sponsored by the National Bureau of Standards. The model has been revised many times since 1911. The Bureau of Standards circulates copies and stands ready to furnish technical aid to any local official who wants it. Less than half the states have adopted even half the provisions of the model law.

Short weight and short measure, whether unintentional or deliberate, may remove only a penny at a time from your pocket. Yet the total take from everybody in the country must run into millions.

Effective protection might cost $12.5 million a year—or 25 cents a year for your family. If it saved just half of what you now lose to shorting, you'd come out ahead.

CHAPTER 29

## Big Supermarket Is Watching You

*What grocery store operators know about the psychology of buying, and how you can turn their ideas to your own advantage*

As you walk through your neighborhood food store picking up a chicken here, a package of frozen beans there, have you ever had the feeling you're being watched? No, it isn't paranoia; it's just Big Supermarket watching you. These days, food store owners know not only *what* you spend for groceries but *why* you spend what you do and what is influencing you to spend it (see Chapter 26, "When a Woman Goes to Market," page 263). With the fierce competition that exists today among supermarkets, an owner will do all he can to find out what makes you tick, in the hope that once you're inside his store you will spend freely the first time around and return to spend again. He has discovered that the layout of the store influences your spending more than any other factor. Quality and quantity do, of course, count when you're first choosing a place to shop, but once you've made the choice it's often the way the products are displayed that determines how much, or how little, you spend. Let's see how this works.

As soon as you have taken your shopping cart, you are expected to proceed into the aisle along the wall (supermarket men call this the first perimeter aisle), lured there by special displays set up along the front window area. If you know that the items you set out to buy aren't located in this aisle, however, you should not let the brightly colored displays deter you from your path.

Whatever the aisle in which you eventually find yourself, the store manager has done his best to make sure you don't leave it without picking up one or two "extra" items. For example, you will notice that perimeter aisles are dominated by the most potent selling items—produce, meat, dairy, frozen foods and bakery goods. Items on shelves across the aisle must vie for your attention, so they're usually shown off by lighted shelving, special prices, blinking lights or bright signs. You need the milk and butter placed along the wall, but if you find yourself drawn to the opposite wall where the blinking neon sign proclaims a special sale on steamed clams, think twice! Is it the clams you want, or the sign?

To allow for maximum exposure of the merchandise (and maximum spending by you) best-selling items are sometimes displayed across from each other. Lettuce may be placed along the wall, and tomatoes on an opposite counter. Thus, you must crisscross the aisle, and in doing so, your eye falls on something you hadn't thought you needed (and probably don't).

Certain items attract shoppers no matter where in the store they are placed. These ten best customer attracters are: (1) coffee, (2) cookies and crackers, (3) canned vegetables, (4) baking needs, (5) paper products, (6) canned soups, (7) laundry supplies, (8) cereals, (9) sugar, (10) salad dressings and oils.

293

By placing these goods in a middle aisle, near items that don't sell as well, the store manager will attract you to that part of the store. Don't forget, you're in that aisle for one reason; anything else you may select is extra money spent.

The store owner may induce you to buy two items instead of one by placing related products next to each other. You'll probably see canned milk with baby foods, powdered cream with coffee, and syrup near pancake mixes. In one large chain store, pretzels and potato chips were not selling very well. When they were placed near soft drinks, sales doubled. A comparable increase in sales resulted when housewares were placed with laundry supplies. Some items do seem to go hand in hand, but only in your mind; and the store owner, in his new role as supermarket psychologist, is well aware of the thoughts that run through your mind as you run through his store.

Candy and health and beauty aids are considered the top "impulse" items. They are usually placed in those areas of the store where customer traffic is heaviest: candy (on lower shelves, for the convenience of children) with cookies and crackers, beauty aids near the dairy department. Items in special displays at the end of the aisle tend to increase impulse buying. Here you'll usually find special foods, discontinued products, magazines and hosiery.

Do you take a shopping list, or do you decide what you need as you walk through the store? Although home economists feel a list helps in careful planning, some surprising supermarket studies have found that if you're a woman with a list, you'll spend about 35 percent more than your neighbor who "impulse" shops. If your husband goes to the store with a list, he'll spend about 50 percent more than your neighbor's husband who leaves the list home.

Now that you're familiar with some supermarket psychology, see if you can out-psyche your store. Are you attracted to items by pretty colors and bright lights? Keep in mind you're there to buy food. The store would prefer it if you lingered in the aisle (the longer you're in the store, the more money you spend); you have better things to do with your time (and money). But, be warned; as soon as a good number of you have changed your shopping habits, Big Supermarket will be right behind you changing his habits to suit your likes, dislikes and pocketbook.

# SPOT YOURSELF SHOPPING

If you've ever stopped to look at yourself or your neighbors in the supermarket you've probably noticed that no two people shop in exactly the same way. People choose stores and brands for a variety of reasons. Does a newlywed look for the same products as the young married shopper? Does the wife of a blue-collar worker have the same gripes against the supermarket as the high-income shopper? Let's see how good a supermarket spotter you are.

The questions and answers in this quiz are based on a survey made by one of the country's largest publications for supermarket managers.

Circle the letter that best completes the sentence. To check your answers, turn to the next page.

1. The No. 1 complaint against supermarkets by shoppers in all categories is:
   (a) lack of service in the meat department.
   (b) spoiled produce.
   (c) broken eggs.
2. You spend the most money in the supermarket each week. You are a:
   (a) newlywed shopper.
   (b) young married shopper.
   (c) small-town shopper.
3. There are more male shoppers in this group than in any other:
   (a) high-income.
   (b) newlywed.
   (c) blue-collar.

4. As a newlywed shopper you look first for:
   (a) low prices.
   (b) brand names.
   (c) large meat department.
5. You select a store for its large frozen food department. You are a:
   (a) young married shopper.
   (b) newlywed shopper.
   (c) small-town shopper.
6. You usually shop alone. You are a:
   (a) young married shopper.
   (b) high-income shopper.
   (c) newlywed shopper.
7. You are a high-income shopper. Your first requirement when selecting a store is:
   (a) fresh baked goods.
   (b) low prices.
   (c) courteous personnel.
8. You are a small-town shopper. The items you're most likely to head for are:
   (a) frozen foods.
   (b) cooking and baking products.
   (c) delicatessen.
9. You are a young married shopper. Your primary consideration when choosing a store is:
   (a) neatness and cleanliness.
   (b) courteous personnel.
   (c) low prices.
10. You will wait for your regular brand to be in stock rather than switch to another. You are a:
    (a) small-town shopper.
    (b) blue-collar shopper.
    (c) young married shopper.

### Answers to "Spot Yourself Shopping," (page 295)

The answers are based on a survey of various social and income groups, and how they shop in supermarkets.

1. (a) All shoppers surveyed agreed on this point. Supermarkets don't provide enough service in determining cuts of meat and advising what each cut should be used for.

2. (b) With a husband, 2.7 children and herself to feed, the young married spends more each week.

3. (c) Because he is engaged in obviously masculine work (construction, factory, and so on) the blue-collar husband doesn't think it belittling to help out with household chores. He also keeps a tighter rein on the purse strings than any other husband.

4. (b) The newlywed shopper is still insecure about her ability to shop wisely so she chooses familiar brand names.

5. (a) Because a young, growing family requires a good deal of her time, the young married shopper looks first for foods that are the easiest to prepare.

6. (b) The high-income shopper, unlike the average newlywed, has the advantage of a second car, and her children are a bit older than those of the young married shopper, so she can shop alone while the children are in school.

7. (c) The high-income shopper doesn't have to worry about prices. Instead she looks for courteous, but not too friendly, personnel.

8. (b) The wife who lives in a small town usually doesn't work, so she has more time to cook and bake.

9. (a) The young married shopper takes her children to the store with her. She can't waste time tripping over boxes in the aisle or slipping on spilled bottle contents.

10. (a) The small-town shopper is more loyal to her favorite brand than anyone else in any social or income group.

## YOUR NUTRITION CHECKLIST

Important as economy is, your family's health comes first. Shop wisely, but be sure that your regular diet contains elements from each of the four important food groups listed below. The minimum daily servings suggested are based on U.S. Department of Agriculture studies.

• Dairy products (including milk used in cooking, butter, cheese, ice cream): two cups for adults, four cups for teen-agers, two to three cups for children.

• Meats and other proteins (beef, veal, lamb, pork, poultry, fish, eggs; dried beans, peas or nuts as alternatives): two or more servings.

• Vegetables and fruits: dark-green or yellow vegetables, at least one serving every other day; citrus fruits or other vitamin C sources, one serving a day.

• Breads and cereals (including all baked goods, pastas): four servings.

# 6
# CLOTHING FOR THE FAMILY

*Knowing sizes, quality and fabrics—
and where and when to shop—will help
you with this big family expense*

## CHAPTER 30

## Ten Cents
## Out of Every Dollar

*Have a good-looking,*
*exciting wardrobe and still*
*keep within your budget . . .*
*Sound impossible? Not if you*
*start with these basics*

"An economical wardrobe is a basic wardrobe," many people will say, "and you can trim your clothing budget to the bone only by dressing yourself and your family in clothes that are 'safe.'" This is not necessarily so. Your clothes reflect the way you see and feel about yourself: A basic, unexciting wardrobe may mean an unexciting person—and that's not you! The family that's budget-conscious can also be fashion-conscious. The key to dressing well on any income— low, moderate or high—is planning.

When setting up a clothing plan for your family you will, of course, take into account the amount of money you can spend and the way your family lives. Let's assume you've followed the advice in Chapter 4, "The Fine Art of Family Budgeting," page 47; you know what your family's expenses are and how much to set aside for them.

Now, take a few minutes to think about your family's life style: where you work, how you spend your free time, your children's activities. If you're a man who works in a suburban factory or a laboratory you do not need as many suits as a city-based businessman, and you can allot a greater amount of money to sports clothes. If you're a housewife you probably need more casual clothing than a working wife. Do you entertain at home, or do you frequently go to shows and nightclubs? If you do go out often, you'll need more formal clothing than your neighbors who entertain at home. Are your children at an age where they're growing rapidly? If so, you won't want to buy expensive clothing or dressy outfits that they'll probably outgrow after one or two wearings. Do they attend schools where uniforms are required? As you'll have saved money on everyday school clothes, you may want to splurge on a few "good" items to make them feel stylish when they're out of uniform. As for babies, it's easy to find pretty, inexpensive clothing, and if you keep the baby's clothing budget down you won't be too upset if he outgrows the new outfit before he's had a chance to wear it.

Fitting the clothes to your family's life should not necessarily lead to conformity. If the women in your neighborhood wear slacks to the supermarket, but you find slacks unbecoming, by all means wear something else. You'll look better and feel more comfortable. If your husband likes brightly colored sport shirts, and the other men in your area have more conservative taste, don't stop him from expressing his individuality. Maybe he'll start a new trend in the neighborhood. Remember, fit the clothes not only to your family's life as a whole but also to the individual needs and tastes of each member of your family.

## Judging Good Workmanship

Get to know quality. Judging workmanship is an important part of an overall clothing plan and will save you time and money. Well-made clothing lasts longer, fits better and is generally more attractive than clothing of poorer quality. In other words, you get what you pay for. If you have faith in the integrity of the stores where you shop, you can be sure of getting quality clothing. Chapter 32, "Smart-Money Clothes Shopping," page 312, tells you about the different types of stores and the kinds of clothing you can find in them.

Once you've determined the quality of the store, get to know the general signs of good workmanship that mark quality clothing:

1. Seams should be wide enough, at least one inch, to allow for letting out and strain (left). A seam sewed too close to the edge of the fabric will rip out easily.

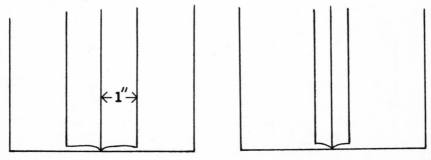

2. Thread should be matched to the color of the garment.

3. Patterns (stripes, checks, plaids) should be precisely matched where they join (left). Check all seams.

4. Stitching along collar and hem should be even (left).

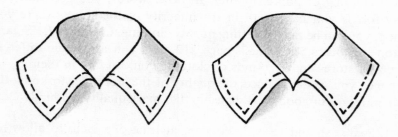

5. Inside seam edges should be finished off neatly (left) and not left frayed (center) or pinked (right).

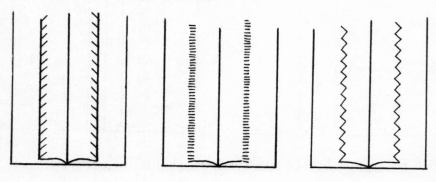

6. Dresses and skirts should have a two-inch hem (left). One inch that may then be let down, with a one-inch hem remaining.

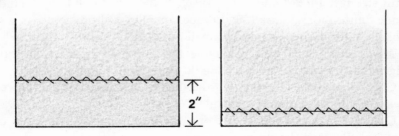

7. Make sure that the teeth of a zipper do not show and that the stitching is even (left).

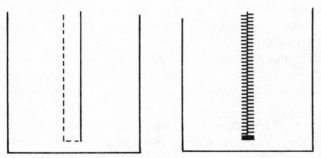

8. Material of quality has resiliency. Squeeze the material; a resilient fabric will feel springy and resume its shape quickly when released.

These are the general signs of quality workmanship. Let's look now at some specific advice on selecting clothes for men, women and children.

*Men's slacks and jackets.* If the store does not have the proper size slacks, buy them one size larger and have them taken in, rather than buying the smaller size that probably can't be let out.

Slacks should have backing within the waistband to stiffen it and keep it from rolling and wrinkling.

Jackets should be *fully* lined, including the sleeves, and the linings should be stitched down to prevent sagging after dry cleaning.

Handmade buttonholes are a sign of quality, since they are made with stronger thread and won't ravel. If the tag doesn't say "handmade buttonholes," ask the salesperson. On well-made coats and jackets, buttons are secured by small opposite buttons on the inside.

*Men's and boys' shirts.* Examine the inside of pockets for raw edges that may ravel; pockets should have reinforcing at edges.

Check the label to be sure that the shirt is Sanforized or guaranteed to shrink no more than 1 percent.

Quality shirts have placket fronts, a reinforcing double layer of material. Buttons should be sewn through both layers.

Pearl buttons are of better quality than plastic.

*Hosiery and lingerie.* Proportioned stockings fit better and last longer because the material is subjected to less strain. When you buy them, give the salesperson your full shoe size—length and width. In a self-service store the label on the hosiery package will have both stocking and shoe size.

If your stockings develop runs easily, try mesh hose. "Runresistant" mesh stockings do run under strain, but not as easily as nonmesh hose. "Runproof" mesh stockings usually won't run, but may develop small holes.

The denier of a stocking is the weight and thickness of each thread; the lower the denier, the sheerer the stocking.

Ask the salesperson if the seams in panties are guaranteed not to ravel. When buying knit panties, ask about runs and shrinkage.

Thermal underwear for both women and men is made of a special knit with innumerable tiny pockets that trap air and provide good insulation.

*Ladies' dresses.* Lined garments hold their shape. Newer fabrics have bonded linings—the lining material is uniformly attached to the inside of the dress. (For more on fabrics, see Chapter 33, page 326.)

Examine labels for fiber content and cleaning instructions.

If you want a long-wearing garment, don't select fragile material.

Check to see that no buttons are missing. Quality dresses usually come with extra buttons.

*Children's clothing.* Many knit and terry cloth stretch suits will fit an infant from birth through the first year or longer.

You can cut costs by purchasing two-piece playsuits and rompers that will expand from birth size to size $2\frac{1}{2}$ years simply by moving the buttons.

When you buy rompers, suits or any garments with snaps at the crotch, look for models with two sets of snaps which will give you an extra inch or two when the second set of snaps is used.

Some wool, cotton and synthetic coats and dresses can be made larger by pulling out or snipping a thread in the sleeves and in skirt hems to release another inch or so of prehemmed material.

Remember, when looking for ways to set up a sensible and realistic clothing budget, bear in mind these points: Plan your family's wardrobe around the way you live and around your family's needs. Know quality: Get to be a judge of well-made clothing that will look and wear better and last longer.

By following these guidelines you should find that you're able to save substantial amounts and keep your clothing budget at a reasonable level.

## SELF-HELP FOR THE YOUNGER SET

When you select your children's clothes, you look for a good buy and for things that are attractive, but there's another feature many mothers don't consider that can ·make life easier for both mother and child. Remember to look for clothes designed to make it simpler for the child to dress himself and become independent. Some garments have self-help features. Clothes with front zipper fastenings are easy for a child to handle. Blanket sleepers come with front zippers, as do coveralls, overalls, jump suits, playsuits and winter and cool-weather jackets. Ski pants with a zipper down the front permit a young child to step into them or to sit on the floor to begin pulling them on.

Dresses that button down the back or side, or have tiny buttons in front, are difficult for a little girl to handle. Select dresses with large, attractive buttons down the front that she can master quickly and easily.

Cotton or synthetic knit outer sport shirts for boys or girls can be obtained with a zipper front closing. Two-piece outfits for boys and girls with elastic in skirt or shorts can be stepped into without your help.

Self-help garments are no more expensive than similar garments without these features, and they'll give you a little leisure and your children a feeling of satisfaction and independence in developing their new-found skills.

## CHAPTER 31

## What You Should Know About Sizes

*Confused by labels such as boys', girls', chubby, petite? Here's a brief look at the mysteries of measurement*

Have you ever bought a pair of shoes too small because the salesman assured you they would "give"? The trouble is that they probably didn't, and after a couple of painful days of cramped, aching feet you decided not to wear them again. Or did the man of the house buy a suit that barely buttoned around the midriff because he planned to take off a few inches soon? Chances are it's still hanging in the closet, waiting for those inches to disappear.

Experiences like these have doubtless taught you the importance of good fit. Garments that don't fit are uncomfortable to wear and never look right, regardless of price. And because they either require costly alterations or tend to wear out rapidly, they can wreck your clothing budget. Proper fit is as important as good workmanship to the thrifty buyer.

To be sure of getting a good fit, allow time to try on suits, slacks, dresses, sweaters, and so on, at the store. Examine yourself critically —preferably in a full-length, three-way mirror—front view, back and sides. Look for straight, smooth lines. If alterations are necessary, be sure there is enough material to let out seams or lengthen the hemline without spoiling the basic lines. Alterations can be costly, too, so be sure they are worth it.

Knowing clothing sizes is the first step to a good fit. In general, sizes are determined by body measurements and overall build. The exact proportions, however, often vary from manufacturer to manufacturer and from style to style, especially for women. You may, for example, wear a size 10 dress with a full skirt but find that you need a size larger in a sheath dress or slacks. Few people are a "perfect" size anything. Use sizes as a guide rather than an absolute.

### Women's Clothing

To assure comfort in the clothes you select always sit down and move your arms in several directions to be sure there is no tightness or pull. If possible, walk around for a while and view the garment in a full-length mirror at some distance. This is a good indication of what it will look like "in action." The lines should be smooth without binding or pinching anywhere. If you have long hair that hangs over your neckline, raise it to check for the fit at the collar, neckline and shoulder. The waist, if defined, should feel neither high nor low.

Always take another look at your purchase to make sure you like the way it looks at a second glance. If this second look requires ten minutes at the mirror, chances are you will never be pleased with it. Once you have found a fit that suits you, look for the same label in the future. Styles may change, but the manufacturer's basic measurements usually remain the same.

Wear the same type of foundation garments that you will wear with the clothes you buy. Different brassieres and girdles can give clothes a different fit. When dress shopping, always wear a slip and a dress that is easy to get in and out of.

Wear shoes with heels of the same height as the ones you intend to wear with the garment. A difference of an inch in heel height can make a dress, coat or skirt look too long or short.

Don't buy a dress that is either too small or large in hopes that you will diet or grow into it. Weight loss or gain, even if you achieve it, can change figure proportions considerably.

## The Rules of Good Fit

Each article of clothing has its own rules of good fit. When you try on a dress, suit, sweater or other garment, here's what to look for:

*Dresses.* Women's sizes can be extremely confusing and mysterious. Some women can wear both junior and misses' sizes, while others require a petite or junior petite. Still others save money by shopping in the teen department. Where do you fit in? To help you determine what size you are, here is a brief description of the different sizes:

1. Junior (sizes 3 to 15): for women of short to medium height (5 feet 4 inches to 5 feet 6 inches) with a youthful, short-waisted figure; small, high bustline; small, defined waist; rounded hips. A junior size 9 dress is normally designed for a woman with these measurements: 32-inch bust, $23\frac{1}{2}$-inch waist, 34-inch hips and $15\frac{1}{2}$-inch back-waist length.

2. Junior petite (sizes 3 to 15): for short women (5 feet to 5 feet 4 inches) with a very small frame and the same proportions as juniors.

3. Misses' (sizes 6 to 20): for women of average height (5 feet 5 inches to 5 feet 8 inches) with well-proportioned figures, longer waists than juniors. The standard measurements for a misses' size 10 are $32\frac{1}{2}$-inch bust, 24-inch waist, $34\frac{1}{2}$-inch hips and 16-inch back waist.

4. Petite (sizes 8 to 20): for short women (under 5 feet 5 inches) with the same proportions as misses.

5. Tall (sizes 8 to 20): for tall women (5 feet 8 inches and over) with longer waist and skirt lengths than misses.

6. Half size (sizes $10\frac{1}{2}$ to $26\frac{1}{2}$): for short women (under 5 feet 5 inches) with short waists and fuller busts, waists and hip lines than juniors. The measurements for a size $10\frac{1}{2}$ dress are 33-inch bust, 26-inch waist, 35-inch hips and 15-inch back waist.

7. Women's (sizes 38 to 52): for medium to tall women (5 feet 5 inches to 5 feet 9 inches) with well-proportioned, mature figures. The clothes are fuller through the bust, waist and hips and longer-waisted than half sizes. A size 38 dress measures 42-inch bust, 34-inch waist, 44-inch hips, $17\frac{1}{4}$-inch back waist.

*Coats, suits and skirts.* Suits and skirts are usually bought in the same size as your dresses. Coats, however, may be different from your dress size, normally a size smaller. Be sure to check all angles of fit in a mirror. Coats and suit jackets must be loose enough to fit smoothly over apparel worn under them, yet not so loose that they don't look neat. There should be no strain across the shoulder or in the armhole when you fold your arms or reach upward. Full-length sleeves should reach the large bone on the wrist as you bend your arm. Be sure the coat or suit jacket fastens smoothly without strain or pull, with enough overlap in front. Coats should fall in a smooth line from the shoulders, unless they are fitted or belted. Full-length coats must be long enough to hide any dress, suit or skirt you plan to wear underneath.

Skirts, when sold as separates, may be marked according to either dress size or waist measurement. A skirt should always fit smoothly with comfortable ease at the hips, and crosswise wrinkles should not form over the front. The waistband must fit snugly but comfortably and hold the skirt in place. In most cases pleats ought to hang perpendicular to the floor and remain closed when you stand still.

*Sweaters and blouses.* These are usually sized according to bust measurement, although some manufacturers size blouses the same as dresses. Sweaters are purchased one or two sizes larger than blouses. A sweater which is the proper size will wear better than one that is too snug, especially in the bust line. Cardigan styles should stay neatly closed between buttons without gapping. Be sure pullovers go over the head easily; if they are stretched too much, the yarns at the neck will break. Shoulders should be wide enough, but not sag. Ribbing at the neck, bottom and sleeves should fit snugly.

Blouses ought to fit comfortably at the neckline and through the bust and shoulders with no strain when the arms are moved. Sleeves must fit freely with no binding at armholes; long sleeves should cover wristbones when elbows are bent. Be sure that tails are long enough to stay tucked into your skirt, slacks or shorts.

*Sportswear.* Pay special attention to fit when you shop for slacks, pantsuits or culottes. You want these garments to look neat and attractive, yet allow plenty of freedom for vigorous activity. It is important to try them on and test the fit by sitting.

Swimsuits may come in dress sizes or be marked according to bust measure. Try them on over panties only. Allow for a little stretching out when the suit is wet, but don't buy one so tight that it cuts into your legs or underarms. See that it is long enough and doesn't ride up too much. By law swimsuits are not returnable, so be very careful in your selection.

Slacks and shorts usually come in dress sizes and feature a variety of styles. Experiment to find the most flattering length of shorts for your particular proportions. A panty girdle can make a world of difference in the way you look in slacks or shorts. The important thing is to be honest in evaluating your figure and always consider the appearance—the rear view is as important as the front.

*Brassieres, girdles, slips and hosiery,* if properly fitting, improve the appearance of your figure as well as the fit of your clothes.

To determine the correct size brassiere, measure yourself before you shop or have the clerk measure you. First determine your chest measurement by placing a measuring tape above your bust under your arms. This figure will be your bra size. If it is an odd number, buy the next largest size. To determine the cup size, measure the fullest parts of the bust (wearing a bra). Then subtract the chest measurement from the bust measurement. Consult the following chart for correct cup size:

| | |
|---|---|
| If bust is the same as chest | Cup is AAA |
| If bust is up to ½ in. larger than chest | Cup is AA |
| If bust is over ½ in. and up to 1½ in. larger | Cup is A |
| If bust is over 1½ in. and up to 2½ in. larger | Cup is B |
| If bust is over 2½ in. and up to 3½ in. larger | Cup is C |
| If bust is over 3½ in. and up to 4½ in. larger | Cup is D |
| If bust is over 4½ in. and up to 5½ in. larger | Cup is DD |
| If bust is slightly fuller than DD cup | Cup is F |

Always try on a brassiere before you buy it. It should fit smoothly at the front and back; should not ride up, squeeze or poke. The straps should never bind.

Girdles are sized by waist measurement. If your waist measures 22 to 23 inches, your size is extra small; 24 to 26 inches, small; 27 to 28 inches, medium; 29 to 30 inches, large; and 31 to 32 inches, extra large. When you try on a panty girdle, the waistband should sit right at the waist (unless it is a high-waist style). The panty crotch should be at a natural level for walking comfort. Test for comfort by sitting, bending and stooping.

Slips are sized by a combination of bust or waist measurement and length. Adjustable straps are used to make minor adjustments in the slip's height under the arms, fit over the bust and length.

A slip should be at least one inch shorter than your dress. For sheer dresses the slip should overlap the top of the hem so there won't be a visible gap between hem top and slip bottom.

Slip lengths fall into three different groups: petite or short, 5 feet 3 inches and under; medium or average, 5 feet 4 inches to 5 feet 6 inches; long or tall, 5 feet 7 inches and over. Waist sizes are: small, 22 inches to 24 inches; medium, 24 inches to 26 inches; large, 26 inches and up.

A slip should cover the bra but not show at the neckline of a dress or at the armhole of a sleeveless dress. It should fit smoothly over the bust to ensure a neat line, and smoothly but easily over the hips. If it hangs loosely or bunches around the top, it is too large. Horizontal wrinkles over the hip area mean that the slip is too tight. To check fit, grasp the skirt of the slip on either side at a point seven inches below the waist and pull up to the waist. When you let go, the slip should fall easily into place over the hips with no tugging. Adjustable straps don't compensate for a poorly fitting slip. If the straps must be pulled up very high in order to have the desired length, other parts of the slip may not fit properly.

Briefs and bikini panties are generally sized according to hip measurement in inches. The chart below tells what size to buy.

| If hips measure | 31–32 | 33–34 | 35–36 | 37–38 | 39–40 | 41–42 | 43–44 | 45–48 | 49–50 |
|---|---|---|---|---|---|---|---|---|---|
| Brief size is | 3 | 4 | 5 | 6 | 7 | 8 | 9 | 10 | 11 |

Stockings and panty hose are usually sold by leg length or height. Manufacturers often include a chart on the package to help you select the correct length. Unfortunately, "medium" in one brand may be shorter or longer than "medium" in another. Since stockings are not returnable after you have tried them on, trial and error is the only way to find the best fit.

## Men's Clothing

When a man shops for clothes he should be as particular about fit as a woman. He should try on coats, suits, slacks and sports jackets at the store and examine them from all angles in a three-way mirror. He should also try on shirts and sportswear (if not in the store, then at home before wearing them). Here are signs of good fit.

*Suit jackets.* These are sized by chest measurement (35 to 46 inches). The collar should hug the back of the neck, with about a quarter of an inch of shirt showing above it. The jacket should fit smoothly across shoulders and back. The length varies with personal preference and styling. Sleeve length should allow for about a quarter of an inch of the shirt cuff to show. The armholes should be comfortable without binding under the arm. If the jacket hikes up when you raise your arm, the armhole is too tight. Lapels should lie flat.

*Trousers and slacks.* These are sold by waist size (28 to 42 inches) and inseam length (28 to 34 inches). (The inseam is the inner leg seam from ankle to crotch.) Trousers and slacks that fit properly should hang straight in the back with a slight break in the front crease. They should be full enough in the crotch, seat and thighs for comfort in sitting. Wrinkles under the hips indicate that the crotch is too long. The waist should be comfortably snug, and any pleats should lie flat.

*Shirts.* Shirt size is determined by neck and arm lengths. If a shirt fits well, the collar will fit closely but not too snugly. The sleeve should cover the wristbone when the arm is bent. There should be no wrinkles or signs of strain across the back or chest. And the shirt-tail should be long enough to stay tucked in.

Men's sizes are far less confusing than women's sizes. All you need to know are your measurements. Slacks come in different cuts designed for fuller or more slender builds. Full-cut slacks, for example, are roomier in the seat, thigh and leg areas than regular-cut slacks. Slim-cut slacks are designed for a close, narrow fit. Men's stores usually have three main departments: men's, boys' and university. While sizes in the boys' shop are smaller, there is no difference in size between the men's and university merchandise. The difference is in price and style; clothes in the men's shop are more expensive and conservative than those in the university shop.

## Infants' and Children's Sizes

New and expectant mothers, as well as friends and grandmothers, are often bewildered by infants' sizes. To unravel the mystery of infant sizes, consult this chart. Remember, go by height and weight rather than age. And pass the information along to Grandma.

| If height is | up to 25 in. | 25½–27½ in. | 28–29½ in. | 30–32 in. | 32½–35 in. | 35½–37 in. |
|---|---|---|---|---|---|---|
| If weight is | 11–14 lbs. | 15–19 lbs. | 20–23 lbs. | 24–26 lbs. | 27–29 lbs. | 30–32 lbs. |
| Order size | 3 mos. | 6–9 mos. | 12 mos. | 18 mos. | 24 mos. | 30 mos. |

As any parent who has ever had to make returns has learned, children are the most difficult to fit correctly. They grow at uneven intervals—often, it seems, just after they've acquired new clothes. Most children's clothes are also sized by height and weight rather than age. This is true of little girls' and little boys' clothing, as well as of infants' and toddlers', except for shoes, socks and infants' pants and shirts. Sizes for older girls and boys are based on height and hip measurement for girls and inseam length for boys. Besides the regular sizes, there are slim and husky sizes for boys and girls.

Subteen and teen sizes are designed for junior high and high school girls whose figures are at an in-between stage—no longer a little girl's but not yet a woman's. These sizes are determined by bust, waist and hip measurements.

No doubt you are often tempted to buy extra-roomy clothes for your growing children, but don't make the mistake of buying things so large that they are uncomfortable to wear. Because a child's growth rate is unpredictable, take his measurements before you shop to be sure he still fits a particular size. If your child cannot try on the article at the store, be sure he tries it before he wears it and before you have removed the various tags and labels. Be careful when you buy a new brand because each manufacturer has his own way of sizing. If possible, buy a brand you know will fit, or measure an unknown brand for size with a tape measure.

## Shoes for the Family

For all members of the family, nothing is more important than buying shoes that fit properly. Shoes that don't fit not only are painful to wear but also can cause lasting damage to the feet. To be sure of getting the best fit, have your feet measured each time you buy shoes. Buy shoes in mid- or late afternoon; feet tend to swell during the day and a shoe that fits perfectly in the morning may pinch later in the day. Warm temperatures also cause feet to swell.

Children's shoes are especially important because their foot bones are still pliable and can be permanently damaged by ill-fitting shoes. Because children's feet grow at uneven intervals, you should check the size every month or two, and be sure at the same time that socks are the right size. The chart below gives the average rate of change of children's shoe sizes.*

| If age of child is......... | 1–6 yrs. | 6–10 yrs. | 10–12 yrs. | 12–15 yrs. | 15 yrs. and over |
|---|---|---|---|---|---|
| Size changes every........ | 1–2 mos. | 2–3 mos. | 3–4 mos. | 4–5 mos. | 6 mos. or more |

*Chart reprinted courtesy of the National Footwear Institute

Shoes that fit properly should be slightly longer than the big toe. Toes should lie flat, and the widest part of the foot should fit the widest part of the shoe. The heel should fit snugly without cutting, and the sides should not gap as you walk. The shoe and foot should bend together as you walk. Don't buy a tight pair of shoes hoping they will stretch. They will never fit properly. Never wear another person's shoes; they have become molded to his foot, not yours.

If you take the time to be sure of a good fit before you buy any article of clothing, you can save yourself time and money and be sure of always looking your best. Be honest as well as critical in evaluating your appearance. Learn the standards of good fit for each item in the family's wardrobe. Why waste your money on baggy pants and skimpy overcoats when you may find a good fit for less?

CHAPTER 32

## Smart-Money Clothes Shopping

*Clothes prices are high
and likely to get worse.
To get the most for your money,
it pays to know the ropes*

Question: What's going up and up with no ceiling in sight? Answer: As any family knows, prices of clothing. Compared with the 1957–59 base years, according to the Consumer Price Index, clothing costs are over 20 percent higher, and there's no sign of leveling off. We spend more than a staggering $42 billion annually for clothes and— down at the family level—about ten cents of every dollar goes to pay for the family wardrobe.

For greatest economy, where should the 10 percent go? Should it be spent in department stores, boutiques, discount stores or the neighborhood shop? That old problem, "I don't have a thing to wear," has a new twist: "Where shall I shop to get my money's worth?"

Unfortunately there is no single quick and easy answer. These days clothes are found everywhere from men's high-fashion boutiques to supermarket counters next to the tomatoes and the canned soups. So where you should go to buy a particular item depends on what the item is and who it is for. It also depends on whether you want to pay cash or use credit; whether you want to buy a brand name or not; whether you need to be fitted; whether you want the assurance of a guarantee or a liberal return policy. If you're going to get the most for your clothing dollar it will pay you to acquire some expertise in the kinds of stores you can shop in, and their advantages and disadvantages.

## Department Stores

One choice is the traditional department store and its not so traditional branch in the suburbs. This is the place to shop when you are looking for a wide range of items and price lines. You may have a daughter, for instance, who is at an awkward age and hard to fit. In a department store you can start in the budget department, and if the dresses there don't fit, proceed to the sportswear, subteen or junior miss shops where the dresses may be cut differently (see Chapter 31, page 304, for information on sizes). You will find brand-name merchandise in all departments. You can also count on the services of a salesgirl, in the better departments at least; use your charge account; be confident that the store will make an exchange or a refund if you have second thoughts; and have your purchase delivered. If the dress shrinks when it's supposedly shrinkproof the store will make an adjustment. Department stores have survived and prospered partly because they do offer these services and because they value their reputations and the goodwill of their customers strongly enough to maintain high standards. They also buy in large quantities, especially if they are members of a chain of stores or a buying group, and can insist that the manufacturers who supply them maintain certain standards of quality.

In recent years, however, the department stores have run into vigorous competition from the discount stores that invaded the clothing field after impressive successes in selling appliances. The department stores have had to charge for some deliveries and to adopt self-service techniques in lower-price departments in order to meet the discount prices. But they are still the place where you will find the greatest variety of merchandise, credit plans and services, though not always the lowest prices.

There is a difference, however, between the main center-city store and the suburban branches. Because the branch stores are smaller and serve a more homogeneous population they usually don't have the variety of merchandise that typifies the center-city store. The suburban branch managers have considerable leeway in selecting stock for their stores. Since of course they choose what they think their customers need and want, their clothes are geared more to the casual, suburban way of life. So if you really want to see *every* dress, your best bet is still the main store.

## Large Chain Stores

Chain stores are other old-timers in outfitting the family, often by way of the postman rather than the salesgirl. The three major chains —Sears Roebuck, J. C. Penney and Montgomery Ward—all sell from their mail-order catalogues as well as from their local stores. They were once the specialists in selling to the farmer and the farmer's daughter and people in small towns, who had no place to shop nearby. Now that the farmer and his daughter have become as style-conscious as the city slicker, the chains are trying to keep up with their taste for fashion while still maintaining the low prices for which they have always been known.

To an even greater degree than the giant department stores, the huge purchasing power of the chains means that manufacturers court them as customers and will make shirts, stockings or sportswear to the chain stores' specifications. Very often manufacturers whose products are nationally advertised, very well known and price-fixed make almost identical items for one of the major chains. The chain sells the product under its own brand name at a lower price than the nationally advertised brand.

In recent years some national chains that used to emphasize selling their clothes by mail have been opening more and more retail stores. These stores compete with department stores by offering the latest fashions, fitting rooms, alterations on men's clothes and the other services that were once the exclusive bailiwick of the department and specialty stores. Since the chains are huge and their clothes are mass-produced, their stores are not the place to shop for the one-of-a-kind fashion—but they are a place to get good values.

In several sections of the country there are local or regional chains that are smaller versions of the big ones and that run their business in the same way. They do not, of course, carry the same weight with manufacturers, nor do they have the same testing facilities that the large chains employ to ensure quality in their merchandise. But they are still important buyers and have considerable purchasing power. They compete with the larger chains and are worth looking into for good buys. This is true too for the smaller mail-order chains without retail stores, particularly those that restrict themselves to a narrow range of merchandise, such as men's sportswear or women's casual dresses. There is no way to judge the quality of either these chain stores or mail-order houses except to try one pair of pants, or one dress, and see how it fits and wears.

## Pros and Cons of Discount Stores

The discount stores are the gadfly of the retail business. These operations got their start after World War II by selling brand-name appliances through stores in the low-rent districts. They could offer the appliances at cheaper prices because they cut out such frills as delivery, attractive store decor, salespeople and services. This same philosophy has been carried over into their retailing of clothing. They sometimes carry name-brand merchandise at lower cost than their competitors, but many manufacturers refuse to sell to discounters and the stores have been forced to turn to less well-known manufacturers, to imports or to buying the odd lots of a supplier left over from his regular stock. Like the other stores, they have manufacturers who will make private-label products for them, and their brands are sometimes good buys.

A discount store is not the place to shop if you want information about sizes or durability—when there are clerks they are not expected to, and usually do not, have much information about the merchandise, except for the price. Since much of their merchandise cannot be tried on, discount stores usually have return privileges. However, their procedures on returns are often cumbersome and time-consuming, and definitely a drawback for the lunch-hour shopper or the mother who takes the kids along when she shops. Within their price range, however, discount stores compare favorably with the bargain basements and the budget shops of the department and chain stores. And one of their big advantages is their hours—in many communities the discount stores, often located in shopping centers, are open long after the other stores have closed.

## Advantages of the Specialty Shop

In contrast to the retailers who emphasize mass appeal, there is the specialty store. As its name implies, it doesn't try to appeal to a broad audience but aims instead for a distinct clientele. Even if the individual stores are part of a chain, as they sometimes are, the merchandise is distinctive and appeals to the same kind of shopper, whether she lives in San Francisco, New York or Atlanta. The store's reputation may have been built on high standards of workmanship or a particular fashion image—young clothes or classic clothes, for instance, with emphasis on good fabrics and fine tailoring rather than the latest style. The store buys from manufacturers who understand the store's market and will meet its demand for clothing that satisfies its customers' taste.

The specialty store that emphasizes classic clothes could be the place to shop for the businessman or woman who wants a suit or coat that will be properly fitted, last for several seasons, hold its shape and always be correct. The coat or suit can be worth its higher price in length of wear and the assurance that it looks and fits well. The higher-priced specialty store is also the place to find styles that have not been mass-produced, if you are willing to pay for a certain amount of exclusivity (but don't count on never meeting someone in "your" dress at a party). Specialty stores usually offer most of the services of department stores.

In addition to these comparatively big operations there are many independent store operators that specialize in shoes, dresses, women's lingerie, men's clothing or women's hosiery. Though they don't have the advantage of big business's buying power, they do have other attractions. When they specialize in one item, such as hosiery, for instance, they too can stock a private brand, or seconds and irregulars, and offer real value. If a store sells only shoes its salespeople can become experts in fitting, especially important for children's shoes. And since the store is local, the staff gets to know your needs and can give personalized service.

## The Boutique

A recent development in retail stores is the boutique. The boutiques originated in a few very elegant and expensive women's specialty stores. They were small shops in the main store, set aside to feature unusual fashions, imports or gift items. Now individual boutiques are springing up in many major cities. Their owners may be designers themselves and even have their own workrooms for producing individualized clothes. They may feature the clothes of one designer or buy from only a few manufacturers. The boutique sometimes offers only a few pieces in each style but is willing to make up any of its styles in the customer's choice of fabrics. It often has unusual accessories—belts, scarfs, jewelry and hats—to go with the dresses. The dresses are not necessarily high-priced—they can start at under $40—but some boutiques carry $1000 clothes as well. The newest development is boutiques for men, featuring prominent designers and high-fashion accessories. A boutique is not the place to shop for a dress or suit to wear to the office; it is a place to try when you want to splurge and get something individual and distinctive—a treat that you deserve for good household management elsewhere!

## Stores That Sell "Irregulars"

A special kind of local store operates in the New York metropolitan area and is spreading into other parts of the United States. This is the store that sells quality "irregulars," that is, goods that better-grade manufacturers have left over after they have completed a selling season. The irregulars may be well-known brand-name merchandise, such as men's sport shirts or women's blouses, that the manufacturer cannot sell to his regular buyers, who want to preserve their stores' reputation for carrying complete and fresh stocks of the latest merchandise. The irregulars may also include designs that buyers rejected as potential duds and on which the manufacturers are trying to recoup a part of their investment. The lot may also include a few samples used to display the manufacturer's line to out-of-town buyers and some merchandise that is not quite perfect.

Regardless of the source of the merchandise, the irregulars store sells its merchandise at well below the prices the dresses, shirts or suits would command if they were perfect, part of a complete range of sizes or in popular rather than off-beat colors. A nationally advertised brand of man's sport shirt, in a complete range of sizes, colors and styles, that might, for instance, cost $12 in a men's store, will sell for half that in an irregulars store, but in just a few styles or sizes. (Some manufacturers insist that these stores remove their labels before the merchandise is put on sale.)

Not surprisingly these stores offer no services—no alterations, no deliveries, no credit, no layaways, no gift wrapping. Some are very lenient about returns; others, which sell fashion goods only, permit no returns. And since they operate on a very low profit margin and have fairly limited stock they don't spend much of their budget on advertising. If one opens in your neighborhood you may read about it on opening day; afterwards ads will be rare. Usually, one woman tells another about bargain stores like this. If you haven't heard of any in your neighborhood, try looking in your classified telephone directory under women's apparel, since such stores are more likely to feature clothes for women, even though they also have some clothes for men and children.

If you know your family's sizes, have lots of time and don't need a dress in a hurry for a special occasion, you can find a bargain in one of these stores. It's a good place to look in on first, since you can always go on to a regular store. But because the labels are often removed and you don't have the store's reputation behind the merchandise, you must be able to recognize quality or you may not end up with a bargain. (Chapter 30, "Ten Cents Out of Every Dollar," page 298, gives you some hints on how to tell quality.)

Finally, added to all these stores are the other places where you can buy items of clothing: women's underwear in the variety store and the five-and-ten; slippers and socks in the supermarket; stockings in drugstores and from vending machines. Here, since quality varies, you can only learn by trial and error.

## Some General Guidelines

Clothing retailers themselves complain that they find the clothing picture confusing, so it's no surprise that consumers are bewildered about the best place to shop. It's impossible to set up any rigid rules, but there are some general guidelines for smart-money shopping which are easy to apply.

If you haven't already done so, start by making a nonshopping tour of the stores in your neighborhood, comparing prices, quality, goods and services. Don't overlook the stores you have not visited in some time. Retailing is a volatile business, and changes in management and merchandising are frequent. You may find, for instance, that a children's shop that never carried the sizes you wanted now has them.

Don't confine yourself, however, only to the stores in your neighborhood. This applies particularly to chain stores, which are not all alike even though they are all operated by a single parent company. Newer stores or stores in the wealthier neighborhoods may carry a more complete stock or better-quality lines than others.

Get to know brand names so that you can compare prices and quality among the well-known brands and between brand-name and private-label merchandise. Learn the brands that a store specializes in, so that when it holds a sale you can tell what merchandise is its own stock marked down and what has been brought in for the sale only. Discover which labels in such standard items as underwear, stockings, shirts, blue jeans are best for your family—for fit and for wear—and then save shopping time by reordering them. Also find out which store's private-label merchandise is as good as comparable nationally advertised brands, which must sell for more to cover the cost of advertising.

Once you have acquired this knowledge about its stock, you should proceed to learn something about a store's operation, particularly about its policy on sales. Sales are a merchandising technique, and to take advantage of them you have to follow a buying technique. Store buyers operate on clothing budgets just as you do. They have to have money "in the bank" in order to place orders for bathing suits while the snow is piling up outside the manufacturer's showroom. One way of getting this money is to have an end-of-season sale, which not only raises cash for the new merchandise but also makes space for the clothes coming in. The stock in the end-of-season sales is merchandise that can't be carried over until the next season— winter coats, men's short-sleeve shirts, flannel nightgowns.

## Saving on Season Sales

There is a rhythm in the retail business—an ebb and flow of quantities of goods in stores—whose highs and lows are due partly to consumer demand, partly to retailers' habits and partly to the reasonable judgment of the retailer.

The intelligent, informed consumer can use this rhythm to her own advantage if she acquaints herself with some of the basic seasonal determinants of retail clothing supply and shrewdly tailors her purchases to the level of goods in the various stores that she patronizes.

She can do this by means of two kinds of analysis, strategic and tactical.

She can use strategy by timing her purchases to the fluctuations of retail supply. For example, don't buy a famous-name bathing suit in June; buy one on sale in July.

The wise shopper can buy tactically by carefully examining the offerings in the retail store. Don't impulsively buy the first bathing suit you see (unless you fall in love with it) but shop through the whole department. Tactical buying demands only a normal supply of common sense and a willingness to shop through a store—both qualities that American women seem to be born with.

Strategic buying, though, requires a knowledge of stores' buying habits that few American women possess and even fewer use.

Stores' buying processes are simple. They are based on climate, season and calendar. Spring coats and suits are shown in great numbers just before Easter. In those years when Easter is early, don't buy beforehand; buy right after Easter, when the inevitable markdowns have been made.

Of course, there are many times when the stores make special efforts to get you to buy. The smart strategic shopper will take advantage of their efforts, such as the traditional annual promotions: January white sales; Columbus Day, Veterans Day and Election Day women's coat sales; back-to-school children's clothing sales; and so on.

Whenever you are shopping, shop carefully. Below are clothing items in nine categories, each with valuable tips to guide you in planning your purchase:

1. *Children's clothing.* Holes in the knees and sleeves suddenly too short are, of course, the big factors here, but the calendar can still be important. The best buying time in the back-to-school period is August, just as soon as the stores start to advertise. The children's departments will be as jammed as they are in the rush around Labor Day, but the stocks will still be in good shape. In the long run you are likely to save most by being able to buy exactly what you want in the proper sizes, allowing for growth, rather than by shopping in the peak period or waiting for late-September markdowns.

2. *Dress fabrics.* Watch for traditional sales in January and Febru-

---

## TYPICAL SELLING PLOYS AND HOW TO AVOID THEM

If you're worried about your willpower when it comes to clothes, and you'd like to stay solidly within your budget, here are some methods that merchandise men and salespeople have learned are almost guaranteed to weaken your sales resistance. Watch out for them!

• Salespersons create an air of excitement and appeal to the customer's feeling that he is an adventurous spirit. Even if you already have as many shirts as you need, you may be tempted by a new color or design that supposedly shows you are a leader, not a follower.

• They create a hectic atmosphere (this works especially well with young customers) and give people a sense of urgency. A saleswoman warns, "You'd better take it while we have it," and although you had planned to buy only one dress, you find yourself with two or even three.

• They call for a "takeover" person. This technique is used especially often when you are buying an expensive item like a fur coat. After the salesperson has answered all your questions and you have had time to narrow down your choices, the manager of the fur department or owner of the store will introduce himself, listen to what has been discussed and add his comments. He may or may not add anything new to the discussion—but he does lend the weight of his personality and authority to the selling pitch.

• They aim for the "multiple" sale. Once you have bought the basic suit or coat, a smart salesperson will suggest shoes, gloves, hats, shirts, scarves, ties and handkerchiefs to match. If you need them, fine. It's a good time to buy. But if you have these things and if you've already spent the money you've allotted for this year's suit, watch out for such selling pitches as, "I know you're not looking for a pink blouse, but see how it picks up the color of your suit and your complexion," or "This suit could really use at least one bright shirt."

ary. Good values in cottons or synthetic-and-cotton blends are available in June. Woolen sales vary greatly. If August and September have been warm, substantial wool values will be available in late September and October, when overstocked stores make markdowns.

3. *Hosiery.* Watch for advertised sales of major brands in October. Ads should be read carefully and merchandise checked. Less-than-reputable stores will sell seconds without identifying them as such. Good stores also sell seconds, but always say so, and more often than not offer prices lower than those of their shady competitors.

4. *Lingerie.* The traditional sale period is immediately after Christmas and through early January. Department stores and shops will offer lower-than-regular prices on famous brands only at this time.

5. *Men's shirts.* November is best for dress shirts. Watch for advertised sales of national brands at this time. Manufacturers like to clear out discontinued numbers in the pre-Christmas period and sell them at discounts to retailers.

6. *Men's suits and coats.* November and December are best for men's winter clothing, and June is best for summer wear. At these times stores have made markdowns, but stocks are still not completely stripped.

7. *Women's coats.* If you aren't able to find the right coat in the October or November sales, then by all means try again in December. This is the month when both stores and manufacturers must clean out their stocks—and most of the winter wearing period is still ahead. Look two or three times for this important acquisition. You'll be amazed at the extraordinary values that turn up in the form of special purchases from overstocked manufacturers or markdowns from overburdened stores.

8. *Women's dresses.* Good buys can be made near the end of different retail seasons while there is plenty of time left to wear. Wools are marked down in November; dressy and cocktail dresses, right after Christmas.

9. *Women's sportswear.* Watch for name-manufacturer sales after the end of the early-season peak selling periods. For example, after the August and September early fall and back-to-school periods, stores are sometimes able to obtain closeouts from overstocked

manufacturers in October or November. If the store is a reputable one, values are likely to be excellent. This is also true for May and June after the early spring season, and July and August for summer sportswear including beachwear.

Bathing suits are tricky to buy on sale. Manufacturers like stores to hold regular prices as long as possible. Stores that carry large selections of major brands watch one another like hawks, and all will usually break prices on the same day—suggested by manufac-

▭▭▭▭▭▭

## TEN SHOPPING TIPS

1. *Avoid impulse buying*. It can be a leak in your clothing budget. Stop a moment before yielding to that half-price sign put out just to appeal to your bargain-hunting instinct and ask yourself, "Will John really wear this psychedelic tie, or will it languish in the closet?" If it is not going to be worn, it's not a bargain at any price.

2. *Returns cost money*. Sit, reach and bend, and encourage the family to do the same when buying such things as coats, suits, trousers and underwear. Your returns to the store will be fewer and you will not only save valuable time but also wear and tear on you and your car.

3. *Study the labels carefully*, especially if they say that a garment requires special care. Save the labels to show to your dry cleaner. If a garment requires special handling consider this before buying—it adds to the cost considerably.

4. *Shop alone if you know what you want*. A friend may be too persuasive and you will regret your purchase.

5. *Don't shop when you are tired*. You'll be tempted to take something that you don't like or doesn't fit just to get out of the store and back home. This is especially true when shopping with children.

6. *Shop early in the season* if you want a wide choice of styles, colors and sizes.

7. *To avoid crowds*, shop in the city between 10:30 a.m. and noon and between 2 and 5 p.m. For the suburbs the best time to do your shopping is 5:30 to 7 p.m.

8. *Go to sales with a specific purpose*, and only buy articles that meet your usual standards even at the reduced prices.

9. *When you need clothes for a special occasion, don't wait to shop at the last minute*. You will probably end up by spending more than you had planned.

10. *If you have a reasonable complaint about merchandise, by all means take it back*. All reputable stores want to know when their merchandise has proved defective—has not worn well, has shrunk or has lost its color. They will try to make an adjustment if you can show that the fault is with the merchandise and not your improper handling of it.

▭▭▭▭▭▭

▭▭▭▭▭▭

## WORDS YOU SHOULD KNOW

**Seconds and irregulars.** Manufactured items that have a slight defect, or imperfection, and are sold at a reduced price. They must be marked "seconds" or "irregulars." The defect may be in the evenness of the dye, or an imperfection in the weave, or thread not quite matched to the material. When you see items marked "seconds" or "irregulars" ask the salesgirl to tell you what's wrong. If it's the dye or thread it may not affect wear, but if it is an uneven weave in stockings they may not wear well.

**Couture and haute couture.** As translated from the French, "sewing" and "fine sewing," respectively. Both these terms refer to the collections of the star designers, whose creations set fashion trends. The couture fashion is produced, mostly by hand, in a workroom and sold in a fashion salon. Most of us can't afford it.

**Line-for-line copy.** A dress or a coat, usually couture or haute couture, that is an exact copy of the original designer's model, is a true line-for-line copy. A few very fine (and very expensive) specialty stores do buy these couture originals and have copies custom-made for individual customers, but this is getting rarer every year. The term is now used to mean that a store has bought a couture original, frequently in Paris or Rome, brought it back and given it to a manufacturer. He tries to duplicate it, but must make changes. Some of the detail and most of the handwork are eliminated. The fabric may not be the same as in the original, which is usually the very best. The style is cut on standard sizes to be put out on the ready-to-wear racks. The final dress, coat or suit is very often a good adaptation of the original, but it's not a true line-for-line copy.

▭▭▭▭▭▭

turers and based on season trend and weather. Stores that blatantly advertise famous-name bathing suits at off prices earlier during the season tend to be mavericks, and their offerings are usually small broken selections of last year's models. Inside tip: Shop on the last Saturday in June and the first two Saturdays in July. Major stores in urban areas first announce sales in Sunday papers, but if you are in the store on the Saturday preceding the ads, the stock will already have been remarked, and you'll be able to select from large marked-down stocks. If you go in the Monday after the ad is run, you'll have to be there bright and early to avoid having to fight your way through a near riot in the swimwear department.

If the garment on sale is a fashion item, such as a highly styled winter coat, it won't be a bargain for you if it's out of style by the time the next Christmas rolls around. On the other hand, staples like pajamas and standard shirts can be bought and put away. Children's clothes may be risky, since it's hard to predict whether Junior will grow just enough to fit the next size or suddenly fill out and have to move into an entirely different size category.

There are also preinventory sales where the buyers stop, catch their breath and see what they have left in their departments before they begin reordering. Here too the store's regular merchandise is on sale, though the sale items are usually odds and ends that have been fairly well picked over, and are often quite shopworn. Again, if you can find a garment you need, it will probably be a bargain. But don't buy something just because it's on sale.

Stores also run promotional sales, which can be the trickiest of all for the customer. Some of the goods may be regular merchandise, marked down or offered at a reduced price to get people into the store so that they will be inspired to buy regular as well as sale merchandise. Some of the sale goods, however, have been specially bought just for the "sale," and may not be the store's usual quality. In the ads watch for the words "marked down from" which usually means the store's regular merchandise, as compared to "special purchase" and "comparable value," which mean that the goods have been bought for this sale and may or may not be up to standard. Special promotions sometimes include some buyers' mistakes— blouses that were drooping on the rack because they lacked fashion appeal, were badly cut or came in hard-to-match or unbecoming colors. Items like these should be approached with caution. If the store has a policy of no returns on sale items, by all means try things on before you commit yourself. If you're not sure, you're probably better off leaving it for some other bargain hunter.

Many stores have clearance racks or tables where they regularly sell the few odd-size shirts they have left, or the soiled baby sweaters, or the dress that has had a few buttons torn off on its way in and out of fitting rooms. If you learn to shop these sale tables first, you will often pick up good buys. But before you buy, make a quick estimate of whether the cost of new buttons or cleaning will not offset the money saved, and whether you can be sure that the soil marks really will come out in the wash.

Finally, remember that shopping for values is a skill that you acquire as you become more and more knowledgeable about the choices open to you. When you have learned how to judge quality, which stores are best for which items, when to pay for services and when price is the best criterion, you will be able to make the buying decisions that are wisest for your family and your pocketbook.

CHAPTER 33

## Fabrics—Facts and Fallacies

*Will they wrinkle? Do they fade? Can they go in the washing machine? —An objective look at today's new fabrics*

With the vast profusion of fabrics, both natural and man-made, and fabric finishes on the market today, it's difficult to know what to select when you set out to buy clothes. The hangtag on a garment tells you both the generic and brand name of the material; but it doesn't tell you if it wrinkles easily, fades in sunlight or is too warm to wear in the summertime. Only by familiarizing yourself with the various fabrics will you know what to expect from them. Once you know that, you'll be able to judge the clothing you buy in terms of performance, cost and care.

Natural fibers such as wool, linen and silk are being supplemented or replaced by synthetics that combine the look and feel of the natural fibers with durability and easy care. For example, wool is warm and doesn't wrinkle, but it must be handwashed. Orlon, a trade name for a synthetic fiber called an acrylic, feels and wears like wool but can be machine-washed and dried quickly. Let's look at both natural and man-made fibers and fabrics to see what they can and cannot do.

*Natural Fibers.* Natural fibers withstand high temperature and because they absorb moistures are comfortable in warm weather, but they may shrink or stretch and they dry slowly.

Wools retain heat, shed wrinkles easily and absorb a good deal of moisture before they feel wet and uncomfortable. They may shrink, however, if soaked in water too long.

Linen is a strong fiber, but it wrinkles easily unless a special finish is applied to the fabric.

Cotton is durable and can be safely washed and dried at high temperatures. However, it soils fairly easily.

Silk absorbs moisture but will waterspot after its saturation point has been reached. It is soft to the touch and has an elegant look, but fades in sunlight and is easily damaged by high temperature and strong soap.

*Man-made fibers.* Man-made fibers, or synthetics, include acrylic, nylon, polyester, spandex, rayon and acetate. Synthetics dry quickly, require little or no ironing and won't shrink or stretch.

Acrylics (trade names: Acrilan, Orlon) are lightweight fibers that feel like wool; they are used in sweaters, socks, knit dresses and shirts. Rubbing causes the fabric to "pill," or bunch together in little balls.

Nylon (Ban-Lon, Agilon) is the strongest synthetic fiber. It is inexpensive and resilient and resists wrinkles, but may melt under a too-hot iron. Dresses, blouses and shirts made with nylon are especially suitable for traveling; they take up little space and come out of the suitcase practically wrinkle-free.

Polyester (Dacron, Kodel) is crease-resistant and quick-drying. It may pill and should be thoroughly rinsed to prevent graying from soil left in the garment. Polyester is found most frequently in men's and boy's shirts.

Spandex (Vyrene) has good holding power and returns to its original shape after being stretched. It is lighter in weight and more durable than rubber, but yellows with age. Most foundation garments today are made with spandex plus another synthetic (usually polyester or nylon).

Rayon is strong and absorbent and holds color well. It wrinkles and may shrink or stretch during laundering unless it has been treated with a special finish. Rayon is used in making men's and boy's slacks and women's dresses.

Acetate (Arnel) has a silklike appearance. It is nonabsorbent and will melt under a hot iron. Acetate dresses are pushing silk out of the picture as the "status" fabric.

The chart on page 329 provides a more complete guide to trade-name fabrics that contain the various man-made fibers.

*Blends.* Blended fabrics, made from combining several fibers, will have all their characteristics. Since blending combines the best features of the fibers used, it creates a fabric of better quality. At least 25 percent of a given fiber must be used in a blend to give it the desirable quality of that fiber, so check the hangtag of the garment you select for fiber content. One of the most popular blends is 65 percent polyester and 35 percent cotton; since the polyester is wrinkle-resistant and quick-drying, it provides easy care, while the cotton adds strength and absorbency. Spandex blends provide elasticity, and nylon blended with another fiber adds strength to the fabric.

*Finishes.* A "finish" is a substance applied to a fabric to change its appearance or performance. The newer finishes that allow for easy clothing care include wash-and-wear, permanent press, soil-resistant. Waterproof, water-repellent and shrink-resistant finishes have been available for some years.

A wash-and-wear fabric requires only touch-up ironing after laundering, since the finish helps the fabric shed wrinkles. Unfortunately, wash-and-wear garments do not have total shape retention and may lose their original pleats and creases. This finish is disappearing as permanent press is being used more and more.

Similar to, but considerably more effective than, its predecessor, permanent press is a special finish that is not finally set until the dress or shirt has been cut and sewn. The completed garment is then baked in a special oven or pressed under high pressure, so that the fabric is given a "memory" of its original shape, the finish is absorbed into the material, and pleats or creases are locked in, wrinkles locked out. Like any innovation, caring for this no-iron feature takes a little know-how. Always read the hangtag for laundering instructions. In buying clothing, be particularly careful to get a good fit, as permanent press isn't easy to alter. If you lengthen a dress, for instance, the crease of the original hemline cannot be ironed out. If you shorten it, you may have to iron the hemline after each washing.

A soil-resistant finish protects the fabric so that stains are not absorbed and can be easily brushed off or blotted away. The longer a stain is left on the material, however, the harder it will be to remove.

Water-repellent finishes slow down absorbency but do not prevent moisture from getting into the fabric. A waterproof finish coats the entire surface of the fabric and prevents any absorption.

# A Guide to Man-Made Fabrics

| CHEMICAL GENERIC NAME | SOME TRADE NAMES | PROPERTIES |
|---|---|---|
| Acrylics | Acrilan, Vyleran, Orlon, Zefran, Creslan | Soft hand (or "feel"), lightweight bulk (warmth without weight); resistant to sunlight; wrinkle-resistant; good dimensional stability. Dries fast. Pleats and creases can be heat-set permanently. Flammable. |
| Modacrylics (modified acrylics) | Dynel, Verel | Similar to acrylics but nonflammable; very sensitive to heat; subject to pilling. |
| Polyesters | Dacron, Kodel, Vycron | Wrinkle-resistant. Pleats and creases can be permanently set by heat. Dimensionally stable; good body, drape and hand. Little or no ironing necessary. Favored for its worsted hand. |
| Nylon | Nylenka, Ban-Lon, Chemstrand, Agilon, Du Pont, IRC | Strongest of all fibers even when wet, yet lightweight. Resists abrasion. Wrinkle-resistant; dimensionally stable; resists perspiration damage; good elasticity. Wear-and-tear resistance. Fast-drying; easy care; pleat retention in many fabrics. |
| Spandex | Tycron, Vyrene | Elastic; softer than rubber but with many of same properties; extremely lightweight. Used in foundation garments and swimwear. |
| Vinal | Vinylon | Useful in a wide variety of textile applications including all forms of wearing apparel, blankets, curtains, sheets, carpets, tire cord, fish nettings, tents and ropes. High softening temperature; high dry strength. |
| Rayon | Tyrex, Fortisan, Super L, Corval, Topel | Absorbent; washable. Will shrink unless treated for shrinkage. Easy ironing with a fairly hot iron. No resistance to wrinkling unless special finish is applied. Flammable if napped; fabric should be treated for flame resistance. |
| Acetate | Arnel, Avisco, Celanese, Estron | Little absorbency, so dries rather quickly. Sensitive to heat, so fabric must be pressed with a cool iron to prevent fusing at thick places. Triacetates will stand higher ironing temperatures. Some wrinkle resistance. Former poor resistance to fume or gas fading (color change due to atmospheric conditions) is being overcome. May accumulate static electricity. |
| Metallic | Lurex, Reymet, Fairtex, Malora, Metlon | Metallic fibers coated with plastic; widely used as ornamental fibers in clothing and household textiles; do not tarnish with wear or use. Plastic coating has tendency to stick to hot iron. |

Shrink-resistant finishes keep the garment from stretching or shrinking during washing. Make sure the hangtag guarantees no more than 1 percent shrinkage.

No matter how familiar you become with fabrics, fibers and finishes, always read the hangtag that accompanies the garment you select. Innovations in fiber content and care are springing up almost daily, and the tag not only will tell you the fiber content of the fabric but will also provide recommendations for proper care.

CHAPTER 34

## Saving on Wear and Tear

*"A stitch in time saves nine" may sound old hat, but thrifty Grandma probably knew what she was talking about*

Does your wardrobe suffer from the ravages of wear and tear? Do the dresses you still think of as "new" look faded and shapeless? Do holes, tears and snags ruin your favorite clothes? Are you spending too much money on clothing repairs and replacements? You can save money and prolong the life of your wardrobe if you treat your clothes with tender, loving care.

Though no garment will last forever, clothes that receive proper care look neater, stay brighter and last longer. Routine cleaning, repair and storage may make the difference, for example, between a pair of shoes that is worn out in a few months and a pair that looks brand-new after a year. Follow these five steps for maximum clothing mileage: (1) Understand what care is required for every item in your family's wardrobe. (2) Keep all your clothes and shoes cleaned and in good repair. (3) Protect your wardrobe against damage, stains and unnecessary soiling. (4) Provide uncramped, well-organized storage, in and out of season. (5) Educate your family to do the same—the children may ignore you during their rebellious years, but some of your advice will stick.

Today's vast assortment of synthetic fabrics and blends, permanent press and spot-resistant finishes can simplify clothing care. To get the desired results, however, you must follow the prescribed cleaning procedure for each fabric and finish. Directions for laundering, drying or cleaning are (or should be) attached to each new garment as hangtags or permanent labels. Unfortunately hangtags usually get thrown away or mislaid, and, unless washing instructions have been attached on a permanent label, it becomes impossible to know the right washing procedure. To help simplify your washday, here is a guide to the sometimes confusing terms that are found on hangtags and labels:

*Washable or machine-washable:* Use any method of washing, hot water, any laundry soap or detergent.

*Cold wash, cold setting or cold rinse:* Use water with temperature of less than 75° F.

*Lukewarm wash, warm wash or warm rinse:* Use water with temperature of 90° F. to 100° F.

*Medium wash or medium setting:* Water temperature can be 100° F. to 130° F.

*Hot wash or hot setting:* Use water temperature of 130° F. to 150° F.

*Hand wash:* Launder by hand in warm water. You may also have garment dry-cleaned unless label specifies "hand wash only."

*Wash separately:* Launder the item by itself or with articles of similar color.

*Delicate or gentle cycle:* Reduce washing time and agitation.

*Durable press or synthetic cycle:* Spinning time should be reduced after clothes are rinsed in cold water.

*No bleach:* Don't use bleach.

*No chlorine bleach:* You may use other than chlorine types of bleach.

*Dry-clean only:* Color, garment construction or finish make dry cleaning necessary. "Professionally dry-clean" tells you not to use self-service dry cleaning.

For best results your general laundering procedure should follow these steps: Prepare clothes for washing by emptying pockets and trouser cuffs; fastening buttons, snaps and zippers; removing any nonwashable trim; making necessary repairs; and presoaking or applying detergent to spots and heavily soiled areas. Clothes should be sorted into groups to be washed together. Separate dark items, whites, delicate fabrics, heavily soiled clothes and lightly soiled ones.

Then follow the instructions for correct water temperature, drying and ironing. Most washable clothes can be washed by machine, but you should wash by hand if the colors tend to run or fade, if the fabric is too delicate for machine action or if the label suggests hand washing only.

## Dry-Cleaning Tips

Nonwashable clothes can be dry-cleaned either by a professional cleaner or at a coin-operated dry-cleaning shop. Whichever you prefer, be sure to clean each piece of clothing before it is heavily soiled and before stains become set. Remember to empty the pockets, fasten buttons, zippers and openings and remove any trim that cannot be cleaned. It is a good idea to remove metal buttons and belt

### HOW TO AVOID DRY-CLEANING DAMAGE

Who's to blame when your best dress is returned from the dry cleaner's unfit to wear?

Sometimes the trouble really is at the source: the garment or textile manufacturer. The dye may fade or streak no matter how well the item is cared for. Buttons, plastic and vinyl piping, special trims, linings and facings can all pose problems for the dry cleaner.

Spots, stains, rips and tears are your responsibility. Always tell the dry cleaner where the stains are and, if possible, what they are. Also, take clothing to be cleaned while the stains are fresh: The longer you wait, the harder they are to remove. In some cases long-standing spots or stains may weaken the fibers and create holes. Rips and tears should be sewn before you take the garment to the cleaner's;

they could get larger and become frayed in the cleaning process.

When the damage is clearly the dry cleaner's fault, he will make a claim adjustment for it. Whether the item was lost or ruined, its value and life expectancy are considered. Logically, an older garment is not worth as much as a brand-new one. To give you a fair guideline for claims, the National Institute of Drycleaning (909 Burlington Avenue, Silver Spring, Maryland 20910) has published a handy pamphlet, *National Fair Claims Guide for Consumer Textile Products*. It has a chart on the life expectancy of clothes, plus a formula to help determine fair settlement. In addition, it defines basic dry-cleaning terms and responsibilities. But the two most important points for good dry-cleaning results are: (1) Purchase quality merchandise. (2) Use a reliable dry cleaner.

buckles as well, because they often become scratched during dry cleaning. If you use a professional cleaner, ask whether he makes it a habit to check pockets, fasten openings and protect buttons and trim, saving you the trouble of doing so.

While the basic methods of professional and coin-operated dry cleaning are similar, there are significant differences between the two. Professional dry cleaning is best for articles that need expert cleaning and pressing, such as men's and women's suits, good dresses, evening gowns, coats and fur- or leather-trimmed items. Hard-to-remove spots and stains also require the expertise of a professional. Be sure to tell the cleaner about any special care requirements and to call his attention to the location and cause of stains.

Coin-operated cleaning is quick and relatively inexpensive. Most everyday dresses, skirts and sportswear clean well in coin-operated machines. For best results, try to remove spots or stains before cleaning and shake and hang the clothes immediately after cleaning to prevent wrinkles.

As a rule, launder or dry-clean your clothes only as needed to remove soil and stains. If a suit or dress merely needs pressing, don't launder or dry-clean it. Overcleaning clothes weakens the fabric and shortens the life of your wardrobe.

## Care After Wearing

Routine care of clothes involves more than proper cleaning. Here are a few additional tips: Put clothes away neatly after each wearing. Iron or press newly washed clothes before putting away (unless they are being stored for several months); make repairs promptly; brush lint and dust off clothes after wearing them; air out your wardrobe from time to time to remove unpleasant odors and kill bacteria. Rotating the articles in your wardrobe also helps maximize their life-span: Clothes will last longer, look better, if given a few days' rest between wearings. A day or so in the closet gives wrinkles time to hang out and lets air circulate through the fabric.

An ounce of care will certainly prolong wear, so use aprons, napkins, bibs and smocks to minimize spots and stains. Look into the new sprays that give shoes an invisible coat of waterproofing. Guard against perspiration stains by using dress shields and antiperspirants.

Hurried or careless dressing and undressing can cause rips, tears, stretching or snags. Pulling trousers on or off when you have your shoes on, for example, will stretch or rip pants legs and cuffs. Jewelry worn while dressing or changing can catch on stockings or knit fabrics. Putting too many items into your pocket will stretch it and perhaps cause a rip. Stuffing a handbag may distort its shape or break the frame.

Make it a habit—and teach it to your children—to hang or fold clothes after each wearing. Throwing clothes on a chair or the floor or cramming things into drawers and closets will make them old before their time. Organize your storage space efficiently to prevent overcrowding. To make room for frequently used clothes, store those

### CHOOSING THE RIGHT LAUNDRY PRODUCT

Cold-water detergents . . . enzyme action . . . low-sudsing products . . . oxygen bleaches. . . . How can you decide which is best? First, read further to learn what each can or cannot do. Then select the one best suited to your laundry equipment, local water conditions, the particular fabric to be washed, amount of soil and the desired results. For best results, always follow the directions on the package.

• Soaps are available in liquid, granular, bar or flake form. They clean effectively in soft water but not in hard water (water containing the salts of calcium and magnesium). Light-duty soaps are designed for light soil and delicate fabrics. All-purpose soaps are suitable for the family laundry and heavy soil.

• Synthetic detergents contain water-softening ingredients and are effective in hard and soft water. They come in liquid, tablet and granular form with a variety of added ingredients. Light-duty detergents are for light soil and delicate fabrics; all-purpose and heavy-duty detergents, for heavy soil and regular wash.

• Cold-water detergents clean in cold water; they reduce the amount of color fading or running and decrease shrinkage. They are not effective on oil stains, which should be treated before laundering.

• Ammonia can be added to the wash water to cut grease and loosen stains and dirt. It also has a slight bleaching effect. It should be thoroughly rinsed away and should *never* be mixed directly with chlorine bleach.

• Bleaches help remove soil and lighten and brighten fabrics. Oxygen bleaches are most common and are safe for all fabrics, finishes and colors, but they may not be as effective as chlorine bleaches. Chlorine bleaches are best used on white fabrics only, as that are worn less often in a dry, ventilated storage space or in the backs of closets. Closet accessories like shoe racks, tie racks, multiple skirt and shirt hangers and garment bags can expand storage space and simplify clothes organization.

When you're putting clothes away, be sure they have enough room to breathe and stay free of wrinkles. Use the correct type of hanger for each item. Heavy coats and suit jackets keep their appearance best when hung on shaped wooden or plastic hangers; wire hangers can distort the shoulders and stretch the fabric. Trousers should be looped over well-rounded hanger bars or hung by the cuffs on spring type hangers. Knitted things should not be hung up because they will stretch. (Never mind the fact that you bought them off a hanger

---

they tend to lighten fabric dyes. They are effective on most fabrics, but should not be used on silk, wool, spandex or nonfast colors. Never pour chlorine bleach directly onto the fabric because it seriously weakens the fibers.

• Bluing is a blue coloring substance that makes white appear whiter when added to the wash or rinse water. It has no cleaning power but counteracts yellowing. Overuse of bluing results in a gray or blue tinge, so avoid use in every wash.

• Enzyme detergents. These recent products contain biological substances called enzymes that work to remove such stubborn dirt and stains as collar and cuff rings, blood and gravy stains without the use of bleach. There are two types of enzyme products: One is conventional detergent with enzymes added; the other is a more concentrated enzyme product designed to remove problem stains or spots when the garment is soaked before washing. Enzyme detergents, however, do not

affect such troublesome stains as ink, grease and certain chocolate and vegetable stains.

Be aware of these facts when using enzyme products: (1) Certain brands are not safe for silk or wool. (2) Enzyme detergents do not work at temperatures over 150° F. (3) Bleaches should not be used together with an enzyme product because the bleach destroys the enzymes; but if a presoak enzyme product is used, bleach may be included in the washing cycle.

• Fabric softeners make clothes feel softer and look fluffier. They contain an antistatic ingredient to prevent static electricity in synthetic fabrics. They should be added to the final rinse water.

• Water softeners and conditioners soften hard water. The size of the wash and hardness of the water determine the amount required. The usual amount of soap or detergent must of course be used in conjunction with your water conditioner.

in the store. During a conference on fabrics held by the National Retail Merchants Association one of its chief executives complained that store clerks, like customers, either don't read labels or pay no attention to them.) Fold knit sweaters, skirts and pants and store them flat on shelves or in drawers.

When you take a vacation or business trip, you can help prolong the life of your clothes by packing carefully. If possible, hang dresses, suits and coats in a garment bag. Placing tissue paper between the folds will help minimize wrinkles and creases.

The warm, sunny days of spring and the chilly days of fall signal the change from one season's weight of clothing to another's. Out-of-season clothes move from the closet to a cool, dry, clean storage closet or to the attic, and in-season clothes take their place. Before storing your wardrobe, see that it has been cleaned and repaired, as dirt and stains become hard to remove or permanently set after several months of storage. Washed shirts, slacks, dresses, and so on, should be folded but not ironed, and then stored. Clothing bags or storage closets are best for storing out-of-season things. Use moth balls, flakes or sprays to protect against moth and other insect damage. Take steps to prevent mildew if you live in a warm, damp climate. Keep clothing, closets, dresser drawers and basements as clean as possible. Ventilate the house and closed areas. Heat the house for a short time or use bags of silica jell or activated alumina usually available at hardware stores to absorb moisture (they can be dried and used over and over). When you find mildew spots, remove them immediately. Don't give the mold a chance to weaken or rot the garment. Brush off surface growth outdoors, if possible, to prevent scattering the mildew spores throughout the house. If you use a fungicidal product on fabrics, wet the surface thoroughly and follow the directions on the container.

Heat is the enemy of fur: Fur and fur-trimmed coats and suits should be stored with a dry cleaner or furrier in fur storage vaults.

Remember, the difference between a neat, fresh-looking outfit and a wrinkled, tired out-one is not always age or price, but proper care. Like everything else you own, the clothes in your wardrobe deserve to be treated well.

# REMOVING COMMON STAINS

Knowing how to remove stains, and tackling them promptly, can save the family budget many a dollar. Most ordinary household stains occur on washables and can be removed with soap or detergent suds and water, if they have not been allowed to set. Before using any chemical, test it on a concealed portion to determine its reaction on the fabric.

Carbon tetrachloride, once an extremely popular and widely used spot remover, is now considered too dangerous for indoor household use.

There are times when a stain is so stubborn or complex, or a fabric so delicate, that it requires the experience and skill of a trained "spotter" at a professional cleaning or laundry establishment. Generally, however, stains can be removed successfully at home by following these rules on washable fabrics:

*Blood.* While stain is fresh, sponge or soak with cold water until it is light brown; wash in warm suds and rinse. If the stain persists, soak briefly in a weak solution of bleach and then relaunder.

*Candle wax.* Scrape off excess wax and press stain between white blotters with a hot iron. Rub spot with lard or turpentine and wash in warm suds.

*Chocolate or cocoa.* Wash in hot suds. Treat any remaining stain with a weak solution of household bleach or hydrogen peroxide. Then relaunder in hot suds.

*Cod-liver oil.* Sponge with glycerin or a commercial cleaning fluid (*not* carbon tetrachloride); rub lightly to loosen the stain and rinse. Then launder in warm suds. Old stains are almost impossible to remove.

*Coffee and tea.* Pour boiling water from a height of three or four feet through fabric stretched taut over a bowl and fastened with an elastic band or string. Wash thoroughly in hot suds.

*Egg.* Scrape off excess egg, soak fabric in cool water and then wash in warm suds.

*Fruits and berries.* Sponge peach, pear, cherry and plum stains at once with cool water and rub with glycerin. After two hours, apply a few drops of vinegar for a minute or two, then rinse and launder in warm suds. For other fruits, stretch the stained portion of fabric over a bowl, pour boiling water through it and then launder in suds.

*Grass and foliage.* Scrub with hot water and suds. If necessary, use a mild bleach. Then wash promptly in warm suds.

*Gravy and white sauce.* Soak in cool water, then wash in hot suds.

*Grease, oil and tar.* Pure fats and oils usually come out after the stain is rubbed with thick soap lather. Rub tarlike or heavy grease spots with lard, then wash in very hot suds.

*Ice cream.* Sponge with cool water to remove sugar and protein, then with warm suds to remove grease. If chocolate or fruit stains remain, follow directions for removing those.

*Iodine.* Warm suds remove fresh stains. If stain has set, moisten and place in the sunshine; or cover it with a paste of starch and ammonia, let this dry and brush it off. Then launder.

*Lipstick and rouge.* Soften with glycerin, then launder in hot suds.

*Mayonnaise.* Sponge with cold water to remove egg, next with warm suds to remove oil; then wash the garment in hot suds.

*Mildew.* Soak through with suds and hang out with mildew exposed to the sunlight. If spots persist, rub them with lemon juice and salt. Then bleach the fabric in the sun and launder.

*Mud.* Allow to dry, then brush off and launder in hot suds.

*Paint.* If fresh, use lots of hot suds; if set, apply turpentine, kerosene or lard and then wash in hot suds. Still-wet water emulsion paint usually comes out in hot suds. There is no practical solvent for dried latex-base or casein-base cold-water paints. Plastic paints require professional treatment with strong solvents. Use a safe commercial solvent (*not* carbon tetrachloride) on spray paints, then launder the garment in warm suds.

*Scorch.* Wash in hot suds. If deep, rub with suds and then bleach in the sun or dampen with hydrogen peroxide; wash again in hot suds.

*Soft drinks.* These stains may turn brown with age, so sponge at once with cool water or equal parts of alcohol and water. Rub stain with glycerin, let stand for half an hour, rinse and then launder in hot suds.

*Tomato and catsup.* Dampen with cool water, rub with glycerin, let stand for half an hour; wash the garment in hot suds.

## HOW LONG SHOULD CLOTHES LAST?

Even with the best of care, clothes will wear out eventually. The National Institute of Dry Cleaning, in its *National Fair Claims Guide for Consumer Textile Products*, gives these average clothing lifetimes:

• **Men's clothing.** Summer-weight suits, 2 to 3 years. Winter-weight suits, 4 years. Wool coats and jackets, 4 years. Leather coats and jackets, 5 years. Dress and plain sport shirts, 2 years. Fancy sport shirts, 2 to 3 years. Wool slacks, 4 years. Cotton and synthetic slacks, 2 years. Vests, 2 years. Socks and ties, 1 year. Shoes, 3 years. Hats, 2 years. Sweaters, 3 years. Rainwear, 2 to 3 years. Sleepwear, 2 years.

• **Women's clothing.** Daytime dresses, 2 to 3 years. Evening gowns and cocktail dresses, 3 years. Skirts, 2 years. Blouses, 2 to 3 years. Wool coats and suits, 4 years. Fur coats, 10 years. Slacks, 2 years. Everyday shoes, 1 to 2 years. Evening shoes, 5 years. Felt hats, 1 year. Fur hats, 5 years. Scarves, 2 years. Slips, 2 years. Other underwear, 1 year. Swimwear, 2 years. Wool and synthetic sweaters, 3 years. Basic suits, 4 years.

• **Children's wear.** Coats, 2 years. Playclothes, 1 year. Dresses, 2 years. Suits, 2 years. Underwear, 1 year. Snowsuits, 2 years.

338

# 7

# THE
# FAMILY CAR

*You can save hundreds of dollars when you buy your car, when you drive it and when you have it serviced. Here's how*

## CHAPTER 35

# How to Save
# Money Buying a Car

*Follow these hints in
picking an automobile
and working out the right
price—they can save you
thousands of dollars
in a lifetime*

Three out of every four families in the United States own a car, and yours is probably one of them. But although the automobile is an accepted part of American life, it is also one of the largest single drains on the family finances. With the exception of your home, your car is the most expensive single possession you are ever likely to buy. And if you add up the costs of buying and operating a succession of cars over the years the total will be staggering.

Because of the amount of money involved and the importance of the automobile in your daily life, you owe it to yourself to approach the purchase of a new car with all the care and thought that such a major undertaking deserves. There are simple rules that can help you to save thousands of dollars during the years you own an automobile:

*Do you need a car at all?* So accepted is the idea that every American family should have a car that this question may not occur to you. If you live in a city apartment with access to public transportation, however, it's a good one to ask—even if you have owned a car until now. The cost of renting a new car for as many as a dozen weekend trips a year will come to less than the installments on a new automobile of your own, quite aside from maintenance, repair, garage and insurance expenses. Many rental companies offer special plans for three- or four-month summer rentals so that you will have a car at your disposal during the good weather months and for vacation trips. Before you buy, therefore, explore the rental possibilities in your area.

Whatever you do, don't wait until your present buggy is on its last mile before you start planning for your new purchase and shopping for prices and dealers—especially if you rely on your car to get you to and from work or for other essential purposes. The pressure of needing something right now or even next week can trap you into accepting an unfavorable deal.

340

*Check the budget.* Of course the cost of a new car has to fit into the family budget, even if that budget is an informal one (see Chapter 4, "The Fine Art of Family Budgeting," page 47). The main points to keep in mind are simple. If you already have a car and are accustomed to making payments, buying a new one probably will not impose much strain on the budget unless you decide to buy a considerably more expensive make or model. The cost of maintaining and operating the new car may even be lower, and your insurance and licensing fees will remain about the same. If you do not now own a car, however, buying one will add very substantially to your total cost of living, and you will have to find additional income or cut back on expenses in some other area—not an easy thing to do! (For more on the cost of owning a car, see Chapter 36, "The Real Cost of Running Your Car," page 348.)

*Know what you want.* The biggest saving you make when you buy a new car can take place before you step into a showroom—at the moment you decide just what it is you want. The size of your family and the way you plan to use the car will generally dictate what you need. A suburban family with young children and a lot of hauling to do may favor a station wagon, while city dwellers with the children off at college will be better served by a compact two-door sedan. Unless you expect to undertake long trips at reasonably high speeds or unless you need a comparatively large car, you may find that the smaller, less expensive 6-cylinder engine will suit your needs better than the larger and more powerful V-8.

Whatever your general requirements, the car manufacturers have seen to it that they can satisfy you over a surprisingly broad price range. If you simply want transportation you can save yourself hundreds of dollars. But if you want extra pleasure from your car purchase—status, glamour, a feeling of achievement—you had better be willing to pay the price.

In a recent model year, for example, the low-priced V-8 in one manufacturer's line carried a recommended price of $3158. The "middle line" model from the same manufacturer was $952 more, and the luxury V-8 was out of sight at $6728. While the economy-minded family is clearly not going in for a new Cadillac convertible, there is a very substantial saving to be made by making a reasonable choice from a manufacturer's lines and models. What's more, you will probably have as good a car at a substantially lower cost if you buy from the top of a manufacturer's low-priced line rather than at the bottom of his medium-priced line. And remember that the same extras usually cost more on middle-line cars than on their lower-priced counterparts. When the basic cost, the extras, the higher operating costs of the bigger, more expensive cars and the additional financing charges on the larger amount of money you may have to borrow are all taken into account, your decision to settle for the most economical car that will adequately serve your needs can save you thousands of dollars.

In deciding on what makes and models you want to look at before you select your new car, it's wise to seek information from sources other than the manufacturers themselves. Several national consumer testing organizations and magazines report every year on the new cars, giving detailed information on price, performance, general convenience and driving characteristics, available extras, inside and outside dimensions and so forth. These reports are on sale at newsstands or can be read at your local library. They will give you an excellent idea of what is available in what price ranges before you start visiting dealers.

Remember, too, that your decision to be sensible and economical is going to be a hard one to stick to. The glitter of a showroom full of new cars, combined with the salesman's plausible spiel about special extras and the advantages of the higher-priced models, has broken down more than one resolute buyer. It will fortify you to link your expected savings to something specific that you can look forward to—a summer vacation trip, new kitchen equipment, a contribution to college funds for the children, a color television set. Whatever it may be, keep your mind on this shining vision when you are tempted to waver, and think of what you'll have to do without if you give in to temptation.

*Shop for the price.* There is no such thing as a fixed selling price for any given automobile. There is the wholesale price—what the dealer paid the manufacturer for it—and there is the manufacturer's "suggested retail price," which appears on a sticker affixed to the left rear window of the car. This suggested price, or "sticker price," is required by federal law and must include an itemized list of standard accessories plus any extras installed at the factory, the federal excise tax and the dealer's makeready fee. A car usually sells for a negotiated price less than the sticker price. So it is important that you shop around for the best terms.

With this in mind, let's go to a dealer's showroom. You have seen a model that seems to meet your needs, and you are ready to discuss price. You have brought with you a price comparison worksheet like the one illustrated on page 345. You have read the sticker price on a car like the one you want. The car you will offer as a trade-in—if any—is outside at the curb or in the dealer's parking lot.

First, ask the salesman what kind of a discount he will offer you from the sticker price. Get him to quote you an exact figure and enter it opposite "Price quoted" on your worksheet. Make sure the figure includes the federal excise tax. Remember that there is nothing in the slightest way tricky or dishonest in asking for a lower price than the one quoted on the sticker. To fail to do this because of mistaken scruples is to throw away money—perhaps hundreds of dollars.

Now continue down the worksheet entering the price quoted you by the salesman for each of the standard options that you have decided you need. He will want to sell you a car the dealer has in stock, if possible, and may press you to accept extras that you don't really want. If you are particularly anxious to take delivery of the new car you will be more likely to succumb to his persuasion, because he will tell you that a car meeting your own specifications will take some time to deliver. But remember that he is as eager to sell a machine he has in stock as you are to drive home your new car. Make it clear to him that if you agree to accept unwanted options you will expect a larger discount from the sticker price than he originally mentioned. Chances are you'll get it.

When all the expenses have been entered on the price comparison sheet in exact figures, the time has come to ask the salesman what trade-in allowance he will give you on the old family car. Be sure the car is accurately described on the sheet, and enter his offer in the appropriate place. A little arithmetic done on the spot or later on at home will give you the real price of your car—the amount you will be borrowing or withdrawing to pay for your new transportation.

Before you leave the showroom, be sure the *dealer* signs the work-sheet. This is your assurance that he will stand behind his salesman's offer to you. *Do not sign anything yourself until you are ready to accept the offer and order a car.* If the dealer refuses to sign the sheet you are better off doing business elsewhere.

If you discuss financing with the salesman, remember that a dealer financing plan is often a source of considerable income to him, but you will almost certainly save yourself money by doing business with a bank if you find it necessary to borrow. (See Chapter 50, "Money When You Need It," page 476, for more details on loans.) A dealer may occasionally use a discussion of financing to confuse you as to the real price of the car. It's best to say you intend to pay cash or finance the car through a bank.

Assuming that there are several different dealers for a particular make in your area or that you are interested in pricing several different makes of car, you should repeat this process at each show-room you have decided to visit, filling out a price comparison work-sheet in each place and having it signed by the dealer. By the time you have completed your research, you should have an interesting range of figures on your "real price" line, and you will be able to evaluate the offers you have had in terms of hard dollars.

*Shop for a dealer.* Before you automatically accept the most economical offer as reflected by your price comparison worksheets, however, give some thought to the dealers involved. The lowest price may have been offered you by a firm whose service facilities are sub-standard or inconveniently located or whose reputation in the community is not what it should be. Always be wary of dealers whose advertising claims seem misleading or exaggerated or of those who have shown a strong reluctance to sign the price comparison sheet. The best guide to a dealer's reputability is the opinion of your friends and neighbors who have dealt with him. Avoid buying from a man with an uncertain reputation even if he has made you the best offer. You may lose more in the long run if he gives poor service or fails to stand behind his warranties.

*Shop for credit if you need it.* If you can afford to pay cash for your car do it. The interest on a three-year loan for a $3000 car may increase its cost by 20 percent or more! Most people, however, have

## PRICE COMPARISON WORKSHEET

Dealer's name and address...........................................

.......................................................................

Make of car ......................................

Model and year ...................................

Body style and color...............................

### Costs

    Price quoted, including federal tax ..................  $_____

    Optional equipment

        Heater........................................  _____

        Radio.........................................  _____

        Automatic transmission...........................  _____

        Power steering.................................  _____

        Power brakes..................................  _____

        Air conditioning................................  _____

        Tires (special)..................................  _____

        Other .......................................

        ............................................  _____

    Shipping cost......................................  _____

    State or city sales taxes.............................  _____

    Registration or transfer fees.........................  _____

    Dealer's undercoating and makeready fees ............  _____

    Total price of car, delivered........................  $_____

Trade-in allowance on................................

.................................................(−) $_____
*(make, model, year and mileage of your trade-in)*

                Real price of your car.... $_____

Dealer's signature.........................................

to borrow at least part of the price of a new car, and if you have to buy on credit you should shop carefully for the best terms. The cost of credit is one of your major expenses when you buy a car.

A full discussion of borrowing money when you need it at the least cost to you can be found in Chapter 50, "Money When You Need It," page 476, and in Chapter 52, "Watch Those Interest Rates," page 493. But there are some specific points about "renting money" to buy a car that you should remember:

1. Make as large a down payment as you can reasonably afford. Your trade-in will count toward most of this, but you would be well advised to throw in some cash if necessary to bring the down payment up to 25 percent or more of the total cost of the car. This will mean fewer or lower payments on your installment loan or other financing plan.

2. Dealer financing plans are almost always more costly than a bank loan. While most such proposals are honest, some are not, and some unscrupulous dealers make more money on their financing than they do on the sale of cars.

3. Unless you're a member of a credit union, a bank loan will probably be your most economical way of borrowing money. You need not have an account to borrow from a bank, and you should shop the banks in your area for the best interest rate you can obtain—there may be some significant differences. In some cities banks will approve a loan for a stipulated sum of money before you go shopping for a car. This way, you know just how much cash you have available and will have a more compelling reason to keep your spending within the agreed-upon limit.

4. When a bank or other credit institution lends you money, it either retains the title or takes a lien on the car you are buying as security for the loan. Because of this, the lender may require you to insure the car against fire, theft or collision damage during the duration of the loan. He may also insure your life for the amount of the note at your expense. Finally, of course, he may repossess the car if you default, and sell it to recover the money you still owe him.

5. Always be sure that the installments you're expected to pay fit reasonably into your monthly budget. Remember that there will be other costs to running your car (see Chapter 36, page 348).

6. Test-drive the car. When you have decided on a car and a dealer and arranged for the necessary financing, the time has come for you to place a formal order. Before you do this, however, you should definitely take a demonstration drive in the automobile you plan to buy, or in one of the same model with the same optional equipment. This will be your last chance to spot any design defects or quirks in the car you will have to live with for several years. If possible, bring along a friend to try out the back seat and add his observations to your own. And by all means make *sure* that the dealer is properly insured if an accident should occur during the test drive.

7. If all goes well on your test drive you are now ready to tell the salesman to fill out the formal purchase order for your new car. This is a printed form similar to your own price comparison worksheet in its general organization and carries the same information. Be sure that the salesman lists everything correctly on the order form and enters the prices you have agreed upon for each item, plus credit for the agreed-upon trade-in allowance. At this point you will be asked to make a down payment on the car, the balance to be paid on delivery. Make sure that the order form is signed by the dealer as well as by you. And to protect yourself fully, you may request that he insert a special clause stating that unless the car is delivered by a certain date and with the specified extras (no more!), your down payment will be returned to you and the order canceled. This will discourage most dealers from trying to persuade you later to take delivery of a car loaded with more optional features than you had ordered, at an extra cost to you.

8. Check your new car carefully when it's delivered. Although the price of most cars includes an item for "dealer's makeready" before delivery, the sad truth is that many people receive their new cars in less than perfect condition. Unless you catch mistakes or imperfections before you get the car home, you may spend frustrating hours and unnecessary money in getting them corrected. So to save yourself grief and extra expense, be sure you have taken the following precautions before you hand over your check for the balance of the purchase price:

*Compare the car with your order*. Make sure you have received the right model and body style, color and optional extras.

*Make a visual check,* keeping a sharp eye out for scratches, dents, bent or broken parts, ripped upholstery. Look in the trunk. It would be quite a shock to open it days hence and discover that you have no jack or spare tire!

*Drive the car at least a short distance* to be sure there are no obvious mechanical difficulties. Check the lights, windshield wipers, horn and heater. Open and close the doors and check the locks. Be sure the speedometer and odometer are working.

*Make certain you have all the necessary papers* to register and insure the car, including a certificate of title in those states that require one. Check to see that these documents carry the correct serial number and description.

*Be sure you have your warranty and service manual.* And read both of these carefully at the earliest opportunity. They can save you costly repair bills later on.

Now you are ready to drive away. Hopefully, you have saved yourself trouble and money by following these simple suggestions. The following chapters offer some hints on how to keep down your operating and maintenance costs.

CHAPTER 36

## The Real Cost of Running Your Car

*Just keeping the old buggy running takes a big chunk of the family budget. Here's what it really costs and how to cut expenses*

The cost of owning and operating a car is the most underrated expense in the family budget. Yet what strikes closer to home in our mobile society?

Eighty million of us own cars. We spend $75 billion annually to pay for them and for the gasoline, taxes, parts, accessories and insurance they require. No one will even hazard a guess as to what we pay for service, repairs and incidentals.

Many of us spend more on cars than on anything else except food and housing, but we think of our transportation costs—if we think of them at all—in terms of the price we paid for the car, plus gas and oil.

This attitude is partly defensive. For most of us there is no alternative to owning a car. Reliable public transportation has become almost extinct in some areas, and seems to deteriorate steadily as our reliance on the automobile increases. Thus the cost of owning and operating a family car is unavoidable, and the tendency is to think as little about it as possible.

This is understandable but self-defeating. The art of money management is based not on doing away with expenses but on keeping them under control and in some kind of reasonable relation to each other. Managing the costs of transportation is impossible if you don't even know what they are.

Before you groan over visions of bits of paper scribbled with "gas $3.32, oil 50 cents," let's take a more practical view. The American Automobile Association has published a booklet on typical expenses. It is based on actual costs incurred by operators of vehicle fleets, thus providing practical averages. They won't match your own outlays exactly, but they'll be close enough.

The AAA uses a 1967 Chevrolet, an 8-cylinder, four-door Impala hardtop, for purposes of illustration. The car is equipped with standard accessories, radio, automatic transmission and power brakes. It's assumed the car will be traded in after three years or at 60,000 miles, whichever comes first. Costs are listed in two categories: variable and fixed.

Variable costs (average per mile)

| | |
|---|---|
| Gasoline and oil | 2.65¢ |
| Maintenance | .68 |
| Tires | .47 |
| Total | 3.80¢ |

Fixed costs (annual)

| | |
|---|---|
| Fire and theft insurance | $ 39 |
| $100 deductible collision insurance | 85 |
| Property damage and liability ($100/$300/$25,000) | 148 |
| License and registration | 26 |
| Depreciation | 684 |
| Total | $982 |

Assuming that the typical motorist drives 10,000 miles a year, this is the way it works out:

| | |
|---|---:|
| 10,000 miles at 3.80¢ ........................................... | $ 380 |
| One year's fixed costs......................................... | 982 |
| Total.... | $1362 |
| (or 13.6¢ per mile) | |

What good does it do you to know that it costs almost 14 cents per mile to drive your car? Not too much, in direct benefits, it's true; but if it only breeds a little respect, it is far from a pointless exercise. Actually, if it keeps you from impulsively buying a second car it could be a godsend. For the sneaky part of the second-car project is that at first it doesn't really seem like an extravagance. For one thing, many people don't actually "buy" a second car; they keep the old one instead of trading it in. That way, it somehow seems as though they got it for nothing, which takes care of the major outlay.

As for operating expenses, the logic is usually crystal clear: If you have two cars, you'll use each only half as much, so, combined, they can't cost much more than one did alone.

Let's take a couple, Joan and Harry, and follow them through the second-car syndrome to see what happens to these two basic ideas:

*Purchase.* Harry's 1965 Chevrolet with 52,000 miles on the odometer was worth $1000 trade-in on the 1969 Ford he wanted to buy. Since Harry and Joan chose to keep the Chevy instead of trading it in, they had to take $1000 out of a savings account paying $4\frac{1}{2}$ percent interest and finance the remaining $2500 due at "$7 per $100 per year." This turned out to be about 14 percent simple annual interest.

*Insurance.* The $124 annual premium on the Chevy was cut to $100 when Harry decided they could drop the collision coverage on the older car. But even so their insurance costs nearly doubled.

*Gas and oil.* When it came to fuel, the couple discovered an eternal truth about motoring: The family that owns two cars just naturally drives more miles than the same family with one. Where they had been averaging 12,000 miles a year in one car, the increased convenience and availability resulted in their driving 17,000 miles after they acquired the second. By now the old Chevrolet was beginning to burn a quart of oil with every other tank of gas. And the new Ford seemed to require a better grade of fuel. The result: Their gas and oil bills doubled.

*Repairs.* Without realizing it, Harry and Joan always had counted on a major budgeting switch to help them over the hump when they traded cars. Buying the new car used to mean they had to start making monthly payments again, but this was balanced out because frequent repair bills disappeared when they turned in the old one. Now that they owned two cars, repair bills and monthly payments began giving them the old "one-two."

*Licenses.* License plates for the new Ford didn't cost any more than the ones for the Chevrolet. But licensing the two did cost twice what one alone had. Another expense doubled.

So, with only the barest idea of what they are really up against, Harry and Joan are now spending close to 30 percent of their income to keep eight wheels rolling.

*Shaving the costs.* Is that too big a bite? Probably, but then only Joan and Harry can decide. What are the alternatives? The obvious one is to get rid of the second car and cut their costs in half. That's a little like saying, however, that they could sell both cars and *really* save money. What Joan and Harry need are a few ways to shave the price of living the way they want to. Here are some possibilities:

1. Rolling stock. Trade in one full-size car and replace it with a compact—the smaller the better. There is no need for a second car big enough to haul a Little League team. The AAA survey shows that Joan and Harry could save about 40 percent of the cost of one car by running a foreign compact in place of an American standard.

2. Insurance. First, both cars should be insured with the same company. This usually means an automatic saving of 20 percent on premiums. Second, the couple who needs collision insurance should carry as big a deductible as they think they can manage on their collision coverage. A policy with a $100 deductible, for example, will cost about half of one with no deductible at all.

3. Tires and parts. If one of the two cars can be assigned to purely local travel it is possible to save money on repair and replacements. A new car that will never be pushed past 40 miles per hour, for example, can survive with third-line tires or retreads. Minimum-grade

tires in standard sizes can be bought for $12 to $15, where turnpike-grade tires designed for prolonged, high-speed driving might cost $25 to $35.

The same theory applies to replacement of parts. Such common parts as water pumps, fuel pumps and carburetors can be purchased much more cheaply in rebuilt form than new. In most cases they'll provide good service, and the odds make it worth the chance.

Above all, however, don't blind yourself to the realities of two-car living. More than one couple has made the jump and fallen right into the trap. They soon find themselves short of money. He blames her for being a poor manager at home, and she blames him for not earning enough at his job. Sometimes they never do get around to blaming the second car.

CHAPTER 37

## Facts You Should Know About Auto Insurance

*Of course you don't expect to be involved in an auto accident. But just in case, it pays to be fully covered*

Your automobile insurance coverage is nothing to "save" money on —at least not in the traditional sense of cutting corners to pare a few dollars from the budget. While there are safe and legitimate ways to reduce your premiums, proper insurance coverage in adequate amounts is absolutely essential to your family's financial safety. If you are ever involved in an accident for which a court adjudges you responsible, crippling financial disaster may result unless you are adequately insured. Awards to accident victims—which include damages for medical costs, loss of income and pain and suffering—often run to many thousands of dollars; and unless you are able to raise the cash, you may find it necessary to dispose of your major assets, hand over your savings and accept a lien on your house and garnishment of your salary. Even if you are not responsible for the accident, your failure to carry the right insurance may result in considerable embarrassment and inconvenience and perhaps the loss of your license for a period of time.

Adequate auto insurance is essential because every state has some form of financial responsibility law, designed to keep off the highways drivers who cannot afford to pay for the possible damages or injuries caused by their driving. In many states these laws simply require that every car owner carry a certain amount of personal liability insurance. To register your car you are required to show proof of this insurance, and if you default on your premium payments your insurance company informs the state bureau of motor vehicles, which, in turn, notifies you that your registration has been revoked. Some states, however, do not *require* that you carry insurance but wait until you have an accident before they lower the boom. If you are involved in a collision resulting in injury or property damage and do not carry adequate insurance, these states may require you to put up thousands of dollars in cash or other assets as proof of your ability to pay damages if it is determined that the accident was your fault. Your inability to satisfy this requirement may result in the suspension of your license, and you may have to wait as long as three years to recover it. In a recent year more than 700,000 people in the United States lost their licenses for not complying with financial responsibility laws— many of them through simple failure to understand what was required of them.

Clearly it's a serious mistake to drive without insurance. To find out whether you have the right coverage, you need to know what kinds of automobile insurance are available as well as what the legal requirements of your own state are. And a word of warning: If a dealer or lending institution advances you money for the purchase of a car and says, "The insurance is all taken care of," be sure to find out exactly what that means. Chances are that the car is covered by collision and comprehensive physical damage insurance to protect the lender's security and that your life has been insured to cover the amount of the note—but you are probably *not* covered by personal liability insurance, which is the most important of all from your point of view.

## The Main Kinds of Automobile Insurance Coverage

*Bodily injury liability insurance.* This is the only kind of insurance that satisfies the financial responsibility laws of the various states, and it is essential that you carry it. This insurance covers you for damages up to the amount specified in the policy if an accident in which you are involved kills or injures passengers or drivers in other cars, passengers in your own car or pedestrians. This type of coverage can be obtained in varying amounts, usually starting with $10,-000/$20,000, which means the insurance company will pay up to

## IF YOU'RE IN AN ACCIDENT

Even a relatively mild automobile accident can have costly and time-consuming consequences. A more serious one can enmesh you in litigation involving hundreds of thousands of dollars. Here are some simple rules to follow if you have the misfortune to be involved in a collision. They can save you time, money and grief later on.

• Even if you think you were in the wrong, *say nothing about who was at fault* to the other driver or to passengers or bystanders. You might regret it later. Simply exchange names, addresses, driver's license and registration information with the driver of the other car.

• Get the names and addresses of everyone involved in the accident, including passengers in both cars. If someone seems to be hurt, make a note of the apparent extent of his or her injuries.

• Get the names and addresses of any witnesses to the accident.

• Take down the names and badge numbers of police officers who arrive on the scene.

• If possible, have photographs taken of the scene of the accident before the cars are moved. Make a sketch map showing the road situation (intersection, curve, bridge), the direction of travel of the cars involved and the positions in which they finally came to rest.

• As soon as possible after the accident, write down the facts while they are still fresh in your mind.

• Report the accident *at once* to your insurance company. This is important, since failure to let them know within a certain number of days may release them from liability. After you have notified them by phone or wire, give them the details of the accident in writing and keep a dated copy for your own records.

• File an accident report with the police or the appropriate state authority as required by law. Keep a copy. Your local police station or motor vehicles bureau office will supply you with the proper forms.

• *Do not* make any statements to the adjuster for the other driver's insurance company, or sign any statements or releases he may show you, or accept any money from him or from anyone else until you have talked to your own insurance adjuster and, if you wish, to your attorney.

$10,000 to any individual injured in an accident and up to a total of $20,000 to all those injured in an accident (assuming, of course, that the fault is yours). Higher coverage can be obtained for relatively small increases in the premium, and, in these days of high court awards for damages, many people feel that it is wise to carry $100,-000/$300,000 liability coverage. When you buy this kind of insurance the insurance company also agrees that its lawyers will defend you if you are sued in connection with an automobile accident. Liability insurance normally covers the members of your family who drive your car as well as friends to whom you may lend it. If there is a young driver in the family, however, your premiums may be substantially increased.

*Property damage liability insurance.* This insurance protects you when your car damages the property of others; it does not cover damage to your own car. Usually the damaged property is the other driver's car, but it may also include lampposts, fences, signs, buildings or anything else you hit in the course of an accident. This coverage is also available in varying amounts.

*Collision insurance.* This covers damage to your own car from collision with another vehicle or a stationary object or as a result of turning over. It is usually sold on a deductible basis: the higher the deductible figure, the lower the premium. If you have $100 deductible collision insurance and your repair bill comes to $320, you pay the first $100 and the insurance company pays the rest. If damages are $100 or less, you foot the whole bill. Collision insurance is expensive. If your car is several years old and you own it entirely, you may want to do without this type of coverage. If, on the other hand, you still owe the bank a substantial amount on your installment loan it is wise to carry it even if they do not require it. (But check to be sure that you are not paying to duplicate collision coverage that's already coming out of your monthly payments.)

*Comprehensive physical damage insurance.* This protects you against loss from fire, theft, vandalism and a multitude of other hazards including falling rocks, flood, collision with animals on the road, and so forth. Like collision insurance, this coverage may be less desirable if your car is old and relatively low in value. But it is worthwhile if you still share ownership with the bank and cannot afford a loss. In many states comprehensive insurance is now available on a deductible basis.

*Medical payments insurance.* The insurance company pays your medical expenses and those of your family and passengers in your car for treatment of injuries received in an accident. It also applies to you and your family if you are hit by a car while you are on foot. The amount of coverage and the premiums are variable.

*Protection against uninsured motorists.* In taking out this coverage you are really insuring yourself against possible loss from an accident caused by a driver who does not have proper insurance. Your own insurance company will pay damages to you and your family and to passengers in your car up to the amount provided in the policy. Although many people consider this an unnecessary form of insurance, it is worth considering. The cost is low, and despite the financial responsibility laws of the states, there are still many drivers on the road without adequate coverage.

## WORDS YOU SHOULD KNOW

**Financial responsibility law.** A statute, in some form in every state, which ensures that the driver of a motor vehicle can pay fair claims to a victim if his vehicle causes property damage, personal injury or death.

**Personal liability.** The legal burden of an individual to make restitution in money for damage done to others through his fault or negligence.

**Liability insurance.** Protection for you and your family against financial loss if you cause injury to the body or property of others. It protects you against court awards for damages up to the amount of the insurance.

**Collision insurance.** Coverage for damage to your car resulting from collision with another vehicle or a stationary object.

**Comprehensive insurance.** Protection against loss from damage to your car by fire, theft, vandalism and many other hazards.

**Medical payments insurance.** Provision for medical and hospital payments up to the insured amount for injuries to yourself or passengers resulting from an accident.

**Deductible insurance.** A form of insurance that pays off only in the amount your loss exceeds a certain figure specified in your policy. Example: You have $50 deductible collision insurance and damage to your car costs $85 to repair. You pay $50 and the insurance company pays $35.

*Towing insurance.* This is strictly for convenience. For a premium of probably not more than $5 a year the insurance company will pay legally incurred towing charges up to approximately $25 per tow.

By checking these categories of insurance against the kinds and amounts provided in your present policy and by consulting with your insurance agent or your attorney, you will be able to obtain a good overall evaluation of your coverage. Remember that to protect yourself you should have substantial bodily injury and property damage liability insurance, and that the legal minimum for your state is not necessarily safe coverage.

## Getting the Best Premium Rates

Shopping for insurance premium rates presents a tricky problem. Rates are determined on a complex basis. Once a company knows what coverage you want, it weighs a number of factors in arriving at an insurance classification and in quoting you a rate. Your place of residence and how you use your car are important factors. A city dweller will undoubtedly find himself paying more than a suburbanite for the same amount of coverage, and a man who uses his car partly for business will probably be quoted a higher rate than one who uses it for pleasure only. The age and sex of the drivers can have an alarming effect on premiums. If you have an unmarried son under twenty-five who uses the family car from time to time, your costs will skyrocket when he first reaches driving age and then will gradually decrease as he grows older. You can usually soften this bite somewhat by seeing to it that the younger members of your family take driver education courses that meet the standards of the National Conference on Driver Education. Insurance companies recognize the value of these courses and charge lower rates for young drivers who have completed them successfully. Some companies also allow discounts for drivers with exceptionally clean records or for drivers of compact cars. Safety features have no effect on insurance rates, but some states authorize lower rates for cars with antitheft devices. Comparison shopping among a few of the leading firms in your area will probably show a small variation in the premiums quoted you.

Choosing the company that offers the lowest premium may be a false economy, however. It is best to deal with a well-known company that has been operating in your state for at least ten years and has a good reputation for settling claims fairly and promptly. You should also find out what a firm's policy is in regard to cancellation of your insurance. If your policy is canceled without apparent cause —as happens all too frequently—you will have to seek insurance under your state's assigned risk plan at a considerably higher rate. (In these quite common plans, state law requires all companies licensed to sell automobile insurance in the state to assume a fair proportion of drivers who have been unable to get insurance or whose coverage has been canceled. The companies are also authorized to charge higher premiums to these drivers.) So try to insure yourself with one of the large firms that cancel only for nonpayment of premiums or for suspension or revocation of your driver's license.

One of the best ways to check a company's reputation for speed and fairness is to consult your friends, acquaintances, local businessmen and perhaps your lawyer. You can also obtain information on any company licensed to sell insurance in your state by applying to your state insurance department.

Remember, above all, adequate coverage with an established company which has a reputation for settling claims fairly is far more important than shaving a few dollars off your annual premium.

CHAPTER 38

## Good Driving Habits That Put Dollars in Your Pocket

*Snowed under by staggering bills for car repairs and replacements? A little tender loving care could make a big difference*

You should know how to operate and care for your car properly to reap a maximum return on your investment. Worthwhile savings are possible in connection with tires, fuel and general car care. Many savings can be accomplished merely by good driving practices.

Driving practices have much to do in determining the life of your tires. Good driving can reduce tire wear, resulting in a minimum cost to you per tire mile. Driving at reasonable speeds helps to preserve your tires. The tread wears almost twice as rapidly at 70 miles per hour as at 45 miles per hour, especially in hot weather or when driving on curved or rough roads.

Avoid striking sharp objects such as curbs, rocks or the edges of holes in the paving. Hitting such objects can pinch the inside of the tire between the rim and the hard object and break the fabric. Any cuts or bruises in sidewalls tend to shorten tire life.

Avoid sudden starts and stops, which scuff off tire tread, and avoid skids, which can leave quantities of rubber on the pavement and take scores of miles off tire life. Keep brakes adjusted correctly so that no tire bears more than its share when brakes are applied. Switch wheels regularly, at no greater than 5000-mile intervals, according to a regular tire-switching plan. This gives every tire a turn in each position. Include your spare in the switching plan.

You should be careful to maintain the tire pressure recommended by the manufacturer. This is a most important way to increase the service your tires will give you.

Check the pressure when your tires are cold and always *before* starting on a trip. Never wait to check pressure until after the tires have been heated by driving, and then "bleed" them to what seems like proper pressure. Correctly inflated tires build up pressure as you drive. If you then reduce the pressure by "bleeding" you will have underinflated tires when they cool, a condition that causes rapid wear. Underinflated tires permit excessive flexing of tire walls. This produces too much internal heat, and the result can be rapid wear and dangerous blowouts. Overinflation also can cause blowouts in weak tires, and excessive and uneven wear, especially on the center of the tread.

Never drive on a flat or soft tire, except to get the car entirely off the roadway for safety.

Inspect your tires frequently for sharp materials picked up from the road and for sidewall blisters or bruises. Remove bits of glass, stone or metal embedded in the tread.

Have your wheels checked regularly for alignment, play and balance. Follow the manufacturer's recommendations on how often the check should be made. Tire life is greatly shortened by wheels out of line or out of balance or by abnormal play in the steering.

## How to Save on Fuel

Some commonsense driving practices greatly help to improve the gasoline mileage you obtain from your car. You will find these suggestions result in savings:

Moderate speeds pay off in saving fuel. Increased speeds can mean appreciably increased gasoline consumption. For prolonged high speeds, you pay in fuel.

You can waste a lot of gasoline by "racing" your engine when starting. "Racing" can burn as much gasoline as speeding, especially when the engine is cold. If you use a manual choke button when starting, push it in as soon as the engine runs evenly. This prevents too rich a gasoline-air mixture from being sucked into the cylinders, which is no help to engine performance and which permits excess gasoline to drain into the crankcase and dilute the lubricating oil.

Sudden, uneven, up-and-down acceleration wastes gas. Start, drive and stop smoothly, and maintain a steady pace. Be a smart driver by planning ahead so you won't use your gasoline to build up speed, only to be forced to brake almost immediately and "kill" the speed. That kind of driving practically throws gasoline away. Screech-brake stops always waste gasoline. Drive in traffic at speeds that enable you to reach consecutive intersections in the green-light interval; you then avoid unnecessary and expensive stops and starts for red lights. Drive gearshift cars in lower gears only as long as is necessary before shifting to high. Driving in the lower gears consumes fuel faster. Shut off your engine during prolonged waits, though never, of course, in traffic. Some drivers fail to realize that an idling engine can use a quart of gasoline in two ten-minute stops.

## Keeping Your Engine in Shape

Having your car engine tuned occasionally will help to keep it operating more efficiently and economically. There is economy in maintaining an engine to give sound performance.

Have a mechanic check the ignition now and then to keep it correctly timed. When the timing is incorrect the spark occurs at the wrong moment, the gasoline-air mixture is not properly burned and you do not utilize the full power of your fuel. A mechanic can also determine whether or not valves are properly seated and operating as they should for high motor efficiency.

An engine running at the proper temperature is easier on fuel. If it runs too hot or too cold the thermostat may be defective or not adequate for the antifreeze being used. Correcting this will save fuel. Too rich a fuel mixture, shown by black smoke from the tailpipe, means wasted gas. Have an experienced mechanic adjust the carburetor—an adjustment that only a skilled person should make.

Overheating takes life out of a car engine. Every time you stop for gas, check to make sure that the radiator is full of water and that the water is moving when the engine is running, showing that the radiator is not clogged. Flush out the radiator every fall and spring. Keep the fan belt just tight enough to avoid slippage, and inspect its inner surface now and then for telltale cracks that show it needs replacement.

If the temperature gauge shows near boiling, stop the engine at once and check the radiator water level. Cool the engine off before you add cold water or you might crack the block or head. Run the engine at idling speed while adding water. Check the fan belt to see whether it is loose, off the pulley or broken. Look for leaks around all hose connections, and tighten loose hose clamps. If the car still overheats, consult an automobile mechanic before further driving.

Correct lubrication helps to guard your car investment. Have the car lubricated regularly, as directed on the manufacturer's schedule and according to its own lubrication chart. Always lubricate well before and during long trips, because sustained driving makes special demands on lubrication. In a car with automatic transmission, check the transmission oil level according to instructions in your owner's manual.

## How Good Driving Cuts Costs

Good driving practices help to reduce the wear and tear on your car. If you drive a gearshift car it will pay you, for instance, to keep the clutch pedal fully depressed while you start the engine, especially in cold weather. This saves the battery, since the starter does not have to work against the cold, stiff grease in the transmission. It will also pay you to warm the engine by letting it run for a short time before starting to drive so that lubricants become more fluid before the engine is harnessed to its load.

If you keep your foot on the clutch pedal or "ride the clutch" when not using it, the result is needless clutch wear. Also, forcing your car to work in the wrong gear for the driving conditions puts it under a strain and results in unnecessary wear.

You help to prolong the life of your car engine by driving with smooth, even acceleration. Avoid sudden speeding up and slowing down. In fact, good car maintenance and all correct driving habits pay off financially, whether in direct economies in operation or by avoiding the heavy costs of accidents.

## BEWARE OF SERVICE STATION GYPS

If you are planning a long auto trip you should be alert to the risk of service station gyps. Although the owners and operators of most filling stations are completely honest, there is a small but growing percentage who are willing to bilk the unwary tourist by tricking or frightening him into accepting unnecessary repairs and then charging him exorbitant prices. These gypsters usually prey on out-of-state drivers, particularly on women traveling without a man, or on younger, less experienced drivers.

Their tricks include: surreptitiously slashing your tires while pretending to check the air pressure, squirting oil on parts of the engine or suspension to indicate a "leak," intentionally damaging your car's fan belt or even crossing or disconnecting ignition wires while checking your oil. In some cases they will simply warn you that your tires are "not safe" for driving conditions

in that part of the country—and your anxiety will do the rest.

To protect yourself against these service station gyps, you should take the following precautions before and during any long-distance automobile trip:

1. Reread your car owner's manual to be sure you are familiar with simple maintenance problems, and have the car itself—including the tires—thoroughly checked and serviced by your regular mechanic.

2. When you stop for service, get out of the car. Watch the attendant's activities under the hood and at the pump. See that he clears the pump before putting gasoline in your car. Make certain you pay only for your gasoline—not a different dollar amount read from another pump.

3. Be watchful if the attendant checks the fan belt; a palmed knife may be used for slashing. It's a good idea, particularly if your car uses an odd size, to carry a spare belt with you.

## Protecting Your Car in Winter

Have your car well prepared for winter weather before the date when the first frost is expected in your part of the country. A complete garage job of winterizing should include:

1. Safety features. Adjust brakes; check tires or shift to winter tires; check windshield wipers; check defroster and heater.

2. Ignition system. Clean and check spark plugs; test condition of battery; check generator, condenser, voltage regulator and distributor; clean and adjust breaker points; inspect starter motor.

3. Lubrication. Change oil and lubricants to lighter winter grades, according to your owner's manual.

4. Watch out to see that the attendant doesn't pour liquid or squeeze it from a syringe over your fuel pump, in order to make you believe it is leaking.

5. Be particularly observant when tires are being checked for proper inflation. A sharpened screwdriver, known in the trade as a honker, can be used for slashing sidewalls.

6. An attendant probably cannot tell by looking at your engine whether the spark plugs need replacing. If you had them checked before leaving home, chances are they do not. The same is true of shock absorbers, points and condensers, especially if the car has been running properly.

7. Take remarks about "unsafe" tires with a grain of salt. If your tires are properly suited to the size and weight of your car, if they were inspected by your own service station before you left home, if they show no cuts, sidewall bruises or blisters and still have adequate tread (a minimum of 1/16th inch in depth in the major grooves), they should get you to your destination with safety to spare.

*Remember that most filling station operators are honest.* If you have watched the attendant carefully while he serviced your car and he recommends a minor repair, he is probably sincerely interested in your convenience and safety.

There should be an extra word of warning, too, for foreign-car travelers. Despite the extensive service organizations set up by many foreign automobile manufacturers, you may find it difficult to get repairs or replacement parts if you break down en route— even from the most honest and up-to-date of the regular service stations. You should be doubly sure to have your car checked before setting out, and you may ask your dealer to supply you with an emergency kit of minor spare parts: a fan belt, spark plugs, points, condenser, fuses, and the like. Ask, too, for a list of service facilities on the route you plan to take.

4. Fuel system. Adjust carburetor; check fuel line.

5. Cooling system. Flush radiator and cylinder block; add antifreeze and rust inhibitor to radiator, following manufacturer's instructions; inspect and adjust fan belt; check all hoses for leaks.

There are two types of satisfactory antifreeze solutions: (1) the alcohol type (low boiling point), which is ethanol (ethyl alcohol) or methanol (methyl alcohol), known as radiator alcohol; and (2) the all-winter type (high boiling point), which is ethylene glycol sold under various trade names and known commercially as permanent antifreeze.

If you use the low-boiling-point type of antifreeze, test it with a hydrometer now and then during cold weather to make certain it has not evaporated, leaving your car unprotected against freezing temperatures.

An antifreeze solution should not be left in the cooling system all summer, because it may cause rust and scale to form. When freezing weather ends, flush the system with clean water and add a rust preventive. Never use antifreezes made from calcium chloride, which corrodes metals, or a petroleum distillate, which causes rubber hoses to deteriorate.

If your car freezes in winter the best policy is to push it inside where it is warm and let it thaw out.

Your car may require a change in the weight of engine oil at low temperatures. After winter is over and warm weather returns, be sure to change back to proper summer lubricants.

## Caring for the Ignition System

Take care of your car's ignition system. When starting the engine, always have car lights turned off; on gearshift cars depress the clutch pedal. These practices decrease the load on the starting motor and save the battery.

Keep battery plates well covered with water. If the battery is weak in turning over the starter motor, have it recharged or replaced. In winter, with a cold engine, stiffened grease, lights used for longer hours and the added load of a heater and defroster, the car battery undergoes greater strain and must be kept well charged. A poorly charged battery is also likely to freeze in winter weather.

Use spark plugs that give a proper spark; weak sparks do not give you the full power possible from your gasoline. Use the kind recommended for your car by the manufacturer.

Have your spark plugs and distributor breaker points checked, cleaned and properly "gapped." If your engine "skips" or pulls unevenly, have it inspected. There may be a poorly adjusted carburetor, a fuel-line break, a bad condenser or a weak high-tension coil.

## Taking Care of Your Brakes

Faulty brakes are found on nearly one third of the cars tested at inspection stations. Too few drivers realize that keeping brakes in condition means economy as well as safety.

When brakes are out of adjustment, tires and brake linings wear out faster. If they "drag," the linings wear out fast, the braking is uneven and control is difficult. Have your brakes checked regularly and promptly adjusted when needed. Replace damaged or worn parts without delay.

The master cylinder must be kept full of heavy-duty hydraulic fluid, and the cylinders at each wheel must be in sound condition. If you sense any decrease in braking power, or if you can press the brake pedal nearer to the floor than an inch and a half, have the hydraulic system inspected at once. Have the brake drums and linings inspected if the brakes squeak, grab or chatter.

Wet brake linings may not hold evenly. Carefully test brakes after you have driven through heavy rain or forded a stream. If they slip, apply them carefully while driving slowly; they quickly dry out.

Avoid overusing your brakes. The so-called brake driver is hard on both the braking system and the tires. Be alert to traffic conditions ahead, and avoid emergencies requiring sudden stops.

## How to Check the Steering Mechanism

If there is any symptom of trouble in your car's steering mechanism, consult an expert mechanic at once. No driver can afford to risk steering failure.

The following conditions warn of possible steering trouble:

1. Too much "play." If you turn the steering wheel two inches before it starts to turn the front wheels, an adjustment is needed.

2. Hard steering. This can be caused by unequal or underinflated tires, inadequate lubrication, improper wheel alignment or worn or improperly adjusted steering parts. Have all checks made.

3. "Shimmy." If the steering wheel shakes rapidly from side to side, check tire inflation and wheel balance. If neither check solves the trouble, have a mechanic tighten connections, correct wheel alignment, replace worn parts or balance the wheels, as needed.

4. Car wandering. If your car wanders from side to side or turns persistently to one side, it can mean unequal tire pressure or poor wheel alignment. Replace worn parts or balance the wheels.

No driver can afford to neglect bad-steering symptoms. Have them attended to without delay.

Good driving and maintenance habits like these not only increase your safety but can save you money over the years.

CHAPTER 39

## Taking the Sting Out of Garage Bills

*Let's face it, some repairs and replacements are unavoidable. Here's a realistic, painless way to cope with these inescapable expenses*

Most people just haven't found a practical way to budget for car care. Automotive repair bills always seem to hit just when your bank account can least stand the strain.

The ideal solution to large and unexpected repair bills is, of course, to prevent automotive problems and anticipate costs. It can be done! Surprisingly, good preventive maintenance is not so complicated or expensive as you might imagine. About $20 a month should do it. Here's how:

To begin with, don't base this year's auto expenses on last year's. (Diagnostic clinic records and state vehicle-inspection statistics show that even the car owner who considers himself extremely conscientious often overlooks the servicing necessary to keep his auto safe as it ages.) Instead, when you make the down payment on your new car, deposit $100 in your checking account. This is your down payment on your family's safety. Each month during the years you will drive your car, you allocate to its preventive maintenance $20 of the family income. This means that you and your mechanic will catch potential problems before they can cause trouble.

To keep track of things, use the chart and accompanying list of car services on pages 368 and 369, which indicate (1) when servicing is necessary; (2) which parts are due for repair or replacement at certain times; (3) approximately how much these items will cost.

Most services, repairs and replacements can be handled at six-month intervals; a few need to be attended to in the interim. All services can be performed at most service stations, garages or car dealers; they are of the sort referred to in owners' manuals as "necessary maintenance." Some parts may not have to be replaced when the chart indicates, but you can ask your mechanic to keep an eye on them from that time on. The $20-a-month budget covers even the cost of five new tires.

The chart is geared to auto expenses and driving conditions in the north-central region of the United States. But you can adjust the chart to your own requirements and set up a workable system.

If you are starting your budgeting with a car that's not new, the chart will serve you equally well. Have your mechanic give the car a complete physical exam or send it through a modern diagnostic center (see "Clinics for Sick Cars," page 370) to find out its condition and make any needed adjustment; then start the chart with the month that corresponds to your car's age.

If your car is more than four years old, however, give it a complete checkup, have repairs made and start at the top of the chart, as if the car were new. But don't expect the chart to predict the timing for replacement of major items; in the health of a car that has done four years' duty, there are just too many variables to forecast when it will show signs of age.

At the end of four years you will probably trade in your car for a new one. If so, the balance in your budget will be more than enough to start a brand-new preventive maintenance plan. If you decide to hold on to your four-year-old, you can carry on from there and keep it in top condition.

Nobody can put a price on automotive safety. But for only $100 down and $20 a month you will have the benefit, without any sudden strains on the family budget, of a safe, dependable car.

## Your Car Care Budget

| AT THE END OF MONTH: | WHEN YOUR BANK BALANCE IS: | PLAN TO INVEST IN SERVICE: | WHICH WILL COST ABOUT: | LEAVING A BALANCE OF: |
|---|---|---|---|---|
| 1 | $120 | A | $ 0 | $120 |
| 2 | 140 | AB | 4 | 136 |
| 3 | 156 | A | 0 | 156 |
| 4 | 176 | ABC | 8 | 168 |
| 5 | 188 | A | 0 | 188 |
| 6 | 208 | ABD | 50 | 158 |
| 7 | 178 | A | 0 | 178 |
| 8 | 198 | ABC | 8 | 190 |
| 9 | 210 | A | 0 | 210 |
| 10 | 230 | AB | 4 | 226 |
| 11 | 246 | A | 0 | 246 |
| 12 | 266 | ABDE | 95 | 171 |
| 13 | 191 | A | 0 | 191 |
| 14 | 211 | AB | 4 | 207 |
| 15 | 227 | A | 0 | 227 |
| 16 | 247 | ABC | 8 | 239 |
| 17 | 259 | A | 0 | 259 |
| 18 | 279 | ABD | 50 | 229 |
| 19 | 249 | A | 0 | 249 |
| 20 | 269 | ABC | 8 | 261 |
| 21 | 281 | A | 0 | 281 |
| 22 | 301 | AB | 4 | 297 |
| 23 | 317 | A | 0 | 317 |
| 24 | 337 | ABDEF | 230 | 107 |
| 25 | 127 | A | 0 | 127 |
| 26 | 147 | ABH | 124 | 18 |
| 27 | 38 | A | 0 | 38 |
| 28 | 58 | ABC | 8 | 50 |
| 29 | 70 | A | 0 | 70 |
| 30 | 90 | ABDG | 85 | 5 |
| 31 | 25 | A | 0 | 25 |
| 32 | 45 | ABC | 8 | 37 |
| 33 | 57 | A | 0 | 57 |
| 34 | 77 | AB | 4 | 73 |
| 35 | 93 | A | 0 | 93 |
| 36 | 113 | ABDE | 95 | 18 |
| 37 | 38 | A | 0 | 38 |
| 38 | 58 | AB | 4 | 54 |
| 39 | 74 | A | 0 | 74 |
| 40 | 94 | ABC | 8 | 86 |
| 41 | 106 | A | 0 | 106 |
| 42 | 126 | ABD | 50 | 76 |
| 43 | 96 | A | 0 | 96 |
| 44 | 116 | ABC | 8 | 108 |
| 45 | 128 | A | 0 | 128 |
| 46 | 148 | AB | 4 | 144 |
| 47 | 164 | A | 0 | 164 |

**What Each Servicing Should Include**

"A" Service
  Have visual inspection made of:
    radiator.
    drive belts.
    transmission.
    oil.
    tires.
    battery.
    windshield-washer fluid.
    lights.

"B" Service
  Change oil.
  Test positive crankcase
    ventilation valve.
  Make under-the-car safety
    check.

"C" Service
  Install new oil filter.
  Clean air filter.

"D" Service
  Have a complete lubrication
    and inspection.
  Test battery.
  Clean terminals.
  Replace windshield-wiper
    blades.
  Aim headlights.
  Have a minor tune-up,
    including:
      servicing spark plugs.
      adjusting distributor.
      adjusting timing.
      chemically cleaning
        positive crankcase
        ventilation valve, choke
        and carburetor.
  Check all wiring.
  Check brake system, including:
    linings.
    drums.
    hydraulic components.
    fluid condition.

Rotate tires.
Check wheel alignment.
Balance wheels.
Polish car.

"E" Service
  Repack wheel bearings.
  Check and flush cooling
    system.
  Replace antifreeze.
  Have a major tune-up, which
    means a minor tune-up
    plus:
      replacing spark plugs,
      positive crankcase
      ventilation valve and
      distributor parts.
  Have a more comprehensive
    test made of engine and
    electrical components.

"F" Service
  Expect to replace:
    fan belt.
    radiator hoses.
    radiator pressure cap.
    thermostat.
    windshield-wiper arms.
    muffler and tail pipe.
    shock absorbers.
  Lubricate universal joints.
  Request a major brake
    servicing, including:
      relining and, if necessary,
      rebuilding wheel cylinders
      and resurfacing drums.

"G" Service
  Expect to replace battery and
    cables.
  Adjust automatic-transmission
    linkage.

"H" Service
  Replace five tires.

369

▭▭▭▭▭▭

## CLINICS
## FOR SICK CARS

Husbands quite often hear complaints from their wives that the family automobile is not running properly. In many cases the wife is at a loss to explain just what the trouble is or what is causing it. For these women modern technology has devised a way to answer their husbands' questions— by getting a report from a car clinic.

These clinics examine almost every working part of the car in much the same way as a physical checkup is carried out at a medical clinic. In the past six years more than 100 such centers have opened in the United States. The clinics have an array of electronic equipment, which is used together with visual and manual inspection. They may have repair shops where any necessary work can be done, but the customer is not required to have the repairs done at the clinic that tests his car. The checkup and diagnosis usually costs about $10. The 100 or more separate tests may take up to 45 or 50 minutes, and a customer can wait while they are being made.

After the tests are completed, the customer discusses the results with the technician and is told what work, if any, is needed. A written estimate of costs is given, and repairs are guaranteed if done at the clinic. However, the clinic report can be taken to another repairman where the needed work can be done or a cross-check made on the estimated cost. In many clinics repair and parts prices are posted where they can be seen before an estimate is made.

An advantage in having a car thoroughly tested for overall problems is that if several repair jobs are needed they all can be made at once, so that a car is not tied up in a shop on several occasions. Besides, making minor repairs when first found can prevent future major overhauls and cut maintenance costs. A car clinic also is a useful place to have a secondhand automobile checked before buying it.

There is, of course, the problem of knowing whether a place that calls itself a diagnostic center really has the equipment to make the tests a good car clinic can offer. Members of auto clubs can check their clubs for approved listings of car clinics. Or the local Better Business Bureau can be checked to see if any complaints have been filed against a car clinic under consideration.

Electronic equipment used in a full-scale clinic is expensive, and just putting a testing machine in a garage or service station does not make it a diagnostic center. The American Automobile Association's clinic in St. Louis cost $200,000 to set up. Centers such as this, where no repairs are made, charge more for diagnostic work. A report from a diagnostic center of this type is taken to a mechanic or repair service, and the car owner knows specifically what needs to be done.

Preventive repair work after diagnosis in a car clinic often saves a car owner money in the long run and increases the safety of his car.

▭▭▭▭▭▭

**8**

# COLLEGE
# WITHOUT BANKRUPTCY

*Advance planning with a knowledge of
scholarships, loan sources and job opportunities
can lighten the family's load*

## CHAPTER 40

## The High Cost
## of Higher Education

*College costs are shooting up.*
*Here's what to expect and how*
*to plan for this*
*big important outlay*

It's no news that college costs are higher than ever and still going up. At some schools basic expenses are three times what they were a generation ago; at others the jump has been fivefold and greater. In another ten years, going to college will probably cost 50 percent more than it does now. Nevertheless, most students who qualify for college, even poor youngsters, can find a way to go—provided they and their families are realistic about costs, about their own ability to pay and about where to turn for help.

On the next page are some current estimates of expenses—tuition, fees and room and board—at an assortment of colleges and universities throughout the country.

Obviously these figures vary widely. Public institutions—community colleges, state colleges and state universities—are generally much cheaper than private colleges, particularly if you live in the area. Costs are often higher in the East and Far West than in the South and Midwest. Living at school, of course, is more expensive than commuting. In some cases a high-cost institution, because of the financial help it can give, may prove just as accessible to a low-income family as a less expensive school.

The cost of a college is not necessarily a guide to its quality. Besides, an expensive place may be wrong for your youngster even if you can afford it; an inexpensive school may offer just the courses and environment he wants.

In any case, you'll need an estimate of costs for each college being considered. Here's how to go about it:

1. Consult the catalogue or a standard directory at the library for the current basic charges: tuition, fees, room and board, and out-of-state charge if there is one.

2. Estimate personal expenses for a nine-month period: clothes, health, recreation, dues, snacks, laundry, travel, telephone, haircuts. Also set down an estimate for books and supplies and a prorated annual figure for such miscellaneous items as a typewriter and room

accessories. If the student intends to live at home, forget about rent or furnishings, but do add up the other items so that you can make a fair comparison of expenses at different types of schools. In a family of moderate means, personal expenses for a student living at home might be around $800 for nine months.

3. That's your estimate of *current* costs. To project ahead, add 5 percent of that figure for each year. Suppose you have arrived at a total of $2100 for the current year, but your son or daughter expects to enter college two years from now. Add 10 percent, raising the figure

## A Sampling of Typical Tuition Charges, Fees and Room and Board Costs Around the Country

| COLLEGE | STATE RESIDENT TUITION AND FEES | OUT-OF-STATE RESIDENT TUITION AND FEES | ROOM AND BOARD |
|---|---|---|---|
| Abilene Christian College (Texas) | $1188 | $1188 | $ 850 |
| Bowie State College (Maryland) | 310 | 560 | 800 |
| Brandeis University (Massachusetts) | 2275 | 2275 | 1200 |
| Clemson University (South Carolina) | 596 | 1196 | 776 |
| Hampton Institute (Virginia) | 950 | 950 | 800 |
| Harvard University (Massachusetts) | 2400 | 2400 | 1300 |
| Hiram College (Ohio) | 2035 | 2035 | 860 |
| Juilliard School of Music (New York) | 1815 | 1815 | Not applicable |
| Lakeland College (Wisconsin) | 1590 | 1590 | 970 |
| La Verne College (California) | 1670 | 1670 | 840 |
| North Carolina State University | 382 | 907 | 766 |
| Northwestern University (at Evanston, Illinois) | 2190 | 2190 | 1197 |
| State College at Lowell (Massachusetts) | 255 | 655 | 850 |
| University of California at Berkeley | 325 | 1525 | 985 |
| University of Chicago | 2100 | 2100 | 1200 |
| University of Nebraska at Lincoln | 433 | 933 | 880 |
| Vassar College (New York) | 2155 | 2155 | 1300 |

to $2310, for the first year; add 15 percent to the current figure for the second year of college, making it $2415; and so on. Thus, a college that now costs $2100 a year will very likely cost over $2600 five years from now. Those are rough estimates; but they're conservative, and it's safer to round them off upward.

## How to Meet Those Expenses

The first source of financial support is current family income. Presumably that already pays for a good part of your child's expenses —food and clothing, for example—and will continue to do so when he goes to college. Perhaps there will have to be some pinching to carry an additional share of the costs. Work out a figure that can be allocated annually.

Savings should be another major source of help. Unfortunately, most families do not save for education, or save far too little. And many that do have assets—stocks, bonds, house equity, paid-up insurance—often are too hesitant about using them for educational purposes.

If college is still some years away, now is the time to start saving up for it. The parents should ask themselves: "How much could we save every week, if we tried a little?"

Could you save 25 cents a day? Half a dollar? Maybe each of you could steal three dimes out of your loose change every day. All right, that's 60 cents a day. Doesn't sound like much of a saving program, but let's see where it gets you.

Every Friday, without fail, you take the $4.20 you've saved from the grocery and odds-and-ends money that week and deposit it in a savings account. Suppose the bank pays you 4 percent interest, compounded semiannually (admittedly this is very low). By the time Timmy or Suzy is ready for college, in 15 years, your six dimes a day will have piled up a $4253.07 balance in the savings account.

If you had spent a little time shopping around for the most interest you could get on your savings, and had put your dimes into an account that paid 5 percent instead of 4 percent, that 1 percent difference would have added $379.33 to the account—pure earned interest, money you didn't have to work for. If you put $5 a week into a savings account paying 5 percent compounded quarterly, at the end of 15 years you'd have $5783.03. That illustrates the importance of careful shopping for top interest on your savings. And make sure it's working for you right from the beginning. Even a half or quarter of a percent can add up, over the years.

But is a simple savings account the best way to build up a send-the-kids-to-college fund? Surveys show that most families use one of four methods: savings accounts, government bonds, insurance policies and mutual funds. How do they compare?

Buying government bonds on a bond-a-month plan, using automatic payroll deductions, is a good method for many families simply because of that word "automatic." When the bills are piling up and you have to pull and tug to make ends meet, it takes a will of iron to wrest a dollar in cash away from yourself and turn it over to a savings teller. But if those few dollars for savings just quietly disappear from your paycheck before you get it, and you never see them in cash, you'll get along without them and seldom be aware that they're missing. In dollars and cents, however, you won't come out quite so well on bonds as you can with a savings account when you've shopped around for a good rate of interest.

Now, what about using life insurance to finance college costs? The type of insurance most often used nowadays is an endowment policy. Endowment policies, like most types of cash-value insurance, consist of two parts. A young father might buy, for example, a $10,000, 15-year endowment policy that would (1) insure his life, giving his family $10,000 at once if he died during the 15 years, and (2) if he lives, pay him $10,000 cash at the end of 15 years. One company's premium for a policy, issued at age twenty-five, is $613 a year. Part of the premium pays for the "pure" insurance, based on the company's calculation of the risk that the policyholder will die, obliging the company to pay the $10,000 death benefit. The remainder of the $613 premium goes into what is, in effect, a savings account that will build up, over the 15 years, to the $10,000 the policyholder will collect if he lives.

The twenty-five-year-old father could buy the "pure" insurance separately (it's called reducing term insurance) for $33.60 a year. Then, instead of turning the remaining $579.40 over to the insurance company to return to him later with interest, he could put it into a

375

savings account of his own. Dividing it into monthly deposits, at a conservative $4\frac{1}{2}$ percent compounded quarterly, at the end of 15 years he'd have, not $10,000, but $12,363.26.

Thus an endowment policy to provide for college expenses is not the way to make the most of your savings. It does have one virtue: Families who can't force themselves to save in any other way will generally scratch up enough to pay life insurance premiums.

If there's plenty of time ahead and you're well covered by insurance and have cash emergency funds on hand, a stock or mutual-fund investment program may be the best way to hedge against inflation and rising college costs. However, no one should attempt to accumulate education funds by "playing" the market as it fluctuates. The aim should be to invest in solid growth stocks on a regular basis. (The periodic-purchase plans offered by the New York Stock Exchange and most mutual funds are useful for this kind of regular investing.) Only a portion of the savings program should be committed to the market, and good professional advice should be obtained. For more on this topic, see Chapter 56, "The ABCs of Stocks and Bonds," page 525.

You've now been exposed, lightly, to the methods most parents use to lay away funds for college expenses. Why not get started on one of them no later than tomorrow?

---

## THE FANTASTIC GROWTH OF THE TWO-YEAR COLLEGE

Nowhere in higher education is the growth more dramatic than in two-year colleges. In 1968, some 50 new two-year colleges opened. In 1969 another 50 or so sprang into existence, bringing the total to 1050 or more. By 1974 there may be 1300 in operation, with probably half of the high school graduates who go to college choosing a two-year college.

But figures tell only a small part of

the story of this uniquely American phenomenon in higher education. What lies ahead for many a high school student who cares to investigate is the discovery that the nearby two-year community college can be an exciting place to go. More important, he's likely to find that it wants him and has a program for him whether he is a mediocre student or a bright one, has special talents or doesn't know what he would do well.

Junior colleges have been around for some time. Most people have thought of them vaguely as private finishing

---

schools for well-off girls, as vocational schools or simply as places to go if you couldn't get into a four-year college.

The new two-year community college that leads the way in the nation-wide junior college movement is far more than that. It is a comprehensive, publicly supported institution where you can learn anything from cooking to advanced chemistry. Its purpose is to open its doors to everyone and keep them open day and evening. Its courses might run six months, two years—or in some cases as long as three years.

Critics say that this kind of school tries to be too many things to too many different people, that it's a smorgasbord with no order to it. But supporters counter that the special function of the community college is to reflect the educational and occupational needs of its community. It's a place where employers can find trained help and even cooperate in the training. And it's a place where students can sort themselves out into academic, semiprofessional or other types of programs that best suit them.

At most colleges you will get an Associate in Arts (A.A.), Associate in Science (A.S.) or Associate in Applied Science (A.A.S.) degree if you take a transfer program that can be continued at a four-year college, or a certificate if you complete an occupational program.

To check on junior colleges and what they teach, see *American Junior Colleges*, edited by Edmund J. Gleazer, Jr., and Paul L. Houts, at your library.

The idea of two-year, low-cost community colleges is attractive, but how successful are they? What are the chances that a youngster who completes a transfer program will be able to get into a four-year college and do well there?

Graduates of transfer programs will have little trouble getting into four-year colleges. Students of Montgomery Junior College, in Maryland, as one example, have transferred to about 200 colleges, including Yale, University of Pennsylvania, University of Chicago, Stanford, Oberlin, Harvard and Columbia.

In a survey of four-year colleges 450 said they were especially interested in graduates of junior colleges. Some examples are: University of California at Berkeley, Wesleyan (Connecticut), Bowdoin, Goucher, Brandeis, Mount Holyoke, Hamilton (New York) and New York University.

Normally, if you have a C average in a regular college-parallel program, you will be able to transfer. The better your marks, of course, the wider your choice.

You may lose some credits when you transfer, and discover, too, that the work load at a four-year college is heavier than you expected. Montgomery Junior College warns its students to expect a "transfer shock" as they get used to the new campus, new teaching and grading policies and new classmates. Many who transfer from two-year colleges find that they have to take more than two additional years to get their bachelor's degrees. And a good many students drop out for financial as well as academic reasons.

But a good proportion do wind up with degrees eventually. And most of them have kind things to say about the teachers and courses they had at junior colleges. This is especially true of bright students who could have entered four-year institutions in the first place but who say that if they had it to do over, they would again start at a junior college.

Not all is smooth running at community colleges. Some are growing so fast that they have little time to catch up with their problems.

Dropouts are a major worry. Many colleges keep only a small fraction of their entering students for two years. There are often good reasons, of course, why students quit. Some get married, some go into the Army, some have family money problems. And many get jobs in their field of training before they finish the program. Too many students, though, sign up for the wrong courses and then quit because the courses are too difficult or because the subjects fail to arouse their interest.

The policy of accepting everyone is sometimes blamed. But it isn't only poor students who drop out. Wenatchee Valley College in Washington found that its incoming freshmen represented almost a cross section of a typical high school graduating class. Half had been in the top 50 percent, half in the bottom 50 percent; 18 percent in the top quarter, 16 percent in the bottom quarter. In the sophomore year the cross section held pretty much the same. In other words, dropouts came from all groups.

The key to the problem is skilled counseling. Junior colleges say this is one of their central services, but an important study shows that three fourths of them have poor guidance staffs.

Finding good teachers is another difficulty. Where the college is treated as a stepchild—in states, for instance, where two-year branches of the state university get priority—staff recruiting for the comprehensive community college is difficult. Where it's given support, finding good teachers is no problem.

Facilities vary widely. In some places—such as Dallas; San Mateo, California; St. Louis; Oakland, Michigan; Chicago; Portland, Oregon; Seattle; New York; and Peoria, Illinois— multimillion-dollar campuses with capacity for elaborate audio-visual equipment have been built or are being planned. But in many other cities the local two-year college is still hardly more than a high school building.

Attending a two-year college is obviously not like going to a private residential college or a state university. For one thing, everyone commutes. Students tend to be older, career-oriented and less intellectual, though many could have entered a four-year college if they had wished.

What the new community college offers, however, besides convenience, low cost and a wide selection of programs, is the chance to escape the mad anxiety about "getting into college."

## CHAPTER 41

How to Go to College on
Almost Nothing a Year

*Believe it or not,*
*it's still possible—*
*if your youngster*
*is lucky enough to*
*get a scholarship*

A scholarship is still the most desirable and most sought-after type of student aid. Scholarships fall into three categories: unrestricted (or general), special and regional. Unrestricted scholarships, such as the National Merit awards, are available to any qualified candidate, and are usually granted on the basis of test scores. Special scholarships are given to students with certain specific connections or qualifications or both: children of union members, children of members of fraternal organizations, sons or daughters of clergymen, members of almost all religious and ethnic groups; the list is endless. Regional scholarships are limited to students living in a particular city or state (for example, the New York State Regents Scholarships). Each year, however, many scholarships go begging because families are just not aware of the number and kind that are available.

The amount of the scholarship your child may receive is usually based on your own financial situation. To find out what you will be expected to contribute, send for the financial statement provided by the College Scholarship Service (the financial division of the College Entrance Examination Board), Box 176, Princeton, New Jersey 08540. Forms are also available at most high schools and colleges. When you have returned the filled-out form, the service will forward it to the colleges you designate, along with an estimate of the amount you can provide. Each college decides for itself the amount it will offer.

In determining your ability to help with college expenses, the College Scholarship Service considers the following: mother's and father's salary; any additional income; business or farm (net worth); other holdings (real estate, savings, investments); special family circumstances (number of dependents); student's savings and other assets; business and medical expenses; debts (for certain purposes).

The table on page 380 shows what a family is expected to be able to pay annually out of income only to support a child at college.

More and more financial aid given to students by colleges these

379

| NET INCOME BEFORE FEDERAL TAXES | NUMBER OF DEPENDENT CHILDREN | | | |
|---|---|---|---|---|
| | 1 | 2 | 3 | 4 |
| $ 6,000 | $ 750 | $ 530 | $ 350 | $ 230 |
| 8,000 | 1,220 | 950 | 720 | 560 |
| 10,000 | 1,690 | 1,350 | 1,060 | 890 |
| 12,000 | 2,150 | 1,730 | 1,400 | 1,190 |
| 14,000 | 2,690 | 2,110 | 1,720 | 1,480 |
| 16,000 | 3,330 | 2,520 | 2,050 | 1,770 |
| 18,000 | 3,970 | 3,070 | 2,360 | 2,050 |
| 20,000 | 4,600 | 3,600 | 2,800 | 2,320 |

days comes in "packages." At Williams College in Massachusetts, for example, if a student needs $1800 aid toward expenses, he'll probably get $1200 in an outright scholarship, $350 as a loan and a $250 campus job. In general, however, the size of the scholarship portion is usually much lower—about $700 on the average at private colleges, $400 at public institutions. At some schools, as many as 40 or 50 percent of all undergraduates are helped financially. Nationally, about a fifth of all students have some kind of aid.

## Figuring the Student's Needs

Good marks are a help toward a scholarship but don't count as heavily as they used to. Financial need has become the central factor, especially in determining the size of the award. Under the 1965 Educational Opportunity Grants program, colleges now have federal money to help many poor youngsters of average ability.

Family assets and the ability of a student to earn some of his own expenses are also taken into account, as are any special circumstances. Look at these two students applying for aid at a college that estimates costs at $2650:

John is one of four children. His father earns $7000. Expectation from family income toward college expenses is therefore about $400. Family assets include $9000 equity in a $13,000 house and $1000 in savings. Debt equals $400, leaving a net worth of $9600, but the father is fifty-five and the college figures that all of that would be needed toward his retirement. John himself has $500 in savings and could earn $300 during the summer. So the total amount estimated

380

to be available to him for college expenses the first year is:

| | |
|---|---|
| From family | $400 |
| Summer earnings | 300 |
| From his savings | 100 |
| | $800 |

Thus John needs $2650 minus $800, or $1850. Some of it will be offered to him in an outright scholarship, maybe as much as $1000, the rest in a loan and a job. If he's an excellent student, an outstanding athlete or attending a well-endowed college, the scholarship portion may be higher.

The second student, David, comes from a home that includes two other children and a totally dependent grandmother. One of his brothers attends a school that costs $1500. His father earns $15,000. Taking all circumstances into account, the college figures that about $1800 can be paid out of the father's income toward David's annual expenses. Family assets include $18,000 equity in a $30,000 house and other savings and investments totaling $10,000. Accordingly, the college decides that about $250 is available annually from assets. David's first-year resources are therefore:

| | |
|---|---|
| From family | $2050 |
| From summer earnings | 300 |
| | $2350 |

His need, as it turns out, is only $300 and probably no aid will be offered. However, if he wishes, he can probably borrow the money, pay the college in installments or get a job.

The largest scholarship awards are made by the most famous private colleges. In fact, about half of all scholarship money is given by about 10 percent of the colleges. Even students from families with higher than average incomes are often aided at these places. But the schools are also the most expensive. At publicly supported colleges, costs are lower, which is in itself a form of aid.

What about an athletic scholarship? Hundreds of colleges give them, though not all schools by any means. Most go to top football and basketball players, but other athletes get them too. According to the National Collegiate Athletic Association, the total amount of the grant can't exceed the cost of room, board, tuition and fees plus

$15 a month for laundry and cleaning. Some regional conferences set lower maximums. A true athletic scholarship is one of the few remaining forms of aid that is often given without regard to need.

Normally, students must meet certain academic standards to qualify for an athletic scholarship, but at many colleges they're quite moderate. In the Atlantic Coast Conference, combined SAT (Scholastic Aptitude Test) scores must total at least 750. In the Big Ten, predicted grade-point average for the freshman year must be about C—. Most conferences say that athletes must maintain passing marks, may not receive pay from other sources, are not to be enticed by heavy entertainment, and so on.

For advice on how to evaluate an athletic scholarship offer, send $1 to the National Football Foundation and Hall of Fame, 137 Church Street, New Brunswick, New Jersey 08901. Ask for the booklet *Making College Count, A College Guide for High School Football Players.* It's helpful for all sports.

## Sources of Financial Aid

The first place to look for financial help—scholarship, long-term loan, time-payment plan—is the college itself. But there are many other sources of aid too:

*National Merit scholarships.* Hundreds of thousands of students take the tests every year. About 14,000 become semifinalists, and most of those—about 97 percent—become finalists. But only about 2400 wind up actually winning National Merit awards ranging from $100 to $1500 a year, depending on need. Average grant is $800.

*National Honor Society scholarships.* Members elected to the society are eligible for over 230 scholarships worth from $500 to $6000. If your child's school has no chapter and would like to establish one, the principal or another faculty member should write to the National Association of Secondary School Principals, 1201 Sixteenth Street, N.W., Washington, D.C. 20036.

*Aid for veterans.* Educational grants are available to the children of veterans who were on active duty after January 31, 1955. Query the nearest office of the Veterans Administration. The child of a veteran who died or was disabled as a result of service may be eligible for as much as $180 a month for education. Check your state department of education and the Veterans Administration for details.

*State aid.* Over 30 states now offer residents some form of financial aid for education. Others are considering doing it. Rhode Island, as one example, gives from $250 to $1000, depending on need, to some 5 percent of its high school graduates each year. Query your state department of education to find out if similar opportunities exist where you live. Be sure to ask whether there is special help for the field the student plans to enter.

*Your community.* Ask your Chamber of Commerce, the library, the board of education, fraternal and service clubs about scholarships and loan funds that local businessmen may have set up for the young men and women in your town.

*Industry.* Many companies have loan or scholarship plans for children of employes or for residents of communities in which they have plants. Don't neglect to check with the firm for which you work about such a plan.

*Labor unions.* The California Labor Federation AFL-CIO, as an example, offers several awards each year to high school seniors, whether or not their parents are union members. Many other unions have similar programs.

*Professional groups.* A number of professional organizations offer aid to students entering their field. For example, the Newspaper Fund, P.O. Box 300, Princeton, New Jersey 08540, publishes a *Journalism Scholarship Guide* for majors in the field. It also lists newspapers that have scholarship programs for newsboys.

*Religious and ethnic organizations.* Query the local and national headquarters of any religious or ethnic group to which the family may belong. The Order of the Sons of Italy, for example, gives several scholarships each year.

*Social Security.* A change in the Social Security Act has extended the age limit for children's benefits from eighteen to twenty-two for full-time students. If this would affect your situation, ask your local Social Security office to give you up-to-date information about the new regulations.

*Federal programs.* For a list of federal programs, write to the Division of Student Financial Aid, U.S. Office of Education, Washington, D.C. 20202.

*Other sources.* The U.S. Bureau of Indian Affairs will supply information about aid for American Indians. The National Merit program has special Achievement Scholarships for Negro students, and here are some other places for Negroes to inquire: National Scholarship Service and Fund for Negro Students, 6 East Eighty-second Street, New York, New York 10028; Office of Economic Opportunity, 1200 Nineteenth Street, N.W., Washington, D.C. 20506; Cooperative Program for Educational Opportunity, 17 Hillhouse Avenue, New Haven, Connecticut 06520; College Admissions Center, 610 Church Street, Evanston, Illinois 60201; Herbert Lehman Education Fund, 10 Columbus Circle, Suite 2030, New York, New York 10019; United Negro College Fund, 55 East Fifty-second Street, New York, New York 10022; Scholarship Information Center, University of North Carolina YMCA-YWCA, Chapel Hill, North Carolina 27514.

□□□□□□

## BUDGETING FOR COLLEGE STUDENTS

When young Robert goes off to college as a freshman, a vital subject in his home, as in millions of homes across the land, is money. "What's the best way for Robert to handle his college allowance?" his mother asks as she gazes fondly at her son. "Should he get a fixed allowance or write home as he needs cash? Open a checking or savings account?"

There are fundamental rules to guide Robert and his parents, you and your youngsters—and these guides apply whether the student is a boy or girl, goes away to school or stays at home, has $5 or $50 per week. Here are the major money ABCs, from the vantage point of the present or future college student:

1. *Decide in advance with your parents what your allowance is supposed to pay for.*

If your allowance is to pay for clothes and important supplies at school, have this clearly understood and allocate funds for these expenses. Don't say, "Sure, twenty-five dollars will do," only to discover a few weeks from now that $25 simply won't do and you must start the weekly "Please, I need more" refrain. If your allowance is to cover just ordinary expenses, such as laundry, cleaning, grooming, have this understood too.

2. *Plan the spending of your allowance as carefully as you plan your study courses—both with your parents and on your own.*

The vital secret to this is a seven-days-a-week plan under which you'll divide your available cash into a spend-

□□□□□□

ing kitty for each day. If you don't do this, you'll be feasting on the first days, in a famine on the last days. You should start your day-by-day plan right after you get to school and be honest with yourself about it. If you know you'll want to spend a certain amount each day at the soda fountain, allow for that amount per day when you set up your budget.

3. *Open a bank checking account as soon as you get to school.* Don't use your desk drawer or pocket as a "bank." The chances of loss or a feast-famine pattern are overwhelming. Open an account, learn how to make deposits, draw checks, balance a checkbook, keep any service charges to a minimum. It will be invaluable training for later life.

4. *If you and your parents can manage it, open a rainy-day account in a savings bank nearby.*

There will always be extra expenses—a special event or a crisis—for which you'll need or want money. This savings account should be earmarked for these extraordinary expenses only, not otherwise touched. If you can't start with this savings nest egg, try to juggle your seven-days-a-week spending plan so you can save a bit and build one yourself.

5. *Don't try to figure your spending down to the penny.*

No plan ever should be that precise. You must have a margin of safety over your regular spending to cover "regular emergencies."

6. *Maintain some simple records on where your money is going.*

Your check stubs will help, but also keep a notebook in a spot where you can easily jot down every day how you're spending your allowance. Don't be too detailed in these records, but don't neglect them either.

7. *Look for ways you can stretch your allowance by free entertainment and by using your leisure time to save on expenses.*

You may be able to save by pooling basic items or dividing up chores with your college friends. You can save a lot with a needle and thread, an iron and a clothes brush.

8. *Learn sensible buying methods and apply them.*

If you're handling your own wardrobe at school, take advantage of neighborhood store sales and off-season clearances. Buying essentials in bulk or on special sales can save you impressive amounts over the course of a term.

9. *During your first reunion with your parents, show your record books, and discuss what's right and wrong with your allowance setup.*

If you're running short despite all your efforts and have records to prove your responsible management, you'll have a good case for a raise. You'll also be able to decide intelligently what you should do if your parents can't afford to give you that raise.

10. *Once you've learned these rules, stick with them!*

Actually, these are money guides for life, not just for college. No matter what your age, you can apply most or all of them.

## CHAPTER 42

## Study Now, Pay Later

*Low-interest government
loans: how they work,
how to get them,
some other sources*

The rising cost of a college education has created a serious dilemma for many parents. Even middle- and high-income families, who are generally considered too well-off for full scholarship aid, have found that the cost of tuition, room and board, clothing, transportation and allowance for a college-age son or daughter takes a large chunk of their annual earnings. Families with two or more children in college or graduate school at the same time are under a tremendous financial strain.

An exceptionally bright youngster may qualify for a full scholarship, a grant or a fellowship. But what about the vast majority of students whose grades are just average?

Thanks to liberal federal legislation, parents in this situation do not have to take out a high-cost loan to cover college expenses or assume the entire financial burden themselves. The government has devised two plans for long-term, low-cost education loans to students, the Federally Insured Loan Program and the National Defense Student Loans. The first is available to students of low-, middle- and high-income families. The second is designed primarily for lower-income students, and loans are allocated on the basis of financial need.

### Federally Insured Government Loans

Here's how the Federally Insured Loan Program works. Any student enrolled in a college, university or other institution of higher learning (such as nursing schools, junior colleges and vocational and technical schools) may apply for a loan. You, the student, borrow the money directly from a commercial bank, savings and loan association, credit union, insurance company or other participating institution. Your signature and proof of your enrollment or acceptance at an eligible school are generally all the bank will require. In some states you must be a full-time student to qualify; in others you must be attending school at least half time.

As an undergraduate or graduate student, you may borrow as much as $1500 a year to a total of $7500. The basic interest rate on the loan is 7 percent a year, but the government may also pay a bonus of up to 3 percent a year to the lender. (In some states the most you can borrow a year is $1000.) Repayment starts 9 to 12 months after your studies are completed. You can pay back as little as $360 a year and take ten years to repay.

If your family's net income is less than $15,000 (after deducting 10 percent for taxes and $600 for each dependent), the government will pay full interest up to 6 percent while you are in school. Thereafter you must pay 7 percent interest, and the government will continue to pay any bonus interest. To give you an idea of how liberal this provision is, a family of four with a gross income of $19,333 a year would be eligible for government subsidy while their son or daughter is in school.

If your family's net income is more than $15,000, you may also secure a guaranteed loan. The only difference is that you must pay 7 percent interest from the beginning.

Repayment of the loan may be deferred if you return to full-time study or if you join the armed services, the Peace Corps or VISTA. Payments may be suspended for this period, and the government will resume the interest payments. The debt is canceled in the event of death or permanent disability.

What is the best way to apply for these loans? You, the student to whom the loan will be made, should write to or visit the financial office of your college and ask for the names and locations of banks or other financial institutions near your home which are participating in the loan program. (If your family has had dealings with the institution so much the better.) Then go to one or more of them and find the appropriate officer who will help you complete the necessary forms. If your college is among the many tied in with the program, its financial aid office may help you with the forms. If it is not, the aid office still will give you the locations of the participating financial institutions in your home community.

Of course, the lending institution is not obligated to give you a loan. And it will determine the amount of money you can borrow. To date, the demand for these loans has been much greater than the supply, and many eligible students have been turned away. If you are turned down by one institution, don't give up until you have tried all the participating banks, savings and loan companies, and credit institutions in your community. If you're turned down by every lending institution to which you apply, write to the state guarantee agency for advice and discuss your problems with your college financial officer.

## National Defense Student Loans

The National Defense Student Loans program is available only to students who demonstrate a definite financial need. The degree of need is determined by calculating the total cost of education—including room, board, tuition, books, clothes and transportation—and subtracting from this the amount of money the family can supply. National Defense Student Loans are offered by individual colleges and universities rather than by private lending institutions.

As an undergraduate attending school at least half time, you may borrow up to $1000 a year to a total of $5000. Graduate students may borrow as much as $2500 a year to a total of $10,000 for both undergraduate and graduate study. The loans are interest free while you are attending school. After graduation you pay 3 percent simple interest each year on the unpaid balance.

Repayment begins nine months after you complete your studies, and you may pay as little as $180 a year for a period of ten years. If you become a teacher, you may cancel up to half the amount owed at a rate of 10 percent of the loan plus interest for each year of teaching. Teachers in schools for handicapped children or in designated low-income areas may cancel their entire debt at a rate of 15 percent of the loan and interest for each year of teaching.

If you join the armed forces, the Peace Corps or VISTA, or return to school at least half time, repayment may be suspended for that period. Again, the debt is canceled completely in the case of death.

## Other Sources of Loans

If you cannot obtain a low-cost government loan or if you cannot borrow enough to pay your expenses, you might consider these possibilities:

1. Many colleges and universities have their own loan and scholarship funds for qualified students. The financial aid officer of the college a student wishes to attend is the best source of details on such funds.

2. Some banks and other lending institutions have special education loan plans under which tuition and expense money is advanced in installments. The simple interest rate under these plans is often well under the bank's rate for ordinary personal loans. Repayment usually begins soon after the loan is made, and borrowers may take up to six or eight years to repay.

3. Many states, too, have special student loan and scholarship funds, as do numerous civic and private organizations. Again, the college financial aid officer is the best source of information on these programs.

4. There are private organizations which lend money to college students or guarantee educational loans. The largest private guarantor of student loans today is the nonprofit United Student Aid Funds, supported largely by private business contributions. The USAF is not only a major participant in the new federally assisted Student Loan Program, primarily as a guarantor of loans made by banks and other lending institutions in more than 30 states, but also has a separate guaranteed student loan program, with over 1000 colleges and universities participating in all 50 states. The USAF's address is 845 Third Avenue, New York, New York 10022.

To be sure to get the best deal when you apply for a commercial student loan, follow these basic rules: Draw up a total budget for all anticipated college costs, including tuition, board, room, books, clothes, transportation, spending money. Divide this amount by the total number of semesters of school attendance. Decide how long you will need to repay the loan. Present these figures to at least two or three different lenders and ask what monthly payments would be required—plus all charges for insurance. Compare each "bid." The lowest monthly charge will be the most favorable to you—assuming equal repayment periods, loan amounts and insurance charges.

Competition for any type of student loan is great, because the demand for loans far exceeds the amount of educational loan funds available. Here are some tips that may increase your chances:

First, apply early. If you know you will need a loan, apply as soon as you are accepted at the college you plan to attend. Many lending institutions use a first-come, first-served policy, so the earlier you apply, the better. The best source for information on student loans will be the financial aid officer at your college. He will suggest all the possible sources of loans, and he may even be able to help you get a loan.

Second, when you apply for a loan, be persistent. If you are turned down at one place, don't give up until you have tried all the other possibilities.

One more point. When you go to apply for a loan, put yourself in the other fellow's shoes. You are asking him to take a big risk and lend you his bank's money to go to college. If you look and sound as if you would be just as likely to drop out of school or not to repay the loan, he probably won't want to give you the money. If, on the other hand, he thinks you look like a mature, responsible person who would really appreciate the bank's help and would honor your obligation, chances are he'll lend you the money. So try to look the part—it will be well worth it!

## THE COLLEGE WORK-STUDY PROGRAM

Nearly 257,000 full-time college students who need financial assistance are being helped by the federally supported College Work-Study Program. Under this program the college or university finds jobs for students either on the campus or with off-campus nonprofit organizations. The government provides 80 percent of student wages, and the college or off-campus agency provides the other 20 percent. Over 1800 colleges and universities participate.

To be eligible for the program, a student must demonstrate a clear financial need. Students in the program may work up to 15 hours a week during the school year and up to 40 hours weekly in the summer and during vacations. Typical on-campus jobs include teaching assistant, library aide, laboratory assistant, maintenance worker and administrative aide. Off-campus employment may be for private nonprofit or public agencies in fields such as health, welfare, education or recreation.

Wages start at $1.30 an hour, with a maximum of $3.25 an hour. While annual earnings average about $1200, it is possible to earn as much as $2000 toward the costs of tuition, room and board, transportation, clothing, books and other necessary college expenses.

## CHAPTER 43

# You Can Still Work
# Your Way Through College

*More students are
working, more jobs are
available, pay
is rising. Here's what
you can expect*

College enrollments are at a record high, as are costs—with the result that more students than ever before are looking for part-time work to help meet their expenses.

But jobs are available in greater numbers too, and pay is up, so most students who want to can earn a substantial part of their college expenses.

Could you? Probably, though it depends to a large extent on where you go to college, what you can do and how many hours you can afford to devote to a job.

To find out what the best campus jobs are and how much they pay, a survey of a number of four-year and two-year colleges around the country was recently conducted. Here is what they report:

The good news is that over 80 percent of all students who apply for jobs get them. At some colleges jobs actually go begging. One out of every three schools reported more openings than they could fill. One reason for the availability of jobs is the federal government's new College Work-Study Program, which gives colleges millions of dollars for employment of needy students.

Do you have to be an above-average student to get a job? Not generally. About four out of ten colleges give some preference to those who have good marks. Do you have to show financial need? Not necessarily, but a great many schools do give priority to those who need aid. The federal work-study program jobs are reserved for students in need.

In general, the bigger the college, the greater the proportion of students who work. At universities with 20,000 or more enrollment, 50 percent of the men and 40 percent of the women work; in small schools the percentages are substantially lower. And the bigger the town in which the school is situated, the greater the chance of finding work. The same proportions hold for two-year colleges.

What is the best way to get a job? Register at the college placement office as early as possible, even before the school year begins. Acquire a skill: typing, shorthand, bookkeeping, gardening, drafting, auto repair, and so on.

"Be willing to try anything. Arrange your class schedule to allow sufficient time for work. Keep your grades up so that you can give your job enough time and energy. Be neat, personable, eager. Learn to type." So says Pratt Institute in Brooklyn, New York, where 90 percent of those who seek jobs get them.

"Plan early and keep in touch with the placement office regularly," says the University of Iowa. Almost everyone there who wants work finds it.

Antelope Valley College, California, where 90 percent of those applying get jobs, advises: "Have a skill. Have transportation. Be dependable, clean-cut."

Catholic University, Washington, D.C., where 70 percent who apply get jobs, says: "Learn a skill. Be businesslike in applying, prompt, neatly dressed, realistic about hours, pay, time off."

## How Much Can You Make?

On the average, students earn about $580 during the academic year and $615 during the summer. But the range of pay is wide. Look at these differences at a few colleges:

*Loyola University,* a large coeducational university in Chicago. Some 42 percent of the undergraduate students work an average of 15 to 20 hours a week. Earnings during the school year average $1600.

*Illinois State University,* a medium-size university in Normal. Approximately 25 percent of the students work an average of 10 hours a week. They earn an average of $475 during the school year.

*University of Texas,* a very large state university at Austin. About 45 percent of the students work. Their hours are about 15 to 20 a week, and they earn some $600 during the school year.

*Clark College,* a small two-year community college in Vancouver, Washington. Some 45 percent of the students work an average of 8 to 12 hours a week. Their earnings average $200 to $300.

*Simmons College,* a small women's college in Boston. More than 50 percent of the students work an average of 10 hours a week and earn $400 to $500 during the school year.

## CAMPUS CAPITALISTS

Jonathan R. Lax, president and chief executive officer of the Odyssey Fund, made an unlikely investment decision in January 1969. Though the small, fast-growing mutual fund was going nicely, he sold its entire common stock portfolio and converted the fund's assets to cash.

It wasn't that Mr. Lax feared the imminent collapse of the stock market. Rather, he had a tough art history exam coming up. "I couldn't very well study and keep on top of the market at the same time," he explained.

A bearded nineteen-year-old, Mr. Lax was a sophomore at Swarthmore College, Pennsylvania. He ran Odyssey Fund from his dorm room. Once exams were over, the fund, with net assets of $5000, was back in common stocks as well as in commodity futures. Shares were held by Mr. Lax, some classmates at Swarthmore and friends and faculty at other schools.

The young fund manager is just one of thousands of student entrepreneurs who are trying their hand at running small, independent businesses. Campus capitalists are flourishing across the country.

Some examples: Girls at Vassar sell each other greenhouse plants, knitting yarn and handmade Ute Indian pottery. Princeton men operate a highly profitable baby-sitting agency called Tiger Tot Tenders. Two co-eds at predominantly black Fisk University in Nashville run a barbershop spe-cializing in "Afro," or natural-style, haircutting. Three students at the Massachusetts Institute of Technology own $30,000 worth of pinball machines, spotted at strategic locations on and off campus. And two lads at Southern Illinois University do a booming business rigging parachutes for local crop dusters.

There's nothing new about a student earning his way through school, but collegians complain that college jobs are often dull, and the going wage of about $1.50 an hour doesn't make much of a dent in soaring education expenses. The students who go into business for themselves say the work is more stimulating and offers a high return for a small investment of time.

The Bureau of Labor Statistics estimates unofficially that 20,000 students between eighteen and twenty-four are running their own businesses. Most of these ventures are small, yielding well under $1000 profit annually. But there's no doubt that the total dollar volume is in the millions. At Harvard alone a group of 20 student businesses grossed $1.3 million in 1968.

Not all schools favor student entrepreneurs. Some administrators feel that business pressures hurt grades; others fear their campuses will be overrun by eager student salesmen. Despite the apprehensions of educators, the academic work of most student entrepreneurs apparently doesn't suffer significantly. Surveys show that the grades of most students remain the same when they begin working.

# A College Job Sampler

| COLLEGE | PERCENTAGE OF STUDENTS WHO WORK | PAY RANGE | AVERAGE HOURS WORKED PER WEEK | AVERAGE EARNINGS |
|---|---|---|---|---|
| Clark College, Vancouver, Washington | 45 | $1.00–2.80 | 8–12 | School year: $200–300; summer: $200 |
| Columbia College, New York City | 60 | $1.60–2.85 | 10–15 | School year: $600; summer: $600–1000 |
| Howard University, Washington, D.C. | Men: 50 Women: 30 | $1.60–5.00 | 15–20 | School year: $700; summer: $700–900 |
| Illinois State University, Normal | 25 | $1.30–3.50 | 10 | School year: $475 |
| Longwood College, Farmville, Virginia | 16 | $1.30 | 10–12 | School year: $400; summer: $100 |
| Loyola University, Chicago | 42 | $1.50–2.25 | 15–20 | School year: $1600; summer: $825 |
| New York University, New York City | 50–55 | $1.75 | 15–20 | School year: up to $1200 |
| Simmons College, Boston | Over 50 | $1.35–2.25 | 10 | School year: $400–500; summer: $650–700 |
| University of Texas, Austin | 45 | $1.30–1.95 | 15–20 | School year: $600; summer: $525–600 |
| Wesley College, Dover, Delaware | Men: 40 Women: 20 | $1.00–3.00 | 12 | School year: $200–500; summer: $600–800 |
| Wharton County Junior College, Wharton, Texas | Men: 25 Women: 5 | $1.00–1.25 | 15–20 | School year: $500–600; summer: $1000 |
| Yale University, New Haven, Connecticut | 40–45 | $1.78–2.14 | 10 | School year: $500–600; summer: $500 |

*Howard University*, a medium-size four-year college in Washington, D.C. Approximately 30 percent of the female and 50 percent of the male students work an average of 15 to 20 hours a week. Earnings average $700 for the school year.

*Yale University*, New Haven, Connecticut. From 40 to 45 percent of undergraduate students hold jobs. Hours average about 10 a week, and average earnings total from $500 to $600 a school year.

Hourly pay varies widely from job to job and school to school. At Wesley, a small junior college in Dover, Delaware, most jobs pay a minimum of $1 an hour.At Howard University, pay runs from $1.60 to $5.

A library assistant gets $1.25 at Wharton County Junior College in Texas; $1.30 at Longwood College in Farmville, Virginia; $1.50 to $1.75 at Simmons College in Boston; and $1.85 at Columbia College in New York City.

## Working Conditions

Here is a rundown of working conditions at a number of colleges throughout the country:

The average student worker puts in nearly 13 hours a week on his job, though many work up to 20 hours or more. What do colleges recommend as a maximum? Most name a figure well under 20 hours. The average comes to 16 hours. At the University of Illinois students are permitted to work up to 30 hours a week for the university while carrying a full course load. But most are advised to put in only 10 to 20 hours.

Sarah Lawrence College in New York suggests a top of 10 hours: "Freshmen are not encouraged to work (other than baby-sitting) unless the need is great."

Gustavus Adolphus in Minnesota also recommends only 10 hours: "Because of increased academic pressure it is becoming more difficult for students to work. We have had many students start work in September only to quit later or ask to have the number of hours cut down."

Instead of working long hours, many students take loans, and some colleges complain about it. Amherst College in Massachusetts reports: "There is good reason to question whether the majority

## TEN RULES
## FOR GETTING
## A SUMMER JOB

Here are ten key rules to help you in applying for a summer job—based on a recent survey of 200 summer employers by the National Directory Service in Cincinnati, publisher of the annual *Summer Employment Directory:*

1. Make a list of jobs for which you want to apply—perhaps a half dozen at most. Your selection should depend on your interests, abilities and specific needs, not just on where you think jobs might be available.

2. Write a letter of application to each employer on a single typewritten page, stating that you wish to apply for a specific job, the period in which you will be able to work and your reasons for wanting the job.

3. State also why you think you will qualify for the job he is offering—and indicate that you have a serious interest in doing the job well.

4. Specify what *you* have to offer the employer—in terms of talents, skills, interests, background, previous experience, willingness to work—not just what you want from the employer. Remember that you want to work for *him*.

5. Attach a concise, one-page "data sheet," giving your name; your address (school and home) and telephone number; personal information, such as your birth date, marital status, father's occupation; a brief educational outline, including the name of your school, your class, major, academic degrees, honors, extracurricular activities; previous work experience; other information such as your special skills, hobbies, travel; and the names and addresses of at least three references.

6. Include with your letter of application a recent photograph and a stamped, self-addressed envelope for your prospective employer to use in replying to you.

7. Make sure that each document is clear, short and neatly typed. The "data sheet" may be duplicated, but the letter itself should not.

8. If the employer sends you an application form to complete, fill it out neatly and completely—and follow all directions regarding extra documents required, references, deadlines, and so on. If you are sloppy on these details, it could easily cost you the job. Your application is a key clue to the employer of the kind of conscientiousness he might expect from you on the job itself.

9. Don't undersell yourself. List *all* the significant pluses that might help qualify you for a particular job. Don't overlook such "little" talents or achievements as "get along well with children" or "worked my way across the country last year."

10. *Apply early.* The longer you wait, the lower your chances of getting the job you want.

Some of these rules may seem obvious. But it's astounding how many job seekers fail to follow them, and thereby forfeit a good job.

of our students need or want to work. Regretfully, we have found that nonscholarship students work harder and earn more money than scholarship students and too many of the latter are prepared to take loans instead of working." As a result, Amherst has increased the figure that it expects scholarship students to earn during the summer and is cutting financial aid accordingly.

The attitude toward loans is quite different, however, at Murray State, located in a poverty area in Oklahoma, where jobs are getting tougher to find: "Loans, especially the government NDEA [National Defense Education Act] program, are a godsend to the low-income, honest student in a nonindustrialized area."

Many educators suggest that students are wise to put only a moderate number of hours into a job and borrow the additional money they need to make up the difference. The result is greater flexibility for course schedules and greater opportunity for participation in worthwhile activities.

## How Colleges Feel

A number of school administrators have reported how they feel about students who work part time in college. Their answers show their generally favorable attitude toward working students:

Wharton County Junior College in Texas: "Generally these students are conscientious and hard-working individuals. Some of the male students, however, work to maintain expensive automobiles and often find themselves in scholastic difficulties."

Loyola University in Chicago: "We use part-time students quite extensively. The students find that working at school is both convenient and a good experience. We have found their work performance good."

Howard University, Washington, D.C.: "Working students develop a strong sense of value and responsibility in college. They appear to be more mature and, surprisingly, show no adverse academic effects as a result of working part time."

Clark College, Vancouver, Washington: "There is a widely held notion that college is somehow a nobler and more worthwhile experience if the student works his way through. This is seldom the case. Being a college student is itself a full-time occupation, and the student's life should include as few outside duties as possible. Gainful employment of up to 20 hours per week need not preclude a full-time college course if both are properly scheduled, but anything approaching full-time employment clearly indicates the wisdom of a partial load in college. The serious student does not accept overlong employment merely to indulge his taste for expensive automobiles or other luxuries. If his circumstances truly require that he work from 20 to 40 hours per week then he should plan—with the aid of his adviser—a course which stretches his two Clark years over three years or even four."

Yale University, New Haven, Connecticut: "Generally students find that part-time work does not interfere with their academic program or extracurricular participation."

Wesley College, Dover, Delaware: Part-time employment provides students with "extra spending money," gives them a "sense of accomplishment" and "increases their appreciation of their education."

## Numbers Going Up

The number of students seeking jobs will increase steadily, but so will the number of jobs. Nearly 70 percent of the colleges say they've already noticed more openings becoming available.

California State at Fullerton says: "Nearby manufacturers need draftsmen, assemblers, lathe operators, etc., and many are willing to hire part-time help and, in some cases, train them. Retail stores use a great many students who are free to work late afternoons, evenings and Sundays. The placement office has more calls than it can fill for typists and salespeople."

The summer job situation is different. Finding suitable openings will probably get harder, especially as more and more high school students look for summer work. See "Ten Rules for Getting a Summer Job," on page 396, for specific advice on finding summer employment.

In summary, there are plenty of student jobs ahead for the school months, and pay is rising. But school work is getting tougher, leaving less time for work, and college costs are rising much faster than part-time pay.

# 9
# HOW
# TO HAVE MORE FUN
# FOR YOUR MONEY

*Whether it's a vacation in Europe
or a camping trip you want, travel today
can be cheap if you know the ropes*

## CHAPTER 44

# Timing Your Vacation to Cut Costs

*Those faraway places may be within reach if you take advantage of off-season rates*

To the amazement of friends and neighbors, the Roger Martins went to Europe last winter. No rich uncle had died nor had they mortgaged their home to the hilt. It was all a simple matter of timing. Like thousands of other Americans, the Martins discovered that a trip they had once dismissed as "too expensive" was actually within reach when they abandoned the traditional idea of a summer vacation. Savings started with their transatlantic transportation and continued right through hotel charges and everyday expenses.

If, like the Martins, you've pondered some "too expensive" trips, it's time you realized there's a high road and a low road to major or, for that matter, "mini" vacations. Because it's paved with fewer bumps in the budget, the low road offers you the quickest, surest way. Europe, the Caribbean, Florida, even your nearest major city —all of these places are geared to high and low periods. By timing your trips to take advantage of favorable rates, you can realize truly impressive savings.

A handful of free brochures from a local travel agent and some simple arithmetic should be enough to encourage transatlantic thoughts. You'll find that, unlike the Caribbean and other close-to-home vacation areas, Europe's greatest off-season bargains are based on transportation costs. For this reason, a table of air fares is the single most important document to study. Looking it over, you'll quickly come across the terms high, or peak, season and low, or off, season. Although peak season varies, in broadest terms it applies to spring and summer rush periods when flights to and from Europe are especially crowded. Late autumn and winter are what is normally considered off season, when popular low-cost fares prevail.

For your first comparison, note that the economy class New York–London passenger in 1969 paid $510 during the summer peak but only $420 during off season—a savings of $90. When passengers use group or excursion tickets the savings accelerate even faster.

For many years the most popular individual fare offered by the airlines has been the 14-to-21-day excursion fare. To take full advantage of this money saver, you should not only fly off season but also between 7 a.m. Monday and 7 a.m. Friday, since a surcharge of $30 each way is added on weekends. Excursion fares, like most of the other special low fares, permit a minimum stay in Europe of 14 days. The maximum length of stay has recently been raised from 21 to 28 days. The New York–London fare for midweek off season is $300, or $120 less than the basic off-season economy fare of $420 and $210 below the peak season economy rate.

Even lower rates are available on the new 29-to-45-day excursion fares. To take advantage of these rates you must remain in Europe a minimum of 29 days; the maximum is 45 days. There is no extra charge for weekend flights. Round-trip New York–London fare runs $250 off season and $295 in the summer.

## IT and GIT Plans

All of the other low airline fares are sold only in conjunction with the purchase of a tour package, and yet each of the fares has significant differences. First, there is the IT (Individual Inclusive Tour) economy fare which, like the 14-to-28-day excursion fare, is offered Monday through Thursday during off season, with return travel occurring between 14 days minimum and 21 days maximum. Although the basic IT rates are $30 less than 14-to-28-day excursion fares, the overall price will run around $40 higher once the tour package is added. But don't let that throw you—the tour is, almost without exception, an excellent bargain and the tour-fare combination easily trims $100 or more from the normal costs of independent travel.

Group Inclusive Tour (GIT) fares are relatively new and strikingly inexpensive. Despite the name, you don't have to be a member of a group to purchase this special fare. Technically you are supposed to be coming and going with at least 15 people who have bought the same GIT fare, but you are in no way restricted to the group and may never even be aware of who the members are. Like other package tours, the GIT is an effort by the airlines to screen out both the man who is traveling on business and the first-trip-to-Europe tourist who plans to see all the major sights. The fares are discounted to an attractive low and the savings then applied to hotel facilities, sight-seeing or special interest activities. These ground arrangements must total a minimum of $70 for 14 days and $7 more for each additional day.

Consider a typical GIT fare. From New York to Amsterdam, the round-trip off-season air fare in 1970 was $260. The additional $70 ground portion might have offered you three weeks' accommodations and a car with 1000 free kilometers. (That's 621 miles and it covers a lot of territory in Europe.) The total of $330 was the same as the 28-day excursion fare to Amsterdam, which did not include ground arrangements.

While it is true that GIT fares are also available during peak season for an additional $50, many of these summer packages are, as a rule, less exciting than those offered in fall and winter. There is one other money-saving advantage. Only a few of the summer package tours include Continental breakfast (coffee and rolls), hotel tips and taxes, which amount to an extra $1 a day, but during off season such charges are likely to be included.

## Package Tours to Look Into

Here are some of the package tours you'll want to investigate.

Two weeks in Paris on a round-trip jet from New York, with all hotels, sight-seeing and tickets to five top night-life attractions included, costs $330.

For a warmer climate you might choose two weeks in Spain and Portugal. The $330 price includes transportation, sight-seeing, hotels with private bath and breakfasts. (Your lunches and dinners will be inexpensive in these two countries.) The package provides for six full days in Madrid, followed by trips to Seville and Lisbon, from which you return on the 15th day of the trip.

If a winter ski holiday is more to your liking, $348 will give you two full weeks in Switzerland at Zermatt, Davos or Innsbruck, with round-trip jet from New York, use of a car, hotel accommodations, and Continental breakfast every morning. When you consider that daily rates at top European ski resorts average from $10 to $25, you realize the savings this GIT fare offers. Incidentally, when consulting airlines or travel agents about snow packages, ask about a bargain called "white weeks"—periods in which rates are greatly slashed and packages include ski lessons, free use of lifts and other extra services and features of the resort.

One of the newest airline sales categories is called the Bulk Inclusive Tour (BIT) fare. The BIT program, which went into effect in November 1969, is divided into three seasons: low, shoulder and peak. While the BIT plan offers perhaps the lowest fares ever available, such as an off-season 14-to-21-day New York–London round-trip ticket for $175, the fare is contingent on the purchase of an additional $100 worth of ground arrangements. With one major airline you can fly round trip to London, obtain hotel accommodations for 13 nights; English breakfast every morning (eggs and bacon, fruit, cereal or juice, fish, rolls and toast, tea or coffee); tickets to eight West End stage shows (guaranteed orchestra or dress circle seats); guest membership in a London casino; a 10 percent shopping discount; loan of a camera; and airport transfers—all for $275, which comes to $25 less than a regular New York–London excursion ticket.

Passengers holding BIT tickets must travel with a group of at least 40 persons but, like the GIT plan, the group can be made up of individuals put together by a travel agent for fare purposes. The BIT plan further resembles the latest GIT packages in that a $7 daily additional charge applies to the packages exceeding 14 days.

Don't be alarmed if, at this point, your arithmetic is no longer simple. Armed with only this working knowledge of airline jargon and bargains, you can approach your local travel agent with self-assurance that a plan or package to fit your budget does exist. Depending on the fare you finally choose, your off-season transatlantic transportation savings will range from $50 to more than $200. Double those figures if you're traveling with a spouse, and the savings really begin to add up.

Another important factor will not add dollars to your pocket but may add to your enjoyment of the trip. As one veteran traveler put it, "When you go in the winter, you really see Europe. In the summer, you only see the tourists." At the same time that several hundred thousand Americans are customarily arriving in Europe, several million Europeans are packing up and moving to mountain and seaside resorts. As a result, the large Continental cities so

## TIPS ON TIPPING

If you are planning a trip in this country or abroad, here are some useful tips that will help you win smiles, not snarls, from the assorted waiters, bellboys, cabdrivers, and so on, that serve you en route.

*In the United States:*

• Tip taxicab drivers approximately 15 percent of the fare, with a minimum tip of 25 cents. If a hotel doorman has summoned a cab for you, he too receives a quarter. Don't tip drivers of airport shuttle buses. If you rent a limousine for some special occasion, tip the driver 15 percent of the fare.

• Tipping a Pullman porter on a train is mandatory if he helps you on or off with luggage or packages, or even if you're just in his car. If he does help you with luggage, you should tip him about 35 cents for each piece he handles. In addition, if you travel in his car for a few hours during the day, tip him 50 cents as you leave, and if you're on for several nights, make it $1 a night.

• At an airport or air terminal the redcap, or porter, should get 50 cents for one small suitcase, $1 for a couple of pieces of luggage and as much as $2 if you're traveling with your family and the luggage is plentiful.

• Tipping in a luxury hotel is obviously more lavish than in small motels or hotels. In a luxury inn the bellhop who carries your suitcase to and from your room should get $1 for a small amount of luggage, as much as $2 for a considerable amount. You can cut that tip in half in a highway motel or an average hotel where you're only staying overnight.

• Chambermaids should be left 50 cents a day per person. When you check out, leave the money in the room in a sealed envelope marked "Chambermaid."

• There is no need to tip bell captains or room clerks unless they do you a very special favor. A bellhop delivering packages to your room should get 25 to 50 cents depending on the luxuriousness of the hotel and the amount of time he had to spend in delivering your package. For example, if he goes to the hotel drugstore to pick up something for you, the tip would be at least 50 cents; but if the store is off the premises, $1.

• If you're staying in a hotel on the American Plan, with three meals a day included in your overall bill, tip at the end of your stay. Give the waiter $1 a day for each member of your family; the busboy 50 cents for each member, and the headwaiter a total of $5 if you've been there for one or two weeks. You can increase that if the quality of the service has been especially good.

• If you call for hotel room service, a tip from 50 cents to $1 is sufficient if the room service waiter merely drops the food off. If he stays and serves you, tip him as you would a dining room waiter.

• Tipping is not limited to dining or traveling. For instance, if you're in a gambling casino, you can tip the dealer or croupier if you happen to be on a winning streak. At a beach resort you ought to figure about 50 cents a day per person for the beachboy or cabana boy who brings you beach chairs and towels, with a top of $1 a day if you're traveling with your family.

• When you dine out at an average restaurant during the course of your trip, the waiter or waitress should receive a flat 15 percent of the bill as a tip. In more elaborate restaurants— or if the service has been exceptionally good—you may want to increase this to 20 percent. The maître d' is tipped only at luxury restaurants where tables are difficult to obtain and he has made an effort to seat you promptly. From $2 to $5 is sufficient, depending on the price level of the establishment. If you accept the advice and services of a formal wine steward in a Continental-style restaurant, he should receive $1 per bottle uncorked. Hatcheck girls customarily expect to receive 25 cents per garment. Rest room attendants should be left the same amount.

*In Europe:*

• Unlike U.S. tipping practices, the bulk of the tip on the Continent is usually included in the bill, as part of the total to be paid, and extra tips—if any—are usually withheld until check-out time and then distributed in one grand sum to each person. The only employes customarily tipped before the final-hour reckoning are the porter who carries your bags to the room and the young bellboy who delivers messages to you upstairs.

• Nearly every Continental lodging automatically adds a service charge and taxes to your statement. They vary from 10 percent to 22 percent, depending upon the country. Most restaurants do the same: Check the next-to-last item on all bills.

• On departure from any but the bottom-budget hostelries, however, certain extra gratuities are expected. In most hotels or pensions—viewing the broad picture of all these lands— give the concierge, or hall porter, a minimum of 25 cents; stretch this to $1 or so if your visit has lasted more than a week and if his service to you has been especially good. Give the maid some small change (5 cents to 15 cents per day should do). The porter who handles your baggage is usually the man who has shined the shoes that you have left outside your door; he rates 20 to 50 cents when you move in and the same when you move out. Never give a concierge or clerk a lump sum for distribution to the rest, because he may keep it for himself (the manager won't).

• In European restaurants, give tips only if your waiter has been unusually attentive; an extra 5 percent is plenty.

• Finally, wherever you are and whatever you do, *always carry a pocketful of assorted small change.* Cash a large bill or two each day before leaving the hotel. If you always have the exact tip on hand, the time and money you'll save will be phenomenal.

popular with foreign tourists are comparatively quiet in midsummer. Strolling along the Via Veneto in Rome, you're likely to discover that the *dolce vita* crowd are none other than your fellow hotel guests. As for Paris, records show that more than 1½ million Frenchmen leave the city by rail alone during the 12-day period from July 24 to August 4 during a typical European summer. And despite recent efforts to stagger summer vacations, the famous *joie de vivre* of Paris may not be all that you expected if you arrive while so many of its regular inhabitants are away.

On the other hand, visiting the capitals in winter can be a memorable experience. In such cities as London, Paris, Rome and Copenhagen, there are operas, plays, concerts and festivals (these events often form the basis for a low-cost package tour). Vienna has 300 balls during carnival season (late January to Ash Wednesday), and Salzburg has special celebrations with music and costumes. The Spanish Costa del Sol, between Málaga and Gibraltar, becomes something of a paradise for golfers. You can spend a week in a good hotel on the Costa del Sol for about $100, including most meals. November to mid-April is the Irish hunting season, and Americans are welcome at the more than 80 hunt clubs located throughout the country.

Some travel authorities insist that to get the best combination of climate and economy in off season you should schedule your trip 30 days before or after the peak tourist season. As far as Europe goes, this might find you in Munich for the *Oktoberfest*, an outstanding beer and food festival, or in the Netherlands for spring tulip festivities.

## Caribbean Bargains

Elsewhere in the world, this reasoning can be a great ego booster. When considering the Caribbean, envy if you must those who flock there for the winter, but don't imagine they're getting out for anything resembling a song. You, however, can come close to it by jetting south after April 14 or a few weeks before December 15. And because the Caribbean bargain season lasts almost nine months don't imagine there's something wrong. Off-season weather is magnificent, since there are only a few degrees of temperature difference between winter and summer. Beaches and restaurants are not crowded and the service is generally better than at the mid-December to mid-April peak.

But most important, all accommodation rates are cut from 25 to 50 percent. Another advantage is that during high season (December 15 to April 15 or May 1), most hotels offer only American Plan (AP) or Modified American Plan (MAP). Under AP all three meals are included with room rates; with MAP, breakfast and dinner. Yet, during off season, you can usually find European Plan (EP), which provides no meals and leaves you free to try different restaurants. Since most tourists inevitably visit the local restaurants anyway, EP saves you from paying twice for a single meal when you decide to try them.

Typical peak-season rates in the West Indies and the Bahamas are about $55 a day MAP for two at a luxury hotel or $30 to $40 a day MAP at a tourist hotel. Off-season rates for two range from $32 to $38 MAP and $17 to $19 EP. In the summer small guesthouses and modest commercial hotels have rooms for as low as $6 single or $5 per person double, with all meals included. Since these hotels seldom offer commissions to travel agents, you'll have to obtain a list by writing the Caribbean Travel Association at 20 East Forty-sixth Street, New York, New York 10017.

Almost all Caribbean air fares remain the same year round. Even so, there are a number of ways you can time your flight to cut costs. Round trip from Miami to Montego Bay, Jamaica, costs $117 economy but only $64 on a 21-day excursion fare. The major restrictions are that you must travel on Tuesday, Wednesday, or Thursday and that you must be back in the States by the 21st day. No tour package is connected with these low fares, nor is there any minimum length of stay required. Also important to remember is that excursion fares permit generous stopovers (called island-hopping in the Caribbean). For example, you can fly all the way down to Trinidad off the South American coast and have more than 20 different islands to choose from in working your way back up (including Martinique, Antigua and St. Thomas). The midweek excursion fare for this colorful flight is $209 round trip from New York, $170 from Miami.

On New York–San Juan flights, where excursion rates do not apply, there is a special thrift fare that provides rock-bottom prices on individual round-trip tickets. To get the lowest possible fare, you must travel on what is called weekday night thrift. Monday through Thursday nights, the New York–San Juan thrift fare is only $114, or $38 below the weekend daytime thrift fare. The night thrift fare is not offered in peak summer, winter and holiday seasons.

## Special Rates for Miami

As long as it's off season, you might consider a combination Miami-Caribbean holiday. A Florida-plus-cruise vacation drops from $371 to $249, a saving of $244 a couple. This two-week package includes hotel room, breakfasts and dinners and an overnight cruise to the Bahamas.

One international airline is offering a new 22-day circle fare from New York to San Juan and Miami. The round-trip fare is $139—a saving of $26 below the lowest previous fare. There are certain restrictions. You must spend a minimum of six days on the trip and travel must be completed by the 22nd day. You cannot fly on Friday and Sunday afternoon or evening. Another airline offers a double vacation package that provides four days in Miami and three days in the Bahamas. The $165 price includes round-trip air fare, Miami Beach oceanfront hotel, breakfasts and dinners in Miami, sightseeing, transfers, round-trip air fare to the Bahamas, two nights' accommodations on Grand Bahama, nightclubs and other extras.

As a jumping-off point for islands of the Bahamas, Miami can't be topped. Popular fares include the $27 round-trip 17-day excursion fare to Nassau and the $27.50 round-trip fare from Miami to Freeport, Grand Bahama. Tourists who only want to gamble in the casino or take a whirlwind shopping and sightseeing tour of Freeport can purchase a special 18-hour excursion fare for $22.50. The fare is offered daily between noon and 6 a.m.

As early as April 1 Miami offers you some of winter's pleasures without the heavy frosting. A number of hotels reduce their rates by as much as 25 percent, and jai alai and horse racing continue until the end of the month. Fishing and camping are also highly popular at this time of year.

The lowest reduction in Miami hotel tariffs comes in May. With rates often 40 to 50 percent below on-season highs, you can save $6 to $10 a day per person, sometimes more. For example, a first-rate hotel charges about $20.50 a day per person, double occupancy, during the peak winter season, but only about $11 per person in May. By taking advantage of package vacations offered by your travel agency, you can even better these rates. A typical eight-day, seven-night package at an oceanfront hotel costs about $70 a person, double occupancy. The price includes hotel bills, airport transportation and a few nightclub outings.

Airlines also offer bargain packages during Miami's off season. One of the lowest-priced of these provides for one full week—eight days and seven nights—in an oceanfront hotel for $22.40 a person, double occupancy, European plan (a slight increase in July and August), plus air fare, of course. Another, with Modified American Plan, sells for $50.50, or about $7 a day.

The best flight bargains to Miami are based on the relatively new "Discover America" excursion fares. These round-trip fares, which have cut most U.S. air fares 25 percent, are applicable from noon Monday to noon Friday, and from midnight Friday to noon Sunday. Further reductions are in effect between East Coast cities and Florida on Tuesday and Wednesday flights during spring and fall months. (Philadelphia-Miami round trip is as low as $84.)

## More Ways to Save

Also investigate fares based on Family Plan. This arrangement enables a family of two or more to travel at greatly reduced rates on certain weekdays or at certain hours anywhere in the United States. The husband pays full fare; the wife pays half or two thirds of full fare; children under twenty-one pay either half or one third of full fare, depending on the area or airline. On a New York–Miami round-trip flight, a family of four will save about $175 by traveling on Family Plan instead of a regular coach class non-Family-Plan flight.

Another economical way to travel long distances is a fly-and-drive combination, particularly when you're interested in seeing more of an area than just the major city or resort. Several airlines and car rental firms now offer special car package rates in conjunction with your air fare. One car rental company charges $99 a week, with 1000 free miles; another company's vacation package costs $88 a week, with 500 free miles and eight cents a mile for additional mileage. On the road, you'll find that the total average cost for a family of four ranges from about $57 to $61 per day. The American Automobile Association breaks down the daily budget this way: $25 for meals and snacks; $19 to $23 for accommodations; $5 for tips and other miscellaneous items; and $8 for gas and oil, figured at 300 miles a day, 14 miles per gallon.

In addition to these special weekly rates, there are numerous budget plans offered by hotels and car rental firms for two- to three-day trips—the increasingly popular "mini" vacation. Here again, the savings are directly related to careful timing. For city dwellers a period in the country is more economical during midweek, while the suburban family will save by sight-seeing in the city over a weekend. The reason is that businessmen fill city hotels during the week, but on weekends hotels have as many as half their rooms empty. In the country the busiest period is a weekend and, consequently, midweek package rates give substantial savings over regular rates. Extras may include sight-seeing, special meals, or both, for city and country packages.

In New York, for example, a couple can spend three days, two nights, in a leading hotel for $26.95 per person for a double room with television and a bar-refrigerator, breakfast in the hotel coffee shop and free hotel parking. The extras included are a sight-seeing tour of the city, admission to Radio City Music Hall and the cover charge at a supper club or dinner show at a top discotheque. The normal rate for the room alone is $24 to $32 daily.

In Chicago a room priced at $39.95 per person for the same three-day, two-night period includes breakfasts, Friday or Saturday dinner, a sight-seeing tour or a boat trip. Free parking or free airport transportation is furnished. Many of these hotel and motel package rates permit children to sleep in their parents' room at no extra charge, an arrangement which also trims family costs.

During winter the most popular country outings are to ski resorts, and Monday through Thursday ski rates drop 25 percent lower than weekend rates. Airlines offer package plans which include a rental car with 500 free miles, tickets for several ski facilities in one area and a room for five days during the week. The cost runs about $97 per person.

One final area of savings is for city dwellers who can only get away weekends. In most large cities (New York is a notable exception), car rental companies, faced with a surplus of cars used by businessmen during the week, cut their rates after Friday noon. On a two-day weekend rental, you can save $10 or more. Some local auto rental companies even throw in the first 500 miles free of charge. Others do not charge for mileage at all but require you to pay for gas and oil yourself.

Although the examples end here, the savings don't. Reduced rates, low-cost packages, off-season and off-hour fares, major and "mini" vacations to the nearest large city, Florida, the Caribbean or Europe—what you've read so far is just the first step to traveling big and saving big at the same time. Heed these things, consult a reliable travel agent and soon you'll be surprising friends and neighbors with a "too expensive" trip of your own at a total cost you will hardly believe.

⎓⎓⎓⎓⎓⎓

## TRAVEL TALK

A table d'hôte lunch may well be cold. The "American Plan" has nothing to do with America, and many Caribbean hotels serve only Continental breakfasts. Confusing? Yes. But that's the language of travel. And if you want to enjoy your vacation this year, you will do yourself a favor by learning some of the jargon that so often creeps into travel literature. Here is a glossary of some of those terms (small capital letters mean that the word is defined elsewhere in this glossary).

**À la carte.** A menu from which items are chosen and paid for individually. This type of meal arrangement is hardly ever included in a tour.

**American Plan** (AP). Hotel accommodations with three meals daily included in the price of the room. This type of arrangement is sometimes referred to as full pension, especially in Europe.

**Carrier.** A public transportation company, such as air or steamship line, railroad or bus line.

**Charter flight.** A flight booked exclusively for the use of a specific group of people who generally belong to the same organization. Charter flights are

⎓⎓⎓⎓⎓⎓

usually much cheaper than regularly scheduled line services but are not open for sale to the general public. They may be carried out by regularly SCHEDULED or SUPPLEMENTAL carriers.

**Conducted tour.** A prepaid, prearranged vacation in which a group of people travels together under the guidance of a tour leader who stays with them throughout the trip. It is also referred to as an escorted tour.

**Continental breakfast.** A breakfast generally consisting of a beverage (coffee, tea, cocoa or milk) plus rolls, butter and jam or marmalade. In Holland and Norway, cheese, cold cuts or fish are generally also provided.

**Couchettes.** Sleeping accommodations provided on some European railroads, mainly French, consisting of a day compartment which may be converted into bunks for four passengers. Pillows and blankets are provided. Since the sexes are not segregated, passengers may not disrobe at night. There is slight additional charge above railroad fare for a *couchette*.

**Coupons.** Documents issued by tour operators in exchange for which travelers receive prepaid accommodations, meals, sight-seeing trips, and so on. Also referred to as vouchers.

**Courier.** A professional travel escort, also called tour leader, tour escort and tour manager.

**Demi-pension.** Hotel accommodations which include CONTINENTAL BREAKFAST and either TABLE D'HÔTE lunch or dinner in the room price. Also called Modified American Plan.

**English breakfast.** The kind of breakfast generally served in the British Isles, including Ireland. It usually includes hot or cold cereal, bacon or ham and eggs, toast, butter, jam or marmalade and a beverage (but not fruit juice).

**EP.** *See* EUROPEAN PLAN.

**Escort.** *See* COURIER.

**European Plan** (EP). Hotel accommodations with no meals included in the cost of the room.

**Final itinerary.** The schedule provided by your travel agent which spells out in detail the exact program mapped out for you, including flight or train numbers, departure times, hotel accommodations, and so on. It is delivered shortly before your departure.

**Full pension.** *See* AMERICAN PLAN.

**Guide.** Someone who is licensed to take paying guests on local sight-seeing excursions.

**Ground arrangements.** All those services provided by your tour operator *after* you reach your first foreign destination. The travel overseas is not included. Also referred to as land arrangements.

**Modified American Plan** (MAP). Hotel accommodations that include breakfast and either lunch or dinner in the price of the room. Also called *demi-pension*.

**Optional.** A word often used in travel literature that means you have a choice of taking or not taking the service mentioned. If you take it, there is always an additional charge over basic tour price.

**Pension.** A French word widely used in Europe meaning guesthouse or boardinghouse.

**Scheduled carrier.** An airline that publishes a tariff and carries out regular flights between given points. In international service most scheduled carriers belong to the International Air Transport Association (IATA). In domestic service most are members of the Air Transport Association (ATA).

**Suggested itinerary.** A preliminary itinerary provided by tour operators for your consideration. It generally shows routings and approximate times, as well as recommended hotels and sight-seeing excursions, and spells out the conditions under which these services will be provided.

**Supplemental carrier.** An airline certificated by the U.S. government to carry out charter flights, but not permitted to engage in regularly scheduled services.

**Table d'hôte.** A complete menu from which deviations may not be made without incurring additional charges. It is the type of meal which will generally be provided when meals have been included in the price of the tour. In Europe, table d'hôte menus hardly ever include coffee or tea after the meal. These are considered "extras."

**Tips.** Gratuities to hotel employes, porters, guides, drivers and others. Be sure to check which tips are and are not included in your itinerary. They can make quite a difference in the cost of your vacation.

**Tour-basing fare.** A reduced, round-trip fare available on specified dates and between specified times, only to those passengers who purchase pre-planned, prepaid tour arrangements prior to their departure.

**Tour operator.** A company which specializes in the planning and operation of prepaid, preplanned vacations and which makes these available to the general public through travel agents.

**Tour organizer.** An individual, usually not professionally connected with the travel industry, who organizes tours for special groups of people, for example, teachers, lawyers, students.

**Tour package.** A travel plan which includes most elements of a vacation, such as transportation, accommodations and sight-seeing.

**Transfer.** The service provided travelers when they arrive at and leave a given city. It takes them from the airport, air terminal, pier or railway station to their hotel, and vice versa, generally accompanied by the local representative of the American tour operator who planned the tour. There is a variation in cost, depending on whether transfers are carried out by private, chauffeur-driven car or by taxi, and whether, in the case of air travel, the transfer is provided between airports and downtown air terminals or directly to the hotels.

**Vouchers.** *See* COUPONS.

**Wagon-lits.** Sleeping cars on Continental European railroads, consisting of a private bedroom (with a sink but no toilet) with accommodations for one or two people.

## CHAPTER 45

## Go Farther
## on Your Travel Dollar

*You can stretch your
overseas travel and see
more—without spending
an extra cent*

Invest a few hours checking the tariffs of overseas airlines, railroads and bus companies before completing plans for your trip abroad, and you can enjoy thousands of miles of additional travel for little or no extra cost. Little publicized, these expanded routings enable you to take advantage of some of the best travel bargains ever as a result of rates which airlines offer for competitive purposes. (Travel prices can change. The figures quoted here are for 1970 and can be used as a guide to approximate savings. But for the most up-to-date prices, check with the airline or travel agent.)

If you're traveling to Rio de Janeiro, Brazil, you can have your year-round economy ticket extended to Buenos Aires, Argentina—1231 miles farther south—for only $20 more. Not only can you enjoy an additional 2462 miles there and back, but you can also add to your itinerary such cities as São Paulo and Pôrto Alegre in Brazil and Montevideo in Uruguay—all on the east coast of South America—and such west coast cities as Santiago, Chile, and Lima, Peru. Cheaper tour and excursion rates are also available.

Few travelers realize that an excursion ticket to Rome also entitles them to visit North Africa and Scandinavia and allows a peek behind the iron curtain in Prague, Czechoslovakia (a country abounding, incidentally, with health spas), at no extra cost. You can stop off to ski in Switzerland and swim on the Riviera—all for the price of a round trip to Rome, which is pegged as low as $409. Two stops in each direction are permitted. There are also cheaper group rates.

For $140, or less than $5 a day, you can travel for one month, first-class, over most of Continental Europe's railroads. Your ticket, known as a Eurailpass, is also honored on a number of bus routes and lake steamers.

If you have a day to spare, 72 cents buys you an unlimited one-day travel ticket valid on a 1500-mile network of country bus routes that emanate from London. Many people, not realizing that this bargain is available, spend five or six times that amount on expensive tours.

There are virtually hundreds of such special deals, some of which will be discussed in detail later in this chapter. But first, how did the air fare bonanza come about?

## Extra Mileage at No Extra Cost

Most of the major international airlines belong to the International Air Transport Association (IATA), a worldwide organization that regulates rates. If you fly the routes of member lines, including those of the iron curtain countries, you are eligible for these special fares.

Suppose you're traveling to Geneva. Nonstop service is available on El Al, Swissair and Trans World Airlines. However, many other lines also serve the Swiss city—via London, Paris, Brussels, Frankfurt and Amsterdam. To remain competitive with the nonstop service and win your business, these airlines are willing to give additional mileage. For instance, instead of flying directly to Geneva for your Swiss vacation, you can stop first in Ireland, wing across to England, continue later to Amsterdam and finally fly to Geneva. Homeward bound, you can travel via Paris, Brussels or a host of other points. The fare for this extended trip is the same as the nonstop round-trip ticket to Geneva. This additional mileage does not apply to special no-stopover or limited-stop tariffs.

On an excursion fare from the West Coast to Sydney, Australia, including stops en route at half a dozen other South Pacific points, the basic round-trip fare is pared down from $1008 (the regular economy fare) to $756. The $252 saving will take care of much of your land portion costs. Also available is a complete tour of the South Pacific for only $995—or $13 less than the regular $1008 air fare.

Africa-bound tourists should examine airline tariffs very closely. A number of companies are promoting camera safaris for Americans who aren't interested in, or don't want the expense of, big-game hunting. One traveler took a camera safari and after spending a few days in Nairobi, Kenya, decided to make a side trip to Johannesburg, South Africa. Because he didn't tell the airline clerk that he held the return ticket on a Nairobi–New York fare, he forked over $323.60 for a separate Nairobi-Johannesburg round trip. He thought this was a reasonable amount for the 3600-mile flight south and back—until he encountered another tourist, who remarked that it was incredible that most New York–Johannesburg fares should be the same as the New York–Nairobi fares. The uninformed traveler had paid for a side trip that could have been included in his original ticket at no extra cost; needless to say, his vacation was spoiled. Only after weeks of negotiation was a refund granted; sometimes it isn't.

The moral is: *Always* check with the airline office or travel agent before purchasing side trips. Most of the time, your initial ticket can be rewritten to include the additional cities at the same price. This principle holds true for Africa as well as Europe, and even for the Caribbean and Pacific.

These are some examples:

If you purchase a New York–Paris ticket, you also can visit Lisbon, although the Portuguese city is much farther south.

If you buy a $161 midweek ticket from New York to Antigua, an island in the British West Indies, an extra $4 will take you much farther south and west to Curaçao. Weekend rates are slightly higher.

If you're bound for the Far East with a ticket to Bangkok, Thailand, you also can fly to Singapore, about 900 miles farther south, for no additional fare. Incidentally, a 12-month round-trip ticket from the West Coast to Bangkok also covers Honolulu; Anchorage, Alaska; Tokyo and Osaka, Japan; Taipei, Taiwan; Hong Kong; Manila.

If India is your destination, you also can include Moscow in your travel plans without paying a penny more. Traveling to India on the northern route via the Soviet Union, you pay the same fare as when you travel via the Mideast.

The basic factor involved in extended routings is the specific maximum mileage (fixed by the airlines) between any two points. (When this mileage is exceeded the passenger pays a prorated surcharge.) Because of this little-known bonus-mileage privilege there are additional miles you can travel for the same price and thus complete your itinerary at no extra cost, most of the time.

For example, the fixed nonstop distance between New York and Rome is 4280 miles. However, the airlines will let you fly a total of 5136 miles—a very handy bonus of 856 miles, which can be used for additional city hopping. Remember—the farther you travel, the greater the bonus mileage!

416

One businessman who travels to Rome quite frequently continues on to Sicily when his meetings are over, on the same ticket, and enjoys a weekend at the beautiful resort of Taormina. If he had to pay for this side trip, it would cost him an extra $55.80, but the 856 bonus miles take care of that. This past winter he continued across the Adriatic from Rome to Dubrovnik, Yugoslavia, and again didn't pay a penny more because he was within the maximum allowance. Next winter, he plans to fly on, at no extra fare, to Tunis or Algiers after Rome.

One of the bonuses well worth investigating is a visit to the Bahama Islands en route to Mexico. This costs only $6.80 more than the regular New York–Mexico City round-trip fare of $270. Look at a map and you'll see that the Bahamas are far off the direct route from New York to Mexico City; yet for the price of a dinner you can cover considerably extra mileage and enjoy another resort area.

Although New York City has been mentioned predominantly in these examples, the same principle is applicable to other North American cities.

## Group Fare Packages

Besides bonus mileage, there are additional types of fares that can be used to stretch your travel budget. Be advised, though, that there are many, many more than it is possible to discuss here.

Most popular of these is the so-called nonaffinity group ticket. Translated from airline parlance, "nonaffinity" means that to qualify for the particular tariff you need not belong to a specific group or association sponsoring a flight. *Complete* responsibility for obtaining the required number (usually between 15 and 40) of passengers to assemble this kind of group rests with the agent or carrier. All you have to do is contact a travel agent or the airline and purchase the nonaffinity group ticket. Then, when you reach your destination, you proceed independently of the others in the group.

For example, there is a special nine-day round-trip package that lets you travel to Israel for as little as $405 (including $45 for hotel accommodations). In spring and summer, the high travel season, the best rates available are $499 and $535 and you can stay up to a year—but hotels are not included in this price. When you consider that the regular high-season economy round trip costs $930 (without accommodations), the $405, $499 and $535 fares are indeed bargains.

Another type of nonaffinity fare is the bulk inclusive tour, known as BIT, which restricts you to a 14-to-21-day stay abroad. When the agent books 40 or more persons for a flight (usually the greater the number of passengers, the lower the flight fare), the New York–London rate, for instance, drops to $175 plus $100 worth of mandatory hotel or sight-seeing vouchers or both. Considering that you pay $420 plus land expenses in winter for the regular economy round trip, $275 is a very good buy. Summer BIT rates are $45 higher. (See Chapter 44, "Timing Your Vacation to Cut Costs," page 400.)

This BIT principle applies to most European points, and passengers often use up the required $70 worth of ground arrangements by hiring a car.

A word of caution on these special tariffs, however. Ask the agent to explain your responsibility should you have to cancel. If you back out of your plans when it's close to departure time, the airline may demand a cancellation fee. This can amount to a rather hefty sum, so get all the details before you place your deposit.

There are other exceptional savings that can be made on BIT trips, especially to the Orient. You can enjoy a complete vacation that includes air fare, hotels, meals and sight-seeing. Prices vary depending on the season, but if you're heading for Japan or any other part of the Orient, ask about BIT, which is rock bottom in price.

For instance, a travel agent or airline can sell you a complete 14-day vacation in Japan, including West Coast to Tokyo round-trip air fare and hotel accommodations, for as little as $500—$184 less than the low-season regular tariff of $684.

Similar deals are available when you travel to Hong Kong, Southeast Asia, Korea and the Philippines. And special low fares are available on South Pacific tours to Tahiti, Australia and New Zealand, as well as Fiji and New Caledonia.

## Bargains on Trains, Buses and Other Side Trips

Going back to Europe now, here are the details of what bargains lie in store for you on Europe's railroads and bus and steamer lines:

There are four versions of the Eurailpass. Besides the $140 pass for one month of roving around Europe, there is a 21-day ticket for $110, a two-month voucher for $180 and a three-month pass at $210. More than 100,000 miles of travel are available on these Eurailpass vouchers —but you must purchase them before leaving the United States.

How about the other extras thrown in with this all-purpose pass? Leave the rails and sail on Lake Constance, if you wish, aboard steamers belonging to Austrian Railways and German Federal Railroads. You also can travel on certain Rhine River steamers and even take a bus from Paris to Nice at the same one-pass rate. In addition, you're entitled to 50 percent off on numerous long-distance buses.

Eurailpass can save you much money and is well worth examining in advance to see if it fits in with your travel plans.

In addition to the Eurailpass, a number of individual countries offer their own plans to visitors. Italy, for example, has a 15-day unlimited rail pass at $52.20 for first-class, $31 for second-class. When you consider that the one-way regular first-class ticket by rail from Venice to Palermo, Sicily—a distance of 930 miles—costs $41.10, the unlimited first-class ticket for only $11 more is a splendid bargain. For those wishing to stay longer in Italy, slightly higher-priced 30-day and 21-day passes are available.

Switzerland offers a Holiday Ticket which is available for one month and allows a discount of up to 50 percent on internal rail, postal bus, lake steamer and mountain bus runs. The Holiday Ticket also allows you five local excursions at half price, plus a basic charge of $9 for first-class or $6 for second-class for each trip.

Belgium, France, the United Kingdom, the Scandinavian countries, Spain and Ireland all have their own programs too.

In the United Kingdom, you can buy a $30 thrift coupon book of British Rail tickets which entitles you to 1000 miles of second-class rail travel. A $45 book gives you 1500 miles. Both are comprehensive enough to permit a circle trip that includes Windsor, York, Edinburgh, Glasgow, Stratford-on-Avon and London. These coupons are also available on Clyde Estuary steamers.

British Rail also offers a 15-day unlimited $60 ticket and a one-month pass for $90, both first-class. There is also a $75 pass for 21 days. Deduct $25 from each pass for second-class, which is usually quite comfortable.

## WATCH OUT FOR
## THESE TOURIST TRAPS

Some travelers make their own arrangements for a trip, and enjoy all the planning and detail work involved. But most of us don't have the time or the expertise and must rely on travel agents—sometimes to our sorrow. Like all human beings, agents differ in their competence, and occasionally there is one who is unscrupulous. But often the source of the traveler's complaints about an agent is a misunderstanding as to what the agent can and cannot do, and what he does and does not charge for.

The Better Business Bureau is frequently the first place to which dissatisfied tourists complain. Here are the most common grievances reported to the bureau, and how to avoid them.

There's nothing like "getting away for a weekend"—only sometimes you can get so far away that you're nowhere near where you thought you'd be. As with every kind of trip or excursion, unless you know exactly what and where the accommodations are, you may be in for a real letdown.

Ski trips and musical festivals have been the source of complaints to the BBB from people who stated that they were put in localities miles away from the scenes of activity or entertainment. This, despite the fact that they had been promised accommodations immediately adjacent to the entertainment facilities. The excuse sometimes offered for this "inconvenience" is that the accommodations in the area of activity were overcrowded. A reputable travel agent, however, would have made this known in advance and would not have oversubscribed the facilities. By dealing with reputable travel agents, you can avoid having a "lost weekend." And always bear in mind that what you don't know *will* hurt you.

Another major area of complaint is the traveler's dissatisfaction or disappointment with accommodations, especially in some foreign countries. A first-class hotel abroad may be the best hotel and indeed *the* first-class hotel of that area. By the traveler's standards, however, it may not measure up to his concept of such a hotel. Not only may first-class hotels differ from area to area and country to country, but the accommodations within the hotel vary from superior to standard to minimum. Be sure to ascertain from the travel agent just what "first-class" or "second-class" means in each city or country to be visited. Your accommodations may entail two in a room; they may not include private bath or other facilities; the rooms may vary in size; dining facilities may differ. The class of transportation varies also; some tours which have been advertised as first-class actually use economy flights or, on land, second-class rail accommodations.

Another source of serious complaint to the BBB is the amount of money deducted from deposits if the traveler cancels. Much of this is attributable to his failure to read the cancellation provisions of the agreement. In the event of cancellation of hotel, air, steamship, rail and Pullman reservations which have been made for you, the amount of the refund or size of cancellation fee depends on the policy set forth by the hotel or the carrier, as well as the terms and conditions set forth by the travel agent. Travelers should always ascertain what the cancellation policy is when making reservations.

Charter flights have been a major area of disappointment to the public. This is sometimes attributable to the deceptive and fraudulent practices of some charter flight promoters. You should recognize that so-called travel arrangers for charter flights are not necessarily travel agents. You should also be aware that some charter flights never materialize. The assumption that a sufficient number of people will actually commit themselves to make the flight economically possible is unfortunately sometimes a miscalculation which ultimately results in cancellation of the flight. Furthermore, the initial price of a charter seat is subject to change depending on the final number of participants in the flight. A person whose plans necessitate travel within a given period should be sure to find out when he will receive a definite commitment that the flight is scheduled to go and what the final price will be.

In order to qualify for, and participate in, a charter flight, government regulations require that you and your family must have been a bona fide member of a bona fide organization for at least six months before the charter flight. Violation of this provision may jeopardize your participation in the flight and could result in a last-minute disappointment.

Read the charter provisions carefully and determine your right to a refund if the flight is canceled. Find out your right to a refund if you decide not to take the flight and the time limit within which you must notify the chartering organization of your cancellation in order to receive a refund. Ask what airline is scheduled to carry the flight and call the airline for confirmation. If there is any question as to whether the airline is certified for charter flights by the Civil Aeronautics Board, contact the CAB or the Better Business Bureau. The bureau may also have information about the reputability and past performance of the promoter or chartering organization.

In conclusion: (1) Check the reputation of the travel agent with the BBB, if you have any doubts. (2) Be as specific as possible in telling your travel agent what your requirements and budget are. (3) Remember that there is a charge involved for certain services provided by travel agents. (4) Make sure you understand the terms and conditions of your agreement, especially cancellation provisions. (5) Since sight-seeing tours differ in extent and detail, find out if the planned tour is a half-day, full-day or just a "drive-by" tour, and whether admission charges are included in the overall cost or will come out of your pocket. You'll reap big rewards in satisfaction as well as money.

There's also a variety of excellent bargains on bus lines in and around London. The country bus routes have already been mentioned: For 72 cents you can travel for a day through the storybook villages and rolling countryside surrounding London. An extra bonus is the local residents who travel these buses daily for shopping trips, school journeys and business visits. The regular and more expensive tours provide you with only overseas visitors like yourself.

The CIE, Ireland's Transport Company, has similar specials. A $28 ticket allows you 15 days of unlimited travel on any scheduled train or provincial bus route. In other words, for approximately $1.85 a day you can roam the gleaming green countryside or cities at your leisure. A first-class ticket is $39.50.

French Railroads will allow 20 percent off on trips from your French border point of entry to your departure point. For instance, you land in Le Havre and then travel by rail at the special discount rate to Paris and Nice, and then turn back to Calais, your exit point. There are two restrictions, however: You must remain at your destination—in this case, Nice—for at least six days, and you must travel a minimum of approximately 1000 miles.

Belgian Railways has Runabout Tickets for 5, 10 and 15 days, starting at $15 first-class and $10 second-class. Thus, for $2 to $3 a day, you can explore provincial towns, main cities and the northern beach resorts. A pass available for any 5 of 14 days costs $18 first-class or $12 second-class and permits unlimited travel.

Spain has an interesting visitor's pass, the Kilometrico, which provides a substantial discount when you travel a minimum of 1864 miles. (Two persons together need only travel a total of 2486 miles to qualify.) Cost of the basic pass is $36 for one or $50 for two. This is a good bargain because, as European nations go, Spain is relatively large and there's much interesting ground to cover from the Pyrenees in the north to the Costa del Sol on the Mediterranean.

Scandinavian Railways also offers special tickets for visitors, with 20 percent off on circular rail and bus routes. Some boat trips are included in this two-month ticket. In addition, Norway, Denmark and Sweden individually have their own discounts. Denmark sells 10-day and one-month unlimited tickets; Sweden grants 15 percent off on midweek trips; and Norway's railroad will grant as much as

25 percent off on some trips, although you may run into a restricted period during the peak summer season.

Other deals to look into are the special unlimited-travel air tickets over the domestic networks of the local carriers in such countries as Finland, Argentina, Colombia and Venezuela. Costs vary from country to country, but for tourists with a specific interest in exploring these nations, the special air fares can prove fine bargains. Finland, for example, offers through Finnair, its national airline, a 15-day ticket for $80 that enables you to fly all over this large country for slightly more than $5 a day.

As you may have concluded, purchasing transportation is every bit as complicated as picking out the best insurance policy. You owe it to yourself to examine the various offerings carefully and determine how you can make the most of them. Quite often, clerks in travel offices need persistent prodding because they aren't aware of some of the bonuses and are apt to shrug off your inquiries. If you do encounter difficulties, ask for the manager and insist on his checking further into the tariff and schedule book, which, by the way, is as thick as the Manhattan telephone directory!

Booking your vacation trip shouldn't be a hit-or-miss exercise. Sit down with a reliable travel agent and tell him what you wish to accomplish. And be sure to let him know that you are aware of the bonuses offered by the different carriers and that you want to find out how to apply them to your needs.

## What You Can Expect from a Travel Agent

A competent travel agent is not merely a ticket seller. He is a specialist whose experience and knowledge enable him to counsel you on how to travel wisely within the confines of your budget.

Most travel agents are appointed by transportation carriers (airline, railroad and steamship companies), after approval by the conferences to which the carriers belong, to issue tickets and officially represent the carriers. To receive such an appointment the travel agent must be able to show financial responsibility and a thorough knowledge of the travel field. Among such conferences are: Air Traffic Conference of America (ATC); International Air Transport Association (IATA); Trans-Atlantic Passenger Steamship

Conference (TAPSC); Trans-Pacific Passenger Conference (TPPC); Rail Travel Promotion Agency (RTPA).

As is the case of responsible elements in any industry, travel agents, as a matter of course, subscribe and adhere to voluntary codes of ethics.

Here are some ways in which the travel agent serves his clients:

1. He arranges for transportation—air, steamship, bus, rail, car rentals and car purchases abroad.

2. He prepares individual itineraries; sells package tours, both personally escorted and unescorted; arranges group tours, books cruises.

3. He arranges for hotels, motels, resort accommodations, meals, sight-seeing, transfers of passengers and luggage between terminals and hotels, and for special features like music festivals and theater tickets.

4. He handles and advises on the details involved in modern-day travel: for example, travel and baggage insurance, language study material, traveler's checks, automobile parking, foreign currency exchange, documentary requirements (visas and passports) and health requirements (small-pox immunization and other types of inoculation).

5. He is familiar with, and has schedules of, train connections and hotel rates; knows the hotel's quality, whether rooms have baths, whether the rates include local taxes and gratuities.

6. He arranges reservations for special-interest activities like religious pilgrimages, conventions and business travel, gourmet tours and sporting trips.

An important part of the travel agent's payment comes from commissions that he receives from transportation carriers and often from hotels. If the service given is simply that of procuring a transportation ticket and making a single hotel reservation, there is usually no additional charge to the customer. The traveler gets the convenience of having his transportation and reservation arranged for him at no additional cost, and the agent is reimbursed for his time and effort through commissions that he receives from the carrier or hotel.

Contrary to popular belief, a travel agent's income is not, however, derived solely from commissions. More complicated travel arrangements—especially prearranged tours and independent itineraries—practically always require a charge for the agent's services. Considering the cost of office overhead (trained personnel, rent, phone calls, cables and telegrams), an agent would find it impossible to remain in business if he did not charge the traveler for these services.

Below are listed the principal services offered by travel agents and the charges, if any, which these entail:

*Air and steamship reservations.* If the traveler requires only a transportation ticket, there is no agency fee. Although the agent is compensated by the carrier, the ticket is the same price whether the traveler deals with the carrier or the agent.

*Rail and Pullman tickets.* The traveler may usually expect to pay a nominal fee, for travel agents generally receive no commission from the railroad company.

*Hotel reservations.* There is usually no agency charge to the client for a resort hotel reservation. If the traveler requests a single hotel reservation at his first arrival city in connection with a transportation ticket secured by the agent, there is usually no agency charge. If the traveler requires several hotel reservations there will normally be a charge.

*Package tours.* A package tour is a prearranged tour designed to fit the requirements of a wide variety of travelers. They may be either escorted or unescorted. They are advertised in brochures, which contain the cost, terms and conditions of the offered package. The responsibilities of both the tour operator and the traveler should be fully understood by the traveler: What happens if you cancel, if you wish to stay longer or leave earlier, if you have last-minute changes in your itinerary both before you leave and en route; what is the amount of the deposit. If you are not clear on any point, ask the agent.

The basic advantage of a package tour is convenience. Also, since the package is arranged by a specialist who buys in large volume, his suppliers—the hotels, sight-seeing companies and others—are anxious to please him by providing high-quality service for those who have bought the package.

A major source of tourists' complaints, and one that has harassed the travel agent, is the matter of the total cost of the component parts as opposed to the total cost of the package. It is unrealistic for the traveler to assume that the travel agent will offer his time, service and professional experience without being compensated. The fact is that if the traveler adds up the total cost of the component parts of the package he will usually find that the price of the package as advertised in the brochure is higher. However, since package tours are arranged for large numbers of people, there may be instances where the cost is actually less than if the individual made his own separate arrangements, including the various services provided en route.

*Group tours.* A group tour is a number of persons, members of a club, business organization or other affiliated group, who are traveling together and have pooled their purchasing power to realize savings, particularly on transportation. Group travel offers the individual some of the same advantages as a quantity discount price. The requirements and regulations as to who may qualify for reduced group transportation rates are subject to change and should be checked with your travel agent.

The itinerary is planned exclusively for the specific group. The emphasis of the group tour may be cultural, religious or just plain fun, according to the interest of the group.

*Independent itineraries.* An individual independent itinerary is like a quality, custom-made suit. It is developed to reflect the specific needs and tastes of the client. This type of tour is designed for those who know where they want to go and what they want to see—whether in this country or abroad. The travel agent sits down with the client and converts his requirements into a special, individually developed itinerary. The total cost of this includes the actual cost of the component parts plus the agent's charge for his professional know-how, time, out-of-pocket expense and services he gives in developing and operating the itinerary. A responsible travel agent will indicate in his contract that there is such a charge for this personalized service.

Because of the obvious work involved, many agents require a deposit prior to tailoring a custom-made itinerary. A statement of the terms should be obtained in advance so that you know what your obligations are. The traveler should familiarize himself with the conditions of the contract—whether they relate to deposits, refunds or additional costs for additional services—and all conditions should be in writing.

Responsible travel agents will gladly provide a copy of the terms and, if necessary, will explain them to you.

Whether you plan your trip with a travel agent or make your own arrangements, you can extend your vacation horizons just by choosing from the many travel bargains available today.

⊏⊐⊏⊐⊏⊐⊏⊐⊏⊐⊏⊐

## HOW TO COMPARE
## TOUR PRICES

Comparing tours is not just a matter of seeing how many days you get for the same number of dollars. Tour operators have to keep their prices competitive, and any substantial variation in prices, therefore, is likely to be based on the fact that the operators are aiming their programs at different markets. Some tour operators concentrate on the luxury traveler and offer only the best accommodations. Others cater to the budget-minded traveler and do away with many of the frills in order to provide economy tours.

There are many factors which determine the price of a tour or a cruise, and you'll find that the operators are fairly meticulous about spelling out exactly what is included. These details usually are covered in the itinerary itself or in a separate section called General Information or Conditions.

For example: Does the tour price include the transoceanic transportation or only the overseas land arrangements? Will you travel first-class, second-class or tourist class? Will you be accommodated in deluxe, first-class, standard or economy class hotels, and will your room include a toilet and private bath or shower? Will you have a single room or share one?

Are all meals included? On many tours, for instance, lunches or dinners are not included in such cities as London, Paris or Rome, mainly because the tour operator feels that the traveler may prefer to explore those cities' restaurants on his own. On some tours only breakfasts are included, and their menus vary from country to country.

Are all sight-seeing trips and entrance fees included? Are tips and taxes included? Will you be accompanied by a tour escort throughout the trip or only by local, English-speaking guides, and at what points? Do the arrangements cover transfers of passengers and luggage between airports, hotels, railroad stations and piers? In the case of cruises, are shore excursions included?

The answers to those questions and the itinerary itself will help you decide which is the right tour for you. As a further guide, see the check lists on the following pages.

⊏⊐⊏⊐⊏⊐⊏⊐⊏⊐⊏⊐

◻◻◻◻◻◻

WHICH OF THESE ITEMS
DOES THE TOUR PRICE
INCLUDE?

HOTEL ACCOMMODATIONS
☐ Single room
☐ Double room (double bed)
☐ Twin-bedded room
☐ Three in a room
☐ More than three in a room; dormitory-type accommodations
☐ Bungalow
☐ Tent
☐ Room with bath
☐ Room with shower
☐ Room with sink only
☐ Room with toilet
☐ Bath or shower in hall
☐ Outdoor sanitary facilities
☐ Air conditioning

STANDARD OF HOTEL
☐ Superior category ("luxury," "deluxe," "four star," "superior first-class")
☐ Medium category (between "first-class" and "superior second-class")
☐ Modest category ("standard class" and other hotels considered suitable for the American traveler)
☐ Pension (boardinghouse)
☐ Student hotel (university student residence operated as hotel during tourist season)
☐ Youth hostel

HOTEL LOCATION
☐ Within walking distance of shopping and entertainment
☐ Away from center of things; taxis needed to main attractions
☐ In suburbs; accessible only by taxi or public transportation

MEALS
☐ Three meals a day throughout
☐ All meals in certain cities
☐ Some meals en route
☐ Breakfast only throughout
☐ Breakfast only in some cities
☐ Breakfast and either table d'hôte lunch or dinner throughout

◻◻◻◻◻◻

- ☐ Breakfast and lunch or dinner only in some cities
- ☐ Type of breakfast:
  - ☐ Continental
  - ☐ American

### TRANSPORTATION BY AIR
- ☐ First-class
- ☐ Economy or tourist class
- ☐ Group fare
- ☐ Excursion fare
- ☐ Charter flight
- ☐ Restrictions on departure days or hours
- ☐ Jet aircraft
- ☐ Propeller aircraft
- ☐ In-flight entertainment

### TRANSPORTATION BY LAND
- ☐ First-class rail
- ☐ Second-class rail
- ☐ Reserved seats on trains
- ☐ Sleeper accommodations:
  - ☐ Single-berth compartment
  - ☐ Double-berth compartment
  - ☐ Three-berth compartment (second-class)
- ☐ Motorcoach
- ☐ Private automobile

### TRANSPORTATION BY WATER
- ☐ First-class on steamer
- ☐ Tourist class on steamer
- ☐ Cabin accommodations
- ☐ Deck accommodations
- ☐ Hydrofoil service

### TRANSFERS
- ☐ All transfers between piers, city air terminals, railroad stations and hotel
- ☐ Some transfers only
- ☐ By taxi
- ☐ By car or limousine
- ☐ By motorcoach
- ☐ Services of an assistant and/or interpreter
- ☐ Porterage at station
- ☐ Number of bags carried free

### ESCORT AND GUIDE SERVICE
- ☐ Assistance of tour operator's local representative on arrival and departure only
- ☐ Guide or tour conductor for whole trip from start in the U.S. to finish in the U.S.
- ☐ Guide on foreign portion only

☐ Guide on part of trip only

☐ Guide at various areas only (miscellaneous local guides)

SIGHT-SEEING AND EXCURSIONS

☐ By deluxe motorcoach
☐ By private car
☐ By sedan with six to eight seats
☐ With English-speaking guide (native)
☐ With multilingual guide
☐ With lecturer at specific sights only
☐ Entrance fees
☐ Theater tickets

TIPS AND TAXES

☐ Usual tips on room
☐ Usual tips on food
☐ Service charges
☐ Tips for porters at airports and stations
☐ Extra tips to hotel personnel
☐ Airport taxes
☐ Seaport taxes
☐ Head taxes
☐ Hotel taxes
☐ Miscellaneous government taxes on tourist services or facilities

BAGGAGE ALLOWANCE

☐ 66 pounds (first-class air travel)
☐ 44 pounds (economy class air travel)
☐ One suitcase, unweighed
☐ Two suitcases, of any weight
☐ Unlimited baggage

MOTORING SERVICES

☐ Motoring itinerary prepared
☐ Unlimited use of late-model, low-mileage car
☐ Automatic shift
☐ Seat belts
☐ Radio
☐ Luggage rack, canvas and straps
☐ Air conditioning
☐ Oil, greasing and initial full tank
☐ Gasoline en route
☐ Oil changes
☐ Maintenance and repairs en route
☐ Unlimited mileage allowance
☐ Mileage charge
☐ Daily charge
☐ Free delivery and collection at specified locations

- [ ] Local government sales taxes
- [ ] All necessary international and registration documents
- [ ] Collision insurance; how much deductible?
- [ ] Fire, theft and glass insurance
- [ ] Driver's insurance, for death or injury
- [ ] Third-party insurance
- [ ] Eastern Europe insurance

TOUR OPERATOR

- [ ] Experienced and reliable professional
- [ ] Member of nonprofit group who has some experience
- [ ] Member of nonprofit group who has no experience

ITEMS TO CONSIDER IN COMPARING CRUISE PRICES

PORT OF DEPARTURE

- [ ] New York
- [ ] Los Angeles
- [ ] San Francisco
- [ ] New Orleans
- [ ] Port Everglades
- [ ] Other U.S. port

- [ ] Overseas port
- [ ] Is transportation to port of departure included?
- [ ] Is return to the U.S. included?

CRUISE VESSEL

- [ ] Tonnage
- [ ] Number of passengers
- [ ] Is it a one-class ship where everyone enjoys the same facilities?
- [ ] Is it air-conditioned?
- [ ] Is it stabilizer-equipped?

ITINERARY

- [ ] Number of days
- [ ] Number of miles
- [ ] Number of ports visited
- [ ] Are shore excursions included?
- [ ] Does rate include boat charges from ship to shore and return when ship is not berthed alongside?
- [ ] Are entrance fees on shore excursions included?

TIPS AND TAXES

Which of these are included:
- [ ] Gratuities aboard ship
- [ ] Tips while sight-seeing
- [ ] Port taxes

▭▭▭▭▭▭

**ACCOMMODATIONS**

☐ Deck location:
  ☐ Upper decks
  ☐ Lower decks
  ☐ Inside cabin
  ☐ Outside cabin
☐ Single-berth cabin
☐ Two-berth cabin
☐ Three-berth cabin
☐ Four-berth cabin
☐ Shower or bath and toilet
☐ Does cabin have porthole?

**MEALS**

☐ All meals included?
☐ Wines and beverages?
☐ Afternoon coffee or tea?
☐ Meals on shore excursions?

**SHIPBOARD AMENITIES**

Are these included or extra?
☐ Deck chairs
☐ Steamer rugs
☐ Cushions
☐ Entertainment
☐ Laundry and valet service

▭▭▭▭▭▭

## GETTING THROUGH CUSTOMS

Don't let a last-minute misunderstanding with the Customs Bureau (a division of the U.S. Treasury Department) spoil your vacation trip.

In a recent year fines and penalties amounting to over $1 million were assessed against residents of the United States who failed to declare articles properly when returning from abroad.

There are simple rules you can follow. You must declare to the Customs Bureau, either orally or in writing, all articles acquired abroad and in your possession when you return. This includes even gifts made to you while you were on your trip. But there is a standard exemption for most tourists. If the fair retail value of your purchases doesn't exceed $100, you may bring them in duty free.

Customs declaration lists are distributed on ships and planes and should be completed before you arrive. Wearing a garment you purchased abroad does not exempt it from duty. You should list all the articles acquired on your trip. Keep the sales slips and have them ready for examination by the customs officer on request.

You can expedite the examination procedure by packing separately the articles you acquired abroad.

For the most recent regulations and rates, send ten cents for a copy of *Customs Hints* to Bureau of Customs, Treasury Department, Washington, D.C. 20226.

## CHAPTER 46

## The Nation's Best Vacation Buy

*Looking for an exciting vacation that won't leave you broke? Why not try camping?*

Until recently camping in the United States meant stuffing a sleeping bag, some warm clothes, a few cooking utensils and first aid equipment into a rucksack, slinging it over your back and hiking toward the hills. But today the typical camper may travel in a fully equipped trailer, usually cooks on a gas stove instead of a campfire and watches television instead of beavers. Today's typical campsite provides living comforts ranging from hot showers to hair driers, clothes washers to snack bars.

The discovery that camping can provide a comfortable, inexpensive vacation, coupled with a greater amount of leisure time, has led to an extraordinary increase in the number of campers. In the period just before World War II about 1 million people a year went camping. By 1960 the total was 20 million. By 1968 it was 40 million.

As one measure of this spectacular growth just in this decade, the latest Rand McNally *Guidebook to Campgrounds* lists 15,000 campgrounds in the United States and Canada (with 500,000 individual campsites), 3000 more than in 1968, up from only 5000 campgrounds listed in 1961. Today 12,000 camping areas are set up specifically to accommodate travel trailers, with 350,000 separate sites for trailers.

By 1980, the Department of Interior's Bureau of Outdoor Recreation predicts, camping will become the second-fastest-growing outdoor activity in this country, outpaced only by water skiing. Between now and the year 2000, the bureau also predicts, camping will grow by a phenomenal 238 percent.

Why this sudden increase in outdoor living? Psychologists say that camping makes people feel important. At home Father has only to turn the dial on a thermostat to heat the house; in the woods he splits an armload of wood and feels more masculine. Mother feels more vital cooking over her husband's fire than in a modern kitchen. Whatever the cause, never before has the American family taken to the woods with such zest and in such numbers.

One of the greatest attractions of camping is its low cost. Your family may or may not have a deep interest in the outdoors, but sleeping in campgrounds and preparing your own meals enable you to take the kind of vacation that might be beyond your means if you had to rely on restaurants and motels.

As an example, the cost of a two-week camping vacation for two adults and two children who travel 1000 miles is likely to range between $150 and $200. A family the same size, doing and seeing the same things but using restaurants and motels, probably would spend between $600 and $800. Here is how costs might compare:

| CAMPING FAMILY'S COSTS | |
|---|---:|
| Food | $ 80 |
| Camping fees | 28 |
| Gasoline, oil | 25 |
| Recreation | 40 |
| Laundry, wood, ice, film, stamps, etc. | 20 |
| | $193 |

| MOTEL FAMILY'S COSTS | |
|---|---:|
| Food | $350 |
| Lodgings | 280 |
| Gasoline, oil | 25 |
| Recreation | 50 |
| Incidentals | 20 |
| | $725 |

Assuming you already have the equipment, here are the major items to take into account in projecting your expenses for a trip:

*Food.* Groceries for campground meals come to about $4 a day for two persons, $6 for four, $7 for six. Cost of restaurant meals runs two to three times higher.

*Lodgings.* Some campgrounds may be used free of charge. In others there is a fee of from $1 to $3.50 a day, depending on the facilities and whether the ownership is public or private. The fee at campgrounds operated by the United States government is $1 a day. If you plan to spend more than a week of camping in federal campgrounds, purchase a "Golden Eagle" permit for $7; it provides admission to all such installations for one year. If you plan to stop at motels en route estimate the cost at $12 to $15 a night for one room, $20 to $24 for two adjoining rooms sharing a single bathroom.

*Transportation.* The price of gasoline and oil may vary substantially from region to region. Generally costs are highest in Canada and in the sparsely populated areas of the western United States. As a rule of thumb, estimate overall expenses of three cents a mile for gasoline and oil if driving a standard car, three and a half cents if driving a camper or a mobile home or towing a trailer. Tolls are about 25 percent higher for a recreational vehicle.

*Recreation, shopping.* Some families spend little or nothing on these activities. Others lay out $5 or $10 a day or more. How you spend depends in part on the enticements. The availability of chairlift rides, rodeos, souvenirs or attractively priced imports is likely to have an impact on any budget. Set aside a reasonable sum for such expenses and try not to exceed it.

*Incidentals.* These include the cost of cigarettes, film, stamps, postal cards, ice, wood, showers (at 25 cents each in many campgrounds), laundry, haircuts, allowances for children and small articles of clothing. Allow about $10 a week, depending on the size of your family.

*Emergencies.* It is reassuring to have funds immediately available in the event there is a need for car repairs, repairs to other equipment or medical expenses. A practical amount to hold in reserve is $50 for each 1000 miles you plan to travel.

To reduce the risk of losing funds many campers rely on traveler's checks and credit cards. Some also record their expenses as they go along, so that they know where they stand at a given point in a trip.

## What to Take Along

Your greatest single expense will usually be camping equipment. When you first try camping your best bet is to buy as little as possible until you decide whether you will continue and, if you do, until you have learned what kinds of equipment best meet your needs. In the meantime there probably is equipment at home you could put to use on a camping trip, like old pots and pans, paper plates and cups, a cooler, a picnic jug, flashlights and blankets that might be used in place of sleeping bags. What you don't have you might be able to borrow, and what you can't borrow you probably can rent.

In most metropolitan areas there is at least one camping equipment supplier who will rent everything a camper needs for a trip. The cost of renting a tent and other basic gear for a family of four for a two-week period is about $80; if blankets are used instead of sleeping bags, this can be pared to about $60. Rental for a recreational vehicle is quite a bit higher. A tent trailer (a tent in a box towed behind the car), with beds and a cooking galley, might rent for between $100 and $150 for two weeks. A fully equipped trailer might cost between $150 and $200 for the same period. The fee for a pickup camper coach (living unit mounted atop a pickup truck) is about $300; for a deluxe motor home, about $500.

If you eventually decide to buy equipment of your own, take your time, since your investment will be sizable. Talk with other campers about their preferences, study the many catalogues available and shop around. Then buy the very best you can afford.

Basic camping equipment includes: a tent or trailer, sleeping bags, air mattresses, gasoline lanterns, a gasoline stove, cooking and eating utensils, a portable icebox and a first aid kit. The total cost for these essentials runs about $300 to $400. Of course you can also select from a huge array of auxiliary equipment. The modern camper can buy a folding toaster, a portable toilet, a gas-operated refrigerator weighing only 24 pounds, an electric fan powered by flashlight batteries, tents coated with aluminum to reflect the heat, tents with nylon screens and picture windows, tents that connect with a station wagon's opened end, camper trailers and buses and deluxe camper coaches. He can pitch a pop-up tent in 90 seconds.

## Prevacation Planning

A camping vacation requires careful planning. You and your family should first decide how much money you can afford to spend, how much time you will have and what kind of camping trip you would enjoy most. Possibilities include a touring vacation in which you stay at a different campground every night or two; a vacation in which you remain at one campground and concentrate on the recreational opportunities; a trip on which some time is devoted to touring and the rest to relaxation; or a backpacking or canoe trip.

Whatever you decide, don't make the mistake of crowding too much into too short a vacation. If you have a two-week vacation, for example, and plan to spend it at one campground, try to find a place within 300 to 400 miles of home. If you want to spend some time touring and the rest relaxing at one campground, extend your range to about 750 miles from home, or about 1500 miles round trip. If you plan to spend all of your vacation touring, think in terms of a journey of up to 2000 miles round trip. Longer distance trips require more time. A 3000-mile journey, for example, requires three to four weeks; a cross-country trip, six to eight weeks.

Once you decide where you are going, map out your travel route

## HOW MUCH WILL IT COST?

The amount of money you spend on equipment will depend on whether you prefer to rough it or travel in style. Plan to spend a minimum of $300 for the bare essentials. To give you an idea of the price range, here is a list of the basic pieces of equipment and their cost. Army-Navy surplus stores can be a good source of inexpensive camping equipment.

- A tent for a family of four or five runs from $75 to $150.
- A simple tent trailer is priced from $450. Pickup campers, travel trailers and motor homes run into thousands of dollars. An elaborate one can cost $5000 or more.
- Sleeping bags sell for between $20 and $25; folding cots cost from $7 to $12; double-decker camping bunks are about $25 to $30.
- Air mattresses cost between $10

and $25. Foam rubber mattresses are priced from $13 to $26.

- A pump for inflating air mattresses sells for $3 to $5. An electrically operated pump that plugs into the ciagrette lighter of your car costs about $8.
- Small heaters run about $15 to $30.
- Gasoline lanterns range from $10 to $30.
- A folding camping table costs about $10 or $20; folding chairs and stools sell for $2 to $10.
- A picnic cooler can be as inexpensive as $2 or as high as $30.
- A portable refrigerator will cost about $30.
- A large water jug runs from $2 for a plastic water can to $15 for a five-gallon galvanized container with a faucet.
- A gasoline stove is priced from $9 to $25; propane and butane stove, $9 to $35; alcohol stove, $10 to $30; Sterno stove, $1 to $2.50.

and find out what recreation, sight-seeing and camping facilities will be available. Most oil companies provide free routing services. For information on camping and recreational facilities, write to the National Park Service and the state government or consult camping guidebooks.

It is important to bear in mind that different campgrounds may serve different purposes. There are four types to consider:

1. *Places to obtain a night's rest.* These are campgrounds close to the route you are following. Although they might have other attractions, their most important feature is a convenient location. Most private campgrounds and those operated by municipalities are in this category. In addition, 14 states have special areas adjoining highways where overnight camping or stopping is permitted. In Canada there is a chain of small campgrounds along the length of the Trans-Canada Highway which are suitable for overnight stops.

2. *Pleasant but not extraordinary places where there may be swimming, boating, hiking or other recreation.* Most campgrounds in state and provincial parks and a small number of private campgrounds are in this category. So are many federal campgrounds, including those operated by the U.S. Forest Service, the Army Corps of Engineers and the Tennessee Valley Authority.

3. *Campgrounds whose main appeal is proximity to a major sight-seeing attraction.* One example is O'Neill Park, which is only 25 miles from Disneyland in California. Some others are Saltwater State Park in Washington, only 18 miles from Seattle, and Prince William Forest Park in Virginia, about 35 miles from Washington, D.C. Tourist information bureaus and Chambers of Commerce are good sources of information on such places.

4. *Spectacular sites which provide unusual sight-seeing or recreational opportunities.* Campgrounds in this category are terminal vacation areas where a family might spend a week or more. National parks and recreation areas in the United States and Canada are in this group, as are the magnificent wilderness parks in such places as Ontario, Quebec, Maine, Michigan and Minnesota.

Try to decide in advance of your trip which parks and campgrounds you will be using. If possible, select also an alternative to each major park as insurance against crowded conditions. Private campgrounds usually provide an excellent hedge, in that, unlike most public campgrounds, they will accept and confirm a reservation on receipt of one night's fee. Fees and descriptions are listed in the standard campground guides.

If there are no other campgrounds near a major park, make a reservation at a motel as a protection against crowding. It can always be canceled if you find you don't need it.

## The Crowded Wilderness

The great upsurge in the number of campers in recent years has created a serious problem of overcrowding. The Great Smoky Mountains National Park, a vast ancient wilderness that sprawls across sections of Tennessee and North Carolina, is a disturbing example of this situation. This park has become so crowded during July and August that it is almost impossible to find a vacant campsite after ten in the morning. Even when one does acquire a place, the thousands of visitors milling about make it hard to truly enjoy the remarkable opportunities for walking, hiking and climbing.

---

### PRIVATE CAMPGROUNDS

There are more than 2000 campgrounds in the United States operated for profit. Some are very satisfactory. They have attractive property and provide a range of facilities (including hot showers, laundry equipment, electric hookups and refills for propane tanks).

A great many private campgrounds, however, are very unpleasant, shabby places, usually a backyard or a cow pasture, where the only objective is to cram in as many people as possible.

Several private campgrounds serve as resorts where a camper may spend all or part of a vacation. Two outstanding examples are the Lake Arrowhead Campground at Myrtle Beach, South Carolina, and the Cherokee Campground on Jekyll Island off Brunswick, Georgia. A great many other private campgrounds, strung along the great vacation routes, function as motels, providing space for overnight stops on long journeys, often where there are no other campgrounds. The most reliable of these are members of the Kampgrounds of America chain, which has about 100 units in operation throughout the United States. A directory is available from Kampgrounds of America, P.O. Box 1138, Billings, Montana. Still other private campgrounds do business outside the big national parks. They frequently are the last resort for campers with no other place to go.

---

The problem is similar at most of the other better-known national parks. At Yosemite, in California, in fact, where probably the worst conditions exist, the campgrounds at the peak of the vacation season are a cross between a teeming slum and Coney Island. The severe crowding that has developed in the national parks in recent years is a source of concern not only to campers but to conservationists, who fear that the unique natural treasures these parks preserve are being jeopardized by the crowds they attract. Some see a day, in fact, when the busiest parks will literally wear out unless steps are taken to curtail their use.

Although there is less of a conservation problem involved, serious space shortages also exist in many campgrounds operated by the U.S. Forest Service and the Army Corps of Engineers. A great many state park systems are also seriously overburdened, including those in California, Florida, Indiana, Michigan, New Hampshire and Ohio.

The problem is essentially one of arithmetic. There are far more people interested in camping during the summer than there are campsites to accommodate them. Although camping facilities are being increased, the process is slow and expensive. The basic cost of preparing and equipping a single campsite is between $1000 and $1500. When land acquisition and the conveniences many campers expect are taken into account, the price rises even higher.

The National Park Service has been adding about 2000 campsites a year to its facilities, some in existing parks where expansion is limited, others in totally new areas. The Forest Service has been adding entire campgrounds of several sites each at the rate of about 1000 campgrounds a year. A number of states also have embarked on large-scale expansion and modernization programs, notably Pennsylvania, Texas, Mississippi, Louisiana, Idaho and Nebraska.

Although conditions are improving, for the foreseeable future it is reasonable to regard the crowded campground as a fact of life. This is not to say that you will find every campground filled to capacity during the summer months. On the other hand, it is a fair assumption that the most popular areas will be filled. This is as true in Canada as it is in the United States. As a result, it is important to plan your camping vacation with this fact in mind and to try to reach potentially crowded sites as early as possible in the day.

# 10
# WHEN SICKNESS
# OR ACCIDENT STRIKES

*Choosing the best protection you can get will
ease the burden on your family and your
finances in times of trouble*

## CHAPTER 47

# What You Should
# Know About Life Insurance

*What's available,
where to get it, how to
estimate coverage,
choosing what's
best for you*

You should buy insurance with the same caution and comparison that you would employ in buying any other major asset, such as a house. If you have bought property, you probably approached several real estate agents and you viewed a number of houses before making your choice. Why buy life insurance differently?

Many people, indeed the majority, play a passive role and let themselves be selected as "prospects" by a neighborhood insurance representative, by a relative who has recently become an insurance agent or broker or by a company coupon advertisement that they have signed without too much—or any—forethought.

You can decide to practice your smart consumer tactics instead. Begin by quizzing your friends. Obtain from them the names of companies and some firsthand experiences of their dealings. But while you make a note of recommended companies, remember that you're not likely to buy the same types of policies your friends have bought—your situation is different and you want only general guidance from them.

Note also the names of advertised companies and those with agencies in your neighborhood. Preferably, drop in at the offices to get an impression of how the organization does business and to obtain information. Undoubtedly you'll be bombarded by agents, but you should certainly resist pressure to sign up until you have compared the life insurance plans offered by several companies.

Moreover, when you have decided on a particular policy, you should not sign until you have thoroughly examined all the clauses and made sure that you understand what is contained in the fine print. If the agent from whom you propose to buy the policy will not provide you with a sample copy, go to another agent.

For your own protection, do business with a well-established company and avoid those that have yet to prove themselves. The giants of the insurance industry do not necessarily offer the most reasonably priced insurance. In fact, a small company may offer you a better deal, but you should check on the company's background. Make sure it is not a newcomer with a similar name to one well known. (See page 455 for comments on mail-order insurance.)

## Stock Companies and Mutual Companies

Basically, two types of policies are available, through two types of company, although there is some overlapping. A *stock company* issues nonparticipating policies, which means that you do not pay as much as you would for a similar participating policy issued by a *mutual company* (usually with the word "mutual" in its title).

In the case of the nonparticipating policy, the company has set the rate at what it expects the insurance to cost. You know in advance exactly what you will pay for your coverage.

In the case of the participating policy, the company has fixed premium rates in excess of what it expects the insurance to cost. Why then should you consider this type of policy? Because in the long run it may prove less costly than a nonparticipating policy, since you will receive dividends after the first two or three years. These dividends are not taxable, for they are actually refunds on your premiums made when the company's operating costs are known. The amount of your annual dividends will, of course, vary with the company's decision and profit. In prosperous times the mutual company's participating policy may pay good dividends, but an economic slump might mean small, or even no, dividends.

Company policies differ on payment of dividends, some tending to increase them in the later years, thus benefiting the long-lived, long-paying insured person. If you have a participating policy, you can accept dividends in a number of ways—from cash payment, which enables you to build your regular savings account, to buying additional insurance. Be sure dividends are paid to you as you want and not automatically applied by the company to the purchase of extra insurance you may not need.

The vast bulk of life insurance is sold by agents. These men are sometimes employes of a company, and may or may not receive a salary in addition to commission. Usually, however, they are self-employed and work only for commission. Bear this fact well in mind, and ask yourself if the insurance the agent is advising for you is for the better protection of your family or if it just pays him better.

When you consider the great importance of life insurance to the security of your family, and the amount of money you will invest, you certainly want to be personally satisfied with the man who will be making far-reaching recommendations to you and to have some background information on him. If you can interview several company representatives and let them suggest certain life insurance planning for you without committing yourself to anyone, you will be in a position to judge both the variations among basic policies offered and the men who describe them to you.

If an agent has been advising and selling to your friends for some years, you know he is no fledgling, but if you are dealing with someone unknown to you, find out how long he has been in the business. While it may be agreeable to give a young fellow a start, let him practice on others. You prefer to know that your man is experienced and has been an agent at least four to five years. If he adds "C.L.U." after his name, you know he is a Chartered Life Underwriter, having successfully met stringent requirements set by the American College of Life Underwriters.

Beware of the man who insists that only some high-priced combination policy will suit your family's needs. It might make you "insurance poor" the rest of your life, while he gains a good commission. Beware, too, of the man who wants you to drop another company's policy to take his. This unethical gambit, known as twisting, has resulted in loss for many people who allowed themselves to be persuaded to drop policies they had held for years. If you meet with this ploy, take the opportunity to review thoroughly what your original company offered, and if changes seem justified, see what it can suggest to meet your present needs. Only if careful investigation proves that the agent had a valid point should you let a former policy lapse in favor of a new one. An agent may be perfectly sincere in his recommendations to you—since he himself is likely to have been very well indoctrinated by his company—but what he offers may not necessarily be right for you. Be ready to provide your own clear-cut ideas on the insurance you and your family should have.

## How to Assess Your Insurance Needs

What type of insurance do you need—and when? In general, your need begins with your financial responsibilities to others. When a young couple first marry, they may live in an apartment and both have jobs. Their money is better directed toward the savings bank than into life insurance unless either must contribute to a dependent.

The real need for life insurance usually begins when the first child is expected. Soon the wife will give up her job; the young husband wants to provide for her and for his child's upbringing in case of his death. At this point he may take out convertible term insurance. If his wife has reasonably good earning potential of her own, his main concern will be for the child's care and education.

The need for life insurance becomes greater as the family increases. The wife is less likely to return to work while the children are young; the couple probably decide they need a house of their own. Now the husband must cover his responsibilities as homeowner in addition to the needs of his family. He can combine whole life with decreasing term insurance under a combination family income policy to protect wife, children and the mortgage. At this point the breadwinner will probably find he needs certain supplementary contracts, or riders. Of particular importance and value is the waiver of premium rider. Should the husband suffer total and permanent disability, the company will pay the insurance premiums.

Another necessary rider is guaranteed insurability; here, the insured protects his right to buy more insurance when he most needs it—regardless of the state of his health at that time.

Although a newly married couple may not really need life insurance, the husband may choose to take his ordinary life insurance policy then. He gains a more favorable premium rate at the earlier age, and that rate continues all his life. If he takes a participating policy earning dividends, he will be that much better off.

When buying insurance, note that the agent receives less commission on term insurance than on the more expensive cash-value policies, which include whole life policies. But if you think your needs can best be served by term insurance, plus your own savings and investment program, you should not allow yourself to be persuaded into taking other policies.

How much insurance do you need? You don't know the true answer, because no one can tell how long you will live. It's a good idea to sit down with paper and pencil to do some very hard, cold figuring. You can assess your needs only by asking, Just where would the family stand if I died now?

A realistic appraisal calls for drawing up two columns, one for liabilities and one for assets. To begin with liabilities, your family would first face the high cost of your death—ask yourself how you stand on medical and hospitalization insurance in case of prolonged illness or injury prior to death (see Chapter 48, "You Can Afford the Best Care," page 459). Would the house be sold? Would your wife be able to work? How long would your children be dependent? Note in your calculations that if your wife survives you she will lose the advantage of filing joint income tax returns.

Consider the funeral arrangements. Do you have a cemetery lot? Would the family have to purchase one or have you stated a preference for cremation? Common sense, not morbidity, dictates that you investigate and make decisions on final arrangements. Note, on the plus side, that Social Security pays toward the funeral costs of an insured worker. (On the subject of funeral cost, the Better Business Bureau of Metropolitan New York, 220 Church Street, New York, New York 10013, will send, free, *A Guide to Help You Arrange Funerals and Interments*. Supply a stamped, self-addressed envelope.)

Now, your death being paid for, where does your family stand financially? In your estimates, you can only use current figures. Figure out your net worth. (The tabulation forms provided in Chapter 3, "How to Appraise Your Family's Security," page 21, will help you here.) You can write down the state of your assets, including any benefits payable at death and amount of family indebtedness.

From your budgeting experience you know basically what it would cost your dependents to live month by month. (For convenience, use a monthly basis in your calculations.) In so many years, some members of your family are likely to be self-supporting, but you may also have to reckon that others, because of incapacity or declining years, may not be. Write down as close an estimate as possible of your financial commitment. For example, a son, already a capable teen-ager, might be able to earn through his college years and need your support for only another five years. But your contribution toward the support of an incapacitated brother might go on for 25 years.

Tabulate the benefits available for your wife and family from Social Security. You have to cover the difference, either through your own assets or through insurance. Essentially, your calculations should take into account these areas exposed by your death:

1. Last expenses. Cash should be easily available in a joint savings account.

2. After-death period. If you can keep about half a year's income in savings you can provide adequately for the readjustment your family would be making.

3. The home. If you are repaying a mortgage, use insurance to cover it.

4. Income for living expenses. In general, this is the main area to be covered by life insurance policies by the breadwinner who does not have other very substantial assets.

5. Education of children. You will use insurance, but the family will have to fend for itself too.

6. Your wife. To cover your wife's lifetime income needs through insurance would be exceedingly expensive. A wife's best insurance is her ability to earn for herself in case of necessity. Where this would not be possible, try to build up other assets such as investments.

Here is a rundown on some of the many types of life insurance available. As your agent explains the combinations his company offers, bear in mind the needs of your family which you have just defined.

## Principal Types of Life Insurance

*Term insurance* offers coverage for a specific span of time, either for a certain number of years or up to a certain age. Usually, term policies do not carry beyond age seventy. Because term insurance carries no cash-value buildup it costs less than whole life insurance. It has been argued that a breadwinner is better off with term insurance than with whole life if he puts the difference between the two premiums into a savings bank where it will earn interest (less taxes, of course). A man who can establish this self-disciplined program may well prefer never to convert to straight life. The nonsaver will combine insurance and savings in the more expensive cash-value policy.

Renewable term insurance is the type to take, because renewal rates will be stated and guaranteed, whether or not rates rise in the meantime, and because the insured person does not have to produce evidence of insurability. Even though his health may have failed he can still renew his policy.

If your preference is for whole or ordinary life, but you cannot presently afford it, make sure that your term policy is convertible. This means that, still without giving evidence of insurability, you may convert to a whole life or endowment policy. However, you may have to inform the company that you intend to convert, and the policy may have a deadline for doing so. Be sure to check on this point. If you have ten-year term insurance, for instance, you may have to announce an intention to convert before the first seven years have elapsed.

Term insurance is often used in addition to whole life insurance by people who have extra risks to cover at certain periods of time. Perhaps a man has covered his family's needs with straight life insurance, and then, unexpectedly, is burdened by helping a brother straighten out his debts or becomes responsible for an aged relative. He finds extra protection for his income in one-year or five-year term.

When the insured breadwinner is handling a heavy debt, such as a mortgage, a decreasing term policy or rider is an extra safeguard. The death benefit decreases during the term of the insurance, but so too does the amount of the debt and the consequent financial responsibility.

A combination plan of gradually decreasing term insurance and whole life is often suggested by an insurance company's agent as the best means of protecting family income.

*Whole life insurance* (also referred to as straight or ordinary life) offers life coverage and other stated benefits. The age at which you buy your policy determines the premium rate at which you will continue to pay. Your policy acquires a "cash value" because the company invests part of the premiums. This cash value is an asset, useful in raising loans, and can help you to cover your insurance if at some time or other you are unable to pay premiums.

There are two kinds of whole life insurance, ordinary (straight) and limited payment. Ordinary life is paid for annually over a whole lifetime. Limited payment is paid for within a stated time, say 20 or 30 years, or by a certain age, such as sixty-five. Because of the higher premiums, limited payment life insurance has the advantage of building up cash value faster, but the cost might prove a burden to the young man who will not reach his highest earning capacity until middle life. For the person whose early years mark the high earning point (an athlete or actor, for example), a limited payment policy may prove useful. But note that early death after completion of premium payments would make this a very expensive policy.

If you eventually wish to discontinue premium payments altogether, several possibilities are open to you: (1) You can receive less insurance protection throughout your life (based on the cash value). (2) You can set an ending date to the full protection. (3) You can obtain a cash settlement for your canceled policy. (4) Instead of life insurance, you have the choice of receiving income for a certain period.

Note that your policy will automatically put some provision into effect if you fail to pay premiums. Find out what it is, because if you cannot pay, you may wish a different provision to be made and you will have to so notify the company.

Whole life carries with it the virtue of being an enforced savings program besides imparting protection to the breadwinner. The cash value accumulated amounts to around 60 percent of the face value. Note that cash value is not an additional sum payable to your beneficiary; it is payable only if the policy is discontinued.

The cost of substantial coverage by permanent insurance may pose a financing problem for a father with young children. Over the next 10 years, his family responsibilities will be greatest. There is still a sizable mortgage debt on the family residence. The cost of children's college education must also be met. After 10 years, though, his need to protect his family against his premature death will gradually lessen. Even so, over the succeeding 15 years, he will still want comparatively substantial insurance coverage. Such coverage under a permanent policy will carry a high premium. Nevertheless, he desires permanent insurance to provide his wife with income-tax-free payment, or "recovery," regardless of when he dies. In effect, he wants (1) highest coverage over the first 10 years, (2) somewhat reduced coverage gradually decreasing in amount over the succeeding 15 years and (3) permanent insurance continuing thereafter, without any further reduction in amount, for the protection of his wife.

He can purchase a whole life policy, with a term rider that offers extra coverage against premature death. Under this rider, extra coverage continues in undiminished amount for an initial 10-year period. Thereafter, over the succeeding 15 years, extra term insurance to be paid in the event of the insured's death gradually decreases to zero. After 25 years, only the face value of the whole life policy is payable to the insured's beneficiary. The insured here ties insurance protection to his actual insurance needs under an ordinary whole life policy with a term rider. Moreover, he benefits from a reduction in premium expense because the extra insurance under the rider is lower-cost term insurance. It is level term insurance for an initial 10-year period and then decreasing term over the succeeding 15 years.

## Policies to Meet Special Needs

*Endowment insurance.* In essence, an endowment policy is a combination of insurance and a savings program. If the holder of an endowment policy dies the beneficiary named collects the stated amount; if the policyholder lives he himself collects on the matured policy. But if before that time he fails to keep up the premiums, he is subject to a penalty and can only recover part of his investment.

Say a person decides against a 20-year endowment policy. Instead, he takes out term insurance for the same period. At the same time, he opens a savings account into which he regularly pays the difference between the term insurance and the endowment policy, which is one of the costlier forms of insurance. If he dies, the term insurance would be paid to his beneficiaries; they would also fall heir to the savings account. If the insured person lives more than 20 years, his term insurance will, of course, lapse, but his savings account plus interest (less income tax on the interest) will amount to much more than the paid-up endowment policy. Had he taken the policy, he would still have to pay income tax on his capital gains.

Since the combination of term insurance and savings produces better results, why do people buy endowment policies? Some undoubtedly do so because they would never save otherwise. The penalty feature forces them to mail their premiums on time; no such spur sends them to the savings bank. Some take endowments because the waiver-of-premium rider can be added to it: In the event of disability, the company would pay the premiums and still fulfill the terms of the contract, that is, pay either a death benefit or a lump sum.

*Combination policies.* Basic life contracts now are combined. On the purchase of life insurance, an individual's choice in the past might have been limited to three basic policies: (1) term insurance, (2) whole life insurance, either an ordinary life or a limited payment contract, and (3) the endowment policy. However, anyone who intends to purchase life insurance now is no longer limited to a choice of one of these basic policies, as we have already seen. Combination insurance contracts are available. For instance, varying straight life–term insurance combinations are available which permit an individual to buy the coverage that most closely meets his insurance needs.

Combined insurance coverage usually joins ordinary life with various forms of term coverage. The variety of coverage is extensive. Some of these policies are directed at younger insureds; others, at the more mature individual.

One new policy combines 50 percent ordinary life insurance with 50 percent term coverage. This reduces the initial premium cost for a higher amount of insurance protection. It has appeal for the father with a growing family. He gets high coverage when his insurance needs are greatest. Term coverage can be converted to permanent insurance up to age sixty-two, but such conversion is not required. Continued high coverage decreases at age sixty-five by 5 percent a year until age seventy-five, when it remains level.

In the case of a young husband, another policy available combines ordinary life insurance with a maximum amount of convertible term. A twenty-five-year-old individual could purchase $100,000 coverage at an initial cost of about $33 a month. At first, the insured gets 10 percent ordinary life coverage with 90 percent term insurance, which decreases every three years beginning at age thirty-one and continuing through forty-six. At any of these ages, however, the insured can convert a portion of the lapsing term insurance into permanent coverage. True, on such conversion, premium costs are increased, but increases in an initial low premium are geared to increases in the insured's earnings.

A graded-premium policy is also available. It is permanent insurance that gears lower initial premiums to anticipated increase in the insured's earnings and future ability to pay. There is a low initial premium which gradually increases over a period (for example, over the first five years) but thereafter remains unchanged. A man currently finds it difficult to finance the permanent insurance coverage he wants at regular rates but anticipates that his income will increase over the next five years. By purchasing a graded-premium policy, he can fit his ability to pay premiums to the actual premium cost.

One form of graded-premium policy uses decreasing term insurance with ordinary life after the first year until at the sixth year the policy becomes a full ordinary life contract. Under this contract, the low

⊏⊐⊏⊐⊏⊐⊏⊐⊏⊐

## WORDS YOU
## SHOULD KNOW

Here is a brief glossary of the terms used in life insurance. You'll find them in this chapter and hear them when you talk with your insurance agent.

**Beneficiary.** The person named in the policy to receive the insurance money upon death of the insured.

**Cash value.** The money a policyholder will get back if he gives up that policy.

**Convertible term insurance.** Term insurance giving the insured the right to exchange the policy for permanent insurance without evidence of insurability.

**Decreasing term insurance.** Insurance that provides for decreasing death benefits during the term of the insurance.

**Disability benefit.** A rider which provides for waiver of premium, some-

times for monthly income also, when the insured is proved totally and permanently disabled.

**Dividend.** The amount returned to participating policyholders as a refund of overpaid premiums; but, being dependent on company operations, it is not guaranteed. It is not taxable.

**Double indemnity.** A policy rider which provides for double the face amount of the policy if death should occur through accident.

**Endowment insurance.** Payment of a definite sum to a policyholder or his beneficiary after a stated number of years.

**Face value.** The sum stated on the face of the policy to be paid on death of the insured or at maturity.

**Grace period.** The time allowed after the premium due date for payment, during which period the policy does not lapse.

⊏⊐⊏⊐⊏⊐⊏⊐⊏⊐

initial premium increases each year for the first five years, but thereafter remains unchanged. In total premium cost, this policy does not promise any premium savings. However, it allows an individual to match premium outlay with increasing income.

A modified life policy has somewhat similar advantages in offering a low initial premium. Under a typical modified life policy, the insured pays an *unchanging* premium lower than the regular rate for the first five years of coverage. Then, in the sixth year, the premium is increased, but it remains level thereafter.

Double life insurance protection until sixty-five is available under combined coverage in a single policy. A father takes out a policy which will pay his family $60,000 if he dies before sixty-five. However, coverage is halved after sixty-five. Thus, if he dies after sixty-five his beneficiary gets $30,000. Presumably, when he is sixty-five his chil-

---

**Insured.** The person on whose life an insurance policy is issued.

**Lapsed policy.** A policy ended by nonpayment of premiums.

**Limited payment life insurance.** Whole life insurance paid for in a specified number of years.

**Maturity.** The date when the policy's face value is payable.

**Nonparticipating policy.** A policy that pays no dividends to the insured.

**Ordinary life insurance,** also called straight life. Whole life insurance with premiums payable until death.

**Paid-up insurance.** A policy for which all premiums have been paid.

**Participating policy.** A policy in which dividends are payable to the insured.

**Policy.** The terms of the insurance contract and the document, issued to the insured, on which they are set forth.

**Policy loan.** A loan made by the insurance company to a policy-holder and secured by the cash value of that policy.

**Premium.** The regular periodic payment made for the insurance.

**Rider.** An endorsement which changes the terms of an existing policy.

**Settlement options.** Alternative ways in which the insured or beneficiary may have policy benefits paid.

**Term insurance.** A policy payable at death if that event occurs during the specified term of the insurance.

**Waiver of premium.** A provision whereby an insurance company will keep a policy in force without payment of premiums. It usually operates as a disability benefit.

**Whole life insurance.** A term referring to either ordinary, or straight, life insurance, on which premiums are payable until death; or limited payment life insurance, on which premiums are paid for a certain number of years only.

dren will be self-supporting adults, with the result that insurance needs will have lessened. The policy, in effect, combined $30,000 permanent insurance with $30,000 term coverage. True, he might buy similar coverage by purchasing a separate $30,000 straight life contract and a $30,000 term policy, terminating at sixty-five. However, this double protection policy carries a reduced premium.

## Income for a Young Widow

*Family income policy.* As noted earlier in this chapter, with a separate policy or rider you may obtain a kind of term insurance running for a certain period (but not beyond a maximum age limit), during which your beneficiary receives a monthly income from the date of your death. If you survive the period, the separate policy pays nothing, although the basic policy to which the rider is attached does pay. Note that if you take out this type of policy, say for ten years, and you live for nine of them, your beneficiary would receive one year's monthly income.

The appeal of a family income policy is greatest for a husband concerned that, on his premature death, he would be survived by a comparatively young widow with minor children. The policy combines permanent insurance with decreasing term coverage. It also provides monthly income that starts on the death of the insured and continues for a specified period—10, 15 or 20 years from the date the policy was originally purchased. This monthly income might be 1 percent per $1000 permanent insurance (for example, $10 per $1000), or 2 or 3 percent ($20 or $30 monthly income per $1000 permanent insurance).

Assume a man buys a $10,000 20-year family income policy, paying $100 monthly income, or 1 percent of $10,000 face value. If he dies one year after purchase, his beneficiary would get $100 a month for 19 years and then $10,000 face value. On the other hand, if he lived for 21 years after policy purchase, his beneficiary would merely receive payment of the $10,000 face value.

Depending on your policy provisions, your beneficiary might receive your basic policy's benefits immediately, with the monthly income being paid until the end of the period; she could split the main benefit, having part paid when the monthly payments start, the rest when they end; or she could reserve payment of the main benefit till after all of the monthly payments had been paid to her.

*Family maintenance policy.* This policy is a combination of permanent insurance and level term insurance. Unlike the family income policy, the period over which monthly income payments are made to the beneficiary does not decrease, regardless of how long a man held the policy, so long as he dies within the specified period. For instance, a husband is thirty years old. He buys a 20-year, 1 percent family maintenance policy with $10,000 face value. If he dies before he reaches fifty, his widow will receive $100 a month for 20 years and then payment of $10,000 face value. However, if he dies after fifty, only the $10,000 face amount will be paid to the widow.

A portion of each monthly income payment will reflect interest yield on the permanent insurance part of the policy left on deposit. This interest is taxable income to the beneficiary. The remaining portion of each monthly payment will reflect installment settlement of term coverage, constituting a principal (tax free) and interest return. The interest portion, though, can be freed from tax—up to $1000 a year—where the surviving spouse is the beneficiary. Lump-sum payment when monthly income ceases is income-tax free.

*Family plans.* There are a number of combination plans offered by various insurance companies, and one is the family policy under which, for example, the husband may have $5000 whole life, and the wife and children $1000 of term insurance. Some consider this as funeral expense coverage, since it would fail to cover the real loss if the wife died and someone had to be employed to care for young children. Insurance on wife and children is offered by some companies as a rider to the husband's insurance.

Variations of the family plan are favorites with the insurance agents who sell them but, in general, do not offer worthwhile protection.

## Other Sources of Life Insurance

*Mail-order insurance.* You may be attracted by a newspaper advertisement in which an insurance company in a distant state offers life or other insurance. Answering such an advertisement may bring a salesman to your doorstep. Because of the distance of the company, you will have little or no chance of checking on its reliability. Maybe it is sound and maybe the salesman can give good advice, but your best move is to do business nearer home and on a direct basis. Besides, you run the danger that the company is not licensed to sell in your state. You lose out on the protection your state law may provide and perhaps open the door to legal complications that will consume time and money after your death.

*Savings bank life insurance.* If you live or work in a state where savings bank life insurance is sold, you have an excellent opportunity. These banks offer advantageous rates. While state law limits the total amount of savings bank insurance an individual may buy (in New York, for example, $30,000), a broad range of straight life, term, endowments and many variations can be obtained. All savings bank plans pay dividends, which further reduce the overall cost of the insurance to your estate.

No salesman will call to urge savings bank life insurance upon you; a substantial reason for the low cost is the fact that you must take the initiative, applying for your policy by mail or in person at the bank. At this writing, New York, Connecticut and Massachusetts are the only states where the law permits savings bank life insurance.

*Group life insurance.* As a member of a union or a professional association or simply as an employe, you may be able to participate in group life insurance coverage. You may have to contribute to the premium (some employers pay the total cost), but your group term insurance will not cost as much as you would pay as an individual. Moreover, no medical examination is required because the risk is spread statistically over a group of individuals.

Usually, upon retirement or on leaving a group, the member can convert to an individual whole life policy or an endowment policy, but it will cost the usual rates, and at sixty-five, for instance, these would be extremely high. "Group paid up" is a plan that helps to overcome such disadvantages. Your contributions go toward paid-up whole life insurance; your employer's go toward term insurance. Upon retirement or leaving the group, you have your paid-up whole life insurance, which you may choose to have remain in force, or to surrender for cash or life income.

In few cases will group insurance provide all the protection a family needs, but it can prove a useful addition to other policies and lower the overall cost of life insurance.

# Insurance Policies Now in Force

**LIFE**

| POLICY NUMBER | COMPANY | PREMIUM | | CASH VALUE | | AMOUNT PAYABLE ON DEATH | BENEFITS | |
|---|---|---|---|---|---|---|---|---|
| | | Amount | When Due | NOW (ENTER DATE) | IN ONE YEAR | | DISABILITY | RETIREMENT AT AGE: |
| | | | | | | | | |
| | | | | | | | | |
| | | | | | | | | |
| **TOTAL** | | | | | | | | |

**ACCIDENT AND HEALTH**

| POLICY NUMBER | COMPANY | PREMIUM | | Cash Value and/or Dividend Credit | REIMBURSEMENT FOR MEDICAL EXPENSES | WEEKLY INCOME | ACCIDENTAL DEATH BENEFIT |
|---|---|---|---|---|---|---|---|
| | | Amount | When Due | | | | |
| | | | | | | | |
| | | | | | | | |
| **TOTAL** | | | | | | | |

**OTHER**

| POLICY NUMBER | COMPANY | PREMIUM | | Dividend Credit if any | TYPE OF COVERAGE | DATE COVERAGE BEGAN | EXPIRATION DATE |
|---|---|---|---|---|---|---|---|
| | | Amount | When Due | | | | |
| | | | | | | | |
| | | | | | | | |

Source: Business News Associates © 1965

## Keeping Your Insurance Up to Date

*Beneficiaries.* You intend the money you are spending annually on life insurance to benefit those financially dependent on you—in most cases wife and children, sometimes parents. A widowed or divorced career woman may have as much responsibility as a father.

The question is, Have you named your beneficiaries correctly? If not, the people you plan to protect may not derive the benefits you intended. The situation may become particularly involved where divorce is concerned. Perhaps, after a financial settlement has been reached, a former wife and children of the marriage should not benefit from a policy already in force. A change in beneficiaries would have to be made.

Note here that when you first take out the policy you should reserve the right to change the beneficiaries. If you do not make this provision, you must have consent in writing from the person formerly named as beneficiary before the company will make the change.

Your insurance company has a legal staff, and if your personal situation is complicated, you should have your agent refer the case to these lawyers. The agent himself should be able to advise you when no unusual difficulties are involved.

If you are consulting an attorney about your will and estate planning, discuss the question of insurance with him. As the years bring changes, you will undoubtedly find that you must alter the names or order of your life insurance beneficiaries.

Servicemen and veterans frequently fail to change the beneficiary's name in their National Service Life Insurance Policy. Originally, the insurance may have been intended to benefit parents. Then the serviceman marries, but he neglects to rename his beneficiaries, leaving his widow to find out that she cannot receive the proceeds of the insurance. Renaming beneficiaries of GI insurance is not complicated; consult the local office of the Veterans Administration. If you are a veteran who has let his policy lapse, inquire if you are eligible to reinstate it. The maximum available is $10,000. Optional coverage for disability is also available.

*Premium payments.* It will certainly pay you to put money aside regularly to meet your life insurance premiums on an annual basis. If you pay every month, quarter or half year, you will be liable for the carrying charges leveled for payments on the installment plan.

To sum up, the insurance needs in your family will differ widely from another's. So, too, will your attitude. If you have the resolve to save regularly and to put aside the difference between renewable term and ordinary life, you may well find the answer in term insurance, which covers the years of your greatest financial responsibility to your family. In your later years, when the need to protect others may have diminished, if not vanished, you can avoid carrying high-priced coverage. A prudent investment and savings program can roll up dividends on money that might have gone into cash-value insurance. On the other hand, you may prefer full insurance coverage until you are sixty-five and also feel safer with the prospect of the return you will get on the cash value of your policy. Your temperament and circumstances will guide your decision.

CHAPTER 48

## You Can Afford the Best Care

*A whopping medical bill could cripple you financially—if you're not covered by a good insurance plan*

Jane Rowley is admitted to General Hospital with pneumonia. She is put in a semiprivate room and placed in an oxygen tent. For four days she requires round-the-clock nursing care, until she is out of danger. After three weeks Mrs. Rowley is well and ready to return home. The cost of her illness exceeds $2000; it could have been much higher if there had been complications or surgery.

Like most American couples, Jane and her husband cannot afford to pay today's high medical costs. If they didn't have adequate medical insurance, they would always be in debt. Fortunately, their insurance protects them.

Medical care is so complex and expensive that everyone must regard health insurance as an absolutely essential part of his life. Getting this coverage is no problem: There are many health plans and insuring organizations ready to provide this service. The difficulty lies in selecting the most sensible and economical plan for your and your family's needs. The choices are broad and varied, apt to confuse or even discourage insurance seekers.

## Group Health Plans

A large number of Americans are included in health insurance plans by virtue of their employment. There are several different arrangements under this heading. One is the compulsory group plan, in which the employer pays all insurance costs and all employes are automatically members. This type of coverage, since it involves no cost to the individual employe, is about the best possible. Sometimes, however, this plan covers only the employe, not his family. For that reason, it is important for the employe to check with the proper person at his place of employment or union to determine if he can, at his own expense, cover his wife and children. The cost of this additional coverage is generally reasonable, and it is well worth it.

The next step is to find out just what is covered by a particular health insurance plan. Full coverage would include costs of hospital, doctors' visits in and out of the hospital, surgery, anesthesia, medication, nursing care and, in a few plans, dentistry and psychiatric care.

If there are important services omitted in the compulsory coverage, the employe may want to take out individual coverage for protection.

On this point a spokesman for the Group Health Insurance Company says: "A group, if it's large enough, can come into an existing insurance organization and more or less write its own ticket. It can buy a standard policy and then say, 'In addition to what you provide, we would like our group to have additional coverage for psychiatric or maternity care,' or something else that might otherwise be excluded. And a group can negotiate with the insurance company and get special features included."

The most common type of group plan is the one in which the employe and employer share the costs, or the employe pays the full amount but the plan is obtained through the company. This type of plan is voluntary, and no employe can be forced to become a member of the group. The advantage of this kind of coverage over an individual policy is in the low cost of premiums.

According to an executive of Greater New York Blue Cross and

Blue Shield: "Blue Cross and Blue Shield are available both as group and nongroup coverage. However, the group premium rate runs approximately 10 to 15 percent less than our nongroup rate for substantially the same coverage and same benefits." Nongroup policies in this area do not include maternity benefits.

As with compulsory coverage, it is recommended that an employe in a voluntary group learn just what benefits he is entitled to. If he has limited coverage, he can buy additional individual insurance.

Plans like Blue Cross and Blue Shield and most (though not all) group plans can be continued individually if a person leaves the group. This means that if a man leaves his job, he can maintain his health policy, but at a considerably higher premium.

Undoubtedly there are many advantages to having group insurance. However, a person cannot get group coverage unless he is a member of a company or organization that carries a group insurance plan. These days most companies offer compulsory or voluntary health insurance as a primary fringe benefit of employment, but there still are millions of people in this country who are insured individually or who carry no health insurance at all.

On this point the Group Health Insurance spokesman remarks: "The group policy is the best health insurance available for your dollar. However, for people who don't have the opportunity of belonging to a group, I would advise buying the individual policy. But, by and large, where a person has the option of participating in a group plan or selecting an individual policy, he's better off with the group plan."

## Policies for Individuals

For the self-employed, for example, there is usually no choice but individual health insurance. There are three categories of coverage that they should consider. The first is hospitalization, which covers the cost of room and board in hospital for a limited stay (21, 90, 120, 180 days, and so on), depending on the particular policy.

The second category is "doctor bill" insurance. The cost of hospital room and board care is only part of the expense of hospitalization. Doctors' and surgeons' fees constitute a good portion of the total and should be covered by insurance.

The final category is the "medical catastrophe" coverage. This is for the time when the patient is ill for a very long period and requires the most technical and intense treatment. Many people feel that they can manage to pay for all the small illnesses but that they would be plunged into debt in the event of very serious illness. The insurance covering this contingency is the major medical plan. It goes into operation only after the expenses reach a certain minimum amount—$300 or $500—and covers up to $20,000, $30,000 or $50,000, according to which plan you carry.

The right combination of medical coverage for you depends on the amount of premium you can afford and the amount of risk you are willing to take.

The average American family, consisting of four or five persons (husband, wife and two or three children), should invest in basic hospital and doctor bill insurance. In the opinion of private insurance agents and group plan executives, the best buy for anyone not eligible for a group plan is individually purchased Blue Cross and Blue Shield.

## Blue Cross and Blue Shield

Operated on a nonprofit basis, Blue Cross, which is the single largest hospital-insurance company in the country, pays out in benefits 95 cents on each $1 collected. This compares favorably with hospitalization plans sold by private insurance companies, which, while they may charge a lower premium, may pay out as little as 55 cents on each $1 collected. Furthermore, Blue Cross is a good buy because in most areas it pays the actual cost of hospitalization, in contrast with most private plans, which pay only a certain amount. With Blue Cross, whether the hospital charges are $10 per day or $50 per day, you are covered for the time specified in your contract. Under many private plans there may be an allowance of, perhaps, $25 per day. Should your cost be that or less, you are covered. But if your cost exceeds the allowed amount, you are responsible for the balance of payment. With these things in mind, it becomes obvious that Blue Cross is the safest bet.

Blue Shield is the name of the plan that covers in-hospital doctors' fees, surgical fees and related expenses. In combination with Blue

Cross, it is the most comprehensive and economical plan an individual family can buy.

Blue Cross and Blue Shield benefits and rates vary around the country. In the New York metropolitan area they are based on income level. For a family with an annual income between $4000 and $6000, the total premium is $312.96 per year, or $26.08 per month. For this amount any member of the subscribing family is entitled to 21 days for room and board in hospital, complete coverage of all medical, surgical, operating room, anesthesia and medication costs in hospital—in fact, all in-hospital expenses. After 21 days, Blue Cross pays 50 percent of hospital expenses. This is total coverage, with doctors and surgeons agreeing to accept the Blue Shield amount as payment in full. And, as almost every doctor you are going to use is a member of the plan, that is really full coverage.

For the family with an annual income between $6000 and $8500, the total premium is $332.16 for the year, or $27.68 per month. The benefits are exactly the same as for the lower-income group, and although the doctor or surgeon will be paid a higher fee in some cases, he again must accept Blue Shield coverage as payment in full.

For the "executive" family, with an annual income exceeding $8500, the total premium is $352.80 per year, or $29.40 per month. The hospital room and board coverage is the same as above, but the doctor and surgeon are paid only a specified maximum by Blue Shield, and the patient may have an additional amount to pay.

To explain the differing rates that Blue Shield pays doctors or surgeons, let us use the example of an imaginary doctor, his three patients and the costs and coverage involved. Dr. Carter has as patients John Jones (low-income bracket), Joe Smith (middle-income) and Frank Clarke (executive). All three have their prostate gland removed, for which service Dr. Carter ordinarily charges $1000. All the patients carry Blue Shield. Blue Shield's allowed maximum for this operation, for the low-income group, is $250. As a participating physician Dr. Carter accepts this amount as his payment in full, and Mr. Jones owes him nothing. The allowed maximum for the middle-income group is $500; Dr. Carter accepts this as payment in full, and Mr. Smith owes him nothing. For the executive plan the allowed maximum is $750, but it does not have the "paid-in-full" stipulation. Mr. Clarke will therefore have to pay Dr. Carter the balance of $250 to discharge the bill.

For all income levels, the Blue Cross coverage is the same, and that part of the premium is the same. After 21 days the amount covered is 50 percent of the hospital bill, up to 180 days. Coverage is renewed with each different hospital confinement, provided 90 days have elapsed since the previous admission. However, as 92 percent of all people hospitalized in the United States do not remain in the hospital for even 21 days, the Blue Cross coverage is almost always total coverage.

## Rates and Benefits Across the Country

If you live in Maryland and want to join Blue Cross and Blue Shield, your premium, regardless of income, for family coverage will be $294.72 yearly, or $24.56 per month. This will guarantee you 30 days of full hospital coverage, and if your family income is less than $7000 per year, full medical and surgical coverage. If your family income exceeds $7000 per year, you will get 30 days of full hospital coverage and an allowed maximum amount toward your medical and surgical expenses.

If you live in Pittsburgh, your family premium will be $311.52 per year, or $25.96 per month, no matter what your income is. Blue Cross coverage for all subscribers is complete for 21 days of the first year you belong. The second year you will be entitled to 3 additional days, or a total of 24 days, the third year 27 days, the fourth year 30 days, and so on, until, after 43 years, you reach the maximum allowed time of 150 hospital days per year. The Blue Shield payment to doctors and surgeons is full for subscribers with annual incomes under $6000. If your family income exceeds $6000 per year, you will be entitled only to a maximum allowance.

If your home is in Illinois, the cost to your family for Blue Cross and Blue Shield will be $278.16 per year, or $23.18 per month. For this, you will be fully covered for 120 days of hospitalization per year. In Illinois income levels play no part in determining Blue Shield payments; all subscribers receive allowances as determined for particular medical and surgical procedures.

Florida families with Blue Cross and Blue Shield coverage pay an annual $212.52, or a monthly $17.71, plus an enrollment fee of $3. For this premium they are allotted $24 per day toward the room expense of the hospital bill for 31 days; all other hospitalization expenses are covered fully for the 31 days. The Blue Shield plan pays the total medical and surgical bill for those with a yearly income of less than $4000 and provides a maximum allowed amount for families with a yearly income exceeding $4000.

Living in San Francisco, your family can subscribe to Blue Cross (which functions as both hospital and medical insurance in northern California) for a yearly premium of $223.80, or $18.65 per month. This pays in full all hospital expenses for 70 days and provides allotted amounts for medical and surgical bills for all subscribers.

The yearly family premium for Blue Cross and Blue Shield in Colorado is $392.40, or $32.70 per month. This pays for 120 days of hospitalization at the rate of $16 per day for the room, with all other hospital expenses covered in full. Medical and surgical bills are paid in full for all families with an income under $9000 per year, with amounts allowed for those with incomes over $9000.

To determine Blue Cross and Blue Shield rates and benefits in your vicinity, contact their local office, which will supply all the information. The foregoing examples show the wide variation around the country. Some plans are cheaper, some are more comprehensive, but all are better than the health policies a private insurance agent can sell you, even though his may look better. The private company is a profit-making organization, and the profit it makes comes from the subscriber—it pays dividends, and they come from you; the agent's fee comes from your premium payments, and so on. Furthermore, Blue Cross and Blue Shield give you coverage anywhere in the country, and in foreign countries as well. There is a new "early discharge" plan that covers many expenses of convalescent care in the home, so that hospital accommodations are available for those who need them. Your policy cannot be canceled at the whim of the company (a proved case of fraud is the one exception). You will not be ineligible after sixty-five years of age; there is a Senior Care plan that supplements Medicare. All children born to you automatically belong to your family plan at no additional cost, and they are covered until age nineteen; thereafter there is a charge for them, but the single-person rate is low, and the benefits are the same as for a family.

## Major Medical Insurance

For those who have basic coverage (Blue Cross and Blue Shield or private-company insurance) and can afford more premium cost, there is another kind of health insurance available: major medical. Because of its expense, it is not recommended for people with incomes of less than $9000 or $10,000 per year. But for our imaginary executive, Mr. Clarke, it is a good buy. Major medical coverage starts to pay only when a certain minimum amount is reached; most policies have a $500 deductible. This means for Mr. Clarke that, if Blue Shield paid $750 toward the total medical bill of $1000, the major medical policy would pay the remaining $250 and all other bills that were not paid by the basic insurance plans. If his bill had totaled less than $500, the major medical policy would not pay anything. At its best, it provides coverage in case of long-term illness, but it does not take the place of basic coverage.

The prospective buyer of health insurance should keep in mind the following points:

1. Find out if you are eligible for membership in a group. Even if your office or factory does not carry a group plan, there may be a group for you through some organization you belong to.

2. If you are covered by a group plan, find out what benefits are due you, what extended coverage you can add at your own expense and whether or not your entire family is covered.

3. If you are not eligible for a group health insurance policy, be very careful about the policy you buy privately. Under this heading is mail-order insurance. Question the company closely, no matter how wonderful the proposition seems. If you do, you are virtually certain to see its failures, hidden costs, lack of meaningful coverage and other drawbacks.

4. If you have any suspicion that you are being cheated in some way by an insurance company, get in touch with your state insurance department. It exists for your benefit and protection.

As the man from the Group Hospital Insurance Company emphasizes: "Many different products travel under the identical label

466

of health insurance or hospital insurance. People say, 'I have hospital insurance,' but that statement conceals enormous differences; it can mean really no insurance or, on the other hand, very substantial insurance. I know of 15 policies that pay $10 to $15 a day. Now, when a hospital bill is at a level of $100 a day and you're in a hospital for ten days, you have a bill of $1000, and if you are going to get back only $100 or $150, in effect you have worthless insurance.

"So people have to examine the content of their insurance policy to determine how much they'll really receive in benefits according to the expenses they expect to incur."

As to the question "When should I take out a health insurance policy?" just remember the answer of our favorite insurance salesman: "If you can tell me when you're going to be sick, then I'll tell you when to buy the policy."

## SOME HEALTH INSURANCE TERMS

Health insurance protects you not against being healthy but against the expenses you incur if you lose your health. Most employes of corporations are covered under a **compulsory group plan** or pay into a **voluntary group plan;** in both the employer usually pays part or all of the premiums. Most such plans cover the family as well as the worker. Many forms of **individual health insurance** are offered by insurance companies, by Blue Cross–Blue Shield or their equivalents. Most of these programs provide for hospital bills, doctor and operating room fees, medicines and convalescent expenses. Another kind of coverage is **major medical insurance,** which protects you against the costs of an expensive illness so colossal that it might wipe out the family's savings.

## THE NEW DENTAL INSURANCE

One of the fastest growing areas in the insurance field is dental coverage. Dental insurance is usually offered as part of a large company group plan, though it has recently been made available to small employers by one of the nation's largest insurance companies.

Such plans are usually offered on a deductible basis—you pay the first $100 of dental expenses and the company picks up the tab for a percentage of the remainder. For a routine oral examination, including X rays, insurance would pay 80 percent of your bill above the deductible amount. It would pay the same percentage for fillings, root-canal therapy, extractions and other oral surgery. Such plans cost from $5 to $10 per month and pay a top limit of approximately $500 per annum.

## CHAPTER 49

## Ten Ways to Cut
## Your Medical Bills

*How to get the same
—or even better—
health protection
for less than you're
spending now*

As a result of skyrocketing hospital charges, doctors' fees and medical insurance premiums, the average American family today spends more than $500 annually on health care. A critical illness, chronic disease or major accident could raise your annual bill to $3000, $5000 or even more. For all of us health care threatens to become an increasingly worrisome part of our budget.

Fortunately, there are simple measures we can take to cut substantial slices off these medical expenses and, at the same time, get better protection for our health. Here are the most practical money-saving moves recommended by leading experts on medical care:

1. Find a family doctor before illness strikes. About 25 years ago, this country had more than 95,000 general practitioners in private practice. Since then, as more and more doctors have gone into specialties, research or administrative jobs, the number of full-time family doctors has shrunk to about 65,000. These remaining GPs have to work an average of 56 hours a week to treat their regular patients. When someone they have never served before phones for immediate help, their secretaries frequently have to turn him away with the advice: "Better go to the emergency department at the hospital." There, a patient usually has to pay both a hospital charge and a separate fee for the services of the doctor on emergency room duty— perhaps two or three times the cost of a visit to the office of your family doctor.

When you select a new doctor, ask him to have your old doctor forward your entire family's medical records. They are a guide to quicker, more certain diagnoses and may prevent duplication of tests or immunization procedures.

2. Discuss fees before you run up a bill. Today many doctors bill their patients—of average income or more—on the basis of so-called relative-value scales. Each doctor sets his own basic fee— $7, $8, $10, $15 or more, depending on where he practices—for

a routine office or hospital visit. Then, for all other services, he multiplies his basic fee unit in accordance with a list of each service's relative value as published by his county or state medical society. If your doctor uses this relative-value scale and charges, say, $5 for a routine office visit, you might expect him to bill you about $10 to $15 for a routine house call and up to $50 or more for a complete physical examination.

Your doctor will sometimes lower his basic fee—and consequently all his other charges—if your circumstances justify the reduction. But don't expect him to pry, unasked, into your finances. If your income is low, tell him about it during your first visit—*before*, not after, he sends you his bill.

3. If possible, see the doctor in his office. Because time-consuming driving is involved, most doctors charge substantially higher fees for house calls. But they have other reasons for discouraging home calls. Away from their offices, for example, they must rely upon only the simple instruments they can carry in their black bags. If diagnosis or treatment requires any more complex equipment, the home visit may become merely a costly time-waster that delays vital decisions.

For the patient too ill or too old to leave home, money-saving alternatives to having the doctor call are often available. For example, many visiting nurse services, which once served charity patients almost exclusively, now provide home visits by registered nurses on a noncharity basis. Fees range from as little as about $6.50 to $10.10 in the smaller towns around the country to $11.50 per visit in the New York metropolitan area. Some insurance plans which do not cover doctors' home visits do pick up the tab for the services of a visiting nurse.

4. Arrange regular checkups. Don't feel that periodic physical examinations will involve a heavy expense and "prove nothing." Even the examination that reveals no hint of illness pays off with peace of mind that makes it worth every penny it costs. If the checkup reveals an incipient illness of the heart, the arteries, the eyes, the kidneys or any other organ, you may be saved from catastrophically expensive doctor, drug and hospital bills. And if an early breast or prostate cancer is detected, the examination may save your life.

5. Investigate specialists' fees. Because specialists must devote

from three to five years to extra training after earning their M.D. degrees, they generally charge more—often much more—for every hour of their services than do general practitioners. But how much any specialist will charge you will depend, in part at least, on what your family doctor tells him about your finances. Thus, if meeting a specialist's bill is going to be a problem, the best time to discuss it is with your family doctor before you see the specialist. He may feel such treatment is not necessary.

Even if a specialist knows your financial situation, he will seldom be able to tell you beforehand how big his bill will be. Your diagnosis may require more tests than anticipated. Medical or surgical treatment may involve unforeseeable, time-consuming complications. And his bill, when you get it at last, may therefore seem very high indeed.

Here again, turn to your family physician if you think you have been overcharged. His phone call to the specialist may bring forth a more reasonable, revised bill.

6. Ask your doctor about a choice of hospitals. The cost of hospital care has been rising even faster than doctors' bills. In New York City for instance, in 1969, increases in wages and fringe benefits for hospital workers plus other expenses raised the daily charges for semiprivate rooms to the range of $50 to $82 per day, in the voluntary hospitals affiliated with the major teaching institutions.

Your family doctor may be able to select the hospital that will be both best for your case and least expensive. He will quite correctly give first consideration to the hospital with which he is personally affiliated, since he is most familiar with your medical record. Large medical centers and university hospitals generally provide special services and costly equipment of great value in the diagnosis of unusual cases and the treatment of critical conditions. They also have to charge the highest rates. For more common illnesses, for an appendectomy or a tonsillectomy, or to have a baby, you might be wiser to patronize your local community hospital with its generally lower room rates. Whichever hospital you and your doctor agree upon, you should share his confidence that it has adequate, modern equipment, and that its staff is well trained and follows the best modern practices.

If your illness or operation is likely to involve a prolonged convalescence, you may find it more economical to enter a hospital with so-called progressive patient care: Patients are moved to less expensive quarters as their need for intensive nursing drops off. Such arrangements are increasingly available, even in the smaller hospitals. In a community health center–hospital setup in an average metropolitan area an intensive care unit for the critically ill could cost $75 per day; an intermediate care unit for a normal hospital case without complications (a routine appendectomy, for instance) could cost from $30 to $40 per day; an intermediate, or extended care, unit could be $20 to $28 per day. Long-term convalescents, those who require only physiotherapy or general diagnostic work-up, could be housed in a motel-like self-care unit at the much lower cost of $15 to $20 per day.

In many hospitals, particularly the smaller ones, X-ray and laboratory technicians don't work on Saturdays and Sundays. Thus the patient who checks in at the end of a week may have to pay full room rates for two or more days before his detailed diagnosis can be established or confirmed. Unless your hospital's technicians process their work on a week-round basis, it may be economical to avoid checking in on a Thursday or Friday.

7. Try to do without that private room. Some people feel that it is worth an extra $10 to $20 a day to enjoy the comfort and prestige of a private room. What they too often overlook is that this self-indulgence may mean paying higher fees to doctors, surgeons and other consultants who, quite properly, see no reason to hold down *their* bills if their patients can afford to pour out money for comforts they don't really need.

Actually, semiprivate accommodations—most commonly two in a room—offer most people distinct advantages: the companionship of a neighbor, more frequent attention from floor nurses and the added safety of having someone present if one should experience some incapacitating emergency.

8. Ask whether the drug prescribed for you has a "generic name." Most widely prescribed drugs have two names: the *brand* name, given to it by its packager or manufacturer, and the so-called *generic* name, which identifies the chemical compound no matter who manu-

factures or markets it. Many physicians prefer to prescribe some drugs by brand name because they place special confidence in the products of particular manufacturers. But if your doctor prescribes an expensive drug for long-term use, feel free to ask him whether a generic name prescription would not serve you just as well. If he agrees, you may be able to cut your medication costs substantially.

In most cases the generic name drug (which must meet the standards set by either the U.S. Pharmacopeia or the National Formulary) sells for less than its brand-name equivalent. A task force on prescription drugs of the U.S. Department of Health, Education and Welfare stated that if doctors made every effort to prescribe generically, patients would realize an overall saving of 5 percent. There are instances in which a patient may save as much as 50 percent in the cost of medication by buying generic name products, but they are rare.

▭▭▭▭▭▭

## SOME HEALTH COST DOS AND DON'TS

1. *Do check on your community health services and the free or low-cost services available through your union or your professional association.* Through local institutions or your group affiliations, you and your family may be entitled to free X rays and vaccinations or low-cost laboratory fees. There may be free diagnoses and services available for handicapped persons.

2. *Don't overlook taking along medical records when you move, go to a specialist or change doctors.* Your new doctor may not be able to use some of these records—the X rays, for instance —but if he can, you will save both him and yourself time and yourself money.

3. *Do be sure that you know your employer's policy on salaries when you* are out because of illness. If it is to pay for a limited amount of sick leave at the beginning of an illness, you may be able to obtain a disability income insurance policy which is cheaper because it doesn't pay until after a given waiting period, or a health insurance policy that pays only after a certain amount of medical expenses have been incurred.

4. *Do keep records of all your bills and expenses.* Keep them not only for tax purposes, as noted in this chapter, but also because you may need them to collect all the money due you under your health insurance or group health insurance plan. At the very least, the records will save time and assure that your claims are settled faster.

5. *Don't neglect to check your health insurance periodically, particularly if you move to a new area.* In addition to

▭▭▭▭▭▭

9. Update your health and hospital insurance. More people than ever before—more than four out of every five of us—subscribe to voluntary health insurance plans. Many of us, however, do not get full value out of health insurance dollars because we sign up for policies that do not fully match our real needs. Young couples, for example, should make sure that they are eligible for obstetrical-care benefits. Older people should be more concerned that their policies will see them through the prolonged treatments needed for arthritis or a chronic heart condition.

Check on the benefits offered to you through Medicaid and Medicare so that you are sure you are getting all the benefits to which you're entitled. In some states middle-income families qualify for Medicaid benefits. And even if you are in a higher income bracket, in the case of a very costly illness you may qualify for Medicaid assistance.

⊡⊡⊡⊡⊡⊡

rising hospital costs everywhere, the cost of a semiprivate room or nursing care may vary considerably from region to region, and you may find that your former coverage is inadequate when you move into a new area.

6. *Do keep up-to-date on changing Medicare and Medicaid benefits,* so that you get all the benefits that you are entitled to and, conversely, can buy more insurance if some of your Medicaid benefits are lowered.

7. *Don't neglect to tell your doctor the whole truth about your symptoms or any medication you have taken, or even that you have been under another doctor's care.* Many patients are embarrassed to tell the doctor that they've been "prescribing" for themselves or visiting another doctor. But it's important, if the doctor is to make an accurate diagnosis and prescribe cor-

rectly, for him to know what you've already taken or what treatment you've had. Without this knowledge he may give you a drug that will counteract one you've taken or result in an unpleasant reaction. And don't overlook minor symptoms that may have disappeared—what appears to be minor to you may not be minor to him. Be as truthful and as accurate as you can, for your own sake.

8. *Do remember that the best cure for illness is not to get sick in the first place.* An ounce of prevention is not only worth a pound of cure—it's also worth money in the bank. Try to get, and see that your family gets, well-balanced meals, enough sleep, daily exercise and regular recreation, so that you all stay healthy. Guard against accidents by observing safety rules in your home and on the job.

⊡⊡⊡⊡⊡⊡

Before you buy or renew any health insurance contract, check it against other available plans. Read the small print to see whether your plan will pay the full semiprivate hospital room rate—or only a fixed number of dollars per day *toward* that rate. Will it cover diagnostic tests and X rays performed in your doctor's office, or will it cover such charges only if you are hospitalized? Does it have a "right of transfer" clause that won't leave you out in the cold if you change employers or become unemployed? And if you are considering adding a major medical or an accident policy to your present plan, will it dovetail with the insurance you already carry or will you be paying extra premiums to cover the same risks?

10. Take all the tax deductions to which your medical expenses entitle you. In figuring your income tax you are allowed to deduct all medical costs that exceed 3 percent of your income, and if drugs or medicines exceed 1 percent of your income they may be included in your medical expenses. Be sure, for example, to deduct not only your doctors' bills but those you have paid to chiropodists, dentists, opticians, physiotherapists, and registered or practical nurses. Add up your expenditures not only for prescription drugs but for aspirin, rubbing alcohol, patent medicines and even tonics or vitamins if recommended by a physician. Count in what you have paid for hearing aids, orthopedic shoes, shoe arches, back supports or elastic hosiery. Include all the premiums you have paid for health and hospital insurance—even that part of your children's camp or college bills itemized as a health service or health insurance fee. Don't forget to include transportation costs that you and your family incurred in going to and from any doctor or hospital for treatment. (For more details, see the special tax section, page 589.)

Keep a running record of all your medical expenses and check it over before the end of the year. If your bills have run low, you might do well to postpone elective expenses, such as new eyeglasses, until the new year. But if you have already spent more than the 3 percent nondeductible amount, you should consider having all needed medical, dental and optical work done before the year ends so that it will all be fully deductible. By taking the fullest advantage of these deductions, you may be able to score a surprisingly large deduction in your total medical expenses.

# 11

# WHAT YOU SHOULD KNOW ABOUT CREDIT

*Almost everybody borrows in one way or another. But you can save substantially if you understand the cost of credit*

## CHAPTER 50

## Money When You Need It

*Shopping for credit—
what's available, where to
find it, how it works,
what it costs*

The coffee-break auto loan, cash-reserve checking account, re-volving charge account and nationwide credit card are here to stay. Ads on subways, buses, television, radio, in newspapers and maga-zines urge us all to buy now, pay later. People are becoming as conscious of their credit rating as they are of their social status. Even the kids have caught on. Last year one six-year-old confided to a department store Santa that all he wanted for Christmas was a BankAmericard.

The lure of easy credit has led some people to the brink of finan-cial disaster. For others, however, it has provided an opportunity to enjoy the car, clothes, house, furniture or vacation they could not otherwise afford. One part of the secret of using credit wisely is knowing how much of a debt burden you can handle. The other is selecting the cheapest, most convenient source of credit. This brief review of the major types of credit, how they work, where to find them, will help you choose the one that's best for you.*

### Bank Loans—For Personal and Business Use

The commercial bank today is a prime source of personal loans, generally at advantageous rates. When you need a loan, you should approach a bank first to check on its terms and your eligibility. The interest rates will vary, depending on your area and require-ments. Terms and interest rates also vary from bank to bank, so visit several to find the ones most favorable to you. Banks offer different types of loans. These include unsecured loans, secured loans, business loans and unsecured short-term notes. Unsecured personal loans are readily available for a wide range of needs, from hospital expenses to home improvement. Provided your credit rating is satis-factory, you may borrow up to $5000 in most cases on your signature alone. The loan is repaid in monthly installments at a true annual rate

---

*The specific interest rates cited in this section are used only as examples and reflect current rates as of early 1970.

of approximately 12 to 13 percent. (See Chapter 52, "Watch Those Interest Rates!" page 493, for more information on interest rates.)

Business loans, of course, continue to be big bank business. With a sound commercial or professional purpose, you can approach a bank for a loan—perhaps $100,000 or more, and you might have five years in which to repay. As a veteran of World War II or Korea, you may still be eligible for a GI business loan. Although you should first apply to the local office of the Veterans Administration, you may find the bank makes your loan through its participation in the GI Bill lending program. Terms are better than those offered to other borrowers.

A secured loan, using stocks or bonds as collateral, permits you to borrow from 50 to 75 percent of the value of the stocks or bonds, depending upon the quality of the stocks or bonds, at a lower rate than an unsecured loan. The bank holds your stocks against cash, and you sign a "time note." This note may become due before you are ready to repay, but if your securities still have high market value, you will probably be able to have your note renewed. You pay only interest. Be aware, however, that you do not get the current market value of your securities as a loan. The bank will offer less, as a protection against possible decline in value. You will not be asked to put up additional security or have your note recalled unless the stock drops to below the actual amount of the loan. If the value of the stock sinks, you will have to provide additional collateral. If, however, you cannot pay the loan, but the value of your stock soars, the bank will sell all or part; it collects the debt, you collect some profit. Your pledged stocks and bonds still bring in the usual dividends, and these may help to offset the cost of your loan. Of course, when you repay a loan secured by stocks and bonds, they are returned to you.

Savings banks and savings and loan associations offer passbook loans to customers with savings accounts. The savings bank will advance you the sum you need (up to the full amount in the account, discounting the interest charges in advance) at the going rate of interest. Some institutions also offer nondiscounted passbook loans, charging 1 percent more than their interest rate on savings. You are required to repay your loan in monthly installments over one to three years at some banks. Other banks leave the manner of repayment largely to the discretion of the borrower. Self-discipline is important here to keep the interest charges from mounting up.

When you take a passbook loan, you have the advantage of not losing the interest accumulated on your savings. Withdrawing savings prior to an interest payment date may result in forfeiture of the interest for the entire period on the withdrawn amount. It may be more economical to postpone the withdrawal and take a short-term passbook loan instead. After the interest is paid on your deposit, you make the withdrawal and repay the loan with interest.

Banks generally extend unsecured short-term notes only to their more valued customers. This type of loan enables you to borrow money at a prescribed rate of interest for a limited period of time, usually two or three months. You repay the loan in one lump sum rather than in installments. What makes this kind of loan so desirable, if you need money for only a short period, is that the rates are comparatively low (8 to 10 percent annual interest) and no collateral is required. If you cannot repay the loan at the due date, the bank may or may not let you renew the loan. Be sure to discuss this possibility with the bank when you take out the loan. Most banks require partial repayment (25 or 50 percent) of the original loan when the loan is renewed. The number of times you will be able to renew the loan will depend on the policy of the bank.

## When You Go to a Small-Loan Company

You will, no doubt, find it easier to walk into your friendly small-loan company—open long after the banks close and on Saturdays too—and to walk out with a $500 loan than you would to get the same money from a bank. But in return for speed and lack of intensive questioning, you will pay their high interest rates. These vary. An interest rate of 3 percent a month comes to 36 percent a year.

In general, go to the small-loan company only if you cannot get a loan from a lower-rate source. If you decide to do so, first check on the company's reputation through the local Better Business Bureau.

## Borrowing on Your Life Insurance

Life insurance policies differ as fund-raising vehicles; the type of policy you own may make a ready loan available to you. Read up on

478

your policy; cash value and loan rate will be stated. If you want the money for a short time your life insurance policy can provide a quick, low-rate method of obtaining money. Write your company, giving your policy number, and state how much you want. (You can borrow most of the cash value.) Usually, a check will be sent within a few days, no questions asked, and you can repay on a system convenient to you. There are no extras on an insurance loan. At 5 percent, for example, you may appear to have a bargain.

But—of course, there is a "but"—you reduce your family's protection against your death by the amount of the loan and the interest charges. The very lack of pressure to repay an insurance loan is not

## THE LOAN SHARK

The reputable loan company operates under state license, which gives varying degrees of protection to the borrower. And since the passage of the Truth-in-Lending Act, loan sharking has become a federal offense. But this doesn't mean that a loan shark cannot still attempt to operate, sometimes under the protection of a large and altogether sinister organization. In these days you may find that he has set up shop in attractive surroundings that are likely to lull the borrower's suspicions.

It would be impossible to list every device an unscrupulous lender might use. As a potential borrower, you should make a prior check on the lender and be aware of the following possibilities:

• You may be asked to sign papers in which there are blank spaces.

• You may not be given copies of all the papers.

• You may not get a chance to read the fine print; an additional document you did not see may be among the carbon copies.

• The amount of the loan may be overstated.

• The date the loan was made may be incorrect.

• The charges may be exorbitant— and they may skyrocket further in mysterious ways if you get yourself involved.

The person who has become involved with a loan shark does not get free easily. Some who have borrowed have accepted lifelong shackles. They don't go to the district attorney because they are afraid that strong-arm tactics may be used against them—and sometimes their fears are realized. The threat alone is a burden no one should carry.

Manage your money so that when you need to borrow your credit is good at reputable sources. Your own handling of your finances is your best protection against involvement with shady characters.

in its favor on a long-term basis. By constantly postponing full discharge of the loan, you shoulder the burdens of a running debt and heighten the risk of being underinsured. You also lack that cushion of financial assurance your insurance policies offer should you have to meet an even greater emergency. If you require an extended and sizable loan you would protect yourself better by offering the insurance policy as collateral for a bank loan.

## Credit Unions and Comakers

Members of credit unions save by purchasing shares in the association. Out of the accumulated savings fund, loans are made to its members. The law permits unsecured loans up to $750 and adequately secured loans in larger amounts, depending on the size of the credit union. Repayments are made periodically, according to an agreed-upon schedule, but they may not extend over more than five years. A credit committee elected by the members of the credit union passes upon the applications for loans. Interest on these loans must not exceed 1 percent per month on unpaid balances, inclusive of all charges incident to making the loan. Each credit union fixes its own interest rate within this limit. The charge for the loan often includes insurance that automatically liquidates the debt if the borrower dies or becomes permanently disabled. (For insurance with other types of loans, see "Insurance of Loans," page 482.)

If, through no fault of your own, you don't have an established credit rating, raising a loan may be difficult. Here, your resource may be a person who has the required financial standing. When you find such a friend or relative to cosign a note at a bank or finance company, you get your loan. Your comaker takes responsibility for settling with the lender if you should fail to do so.

## Charge Accounts

Charge accounts are another source of credit. There are several types, of which the most usual is the open, or regular, account. You buy from stores in person, by mail or by telephone without down payment or service charge. But the statement you receive is invariably marked "Payable within 10 days of receipt of statement." In practice, this works out as a 30-day period, and some stores will, protestingly, carry unpaid balances forward for several months for the customer with a good credit rating. Ultimately, of course, if you continue to be delinquent for a long period of time, they will threaten to sue, and you should certainly settle the account in a hurry to avoid such proceedings. In the meantime, you are likely to have been labeled a poor risk at the central credit bureau.

Other stores impose a service charge on the past-due balance. The amount of this charge depends on the type of contract you signed in the first place. If you find it hard to settle regular charge accounts in 30 days, you can open a service charge type of account.

Titles of accounts vary from store to store and it is not always possible to say which title fits which method. Some retailers combine different forms of payment in their installment contract. For example, one national company's "revolving charge account" contract permits the customer three choices: He may pay within 30 days, no penalty, or, if he fails to pay, he automatically becomes liable for a charge of

---

## LOANS AT THE SIGN OF THE GOLDEN BALLS

The sign of the three golden balls, hanging over dingy stores on back streets and in run-down neighborhoods, denoted the local pawnbroker to generations of borrowers throughout the western world.

In 20th-century America, the dusty little shop has, in many places, blossomed into handsome establishments run by corporations. The principle of lending remains the same. The customer takes his security, in the form of jewelry, furs, a camera, a musical instrument, to the pawnbroker; in return, he receives a loan and a receipt. If he is unable to repay the loan, plus interest, he will never return to redeem his pledge. In time, the article will be sold and the pawnbroker gets his money back.

Hopefully you will never need the pawnbroker, but if you ever use such services, seek out the reputable man who allows you to seal your pledge of jewelry in a bag or to write the serial number of equipment on your receipt as a guard against substitutions.

Interest rates vary—perhaps as low as 2 percent a month, or they may be five times higher—but they all end with the month in which the customer repays his debt.

"No questions" is the rule at the pawnbroker's and, for the short-term need for ready cash, the establishment still has a place in the complex society of today.

$1\frac{1}{2}$ percent a month on his outstanding balance. He then remits whatever installment payment is due according to a set schedule. That is, if he owes $50, he may have to pay $10 a month, but if he runs his account to $200, he pays $20. He can also pay off the rest of his debt before the final installment is due.

Another form often described as the revolving credit account works this way: The customer agrees with the store's credit department on an amount to be paid monthly. The store then sets a limit on what he is allowed to buy, so that the amount of outstanding debt will not exceed the level originally agreed on. This type of account is helpful to those who are too easily carried away by the array of merchandise in a store and the magic-wand effect of the words "Charge it!" Debts above the agreed amount must be paid immediately.

The "Retail Installment Credit" agreement of a famous coast-to-coast store operates as a regular charge account when the bill is paid before the next statement date. Otherwise, the customer has to pay a service charge of $1\frac{1}{2}$ percent per month and at least one sixth of his current balance. The minimum monthly payment is $10.

---

## INSURANCE OF LOANS

With many types of loans you automatically acquire life insurance—for which you may or may not pay directly, according to your source. The life insurance buys protection for the lender against your death and consequent inability to pay the debt. It does not, however, protect your family. It may sometimes appear that you are getting a particularly good deal—a competitive rate of interest plus insurance. A closer look at the terms of the contract, however, may prove otherwise. You and your family would derive no personal benefit from the insurance—except for the coverage of the debt in case of death—and taking full cost into consideration, you may find that the overall contract is no bargain.

You may be offered "free insurance," which is part of the agreement, but the cost may be built into the interest charge you pay. Sometimes, in addition, you will be offered the benefits of accident and health insurance for "pennies a day." In either case, the insurance is often badly overpriced. Should you protect your responsibility for the loan to this additional degree? Before doing so, check on whatever coverage you already have in case of accident or disability and what the general state of your finances would be in such an eventuality.

---

The "Flexible Charge Account" of one New York City store operates as a regular account or as an approved limit type of account. The customer pays according to schedule: If he owes $50, he pays $10; if he owes $200, he pays $40. Interest charges are included.

The "Optional Account" of a well-known western store also can be used as a regular account, or the customer pays according to the current extent of his debt. When his balance is $50, he pays $5; when he owes $200, he pays $10. Of course, he also pays an interest charge of $1\frac{1}{2}$ percent per month.

A $1\frac{1}{2}$ percent monthly interest charge is usual in the retail business on bills to $500. Over that amount, it is reduced to 1 percent a month. Note that $1\frac{1}{2}$ percent a month is 18 percent a year.

One difficulty that arises in these multiple-type agreements is that the customer who mailed his check to settle on the regular 30-day basis may get a bill with a $1\frac{1}{2}$ percent service charge. The reason is that his payment did not reach the company's accounting department before the next billing period. If this happens to you, write the store at once.With some revolving charge account agreements, the customers' partial payments are not deducted when interest is computed, and your further purchases may extend the amount of a service charge debt you do not even owe.

Many companies besides department stores set up "easy payment" plans, which do not have the optional regular account feature. The customer pays a presettled amount each month until the specific merchandise is paid for. The time periods of installment contracts will vary and the carrying charges also. You must also keep in mind the percentage you would actually be carrying. Your pocket might be better served if you get a loan and buy the goods outright.

A large initial payment will reduce the spread of payments and the charges you will be paying. Be sure to leave yourself a cash margin for emergency. Certainly it is not possible to safeguard against all eventualities, but it is the too heavy load assumed for too long a period that drives many families to seek community counseling agencies' advice. Interest charges mount up during a spread-out paying period. Such advertising as "Easy terms! No down payment, three years to pay" may involve you in a prolonged and inflated debt. Pay as quickly as you can, to reduce the overall cost.

## Credit Cards and Bank Credit Plans

Some invitations to use credit cards are, in effect, invitations to take a loan at a high interest rate. Do you need this type of advance? The smart money manager uses credit cards instead of paying cash. But he does so knowing that he could have paid cash if he so wished; and he does not charge items or services he would not otherwise have bought. Billing is either through a specific company, as when you charge at a department store or buy gasoline, or may be consolidated, as when you use one type of card for a variety of services or purchases.

Some organizations issuing credit cards do so on payment of an annual fee; they will add a service charge on delinquent accounts. Your need for such services in the course of your business or social life will dictate whether or not you apply for membership. If and when you do so, weigh the specific charges made by the particular organization against your expected benefit from the services offered. (See Chapter 54, "The Credit Card Revolution," page 509, for more information on credit cards.)

Currently, bank credit plans are blossoming overnight. They vary in detail, but not in substance—the people who use them pay interest, and that adds up to good business for the banks. One plan establishes the borrower's right to credit of up to $5000. The borrower does not actually receive any money. He makes use of the available credit whenever he pays his bills with the special checks issued to him. He pays a monthly interest charge on the amount of credit he actually uses, and he pays for the checks. As he repays the amount borrowed, plus interest, he establishes his right to use the credit again.

Another system does not require special checks. A borrower of good standing may write a check for more than he currently has in his account. But because he has arranged for the bank to set up a credit reserve of from $400 to $5000, his check is met. In multiples of $100, the bank will move money into his otherwise overdrawn account. The borrower repays on a 12-month or 24-month basis, plus a monthly interest charge of 1 percent on the *daily unpaid* balance. If he repays in less than a month, the interest is proportionately reduced. If he does not draw on reserve by overdrawing his account, he pays only the normal charges for checks and service.

In both of these credit plans the borrower must meet standards of credit eligibility similar to those required by a bank in making conventional type loans. The loan proceeds are not turned over to the borrower under either of these plans. Instead, the loan comes into existence when the check is written.

In another type of plan, banks issue credit cards honored by participating merchants in an area. The statement of your various bills comes to you from the bank, and if you pay within a stated period, there is no penalty. However, the plan also works on a budget basis, so that you can spread payments over two years at an interest rate of $1\frac{1}{2}$ percent a month on your unpaid balance. The bank is, of course, running a plan similar to a department store charge

---

## WORDS YOU SHOULD KNOW

**Personal loan.** A sum of money borrowed from a bank or loan company at high interest rates, usually for a short time, for some personal need of a temporary nature. The borrower customarily promises to repay the money plus interest in regular installments by a specific date.

**Unsecured loan.** A personal loan granted with no security other than the borrower's signature on a promissory note. Most institutions lend small amounts to regularly employed people.

**Secured loan.** A personal loan for which the lender protects himself by securing from the borrower a collateral of stocks, bonds, real estate or other assets, worth more than the loan. The collateral is forfeited if the loan is not repaid with interest at the time agreed upon.

**Passbook loan.** A personal loan secured by your own savings account, which must exceed the amount of the loan.

**Collateral.** The assets put up by a borrower as a pledge for his loan.

**Loan shark.** An unscrupulous lender, usually a private individual rather than a company, who charges exorbitant interest and often uses physical violence to enforce collection of the debt.

**Service charge.** An amount, usually 1½ percent per month (that's 18 percent a year), due on unpaid balances of credit card and department store charge accounts.

**Revolving credit.** A system of flexible indebtedness with a top limit geared to the borrower's income. Example: A department store charge account against which additional purchases may be made while old charges are being paid off.

account, but through the participation of dozens of merchants and services in a specified area. Moreover, it will issue loans of between $25 and $150 to its cardholders without a loan application.

The loan application can be dispensed with because, in the credit-card plan, as with the special-check and reserve accounts previously described, the bank customer has had to fill out a detailed application form in the first place. In reality, he is processed like any other type of borrower although he does not get a loan as such. With a regular bank loan the borrower describes his purpose, which must be approved; under the other systems he spends or charges as he pleases.

If you need money today, for almost any reason, the problem is not where to get it but which of the many types of loans or credit to use. Shop around until you find the one that is least costly and most convenient for you.

## HOW TO HANDLE A DEBT CRISIS

What happens when the unexpected happens—someone in the family has an accident or becomes sick, or your home furnace finally gives up, or your car motor needs an overhaul? And you find that because of this unplanned-for expense you cannot meet your regular installment payments.

Above all, don't panic. Reliable lenders will try to cooperate with you if you explain your situation to them honestly, before you have become delinquent. They have almost as much stake as you have in seeing that you meet your obligations, since they really don't want to be in the business of trying to sell houses, used cars or repossessed television sets. Get in touch with them, and tell them why you are in a financial bind and how you propose to extricate yourself. Tell them when you believe you will be able to start regular payments again and how you propose to handle the interim period. Perhaps you can give each creditor a regular fraction of what you owe until you can resume full payment. Maybe you can continue to pay the interest on the loan until you are in a position to begin repaying the principal. If you can show that your intentions are honorable and that you've been caught in a situation that you hadn't foreseen, you will find your creditors not only willing to go along with you but also helpful in working out a debt schedule that you can handle.

Of course, this will be much easier to do if you have a record of meeting your payments promptly so that you have established yourself as a good credit risk.

## CHAPTER 51

## How's Your Credit?

*Here's how to rate yourself
the way the credit bureaus rate you—
and how to keep in
their good graces*

Imagine what it would be like if everyone had to pay cash on the barrelhead for everything he owns or uses—house, car, fuel, electricity, milk, furniture, washing machine, television set, and so on. Not long ago most people did have to pay on the spot, and as a result only a few were able to own the goods or enjoy the multitude of conveniences that are now available to just about anyone—that is, anyone whose credit is good.

How is yours? If you wanted to open a charge account at a department store, buy a boat on the installment plan or obtain a national credit card, would you have any trouble? Sit at the credit manager's desk and see yourself as he sees you before he initials the card that says you're OK for credit.

The merchant is after profits. He wants you to buy and buy and buy. And he's anxious to give you credit to help you do so. But he wants you to pay your bills too, for most of what you owe him he very likely owes elsewhere.

Some merchants are afraid of credit. They restrict it so rigidly that it doesn't boost sales much at all. Others are too greedy. They encourage customers to overbuy, let them get into a jam and perhaps eventually get into one themselves.

A good businessman will encourage you to open an account with him but will check you carefully when you do. Half the job of collecting an account, according to credit people, goes into the effort of checking on it when it's opened. The more carefully the checking is done, the less trouble later.

Here are the basic questions a credit manager tries to answer when he opens an account. Some of the information will come directly from you when you fill out an application blank or are interviewed. Much of it will come from other sources: your bank, your employer, regional or national credit bureaus, other merchants, your personal references, maybe your neighbors and landlord.

*Who are you?* Name and address are not sufficient. The account must show enough identifying information that you won't be confused with anyone else. One credit bureau reports 1350 variations on the name John Smith (J. Smythe, Jon Smith, John Smit, and so on) in its files. But even if you have an unusual name there's always a chance that someone else will turn up with one like it, so your spouse's name and your middle initial or name are needed too.

Who you are includes age and family status, for the credit analyst is trying to determine what sort of person you are. Stability is thought to increase with age. From the mid-twenties on, you're likely to be less impulsive, less daring, more conservative. Until recently few companies granted credit to teen-agers, though stores are beginning to do so now under limited conditions.

The most stable age bracket is thirty-five to sixty-five. If you're older, you may be turned down for credit unless you can offer security, have had an active account for a long time or clearly have wealth or a good income. Married people are considered better risks than single people or those who have been divorced or are separated.

*Where do you live?* If your neighborhood is respectably "middle class," fine. If you've lived at the same address three years or more, so much the better. If you're a renter that's all right too, but if you own your home you're tops.

The credit man's smile isn't quite so bright, on the other hand, if your address tips him off to any of the following: The neighborhood is run down or has an unsavory reputation. You receive mail in care of a friend. You live in a furnished apartment, rooming house or cheap hotel. You've been living at your address less than a year. Worst of all, you're a transient with half a dozen addresses in your recent past. Any of these will alert the credit man to dig deeper.

*What's your income?* Now you're getting close to the nub of the matter. The credit man will undoubtedly ask you how much you make. He'd also like to find out, if he can, what other income and assets you have, as well as how much members of your immediate family bring in. But the figure that he will basically be interested in is how much you earn.

The stability of that income is very important too. How long have you been on your job? Five years or more—good. Less than two years—caution.

As for your future prospects, he may not come right out and ask you what they are, but he will make a judgment based on the type of work you do.

Here's a list of occupations in the order in which many credit men rate them. The first nine are jobs that are pretty secure and require experience and seniority to get ahead. From No. 10 on, the occupations are those that the credit man may worry about, with the shakiest ones at the end of the list.

1. Executive
2. Officer in armed services
3. Professional
4. Employe of financial institution
5. Civil service worker
6. Office worker
7. Farmer (owner)
8. Small retail proprietor
9. Employe of public utility
10. Insurance agent
11. Traveling salesman
12. Unskilled factory worker
13. Nurse
14. Building-trade worker
15. Tenant farmer
16. Laborer
17. Worker in service trades: barber, waiter, tailor, beauty shop operator, bartender, domestic, entertainer

*Will you pay?* This is the single most important determination that the credit man must make. People with moderate incomes are often far better credit risks than people with high incomes but expensive tastes and little sense of responsibility.

Your character is what counts, and to assess it the credit man must study all the information he has gathered and match the strong points against the weak ones. But the important item is your past record. If you have paid promptly in the past, particularly the recent past, then presumably you will continue to do so.

Many credit managers can make a pretty good judgment based on just two factors: reports from other merchants and your occupation. If reports say "prompt pay" and you are in a highly secure job, fine. This opinion is subject to reversal, however, if some strong negative information should turn up.

What if you have never had credit before? The merchant will look more carefully at your position, earnings, capital assets and general reputation.

What happens if you have had some tough times in the past and were slow in paying a few old bills? That depends upon what the reasons were and how you handled the situation. If your trouble came during a general depression or because of some personal emergency, such as job loss, it will probably be discounted—especially if your more recent record is good and if when things were tough you took every care to preserve your reputation, as described later in this chapter and in "How to Handle a Debt Crisis," in Chapter 50, on page 486.

Nationally, bad-debt losses on monthly charge accounts range from 1/10 of 1 percent to 1 percent of credit sales. Installment bad-debt losses range from 1 to 2 percent of installment sales. That doesn't seem like much at first glance. The trouble is that many people who do eventually pay up are slow and that's expensive to the merchant. He figures a cost of 4 to 9 percent of gross credit sales to set up and run his credit department. Slow payers boost that percentage.

As an account ages—that is, remains uncollected—its dollar value gradually declines. The cost of collecting it goes up, the chance of its being completely defaulted increases and the merchant cannot offer it to a bank as collateral for a loan. According to some credit people, the average dollar that is owed is likely to shrink in the process of collection as follows:

Current....$1.00
2 months....90
6 months....67
1 year....45
2 years....23
3 years....15
5 years....01

## Staying Out of Trouble

Small wonder that a merchant worries when payments fall off and wants to help protect other businessmen by warning them of accounts that are likely to be risky.

Does that mean that he'll put the sign on you the moment you delay a remittance? No. But he does have some reasonable expectations. Here are five simple rules you should be sure to follow in order to stay in his good graces:

1. *Don't get in over your head.* Just because credit comes easily doesn't mean that you should overuse it. A pattern of continuous high debt in relation to income doesn't look good, even if you've been managing to keep up with your payments.

2. *Keep up your payments.* Know what and when you're supposed to pay. An occasional delay won't hurt. Chronic delays might dub you as "OK but slow." National gasoline companies, credit card people and many others are leery of slow payers and drop them quickly.

Generally, you're expected to pay within 45 to 50 days for a charge purchase. Half of all credit customers do so, and most of the rest pay within 90 days. If you habitually let things go to 90 days, though, you're tagged as slow.

The credit bureau, which is a central clearinghouse of information for merchants, may receive a report on you if you don't clear up a charge account debt after several statements or if you miss two or three installment payments.

3. *Don't become a collection problem.* Ten percent of the people who buy on credit cause the headaches of credit men. They don't pay and don't say why. Eventually most of them do pay, but only after dunning. The result is a spoiled credit record.

4. *Tell creditors when you move.* If you're moving out of town, pay up first.

5. *Track down errors.* If you are denied credit, find out why. There may be a mistake, and if so, you'd better get it straightened out before your reputation as a credit risk suffers further.

Remember, good credit is your key to a world of material comforts. Lose it and you lose a tool that greatly magnifies the power of your dollar.

## KNOW YOUR
## CREDIT RIGHTS

The consumer should know that there is nothing private about his credit rating and that threats to "report" him as a bad risk are next to meaningless. The fact is that there are a number of big "information organizations" that began keeping track of him almost from the moment he made his first credit purchase at any store, anywhere—such organizations as the Associated Credit Bureaus of America, the Retail Credit Corporation and the Credit Data Corporation.

As the New York *Times* reported not long ago, the business of these centers is simple: the exchange of facts, facts, facts. They know how old you are, what your earning schedule has been, what you do in your spare time, what your spending practices are, how your family lives. Just remember how much information you have given out about yourself in casual surveys, in filling out application forms, in recording your opinions and proclivities. That is where the information has come from. And it is available—either on an exchange basis of one organization trading favors with another or for a slight fee—to any legitimate applicant for the dossier.

While it may give you an uneasy feeling to know that somebody is keeping track of everything you do, it should also reassure you that any threat that you will be reported as a bad risk is meaningless. Your credit rating stands or falls on legitimate past and present performances. It is not going to be destroyed with a single complaint of credit difficulty in which you may be the innocent—or at least the unwitting—victim of circumstance. The record is there to back you up as well as to take you down a peg or two, depending on how you've conducted your personal financial affairs.

And there are, according to a consensus of legal advisers and credit experts, some simple rules for that:

1. If you're broke and up against the financial wall, make minimal payments of whatever you can scrape together to demonstrate your good intentions—and to avoid the vulnerability that goes with appearing to be irresponsible. Once you do that, it's a matter of record, and you can't be sued.

2. Find out what your rights are in a credit dispute, possibly by spending a few dollars for half an hour of a lawyer's time or by going to the Legal Aid Society if you can't afford help.

3. Don't be bullied by an "official notice" unless it really is official and comes in the form of a summons. Anything else you may receive is just a piece of paper or warning of possible future action.

4. Try not to overextend yourself in the first place when that payment plan looks so easy. But if you do, keep your head in the crisis that follows, no matter how many threats you get.

We're all responsible for our debts, but undue worry and anxiety aren't among the debts anyone has to pay.

## CHAPTER 52

## Watch Those Interest Rates!

*Credit costs vary. Whether you're borrowing or buying, be sure to check the price tag on the money itself*

When we pay cash for a product or service, we know exactly how big a hole the purchase is going to make in the pocketbook or the bank account. But until the passage of the Truth-in-Lending Act, "buying" money was something else.

The cost of consumer credit was usually disguised, and the borrower would often unwittingly pay a staggering rate of interest, as these citizens discovered:

A federal employe in New Mexico bought a television set for $285.55. When he asked, he was told he could pay for it at the rate of "about $14 per month." Since not a word was said about interest, credit or finance charges, he assumed the installment arrangement was simply a courtesy extended by the dealer. Over the course of ten months he paid $147.30. Only then, looking at the paper he'd signed, did he discover that he still owed $206.22; he had been charged $67.97 to finance the purchase! The annual interest rate came to more than 33 percent—a rate which could make him bankrupt.

A mechanic in Texas bought $1812.80 worth of household furniture, for which he made a down payment of $261.80, and contracted to pay 36 monthly installments of $56.34 each. Only after he was unable to meet all his obligations did he stop to figure out that the furniture was costing him $477.24 in finance charges—a true annual rate of 19.4 percent.

A clerk-typist in Washington, D.C., in need of money because of a family illness, borrowed $1000 from a bank. Her other debts made it difficult to repay. So, just to meet installments on the loan, she obtained another loan—thus paying extra interest on money to pay interest. In a few months, in a series of Peter-to-Paul operations, she ended up with three bank loans totaling $2000, a finance-company loan of $800 and some $800 in other obligations. Her local credit union, to which she took her troubles, calculated that she was paying credit charges at the rate of well over 40 percent a year.

These borrowers, like millions of others, were victims of a credit system that was a model of contrived confusion—and sometimes deception. Enormous sums were involved. Consumer debt, both installment and noninstallment, in the first half of 1969 amounted to over $112 billion. How much of that outlay represented overcharges is anyone's guess. It is plain that any consumer seeking credit used to need a detective's persistence and a mathematician's skill to determine what he actually paid in interest.

## Interest Rates in Disguise

The traditional way of stating the cost of credit is in terms of the *annual* interest—the custom in business and in home mortgages. In consumer credit, however, lenders frequently used slick techniques to make the cost of borrowing seem cheap. There were five main methods; some are still being used, but now the true interest rate must be stated:

*The add-on.* A bank may offer a loan at the cost of, say, $6 per $100, adding the interest charge right away on to the principal, which is then repaid in 12 monthly installments. This sounds like 6 percent annual interest. Actually, it is about 11.1 percent. Because the borrower is steadily paying it off, the average amount of his loan over the course of the year is only about $50; yet he pays out a full $6 interest on $100.

*The discount.* In this case the interest charge of $6 per $100 is deducted when the loan is made, so the borrower receives only $94. He's being charged $6 not on a full $100 but on only $94, in addition to paying interest on parts of the loan after they have been repaid. Thus he pays still more for his money than the borrower who gets a comparable add-on charge.

*Monthly rate.* Small-loan companies often quote interest rates of 1.5 to 3.5 percent per month. Such rates make borrowing sound very cheap, but the loan is usually for a year or more. To figure the true annual rate multiply by 12; it will range from 18 to 42 percent.

Department stores levy a service charge of, usually, 1.5 percent per month, on "revolving credit" charge accounts. "Service charge" sounds more trifling than "interest rate," but customers are really paying 18 percent interest for the convenience of charging.

*No interest rate quoted at all.* Here the seller would merely indicate the size of the down payment and of the installments to be paid for 12, 24 or 30 months. The total credit cost, in a lump-sum figure, might or might not have been mentioned in the contract—before Truth-in-Lending.

*"Loading" the contract.* The credit charge would be inflated by extras—investigation fees, processing charges, service charges, high premiums for insurance (even though the borrower might already have insurance that would cover the loan). Many of these fees were merely disguised interest charges.

By no means all lenders were out to fleece the consumer. Many avoided mention of annual interest rates because of the widespread public impression that more than 6 percent a year is usurious—a belief that traces back to medieval church doctrine. When home mortgage credit became widely available at the beginning of this century, ethical lenders held to the historical "fair" rate of 6 percent. But as a former Commerce Department official has pointed out, "Under the conditions applying to a modern installment credit system, the idea of only a 6 percent credit charge is a myth—and the public should be aware of it."

For a $10,000 mortgage, 6 percent annual interest was long a reasonable limit—because a building is offered as collateral and because the loan is large in relation to the bank's administrative costs. But in installment loans of only a few hundred dollars (often with no collateral) the expenses involved in extending credit are relatively high. For one thing the merchant must borrow his money from a bank—often paying 6 percent or, in recent years, much more. Then he has the costs of credit investigation, bookkeeping and billing, sometimes of dunning his customers or hiring a collection agency; also he has an occasional uncollectable account. When all these expenses are taken into consideration, a charge of 12 percent a year— or more—is by no means unreasonable. The customer, however, has a right not to be kept in the dark.

## Truth in Lending—Honesty by Law

Since July 1, 1969, when the Truth-in-Lending Act became effective, much of this has changed, and comparison shopping for "buying money" is now possible without slide rule, instant calculator and a degree in advanced math. The law was planned to ensure that all borrowers and customers know what they are paying to "buy" money so that they can compare costs and avoid the uninformed use of credit. The two most important parts of the law deal with the finance charge and the annual rate of interest. They are the ones that tell you, at a glance, how much you are paying for credit and its relative cost in percentage terms. All banks, savings and loan associations, department stores, credit card issuers, credit unions, automobile dealers, consumer finance companies, residential mortgage brokers, and their helpers—the plumbers, electricians and automobile mechanics—are regulated by the law. So is your doctor, dentist, lawyer and any other professional person you deal with. Hospitals are included too—in fact, any individual or organization that charges

## WHAT TO KNOW ABOUT SIGNING AN INSTALLMENT CONTRACT

Whether a contract is offered to you by a ready-money lender, by a store where you wish to buy "on time" or by a door-to-door salesman, you should know that this person or his company is likely to sell the installment contract to a third party.

That third party may be a bank or a sales finance company and the matter may well be in order. You pay on time; no trouble, no repercussions. But when you do not pay, the buyer of the contract has the legal rights set out in that contract: He may repossess the property, take over your security, have your wages garnisheed or take you to court. You have signed; you are definitely committed to whatever terms you so accepted. It's your re-

sponsibility, therefore, to know what you are signing and what will happen if you fail in payment.

Since your legal commitment will be what the contract says and not what the salesman or lender says (unless those statements are written into the contract), your first step is to read the fine print of the contract before you sign it and to see that full information is given. Examine these points:

Does the contract spell out in detail what you are buying? The price of the merchandise or the amount of cash lent? What your allowance is from the trade-in (when you're buying a car, for example) or the sum of the down payment? The total amount of your debt and how payments have been divided? The number of your installments and when they occur? And, very important, what the credit charges are?

What happens if you cannot pay?

for giving you credit that must be repaid in more than four install-ments. There is, however, an upper limit of $25,000 on the credit extended—the Truth-in-Lending Act does not apply to loans beyond this amount—except for mortgages, which can exceed the $25,000 limit.

The law has divided consumer credit transactions into two cate-gories: open-end and nonopen-end. Typically, open-end credit is the kind you get from retail stores that offer you a revolving charge ac-count, or from banks or other institutions that offer you a credit card. An open-end account means that you can keep on buying on credit while you are paying off old bills. By contrast nonopen-end credit is for a specific amount, for a specific period of time, with an agreement on the number of payments you will make and their due

Are the goods repossessed? If so, are there terms under which you can re-deem them? What are the details on nonpayment penalties? Note that re-possession of the goods may not relieve you of commitment to pay.

Can your pay be attached if you fail to meet installments? Does the con-tract include an assignment of part of your wages?

Has the salesman or lender filled out all the spaces in your contract? Sign nothing till blanks are satisfactorily completed or you may become liable for charges or goods you did not con-sent to accept.

To whom will you make your pay-ments? You may suppose that your contract is with a certain store or dealer when, in fact, you will be deal-ing with the bank, finance corporation or some other central organization that has bought up the contract or acts for your merchant or lender.

Will the monthly payments com-pletely cover your indebtedness for the goods or loan and interest? If not, you might find a lump-sum balance still has to be paid, and without delay. This type of provision is being elimi-nated by merchants and lenders of good standing, but may still occur and prove a trap for the unwary and ill-prepared customer. Check to make sure it is not in your contract.

Credit laws vary considerably from state to state. Inquire if your state's banking department issues information for the consumer.

When you have signed your con-tract, make sure you have a copy and that you keep it safe for reference. Moreover, changes designed to protect the consumer are taking place in both state and federal laws. Be alert for these developments and see that you receive all the protection the law af-fords in your credit dealings.

date. This is the kind of credit you get when you buy what retailers call "big ticket" items—washing machines and other major appliances, television sets, automobiles, boats—or when you get a bank installment loan.

## What the Merchant Must Tell You

What is a merchant required to tell you when you open a charge account or some other kind of open-end account? Lots of things that he may or may not have told you before: how long you can defer paying your bill without incurring a finance charge; the method used in determining the unpaid balance on which the charge is calculated; the periodic rates used and the amount of unpaid balance to which each applies; the conditions under which additional charges can be made, plus the details of how these charges are calculated; the minimum payment that must be made on each billing; and any liens that may be acquired on your property.

In addition to telling you these things *before* you open the account, the merchant should supply this information on your monthly statement: the unpaid balance at the start of the billing period; the amount and date of each extension of credit and a statement of each item bought; payments made and other credits, including returns, rebates and adjustments; the finance charge in dollars and cents; the rates used in calculating that charge and the range of balances to which the finance charge was calculated; the closing date of the billing cycle and the unpaid balance at the time.

How is the annual percentage rate determined on open-end credit? The finance charge is divided by the unpaid balance to which it applies to get the rate per month (or whatever time period is used). If it is the usual monthly rate it's multiplied by 12 to get the annual rate.

Note that the new law *does not establish any maximum or minimum charges for credit;* presumably these will continue to be set by that old reliable "law" of supply and demand. All Truth-in-Lending does is require that the creditor tell you, in plain English and in large type, what you pay for the credit and how the charge is computed. It is still up to you to learn who offers what credit terms, and which are the most advantageous. Consider the variety of charge accounts available, for instance, and you'll see why it pays to be informed.

*Thirty-day, or regular, accounts.* The store bills its customers on a regular cycle so that your bill comes due the same time each month. Since there is an inevitable delay between the time you charge something and the time it takes the charge to go through the store's bookkeeping and appear on your monthly statement, you get about a month of free credit. If you pay your bills promptly—within 30 days is the accepted standard—you can continue to have this free credit indefinitely.

*Revolving accounts.* The store bills you for the entire balance due, but you are only required to pay part—how much depends on the terms set up by the store—either a given percentage of the total bill or a set amount. When you have made the required monthly payment, you are free to add on new charges, up to a maximum that the store has set for you. The unpaid portion of the bill is subject to a percentage service charge, usually at an 18 percent annual rate. But the *amount* you pay at this annual rate depends on whether the store calculates the percentage due before or after deducting the regular monthly payment and any returns you have made. If the percentage is figured before payments and returns it will, of course, be a larger amount and more money out of your pocket. So when you decide to open a revolving plan, by all means check on the store's billing method, which it is now required to explain.

*Optional revolving accounts.* The store bills you on a regular monthly cycle, and you have the choice of either paying immediately, as with a regular charge account, and getting "free credit," or paying part of the bill on a revolving credit arrangement and incurring a service charge. As noted before, find out how the store calculates the amount of the bill on which a service charge is due, before you commit yourself to any optional revolving credit plan.

Not all stores offer a choice of accounts, so if you find something available in one store only—for instance, a particular style of coffee table that just fits the space you have—and you plan to buy it on credit, you will of course have to accept the terms that store offers. But don't accept any credit plan without first inquiring if there are other plans available, and then pick the one that offers the best terms. And if you have your choice of stores all offering about the same merchandise, shop around for the one that offers the best credit plan.

## What's Required on Bigger Loans

How about nonopen-end loans and credit? These often add up to large sums, since this category includes the expensive appliances, automobiles and mortgages. Here are the things that the lender must tell you, in writing: the total dollar amount of the finance charge, except in the case of mortgages; the date the finance charge begins, if it's different from the date of the transaction; the annual percentage rate (unless the finance charge is less than $5 or the total amount borrowed is less than $75); the number, amounts and due dates of payments; the total amount of the payments, except in the case of first mortgages on houses; the amount charged for delinquency or default and/or the method used for calculating the amount charged; a description of any penalty charge for prepayment of principal and how the balance of the unpaid finance charge is calculated in the case of this prepayment; and finally, a description of the security the creditor will collect if you default on your loan.

▭▭▭▭▭

## HOW TO
## BEAT THE HIGH COST
## OF MONEY

Question: Can you beat the high cost of money today? Answer: *Yes.*

Borrowing costs, already at the highest levels in modern times, are still climbing. When "fringes" are added to basic rates, even the nation's top-ranking giant corporations are paying record-breaking rates for bank loans, and small installment-loan rates are scaled way up from these prime rates. Mortgage money is brutally hard to get and, where available, even more brutally expensive. But you can beat this high cost of money and here are five ways to do it:

1. If you're buying a house it's usually best to put down the largest down payment you can, arrange to pay off your mortgage in the shortest feasible time and shop as never before for the best terms for you.

2. When buying a car or any "big ticket" item, follow the same basic down-payment–repayment rule. This is the worst possible time to look for "easy credit"—meaning loose credit—terms. The axioms are:

The cheapest way to buy any major item is to pay for it with your own cash; the next cheapest way is to put down as much as possible and pay off the balance as quickly as possible; the most expensive way is to pay down as little as possible and stretch out repayment as long as possible.

3. Shop for loans of any type among the many sources of credit, and avoid apparently easy but costly forms of

▭▭▭▭▭

This last point is a tricky one that you should understand. It means the creditor has to spell it out if, under the terms of the loan, he is entitled to repossess your car, for instance, or deduct a certain amount from your checking or savings account, or have a claim on payment before your other creditors.

There's more too. In the case of a loan you must be told the amount of credit you are getting, including all charges that are part of the amount of credit extended but are not a part of the regular finance charge. These extra charges must be itemized and might include such things as points (for securing a mortgage); an appraisal or credit report fee (except in a real estate transaction); or a premium for insurance, if this is one of the conditions on which credit is being extended to you.

In the case of a purchase of an item on credit you must also be told, in writing, the difference between the down payment and the cash price, including the value of a trade-in if it's used as part or all

borrowing. As an illustration, if you borrow money on which you agree to pay a seemingly low monthly rate on the unpaid balance, you may actually be paying a very stiff rate. A rate of $1\frac{1}{2}$ percent a month on an unpaid balance becomes 18 percent over 12 months; a rate of $2\frac{1}{2}$ percent a month on an unpaid balance becomes 30 percent.

As an illustration on the other side, individuals across the nation have discovered the virtues of borrowing against the cash value of their life insurance policies. In many cases the rate is as low as a simple 5 percent a year. If you choose this method, though, pledge to yourself that you'll put aside a specified amount each month in a savings institution to retire your loan at the earliest feasible date.

Don't let this loan run on and on; you may be risking your family's welfare.

4. Borrow precisely what you need— no more, no less. If you need $300, don't borrow $500 to have extra cash in your pocket—not at these interest rates. But if you do need $500 don't borrow $300—and make it necessary for you to return for another loan.

5. Make regular savings an absolute "must" in your budget so that you can share in the high rates being paid on savings today. If you can earmark funds from your pay to meet an installment each month, you can, if you try, earmark the same funds to build a nest egg.

These are only five of the fundamentals—but these five alone will help you come out ahead in this era and any other.

of the down payment; the amounts deducted as prepaid finance charges or required deposits; the amount being financed; and (except for houses) the total cash price plus the finance and all other charges.

On loans and credit in this nonopen-end category the annual percentage rate is calculated by the actuarial method—the same method used to compute your mortgage payments. Your payments go first to pay off the interest due and then to pay off the principal. Don't even try to figure out these payments; the method is so complicated that the Federal Reserve Board has prepared tables for a variety of charges, times of payments, and so on, and whomever you buy from uses either these tables or others, equally accurate, that he has obtained from banks or his own trade associations. (You can, of course, ask to see the tables if you have any doubt about the charges, but a reputable creditor will use reliable tables.)

There are, however, differences in computing this actuarial rate that you should know about, to be sure that you are getting the most use from your money. The question is: Is the actuarial table based on an add-on finance charge, or is the finance charge discounted in advance? Let's say, for example, that you have borrowed $1000 at 6 percent, to be repaid in 12 monthly installments. You have to pay back $1060, but you only have the full use of that $1000 for the first month. After that you have less and less of that $1000 as you pay back more and more, so the 6 percent of $1000 for the first month becomes 6 percent of less and less each month—which in effect is a higher interest rate. It is, in fact, an annual rate of 11.1 percent when the figures are worked out for the loan as a whole.

If the table is figured with the finance charge discounted in advance, you borrow $1000, but you only get the use of $940 to start, and less and less each month. In this case the annual percentage rate is actually 11.8 percent. As always, when it comes to money, it pays to ask first, since it may mean to pay less later.

## New Real Estate Rules

Real estate is another area that's less mysterious now that Truth-in-Lending is in effect, but here the consumer has not fared so well. Unlike other loans, as we've noted above, there is no requirement that your mortgage banker tell you how much your house is going to cost when you add up the principal and the interest over the 20 or 25 years that you send in those monthly checks. As pointed out in Chapter 12, "Taking the Mystery Out of Mortgages," page 137, in some cases the interest over the years may actually be more than the principal. Whether this is so or not, the interest is usually a very, very large sum that most of us just don't stop to think about.

In other aspects of real estate transactions, however, the consumer has benefited from the new law. If you decide to borrow money using your house as collateral and you sign a contract for a loan, you now have the right, within three days, to change your mind, cancel the contract without any penalty, get your down payment back in full and insist—if any merchandise, such as a pile of bricks or a heater has been delivered—that the seller pick it up within ten days or forfeit his claim to it. No work can be done on your property until your time for canceling has passed.

This part of the law was passed primarily to protect homeowners who had previously been induced by unscrupulous home repair racketeers to sign what the owners thought were ordinary installment loan contracts, only to find out to their sorrow that they had actually signed for a very expensive second mortgage. It was also designed to protect against lenders who promised people deep in debt that they could solve their troubles by consolidating their debts into one "easy" loan, using their homes as security. Here, too, the unwary found that they had simply exchanged one set of problems for another, and were in danger of losing their house if they didn't keep up the payments on the expensive second mortgage they had signed in order to obtain the consolidation loan.

The law now says that the creditor must explain that the contract may result in a lien or a mortgage on the customer's house. Only after this explanation is given to the customer in writing, in large type, can the contract be signed.

So if you find that you have signed a contract that you regret, you still have three business days in which to change your mind. To be sure that you get your release, you must state your wish to cancel on your copy of the contract; sign and date it within the three-business-day limit; and either mail the notice to the creditor at the address shown on the contract, or deliver the notice personally or by messenger, or send a telegram or letter stating your intentions. A telephone call is *not* acceptable; your cancellation must be in writing. Both mortgage brokers and craftsmen are expected to allow a reasonable time to expire—allowing for delays in the mail or other circumstances—before they assume that they have a firm contract that can be enforced against you.

The present provisions of the Truth-in-Lending Act provide more protection for you, the credit user, than has ever existed before. It's now possible to shop around for money and credit terms forearmed with knowledge that can help you make the best choice. But even though you now know what money costs, and find it much easier to be a comparison shopper, money doesn't cost any less. It is still up to you to make the right decision about what kind of credit to use and which is most advantageous in your own individual family situation.

▭▭▭▭▭▭

## HELP FOR DEBTORS

There are two provisions of the Truth-in-Lending Act that are especially important to the consumer who finds himself heavily in debt: the anti-garnishment provision and the regulations on loan sharking. Hopefully, they will not apply to you, but it's good to know about them.

The law prohibits garnisheeing (that is, having an employer automatically make deductions from a paycheck before the employe receives it in order to satisfy a judgment against the employe) more than 25 percent of a wage earner's take-home pay. A weekly paycheck of under $48, after deductions, cannot be garnisheed at all. The law also says that the employe may not be fired simply because his wages are being garnisheed for the first time. This is good protection for people (frequently in unskilled, low-paying jobs) in states where they have been under little or no protection. Garnishment has not been permitted at all in Florida, Pennsylvania and Texas. In Nebraska, New Jersey and New York the upper limit has been 10 percent of the paycheck; other states have been more severe with debtors, who will now have some relief.

The law also prohibits loan sharks from charging interest rates of more than 45 percent per year. There have been instances where a rate of 1000 percent was enforced, frequently through strong-arm methods. The loan shark business has been estimated at $350 billion per year, much of it channeled into the underworld.

▭▭▭▭▭▭

## CHAPTER 53

# When You
# Borrow on Your Assets

*Secured loans are easy
to get and bear lower
interest rates—
but they do have
some drawbacks*

What's the ideal financial situation? How about enough money in the bank to meet all needs and wants, and enough left over for emergencies? Unfortunately, few of us achieve this happy state of affairs. More usually, the time comes when borrowing is a must—and the real question is how to go about it as painlessly as possible, with the least amount of risk. One way is to use your assets as collateral—to borrow using a savings account, your life insurance, stocks and bonds or your house as security for a loan. There are various kinds of loans against these different assets, and each has its advantages and disadvantages. Here's a review of the alternatives, to help you decide which is possible—and best—for you.

*Passbook loans.* Your collateral is your savings account in a savings bank or savings and loan association. So you are in effect borrowing your own money. A bank will lend you the amount you need up to the limit of your account, keeping your passbook until you have completely repaid the loan. What you will be charged depends on the bank; some charge the going interest rate on loans, while others charge 1 percent more than they pay as interest on savings. How long you can keep the money and how quickly you repay also varies from bank to bank. Some will leave it up to you to set the terms you want (within reason); others will arrange monthly installments.

What's the advantage of borrowing your own money? (You do not, incidentally, have to borrow from your own bank, though most people do.) If you were simply to withdraw the money that you needed, you would lose the interest on that amount. By borrowing, you leave the account and the interest intact. You get a comparatively low-cost loan, since you are paying only the difference between the cost of the loan and the interest your money earns from your savings account. Actually, the cost amounts to even a little less than this because the interest on the loan is tax deductible.

There are two things to watch out for: (1) If your bank pays interest from day of deposit to day of withdrawal you aren't going to lose any interest by taking out the money, so of course there is no need for a passbook loan. (2) Some banks have a minimum required fee, regardless of the size of the loan. If you want to borrow a small amount for only a short time, find out in advance if there is a minimum fee. You may find that the fee is larger than the interest you would lose by withdrawing, and it would be cheaper just to withdraw.

*Stock and bond loans.* The stocks and bonds you own are your collateral. How many and which ones you want to pledge will depend, of course, on the size of the loan you need and the market value of the stocks or bonds you are offering. The bank accepts your stocks in return for the cash you need, and you sign a note agreeing to repay the loan either by a specified date or on demand.

The terms of a loan with stocks and bonds as collateral are usually quite liberal. The cost is the going interest rate, and it is not discounted (subtracted from the principal in advance), so that you have full use of the principal for the length of the loan. Usually only the interest is paid, in regular quarterly payments, until the principal comes due, either on the maturity date or on demand. Many banks will allow up to three years for repayment.

This type of loan offers several advantages: a lower interest rate than other loans on which the interest is discounted in advance; flexible repayment terms that can often be set for your convenience; and the use of money without permanently giving up an asset. Though the bank holds the stocks they still belong to you, and you continue to collect dividends.

But there are disadvantages too, and they can be significant. The interest rate is not fixed for the length of the loan. When money market rates change, the bank has the right, which it usually exercises, to raise your interest to conform to the new higher rate. And the flexibility of the "on demand" terms works to the banker's advantage as well as to yours. He probably won't bother you as long as the price of your stocks remains stable, but should their value drop, he will be on the phone asking for more collateral or even for repayment of the loan—at a time that may prove to be very inconvenient.

*Life insurance loans.* Your collateral is any life insurance policy that has a cash value, including ordinary life policies, endowments and some annuity policies. (Term policies are excluded since they have no cash value.) How much you can get depends on the age of the policy; policies usually begin accumulating cash value in the second year. The insurance company will lend you up to about 95 percent of the cash value, deducting only the interest due between the time the loan starts and the anniversary date of the policy. (If you want to know how much you can borrow and at what rate, check your policy—you'll find a schedule in it that tells you.)

The terms of the loan are generous. There is no limit on the length of the time for repayment, unless you decide on one yourself. You can pay whenever it's convenient. If you choose not to pay the principal you can pay the interest, and continue to use the principal indefinitely. (Interest is usually paid at the time of the premium payments.) If you choose to pay neither, the interest will simply be added onto the loan, increasing your indebtedness. Even if this goes on until finally principal and interest are equal to the cash value of the policy, the company will not close out the policy without giving you some advance notice—a month or more—so that you have time to repay enough to keep it active.

A loan on your insurance policy doesn't mean that you have lost the protection of the policy, but it does mean that your benefits are reduced by the amount of the loan (both principal and interest). If you should die before the loan is repaid your beneficiary would not receive the original value of the policy, but only what was left after paying off the loan. And since the cash value is diminished by the amount of the loan, you have less to offer as collateral should you need another loan.

You might, for instance, have major medical bills that make it difficult to keep up your premium payments. You could take out a second loan, but only against the remaining cash value of the policy. In other words, every time you borrow against your life insurance policy you reduce its value as an asset. All that you have to spend for emergencies is the uncommitted cash value of your policy. And, unfortunately, though the cash value of your policy declines while there is a loan outstanding against it, your premiums don't. So you are really paying the same amount of money, for less protection, until the loan is paid off.

*Mortgage loans.* Your collateral is your house, which has, of course, already served as the collateral for your mortgage. If you have an open-end mortgage—one that permits you to borrow back the principal that you have already paid in—you can add this money onto the mortgage again and continue to pay as before in monthly installments. However, you have lengthened your mortgage by the time needed to pay off the new loan. Usually the interest rate is the same as, or not much higher than, the one on your mortgage. If you were fortunate enough to get a mortgage when rates were comparatively low, a loan like this is most economical. (For more detailed information on mortgages, see Chapter 12, "Taking the Mystery Out of Mortgages," page 137.) Although this kind of loan is most often given for home improvements, there is no requirement that the money has to be used for such purposes.

A variation of the mortgage loan is straight mortgage refinancing. The idea is similar to the open-end mortgage, but the terms are not as advantageous. Instead of adding onto your present mortgage you apply for a new one—for the amount you want to borrow plus what you still owe on your old mortgage. Since it is a new mortgage you will probably have to pay a higher interest rate, in line with the current mortgage market. You will have to pay some fees again, for various bank and legal services, though they may not be as high as the first time. You go on paying in monthly installments as before, but the payments are greater since they include payment for the new loan and a higher interest rate.

It is possible to refinance your mortgage regardless of who granted it originally and whether or not it was guaranteed by the Federal Housing Administration. However, sometimes the gap between possibility and actuality is wide, particularly in a period of tight money. When mortgage money is scarce many commercial banks are not willing to provide this refinancing. And when savings banks do it they usually insist that the money be used only for home improvement loans. You must come to them with a detailed estimate of the cost of materials, if you are going to do the job yourself, or an estimate from a contractor, if you are planning to have someone do the job for you. In any case allow a minimum of a month, and possibly several months, before you get an answer.

If you don't have the privilege of an open-end mortgage, with its low interest rates, compare the costs of refinancing your mortgage with the cost of getting an ordinary loan. It may not be economical unless you want to borrow several thousand dollars.

As you can see, there are advantages in borrowing against your assets. In general you can get lower interest rates than on conventional unsecured loans. Since the collateral you offer is valuable, the loans—except for refinancing mortgages—are generally quick and easy to make. In some cases little more is needed than a call to your broker or your life insurance agent. For the most part you can use the money as you choose, whether your purpose is as serious as a major medical bill or as indulgent as a mink coat. But there are hazards on borrowing on these assets, and one of the major drawbacks is this very ease. Just because the penalties are few it requires discipline to pay off the loans and not let them slide—always planning to pay off next week or next month. With a life insurance loan, this could actually result in a financial loss to your family at the very time when they may need money most. In any case, you may find that you are paying far more interest than you should, simply because you are continuing to maintain a long-term debt. So look on your assets as just that—to be kept against emergencies and borrowed against only when absolutely necessary.

CHAPTER 54

## The Credit Card Revolution

*The proliferation of cards brings great advantages— and great temptations!*

Is cash money obsolete? And are checks on the way out too? Are we headed for a society where everyone uses only credit cards and the man who wants to pay with dollar bills is looked on as very old-fashioned, if not out of it altogether? Not quite, but credit cards, especially bank credit cards, seem to be increasingly the passport to our financial future. Basically there are three types of credit cards, which serve overlapping but different functions: the "T&E" card, the specialized card and the bank credit card.

The ubiquitous travel and entertainment card, popularly called the T&E card, is used primarily by business and professional people. Before he is issued one of these cards the businessman's credit is carefully investigated. Usually, unless his company guarantees the card, he must be earning a fairly good salary and have a good employment record. Membership in one of the three major T&E credit card groups—Diners' Club, American Express and Carte Blanche—usually costs about $12 per year. Bills are due on receipt, and for a period ranging from 25 to 50 days, depending on the issuer, no interest is charged for delinquent payment. After this period the cardholder may be charged up to 18 percent annually or he may lose the charge privilege; T&E cardholders are expected to pay promptly.

It's important to realize that the use of T&E cards is *not* conducive to economy. Because of the annual cardholder's fee and interest charges on overdue bills, you are paying a premium for the convenience these cards afford. They also represent a temptation to splurge on an expensive restaurant dinner or a weekend trip you may not be able to afford. T&E cards are primarily geared to the spending habits of businessmen whose expenses for travel, entertainment and services are often reimbursed by their employers. The economy-minded family should approach them with caution.

The specialized, or private label, card—for charging such things as gasoline and oil, airline tickets, telephone calls or car rentals—is also well known. A specialized credit card is customarily issued by the oil company, car rental agency or airline itself. Payment is due as soon as the bill arrives, and there is no interest charge unless the credit is extended for more than a month.

The holders of both T&E and specialized cards have always been primarily men, since they are the ones who travel and entertain in the course of their business or professional activities. The scope of the cards has been extended in recent years, however, by making them "his and hers," that is, allowing the husband to take out a card for his wife, at a somewhat lower membership fee so that she too can charge meals, flowers, elephant hide wallets and all the other things on the growing list of special items available to members of these credit card clubs.

The real credit card revolution, however, has been the rapid ex-

510

pansion of bank credit card plans, extending credit card privileges to that huge (and willing) market—the American housewife. The minimum income level for admittance to the "club" is lower than that for other cards (about $6000 compared to $10,000 or more for the T&E cards); there is no membership charge; and a person doesn't have to be a depositor of a bank in order to get one of its cards. When the card is issued, the bank usually assigns to the cardholder a maximum amount of credit, based on the family's credit rating, which can range from $100 to $400, or more in the case of customers with very good credit rating. The cards usually expire at the end of a year and are renewable.

Most banks set a ceiling on the amount that can be charged without having the merchant check with the bank. The usual limit is about $50, but this varies with the bank and the store. The limits on charges for services are more flexible and can go as high as $500 for an airline ticket. Many banks add on a "cash advance" privilege to their credit cards; that is, they'll let the cardholder borrow on the credit card, and add this advance to his bill.

These bank cards are honored by thousands of merchants and businessmen who have not been willing or perhaps able to extend charge privileges to their customers. They are not usually accepted, however, in the major stores that have their own revolving credit plans. (For information on this type of credit, see Chapter 50, "Money When You Need It," page 476.) When people use their bank credit cards the merchant forwards the bill to the bank issuing the card, which then credits the merchant's bank account and deducts a service fee of from 3 to 7 percent. The bank then takes on the job of billing and collecting from the customer. The shopper has the advantage of credit in many places where he had no credit before, the merchant gets his money quickly, sometimes at a cost lower than that of maintaining his own charge system; and the banks have the advantage of a whole group of new customers.

## How to Use Credit Cards to Your Advantage

Obviously credit cards offer many advantages:

1. They're time-savers: Instead of applying for credit in many stores and filling out many forms, you make one application and you

have a card valid in many places. And, instead of long check-writing sessions every month, you pay only one monthly bill.

2. They're credit extenders: You can shop in many places not previously available because you didn't have credit there. You can get services in local places, such as restaurants, that don't usually extend credit to strangers. And you can use this privilege in places outside your usual shopping grounds—in other towns and states, and even outside the country.

3. They're money savers: You can take advantage of sales, when your bank account is low, by using your credit. You have the use of money while you are being billed: You can charge when you are on vacation, for instance, and not pay until the bill arrives, which can be quite some time if you've been traveling outside of the United States. If you charge an emergency expense, such as a car repair, and don't have to pay for it until you are billed in about a month, you have, in effect, received a very short-term loan.

4. They add convenience and safety. You don't have to worry about being caught without lunch money and, perhaps more im-

---

## A QUESTION OF IDENTIFICATION

With so many bank cards in use, there is always the possibility that some will get into the wrong hands. When this has happened, according to a spokesman for the American Bankers Association, banks have not considered the cardholder liable, even when he may have been at fault by not notifying the bank promptly enough that his card was lost or stolen. However, banks are continually working on new ways of making the cards more personalized, to avoid the problems created by their loss or theft.

One method that seemed almost in-
fallible backfired. One city bank used photographs with its cards, and was then very embarrassed when young housewives, with their hair in curlers, were refused cash advances at their own banks and were told by several stores that they must have stolen cards.

Another solution the banks are working on would have each credit card magnetically coded. When the cardholder presents his card the merchant slips it into an electronic box supplied to the store by the bank. The cardholder then presses down three numbered keys in a combination known only to him. If the circuit is correctly completed, a green light shows up on the box. If not—no credit!

512

portant, you don't have to carry large sums of cash with you.

The trouble with credit cards is their very convenience. In addition to the advantages listed, many bank credit cards have a line of credit attached to them that makes it easier than ever not only to charge goods and services but also to "charge" money—to get a loan on the basis of the card with very little red tape. There's also the temptation to keep on using the credit card, adding new bills even before the old ones are paid. The banks that offer cards know this very well. Their own surveys have shown that only about a third of their customers pay in full on the first billing, within the time limit that credit is allowed without any interest charges. The other two thirds "roll over," that is, pay only part of the bill and continue to add new bills, which means that they have to pay interest on the unpaid balance.

It's these interest payments that make the bank credit card business profitable. The credit card becomes a revolving credit account, with an interest rate that can range from 15 to 18 percent or more annually. Using the card is so convenient that it's easy to exceed your budget without realizing it, especially if more than one member of the family has a card. At the very least, you will sometimes incur interest charges that you might not have incurred if you had stopped to think that you probably couldn't pay the bill within 25 days and should therefore either defer your purchase or shop around for better credit terms.

Does this mean that you should take out your scissors, cut up that neat little plastic card and forget the whole thing? Not at all. Why deprive yourself of the many and real advantages of this portable bank account? It does mean that the credit card has to become part of your family budget—that you have to set limits on its use, consider it as another credit "tool" and be aware of how much you are paying for the credit you are getting. (For more on credit see Chapter 50, "Money When You Need It," page 476, and Chapter 52, "Watch Those Interest Rates!" page 493.) If you can manage to pay within the no-interest-charge billing period set by the bank, you're really ahead. If you cannot, then be sure that the advantages of the credit card are not offset by the temptation to overextend yourself or to use an expensive form of credit when a cheaper one would do.

513

## Credit Card Dos and Don'ts

Here is a list of "dos and don'ts" that should help you have all of the conveniences of a credit card, without incurring any of the headaches.

*Do* set a reasonable limit on the amount you will allow yourself to charge on your card, and stick with it.

*Do* check each charge slip before you sign it to be sure that the charge is correct and isn't written in such a way that it could be altered after you have left the premises.

*Do* save your receipts so that you can check your statements. Mistakes are apt to occur, even in the day of the electronic computer.

*Do* keep a record of your credit card number in a safe place, and if it is lost, let the issuer know at once.

*Do* be sure to get your card back whenever you use it, and don't leave it lying around in places like the glove compartment of your car. There is a big market for stolen credit cards.

*Do* consider taking out credit card insurance. There may be a very low-cost (usually about $5 or less) policy available through card registry services being established around the country. You may also be able to get insurance through the corporation issuing the card or add it on to your homeowners' policy.

*Don't* sign up for a bank credit card before finding out how much the bank charges for extending credit after the no-charge period has ended, and how the bank computes the service charges. Banks charge different rates of interest, and they also differ on the basis on which the rate is computed.

*Don't* lend your card except in very exceptional circumstances. You are legally responsible if the other person loses or misuses it.

*Don't* keep an unsolicited credit card unless you plan to use it.

*Don't* count on your credit card to get you everything or everywhere when you're abroad. You should always have some cash and some traveler's checks with you.

*Don't* use your credit card in a foreign country until you have checked the exchange rate of the native currency for the American dollar. You may be cheating yourself if the free-market exchange rate is more favorable to the dollar than the official rate you pay when you use your credit card.

# 12

# MAKING YOUR MONEY WORK FOR YOU

*Learn the advantages and disadvantages
of savings accounts, the market,
the mutual funds—and pick accordingly*

## CHAPTER 55

## Watching
## Your Savings Grow

*Want to put your money
to work? One of the easiest,
oldest, safest ways
is to open a
savings account*

Depositing a certain sum in a savings account every month is a traditional way of putting your money to work, and one of the safest. In recent years Americans have been saving greater amounts than ever before—despite the simultaneous growth in ownership of stock and mutual funds and in other forms of investment. Savings institutions offer various interest rates and special plans to their depositors, and selecting the one that best suits your resources and goals can increase your profit.

In deciding where to place your money, you can choose between commercial banks, savings and loan associations and savings banks. In addition, your savings may go into U.S. Savings Bonds or certificates sold by banks.

Commercial banks are the largest holders of savings in this country. In some communities a commercial bank is the only institution in the area that accepts savings. Interest paid by commercial banks on savings accounts varies, but it is usually lower than the rate offered by other savings institutions. Commercial banks, however, offer certain banking services not available at other banks—for example, checking accounts, the most popular service available.

Christmas Club accounts are available at commercial banks as well as at other banking institutions. Anyone who joins a Christmas Club signs an agreement to make a regular weekly deposit for 50 weeks. The amount is up to the saver—it can be 50 cents, $1, $2, $3, $5, $10 and in some cases as much as $20. Christmas Club, a corporation, is the organization that sponsors most club plans and supplies coupon books and promotional material to participating institutions.

Each year's "club" comes to an end in November when the savings checks are mailed out. There is, of course, nothing to prevent a person from redepositing a part or all of his savings into next year's club, and the accumulation process then begins all over again.

As a rule, the money put into a club account can be withdrawn at any time. Some commercial banks exact a penalty, however, for early withdrawal before the full 50-week period of payments has been completed. Partial withdrawals before the expiration of the 50 weeks generally are not allowed—you must either leave it all in or take it all out. Unlike regular savings accounts, most Christmas Club accounts do not pay any interest. Some banks pay partial interest, and a few pay full interest.

Often employes in a company join a Christmas Club together. One member is delegated to take the weekly payments and coupon books and make the deposits for the group.

## Special Savings Programs

A certificate of deposit, also called a savings certificate, is a document offered by commercial banks to depositors who agree to keep a specified amount of money in the bank for a specified period of time. In return the bank pays a higher rate of interest than the depositor would receive from a regular savings account. The certificate is used to attract money and keep it available longer to the bank for loans.

Generally, certificates cover large deposits; depending on the bank, the minimum may be $500 or more. The larger the amount deposited, the longer the fixed time period and the higher the interest rate paid. Maturity dates for certificates of deposit range from 30 days to five years, and although you can take your money out before the date of maturity you'll receive less interest than if you had waited until the certificate reached full maturity. If your money is in a regular savings account you can withdraw at any time without a penalty.

The major benefit of certificates of deposit is that they offer high interest rates. The main drawback is that you need a large sum of money which you can keep in the bank for a long time.

Many commercial banks offer an automatic deduction plan. Under this plan you authorize the bank to transfer a specified sum from your checking account to a savings account at fixed intervals. You will receive the bank's stated interest rate on the amounts you accumulate in your savings account.

Payroll savings plans are offered by both commercial and savings banks. With this plan you authorize your firm to deduct automatically a specified amount from your paycheck each payday and invest it in U.S. Savings Bonds. An advantage to buying bonds instead of putting your money into a savings account is that you don't have to pay income tax on the interest until you cash in the bonds.

Both the automatic deduction plan and the payroll savings plan are excellent methods of "forced" savings, especially if you are one of those who find it so difficult to save.

## Savings Associations and Banks

A savings and loan association, either state or federally chartered, accepts savings with which it makes mortgage loans for the construction, purchase and repair of homes. There are nearly 6300 of these specialized financial institutions in the nation, of which nearly 2000 are federally licensed and the rest state licensed. Though there may be periodic exceptions, the associations generally pay a higher interest rate on savings than do either savings banks or commercial banks. This is because the associations have most of their assets—up to 85 percent—on loan in high-yield mortgages. Like savings banks, which are discussed below, the majority of the associations are "mutuals," being owned by their shareholder-depositors.

A depositor in a savings and loan association technically is buying savings shares on which he receives dividends (interest), and legally he is a shareholder. The commercial bank's checking or savings account depositor, by contrast, is a creditor of the bank, which owes him the money he has left with it.

Passage of the Federal Home Loan Bank Act in 1932 created a system of regional reserve banks. The system's member associations have greater financial flexibility because they may borrow from the 12 reserve banks, using as security the mortgages they hold. Federally chartered associations must be depositor-owned and must belong to the system, as well as to the Federal Savings and Loan Insurance Corporation, which insures savings accounts up to a maximum of $15,000 each. State-chartered associations may subscribe to these federal agencies, and in some states they must to meet their charter requirements. As a result, state and federally chartered members of the Federal Home Loan Bank system account for more than 95 percent of all savings and loan association assets, and more than two thirds of the nation's savings and loan associations carry deposit insurance.

As is the case in commercial and savings banks, an individual or family may have insured accounts in several associations, or several accounts under family members' names in one association, though some institutions impose restrictions.

Aside from home mortgages and home improvement loans, associations provide a variety of other services. Among them are passbook loans (see Chapter 50, "Money When You Need It," page 476), banking by mail and the mailing of dividend checks to owners of certain types of savings certificates or savings accounts.

Savings and loan associations also are known as savings associations, as building and loan associations, in New England as cooperative banks and in Louisiana as homestead associations.

Although savings banks, which are mostly mutual banks, have been in existence in this country for more than 150 years, there are still many states in which these institutions are not permitted to operate. Government regulations restrict the maximum interest rate banks are allowed to pay on savings accounts. Some savings banks pay the maximum, others less. Mutual savings banks also offer other services, such as late banking hours one evening of the week, banking by mail with free postage for depositors, Christmas Club accounts and, in a few states, savings bank life insurance. (See Chapter 47, "What You Should Know About Life Insurance," page 442.)

Some banks offer packaged savings plans, which combine a savings account with life insurance and purchase of U.S. Savings Bonds. Under a triple package plan, all three are obtainable through regularly made deposits in the bank. One bank, calling its plan a triple thrift superhighway to financial security, illustrates the results of ten years of regular deposits as shown in the table on the next page.

Note that the cash-in-bank figures do not include the interest that the savings earn. The term insurance decreases in coverage to 90 percent in the fifth year, 70 percent in the tenth year. However, the policy pays cash dividends and can be converted to permanent insurance without medical checkup, or may be kept in force ten additional years at the same premium. (For complete information on insurance, see Chapter 47.)

| TEN-YEAR RESULTS OF A TRIPLE PACKAGE SAVINGS PLAN | | | |
|---|---|---|---|
| DEPOSITS OF $5 A WEEK | | | |
| STARTING AGE | CASH IN BANK | SAVINGS BONDS (FACE VALUE) | DECREASING TERM INSURANCE (INITIAL AMOUNT) |
| 20.............. | $1910 | $500 | $10,000 |
| 25.............. | 1880 | 500 | 10,000 |
| 30.............. | 1830 | 500 | 10,000 |
| 35.............. | 1740 | 500 | 10,000 |
| 40.............. | 1570 | 500 | 10,000 |
| 45.............. | 1500 | 500 | 10,000 |
| 50.............. | 1070 | 500 | 10,000 |
| DEPOSITS OF $10 A WEEK | | | |
| 20.............. | $3900 | $500 | $30,000 |
| 25.............. | 3820 | 500 | 30,000 |
| 30.............. | 3670 | 500 | 30,000 |
| 35.............. | 3370 | 500 | 30,000 |
| 40.............. | 2870 | 500 | 30,000 |
| 45.............. | 2720 | 500 | 20,000 |
| 50.............. | 2150 | 500 | 20,000 |

A packaged plan can be worked out calling for deposits at other intervals, such as monthly or semimonthly. Instead of term insurance, a plan can be arranged with straight life or 20-payment life insurance. Or a savings plan may include only two of the elements, omitting either the insurance or the Savings Bonds.

Even if you have other assets—stocks, bonds, real estate—a savings account is a necessary part of every family's financial plan. It makes your money available to you in the event of an emergency in the way that investments do not. Sale of stocks and liquidation of assets take time; a savings account provides ready cash. With a savings account at least part of your money is at your disposal at all times.

Once you have decided to open a savings account, try to keep a minimum amount of five to six months' income in the account. This will provide you with an emergency, or reserve, fund in the event the breadwinner's income is curtailed or cut off for any length of time. The fund will allow you to live in the manner to which you are accustomed until financial matters are restored to normal.

The interest rate alone is not the sole criterion for people in choosing where to maintain a savings account. The convenience of banking near one's home or office and using one bank for both checking and savings accounts are often determining factors.

## When You Open an Account

Before opening a savings account, check these points:

1. Safety of your savings. How will you be protected against loss of your savings? Membership of a bank in either the Federal Savings and Loan Insurance Corporation or the Federal Deposit Insurance Corporation guarantees the safety of your savings. Each is an agency of the United States government and insures up to $15,000 of your savings in an account. An individual may have only one account insured up to $15,000 in a single institution.

However, where state laws permit, two or more persons may have individual insured accounts of $15,000 each and, in additon, have an insured joint account. In this way, a husband and wife may have insured accounts in one bank totaling $45,000: $15,000 insurance protection on wife's individual account, $15,000 insurance protection on husband's individual account, and $15,000 insurance protection on joint account of husband and wife. It is also possible to have additional insurance protection when savings accounts are owned in conjunction with one's children or other relatives.

If your funds exceed the insurance limit, you should maintain accounts at more than one savings institution to assure complete insurance protection for all your savings. In even a small city you should be able to find several banks with equally favorable interest rates.

There is no cost to the individual saver for this insurance protection. Rather, each member bank pays premiums directly to the insuring corporation. In Massachusetts, Maryland and Ohio, savings are protected by state insurance agencies.

2. Compounding of interest. Two banks may pay the same rate of interest; nevertheless, your savings might earn more money in one bank than they would in the other. The reason: Some banks compound interest more frequently than do others.

Many banks compound and pay interest four times a year; at a 5 percent interest rate, it takes 14 years for money to double. Of course, all interest earned is subject to taxation.

Regular monthly deposits in a savings account paying 5 percent interest, compounded quarterly, would grow as shown below:

| IF YOU DEPOSIT MONTHLY | $25 | $50 | $100 | $200 |
|---|---|---|---|---|
| In 5 years you deposit............. | $ 1,500 | $ 3,000 | $ 6,000 | $ 12,000 |
| With interest you have............. | 1,706 | 3,412 | 6,825 | 13,650 |
| In 10 years you deposit............ | 3,000 | 6,000 | 12,000 | 24,000 |
| With interest you have............. | 3,893 | 7,787 | 15,575 | 31,151 |
| In 20 years you deposit............ | 6,000 | 12,000 | 24,000 | 48,000 |
| With interest you have............. | 10,292 | 20,585 | 41,175 | 82,351 |
| In 30 years you deposit............ | 9,000 | 18,000 | 36,000 | 72,000 |
| With interest you have............. | 20,809 | 41,621 | 83,250 | 166,504 |
| In 40 years you deposit............ | 12,000 | 24,000 | 48,000 | 96,000 |
| With interest you have............. | 38,095 | 76,196 | 152,407 | 304,819 |

3. Withdrawal penalties and restrictions. Banks can legally require 30 days' notice of withdrawal from their depositors. Some banks impose a service charge for each withdrawal over a prescribed number.

Find out if the bank's practice is to require notice before a withdrawal is made. Ask whether it places any restriction or penalty on the withdrawal of funds, such as not permitting withdrawals within a certain period of time after an account has been opened. Inquire if it imposes a service charge for extra withdrawals. It is also wise to check on how withdrawals can be made: Will the bank honor a request for withdrawal of funds by mail? This is particularly important in today's mobile society, with the frequent transfers of company personnel and their families.

Some years ago, a large commercial bank followed the practice of imposing a charge if a bank check was requested by a depositor withdrawing funds from a savings account. Be sure yours does not.

4. Loss of interest. Ascertain the bank's timetable for paying interest. Then you will be able to time your deposits to earn the maximum interest. A few banks pay interest from the day of deposit to the date of withdrawal. Some banks pay interest from the first of the month on deposits made during the first ten days of the month. Money deposited after the ten-day grace period may not begin to earn interest until the next period. If funds are withdrawn from the

bank before the end of the interest period, the entire interest for the period on the withdrawn amount may be lost.

5. Responsibility of depositor. Do not be misled into thinking that a bank passbook is sufficient and perpetual proof of your ownership of funds on deposit at the bank. It is not. Every state, to some extent, practices "escheat," or state seizure of property with no apparent owner. One of the most common forms of escheat is acquisition by the state of unclaimed bank deposits.

How can such a thing occur? Enticed long ago by a premium offer, someone opened an account at a distant bank, placed the passbook in a "safe" place and forgot about it. The birth of a baby inspired the opening of a now long-overlooked bank account. A husband or wife started building a private nest egg in a secret bank account, the evidence of which was tucked away and forgotten.

Depending upon the state in which the bank is located, an account that has been dormant for a number of years becomes vulnerable to the laws of escheat. In New York, the time is ten years. If a bank fails to reach a depositor through the mails at his last known address and through advertisements and public notices, it must turn the funds over to the state after ten years, in accordance with that state's law. Once the money has been handed over to the state, securing its return is quite costly.

To safeguard your savings you should keep a record of all your accounts: the number of the account, the bank and its location. At least once a year, have the bank interest entered in each passbook you own. If you move, notify the bank of your new address.

Another little publicized fact is that savings accounts dormant for a number of years may cease earning interest. In addition, a bank may, under its rules, pay no interest on balances below a set amount, and this amount can change without a depositor's knowledge.

## U.S. Savings Bonds

United States Savings Bonds play an important role in the financial security programs of millions of American families; more than $50 billion worth of these securities are currently outstanding. The popularity of Savings Bonds reached a ten-year peak in 1966; sales of Series E Bonds alone were the highest since the end of World War II.

In addition to patriotism, people have been attracted to investing in Savings Bonds for one or more of these reasons:

1. Savings Bonds are considered to be a riskless investment because they are backed by the credit of the U.S. government.

2. They are liquid reserve, quickly and easily translated into dollars and cents when needed. They always can be redeemed at a stated value on demand after two months from the issue date.

3. Unlike other types of investments, they are not subject to market fluctuations; they are never redeemed for less than the amount invested.

4. Interest on Savings Bonds is not subject to state or local income or personal property taxes.

5. The federal income tax on Series E Bond interest can be deferred, and the annual increases in value need not be reported on the federal tax return until the bond is cashed.

6. If Savings Bonds are lost, stolen or destroyed, they can be replaced without cost.

7. Savings Bonds are easy and convenient to buy. They are sold at neighborhood banks, and many corporations have established payroll savings plans.

On the other hand, there are certain disadvantages to Savings Bonds as a form of investment:

1. Although the U.S. Treasury has raised the interest rate for Savings Bonds several times in the past, and again in 1969, bond rates have always lagged behind savings bank rates. When the Savings Bond rate in June 1969 was increased to 5 percent, many banks and savings associations were offering 5 to $5\frac{1}{2}$ percent interest.

2. Although people are allowed to report Series E Bond interest annually on their federal income tax returns, it is more usual for them to defer the reporting of interest. As a result, when funds are needed and the bonds cashed, all the accumulated and current interest becomes taxable in one year. If this occurs in a high-income year, the resulting tax may prove to be onerous.

3. Savings Bonds cannot be used as collateral and cannot be pledged. If the money is needed, the bonds must be cashed and an immediate tax incurred on both the current and any accumulated interest on which tax has been deferred.

4. Compared with other investments, like securities or real estate, Savings Bonds offer neither growth potential nor capital gain possibility.

5. Because of inflation, bonds tend to shrink in value. The dollars returned at maturity are worth much less than the dollars invested.

U.S. Bonds at present pay an interest rate of 5 percent if they are held to maturity. The Series E Bond matures in five years, ten months, and the Series H in ten years. The Series E, which is sold in various denominations with maturity values from $25 to $10,000, accrues interest payable when the bond is cashed. The Series H is sold in denominations of $500, $1000, $5000 and $10,000; interest is mailed to bondholders every six months.

Once you have decided to put your money to work in a bank keep in mind the following points: (1) Find out about the different kinds of banks in your area—commercial, savings or savings and loan. (2) Determine which one is the most convenient, and which one offers the best services for your needs. (3) Learn about interest rates, and when and how often interest on your account is compounded. (4) If you need more self-discipline when saving, find out about automatic deductions and payroll savings. (5) Find out what U.S. Savings Bonds can offer you in the way of a savings plan.

As soon as you are ready—and the sooner, the better—decide on a bank, open your account and watch your savings grow.


CHAPTER 56

**The ABCs
of Stocks and Bonds**

*Before you step into the exciting, uncertain world of investment, it's wise to know the basic facts about the securities market*

At least 1 million people will become first-time stockholders in 1970, joining the 27 million of us who already hold shares in publicly owned companies and mutual funds. By 1980, the authoritative estimate is, there will be at least 35 million stockholders in the United States alone.

If you are not already a member of this vast army of investors, there are a number of reasons you may want to consider joining it. You may be looking for a way to increase your income and help finance your children's college education. You may want to build a comfortable nest egg for your retirement years. Or you may be itching to try your hand at the excitement, uncertainty and challenge of the market.

But whatever your reasons, don't plunge into the world of high finance without learning a few ground rules. Investing in securities is never a "sure thing." Even the most experienced analysts cannot be absolutely certain about the future of a particular stock. Prices go up or down for any number of reasons, some logical, others incomprehensible. Some companies continue to grow and prosper, while others fall by the wayside. A few promising industries flourish, while others never get off the ground.

Given the amount of risk involved, it pays to be cautious. Successful investment is essentially a matter of minimizing your losses and maximizing your gains. It is also highly individualistic. What's best for you and your family may be quite different from what's best for your neighbor or your boss. There are basically four steps to success on the stock market:

1. Determine your personal investment objectives.
2. Decide the best way to meet your goals.
3. Choose a good broker to advise you and manage your portfolio.
4. Keep informed.

Before you make your first investment, be sure that you can afford to take a loss if your stocks decline in value, that you have set aside enough funds for regular living expenses and unexpected emergencies. Invest only excess capital in stocks and bonds. According to the New York Stock Exchange, some people should never buy stocks, no matter how much money they have: "The person who can be seriously upset by a slight decline in prices—or who goes off on a shopping spree at the first sign of a price rise—is better off staying out of the stock market."

What do you want from your investments? Is your aim a steady income in dividends every three months? Are you looking for a handsome profit within a year or two, or do you need maximum safety for your investment? No single stock or bond will satisfy all three requirements. If your aim is a quick profit, you'll choose a more risky stock than if your goal is maximum safety. You won't buy the same stock for highest income as for a steady income.

For instance, if you're an elderly widow who must live on the returns from your investments, your chief goals will be stable income and preservation of principal. You'll therefore buy good "income securities"—bonds with high-interest returns and high-quality stocks that will give you a relatively substantial dividend return each year. Stocks with long-term growth potential and speculative stocks are not for you.

But if you're a young man earning more than enough to meet your family's current expenses and with funds set aside to cope with financial emergencies, your objective will be capital gains. You'll buy stocks that promise to grow in price along with the growth of the economy over the years. You may take greater-than-average risks in the hope of getting higher-than-average profits. While you may lose on a stock in which you speculate, you can afford the risks at your age; you have time to recoup.

Successful investing also calls for a basic understanding of investment terminology. Do you, for example, know the difference between preferred and common stock? Convertible and nonconvertible bonds? Certain types of securities will be better for you than others, so learn what each means and how each one works.

When you buy the stock of a corporation, you are investing money in the venture and, in a sense, you become part owner of it. In return for your investment, the corporation generally pays you dividends out of its earnings and profits. If the corporation is very successful, you may profit by an increase in the value of your stock and receive dividends at the same time. (Any increase in the value of your shares is not taxable until you sell them.) On the other hand, if the corporation does poorly, you may receive little or no dividends and your shares of stock will decline in value.

## Commons vs. Preferred Stock

There are two classes of stock, common and preferred. Holders of common stock participate in the company's profits and most of its losses. Preferred stock is the senior stock of a corporation and its dividend is usually set at a fixed amount. The claim of preferred-stock holders on company earnings is second only to that of the company bondholders and takes precedence over that of common-stock holders. High-grade preferred stock provides a steadier dividend income than does common stock, but the value of common stock fluctuates more widely, offering greater chances for appreciation. If the company has a good year, the dividend of the common stock may be higher than that of the preferred, and many preferred stocks can be called in by the company at prices set when they were issued.

Some preferred stocks and certain bonds are convertible; that is, they can be converted into common stock of the issuing company at the discretion of the investor. Generally, the convertible privilege is included in a provision which appears in print on the bond or preferred stock itself.

## INVESTORS' MOST COMMON MISTAKES

One of the most common mistakes made by inexperienced investors is disregarding the fundamental investing rules and buying blindly on tips or rumors. Usually, these situations involve extreme risk, and when the buyer is badly hurt, he is likely to become completely disillusioned about stock investment.

Here are other misconceptions and errors of new investors:

• *Expecting too much, too soon.* Many inexperienced investors become fidgety when their stocks rise only a little or decline soon after they buy. They refuse to allow time for their stocks to perform as expected. Millions who have taken short-term losses would have shown handsome profits if they had had more confidence in their own judgment, or that of their brokers, and been more willing to give their stocks a chance to move.

• *"Hit or miss" investing.* Most new investors overlook the importance of family investment planning. What they *should* do (and don't) is develop a diversified financial program which allocates funds to major types of investments—savings in cash or its equivalent, life insurance, real estate (a home), as well as stocks and bonds.

There is no formula under which you can automatically put a proper percentage in each type of investment. Your individual allocation must depend on your income bracket, your age, your family responsibilities—and, of course, your considered judgment about the economic outlook. The key point, though, is to have an invest-

Conversion privileges and terms vary. The convertible preferred stock or bond of one company might be convertible into one share of its common stock, while that of another company might be convertible into three shares of its common stock. Also, the conversion privilege might continue indefinitely or be limited to a period of time ending on a specific date.

You might want to invest in convertible securities for capital gains and as a hedge against a market decline. Convertible securities (bonds or preferred stock) have a senior position in the company's capitalization before common-stock holders are paid off. So if the stock market drops they are less vulnerable to the decline. Thus danger of a large capital loss is minimized. And since the convertible can be converted into the common stock, its value moves up as the value of the common rises.

〓〓〓〓〓〓

ment plan. "Hit or miss" is a widespread error.

• *Deceiving yourself and your broker.* Many investors give lip service to what they believe are the "right" objectives—long-term gains or dividends—when, in reality, they are interested only in short-term profits. This deception puts both the investor and his broker at a serious disadvantage in selecting suitable stocks and in timing transactions.

Many investors also often act against their own investment convictions. For instance, the stockholder who knows his goal is long-term capital gain may be too anxious to realize a quick profit and may sell out far too early. Or he may be reluctant to sell even in the face of convincing evidence that he should and, despite his broker's advice, may hold on far too long.

• *Buying "the stock market," not individual stocks.* While stocks generally will follow the same major trend, a costly common error of the amateur is to justify buying and holding an inexpensive, little-known issue simply because the overall economy is growing or the stock averages are climbing. In the greatest bull markets, though, many stocks slide, and in today's viciously selective market, what you own is particularly important in determining growth.

• *Ignoring the broker.* Too many shareholders feel that because their money is involved, they have to know all the answers. They would consider a person trying to be his own physician or lawyer a fool, but it is just as foolish to shrug off a broker's experience and skill when reaching vital investment decisions.

〓〓〓〓〓〓

In fact, when the value of the common and preferred stock is equal, the preferred's capital gain potential is enhanced over that of the common stock. A convertible preferred that can be exchanged for three shares of the common stock, for example, will jump three points on every one-point rise in the common stock once the parity point, or point of equalization, is reached.

A convertible generally will command a price over and above its intrinsic worth. You must pay something for the conversion privilege. Also, dividends are paid at a set rate, which may be lower than that offered by the underlying common stock.

## Pros and Cons of Bonds

When you buy a bond, you are lending money to the issuer of the bonds. You become a creditor, not an owner. The borrower pledges to pay you a specified amount of interest on specified dates and to repay the principal on the date of maturity stated on the bond.

Some bonds mature in a few months or years. These are short-term issues. Long-term issues mature after many years. Bonds often have two rates of interest: a stated rate and an effective rate. The stated rate is printed on the bond; the effective rate is the actual amount you receive and depends upon the price you paid for the bond. If the stated interest is 4 percent and you pay the full (or par) value of the bond, you will receive 4 percent interest on your investment. On the other hand, if you purchase the bond below par, it will return more than 4 percent of your investment because interest is figured on the par value of the bond.

The tax status of the bond is another important feature. Income from corporate bonds is taxable. But income from state and municipal government bonds is tax exempt. Persons in the higher income tax brackets naturally prefer the tax-exempt income. Depending on your tax bracket, the return from a tax-exempt bond can be as high as, or higher than, the net return, after taxes, from other investments.

Most bonds are publicly rated by well-known financial and advisory services, such as Standard and Poor's or Moody's. (Standard and Poor's ratings are AAA, AA, A, BBB, BB, and so down to D; Moody's ratings are Aaa, Aa, A, Baa, Ba, B, and so on to C.) You may get these ratings at your bank or library. Consider all the facts and get any necessary advice before investing in bonds. They are a safer investment than stocks, but the return may be less and they do not generally increase in value. Marketability or liquidity (the ease with which you can convert your bonds into cash) is also important. If your bonds are bought and sold frequently, it is likely that you can get a fair price if you should have to sell in a hurry.

What bonds should you buy? If your objective is a high degree of liquidity—meaning you may need your cash on short notice—you should invest in top-grade, short-term bonds. If your objective is a steady income plus relative price stability, your best bet is to invest in high-to-medium-grade bonds with longer maturities.

Bonds with the highest yield may not be the safest investment. Higher yield generally means greater risk. For example, government bonds find willing buyers even though they carry relatively low interest rates. Bonds of new or unstable corporations are more speculative, and the corporations must pay a high return to attract investors. Long-term bonds generally have higher yields than short-term bonds for two reasons: (1) A distant maturity date makes it difficult to predict the financial strength of the borrower at the time the bonds will fall due. This uncertainty makes it necessary to offer some bonds at a higher yield. (2) Informed investors may expect interest rates to rise and thus may be unwilling to buy long-term bonds with a low yield. To attract investors, issuers of long-term bonds must therefore pay higher rates.

## "Getting into the Market"—The Right Way

Let's assume you have decided to make your first venture into the stock market. You have a few hundred dollars and you want to buy some shares of stock. Where do you begin? The first step is to get in touch with a reliable broker and ask his advice on the best type of investment program for you. Here are four key rules:

1. Deal preferably with a firm that is a member of the New York Stock Exchange. Of course, there are nonmember firms which also rank at the top—but you're a beginner, you may be taking a chance. A NYSE member firm must meet the highest standards established to date: fulfill minimum capital requirements and undergo both an annual surprise audit by an independent CPA (certified public ac-

▭▭▭▭▭▭

## WORDS YOU
## SHOULD KNOW

**Annual report.** The formal financial statement issued each year by a corporation to its shareholders. The annual report shows assets, liabilities, earnings—how the company stood at the close of the business year and how profitable it was during the year.

**Averages.** Various ways of measuring the trend of securities prices, the most popular of which is the Dow-Jones average of 30 industrial stocks listed on the New York Stock Exchange.

**Bear market.** A declining market.

**Big board.** A popular term for the New York Stock Exchange.

**Blue chip.** Common stock in a company known nationally for the quality and wide acceptance of its products or services and for its ability to make money and pay dividends. Usually such stocks are relatively high priced and offer relatively low yields.

**Bond.** Basically an IOU, or promissory note, of a corporation, usually issued in multiples of $1000, although $100 and $50 denominations are not uncommon. A bond is evidence of a debt on which the issuing company usually promises to pay the bondholders a specified amount of interest for a specified length of time and to repay the loan on the expiration date. The bondholder is a creditor of the corpora-tion, not a part owner as is the shareholder.

**Broker.** An agent, often a member of a stock exchange firm, who handles the public's orders to buy and sell securities.

**Bull market.** An advancing market.

**Capital gain or capital loss.** Profit or loss from the sale of a security or other capital asset.

**Certificate.** The actual piece of paper which is evidence of ownership of stock in a corporation.

**Commission.** The broker's fee for purchasing or selling securities for a client. Fees average 1 percent for stocks and $\frac{1}{4}$ of 1 percent for bonds.

**Common stock.** Securities which represent an ownership interest in a corporation.

**Convertible.** A bond, debenture or preferred share which may be exchanged by the owner for common stock or another security, usually of the same company, in accordance with the terms of the issue. Non-convertible securities do not have this feature.

**Dividend.** The payment designated by a corporation's board of directors to be distributed among the shares that are outstanding.

**Earnings report.** A statement issued by a company showing its earnings or losses over a given period.

**Floor.** The huge trading area of the stock exchanges where stocks and bonds are bought and sold.

**Growth stock.** Stock of a company whose earnings are expected to

▭▭▭▭▭▭

▭ ▭ ▭ ▭ ▭ ▭

increase at a relatively rapid rate.

**Mutual fund.** A company which uses its capital to invest in other companies. There are two main types: the closed-end and the open-end. (See Chapter 57, "Mutual Funds and Your Family," page 542.)

**Odd lot.** An amount of stock less than the established 100-share unit of trading.

**Offer.** The price at which a person is ready to sell a security. Opposed to "bid," the price at which one is ready to buy.

**Option.** A right to buy or sell securities or properties at a specified price within a specified time.

**Over-the-counter.** A market for securities made up of securities dealers who may or may not be members of a securities exchange. Over-the-counter is mainly a market over the telephone rather than on the floor of an exchange. Thousands of companies have insufficient shares outstanding, stockholders or earnings to qualify for listing on a stock exchange. Securities of these companies are traded in the over-the-counter market. Most U.S. government bonds and municipal bonds are traded over-the-counter.

**Portfolio.** The total holdings of securities by an individual or institution.

**Preferred stock.** A class of stock with a claim on the company's earnings before payment may be made on the common stock, and usually entitled to priority over common stock in the distribution of assets if the company liquidates.

**Price-earnings ratio.** The current market price of a share of stock divided by earnings per share for a 12-month period. For example, a stock selling at $100 per share and earning $5 a share is said to be selling at price-earnings ratio of 20 to 1.

**Prospectus.** A circular which describes securities being offered for sale to the public. Required by the Securities Act of 1933.

**Quotation.** The highest bid to buy and the lowest offer to sell a security in a given market at a given time. If you ask your broker for a "quote" on a stock, he may come back with something like "$45\frac{1}{4}$ to $45\frac{1}{2}$." This means that $45.25 is the highest price any buyer wanted to pay at the time the quote was given on the floor of the exchange and that $45.50 was the lowest price any seller would take at that time.

**Split.** The division of the outstanding shares of a corporation into a larger number. A 3-for-1 split by a company means that each holder of 100 shares will have 300 shares, although his proportionate holding in the company will remain the same.

**Ticker.** An instrument which transmits to subscribers throughout the United States prices and volume of security transactions, usually within minutes after each trade on the floor of the New York and American stock exchanges.

▭ ▭ ▭ ▭ ▭ ▭

533

countant) firm and spot financial checks by the Exchange. Its employes must complete a minimum training period of six months, pass an Exchange exam and work at their jobs full time. These requirements give you protection, and it's only common sense to accept it.

2. Shop around, as you would shop for any service as important as this. Call on at least three or four firms in your area, and find out if they will open an account for a person with your available funds.

3. Ask each firm for its investment recommendations for a person in your financial position and for its research reports on the companies suggested. (The person to whom you'll speak will be variously called a registered representative, customer's man or account executive—but you'll call him your broker.)

4. On the basis of your comparisons of the firms and their advice to you, select your broker and then give him all the pertinent facts about your financial circumstances and goals. The more he knows about your situation, the better he can advise you.

We often create for ourselves one of the toughest problems involved in choosing and using a broker to help us manage our stock investments wisely. We expect our broker to be right all the time, and when he isn't we become disenchanted and are tempted to follow the tips of those who claim to be making a fortune. This way leads to disaster—every day a dismally large percentage of Americans are taking this course. Even the most astute professional will not be right all of the time. In fact, in some periods, his advice will range from indifferent to downright bad.

Your broker should be right enough of the time to help guide you toward your investment objectives and to help you enlarge your overall nest egg. You should be able to trust his experience, research and judgment. But that's all. It's your money, your investment program and, basically, your responsibility.

Don't rely entirely on your broker's judgment about which companies are good investments and which are not. Ask him for any research reports his firm has made on the companies he recommends. Answer for yourself the key questions about the companies: What are their earnings prospects? How good is their management (a vital factor)? What are the potential markets for their products and services?

## How to Choose Good Stocks

You wouldn't dream of buying a house simply on the basis of how it looks from the outside. You'd examine the inside thoroughly, check on the quality of the construction, the reputation of the builder and so forth. The same thoroughness must be applied to buying stocks; for, next to buying a house, investing in the stock market may be the most important financial decision you make.

You also probably wouldn't dream of trying to trade in and out of real estate and speculating against the real professionals in this field. Again, the same rule must be applied to stocks. In the long run, as a long-term investor you will almost surely make out better than the in-and-out trader.

One of the best ways to select a stock is on the basis of your own familiarity with, and respect for, the company's products or services. If you are a housewife and find a company's products highly satisfactory, this may be a clue to an excellent investment. Or if you're a businessman and find a company's services particularly useful, this might be an indication.

Get the facts and study the company with the help of a qualified broker, and then make your decision. This is the process which distinguishes investing in stocks from gambling.

Here are some additional suggestions for choosing a stock:

1. For investment, choose sound, essential industries. Food, transportation and utilities are basic industries and can more readily hold their values during economic declines than nonessential industries that provide services and luxuries. Of course, essential industries can change. What is an essential today may not be one a year from now. For example, the production of steam locomotives was once an essential industry. Today, it doesn't exist.

2. Invest in companies that are recognized leaders in their industries. True, some analysts do not agree with this advice and hold that the only substantial profits are made in new, unknown companies. But you are investing, not trying to "get rich quick." Some smaller companies may turn out to be more profitable than well-known firms, but your chance of choosing such a company is often a matter of luck. The advantages in selecting the recognized companies are that they have proved their ability, their management

## HOW TO READ
## AN ANNUAL REPORT

If the price-earnings ratio of the company in which you own stock is seven to one, what does this suggest about its prospects—and your prospects—for future profits? What key clues to the financial health of a company can you get from its annual report? Here is a listing of the major items found in today's typical annual report—and brief guidelines on how to interpret them:

1. The *president's letter to stockholders* is the first place to look for a summary of your company's financial highlights for last year, plus the reasons why profits were up or down. This letter or the subsequent text also should give you the company's own assessment of its long-term outlook, with supporting facts.

2. The *income statement* or *earnings report* is a summary of last year's sales volume, other income, costs, profits or losses with comparative figures for the prior year. The initial figure is the company's net income or net profit; this figure should be compared with profits over the previous five or ten years (usually summarized separately).

3. The *net profit ratio* is a prime indicator of your company's efficiency, and you can figure it by dividing total net profit by total net sales. This ratio today may range from 1 percent to 30 percent or more, so you must compare last year's record against the record for previous years and against the

performance of other companies in its industry.

4. The *price-earnings ratio* is a measure of how the overall investment community views your company. The ratio won't appear in an annual report, but you can calculate it by dividing the current market price of a share of your stock by the company's last year's per-share earnings noted in the earnings report.

5. The *retained earnings statement* tells you what share of company profits are being returned to you as dividends and what share is being held back. If the proportion going to you in dividends declines sharply, look for an explanation of how the extra funds are being reinvested.

6. The *ratio of current assests to current liabilities* tells you how much of a financial cushion your company would have left if it paid off all current debts. As a rough rule of thumb, many industrial corporations maintain twice as large a volume of current assets as the volume of current liabilities.

7. The *debt-to-equity ratio*, or *leverage factor*, is a measure of the amount of long-term debt your company is carrying in relation to stockholders' investment. This ratio is figured by adding total stockholders' equity. Normally, this ratio is above 50 percent for manufacturing companies.

8. *Footnotes* often reveal important information. A footnote might tell you, for instance, that an unusually high profit stemmed from a "one-shot" (nonrecurring) financial windfall.

is experienced, they will have resources for research and they can finance their needs more easily than smaller companies.

3. Invest in several different companies, each in a different industry. Over a period of time you will probably make a bad investment. If you invest in only one company, this error may be costly; if you have, say, six different stocks, your good judgment on four of them may more than offset a bad decision on one or two. Of course, such hedging can also be achieved by investment in mutual funds (for information on mutual funds, see Chapter 57, page 542).

4. Invest about the same amount in the shares of each company you select. Don't make a favorite of any one stock. There are many sound industries.

5. Invest in shares listed on one of the two major securities exchanges, the New York Stock Exchange or the American Stock Exchange. Before its stock may be listed on either of these exchanges, a company must file information with both the private financial authorities and the federal government. Specific standards must be met; regular reports must be published; transactions are under the constant surveillance of the exchanges, the federal government and expert investors and bankers. Furthermore, a listing on the exchanges makes it easier to buy or sell stock. Listing, of course, is no guarantee of merit, but it is a fairly substantial guarantee that the company will operate according to the established current business standards.

6. Invest in shares that can show an unbroken earnings record or a dividend record or both for the last ten years. Such a record indicates that an enterprise is sound.

7. Buy shares that over the past ten years have earned at least $5 for every $4 paid out in dividends. A company should not pay out all it earns, but should build up a reserve to handle emergencies or to ensure its ability to take advantage of future opportunities. A company that earns considerably more than its dividend is preferred to one that just about earns it.

8. During a period of a year or two, sell at least one stock, choosing the weakest on your list without considering its original cost. Invest the proceeds in a more profitable security.

9. When you place an order with your broker to buy or sell, don't set a fixed price; buy or sell "at the market." Buying or selling

at the market means your order will be filled at about the price of the next transaction in your stock on the exchange. This is a better approach than giving your broker a fixed price—even an expert cannot fix the value of a stock to within fractions of a point. Since you are investing for the long term, it will be completely unimportant over that period whether you paid $20 or $21 for a specific share of stock.

10. Don't buy on margin (a loan from your broker to pay a portion of the cost of a security). Stocks can decline and you can lose your investment if it is financed by margin loans. Buying stock on margin is primarily for the in-and-out trader who is shooting for short-term profits.

An important part of investing in securities is keeping abreast of developments in the companies in which you have invested and learning about other companies with potential investment opportunities. It is equally essential to review your investments from time to time, to weed out any unsatisfactory choices and to determine whether your investment objectives have changed.

Sources of investment and financial information include the business sections of newspapers and periodicals devoted to financial news. The companies themselves issue prospectuses and annual reports on their earnings, losses, dividends and other matters of interest to stockholders.

If you are not familiar with the form and contents of a standard annual report, see "How to Read an Annual Report" on page 536. If the annual report you receive from a company in which you own stock does not contain at least the basic items of information listed there, or the facts from which to calculate them yourself, ask your broker for further details. He can also provide you with the industrywide record. This is the minimum you should know about the company and the industry in which you are investing your savings.

Newspaper stock tables can seem formidable to the beginning investor, but they are important in keeping abreast of the changes in the market. "Reading a Stock Table" on pages 540–541 will give you the basic information you need to decipher the columns of figures you will find daily in the financial section.

Many brokerage firms maintain large research departments that prepare extensive reports on various companies. You might even want to enroll in a basic course on investment. Such courses are offered in major U.S. cities by member firms of the New York Stock Exchange, by other individual brokerage houses and by adult-education institutions. Educational pamphlets on the stock market can be obtained at no charge from both the American Stock Exchange and the New York Stock Exchange.

## The Unimportance of Timing

What is the best time to buy or sell a stock? This is easy to say in retrospect but impossible to predict for the future. A review of the stock market's history indicates that there is a cyclical character to prices. The low and high markets of the past stand out clearly on charts already drawn—charts showing where the market has been, not necessarily where it is going. True, the expert studies the current market to determine whether it is advisable to buy or sell at current market prices and to predict the future moves of a particular stock. But for the average investor, market analysts suggest, "Give up any idea of 'beating the market,'" and develop a program of paying current securities prices with current earnings.

The advice is based on the assumption that securities will tend, in market value as well as yield, to keep step with current living costs. Since the long-term trend of prices has been upward, it follows that a safe rule of thumb would be to buy quality securities on a regular basis and to trust that the long-term uptrend will continue in the next 20 to 40 years, just as it has over the last 150 years. Let the day-to-day, month-to-month and perhaps even the year-to-year price swings average themselves out.

The successful investor is not the slick gambler who makes a quick killing on the market. Long-term profits are more than a matter of luck. They call for forethought, wise judgment and expert advice. Before you put your money into securities, analyze your investment objectives, study the alternatives, consult a good broker and select stocks and bonds that will best fulfill your objectives. Keep well informed; follow the movement of your securities; read prospectuses, annual reports and other financial news. In the field of investment, knowledge and sound judgment—not luck—pay the best dividends.

□□□□□□

## READING
## A STOCK TABLE

A basic tool for the investor is the daily record of transactions on the New York Stock Exchange. There are numerous securities tables, ranging from transactions on other exchanges to quotations in the over-the-counter market and prices from foreign markets, but the NYSE table is commonly regarded as the most important for the average investor.

Some people, notably newcomers to the financial scene, have trouble reading the table. With a little practice, however, you can read the NYSE table as readily as the news columns of your newspaper despite its confusing appearance.

Here is the information presented in each line of the table: the stock's high and low for the year, name of the company, common or preferred stock, dividend, volume of transactions, the opening and the high, low and closing prices for the day and the net change from the closing price of the preceding day.

Each column is identified at the top of the table as shown below, using the well-known "XYZ" corporation as an illustration. (Not all newspapers follow the same style of presenting the table.)

| High | Low | Stocks | Div. |
|---|---|---|---|
| 60 | 50 | XYZ | 1.50 |

| Sales in 100s | Open | High | Low | Close | Net Chg. |
|---|---|---|---|---|---|
| 70 | $54\frac{1}{8}$ | $55\frac{1}{2}$ | 54 | $55\frac{1}{4}$ | $+1\frac{1}{4}$ |

Under "High" we learn that XYZ's top price for the current year was $60 a share and the low $50. But there's a qualification to that statement. Up to around mid-March of any year, the high-low is based on the price range of the current year and of the preceding year.

Under "Stocks" we discover that XYZ is a common stock. If it weren't, XYZ would be followed by *pf* to indicate a preferred stock. Most of the names are abbreviated and, admittedly, some of the abbreviations are somewhat cryptic. We would have considerable sympathy with the novice investor trying to figure out the meaning of Coop T&R (Cooper Tire & Rubber Company) or Miss Riv (Mississippi River Fuel Corporation) or other abbreviated corporate names.

Then we come to "Div.," a figure which follows immediately after the name of the issue. The 1.50 after XYZ indicates that XYZ has had a regular dividend rate and has been paying $1.50 a share annually. It should not be assumed, however, that XYZ will not raise, lower or omit its dividend in the future—the $1.50 refers only to the company's past performance in paying dividends.

A number of companies, for their own reasons, pay dividends somewhat erratically. If there were an *e* after 1.50, it would mean that $1.50 is the total amount of dividends declared or paid thus far in the current year. The *e* is one of the most frequent added notes, but you may find any one of an

□□□□□□

assortment of letters following the dividend figures.

If 1.50 were followed by *a*, it would mean that XYZ also had paid or declared one or more extras not included in the 1.50. Or it might be followed by *b*, which would mean that the company paid a stock dividend in addition to its annual dividend rate of $1.50 a share.

Going down the alphabet considerably further, you may run across a *p* after a dividend figure; we hope you don't if it is stock in which you have an interest. The *p* means that $1.50 has been paid thus far in the year, but that at the last dividend meeting of the directors the dividend was omitted or deferred, or no action about payment was taken.

A quite infrequent letter in the notations is *y*, which means that the amount is a liquidating dividend. In other words, the company is going out of business and this is what they have paid their shareowners as a settlement on the way out.

A very frequent notation after the dividend is *xd*. This means, in effect, that in the recent past XYZ has declared a dividend, but it also means— more importantly—that the person buying XYZ on that particular day will not receive the dividend. The abbreviation *xd* stands for "ex-dividend" and means that the dividend will be paid to the previous owner of the stock and not the new investor. This fact, of course, is reflected in the day's price of the stock.

Our next column is "Sales." As the heading indicates, "70" shows that 7000 shares of XYZ were traded on that particular day. The figure also tells you that the unit of trading in XYZ is 100 shares—otherwise it would have a *z* in front of it. The letter *z* means—and footnotes to the table tell you this—that the figure represents total sales. Some stocks are traded in 10-share units, so if there were a *z* in front of 70 it would mean that only 70 shares were bought and sold on that particular day.

So much for abbreviations. In the column after "Sales" we find that XYZ opened at $54\frac{1}{8}$. Here again a little translation is necessary, Actually, XYZ opened at $54.12\frac{1}{2}$ a share. Stock prices on the floor of the exchanges are established in $\frac{1}{8}$s and they are published that way. Now, during the day XYZ sold up to $55\frac{1}{2}$, or $55.50. Low for the day was 54, or $54 a share. The issue closed at $55\frac{1}{4}$, or $55.25 a share.

Net change was $+1\frac{1}{4}$, or $1.25 a share higher than the preceding close. This does not necessarily mean the preceding day but could be days earlier, the last day the stock was traded —that's the basis for the figure in the net change column.

The stock table may also be helpful in figuring out indicated yield or return on investment. This is figured very simply by dividing the dividend by the present price. In the case of XYZ, divide $1.50 by $55.25. Your yield is 2.7 percent.

## CHAPTER 57

# Mutual Funds and Your Family

*An objective look at these popular funds—what they are, how they operate, how they could affect your financial future*

In the past decade the number of mutual funds—also called investment trusts—has mushroomed. Ten years ago there were only 450 of these mutual funds. Today there are nearly 1000. Their total assets have grown from $17 billion to $70 billion.

What's behind this tremendous growth? For one thing, in some years mutual funds have performed better than the stock market as a whole. Perhaps equally significant, the funds offer advantages to you if you are a family with relatively small amounts to invest and little time or knowledge to manage investments on your own. When you invest in a mutual fund your money is pooled with the money of other investors and used to buy a broad spectrum of securities. No matter how little you invest, you have a share in the performance of 100 or more companies rather than just 1 or 2. What's more, your investments receive full-time professional supervision.

No two mutual funds are the same. They vary considerably in size, type of fund and caliber of management and in investment objectives. Their assets vary from a few million dollars to well over $2 billion.

Basically, there are two different types of mutual funds, closed-end and open-end: A *closed-end* company is simply a corporation that invests in the securities of other companies. You buy shares in the mutual fund company as you would buy shares of U.S. Steel or General Motors. An *open-end* company is so named because its capitalization is open: It can create and sell new shares in itself whenever there is a market for them; then buy back and retire the shares whenever a shareholder wants to cash them in. In other words, when you put your funds in the company, you receive newly created shares which represent your proportionate share of the entire fund. Open-end mutual funds today control nearly $40 billion of investments for both small and large individual investors, pension funds, corporate groups and institutions.

The shares of the most active closed-end investment companies are traded on the stock exchanges. Others are traded "over the counter." In either case, you will pay a commission computed in exactly the same way that your commission would be figured in buying shares of any industrial corporation. These range from 6 percent of the total amount of money involved down to around 1 percent on larger purchases. Closed-end funds often sell at either a premium or a discount—that is, either at a higher or a lower price than the net asset value per share. If, for instance, the asset value per share (the fund's total assets divided by the number of shares outstanding) is $15 and the stock is selling at a premium, you may have to pay $18 to buy that $15 share. If, on the other hand, the stock is selling at a discount, you may be able to buy the $15 share for only $12.

You buy most open-end mutual funds through brokerage offices or through selling organizations set up to handle one or more funds. Commission costs will vary, from as high as 8.5 to 9 percent of the total cost of the shares for small investments to half that rate or even less for sums running into the tens of thousands of dollars. Each fund has its own schedule of fees.

You can tell at a glance what the maximum fee is by checking the price of the fund in the special list of mutual fund quotations carried by many newspapers and financial publications. The fund will be listed thus:

|  | BID | ASKED |
|---|---|---|
| XYZ Fund | $11.34 | $12.26 |

The fund's asset value stood at $11.34 per share on this day. The asked price is the price you would pay per share. The 92-cent difference represents the commission cost per share, which in this case comes to 8.1 percent. Another fund might be listed as: $13.12 bid, $14 asked—the 88-cent difference here representing a commission of about 6.7 percent.

The so-called front load funds use 50 percent of the first 13 monthly payments to prepay salesmen's commissions. The percentage of commission deducted from each payment then falls to a lower figure for the remainder of the plan. As a result, only half of the early payments goes into the fund for investment. Anyone who signs up for a ten-year plan and drops out before the plan is completed—especially if he withdraws within the first few years—actually has a small investment in the fund itself, since so much has gone for commissions; he is heavily penalized for dropping out.

Mutual fund sales charges have been criticized as being excessive by the Securities Exchange Commission. Legislation has been proposed in Congress to reduce these charges.

There are over 50 funds that charge no sales commission, because they have no salesmen or sales organization. Most of these "no-load" funds grew out of investment advisory services, which originally managed the investment of large sums for individuals but were prevailed upon by smaller investors to open their services to them as well. If you want to buy into a no-load fund, you must take the initiative. While these funds also do some modest, low-pressure advertising, any inquiry on your part will not be followed up by a salesman. You can always identify a no-load (no commission) fund merely by running your finger down the mutual funds list in any financial publication: The "bid" and "asked" price will be identical.

## A Fund to Meet Your Needs

There are mutual funds for every type of investment objective. Some aim for high current yield; some seek capital growth; some strive for a combination of both. You'll want to choose a fund that has investment goals similar to yours. Here are the main categories:

*Growth funds.* Their objective is to achieve a growth in the value of shares, which eventually leads to growth in income. Growth fund assets are usually invested in common stocks up to about 90 percent. Generally, growth funds appeal to younger persons.

*Balanced funds.* These funds invest in common stock, bonds and preferred stock. The idea is that these three kinds of investment provide defensive strength in a declining market. Investments are divided approximately into common stocks, 60 percent; bonds and preferred stocks together, 40 percent. In a rising market, balanced funds generally do not show the increase of a growth fund in value.

*Income funds.* Investments here are primarily high-yield securities. There are differences even within this category, as some income funds will take slight risks in order to give shareholders a higher yield.

⊏⊐⊏⊐⊏⊐⊏⊐⊏⊐⊏⊐

## INSURANCE ON YOUR
## FUND INVESTMENTS

Many funds provide life insurance with their monthly contractual plans at low rates. Don't confuse this protection with lifetime insurance. It's in the form of declining-balance term insurance and assures only the completion of your investment program should you die before the entire plan is paid up. It might not adequately provide for your family in the event of your death. So don't let a salesman talk you into canceling your life insurance policy and substituting this form of mutual fund coverage. In a ten-year, $50-a-month program, the protection in mutual fund insurance is $5950 during the first month, but only $50 in the last month of the tenth year, and after that, zero.

⊏⊐⊏⊐⊏⊐⊏⊐⊏⊐⊏⊐

Investments are in preferred stocks, bonds and common stocks with a high yield in dividends and interest.

In addition to the three basic types of mutual funds, there are funds which attempt to combine two or more of these basic objectives and others which may be described as specialty funds.

*Bond funds.* Securities purchased in this kind of fund generally provide a fixed income and do not increase substantially in value.

*Industry funds.* Investments are concentrated in a single industry, including subsidiaries. On occasion, sponsors of industry funds offer funds from several industries. You may switch from one industry fund to another in the sponsor's portfolio for a small sales charge.

*Real estate investment funds.* These are designed to encourage small investors to participate in diversified real estate ventures. As an investor in a real estate fund, you may enjoy a slight tax advantage, for you will have nontaxable distributions from depreciation reserves. (For more on real estate investments see Chapter 58, "What You Can Do About Inflation," page 549.)

If you are young and want capital gains, select a growth fund—one invested in fast-growing industries like aviation, electronics, chemicals, life insurance and synthetics. If you are approaching retirement and will soon need a steady source of income, consider only funds which are aimed at providing maximum income—funds which concentrate their investments in coppers, rails, utilities and cyclical manufacturing concerns. Do not let a salesman talk you into a growth type fund with the argument that his fund has been successful in accumulating large annual capital gains, making dividend income unimportant. Capital gains are welcome, but dividend income is steadier.

Most mutual funds pay quarterly dividends each year. These will, of course, vary in amount from time to time depending on fund earnings. The fund receives many dividend and interest checks from the securities it holds, and each member receives a proportionate share of these after management fees and operating expenses are deducted. In addition, you may receive capital gains distributions resulting from profitable security sales by the fund. If you were to invest in several mutual funds with different dividend payment dates it would be possible for you to receive a dividend check each month.

Once you select the general type of fund you seek, indulge yourself in some comparative research. Periodic reports on the market performance of mutual funds, including management results, are available in various publications prepared by Arthur Wiesenberger Services Corporation.

Each year a certain number of funds outperform the competition,

---

## PROVIDING FOR RETIREMENT INCOME

Let's assume you have completed a ten-year contractual mutual fund program. You have several options:

1. You may cash in your shares.

2. You may make no further payments, but allow dividends and capital gains to be reinvested in acquiring more shares.

3. You may take your dividends and capital gains in cash.

4. You may set up a level withdrawal plan which will give you so many dollars a month to live on.

The level withdrawal plan can provide a steady source of retirement income. It works this way: Most funds in which you have $10,000 invested (a few set the level at $5000) will allow you to make a regular monthly withdrawal from the fund, measured in dollars or shares.

The widely accepted rule of thumb for this level withdrawal program— which can be helpful in financing retirement—is that $50 a month can be withdrawn from a $10,000 investment, beginning around retirement age, with little danger that the investor will run out of money in his lifetime. To make this payment, the fund will redeem enough of your shares every month to provide a payment of $50. Then, when it declares its dividends but an investor is well advised to take a look at the five- and ten-year records carved out by the respective managements. This history of achievement, while by no means a guarantee of future performance, is a factor in determining whether one common stock fund, or a certain balanced fund, seems a relatively desirable choice for the investor. The objectives of a fund and the caliber of its management are equally important factors in selecting a mutual fund. This information is included in the fund's prospectus and should be compulsory reading for the would-be investor.

You can buy a mutual fund by making a large single investment, or you can invest fixed amounts over a set period of time. You can make the periodic investments under either a contractual or a voluntary plan. Under a voluntary plan, you are not legally bound to a monthly payment. A voluntary mutual fund plan charges commission at a given rate on each monthly purchase as you make it. You do not prepay commissions as in a contractual plan, which is discussed below. The voluntary plan commission is generally a flat 8 percent on each purchase of shares and for each reinvestment of

---

and capital gains, it will repurchase shares.

A well-run income type fund will generate enough dividends and capital gains to keep your investment at least fairly level—offsetting your withdrawals with quarterly and annual reinvestments of the dividends and capital gains. Some funds, in fact, can boast that over various periods of time they have actually been able to increase the $10,000 investment, all the while paying out $50 a month to the investor. In some cases and at other times the $50 monthly withdrawal will cut into assets a bit. In any event, this plan is not a guaranteed annuity. You are drawing $50 a month from invest-

ments in securities that may fluctuate.

Instead of fixing withdrawals at a dollar figure, the withdrawals can be expressed in terms of shares. If, let us assume, your mutual fund asset value now stands at $10 a share, you might ask the fund to sell five shares a month and send the proceeds to you. If the price goes to $11, you will receive $55; if it falls to $9, you will get only $45. If you need exactly $50 a month, this type of withdrawal is not for you. But if your budget can stand some slight variation from month to month, then the share plan works out slightly better over the years since you will not have to sell more shares when the price is low and fewer when the price is up.

---

dividend income over the years. Capital gains are reinvested at no charge. Life insurance is not available with the voluntary plan. You cannot replace withdrawn funds without paying another commission.

Under a contractual plan, you agree to invest a fixed monthly amount. It can be as small as $25 a month. A fixed contractual plan allows you to dollar-average your investments over the years, taking advantage of market changes. The plan can be tied to a declining-balance term insurance. Then if you die during the investment period the insurance will pay the remaining balance under your plan.

A contractual plan requires the prepayment of a substantial part of the commissions in the first year of the plan. For example, a fund would deduct half of your first month's investment to prepay commissions. Afterwards, the commission rate would drop. Over the years, you would be paying commissions of 8.5 percent or more. As noted before, if you were to drop the plan before the commissions were averaged out, you would dissipate your investment in the commission expense. However, the contractual plan does allow you to reinvest both dividend income and capital gains over the years without paying any additional commission. (There may be a small "custodian" charge for reinvesting dividend income.) If you need funds in an emergency, the contractual plan allows you to withdraw up to 90 percent of your funds and reinvest them later without payment of commissions.

It is difficult to calculate whether a voluntary or a contractual plan is less expensive if both are completed over the same period of

## FACTS ON FUNDS

A **mutual fund** is a pool of money from many investors which is used to buy securities under the supervision of professional managers who are paid for their services. The purchaser invests in shares in this pool. An **open-end** mutual fund sells new shares in itself if a market exists, then buys these shares back from owners who desire to cash in, paying them a proportion of the total fund existing on that date. The sales commission charged when you purchase fund shares is called the **front-end load.** Some **no-load funds** charge no commission. A **growth fund** invests in securities expected to gain in value, with little emphasis on current income; an **income fund** emphasizes high cash yield. Specialized funds invest only in common stocks, in bonds, in real estate or in a single industry.

time. The contractual plan's commission charges may be offset by the reinvestment of dividends at no charge. The lower commission of a voluntary plan may be offset by the fees for reinvestment of dividend income.

In making your decision, consider your ability to make regular payments and your other resources to meet emergencies so that you can always make the fund payments. Above all, do not commit yourself to a plan unless you know the privileges and charges involved.

If chosen carefully, a mutual fund can be a sound and profitable source of income. Look first for a fund that satisfies your investment objectives. Be sure the men who will be supervising your money are well qualified. Review a fund's performance over the past five or ten years. Learn about the management fees and sales charges, the average size of dividends and capital gains. Find out whether you will be able to invest conveniently and whether you will be able to reinvest dividends inexpensively. The results will be well worth the extra time and effort. A topnotch mutual fund could help your family achieve financial security and a brighter future.

CHAPTER 58

## What You
## Can Do About Inflation

*You can't stop it, but you can take steps to outsmart it—here's how you can fight back*

Up, up, up go the prices! On any day of the year, Americans all over the country are paying more for food, clothing, rent, appliances, haircuts, bus fares, television and auto repairs and almost every other type of goods and service than they did last year, and a whale of a lot more than they did a decade ago.

If you want to see how inflation has affected you, consider these facts:

The government has set the year 1939 as a so-called base year from which the purchasing power of the dollar is figured, using the Consumer Price Index, or CPI. This economic barometer, published monthly by the U.S. Bureau of Labor Statistics, measures the average change in costs of goods and services bought by wage earners in

56 cities. It tells you that since 1940 the buying power of the dollar has gone steadily downhill.

## The Shrinking Dollar

The $1 that bought you 100 cents' worth just before World War II will buy only 37 cents' worth today. The dollar you spend today will buy only 76 percent as much as it did in the 1957–1959 period.

For the past three years prices as recorded by the CPI have been rising at the rate of more than 4 percent annually, continuing to chip away at the value of your money. In 1969, consumer costs jumped 6.1 percent, the sharpest increase since 1951.

If the CPI keeps moving upward—and all signs indicate that it will—by 1980 your dollar may purchase only two thirds of what it does right now.

What's causing it all to happen? There's no big mystery. Inflation comes about when, as the Chase Manhattan Bank explains, "the rise in total spending exceeds the rise in production and services. When demand starts to chase supply, prices start going up. The more demand and the less supply, the higher the price tags."

When prices are high, unions demand wage hikes so that employes can meet the increased cost of living. When management must pay out more in wages and salaries, cost of production is increased and therefore prices of finished articles have to be raised. Higher pay also puts more money into circulation to keep chasing scarce goods and services. These in turn are increased in price as the demand grows. This is called the wage-price spiral.

What can you do to protect yourself against this relentless erosion of the purchasing power of your hard-earned dollars? While no method is guaranteed, there are some specific measures you can—and in fact must—take to minimize the potentially ruinous effects of inflation. Moreover, a little thoughtful planning can put you ahead of the game.

The starting point for anyone, whether single or the head of a family, is to put himself at once on "inflation alert." This means that from now until inflation ebbs—which may be a very long time indeed—your personal economics must be geared to, and dictated by, an inflation economy. All your money dealings, large and small,

## The Costs Go Up

**1957-1959 = 100**

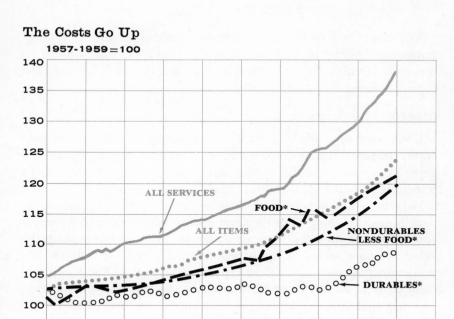

*SEASONALLY ADJUSTED          Source: U.S. Department of Labor, Bureau of Labor Statistics

*The ugly profile of inflation appears graphically on this Bureau of Labor Statistics chart of soaring costs in the 1960s. The chart uses the average cost of the various goods and services in 1957–1959 as a base line of 100. In the face of a continuing inflationary trend, careful financial planning is necessary to protect your family's financial well-being.*

all planning and all spending, must be weighed with inflation in mind.

This mental conditioning is more important than you may realize. Too many people moan and groan about high prices but go right on spending as before. If you convince yourself that you must manage your money in terms of the lessening value of the dollar, you are more apt to come out ahead.

The first step is to make a systematic check of your basic security programs. This is the first principle of sound economic strategy. It is essential to make sure you have an adequate line of defense against the unexpected.

## Closing the Gaps

Look over your life and health insurance and your savings program, because those up, up, up prices may have opened dangerous gaps. Your wife and children may not be able to get along at today's prices on yesterday's insurance, should you die.

How long has it been since you reviewed the fire insurance on your house, covering both dwelling and personal property? Even if you have done only ordinary maintenance, inflation has sent up the value of your home. A split-level home bought for $20,000 ten years ago may cost $30,000 to replace today. In addition, replacement costs of clothing and furnishings are higher. If trouble comes, you may find yourself holding an insurance check that cannot begin to cover what you lost.

Long-range savings goals will probably have to be upgraded as well. College funds for children, for example, will require expansion. Basic college costs are marching in advance of average price rises. Retirement programs which include savings, life insurance and other fixed-dollar guarantees may also require some hikes.

As you revise and adjust your long-range security program, it might cheer you to learn that the dollars you have in savings and investments are helping to curb inflation. They are not out in the marketplace bidding up the prices of goods and services. They are working in the economy, as capital, to increase productive capacity, which in turn also tends to stabilize prices.

The next phase of your action plan to beat inflation is to make the dollars you have cover as much territory as possible.

This calls for prudent buying. Inflation means an average rise in prices, but not everything goes up and certainly not all costs go up at the same rate. This is true especially of food prices, despite some sharp upswings. Certain foods, at certain seasons, are cheaper because of abundant supplies. Many out-of-season foods are strictly luxury items. Watch your local newspapers for supermarket specials and, when shopping, try the store's own brand, which can be up to 20 percent cheaper than those advertised nationally. (For more on supermarket shopping, see Chapters 26 and 28, pages 263 and 288.)

Clothing also varies in price according to the season. Watch for annual and semiannual sales. (See Chapter 32, "Smart-Money Clothes Shopping," page 312.) The same goes for household furnishings and some major appliances such as refrigerators, washing machines, television sets and air-conditioners.

Check prices at discount stores, where you can sometimes find bargains if you are willing to shop around a little. Discontinue magazines that few members of the family read. Insist on firm prices for repair jobs by auto mechanics, plumbers and furnace repairmen and compare their charges. Eat out less often. Take buses rather than taxis.

Pay life insurance premiums once a year instead of quarterly (there's a slight extra charge for making payments monthly, quarterly or semiannually). Operate a car a year longer than usual; this can save money if repair costs don't mount too fast. Switching from a regular checking account to the special kind that costs 10 cents a check plus a maintenance charge may help save money. The $500 or so required to avoid service fees in a regular account might be more profitably put into a savings account, so check your costs if you now have a regular account.

Now the third step: specific hedges against dollar shrinkage. The fundamental principle underlying all inflation-proofing moves is converting extra fixed dollars—cash or its equivalent—into other types of assets that can reasonably be expected to increase in dollar value as the general level of prices continues to mount.

## Four Ways to Fight Shrinking Money

Here are four ways to put this rule into practice:

*Buy real estate.* Because the supply of real estate is fixed, while demand increases as the population expands, the value of real estate is bound to increase in the long run. In certain areas property values increase at a faster rate than inflation. Some experts advise buying and holding land in the path of urban or industrial expansion. Others consider farmland or resort property a wise long-range investment. Before investing in real estate, study the area carefully and seek sound advice.

Of course, you need a great deal of capital to buy large tracts of land, and most of us just don't have that kind of money. One way to invest smaller amounts is to buy stock in a real estate investment company or trust. Most of these have their money tied up in office buildings, apartment houses, retail stores and shopping centers in or near large cities. Since many cities are plagued with problems stemming from riots, poor transportation and the flight of people and businesses to the suburbs, you need to examine carefully the properties the company or trust has invested in. (Some trusts, it should be noted, invest in construction loans and mortgages, rather than land.) Also, keep in mind that the turnover in the stock of small

---

## A SELECTIVE SPIRAL

In just ten years, the buying power of the dollar has dropped by well over ten cents.

This is the overall measure of what price rises in this period have done to the purchasing power of your earnings. But it is far from the whole story. You don't spend one single $1 for one fixed market basket of "things" and "nonthings"—you spend many dollars for many different market baskets, and there is a spectacular variation in how much each of your dollars buys in comparison with ten years ago.

For instance, the $1 you budgeted a decade ago for the purchase of food to eat at home now buys you 79 cents' worth of food. But the $1 which went for your restaurant meals in 1960 will now buy you only 67 cents' worth of food. The cost of eating out has climbed much faster than the cost of eating in.

The $1 you put aside in 1960 for furniture will buy you 83 cents of furniture today. But the $1 you put aside for mortgage payments, taxes, insurance, repairs and other home-ownership costs will now cover only 69 cents' worth of these costs. The rise in the price of furniture has been picayune against the rise in other vital costs that are involved in owning a home.

Again, the $1 you spent to buy and maintain your car ten years ago will pay for 81 cents of these costs now. But the $1 you spent during the earlier period for bus fares, subway tokens and other forms of public transportation is worth only 61 cents.

Inflation, in short, is choosy in how it attacks the various items which make up our cost of living. And behind inflation selectivity are powerful fundamental forces.

Most significant is the relentless increase in the cost of services year after

real estate investment trusts is usually slow, so there's often a wide spread between the prices sellers ask and those that buyers will pay. For information on specific real estate investment companies or trusts, consult a stock broker and ask him to get you some comparative reports on various real estate trust funds. Some of the major investment banking companies have real estate divisions which may also be a source of information.

Just owning a home can be an excellent hedge against inflation. Homeownership will shield you against rent inflation. Taxes, heating fuel, services and other costs are bound to rise, of course, but remember that you will be repaying your mortgage loan in dollars that are cheaper than those you borrowed. Moreover, your house probably will increase in value over the long run.

year, an increase which has dwarfed the rise in the cost of goods. Our demand for services of all kinds is expanding without interruption. Meanwhile, the cost of the services is being pushed up by rising wages and materials in all the major categories of services.

One single comparison dramatizes this point. The $1 you spent for products in 1960 still will buy you 81 cents' worth of things today. But the $1 you spent a decade ago for medical care, haircuts, auto repairs, and other services will buy you only 67 cents' worth of the same services now.

The prices of goods generally have been rising, too, under the pressures of higher demand, higher wages, higher material costs. The increases here, however, have been tempered by rapid improvements in the productivity of workers in goods-producing fields, spectacular advances in the efficiency of factories and machines, intense competition among makers and sellers of goods. In many services these factors have had little effect in keeping prices down.

Although, comparatively speaking, things today are a much bigger bargain than nonthings, there also are sharp differences within the products category, that is, between price trends of durable goods and of nondurable goods.

Again, one single comparison will tell the tale: The $1 you spent a decade ago for clothes will buy 76 cents' worth of clothes today, while the $1 you spent for electrical appliances and other household durables will actually purchase 94 cents' worth of these items today.

This glance behind the overall decline in your dollar's value may give you scant consolation as you try to make a penny do 2 cents' work. But at least it's a guide to what type of dollar has lost the most pennies and why.

*Buy shares in American business.* Ownership of common stock is one of the most effective safeguards against dollar erosion. Despite dips along the way, stocks on the whole have climbed upward for decades. If you had invested in an average group of good issues at the close of World War II, you'd be sitting pretty today. The Dow-Jones average, which records the performance of 30 of the nation's blue-chip industrial corporations, rose from 175 in 1948 to 800 in 1969. That doesn't mean that every stock increased fivefold or that there weren't some which lost. It *does* mean that wise investing generally can be expected to pay off. And don't forget, stock ownership pays interest in the form of dividends.

A final word about stocks. They go up; they also can go down. There are risks, of course, although some are less risky than others. (See Chapter 56, "The ABCs of Stocks and Bonds," page 525.)

*Carefully and selectively accumulate rarities.* Anything that can no longer be duplicated is bound to increase in value, and with a little expertise you can derive profit as well as pleasure from many kinds of collections. (See "Better Than Money?" on the next page.)

*Look into home refinancing.* If you borrow now on a long-term basis, you will repay your debt in cheaper dollars. Thus, after analyzing your particular situation, you may find it to your advantage to refinance your house and obtain a larger mortgage, especially if your house has increased in value and you have a sizable equity in it.

Weigh carefully the costs involved: higher interest rates, repayment penalties and the like. Refinancing will make available to you a large sum of cash that can be put into investments that are more or less inflation-proof.

One of the best protections against inflation is so obvious it needn't be put into a list of things to do: Hold a steady job. People who receive paychecks regularly will find them fatter as the years go on, thus increasing buying power. Even though prices go up, wages and salaries generally have been keeping pace. The people who really suffer from inflation are those on fixed-dollar incomes.

The worst thing you can do in these dollar-dwindling days is to sit there and watch your money melt. No magic economic pill exists to set things right, but you can take some giant steps that not only can minimize the effects of inflation but can even help you beat it.

## BETTER THAN MONEY?

As the value of the dollar declines, growing numbers of Americans are finding ways to protect themselves against inflation. A random sampling of bankers, brokers, investment counselors, speculators and collectors reveals a vast array of techniques, all directed toward the same end: to avoid holding on to paper dollars at a time when their value is diminishing, and to accumulate items of real and enduring worth that will increase in rarity and monetary value.

Besides the classic inflation hedges of buying real estate and common stocks, ingenious investors have exchanged their money for valuables like these:

*Stamps and coins.* These are the collector items most traditionally associated with inflation protection. Value to collectors increases greatly during periods of inflation. Many rare postage stamps have doubled in value since 1965. Benjamin Stack of Stack's Coin Company in New York City recalls a 1700-year-old Roman coin he sold for $200 in the early 1940s. He recently re-sold the same coin for $13,500, and its value will doubtless increase with time.

United States silver coins (the old variety, now superseded by the copper-alloy coins) are worth 40 or 50 percent more than their face value. One ambitious New York accountant has $10,000 tied up in such coins. But to cash them in he would have to melt the coins down, a messy and expensive process.

*Platinum.* This metal has attracted investors despite its high price (nearly $235 an ounce) because of its growing industrial value (in electronics, alloys and fuel cells) and because, ounce for ounce, it is 15 times scarcer than gold. Its value seems bound to go up.

*Fine paintings.* Art works usually increase in value during periods of inflation because more and more investors are attracted to them. One reliable study shows that the value of old masters rose about 15 percent in both 1966 and 1967. But the biggest recent price increases have been in the works of lesser-known artists of the impressionist and postimpressionist schools. One shrewd collector has purchased 14 paintings by lesser-known postimpressionists since the early 1960s and watched their value increase 150 percent. The early works of the "Pop" artists have also skyrocketed in value.

*Gems.* Some people feel that precious gems are good inflation protection. The family diamond, however, may not be as precious as it seems. Much of the value of diamonds grows from scarcity, but no one knows just how scarce they are, since a South African syndicate controls virtually all the places where diamonds are found. The syndicate supports the price of diamonds year after year by making sure that not too many are mined.

*Autographs and letters of famous people.* These, too, are collector items that have benefited substantially from the flight from cash. In a similar category are *rare books*, which include first editions of now-famous writers and works of great antiquity and historical interest.

In fact, it seems that during periods of inflation almost anything of interest to collectors will increase in monetary value faster than the dollar declines. The last few years have seen striking increases in the prices of antiques, tapestries, vintage autos, old weapons, player pianos, even overstuffed Victorian furniture. An early issue of *Superman* comics can bring as much

as $150, and a 1953 issue of *Playboy* fetches $100.

Of course, to profit from a collection, you must be careful what you collect. When a Canadian collector died a few years ago, his stamp accumulation realized considerably more than he had paid for it. His first love, however, was millstones. He left what was certainly the finest collection of millstones ever assembled—most likely it was also the only collection. A buyer was never found, and the collection has now disappeared.

---

## VALUE OF THE DOLLAR OVER THE PAST 30 YEARS

The Bureau of Labor Statistics in the Department of Labor has compiled the following "Value of the Dollar" table based on the Consumer Price Index. It is assumed that the 1939 dollar was worth 100 cents. All figures are the average for each year.

| Year | Value | Year | Value |
|---|---|---|---|
| 1940 | 99.2 cents | 1955 | 51.9 cents |
| 1941 | 94.4 cents | 1956 | 51.1 cents |
| 1942 | 85.3 cents | 1957 | 49.4 cents |
| 1943 | 80.3 cents | 1958 | 48.1 cents |
| 1944 | 79.0 cents | 1959 | 47.7 cents |
| 1945 | 77.2 cents | 1960 | 46.9 cents |
| 1946 | 71.2 cents | 1961 | 46.5 cents |
| 1947 | 62.2 cents | 1962 | 45.9 cents |
| 1948 | 57.8 cents | 1963 | 45.4 cents |
| 1949 | 58.3 cents | 1964 | 44.8 cents |
| 1950 | 57.8 cents | 1965 | 44.1 cents |
| 1951 | 53.5 cents | 1966 | 42.8 cents |
| 1952 | 52.3 cents | 1967 | 41.6 cents |
| 1953 | 51.9 cents | 1968 | 40.0 cents |
| 1954 | 51.7 cents | 1969 | 37.5 cents |

# 13
# PLANNING
# TO ENJOY YOUR
# RETIREMENT YEARS

*Now is the time to review or initiate*
*your retirement program for your future*
*comfort and independence*

CHAPTER 59

*Wondering how it all works?*
*Who's eligible? When payments*
*start? How much you'll get?*
*Here's the whole story*

## What You Can Expect from Social Security

Today, nine out of every ten wage earners and their families are covered by Social Security. This means that when they retire or become disabled they can count on a steady source of income, and when they die their families will have something to fall back on. Chances are you will need—and receive—Social Security someday.

Do you qualify for Social Security benefits? How do you apply? What benefits are you and your family entitled to? Here is a complete, up-to-date explanation of how the program works.

Becoming eligible for the Social Security program is easy, since all you have to do is work at a job that is covered by the Social Security law. Today, most jobs and self-employed activities *do* come under Social Security. You must have a Social Security card, which you can get at any Social Security office; the number on your card is used by the government to keep a record of your earnings and of any benefits to which you and your family become entitled.

To qualify for retirement benefits you must have worked a given number of years. Anyone who works for ten years or more is eligible for full benefits. Most wage earners receive credit for one-quarter year of work for any three-month period in which they receive $50 or more in wages. They are credited for all four quarters if they earn $7800 or more in a year, regardless of how much they earn in any one quarter. A self-employed person who earns $400 or more in a year receives credit for a full year. A wage earner who receives farm wages is credited with one-quarter year of work for each $100 he earns in a year, up to $400.

If you were born before 1930, you will need the amount of work credits indicated in the table on the opposite page to receive full benefits.

Wage earners born after 1929 are entitled to death benefits at age twenty-eight if they have worked at least one-and-a-half years. For each subsequent year, an additional quarter year of work credit is

| IF YOU REACH 65 (62 IF A WOMAN) OR DIE OR BECOME DISABLED IN: | YOU WILL BE FULLY INSURED IF YOU HAVE CREDIT FOR THE FOLLOWING NUMBER OF WORK YEARS: |
|---|---|
| 1965 | 3½ |
| 1967 | 4 |
| 1969 | 4½ |
| 1971 | 5 |
| 1975 | 6 |
| 1979 | 7 |
| 1983 | 8 |
| 1987 | 9 |
| 1991 or later | 10 |

required. This means that a thirty-year-old wage earner needs two years of credit, a thirty-one-year-old needs two-and-a-quarter years, and so on.

A person is also fully insured if he has credit for one-quarter year of work each year after 1950 up to the year he retires, becomes disabled or dies. Wage earners who are not fully insured may still qualify for death benefits if they are currently insured. To be currently insured, a worker must have credit for one-and-a-half years of work in the three years before he dies.

If you are fully insured, other members of your family may also receive benefits when you retire. These include: any unmarried children under eighteen, or between eighteen and twenty-two if they are full-time students; unmarried children eighteen or over who were disabled before they reached eighteen and are still disabled; a wife under sixty-two who is caring for a child under eighteen or a disabled child; a wife or a dependent husband over sixty-two.

Your survivors will be entitled to benefits when you die if you are fully or currently insured. These survivors are: a widow under sixty and caring for either a child under eighteen or a disabled child; a widow over sixty, even if there are no dependent children; a disabled widow over fifty; unmarried children under eighteen or between eighteen and twenty-two if they are full-time students; unmarried children over eighteen who were disabled before age eighteen; a dependent parent sixty-two or over. In addition, your family will receive a lump-sum death benefit of up to $255.

To qualify for disability payments a wage earner must have a

561

severe physical or mental condition that prevents him from working and is expected to last at least 12 months or to result in death. If you become disabled before you are twenty-four you may collect disability payments if you received credit for one-and-a-half years of work in the three years before you became disabled. If you become disabled between twenty-four and thirty-one, you need credits for half the time after you became twenty-one and before you were disabled. After age thirty-one, you must be fully insured and have credit for five of the ten years before you were disabled.

The amount of your disability benefits generally equals the retirement benefits you would receive if you were sixty-five. Payments will also be made to any dependents who would qualify for retirement benefits (see above).

How much will you and your family receive when you retire or if you become disabled? That depends on your average annual earnings over a period of years. You can figure out the amount of your benefit by using this set formula:

1. Count the number of *base* years. That is, if you were born before 1930, start counting with 1956; if you were born after 1929, start with the year you reached twenty-seven. Count from this year up to, but not including, the year you will become sixty-five if you are a man, or sixty-two if you are a woman. To figure death or disability benefits, count up to, but not including, the year the worker died or became disabled.

2. Make a list of your earnings for each year after 1951, including the year you will retire, became disabled or, if you are widowed, your insured husband or wife died. Do not list more than: $3600 for any year from 1951 to 1954; $4200 for any year from 1955 to 1958; $4800 for 1959 to 1965; $6600 for 1966 and 1967; and $7800 for 1968 and later. Put down a zero for any years you had no earnings.

3. Cross off your list the years of lowest earnings until the number of earning years on your list is the same as the number of base years. If, for instance, your list of earnings years has 12 entries and the number of base years is 9, you cross off 3 earnings years from your list. No more than 5 years of low earnings can be excluded, however.

4. Add up your earnings for the years left on your list and divide by the number of base years. The result will be your average yearly

## Examples of Monthly Cash Payments

| AVERAGE YEARLY EARNINGS AFTER 1950[1] | $923 OR LESS | $1800 | $3000 | $4200 | $5400 | $6600 | $7800 |
|---|---|---|---|---|---|---|---|
| Retired worker—65 or older / Disabled worker—under 65 / Disabled female worker—under 62 | $64.00 | $101.70 | $132.30 | $161.50 | $189.80 | $218.40 | $250.70 |
| Wife 65 or older | 32.00 | 50.90 | 66.20 | 80.80 | 94.90 | 109.20 | 125.40 |
| Retired worker at 62 | 51.20 | 81.40 | 105.90 | 129.20 | 151.90 | 174.80 | 200.60 |
| Wife at 62, no child | 24.00 | 38.20 | 49.70 | 60.60 | 71.20 | 81.90 | 94.10 |
| Widow at 62 or older | 64.00 | 84.00 | 109.20 | 133.30 | 156.60 | 180.20 | 206.90 |
| Widow at 60, no child | 55.50 | 72.80 | 94.70 | 115.60 | 135.80 | 156.20 | 179.40 |
| Disabled widow at 50, no child | 38.90 | 51.00 | 66.30 | 80.90 | 95.00 | 109.30 | 125.50 |
| Wife under 65 and one child | 32.00 | 50.90 | 70.20 | 119.40 | 164.60 | 177.20 | 183.80 |
| Widow under 62 and one child | 96.00 | 152.60 | 198.60 | 242.40 | 284.80 | 327.60 | 376.20 |
| Widow under 62 and two children | 96.00 | 152.60 | 202.40 | 280.80 | 354.40 | 395.60 | 434.40 |
| One child of retired or disabled worker | 32.00 | 50.90 | 66.20 | 80.80 | 94.90 | 109.20 | 125.40 |
| One surviving child | 64.00 | 76.30 | 99.30 | 121.20 | 142.40 | 163.80 | 188.10 |
| Maximum family payment | 96.00 | 152.60 | 202.40 | 280.80 | 354.40 | 395.60 | 434.40 |

[1] Generally, average earnings are figured over the period after 1950 until the worker reaches retirement age, becomes disabled or dies. Up to five years of low earnings can be excluded. The maximum earnings creditable for Social Security are $3600 for 1951–1954, $4200 for 1955–1958, $4800 for 1959–1965 and $6600 for 1966–1967. The maximum creditable in 1968 and after is $7800, but average earnings for retirement benefits cannot reach this amount until later. Because of this, the benefits shown in the last two columns on the right generally will not be payable until later. When a person is entitled to more than one benefit, the amount actually payable is limited to the larger of the benefits.

563

earnings over the period. Once you know your average earnings, you can calculate your benefits by referring to the table on page 563. The average yearly earnings figures on the top line go only to $7800 because that is currently the maximum amount that can be credited to your Social Security account. It is to be expected however, that as benefits increase, so will the maximum contribution.

If a person is entitled to benefits as a wage earner as well as a dependent, he receives whichever payment would be larger. A working wife, for example, would be eligible for more money if she applies for retirement benefits in her name rather than as a dependent of her husband. The maximum benefit for a dependent wife over sixty-five is $125.40, while the maximum for a retired or disabled worker is $250.70. The total monthly amount a family receives, however, may not exceed the amount of the maximum family payment (see the chart on page 563).

The wife and dependent children of a retired wage earner are entitled to monthly payments of half the amount paid to him. When he dies, his widow receives $82\frac{1}{2}$ percent of his monthly benefits, and his children and other dependents get 75 percent. The total benefits paid to a wage earner and his family, however, may not exceed $434.40 a month, no matter how many dependents.

A man may begin collecting retirement benefits when he becomes sixty-two if he wishes, but his benefits will be reduced somewhat. For each month before he reaches sixty-five, payments are lessened by 5/9 of 1 percent. His wife's benefit will be reduced by 25/36 of 1 percent for each month before she reaches sixty-five. A woman worker applying on her own behalf is entitled to full benefits when she reaches the age of sixty-two.

If you (or your survivors) continue to work after beginning to collect benefits, you may collect full benefits if you earn less than $1680 a year. If you earn between $1680 and $2880 a year, $1 in benefits will be withheld for every $2 you earn over $1680; $1 will be withheld for every $1 of earnings over $2880. There is one important exception to this rule. Regardless of your total earnings for the year, you can receive benefits for any month in which you earn less than $140. So if you hit the jackpot financially one month, you can still collect during the remaining months of the year. After you reach seventy-two, any earnings in excess of $1680 a year will not reduce your benefits.

Income from savings, investments, pensions, insurance or any royalties you receive from copyrights or patents you obtained before retiring are not counted as earnings. No matter how much money you receive from these sources, you can still collect your monthly Social Security check.

When you begin to plan for your retirement years or your family's future in the event of your death or permanent disability, take your Social Security benefits into account. While they certainly will not provide complete support for you and your family, they can be a valuable cushion during the years when the family breadwinner no longer brings home the bread.

## HOW MUCH WILL YOU PAY?

Every person whose job is covered by Social Security must contribute part of his earnings to the Social Security program. The employer deducts a given amount from each worker's paycheck and sends it, along with an equal amount (the employer's share of the contribution), to Internal Revenue.

Any earnings in excess of $7800 (the maximum amount covered by Social Security) are not taxed. The percentage of earnings to be deducted for Social Security is fixed by law. Look at the chart below for the amount you will have to contribute in future years.

### CONTRIBUTION RATE SCHEDULE FOR EMPLOYES AND EMPLOYERS (EACH)

| | Percentage of Covered Earnings | | | |
|---|---|---|---|---|
| YEARS | FOR RETIREMENT, SURVIVORS AND DISABILITY INSURANCE | FOR HOSPITAL INSURANCE | TOTAL | MAXIMUM CONTRIBUTION |
| 1969–70 | 4.20 | .60 | 4.80 | $374.40 |
| 1971–72 | 4.60 | .60 | 5.20 | 405.60 |
| 1973–75 | 5.00 | .65 | 5.65 | 440.70 |
| 1976–79 | 5.00 | .70 | 5.70 | 444.60 |
| 1980–86 | 5.00 | .80 | 5.80 | 452.40 |
| 1987 and after | 5.00 | .90 | 5.90 | 460.20 |

## LEAST-KNOWN FACTS ABOUT SOCIAL SECURITY

A staggering total of more than 16 million questions come into Social Security offices across the nation every year—ranging from "Can my cat get a Social Security card?" (no) to "Send me everything on Social Security" (the data would fill a couple of railroad cars).

What are the questions pinpointing the least-known and most misunderstood details of the whole system? Here they are—with the answers:

*Q*: Just who is *not* covered by Social Security today?

*A*: Railroad workers and federal civilian employes, both of whom have their own retirement systems, and an uncounted number of parents who help their children with domestic work. Parents actually employed by their children in a regular business, however, are covered.

*Q*: To what extent are household employes covered?

*A*: They are covered if they earn at least $50 from the same employer in any given calendar quarter—or about $4 a week. This includes maids, cleaning women, baby-sitters, cooks, gardeners, handymen.

The employer must report quarterly wages over $50 to the District Director of Internal Revenue within a month of the end of each quarter and pay taxes of 4.8 percent (1969–1970 rate) of the wages earned. The employe pays a matching payment of 4.8 percent.

*Q*: Are ministers and clergymen covered by Social Security?

*A*: Yes—unless they file an application with the Internal Revenue Service to be excluded. They must report earnings as a self-employed person, even though they may be employed by their church.

*Q*: Can a worker in a nonprofit organization receive benefits?

*A*: Yes—if the organization is operated exclusively for religious, charitable, scientific, literary, educational or humane purposes, he can be covered provided (1) the organization waives its exemption from payment of Social Security taxes by filing a certificate with the Internal Revenue Service and (2) the employes who wish to be covered sign that certificate.

*Q*: Can a divorced wife get wife's benefits when her ex-husband retires?

*A*: Yes, if the wife is sixty-two or older and the marriage lasted at least twenty years before the divorce.

*Q*: Can a divorced wife get survivor's benefits in the event of her ex-husband's death?

*A*: Yes—if she was married to the worker for twenty years and if she had been receiving at least half of her support from her ex-husband under court order or divorce agreement. But she is eligible *only* for monthly mother's benefits and those only if she has in her care children of her divorced husband who are unmarried and under eighteen.

*Q*: Can a woman collect benefits

both as a worker and as a wife?

*A*: No. She collects only the benefits based on her work unless her benefits as a wife, based on her husband's earnings, would be higher. In that case the difference is automatically added to her monthly check.

*Q*: What happens to his or her Social Security benefits if a man or woman stops working before retirement age?

*A*: The benefits stay in his or her Social Security account. If he or she has worked at least one fourth of the time since December 31, 1950, or since his or her twenty-first birthday if it fell after that date, he or she is eligible for insurance.

*Q*: What if a worker becomes disabled before retirement age?

*A*: If he worked at least five out of the ten years before he became disabled and if he falls within Social Security's definition of disabled, he qualifies for monthly payments both for himself and for his dependents who qualify. If he became disabled between ages twenty-four and thirty-one, he must have worked half of the time between age twenty-one and the time he was disabled. A worker who becomes disabled before twenty-four needs credit for one-and-a-half years of work in the three years during which he was disabled.

*Q*: How does Social Security define disabled?

*A*: A person is considered disabled if he cannot work because of a severe mental or physical impairment that has lasted (or is expected to last) for 12 months or longer. Benefits can be paid even if he expects to recover and return to work, as long as the impairment is severe enough to keep him from working for a year or more.

## YOU MUST APPLY FOR BENEFITS

Social Security payments do not begin automatically. You must first file an application at your local Social Security office. (Look in the telephone book under "U.S. Government, Social Security Administration.") Unless you notify that office several months before your retirement, you may lose out on payments between the time you retired and the time you notified the Social Security office. For the same reason, the local Social Security office should be notified immediately if a worker dies or becomes disabled.

When you apply for benefits, take along your Social Security card and proof of your age (a birth certificate, for example). A widow applying for death benefits should take her husband's Social Security card, her marriage certificate and birth certificates of any children eligible for benefits. If you do not have these documents, contact the Social Security office. They will tell you about other proofs you may substitute.

*The right pension plan
could make
all the difference
in your retirement
years*

When you start your business career, a pension plan may be at the bottom of the list of things you want from a job. But as you get older and find that two can't live as cheaply as one—especially when the two acquire offspring, house, car and stacks of bills, you begin to realize that pension plans are a very important part of your future. A good plan can make the difference between living in comfort and living on the thin edge of financial insecurity. And the time to judge a plan is while you still have some choices, either in the way you decide to take benefits under an existent plan or—if you are changing jobs—what gains or losses you will have in the new company's pension plan.

Since pension plans are set up on several different principles, there are countless variations in what they offer or provide. To make an evaluation, here are the questions you need answered:

1. What are your guaranteed rights under a given plan?

2. How much pension will you receive when you retire?

3. Will your benefits continue without reduction as long as you live?

4. Can you take an early retirement and, if so, is there a financial penalty?

5. Can you continue to work after the retirement age or is retirement compulsory at a stated age regardless of your physical and mental condition?

6. At what age do you acquire a vested right in the pension; that is, the right to part or all of the pension benefits that have been set aside for you in a fund?

7. What are your rights to a pension if you either leave your job or are fired?

8. Is the pension set up so that your financial rights are maintained irrespective of what happens to the company?

9. What are your rights if your employer discontinues the plan?

There was a time when all these questions would have been extraneous, since pensions were dependent on the goodwill of the employer or the profitability or solvency of the company. But these days pensions are increasingly becoming a standard part of the fringe benefits that go along with a job. So now the important thing is to consider how the various plans answer these questions, to either your benefit or your detriment.

In general, pension plans are set up to assure future payments either by means of a trust fund that is separate from the operating funds of the business or by the purchase from an insurance company of annuity plans that make you, the employe, the beneficiary. (For more information on annuities, see Chapter 61, "All About Annuities," page 574.) In either case the plan may be contributory or noncontributory, and there are variations even in these categories.

Under the contributory plan employe and employer each put some money in the plan, usually at an agreed-upon rate; usually the employer's contribution is larger, but this is not necessarily so. Frequently the contributory plan is voluntary, and you, the employe, choose whether or not to join. If you don't, however, the employer does not put money aside for you anyway—you simply are not a member of the plan. Should you join and later decide to leave your job, your contribution will be returned to you, possibly with interest. But your employer's contribution remains in the fund, unless you have acquired a vested right in the fund. (More about this later.)

In a noncontributory plan your employer pays a given amount into the fund annually and you contribute nothing. Whether or not you receive part of this if you change jobs depends on how the plan was set up.

Since the pension you receive very often depends on how many years of work "credits" you have earned, *when* you are eligible to join a plan is one of its most important provisions. In some companies you become eligible as soon as you are hired, or within a very short time. In others you have to have a specified number of years of continuous employment before you are eligible; this may be as much as 15 years.

Some companies are reluctant to accept older but newly hired employes into their pension plans, since the employes become eligible for benefits fairly quickly. Other companies, besides specifying a given length of employment before eligibility, rule out eligibility beyond a certain age. If you are hired at age fifty, for instance, you may not be able to join a pension plan, unless the company bends the rules or makes some special provision. This is one of the aspects of discrimination in hiring because of age that is not yet covered by the Age-Discrimination-in-Employment Act—but it has been noted as a trouble spot that Congress does plan to investigate.

## Computing What You Get

Another very important aspect of a plan is how the company computes how much pension you will get. There are many ways of doing this, such as: providing a specific sum for each year of eligibility; taking a given percentage of yearly base pay, excluding bonuses, commissions and overtime; or using a fixed percentage of earnings. If a fixed percentage of a given base is used, the base can vary considerably, depending on how the plan is set up. The base may be anything from an average of your earnings from the day you became eligible to an average of your earnings for the last five or ten years of your employment.

As inflation has become more and more of a problem, some companies have tried to set up their plans to offset the rising cost of living. If the pension plan is based on an annuity at retirement the company will attempt to adjust the annuity you will receive, either by increasing it according to a set formula so that it makes allowance for the rise in the price index or by adding to the basic annuity in accordance with the rise in the price index. The adjustments are usually made from an extra fund, based on the return from common stocks, rather than from the annuity payouts.

A pension plan may or may not take into account your dependents. Under some plans your widow or other dependents would receive only your contributions plus interest if you were to die before retirement. Under other plans your widow or dependents would receive the benefit of whatever funds have been built up to your credit under the plan. Usually you may arrange to have your pension paid as long as either you or your widow is alive, though this might somewhat reduce the amount of each payment. This is like an annuity that is payable as long as either of the annuitants lives. Under a typical plan you must decide *before* your retirement whether you want the pension payable to you alone for as long as you live or whether you want it payable to you and your wife as long as either of you is living.

As part of some plans, or as a collateral benefit, there may be a life insurance provision. If the pension plan itself does not provide for any death benefit to dependents in case of an employe's death,

## THE CHOICE AMONG ANNUITY PLANS

Most pension plans based on annuities offer some kind of choice as to how you take the annuity provided.

• *Straight life annuity.* Usually the basic provision is for a fixed sum as long as you are living—the straight life annuity. However, you may decide that this is not the best idea for your family. If so, here are some other possibilities you might consider.

• *Refund annuity.* Under this plan you choose to take less total income, but you name a beneficiary who is entitled to receive the equivalent of an insurance payment when you die. The amount of payment is the difference between the total value of your pension at the time you retired and the amount that had already been paid out to you at the time of your death.

• *Installment annuity.* This guarantees a given number of years of payment. Although the total you receive may be less than if you had chosen to take a straight life annuity (depending on when you die) you have the guar-

antee of a specified number of years of payment and—more important—if you die before the guaranteed number of years your beneficiary receives the remaining number of installments.

• *Joint and survivor annuity.* This guarantees a lifetime income for you and the person you name to share your annuity on a joint basis. If you die, your survivor is guaranteed the remainder of the annuity, although often at a reduced rate. This plan usually has to be arranged for at least several years before retirement; or if you delay your choice, you have to be able to prove good health at the time you specify. Very often, if you choose the joint and survivor (also known as the contingent annuity) plan and then want to change your mind you cannot switch to another plan without the consent of the insurance company. Furthermore, the choice is canceled if either you or your wife dies before your retirement.

With all of these options, it's wise to check with an expert on pensions within your own company before you commit yourself.

the company may arrange for a collateral life insurance program. Such a plan may provide life insurance in an amount equal to your annual salary or some related figure.

Many plans make provision for the vesting of your rights under the plan after you have accumulated a specified number of years of service. There are several ways in which these vested rights may be allowed. Under one such plan, if you have accumulated at least ten years of service and have reached the age of fifty-five you will keep your rights even if you resign from the plan or leave your job. In such a case whatever money has been accumulated to your credit will be held until you reach retirement age (usually sixty-five). You will then get whatever pension has accumulated to your credit. Another possibility would be allowance for early retirement at a reduced pension, after a specified number of years and at a specified age.

Many plans don't allow you to withdraw any funds when you leave the company except those that you have contributed to the plan yourself. Others include funds put in by the company, but only up until the time of your departure. Some hold your share for you after you leave, but allow you only a percentage of any increase in the value of the fund when you reach retirement age—a situation that might occur, for instance, if part of the fund was invested in stocks. Other plans allow the benefits to accrue even though you are no longer an employe. The vesting provisions are so varied that a careful study of your company's plan is the only way to make sure what your benefits are, when you can leave or retire without sacrificing them and when you are eligible to receive them. Then, if you have any questions, ask *before* you have made a decision. This is particularly important since you may otherwise forfeit benefits.

Some pension plans are coordinated with Social Security payments, so that your pension plus Social Security will equal the retirement amount your plan has provided for. (For more on Social Security, see Chapter 59, "What You Can Expect from Social Security," page 560.) In estimating how much you will actually have to live on, you have to remember that pension benefits under most plans are in fixed-dollar amounts. So, as long as we have inflation the dollar you receive when you begin to collect a pension will not buy as much as the dollar that was originally paid in, even if your company has made some provision for a cost-of-living allowance. You may still need your savings, in addition to a pension and Social Security, in order to maintain the standard of living that you have reached before retirement.

## Seven Vital Dos and Don'ts

To be sure that you take full advantage of pension benefits and that you know what to look for—if you are considering changing jobs and want to compare the advantages of two different plans— here's a list of dos and don'ts that should prove helpful.

*Do* ask the company you work for to explain its pension plan and give you a copy of it so that you can study it carefully.

*Do* ask questions about any aspect of the plan that is not clear. Usually there is at least one person in the company who is a special-

### BE SURE OF YOUR VESTED RIGHTS

Your "vested right" is that portion of an accumulated fund which belongs to you at any particular time. In a pension plan this may be nothing unless you have served for a certain number of years. Usually a company pension plan, if liquidated by a job change before retirement, includes as a vested interest only such money as the employe himself paid in, sometimes plus interest. The company's matching money remains in the fund for the benefit of those who work to retirement age. Some vested rights are frozen and "thaw" only at retirement. This scheme is designed to encourage a lifetime of service to the company, so the penalty for early liquidation is severe. Another form of vested right is a life insurance policy owner's surrender value in his policy.

### TAX ADVANTAGES OF COMPANY PENSIONS

The availability of a company pension plan has many advantages to you as an employe. It helps you plan for retirement, and it relieves you of a considerable part of the financial responsibility of this planning. There are tax advantages, too, under our present system of income taxation. A pension plan that has the approval of the U.S. Treasury Department relieves you of any income tax obligation for its benefits until you actually receive them after retirement. If you were to be paid the amount of money necessary to set up an equivalent retirement fund of your own, you would have to receive considerably more additional salary than your employer pays to maintain the pension plan. This is, in effect, a deferred salary on which you pay no tax at the time it is earned.

ist in pension planning and will be able to give you advice and clarify any provisions that confuse you.

*Do* look into the various options that are open to you in the way that you can take your pension; that is, should your dependents receive it or just you, should you have a guaranteed number of years of payment but less income, and so on.

*Do* decide on the options early in your career, while you have a choice, and then review the options if your family situation changes.

*Don't* pick a time to retire without checking on your pension plan. You may find that it will be more advantageous to delay or advance it, depending on the terms of your company's pension plan. If, for instance, the plan is composed of an annuity plus a supplement based on the return from a common stock portfolio and the market is in a slump, it may be possible to delay your retirement until the stock market has recovered.

*Don't* count on the company to keep in touch with you if you leave and have a vested interest in your pension plan. Find out when and how you must file a claim for your interest in the plan, and let your family know about your rights. Keep a record of your claim.

*Don't* ignore proposals for pension plans in an industry in which you work. Be sure that the plan will be administered by responsible trustees and that your interests are protected.

CHAPTER 61

## All About Annuities

*You can set up your own retirement income program by investing in one of these plans*

An annuity is an investment that generally guarantees a fixed income for the remainder of a person's lifetime. The principle underlying annuities is simple, although policy combinations themselves can be confusing. In return for payment of a premium, you are promised a guaranteed annual income beginning at a designated age and continuing for the rest of your life, no matter how long or short that time might be. The amount of annuity income you will receive depends on the amount you invest in premiums and your age at the date of the contract and at the time payments are scheduled to begin.

Although annuity income is often referred to in annual terms, installments may be paid monthly, quarterly, semiannually or annually, depending upon the arrangement you make with the company.

The price of an annuity can be figured in either of these ways: You can find the amount it would cost to buy an annuity paying a stipulated annual income of, say, $2400; or if you have a specific sum to invest—perhaps the cash value of life insurance policies or proceeds from the sale of a home—you can find how much income you would receive if you were to invest the sum in an annuity contract.

Annuities may be purchased either on an individual or a group basis. They are available on a group basis under tax-protected plans set up by employers. Some employers pay the full cost of the annuity in behalf of their covered employes. Under other plans, both employer and employe share the cost of the annuity; the employe's contribution may be deducted from his paycheck.

## What Kind of Annuity?

There are several kinds of annuity contracts to choose from. All provide guaranteed payments for the life of the annuitant. Some annuities contain additional guarantees and coverage; these are more expensive and pay a lower income in relation to the premium paid.

*Straight life annuity*. This is a "pure" annuity paying regular installments of income to the purchaser for his entire life. At his death, all payments cease. An annuitant may receive only one installment, or he may receive hundreds, depending on how long he lives and how often the payments are made. He will, however, receive the largest amount of income for his investment. A straight life contract is the most economical annuity you can purchase, but it has this drawback: The possibility always exists that a person may not live long enough to recoup his investment—he may just have started receiving annuity installments when he dies. No further payments would be forthcoming to his heirs, for the company would have completely fulfilled its obligation. This is a gamble many persons are reluctant to take. Other, more expensive types of annuity contracts are available offering more liberal terms.

575

*Life annuity with installments certain.* This type of annuity specifies that if the annuitant dies within a certain time, such as 5, 10 or 20 years, a beneficiary would continue to receive the installments of income for the remainder of the guarantee period. If the annuitant survives the specified period, no payments would be made after his death. The longer the period of guarantee, the lower the annuity income.

*Refund annuities.* These promise that the amount invested in the contract will be returned to the annuitant or his beneficiary. If the annuitant recovers his investment during his lifetime, no further payments will be made. There are two basic types of refund annuities.

An installment refund annuity provides that if the annuitant dies before collecting what he paid in, his beneficiary will receive the installments from the company until the annuitant's investment has been refunded.

A cash refund annuity provides that, instead of installments after the annuitant's death, the beneficiary will receive the balance of the annuitant's investment in a lump-sum payment.

Refund annuities should not be considered a means of leaving an estate to one's heirs. If you, as the annuitant, live long enough to recover your investment, there will be nothing left for your beneficiary. Under an annuity contract promising payments for at least a certain number of years, once the annuitant survives the guarantee period the heir has no expectancy.

Remember, these clauses in the annuity contract are not purchased cheaply. Annuities with guarantees give less income per cash investment than straight life annuities.

*Joint and survivor annuity.* An annuity contract may provide income for more than one person's lifetime. It may be based on the lives of two or more persons, usually a husband and wife. Where more than one life is covered, the contract is called a joint and survivor annuity. Under such an annuity, the income is paid as long as one of the persons remains alive. Payments cease after the death of the surviving annuitant. The contract may provide for a constant amount of income during the lives of the annuitants covered, or it may call for a reduction in the amount of the payments after the death of one. Per cash investment, the joint and survivor annuity provides less income than a straight life annuity, particularly if there is a great disparity in the annuitants' ages.

## How to Buy Annuities

There are two methods of purchasing annuities. They may be bought with a single lump-sum payment or on the installment plan. An annuity can be purchased to start paying income immediately, or the contract may provide for installments to begin sometime in the future.

*Immediate annuity.* This provides for income to begin shortly after the contract date. Income payments may start one month from the date, if payments are to be made on a monthly basis, or one year from the purchase date, if payments are annual. Widows, retired persons or people who are planning to retire soon are most likely to purchase immediate annuities.

*Deferred annuity.* With this kind of contract, payments begin at a future date. A deferred annuity may be purchased by a single premium; however, it is more likely to be bought over a period of years in annual or more frequent installments. Should the purchaser of a deferred annuity die before payments start, the amount invested or the cash value, whichever is higher, can be recovered by his beneficiary.

Many retirement plans that are referred to as deferred annuities are actually savings plans. Some include insurance coverage but contain no annuity element during the deferred period. Under these plans a fund is accumulated which may be used to buy an immediate annuity at the end of the deferred period.

The standard annuity is supported by fixed-dollar investments, such as bonds and mortgages, and it pays a fixed-dollar income; the variable annuity holder's payments are invested primarily in common stocks. Ultimately the income payments he will receive will depend on the value of his accumulated investment at the time he begins to collect the annuity and the performance of the stocks in the company's investment fund.

Variable annuities are designed to overcome a principal drawback of the conventional annuity, the erosion in the value of its fixed payments owing to inflation. The shrinkage in the purchasing power of the dollar is strongly felt by persons living on fixed annuity income. They are prime victims of an inflationary economy. (For more on counteracting the effects of inflation, see Chapter 58, "What You Can Do About Inflation," page 549.)

The variable annuity, like the standard annuity, guarantees an income for life, but unlike the conventional annuity, the amount of the payment is not fixed. If you buy a variable annuity, you are actually purchasing an interest in an investment portfolio comprised of stocks. You are credited with "accumulation units" representing your proportionate interest in the fund. If you pay $100 into a fund worth $50 million, with 500,000 accumulation units outstanding, you receive 1 accumulation unit. If the value of the fund is $60 million a $100 payment entitles you to 5/8 of an accumulation unit; if the fund is worth $40 million, $100 buys $1\frac{1}{4}$ accumulation units. Reinvestment by the fund over the years of its dividends and capital gains entitles participants to additional accumulation units.

In connection with the operation of the fund, there are commission and administrative costs; these charges range from about 8 percent to 15 percent.

You generally buy accumulation units until the time your annuity income is slated to begin. You then receive a fixed number of "annuity units." This is the number of units you receive on the first payment date, and it does not change thereafter. However, the value of each annuity unit, representing a proportionate interest in the fund itself, will fluctuate in value, reflecting the changing values of the investment fund. You are given on each payment date an amount equal to what the annuity units being paid out to you are worth at that time.

At present, variable annuities are not widely available; few companies write these contracts. Many states prohibit the selling of variable annuities to individuals; others impose many restrictions. Up to now, these contracts have been sold mainly to groups, such as the Teachers Insurance and Annuity Association. Their plan, CREF (College Retirement Equities Fund), combines the variable annuity with the fixed-dollar annuity. An annuitant, under this plan, must put at least part of his contribution into a fixed annuity. He may put only 75 percent of his contribution into the variable annuity. The combination of the variable annuity with the standard annuity is for the protection of the participant in case of a protracted depression. He would have the assurance of receiving at least a guaranteed amount from the fixed-dollar segment of the plan.

Annuities are a conservative method of financing retirement. The chief advantage of the annuity is the assurance that you can never outlive your capital. You can depend on the annuity as a source of income during your entire lifetime and have complete freedom from investment management.

On the other hand, the type of financial security offered by the conventional annuity has the drawback of being vulnerable to inflation. Whereas the fixed-dollar payments are guaranteed, their purchasing power is not. As an investment, annuities earn a low rate of interest. Once payments begin, the annuity has no cash or loan value and cannot be used as a source of funds in an emergency. Annuities should not be purchased if you seek a return on your investment. But if you are looking for a safe, methodical way to obtain a secure lifetime income, you may decide to invest in one.

CHAPTER 62

## Pros and Cons of Joint Ownership

*Before you put everything in both your names, be sure the arrangement will work to your advantage*

"Of course we both want to be named as owners," said the young man, as he and his wife were about to take title of their new home.

This is the almost automatic declaration of most couples purchasing real estate or securities or opening a bank account. But—is it the right one to make about ownership?

Not necessarily. While most couples assume that joint ownership is a good thing, it can generate costly, sometimes distressing, problems. These may include loss of control of the property, loss of the right to dispose of it at death, loss of income and an increase in tax liability. People are often misled by certain illusions about joint ownership. They assume, for example, that it eliminates the need for a will. It doesn't. Or they assume that jointly held property is not subject to estate taxes. Like all inherited property, property held in joint ownership is taxable.

Whether joint ownership is best for you will depend on where you live, how much property you own and whom you want to inherit it. The forms and rules of joint ownership vary from state to state. To be sure it will be advantageous, you would be wise to consult with a lawyer and perhaps a tax expert before making a decision. They may suggest substitute legal arrangements that would more effectively achieve the desired results.

Joint ownership may take several forms, each with its own set of rules. The principal kinds are:

*Tenancy by the entirety.* This kind of joint ownership applies only to husbands and wives, and in most states only to their ownership of real estate. A common example is when the deed to a house is made out to "John Smith and Mary Smith, his wife." Neither John nor Mary can sell or give away any of the property without the other's consent, and when one of them dies the other automatically becomes the sole owner of the property. Regardless of what his will might say, John cannot leave any part of the property to anyone but Mary if she is still alive at the time of his death.

*Joint tenancy.* This kind of joint ownership allows either owner to sell or give away his share of the jointly owned property during his lifetime. Unless he does this, however, the entire property goes automatically to the other joint owner or owners—again regardless of any provisions to the contrary in the dead man's will.

*Tenancy in common.* A share of property owned in common with others may also be sold or given away without the consent of the other tenants. The great difference in this case is that when any of the tenants in common dies, his share passes directly to his heirs or as directed in his will, not to the other tenants in common (unless, of course, they happen also to be his heirs or legatees).

*Community property.* These laws (which apply only in the states of Arizona, California, Idaho, Louisiana, Nevada, New Mexico, Texas and Washington) presume that the properties acquired by a husband and wife through their mutual efforts belong to them equally. There are variations in the way these laws are applied, but in general a married couple's house would belong half to the husband

## SOME DANGERS OF JOINT OWNERSHIP

Some people, trying to avoid the costs of probate, think that they can arrange for joint property ownership and so eliminate the need for a will altogether. This maneuver may have the most unfortunate results, however, because joint ownership does not adequately meet all the eventualities that take place after death. The principal objection is that jointly owned property may pass to people who would not have been named as sole heirs.

Here is an example: A childless couple put all their property in joint names; neither made a will. The husband died in an automobile accident that left his wife seriously injured. A few weeks later she, too, died. Because she was sole owner of the property for those weeks, all of it went to her brothers and sisters. Her husband's parents received nothing. Had the couple made a will naming heirs in the event of both their deaths, the property would have been distributed fairly between both families.

The popular notion that joint ownership frees property from estate tax is incorrect. *Under federal estate tax law it is assumed that all property held in joint names belongs to the owner who dies first.* Say the survivor paid for, inherited or otherwise acquired the property which was held as joint property. But the law assumes that the property belonged to the person who died.

For example, a husband buys property and names his wife as joint owner with him. On his death, the full property, not half, will be included in his taxable estate. If the wife was to die first, the federal government could claim that she was the original owner of the property and that consequently it is taxable in her estate. The surviving husband would have to prove that he alone bought the property.

Jointly owned property may sometimes be subject to *increased* estate tax liability, as the following case illustrates: Over a period of years, the wife received over $40,000 from her parents. She turned all the money over to her husband so that he could invest it for her. He bought some municipal "bearer" bonds, on which the owner's name does not appear, and placed them—together with his own securities—in a safe-deposit box. The box was rented in the names of both.

The husband died and, as required by state law, a representative of the state tax commission was present when the safe-deposit box was opened. The wife was unable to show that she was the true owner of the bonds, which were listed among her husband's assets. Because she was the sole beneficiary, she recovered the bonds, but only after tax from her husband's estate had been paid on them.

To avoid confusion about the real owner of jointly held property, husbands and wives should keep complete and accurate records of each of their contributions to the purchase of any property or stocks.

and half to the wife, even if his name were the only one appearing on the deed. While he might bequeath his half share to someone else, his will could not dispose of his wife's share.

Of the several joint ownership forms, the most widely used are "tenancy by the entirety" and "joint tenancy."

The prime advantage of a joint ownership form that includes the survivorship right is that property passes to the surviving co-owner directly and is not part of the deceased joint-owner's probate estate which passes under his will. This can save executor's fees and other administrative costs and time. It does not eliminate federal and state estate taxes.

Further, jointly held property—including bank accounts and securities—can be sold quickly by either co-owner in an emergency. In many states, creditors may not have access to jointly owned property, though the same property may be available to them if it is individually owned.

To many people, jointly held stock provides an appealing tax advantage. There is an exclusion from taxable income of up to $200 on dividends on such stock, compared with a $100 maximum on individually owned stock.

Joint ownership of property also permits splitting of income or gains. This would benefit unmarried co-owners or couples who find it more advantageous to file separate federal and state returns. It also helps couples in states that do not allow joint filing of state income tax returns.

Income of real estate jointly owned by a couple may be split between husband and wife without gift-tax liability. If the property were owned by one spouse, who transferred half the income to the other, the excess over $6000 a year would be subject to the gift tax.

On the other side of the ledger are the disadvantages of joint ownership, one of which is loss by the individual of control of the property. This poses little difficulty unless the co-owners are in dispute or, in the case of married couples, become separated or divorced.

Income can be lost by one of the co-owners because joint ownership frequently gives the other a legal right to his fractional share. This would not seem a problem for a married couple, however.

A person who places property in joint ownership generally gives up his right to dispose of it in his will. Where there are enforceable survivorship rights, the surviving co-owner would receive the property outright. But even where there are not such rights, a co-owner may dispose of only his partial share by will.

Among tax disadvantages are the creation of a possible gift-tax liability upon establishment of joint ownership and termination of joint ownership while the co-owners are alive. In both cases, the transfer of property might be viewed as the giving of a gift.

There generally is no particular estate-tax advantage to joint ownership, but there could be disadvantages. When a co-owner dies, for example, the *total* value of jointly owned property is included in his estate for tax purposes, just as if he had owned it alone, unless the surviving co-owner can prove the extent of his contribution. The total value may be subject to estate taxation once again when the surviving co-owner dies.

If you own property jointly or if you are planning to place some of your things under joint ownership, ask yourself whether it is the best way for you to hold your property. Will it be a painless, inexpensive way to provide for your survivors? Or will it destroy your freedom to dispose of your property as you wish? You should now have a general idea of the pros and cons, but don't make a final decision without consulting a lawyer. Only an expert can advise you on the complicated legal and tax aspects of joint ownership.

⊏⊐⊏⊐⊏⊐⊏⊐⊏⊐

## WHO OWNS WHAT?

Most people assume that all jointly owned property automatically passes to the surviving partner when the co-owner dies. This is not always the case.

If, for example, real estate is held by tenancy in common, the tenant's share of the property goes to his heirs, not to the co-tenant(s). Real estate that is held by joint tenancy or tenancy by entirety, however, must go to the surviving partner, even though the will of the deceased specifies otherwise.

Household effects are held by tenancy in common and do not pass to the surviving owner unless stated specifically in the will. In the absence of a will, they are distributed among the heirs according to the laws of the state.

To be sure any property you hold jointly will be disposed of as you wish, check with a lawyer before you place anything under joint ownership. And, of course, don't let joint ownership take the place of a will.

⊏⊐⊏⊐⊏⊐⊏⊐⊏⊐

CHAPTER 63

## Can Your Wife
## Afford to Be a Widow?

*Every family's situation is
different and state laws
vary, but there are
general rules important
to know*

For years Mr. Smith lived with the delusion that should he die abruptly, his house was in order. His will was up to date; his life insurance was paid up; he owned his home outright; he kept ready cash in the bank; a few easily salable securities were tucked away in the safe-deposit box, along with other documents that might become important upon his demise.

The sudden death of several longtime acquaintances jolted Mr. Smith out of his complacency. In some cases the carefully laid plans of these friends fell apart. Their widows suffered frustrations and heartaches waiting to gain the use of their own property. In two instances widows who eventually received ample estates had to borrow money in the meantime for household expenses. After hearing about the legal pitfalls that these husbands had failed to anticipate, Mr. Smith determined to take another look at his own affairs.

This was an eye-opening experience. He questioned estate lawyers, bank trust officers, tax accountants and other authorities. And he soon discovered that he had unwittingly set some legal booby traps for his heirs. His will was all right. But he had not arranged his goods and chattels so that, during the trying few weeks or months immediately after his death, his wife would have cash for her living expenses. His wife simply could not afford to become a widow.

Like many of us, Mr. Smith thought it was an easy procedure to transfer money in bank accounts, insurance, real estate, securities and other simple assets of a dead husband to his widow's ownership. He found out that it is not. Administrators and executors of estates must deal with ever-changing statutes different in each state.

Misconceptions about the administration of estates are common. For example, it's a common belief that an "estate" is something involving considerable property. This is just not true. For tax purposes, whatever you own constitutes an estate.

Life insurance builds many a small estate into one big enough for the tax collector to eye with interest. An estate is subject to a federal estate tax only if it is in excess of $60,000. But since life insurance proceeds are not legally part of your estate, up to $60,000 more can be left to your wife in this way without incurring a federal tax. But state inheritance and estate taxes are also imposed, and for these the exemptions are much lower.

What happens to your estate after your death? The morning your name appears in the obituary column your banker is required by state law to seal up your safe-deposit box. He also impounds your bank accounts, both checking and savings. If they are joint accounts your wife can no longer draw money from them, even if they include her own funds. Nor can she freely sell or transfer your jointly held securities or remove any personal valuables she may have put into the box while you were living. She won't even be able to cash your salary check. These are safeguards to make sure that your creditors and the various tax collectors get their due before your heirs divide up the leavings.

In the usual case, these assets remain tied up until your executor presents to the bank the necessary tax waivers and other documents. But no one can officially act as executor until your will has been properly presented to the probate court and an executor approved by the court—a process which may take several weeks. Nor is this the end of the business. Your executor now proceeds to settle the estate. He collects the assets, pays creditors and funeral and administration expenses, settles taxes and distributes the assets to the proper legatees. Finally he prepares and files an accounting in the probate court for its approval. The whole process usually takes from seven months to a year, and often much longer.

## Access to Ready Cash

So the first problem your wife will face is how to put her hands on enough ready cash to meet day-to-day expenses while your bank accounts are impounded and later while your estate is being administered. One solution is for the wife to have a savings account in her name alone.

These funds for immediate needs can be supplemented relatively soon by those of your assets which do not pass under your will but pass directly to your wife, such as U.S. Savings Bonds and life insurance payable to her as beneficiary, her share of jointly held U.S. Savings Bonds and joint bank accounts. Since these assets do not become a part of the probate estate which must be administered by your executor, it is usually possible to have them distributed to your wife after only the delay necessary to obtain tax releases, copies of the death certificate and other documents required by the bank.

## WATCH OUT FOR "FRIENDS" AND ADVISERS

The widow who has spent her life shopping carefully for values when buying clothing, household goods, furnishings, food and services should use the same caution when investigating advisers after her husband's death. It is one of the seamier facts of life that there are people who specialize in preying on widows. They check the obituary columns and find out all they can about the size of an estate and the knowledgeability of the widow. Then they attempt to "share" in her estate through a variety of schemes, including investment advice, insurance and retirement plans and whatever other new plan they can come up with to part the widow from her inheritance. Even if these are within the letter of the law, they are often not beneficial to the widow.

Before giving any information about her financial affairs and certainly before accepting advice, a woman should carefully investigate *anyone* who gets in touch with her after the death of her husband—including strangers who claim to have been friends or business associates of her husband and recent friends, even if she has met these people under circumstances that are completely valid.

Sometimes, however, it is not outsiders but close friends who, with the best of intentions, are the widow's worst enemies. They may offer advice on buying stocks, making investments, getting loans or on other business matters—often very bad advice, though it is well meant. The widow is better off consulting an outside, impartial observer who is experienced and has no emotional ties with her or her late husband. The family banker is a good source of advice if she needs it; if he cannot give an opinion himself he can refer her to someone who can.

One of the best legacies a husband can leave his wife is to tell her where she should turn for advice if she needs it. During his lifetime he should see that she gets to know the people and the organizations he trusts. He might even find it advisable to leave a statement with his will, specifying who should be consulted if questions arise. Unless the widow is both well informed and wary, all a husband's careful plans for her future may be undone by incompetent or unscrupulous advisers.

In addition, in many states, small accounts—for example, those under $500—may be released by the bank to the wife as surviving joint depositor without the usual formalities. An alert probate attorney can usually get such needed funds released in a few days. If there are sizable claims against an estate and the settling of it is going to be delayed, the executor may have to ask the court to grant the wife a "widow's allowance." This permits payment of a monthly allowance to a widow during the period of administration. In some states this payment takes precedence over claims of creditors.

One important thing to remember: Don't take a shortcut to get cash. Fearful that she might lack funds to pay funeral, medical and other bills, one worried widow slipped into the bank the morning after her husband died and drew most of the cash out of their joint account before the bank heard of the death. When the court's appraiser learned of this, he tied up the estate for weeks until he satisfied himself that she was not trying to cheat the tax collector.

"She made two mistakes," a probate attorney points out. "First, she should not have taken the money from the bank. Second, she should not have paid the funeral and medical bills. The executor will pay them out of the estate's assets before taxes are computed. They're deductible expenses."

Another widow compounded her troubles by giving a valuable camera to a family friend, carrying out her late husband's wishes. The tax appraiser delayed his report to the court until he was satisfied that she had not similarly disposed of other assets. Meanwhile, she was strapped for cash.

"Never give away anything, not even a necktie, until the will is probated and the approval of the tax authorities has been obtained," one attorney warns.

## More Points to Remember

Where should one keep his will, insurance policies, deeds and other papers that suddenly become all-important when he dies? Is a safe-deposit box the right place, since the box might be sealed just when the papers are needed?

Ordinarily, the lawyer who draws the will likes to keep it, or a facsimile, in his safe, because he may be the executor or the executor's attorney handling the probate. The banker also likes to have a copy if his bank is named executor or trustee. One solution is to keep the paid-up insurance policies in the wife's personal safe-deposit box; the will can be left in the attorney's safe, with a copy for the husband's own files. The deeds to any plots of land and stock certificates can remain in the husband's safe-deposit box.

Thousands of families have moved from one state to another in recent years—as a result of business transfers, in search of new opportunity or for retirement. Many are caught unknowingly in the tangle of conflicting state regulations. In California, for example, their accumulations since the time they settled in the state are community property, but what they had accumulated before they became Californians is not. Bank trust officers and attorneys emphasize that families who have moved from one state to another should find out from their lawyers how the move has affected the ownership of their possessions.

How can a husband make sure he is not setting legal traps for his widow by well-intentioned but unwise planning? Obviously, it would take a whole book or more to point up all the pitfalls in 50 states. However, a composite of suggestions from many authorities would read like this:

1. Make an inventory of your assets—home, insurance, cash, securities, personal possessions—listing their approximate value. Update it each year.

2. If you have not already done so, draw up a will, with the help of a competent attorney. This is of crucial importance. Discuss matters with the attorney to make sure that your wishes, your assets and the law all mesh. Double-check with a trust officer of your bank.

3. Evolve a plan whereby, if you should die suddenly, your wife will have access to expense money.

4. Make sure your wife—before she is thrust unexpectedly into the problems of being a widow—knows what the family assets are and where to find records of ownership.

"I often think what a lot of time and money and grief for the widow might be spared," a probate attorney says, "if a departed husband could return for 20 minutes to answer a few simple questions about how he had intended her to handle his affairs."

# HOW
# TO SAVE MONEY UNDER
# THE NEW TAX LAW

*Learn the key points of the new law and
how you can cut your income tax bill when you
fill out your  federal returns*

# The New Tax Law— And What It Means to You

*The income tax reform bill passed by Congress in late 1969 provides a variety of ways in which the taxpayer can lighten his burden. This special section tells you how to take advantage of these new provisions and what you can expect to save.*

During the last few hours of 1969 President Richard M. Nixon signed the first major tax reform bill to pass Congress in 15 years. "Reform" it is called, but actually the new law is a combination of tax reform and tax relief. The reforms plug some of the loopholes and attempt to deal with some of the more glaring inequities. Tax relief is provided by shifting part of the tax burden upward, from low- and middle-income groups to those in the higher brackets. The result will be lower tax bills for a great majority of the country's individual taxpayers.

The relief doesn't come all at once, however. It is spread out in stair-step fashion over the four tax years starting with 1970. Until the April 15, 1974, tax deadline on 1973 income, most taxpayers will find that each year brings a different set of figures to be used in their calculations, affording some smaller or larger degree of additional relief. By the end of that time most will find that since 1969 there has been a change in the methods used to determine the tax owed and to ensure that everyone pays only what tax codes require, and no more.

## THE KEY CHANGES

Most of the reduction in tax payments has been brought about by two basic parts of the law:

- The *exemption* allowed each taxpayer for himself and for each of his dependents—generally but not very accurately known as the personal exemption—has been raised in four steps by 25 percent. For 1973 it will have risen from $600 to $750 per person in your immediate family.

The increase is the first in 22 years. Although the exemption was presumably created to lighten the tax burden of those less able to pay because of the number of mouths they had to feed, it had never been increased even while the cost of feeding mouths was rising inexorably. A principal beneficiary of tax relief cast in the form of greater exemptions, therefore, is the large family.

• The *standard deduction*, used by taxpayers who haven't enough tax-deductible expenses to make itemizing them worthwhile, has been increased in three steps to roughly half as much again as the old 10 percent of income with its maximum allowance of $1000. By 1973 you will be entitled to a standard deduction of 15 percent of your family income with a ceiling of $2000.

Chief beneficiaries of this measure are taxpayers at middle-income levels and below, especially single persons, young marrieds, apartment dwellers and renters. The effect is to give such taxpayers an automatic deduction equal to that previously enjoyed by homeowners, who could itemize up to $2000 in deductions of such major cost-of-living items as mortgage interest and real estate taxes. Conversely, it means that, in general, the mortgaged homeowner will benefit proportionately less from this provision of the tax bill—or not at all, if he has been itemizing deductions equal to 15 percent of his income, or more.

These are the two measures responsible for most of the tax relief. There are two others that will reduce or even eliminate tax bills for some taxpayers:

• *Single persons*—unmarried men and women, widows and widowers and the divorced—benefit by a narrowing of the spread between their tax rate and that of married couples filing joint returns. Before the new law single persons paid up to 141 percent of the tax called for by a joint return on the same amount of earned income. The new law limits the single person's tax to not more than 20 percent over that paid by a couple.

• A new *low-income allowance* wipes out taxes altogether for many subsistence-level families, provides sometimes substantial tax savings at income levels up to about $6667 and cuts taxes on the earnings of working students. If the allowance amounts to more than a taxpayer's percentage standard deduction, it can be claimed instead of the deduction and in addition to his exemptions. For example, a man making $5000 in 1973 would have a standard deduction of $750, figured at the new 15 percent rate. But the low-income allowance for that year is $1000. He is therefore entitled to reduce his taxable income by an additional $250 simply by substituting the allowance figure for the standard deduction figure. (For more information on limitations in the application of the low-income allowance, see page 602.)

## HOW RELIEF WILL COME

Here's how tax relief is scheduled to arrive, a bit at a time, from 1970 through 1973:

**1970**

• For most persons there was no effect on returns filed by April 15, covering 1969 taxes.

• At the first of the year, a drop in the surtax (10 percent in 1969) to 5 percent for the first half of 1970. After midyear, no more surtax (but there is a $2\frac{1}{2}$ percent surtax for the entire year when the return is filed).

• Effective July 1, an increase in the personal exemption from the old $600 to $650. Against income earned over the entire year, figure it as $625. This (along with the phasing out of the surtax) shows up in pay envelopes as more to take home; the increased exemption, as well as the dropping of the surtax, will be reflected in lowered withholdings for income tax beginning with the first pay period after July 1.

• Maximum low-income allowance is set at $1100 for all of 1970. The allowance is phased out as income increases.

**1971**

• Standard deduction increases to 13 percent of income, with a limit of $1500.

• Personal exemption of $650 is effective for the full year.

• Low-income allowance drops to $1050 (as increased deduction and exemption afford more relief).

**1972**

• Standard deduction increases to 14 percent of income, with a limit of $2000.

• Personal exemption increases to $700.

• Low-income allowance drops to $1000.

**1973**

• Standard deduction increases to, and remains at, 15 percent of income, with a limit of $2000.

• Personal exemption increases to, and remains at, $750.

## YOUR SHRINKING TAX BILL

Here's how these successive changes affect the tax bills of a family of three, using the standard deduction, at income levels up to $11,000:

FEDERAL TAXES DUE

| EARNED INCOME | 1969 INCOME | 1970 INCOME | 1971 INCOME | 1972 INCOME | 1973 INCOME | REDUCED FROM 1969 TO 1973 BY |
|---|---|---|---|---|---|---|
| $ 4,000 | $ 249 | $ 226 | $ 220 | $ 191 | $ 163 | 40.5 % |
| 5,000 | 424 | 399 | 354 | 322 | 290 | 34.4 % |
| 6,000 | 604 | 556 | 496 | 460 | 426 | 29.8 % |
| 7,500 | 881 | 811 | 729 | 687 | 644 | 26.9 % |
| 9,000 | 1163 | 1073 | 977 | 932 | 886 | 23.8 % |
| 11,000 | 1566 | 1443 | 1308 | 1258 | 1209 | 22.8 % |

Tax tables for 1971–1973 had not yet been issued at press time. Figures for these years may be lower than those given above.

At higher income levels, tax cuts are considerably smaller in terms of percentage reductions. The table below shows the amount that tax bills are down, after the four years of changes, for a family of three using itemized deductions, which average about 18 percent of income:

| EARNED INCOME | TAX ON 1969 INCOME | TAX ON 1973 INCOME | REDUCED BY, |
|---|---|---|---|
| $13,000 | $1726 | $1470 | 14.8 % |
| 15,000 | 2123 | 1830 | 13.8 % |
| 17,500 | 2638 | 2285 | 13.4 % |
| 20,000 | 3201 | 2798 | 12.6 % |
| 25,000 | 4418 | 3890 | 12.0 % |

To illustrate how the increased exemption works as a particular boon to large families, here is the way the tax bill falls, from 1969 to 1973, on family income of $10,000 as the number of dependents increases:

| | TAX ON 1969 INCOME | TAX ON 1973 INCOME | TAX REDUCED BY |
|---|---|---|---|
| Family of 3 . . . . . . . . . . . . . . | $1351 | $1048 | 22.4 % |
| Family of 4 . . . . . . . . . . . . . . | 1225 | 905 | 26.1 % |
| Family of 5 . . . . . . . . . . . . . . | 1100 | 763 | 30.6 % |
| Family of 6 . . . . . . . . . . . . . . | 975 | 620 | 36.4 % |

## OTHER IMPORTANT FEATURES

Many taxpayers will be affected by some of the additional provisions of the bill listed below. More information on these changes in the law will be found on the pages indicated.

• Filing and withholding procedures have been changed to help the taxpayer (see page 598).

- More buying power for retired people results from several features of the bill (see page 619).
- There is a new ceiling on the capital gains tax limit (see page 604).
- Taxpayers in high-income brackets both gain and lose (see page 607).
- It's easier to qualify for "income averaging" (see page 596).
- Rules for depreciating commercial real estate have been tightened (see page 608).
- Wealthy "hobby farmers" will find that they can no longer profit by operating at a loss (see page 616).
- A more liberal deduction is allowed for moving expenses (see page 613).

## How to Save Money Under the New Tax Law

*Follow this up-to-date advice to make sure you don't pay a penny more than you owe*

*Wherever examples and illustrations are used, the arithmetic has been based on tax rates, deductions, exemptions, and so on, as of 1973, when all provisions of the new tax law become fully effective. Note that a number of changes take place in a series of steps, leaving some discrepancies between the examples as given and the figures that would apply during these interim years from 1970 to 1973.*

After a June wedding in the Indiana town where they'd grown up together, Jerry and Lois set off on a honeymoon trip across the country. Before graduation Jerry had signed up with one of the company recruiters who had visited his college campus in Ohio, and the newlyweds had nearly a month before he was due to report for work on the West Coast.

It was a joyful, never-to-be-forgotten trip across the great American West, even though they did arrive on the Coast nearly dead broke. They didn't mind penny-pinching for the next couple of months; every time they had to dine on beans and franks they agreed it had been well worth it. And they might have enjoyed the trip even more if they'd known they could recover a good part of the cost the following

April, with tax savings. But, like most young people, they didn't pay that much attention to the subject of income taxes.

It's easy to fall into the habit of using the one-page form, and so avoid involvement with the extra "schedules" on the other pages of the tax form, which look so formidable—though actually their bark is worse than their bite. It's tempting to do it the short way: Take your standard deduction and your exemptions and look up the amount of tax you owe. Maybe you have to send in a few more dollars, or maybe you get a few back. No headaches, no long evenings sweating over your records for the year, no long columns of figures and hours of arithmetic.

Easy can be expensive, however. Many families, once they fall into the habit, continue doing it the easy way long after they could add together enough itemized deductions to cut their tax payment substantially. And even before that, there may be years when it's an expensive mistake for a young couple to assume that their finances are too simple and uncomplicated to yield any tax-saving possibilities. Here's how much that mistake cost Jerry and Lois:

When they made out their first joint return, after ten months of married life, they were so happily surprised by the results that they treated themselves to a candlelight-and-wine dinner. Jerry had two sources of income for the year: one a well-paid job he had held in college and then, beginning in July, his six months' employment in California. Between the two jobs, just a little less than $1100 had been withheld from his salary. With Lois looking over his shoulder, it took Jerry only a few minutes to add the two income figures together, enter the standard deduction, take their two exemptions and find in a table the amount of tax owed—only $938. The refund of $158 sounded like something to celebrate, so they celebrated. Most inappropriately, since they were paying about $130 more than they actually owed.

You'll nearly always have excess tax withheld when you work a short year. The amount withheld from each paycheck by your employer is determined by a Treasury Department withholding schedule. If your salary is $10,000 a year, the amounts withheld are based on the tax you'd ordinarily pay on $10,000 of earnings. If you work only half a year and earn $5000, you're in a much lower bracket, and the amount withheld during the six months will be considerably more than the amount of tax owed.

The reductions to which Jerry was entitled, but either didn't know about or missed because he did his return the short, easy way, illustrate a number of the more commonly neglected tax savers:

*Overpayment of Social Security tax.* During the five months that Jerry worked at his part-time job in college, his employer withheld from each paycheck the required amount for F.I.C.A. (Federal Insurance Contributions Act), or Social Security, tax. The W-2 form that was mailed to him shortly after the end of the year by his college employer showed the total withheld as $145.20. The W-2 form supplied by his new employer showed what had been withheld during the latter half of the year: $260.00

The two figures came to $30.80 more than the Social Security tax required on Jerry's earnings for the year—and he should have subtracted that amount directly from the "total tax" figure near the end of his return. An overpayment of your F.I.C.A. is not a "deduction," so you don't have to itemize your deductions to get the benefit.

This is an easy one to miss. There is a line on the tax form that invites you to subtract "excess F.I.C.A. tax withheld"—but the form doesn't lead you through the figuring that tells you whether or not there was an excess. For that you have to read the instructions that come with your form. If you have had more than one employer during the year, you may have overpaid Social Security taxes,

□□□□□□

## THE NEW TAX LAW:
## EASIER INCOME AVERAGING

If your income takes a big jump in one year, it's often possible to avoid paying your tax in the bracket that you've reached by a method that is called income averaging.

Simplified, this means treating your peak-year income as if it had been spread over the past five-year period, along with the previous income you received during that time. This can result in considerable savings. The new law eases the conditions you must meet in order to "average," mainly by reducing the amount your income must increase before you qualify. Prior to the new law, the peak-year income had to be more than $3000 and a third more than the average of the earlier four years; now you can average if it's only a fifth more and more than $3000.

Income averaging entails complicated tax computations and you may need expert help. Many tax advisers are reluctant to suggest income averaging unless the potential saving is quite large, because it may expose four years of past income tax returns to critical examination.

□□□□□□

because each employer is required by law to withhold for Social Security as if beginning from the first of the year—regardless of how much may have been withheld by another employer earlier in the year. You should always have a credit coming for excess withholding, therefore, if you have two or more jobs during the year and your combined income from them is more than the amount subject to F.I.C.A. withholding.

*Moving expense adjustment.* If you move to a new residence during the year because of a new job location, you're entitled to an adjustment to cover moving expenses—if you bear the cost yourself and aren't reimbursed by your employer.

This applies not only to someone who's changing jobs but to anyone who changes his residence in going to work for the first time. A young person starting out on his first job will usually have had his parents' home as his legal residence. He or she is entitled to deduct allowable moving expenses if the general requirements are met: The move must be at least 50 miles (measured by the shortest of the more commonly traveled routes between two points), and the new job has to be permanent—meaning that you must work in your new location at least 39 weeks out of the next 12 months—or Uncle Sam will take your moving allowance back next year.

Jerry was entitled to deduct the "reasonable costs" of getting himself, other members of his family (Lois), their household goods, personal effects and pets from his former residence in Indiana to his new one on the West Coast. Since they went by car, they had a choice between five cents a mile (over the shortest, most direct route—not all of their honeymoon ramblings) and actual out-of-pocket expenses for gas, oil, repairs and other normal expenses. They could have deducted the cost of meals and lodging while traveling, for those days required by a direct route, and the $40 shipping charges on the trunks and cartons that followed them to their new home. Finally, their motel room and meals during the four days they spent looking for an apartment were deductible expenses.

So there was nearly $400 that Jerry could have taken as a deduction from gross income. He needn't have itemized his deductions to get this sizable tax break; while taking the standard deduction, he could have deducted moving costs and had that much less income to pay tax on.

Missing this one resulted in Jerry's paying $63 more tax than he needed to. That's $93.80 that he's donated to the government so far.

━ ▭ ▭ ▭ ▭ ▭

### THE NEW TAX LAW: CHANGES IN FILING AND WITHHOLDING

When the amounts withheld from your earnings are more than enough to pay your tax bill, you are in effect making an interest-free loan to Uncle Sam— poor financial management, from the taxpayer's point of view. The new law makes it easier to avoid this. For example: You know that unusually large medical expenses are going to result in a deduction lowering your tax payment well below your normal withholding schedule. While formerly you could avoid excess withholding because of large itemized deductions by filing a Form W–4 Schedule A, with your employer, the new law eases the requirement that must be met to qualify for additional withholding allowances.

The reverse of this situation occurs when you receive income from supplemental employment benefits or taxable income from annuities or pensions not covered by withholding. To avoid having to cover these at tax time, you may now request an employer or the source of your annuity payments to withhold as much as necessary.

Many college students with part-time jobs will benefit from the new regulations regarding who must file a return. Under the old rule anyone under sixty-five with income of $600 or more in the year had to file. With exceptions for some married couples, filing requirements were raised to levels more nearly reflecting the low-income allowance and the taxpayer's own personal exemptions. For 1973, for example, a single person with income less than $1750 ($1700 till then) is not required to file. And where the earnings of such a person would normally be subject to withholding, making it necessary to file a return to secure a refund, the new rules allow an employe to file a statement certifying that he had no tax liability for the previous year and will have none for the year. The employer is then not required to withhold for taxes and the wage earner will no longer have money "borrowed" from him, only to be returned the following year as a refund.

▭ ▭ ▭ ▭ ▭ ▭

*Sick pay you can exclude.* In September Jerry agreed to let a couple of his new friends introduce him to the sport of mountain climbing. He fell off a ledge, broke his leg, spent 2 days in the hospital and was laid up at home, for a total of 15 working days. Company policy provided that he receive 70 percent of his regular pay during this period.

If Jerry had shown more interest in his tax forms he might have noticed a section that allows for excluding sick pay, and if he'd investigated this deduction from gross income (treated the same way as moving expenses), he'd have found that he could exclude $225 from the amount of income he was required to pay tax on.

The sick pay exclusion is a bit complicated, but it's worth making the effort to understand it.

1. You must be absent from work because of sickness or injury, but whether either was incurred in connection with your work is immaterial.

2. You must be absent from work longer than the prescribed waiting period (see below).

3. Your employer must have a regular, established policy concerning sick pay. It doesn't have to be an insurance plan; there doesn't even have to be anything in writing concerning the plan: It need only be an established, consistent practice.

If these conditions are met, you can exclude from taxable income pay received while sick, as follows:

If you receive more than 75 percent of your regular pay while absent, there is a 30-day waiting period before you start excluding sick pay.

If you receive 75 percent or less of your regular pay, there is no waiting period if you're hospitalized for at least one day (at any time during the period of absence). If you're not hospitalized, there's a seven-day waiting period before you begin excluding your pay.

For the first 30 days of absence, you can exclude up to $75 a week of sick pay after your waiting period, if any. After 30 days the limitation rises to $100 a week.

It's made somewhat more complicated than this by rules concerning holidays, work days, and so forth, but simply doing the step-by-step arithmetic on the required form is less difficult than it sounds. You fill out tax form No. 2440, "Statement to Support Exclusion of Sick Pay," when you claim this one.

If Jerry had taken the exclusion he was entitled to, it would have lowered his tax payment by another $36. He has now charged himself $130, less a few cents, for taxes he wasn't required to pay.

## Claiming Your Deductions

Within a few years Jerry's position with the company was secure, and with a first child on the way he and Lois became the owners of a modest split-level house in the suburbs. Now Jerry was prepared to take seriously the question of itemizing his deductions, for he was well aware that the tax advantages of homeownership are one of the attractions cited by both those who have houses to sell and those with a desire to own.

Once you've become a homeowner, as Jerry and Lois discovered, it's impossible to ignore that section of the tax return where you itemize your deductions. For the family with a typical suburban mortgage, acquired within the last ten years or so, two items alone— mortgage interest and real estate taxes—will bulk larger, together, than their standard deduction. It's because they can't claim these two major and best-known deductions that many nonowners make little or no effort to keep track of, look for and total up individual deductible items. They assume it's only a matter of a few dollars here and a few there, which never add up to anything very impressive. But you'll find in fact that they frequently exceed the standard, if you know your deductions and what to look for.

There is no attempt here to cover the exotic items that may apply to one taxpayer in a thousand. We're concerned mainly with the individual or family on a salaried income, whose finances are fairly simple and straightforward—no investments in oil-prospecting syndicates, no portfolio of tax-exempt securities, no equipment leasebacks or similar arrangements that are a comfort to those in the upper tax brackets. Forgetting such as these, your deductions fall into a few major categories.

*Interest.* If you're making much use of credit, borrowed money or installment buying, the amount you're laying out for interest charges may surprise you when all the items are added up.

Aside from the home mortgage, the biggest and even more common item in this era of mobility is the cost of financing an automobile. If you've financed $2500 of the purchase price, for example, you're going to pay from around $120 to perhaps twice that as interest, depending on who's doing your financing and whether it's a new or used car. A revolving charge account, where there's an average of $150 a month on the books, will typically cost around $27 a year, usually designated as "finance charges." Where the interest charge is not stated separately, the deduction for finance charges is limited to 6 percent of the average monthly unpaid balance.

The same is true for educational services where carrying charges are separately stated but interest charges cannot be ascertained. For example, when educational costs such as tuition, fees and lodging are paid on an installment plan, you may assume that carrying charges include interest of 6 percent on the average unpaid monthly balance and include this among your deductions for interest.

Financing "big ticket" items often involves signing a note for the purchase price plus interest. Interest may be charged either by the "add on" method or by discount. In the latter case, what shows as the amount you received will be less than the actual amount of the loan. With 7 percent interest being charged, for example, you would receive only $1116 on a face amount of $1200 if repayment called for 12 monthly installments. The one year's interest of $84 would be subtracted from the $1200 you theoretically borrowed. In calculating your deductions for interest, you claim not 7 percent of the $1116 you received ($78.12), but 7 percent of the $1200 face amount, $84. This is not considered interest paid in advance and is deductible only as the loan is repaid.

*State and local taxes.* The homeowner is by no means the only one who pays deductible taxes in substantial amounts. Especially in view of the growing use and rising rates of state income taxes, and the sales and use taxes now levied by both state and city, almost anyone can add up enough open and hidden taxes to constitute a major deductible item.

What kinds of taxes are deductible? They must fall into one of these categories:

1. Income tax imposed by a state or local taxing authority or paid to a foreign government.

2. State or local general sales tax. The word that tells you whether or not it's deductible is "general." That means it is imposed at a uniform rate on retail sales of all tangible personal property. A tax that's imposed only on cigarettes, for example, or theater admissions or specified luxury items is not general. Certain items may be excepted, however, from the general tax—food, for instance—or taxed at a lower rate. It's when a tax is selective that it fails to qualify as general.

3. State or local gasoline sales tax. This is deductible so long as it is stated separately from the retail price and passed on to the consumer.

4. Personal property taxes, state or local, only when they are ad valorem, that is, based on the value of the property taxed.

5. Real property (real estate) taxes, imposed by a state, local or foreign government, when levied for the general public welfare. That eliminates, generally, assessments for local benefits and improvements—but see comments on this in the section below on the homeowner's taxes.

Taxes that don't fit one of the above descriptions generally are not deductible for federal income tax purposes. Fees for driver's licenses, hunting and fishing licenses, dog taxes, marriage license fees and such—even though they may bear the name of tax—are not generally taxes and don't qualify.

You may be able to increase your deductions for taxes if you're willing to keep careful and detailed records of your expenditures. Federal income tax instructions, for example, include each year a guideline table indicating what the IRS considers a reasonable deduction for sales tax paid during the year, state by state, for family units of different sizes in the various income brackets. You're told here that if you bought an automobile during the year you can add its sales tax to the figure given in the table. Other items for which the tax can be added, if taxed at the general rate, are airplanes, boats, mobile homes and material to build a new home. Other "big ticket" items bought during the year are included in the sales tax table. By keeping receipts and records covering every penny of expenditure, a number of taxpayers have found that sales taxes cost them considerably more than the table allowed. Be prepared to support your deduction with the necessary records if it is much higher than the

▱▱▱▱▱▱

## THE NEW TAX LAW:
## LIMITS ON THE LOW-INCOME ALLOWANCE

You can't take advantage of the new "low-income allowance" unless you have a relatively low income. For example: The allowance is set at $1100 for income earned in 1970. Does this mean that a taxpayer with an income of $9000 in this year, who is limited to 10 percent or $900 as his standard deduction, can claim the low-income allowance and a deduction of $1100? The answer is no.

The low-income allowance was designed primarily to eliminate income tax for people with poverty-level

income. For 1972 and later years the low-income allowance is a flat $1000, but special conditions apply during the 1970 and 1971 tax years. In those years the low-income allowance consists of the "basic allowance" and an "additional allowance." The additional portion of low-income allowance is reduced by $1 for every $2 for 1970 and $1 for every $15 for 1971 that your income exceeds the "no-tax" level. That is determined by adding together the maximum low-income allowance and the personal exemptions that can be claimed by the individual or family. For the 1970 tax year, with the allowance at $1100, income tax is eliminated as follows:

▱▱▱▱▱▱

table allows. The IRS hasn't any use for estimates or what you remember.

Another possibility is that you're paying more gasoline tax than the IRS tables estimate for you, based on miles driven during the year and the tax rate in your state. The tables seem to assume that everybody gets around 14 miles per gallon—though if "all or part" of your mileage was driven in a four-cylinder car, you're instructed to deduct half the amount shown in the table, which presumably means that you should average 28 miles per gallon if you drive a beetle half the time and an Indianapolis 500 Offenhauser the other half. At any rate, if you drive a gas hog, do a thorough job of record keeping on gas purchases and you'll cut your income tax. Good gas records are particularly necessary when you cover a substantial amount of mileage in high-tax states and live in a low-tax state. Let's say you live in Missouri (five cents a gallon) but do half your driving for the year in North Carolina (nine cents). If you file your tax return from Missouri, you'll have to take the five-cent allowance unless you're prepared for the possibility of a tax examiner turning a cold and disbelieving stare on your deduction. Keep good records, and let him stare.

Single person, $1100 allowance + $625 exemption = $1725.
Two in family, $1100 allowance + $1250 exemptions = $2350.
Three in family, $1100 allowance + $1875 exemptions = $2975.

Applying the rule of $1 reduction for each $2 of excess income, a family of three with a 1970 income of $3975—$1000 above the no-tax level—would have to reduce the low-income allowance by half of $1000, or from $1100 to $600. That's still an advantage over the regular standard deduction, but the advantage for the family of three is wiped out when income reaches $5000. At this point the percentage standard deduction (10 percent) is equal to the low-income allowance of $500—the basic allowance for a family of three and not subject to reduction.

The rule on reduction applies only to 1970 and 1971 income, though; thereafter, any taxpayer can use the $1000 low-income allowance if it's to his advantage. When his income reaches $6667, the 15 percent standard deduction will give him a deduction of $1000.05. The low-income allowance generally will not have to be computed by taxpayers. Tax tables, which cover incomes up to $10,000, give the taxpayer the larger of the percentage standard deduction or low-income allowance.

*Medical and dental expenses.* If you add up only your payment of doctors' and dentists' bills for the year, you may be ignoring a good share of your allowable expenses. Among the items that have been ruled deductible as medical expense are elastic hosiery, whirlpool baths, plywood bedboards to relieve back ailments, arch supports, back supports, reclining chairs, a wig for a woman who was emotionally upset over loss of her hair, payments to unlicensed healers. Some aids to health of this type may be disallowed by the IRS unless prescribed by a physician, it's true, but the list may suggest deductible expenses that you'd otherwise overlook. If they're on the doubtful side, you would be wise to check them out with a qualified tax adviser.

One item in medical and dental expenses that's often missed is transportation. The Treasury Department doesn't expect you to walk to and from your appointments. When you take a bus or a cab the fares are a legitimate part of the cost of seeing the doctor or dentist. If you drive your own car, you can deduct either actual out-of-pocket expenses for gas, oil and other operational costs or five cents a mile. Where an adult or attendant has to accompany a child, that transportation expense is also deductible as a medical expense.

Until fairly recently the average family wasn't able to claim a deduction for medical and dental expenses until the year's bills climbed well above normal. The reason was the reducible feature of this deduction. You added up actual expenses and then deducted from that total 3 percent of your income; what was left—if anything— you could take as your income tax deduction. If the family income

━━━━━━

### THE NEW TAX LAW:
### CHANGES IN
### CAPITAL GAINS RATES

The new tax law does lop off some of the advantage of long-term capital gains treatment—but only for those in exceptionally high tax brackets. The old law said that no matter how high your tax rate on ordinary income, you never had to pay more than 25 percent on long-term capital gains. That rule now applies only to the first $50,000 of such income. Above that, long-term capital gains are taxed at half the taxpayer's ordinary income rate, beginning with 1972. The rate for 1970 is 29½ percent and for 1971, 32 percent of your long-term capital gains above the $50,000 annual limit.

━━━━━━

was $10,000, for example, you subtracted $300 from your total medical-dental expenses of $305, leaving $5 as the deduction.

That situation has been greatly improved, from the taxpayer's point of view, by separating from other medical-dental expenses the premiums paid for medical insurance. Notice on your tax form that now you list one half of your insurance premiums (up to $150), and then your other expenses less a percentage of income. One half of what you pay for insurance is *not* whittled down by the percentage-of-income deduction; you can use it to reduce your income tax payment even if you don't have a dime's worth of doctor or dental bills during the year. You may not even be aware of how much you're paying for medical insurance if you participate in a company plan where you pay part of the cost and your employer the other part, with your share taken out of paychecks. In one typical plan the employe has $7.15 deducted from each semimonthly paycheck. That's a yearly total of $171.60, of which he can take half, $85.80, as an income tax deduction independently of any other medical or dental expenses for the year. You can add the excess premiums to your other medical-dental expenses, which are subject to the percentage reduction.

Caution: Medical insurance, to qualify for this deduction, must be of the type that specifically reimburses you for medical, dental and hospital bills. The so-called hospital policy that pays you a specified sum of money each week when you're hospitalized, without regard to your actual bills, does not qualify.

You *can* deduct premiums for: (1) policies that reimburse either you, or the doctor, hospital or laboratory direct for billed fees and charges; (2) membership in an association providing cooperative or "free choice" medical or hospital care; (3) group clinical and hospital care; (4) the medical-care portion of a policy that provides more than one type of reimbursement; (5) policies that reimburse the cost of prescription drugs; (6) policies that reimburse for dental services or group plans providing for services; (7) the supplementary medical insurance available to Medicare beneficiaries—but not the part of the Social Security tax that covers Medicare itself.

*Contributions.* Many taxpayers fail to claim deductions for contributions to which they're actually entitled, because of the widespread misconception that only contributions to church and charity qualify. The tax code is, in fact, much more flexible.

You may deduct contributions to a nonprofit organization

605

operated for religious, charitable, scientific, literary or educational purposes or for prevention of cruelty to children or animals. You may deduct contributions to the United States, a territory or possession, or any state, city, town or other agency of local government for "public purposes." Those two words cover a wide range of worthy causes: public works (the construction of highways, parks, dams), highway safety programs, conservation, wildlife preservation and public welfare, to suggest only a few. Agencies created by federal or local governments are included: civil defense units, police departments, fire departments, park districts.

You may deduct contributions to a fraternal organization operating under the lodge system if contributions are used for any of the principal purposes enumerated above. Contributions to nonprofit war veterans' groups and auxiliaries are deductible. So are contributions to nonprofit cemetery and burial associations if they benefit the whole cemetery and not your individual plot.

The contribution need not be in cash; it may be in kind. Let's take a few everyday examples:

You're a den mother. The Boy (Cub) Scouts is an approved organization. The cost of the uniform you buy or make is a deductible contribution. So is the cost of laundering or cleaning. Both the cost and the upkeep of uniforms worn while performing donated services are deductible.

You buy a ticket, for $10, for a benefit performance with proceeds going to the Weehawken Committee to Preserve the Pie-Billed Grebe. If you bought it on the open market, this ticket would cost you $2. The difference—$8—is a deductible contribution.

You buy a chance on a station wagon being raffled off by St.-Eustasius-on-the-Moor, for $2. Deductible? Sorry, no. (But you can offset the $2 gambling loss against gambling profits you may have had during the year.)

Every Thursday night you spend three hours as a volunteer, unpaid worker at your local charitable family service agency. Do you have a deduction? Yes. Not for the value of your time but—unless the agency is within walking distance—for your transportation.

Contributions of property other than money are just as deductible as cash—except that you must include with your return a statement of (1) the kind of property donated and (2) the method used to determine the fair market value of the property, which is the amount you may deduct. If the market value is more than $200, considerably more elaborate information is required. Details are given in IRS Publication No. 526, *Income Tax Deduction for Contributions.*

The opportunity to make a deductible gift of property that's undoubtedly missed by thousands of taxpayers every year is the contribution to your favorite appropriate charity of used clothing, household goods or furniture. Concerning the latter two, you'll have to let your conscience be your guide in valuing your contribution. In the case of used clothing and household textiles there's a formula for arriving at fair market value, developed by the National Institute of Drycleaning. Its *National Fair Claims Guide for Consumer Textile Products* is primarily for use in the cleaning trade in adjusting claims for lost, stolen or damaged clothing or textiles. Although use of the guide is not officially sanctioned, tax experts say it may be helpful in establishing the value of donated clothing for tax purposes. To simplify calculations, however, the nationally sponsored Textiles for Charity program has adopted the single formula of 15 percent of *replacement* cost as a basis for valuation.

Ordinarily you should have receipts to support claims of contributions. If contributions of clothing or other property are picked up by the organization you're donating them to, list the items and their value and have the collector sign for their receipt. If the value involved is modest, however, you can put them in a collection box maintained by an organization, keeping for your tax records an

=========

## THE NEW TAX LAW:
## FOR THE AFFLUENT—
## BAD NEWS AND GOOD

Taxpayers in the higher brackets find both bad news and good in the new tax law. It is bad for the small group that has made such cunning use of tax shelters that they've paid no income tax whatever, although their actual income ranged from $250,000 to $1 million or more. Now they must pay at least a minimum tax, established as a percentage of income that was formerly shielded by so-called tax preferences.

The news is better for those who receive primarily earned income—as opposed to investment income—but enough of it to push them into very high tax brackets. Well-paid executives and self-employed persons are most affected. Where previously they might be subject to the maximum 70 percent tax rate on earned income, the new law limits this to a maximum of 60 percent in 1971 and 50 percent in succeeding years.

=========

itemized list as above, with a notation on the location of the collection box and the date deposited.

If there is any question in your mind about whether a given organization qualifies for deductible contributions, the organization itself can tell you whether it's on the Treasury Department's list of approved organizations.

Up to this point we've covered the deductions that are spelled out on your tax form, each with a section of its own where you can furnish the required information. Then, almost as a footnote, there's a reference to "miscellaneous deductions." Only those who are curious enough to give the instructions a careful reading or dig into an income tax manual can unravel the mysteries of the miscellaneous deductions. Like a majority of taxpayers, you may not even know their names and so may be overpaying your tax because you don't know when to take advantage of them.

*Employe business expenses.* Even though you are a salaried employe or an hourly wage earner, certain required job expenses may be deductible. Here are some examples.:

● Union initiation fees and dues; union assessments for pension funds and for unemployment benefit funds, but not assessments for sickness, accident or death benefits.

⸺⸺⸺

## THE NEW TAX LAW: REAL ESTATE REFORMS

The high profits enjoyed by some real estate developers and operators in the past, through the aid of the "rapid write-off," are severely curtailed by the new law. Owners of new residential property are little affected, but office building centers and other commercial real estate, where most of the lush profits were to be found, must now be depreciated at lower rates. By using accelerated depreciation (coupled with a high debt ratio to create large mortgage-interest deductions), a real estate investor was formerly able to bunch together such large deductible expenses in the early years of ownership that, for tax purposes, he could show he was operating at a loss or at only a small profit. Actually, however, enough cash might be flowing in to give him an extraordinarily good rate of return on his own relatively small investment. As a result of the new tax law, it's no longer possible for the developer of commercial real estate to realize profit in this way. From now on, accelerated depreciation is available only to owners of new residential construction for rental use. New commercial property and used residential rental units get partial benefits.

⸺⸺⸺

● Service charges—equivalent to union dues—paid by non-members as a condition of employment.

● Fees paid to an employment agency to get a job.

● Membership dues in professional societies.

● Subscriptions to technical or professional publications, and books of a similar nature, if they have a short useful life (otherwise—and it's hard to pin a definition on "short"—you depreciate them).

● Uniforms and work clothes, under certain conditions. As a rule, the cost of work clothes is *not* deductible—but if your job requires you to wear a distinctive uniform or clothing that's not suitable for ordinary wear, the cost probably is a deductible expense. "Distinctive" is important. A painter, for example, was not allowed to deduct the cost of his "uniform" because his white overalls, cap, and so on, even though required by job rules, were just plain white overalls.

● If the cost of your work clothing qualifies as deductible, then so does the cost of keeping it cleaned or laundered and repaired.

● Protective clothing—such as safety shoes and helmets, a commercial fisherman's oilskins and boots.

● Small tools and supplies not furnished by your employer.

● Laboratory breakage fees paid by research workers.

● Premiums for surety or fidelity bonds, if required by your job and paid by you.

● Substitutes paid by teachers and others required to reimburse replacements when absent.

● Periodic physical examinations required by your job, if they are paid for by you.

● Transportation, under certain circumstances. If you're moonlighting, or working at two places the same day, the cost of getting from one job location to another is deductible. If you go home in between, say for dinner, you can still deduct what it would cost to go directly from one job to another. Otherwise, however, the cost of travel from home to work and vice versa is not deductible, with some few exceptions. Transportation and travel expense are deducted from gross income rather than under miscellaneous expense. Thus, you can deduct them while claiming the standard deduction.

● Educational expenses. These are a special kind of employe business expense, deductible in certain circumstances. They are if the education or training maintains or improves the skills required by your job duties. That is, if you're improving your ability, making yourself promotable in your present job, educational costs are deductible. But if they're to qualify you for a new kind of job, business or profession, you'll have to pay your own way.

*Casualty losses and thefts.* Here is another type of claim to a miscellaneous deduction. A casualty is defined by the IRS as damage to property resulting from an "identifiable event of a sudden, unexpected or unusual nature." Thus, if lightning strikes a tree, it's a casualty loss. If the tree is toppled by Dutch elm disease it isn't a casualty, even if it falls over in the middle of the night, quite unexpectedly. If your house is knocked off its foundations by a runaway bulldozer, it's a casualty loss—but not if it falls off some night, to your sudden dismay, because erosion has been gnawing away at the foundations for two or three years.

You can deduct nonbusiness casualty losses to the extent that they exceed $100 per claim and are not reimbursed by insurance. Your car is damaged in a collision, and repairs cost $450. An insurance company settles with you for $200. Of your $250 loss, you bear the first $100 alone; the remaining $150 you can deduct as a casualty loss.

*Child care.* Women (and in some cases men) who have to pay for child care while they're at work—or for the care of an incapacitated adult—can claim a deduction for this expense, subject to certain limitations. Any working woman may claim the deduction—whether single, married, widowed, separated, divorced or deserted—but it's available only to men who are widowed, divorced or legally separated, or whose wives are incapacitated or institutionalized.

The deduction is allowed for care of a child under thirteen years of age, to the extent of actual expenses incurred, up to the limitation set by the tax code. (If there are two or more children under thirteen, the limitation is increased by 50 percent.) In the case of a married woman, when family income exceeds a certain figure, the child-care deduction is reduced dollar-for-dollar by the excess. If there is no husband, or if he's incapacitated, the full deduction is allowed regardless of the amount of the woman's income. For the rules governing reductions in relation to income, refer to the instructions accompanying current tax forms. Form 2241, which may be filed if the deduction is claimed, takes you through the computing. These rules also apply to someone who is looking for work.

*Alimony payments.* It's doubtless unnecessary to tell anyone who's making them that these are included in miscellaneous deductions. They are deductible by the former husband and reported as income by the former wife. A lump-sum settlement payment to a former spouse is not deductible, however. Child support is neither deductible nor reported by the former wife as income.

*Safe-deposit box rental.* This is a deductible item if it's used for safe-keeping of securities certificates or other paper relating to investment income, in which case it's part of the cost of generating income. If it's used only for storing "valuable papers" that do not generate taxable income, the rental is not deductible.

*Cost of preparing tax returns.* Fees charged for tax counsel or assistance in preparing returns are deductible, as are tax manuals, handbooks, guides and other explanatory material. A good manual at a bargain price is the one published yearly by the Internal Revenue Service, *Your Federal Income Tax*, which sells for 60 cents. Ask for "the Blue Book" at your district IRS office. You can deduct the price.

## Joint or Separate Returns?

When a married couple like Jerry and Lois itemize deductions, in some circumstances it's to their advantage to file separate returns.

Ordinarily you'll pay less tax on a joint return, because what it does is split the family income down the middle and attribute half of it to each of you. For example, if the total family income is the husband's salary of $10,000, a joint return will result in the same amount of tax that's paid by two individuals, each earning $5000. You benefit from the lower tax bracket.

Separate returns sometimes result in paying less tax when both husband and wife have taxable income and they have one or more large, deductible expenses during the year, such as a hospital bill. For example, this family of three: Jerry's income is $9000, Lois' is $5500. Medical-dental expenses for the year total $800—$775 incurred by Lois, $25 by Jerry. Other itemized deductions come to $2500. By filing separate returns instead of jointly, they can cut their tax payment by about $43. Lois lists only her own medical-dental bills under deductions, and takes her personal exemption. Jerry takes his $2500 of itemized deductions, his personal exemption and that of their child. Their tax is less because the medical expenses are reduced, not by 3 percent of the $14,500 family income, but by a much smaller amount, 3 percent of Lois' $5500.

Note that when separate returns are filed, if either the husband or the wife itemizes deductions, the other must itemize also. Regulations prohibit one itemizing and the other taking a standard deduction.

611

If both choose to use the standard deduction when filing separately, the maximum is $500 for 1970, $750 for 1971 and $1000 for 1972 and later years. The maximum standard deduction allowed on a joint return is double the above amounts.

## Tax Tips for Homeowners

*Mortgage interest.* Traditional advice concerning a mortgage is: Pay it off as quickly as you can, to spare yourself as much as possible of the enormous interest cost that piles up on a long-term mortgage. It will be pointed out, as an example, that if you pay off a 7 percent, $18,000 loan in 20 years your interest costs are $15,493, while if you pay it off in 12 years they are $8654—and doesn't it make sense to save nearly $7000 if you can? It sounds like an irresistible argument; the only thing wrong with it is that it leaves out some of the facts. Using your spare money to get the mortgage paid off as rapidly as possible is not always to your advantage.

Let's say that Jerry and Lois have just become the proud mortgagors in the loan referred to above—$18,000 at 7 percent, 20-year term. After making mortgage payments for a year, Jerry has $1000 left over from a Christmas bonus. Should they apply it to paying off the mortgage?

1. If they do, the mortgage will be paid off about three years earlier than the scheduled 20 years, and total interest costs will be about $2489 less. In effect, they give up $1000 of cash-in-hand now in order to have $2489 more in the family accounts 16 years from now. That's a good deal, isn't it?

Not particularly, in comparison to how they'd come out if they took their $1000 cash-in-hand and put it, instead, into a savings account paying 6 percent compounded quarterly. On mortgage-burning day the account would have a balance of about $2593. That's only about $100 more than Jerry and Lois would save in interest charges on the mortgage, to be sure, but . . .

2. By applying the extra $1000 to reducing the principal of the mortgage loan, they reduce the amount of interest paid during the coming year, and hence their income tax deduction for interest—by $72. The effect of this is a loss of $14 in tax savings for the year, given their taxable income of $9000, for by this time Lois has stopped working. (The higher the tax bracket, the more is lost in tax savings, of course.)

In each succeeding year, the effect of the lower interest payment will be reflected in the lower deduction and a slightly higher tax bill. It would be fictional to calculate the difference in taxes 16 years ahead, since both tax rates and Jerry and Lois' tax status are sure to change. But, neglecting that, the difference can be estimated at around $150. That, added to the $100 advantage noted above, puts Jerry and Lois about $250 ahead. And in addition . . .

3. There is the familiar argument that as the years go by you're paying off a long-term loan with "cheap money" because of inflation. What course inflation will take in the next 16 years is anybody's guess, but most economists seem to agree that in an economy posited on growth, at least a mild accompanying rise in prices and wages is a built-in feature. So it's probable that Jerry and Lois will find it easier, and "cheaper," to come up with the $139.55 monthly payment ten years from now than they do today.

4. The final factor Jerry and Lois have to take into consideration is how successful they are at managing surplus funds. We've only assumed that their alternative use of the $1000 would be to put it in a savings account paying somewhat less than the top rate. If Jerry has the knack of finding places to put a spare $1000 where it will yield a return of 8, 10 or 12 percent a year, then they ought to invest the $1000. When you take into account the tax savings because of the

═ ═ ═ ═ ═ ═

## THE NEW TAX LAW:
### YOUR MOVING EXPENSES

The new tax law considerably liberalizes the rules on job-related moving expenses. First of all, if it's necessary to make a house-hunting trip to the site of a new job, costs of transportation and lodging and meals away from home are now allowed as part of your moving expenses. Formerly they were not.

Second, if you do your house hunting after you move to a new job location, or if for some reason you can't occupy your new home at once, you may also include as a moving expense your meals and lodging, near your new job site, for a maximum of 30 days.

Third, expenses "incidental" to the sale of your former house or to the purchase or lease of a new home may also be included. There is, however, a limit of $1000 on the amount you can claim for the first two of the above expenses and an overall limit of $2500. Note also that where a 20-mile move used to qualify for an adjustment to income, the new law says your move must be at least 50 miles. For details about other conditions concerning moving expenses, see the instructions included with your tax forms.

═ ═ ═ ═ ═ ═

interest deduction, Jerry and Lois are paying their mortgage lender not his 7 percent, but an effective rate of about 6.6 percent. If Jerry, as an investor, can better 6.6 percent, then he's ahead when he continues using the mortgagee's money instead of paying it back.

*Real estate taxes.* Those that are general and levied for the public welfare are deductible. Taxes such as special assessments to provide local benefits and improvements, which tend to increase the value of the assessed property, are not deductible. However, if the tax is levied to cover costs of maintenance or repair of a "local benefit" or to pay interest charges, the tax is deductible.

*Tax savings when you sell your house.* One occasion on which many homeowners fail to take advantage of tax savings they're entitled to is when the home is sold.

When you sell a house for more than you paid for it, the profit is taxable income. Specifically, to the tax people, it's a capital gain. There are two kinds of capital gain, taxed at different rates. Short-term capital gains are treated like ordinary income; long-term capital gains are taxed at a lower rate. It's a long-term capital gain, by current definition, if you've held it more than six months from date of acquisition to date of disposal. Such gains or profits are taxed at half the rate of your ordinary income, but at no more than 25 percent for most taxpayers. If you realize a gain of $2000 on a house you've owned longer than six months, you include only half the gain, $1000, in your taxable income.

Homeowners get a special break in being able to defer payment of the tax when they sell at a profit. If you buy and occupy another house within 12 months after sale of the old one, and it costs at least as much as the adjusted sale price of the one that you sold, you report the gain but don't pay it, for the present. But it's only postponed, not forgiven. Whenever in the future you take any profit out of the sale of a house, Uncle Sam will be waiting to collect. If you're between houses longer than 12 months (18 months if you build), the tax falls due. The idea that the tax is forgiven has made many homeowners careless about doing everything possible to reduce their tax liability when they sell—and a great deal is possible.

The word you have to learn is "basis." The selling price of your house is not what determines your gain (or loss). Basis is all-important. There's nothing difficult about it. Let's say you buy a house for $18,000 and a year later add on another room at a cost of $2000. From the tax collector's point of view you just bought another

$2000 worth of house. When you sell the house you will report, for tax purposes, that you paid $20,000 for it. Or, more correctly, your basis has now become $20,000; it will probably change from time to time.

You needn't do anything so obvious as adding another room to acquire "more house," however. Any improvement that results in a better, more valuable house is considered to give you "more house," and the cost of the improvement is added to your purchase price, or your basis, to give you in effect an increased cost. Let's say the cost of improvements you've made to your $18,000 house over a ten-year period add up to $3500. You sell the house for $21,000. You have no gain and no tax to pay, because your basis is $21,500; you've actually sold at a $500 loss. Improvements, obviously, are important to you as a taxpayer.

The IRS distinguishes an improvement from a repair this way:

"A repair merely maintains your home in an ordinary efficient operating condition. It does not appreciably add to the value of your home or prolong its life. Repainting your house inside or outside; fixing your roof, gutters or floors; mending leaks; replacing broken windowpanes, etc., are examples of repairs.

"An improvement materially adds to the value or usefulness of your home, appreciably prolongs its life or makes it adaptable to new uses. Putting a recreation room in your unfinished basement, adding another bathroom or bedroom, putting up a fence . . . or paving your driveway are improvements."

One way to add to your basis is to think creatively when there are repairs that need doing. The living room walls are cracked and badly in need of patching and painting. That's a repair, which won't do anything for you as a taxpayer. Perhaps it wouldn't cost much more to install paneling—an improvement. And though painting is a repair if you *just* paint, if it's done as "part of an extensive re-modeling or restoration of your home, the entire job is considered an improvement." So it pays to think big when you're faced with repairs.

Improvements are only one of the items that add to your basis. Additions generally begin on the day you buy the house—at the closing. Many items charged to you here are part of your cost of acquiring the house and are added to the stated purchase price to arrive at your basis. Attorney fees; the cost of abstracts, surveys and title insurance; transfer taxes—all these add to your basis. So do items which are owed by the seller, but which you agree to pay, such as back taxes or interest, recording fees, sales commissions. It's quite possible that your $18,000 house cost you closer to $19,000 by the time you got the keys.

"Local benefit taxes," it was noted earlier, are not deductible as taxes. But if they improve your property, they add to your basis. Assessments for things like streets, sidewalks, water and sewer systems are part of the cost of your property and reduce the gain you report when you sell at a profit.

Taking advantage of all your additions to basis obviously requires good record keeping. You should start a tax file on your house even before the closing, and collect in it all bills, receipts, canceled checks and other material affecting your basis. It's important to be able to document your report of gain or loss when you sell.

Let's say all these additions to basis now have the tax cost of your $18,000 house up to $22,700. You find a buyer who's willing to pay $23,700. That doesn't necessarily mean that you'll be taxed on a gain of $1000. There is still another item, used in arriving at the gain or loss, that can reduce your tax liability.

The "selling price"—unadjusted—is the figure at which you and

---

## THE NEW TAX LAW: HOBBY FARMS

The "hobby farm" has been a favorite tax saver among high-income individuals in past years. Using the kind of deductions allowed to genuine, dirt-on-their-shoes farmers—but without the latter's attention to profitable farming—the hobby farmer could operate at substantial yearly losses. Those losses could be used to offset high income from other sources and reduce taxes. Meanwhile the value of the hobby farm would be appreciating, and at the appropriate time it might be sold at a handsome profit, which was subject only to the favorable rates that were then applied to long-term capital gains.

But now, under the new tax law, a farm or other activity must show a profit for at least two years in five (or two in seven for certain kinds of farms), or the law assumes it's a hobby—not an honest, profit-oriented farm—and losses can't be deducted. Other restrictions are being enforced to discourage operation of farms merely for tax savings. Among these is the farm recapture rule which applies to an owner with $50,000 or more of non-farm income and a net farm loss over $25,000. Such rules make it impossible today to milk large tax advantages out of a hobby farm.

---

the buyer agree to deal. From that figure you subtract your selling expenses—broker's fees or sales commissions, advertising costs, legal fees, and so on. What is left is the "amount realized." This figure, when compared with the "selling price," gives you your profit or loss. While "fixing-up" expenses are not taken into account in figuring your gain, they are included in computing how much profit you currently pay tax on if you are entitled to defer paying tax on the gain. For example, if you replace the residence within the required period of time, fixing-up expenses are deducted from the "amount realized" to arrive at the "adjusted selling price." They are quite special because this is the one circumstance in which repairs can be used.

Fixing-up expenses are allowable as an adjustment only when they are patently for the purpose of making the property more salable or more presentable, immediately prior to sale. The work must be performed during the 90 days previous to the date on which the contract to sell is made, and they must be paid for within 30 days after the date of sale. They must be repairs, not improvements, and otherwise nondeductible for tax purposes. If your fixing up meets these tests, you can deduct the cost from the "amount realized" to arrive, finally, at your "adjusted selling price." It may help you to eliminate paying tax on your profit currently.

## How to Get the Most Out of Savings for College Expenses

If you're a homeowner, the statistics tell us, the odds are better than ten to one that you're also a parent. At about the same time that you acquire one of life's major expenses—a house—you acquire a future commitment to another of life's major expenses—the cost of putting one or more children through college. You need every help you can get with this one, and fortunately there are ways of laying up treasure against the college years that reduce taxes and make the educational dollar go farther.

Conscientious parents like Jerry and Lois who begin putting $10 a week, or $40 a month, into savings when Junior is six years old, will have at least a start on paying college costs by the time he's eighteen—around $8430, in an account paying 6 percent compounded quarterly. But if they're a $10,000-a-year family, they will meanwhile pay about $525 in income tax on the interest the fund is earning while building up. It's easy to avoid this kind of erosion.

617

One, you simply give the money to Junior. If you do this in such a way that it's legally *his* money, the interest earned will be his, and the tax liability his. Until his income exceeds $1750 a year he pays no tax, however, so he can accumulate more than $34,000 in his savings account before this becomes a problem. Under the Uniform Gifts to Minors Act, now adopted by all states, you can give not only cash but bonds, stocks and other securities and retain the right to manage the account, as custodian, until the minor reaches age twenty-one, when he takes sole ownership and control. Be sure your gifts are made in proper legal form—any bank or savings institution should be able to tell you how to satisfy the requirements—and obtain a Social Security number for Junior so that you can begin filing tax returns for him as soon as required.

Another method is to place Junior's money or income-producing assets in trust. This can be as simple as establishing a custodial bank account or considerably more elaborate, as called for by the circumstances. There are two kinds of trusts. When you establish an irrevocable trust, you surrender completely and forever the ownership and control of the assets involved. In this case the property is no longer yours, none of the income is yours and so of course you're relieved of any tax liability. Taxes are paid either by the trust, which legally owns the assets, or by the beneficiary, to whom the trust passes on all or part of the income. Under the throwback rule, for trusts that accumulate income, distributions of accumulated income are taxed as though they were actually distributed to the beneficiary in the year earned by the trust. As distinct from this kind of trust, there is the revocable trust. When you establish it, you retain the right to revoke or dissolve it if you choose. You haven't really given the assets away, since they're yours any time you want to revoke the trust, and so far as tax treatment is concerned, it's the same as if the money were in your pocket.

There is *no tax advantage in a revocable trust.* There are other reasons for establishing one, but rearranging the ownership of assets so as to reduce taxes is not one of them. Remember that when we talk about a trust for tax purposes we're talking about an *irrevocable* trust, where you dispose of ownership and control completely and permanently.

Establishing a trust savings account can be as easy as opening a checking account. Many of the larger savings banks have prepared trust indenture forms for this purpose, and though you should consult your lawyer on such a matter, you're spared the expense of having the legal papers prepared. How much control the parent can exercise over use of the funds varies from state to state. Consult your banker or lawyer or both about the terms of a trust savings account in your state.

If your thinking runs to a type of investment that has more potential for growth, in building up college funds, it's a simple matter to make Junior the owner of mutual fund shares or stock certificates under the Uniform Gifts to Minors Act. Any dividend income belongs to Junior, and it's his responsibility to pay income tax when it's owing, even though he may be only six years old. But he, like anyone else, first gets his dividend exclusion, and he can receive up to $1750 of income beyond that before he begins paying tax. Capital gains distributions from a mutual fund are taxed to the minor in their entirety, but again will have to exceed, with other income, $1750 before tax becomes due.

Parents individually can give up to $3000 a year, or $6000 jointly, before filing a gift tax return is required. The gift itself is not taxable income to the child—only the income from it.

There is one possible legal pitfall concerning trusts and custodial arrangement under the Uniform Gifts to Minors Act that parents should be wary of. Even though you have divested yourself of certain assets or property by putting them in trust, you may still be

▭▭▭▭▭▭▭

*THE NEW TAX LAW:*

**MORE SPENDABLE DOLLARS FOR THOSE IN RETIREMENT**

Three features of the new tax law combine to give retired people a substantial increase in spendable dollars. First, since those over sixty-five may enter a double personal exemption on their tax returns, the increase from $600 to $750 in steps over four years means $300 per person. Thus in 1973 a retired couple will have an additional $600 escaping income tax.

Second, the new tax law includes a provision that raises Social Security benefits by 15 percent across the board. Third, by using the low-income allowance in conjunction with the increased exemption, in 1973 couples aged sixty-five and over may have as tax-free income up to $4000 in addition to their nontaxable Social Security payments.

A chart, "Examples of Monthly Cash Payments," showing Social Security benefits under the new law appears in Chapter 59, "What You Can Expect from Social Security," page 560.

▭▭▭▭▭▭▭

held liable for paying taxes on the income from the fund if it is used to discharge the obligations of support that you have as a parent. You can't, certainly, use such trust income to pay the cost of your child's food, clothing and lodging. Is providing your child with a college education one of your legal obligations of support? The answer to that varies according to individual state laws, and it's advisable to consult a lawyer on this point. There is, in any case, a method of giving educational funds to Junior or Suzy in such a way as to obviate this difficulty, when it exists.

There is an exception to the distinction made earlier between revocable and irrevocable trusts, where the latter was said to be absolutely permanent. Provision is made by law for a short-term trust—it's known to the profession as a Clifford trust—which receives the same tax treatment as an irrevocable trust but need not be permanent. Its terms provide that the original owner of the assets gets them back either (1) upon the death of the beneficiary or (2) at the end of a period that must be more than ten years—for example, ten years and one month.

A plan designed by Jack Crestol and Herman M. Schneider, attorney-accountants who are authorities on trusts and estates, makes use of the Clifford trust in combination with a custodian bank account in a way that offers the best protection in those states which require that trust income not be used to pay for college expenses if it's to escape taxation to the donor. The Crestol-Schneider plan calls for a short-term trust that owns the income-generating assets and a custodian bank account that serves as a receptacle of the income, which is "emptied out" of the trust into the bank account at least once a year. The trust has the tax liability of an individual taxpayer, but it accumulates no income that is subject to tax, unless securities owned by the trust realize capital gains of more than $300 a year. Distribution of income from the trust and subsequent earned interest of the custodian account are taxed to the child, but he pays no tax until his income reaches $1750 a year.

If the trust fund is set up to run its ten-years-plus term before a child reaches college age, it is terminated before he begins using its funds for college expenses. Thus the trust, which no longer exists, is not directly paying for educational expenses, and the legal question of whether it is discharging a parent's legal obligation is avoided. The Crestol-Schneider combination provides sufficiently broad tax shelter that a fund large enough to pay for college expenses, and graduate school beyond, can in most cases be accumulated virtually tax-free. It has the added advantage that the original assets, having performed their function, revert to the parent to be incorporated into his own program of building up retirement funds.

This is not exactly a simple plan for financing college costs. You'll need the services of an attorney well versed in trusts and tax laws, but if the amount of assets involved is large enough, the tax savings can make it well worth your while.

## Tax Savings on Retirement Income

Consumer data on income and expenditures show that it's not until age forty-five that the average breadwinner begins to accumulate any substantial amount of discretionary savings—that is, available, usable surplus money which you bank or invest, as distinguished from savings committed to paying off mortgages or other fixed obligations. Raising the kids and getting them through school obviously takes just about all the resources of the average family. It's from about age forty-five on to the end of the working years that there is a surplus available, and parents turn their attention to accumulating funds for some of the amenities of life and for use as retirement income.

There are principally two ways—leaving out the ultrasophisticated devices of those who have a cook, chauffeur and tax lawyer on their household staffs—of avoiding the payment of unnecessary taxes on such funds. One is to defer receipt of the income your savings and investments are earning—postponing it until after retirement, when most families are in a lower tax bracket. You can then receive the income with much less erosion by taxes. Another way is to break up income that would come to you in large, highly taxable chunks— as when you have unrealized capital gains on investments that have appreciated—and arrange to receive it in smaller, less taxable chunks. Installment sales are one example of the second method.

There is, in addition, one circumstance in which current earnings, as well as unearned income from savings and investments, can escape taxation. Tax-sheltered pension and retirement plans, available both to salaried individuals and to the self-employed, offer an opportunity to build up retirement funds at a much faster rate than when your building is subject to normal tax erosion.

The annuity is a common method of deferring investment income until retirement years. Its only tax advantage, generally, is that the interest is not paid out to you now, but later. For example, you make payments of $60 a month on an annuity, for 15 years, giving you a total investment of $10,800. If you put the same $60 a month into a savings account, you would pay income tax on more than $5000 of earned interest, at the tax rates of your relatively high earning years. When you put the money into an annuity, you pay no taxes on interest until you begin getting your capital and interest back as income at retirement; then you pay taxes on the interest portion of your monthly income.

If this annuity provided an income of $100 a month for life, for instance, you multiply the annual payment ($1200) by your life expectancy, as given in tables of the Internal Revenue Service (if your annuity falls under the Treasury Department's "General Rule for Annuities." There are many exceptions; tax treatment of annuities is in fact a complex and difficult subject). Let us say it's 15 years. Of the total $18,000 it's anticipated you will receive, $10,800 is "return of capital"—the amount you spent to buy the annuity. That is not taxed. It amounts to 60 percent of the total, so 60 percent of each year's annuity income is not subject to tax. The remaining 40 percent is taxed as interest paid to you. The tax advantage lies in its being paid when you are most likely to have dropped down a few tax brackets.

For those who prefer a do-it-yourself annuity, a number of the large banks offer the deferred-income savings account. Don't start one of these unless you're certain you can get along without the money until it's released, because it's pretty well padlocked meanwhile. Your interest is retained by the bank and added to your bank account.

Receipt of income can be deferred to a period of up to 14 years in some banks (a shorter time in others), and top savings rates are generally paid. One New York bank pays, at the present time, $5\frac{3}{4}$ percent compounded monthly, the equivalent of 8.81 percent average annual interest over the maximum period of deferral. An initial deposit would more than double in that time (it would grow to nearly $2\frac{1}{4}$ times the original amount), so the depositer is escaping tax, for the present, on an amount more than equal to his deposit. A large initial deposit is generally required, after which smaller increments can be added.

The Keogh retirement plan for self-employed individuals (named after the act sponsored by New York Congressman Eugene Keogh) is an example of how taking advantage of tax shelter opportunities can greatly increase the investment potential of your earned income. Under this plan, the lesser of 10 percent or $2500 a year of your current income can be excluded from the amount on which you are taxed. Both this amount and all its earnings, as interest or investment income, escape taxation until you begin making withdrawals for retirement income, at age fifty-nine and a half or later.

The leverage this applies to growth of investments goes beyond the deferred taxation alone—though that's a considerable advantage in itself. Take, for example, a self-employed man who for 15 years contributes the maximum permissible—$2500—to a Keogh plan. Each amount he invests averages, over the years, annual growth of 6 percent. After 15 years he will have in his account approximately $22,500 that has not been taxed—and in his tax bracket he would have paid a total of at least $8100 in taxes. But probably more important than the fact that he's deferred taxes on this amount is the fact that he's had this money available for investment and growth, almost like an interest-free loan. That $2500 he invested at the end of the first year grew to $6500. Without the shelter of his Keogh plan, income tax would have cut his $2500 to $1600 or less, which then invested would have grown to $4160 at most. It's having *all* of this earned income growing and multiplying—not just the part that's left after taxes have whittled away their share—that makes something like the Keogh plan so advantageous.

The Keogh plan is relatively new and, evidently, relatively unknown to the self-employed, judging by the small percentage who have applied for the necessary IRS approval. The Keogh Act was voted by Congress in the 1960s to remedy an unfair advantage given by the tax laws to corporation employes. Many good corporation fringe-benefit programs provide a tax-sheltered investment plan similar to the Keogh plan—an advantage denied to the self-employed until the Keogh Act. Whether you are a corporation employe or self-employed, you'll do well to strain yourself to contribute up to the maximum allowable in such a plan, if you want investment dollars to flex their muscles unimpeded by tax restraints.

## Support of Dependents: Claiming All Your Exemptions

For elderly parents past their earning years to rely on sons or daughters for support, wholly or partially, is no new phenomenon. It's an age-old and worldwide prerogative of parents, supported in some states by law. Social Security and union and corporate pension plans have reduced the necessity in this century, but studies by the Social Security Administration and congressional committees show that most retirees need, at least eventually, supplementary support. The tax laws, fortunately, are fashioned to ease the burden of working families who support, or help support, dependents either young or old. How they are so fashioned is probably not so well understood as it might be, and opportunities to cut tax bills by taking advantage of dependency exemptions are frequently missed.

You need not contribute money to the support of a dependent to qualify for a dependency exemption. Support can be provided by furnishing food, lodging, clothing, taking someone shopping in your car—even financing a trip to the beauty parlor or a card party.

The definition of a dependent is clearly spelled out in the tax code. To qualify as a dependent, a person must meet five tests:

1. *Gross income.* A dependent must have a "gross income" of less than $750 a year for 1973 and later years (the amount varies from $600 for 1969 to $700 for 1972). What "gross" means here, however, is essentially "taxable." Social Security benefits, which are not taxed, are not included in gross income. Neither is the tax-free portion of an annuity income, as described earlier, or other retirement income from pensions or earlier investments where an untaxed "return of capital" constitutes part of the installment.

The income test does not apply to your minor children who are under nineteen or who, regardless of age, are full-time students at a recognized school for some part of each of five months of the year or are taking a full-time on-farm training course. Note that so long as one of your children continues in school as a student, no matter how much he earns you may continue to claim a dependency exemption for him provided that you contribute more than one half his support—and he may, at the same time, claim his own personal exemption when he files a tax return.

2. *Support.* You must provide more than 50 percent of the dependent's support. How this is calculated is explained below.

3. *Relationship.* Something of a misnomer, since a dependent need not be related to you. A dependent can be anyone, meeting the other tests, who is a "member of your household," living under your roof for the entire year except for temporary absences. (Housekeepers, maids, anyone who works for you cannot be claimed as a dependent.) If a person is not a member of your household, however, he or she

can be claimed as a dependent only if related to you in one of these ways: (a) a child (including one legally adopted or placed with you for adoption), grandchild, great-grandchild, and so on, or stepchild—but not a descendant of a stepchild; (b) your parent, grandparent or other direct ancestor, or a stepmother or stepfather—but not a foster parent; (c) a brother or sister, half brother or half sister, stepbrother or stepsister; (d) a brother or sister of your father or mother; (e) a son or daughter of your brother or sister; and (f) six relations by marriage: father-in-law, mother-in-law, son-in-law, daughter-in-law, brother-in-law, sister-in-law. Once the relationship is established, it isn't changed by divorce.

4. *Citizenship or residence.* Your dependent must be a citizen or resident of the United States or a resident of Canada, the Canal Zone, Mexico or the Republic of Panama.

5. *Separate return.* A dependent may not file a joint return. You support a daughter, for example, while her husband is in military service. Even though you provide more than half her support, you may not claim her as a dependent if she and her husband file a joint return. Or: Your daughter marries late in the year, and prior to April 15, without consulting you, she and her husband file a joint return. Though you provided support during the year, and she otherwise qualifies as a dependent, you lose the exemption.

The support test, No. 2, is the one that requires the most attention. To determine whether you provided more than 50 percent of a dependent's support, it's necessary to itemize living expenses—and you may be asked to produce records of expenditures if a dependency claim is questioned. What's important is that some expenditures are considered items of "support," and others are not—capital expenditures, for example, which include the purchase of a car (though the cost of transportation is included in "support") and life insurance premiums. And when you are calculating support, Social Security benefits spent for the dependent's own support are taken into consideration, though they are *not* counted as part of gross income in the income test.

That may sound forbiddingly legalistic, but let's take an example of how it can affect your pocketbook. Bill and Sally Moore contribute to the support of her mother. Mrs. Samson receives Social Security benefits of $156.50 a month and $36.50 a month as beneficiary from a pension of her late husband. What is her gross income? Nothing, from Social Security. The pension payments consist of 40 percent nontaxable return of capital and 60 percent taxable income; of the $438 a year, $262.80 is taxable and an item—her only item— of "gross income." It's less than $750 a year, although she actually has an income of $2316 a year, so she meets the gross income test of a dependent.

What about support? Bill and Sally send Mrs. Samson a check for $125 every month, and that's all they feel they can squeeze out of their budget. Their $1500 brings Mrs. Samson's total support to $3816, assuming Mrs. Samson spends all her income on support. Half of this is $1908, so Bill and Sally are $409 short of the amount that would make their contribution more than 50 percent of Mrs. Samson's support. That much extra wouldn't be easy to find, and in any event it wouldn't make sense from a financial standpoint to lay out $409 to get a $750 exemption that would reduce their tax payment by $165.

But a little study of the rules on support would repay them—to the extent of that $165 tax reduction, which they can have without increasing their contribution by a penny. All it calls for is some rearranging.

Mrs. Samson has refused to surrender for its cash value an insurance policy she's had since she was eighteen. Determinedly maternal, she's always told Sally when it comes up, "No, I want you to have something when I'm gone." Sally and Bill feel the least they can do is pay the premium, so every year they write out a check for $188. Life insurance premiums are a "capital expenditure," not an item of support, so this doesn't count toward their contribution.

Then there was the sofa at Christmas. For a long time Sally had been saying, "Mother, that sofa is a disgrace"—but Mother lives on a tight budget and new sofas are expensive. The new sofa appeared at Christmas, a present from Bill and Sally. And again, furniture is a capital expenditure and the $249 it cost isn't included in their yearly contribution.

Here's how things could have been rearranged: While Mrs. Samson receives $1878 a year in Social Security benefits, only that part which is spent on items of support is taken into account in calculating "total support" on tax form No. 2038, which you may be asked to fill out if an examiner wants more information about a dependency claim. If Mrs. Samson uses part of her Social Security money for capital expenditures, that much less has been spent during the year for her support. So all Sally and Bill had to do was make out a check to Mrs. Samson, instead of to the insurance company, and let Mother pay the premium out of her own funds. The same with the sofa: "Mother, here's a check for $249, and we're going with you while you pick out a new sofa."

Now Mrs. Samson's income consists of:

| | |
|---|---|
| Social Security benefits | $1878 |
| Mr. Samson's pension | 438 |
| Bill and Sally, $175 a month | 1500 |
| Extra check, Bill and Sally | 188 |
| Extra check, Bill and Sally | 249 |
| | $4253 |

But *Mrs. Samson spent* $188 plus $249 of this—$437—on insurance premiums and furniture, which are not items of support. Her total support therefore consisted of:

$4253
$- \ 437$
$3816

Bill and Sally contributed

$1500
188
249
$1937

This is more than 50 percent of Mrs. Samson's total support, and Bill and Sally are entitled to an additional exemption of $750 on their tax return.

It's also possible sometimes to rearrange items of income so that a dependent meets the gross income test. Albert N. contributes more than 50 percent of his mother's support, but can't claim her as a dependent because she has more than $750 of gross income. Included in it is about $175 a year in dividends from 75 shares of an heirloom blue-chip stock left to her by her late husband. Can Albert persuade Mother to sell her stock and buy municipal bonds with the proceeds? That shouldn't be hard, since it would actually increase her income by $50 or more a year—and the interest from municipals is not taxed. Eliminating $175 from her taxable income would bring her "gross income" below $750 a year and allow Albert to claim her as a dependent.

Relatives who jointly support a dependent, none of them contributing more than 50 percent, may neglect tax savings that could be realized through a multiple-support agreement. This is the exception allowed to the support test. Anyone who contributes more than 10 percent of the support of an otherwise qualified dependent may claim the exemption if others who contribute more than 10 percent sign a "Multiple Support Declaration," form No. 2120, which must be filed with the return of the person claiming the exemption. Two brothers and a sister contribute equally to the support of their parents—none more than 50 percent of their total support, but all more than 10 percent. By agreement, one of them can claim the exemption this year, the others in succeeding years.

You contribute to the support of a dependent who lives with you as a member of your household by furnishing food and lodging, the latter treated as the dependent's expense for rental. To determine how much of his or her support goes for rent, if you own your home, you establish the fair rental value of the property. Find out what comparable houses are renting for, or get a statement of the fair rental value from a qualified real estate broker. House rentals are generally based on the unfurnished rate. If that's what you have to go by, don't neglect to add the fair rental value of furnishings. A fair share of utilities is also part of the dependent's expense for rent. Your contributions to support include not only allowances or spending money furnished in cash but items of support paid for or furnished by you: medical and dental services, including premiums on medical-hospital and accident insurance; transportation (but not the cost of a car, a capital expenditure); personal care such as barber or beauty shop services, cosmetics and entertainment, which includes sports activities, recreation, vacations, parties and social events. For an adult dependent, alcoholic beverages are included in entertainment costs.

Finally, there is something called the retirement income credit available to retired persons, which evidently needs wider understanding, since those who prepare tax returns professionally say it's a frequently neglected tax saving. Nevertheless, anyone receiving retirement income should know about it, since it may result in lower tax payments by those whose income includes dividends, interest, income from rental property or taxable pensions or annuities. Your local IRS can help you understand this complex provision of the law.

## Professional Help with Taxes

As the foregoing suggests, the preparation of even a simple, individual tax return has become so complex and demanding that it's akin to trying to fix your television set on the basis of what you learned in a general science course. Aside from the vexations, you're probably missing some possible tax savings when you make out your own return, since it's almost impossible for a nonprofessional to bring enough knowledge to the job to effect all the possible reductions and savings. The evidence is, professionals say, that up to 75 percent of their first-time clients have been neglecting to take advantage of some saving or other.

Having a professional prepare your return probably doesn't cost as much as you imagine, if you've never looked into it. Fees are as low as $5 to $10 for an uncomplicated individual return. As in most instances, you get what you pay for, and if you take a bundle of complicated tax problems to a part-timer who rents a vacant storefront during tax season—who may handle a simple return quite adequately—you may find it expensive in the long run, no matter how low the fee. On the other hand, a taxpayer with the kind of return that would take a week's work if he did it himself is often happy to pay a substantial fee to a good certified public accountant who specializes in individual or small-business tax work.

Finding the tax man or tax service you're going to be happy with presents much the same problem as finding a good family doctor or neighborhood handyman. The large organizations that maintain year-round tax offices generally have systematized procedures that are adequate for the person with no unusual tax problems. The computerized services are whizzes at doing your calculations and arithmetic, but all the machines know is what you tell them, and they won't do much creative thinking for you. For that, you need your own tax adviser—which, again, need not be as expensive a luxury as it sounds. By shopping around you'll find quite a range of fees.

If you're not sure whether it's worth the fee to have your return prepared, try this: The next time around, work out your tax for yourself, then take your records and summaries to a professional who'll prepare the return for a modest fee. That may be the only fee you'll ever have to pay. If he turns up deductions, adjustments or credits that you didn't know about, you can effect the same savings in subsequent years, making out the return yourself. And you won't even be out the full fee, since it's deductible.

# Acknowledgments

WHERE DO THE DOLLARS GO?, from "Where the Family Money Goes," *Changing Times, The Kiplinger Magazine* (Aug. 1966), © 1966, The Kiplinger Washington Editors, Inc. HOW DO THOSE JONESES DO IT?, excerpts from *Changing Times, The Kiplinger Magazine* (April 1968), © 1968, The Kiplinger Washington Editors, Inc. HOW TO APPRAISE YOUR FAMILY'S SECURITY, from "A Do-It-Yourself Financial Checkup," *Changing Times, The Kiplinger Magazine* (July 1967), © 1967, The Kiplinger Washington Editors, Inc. SEE HOW YOUR FAMILY COMPARES, from "How Do You Compare?" *Changing Times, The Kiplinger Magazine* (Aug. 1966), © 1966 The Kiplinger Washington Editors, Inc. THE FINE ART OF FAMILY BUDGETING, from "Steps in Making a Budget," *U. S. Dept. of Agriculture Guide to Budgeting for the Family*, 1968, U. S. Dept. of Agriculture. THESE BONERS WRECK BUDGETS, from *Changing Times, The Kiplinger Magazine* (Sept. 1968), © 1968, The Kiplinger Washington Editors, Inc. TEACHING CHILDREN TO MANAGE MONEY, excerpts from "Managing Your Money," by Carlton Smith and Richard Putnam, *The Pharmacist's Management Journal* (Feb. 1968), © 1968, Professional Communications. WHEN MOTHER BRINGS HOME THE BACON, excerpts from "Special Situation," in *Sense with Dollars* by Charles Neal, copyright © 1965, 1967, Charles Neal; reprinted by permission of Doubleday & Company, Inc. FAMILY RECORD GUIDE, from *Changing Times, The Kiplinger Magazine* (Aug., 1963), © 1963, The Kiplinger Washington Editors, Inc. YOUR PERSONAL AFFAIRS, from "My Personal Affairs," *Family Money Management—A Modern Guide to Family Finances from First Federal Savings*, © 1965, Business News Associates, Inc. WHAT RECORDS TO CHANGE AT MARRIAGE, from *Good Housekeeping* (Feb. 1968), © 1968, The Hearst Corporation. TRICKS TO HELP YOU SAVE, excerpts from *Changing Times, The Kiplinger Magazine* (Jan. 1969), © 1969, The Kiplinger Washington Editors, Inc. YOU CAN BUY AND BUILD, from "Today's Development House—all but custom built," by John H. Ingersoll, *House Beautiful* (Sept. 1968), © 1968, The Hearst Corporation: reprinted by permission of *House Beautiful*. HOW MUCH HOUSE CAN YOU AFFORD?, from "What Can You Afford to Pay for a House?," *Changing Times, The Kiplinger Magazine* (June 1968), © 1968, The Kiplinger Washington Editors, Inc. WHEN YOU BUY A HOUSE, excerpts from "The Science of Sizing Up a House," *Changing Times, The Kiplinger Magazine* (April 1967), © 1967, The Kiplinger Washington Editors, Inc. TWENTY-TWO COMMON LITTLE TRAPS, from "The Garbled Floor Plan," in *How to Avoid the 10 Biggest Home-Buying Traps* by A. M. Watkins, © 1968, A. M. Watkins; reprinted by permission of Meredith Press. HOW MANY OUTLETS? from *Home Buyer's Guide*, 1960, The Southern Pine Association, New Orleans, La. THE VANISHING BUILDER, excerpts from *How to Avoid the 10 Biggest Home-Buying Traps* by A. M. Watkins, copyright 1968, A. M. Watkins; reprinted by permission of Meredith Press. GET A LAWYER BEFORE YOU SIGN ANYTHING, from "Don't be a Dupe when You Buy a House," by Jerome Beatty, *Suburban Life in New Jersey* (Jan. 1953), © 1953, Suburban Life, Inc. THE COST OF BUYING A HOUSE, from *Consumer Close-Ups* (March 1969), Dept. of Consumer Ed., Cornell University, Cooperative Extension, N.Y.C. BUILDER'S WARRANTY, excerpts from "Home Mortgage Insurance," *HUD Consumer Bulletin* (Sept. 1967), U.S. Dept. of Housing and Urban Development. MOVING WITHOUT TEARS, excerpts from *Help Your Family Make a Better Move*, by Helen Giammattei and Katherine Slaughter, copyright © 1968, Helen Giammattei and Katherine Slaughter; reprinted by permission of Doubleday & Company, Inc. HOW TO GET MORE WHEN YOU SELL YOUR HOME, excerpts from *Help Your Family Make a Better Move*, by Helen Giammattei and Katherine Slaughter, copyright © 1968, Helen Giammattei and Katherine Slaughter; reprinted by permission of Doubleday & Company, Inc. HOW TO TURN DISCARDS INTO DOLLARS, by Jane Ratcliffe, condensed from *Family Weekly* (July 1966), © 1966, *Family Weekly*. TAX ASPECTS OF SELLING YOUR HOME, excerpts from "Buying and Selling a Home," by Jacquin D. Bierman, *Parents' Magazine and Better Homemaking* (April 1967), © 1967, Parents' Magazine Enterprises, Inc. YOUR HOME: A HAVEN OR A HEADACHE?, excerpts from "Avoiding High Repair Bills: A Maintenance Program for your House," in *The Complete Book of Home Remodeling, Improvement and Repair* by A. M. Watkins, © 1962, 1963, 1969, A. M. Watkins; reprinted by permission of Doubleday & Company, Inc. Excerpts also from "Save Cash on Home Maintenance," in *How to Get More for Your Money in Running Your Home* by Merle E. Dowd, © 1968, Merle E. Dowd; reprinted by permission of Parker Publishing Company, Inc. YOU REALLY CAN SAVE ON UTILITIES, excerpts from "How to Control Expenses for Heating and Cooling," in *How to Get More for Your Money in Running Your Home* by Merle E. Dowd, © 1968, Merle E. Dowd; reprinted by permission of Parker Publishing Company, Inc. HOME IMPROVEMENT: A GOOD INVESTMENT OR A POOR ONE?, from "Home Improvement" by Dick Pratt (Unpublished material); reprinted by permission of The Family Circle, Inc. FURNISHINGS THAT ARE RIGHT FOR YOUR FAMILY, from *American Home's How to Buy: Home Furnishings Guide*, © 1968, Downe Publishing, Inc.; reprinted by special permission of *American Home Magazine*. HOW TO BUY APPLIANCES, from "From a Frosty Refrigerator to . . . a Drier Dryer: A Guide to Appliance Buying," *McCall's Magazine* (Jan. 1969), © 1969, The McCall Corporation. HOW MUCH DO YOU SPEND FOR GROCERIES? excerpts from "What Other People Spend for Food," *Changing Times, The Kiplinger Magazine* (June 1960), © 1960, The Kiplinger Washington Editors, Inc. COMMON CONTAINER SIZES, from *Home Economics—Consumer Services*, 1968, National Canners Association, Washington, D.C. THE COST OF CONVENIENCE FOODS, excerpts from "The Saving Graces of Convenience Foods," *McCalls Magazine* (May 1965), © 1965, The McCall Corporation. ANSWERS TO SOME QUESTIONS

# INDEX

À la carte, defined, 411
Accidents, car, 354
Accounts
  charge, regular and
    revolving, 498, 499
  savings, 516–25
Add-on interest rates, 494
Adjusted sales price, 166
Advertising, bait, 238
Agents
  real estate, 159–160
  insurance, 212
  travel, 423–27
Air travel, 400–09
Alcoholic beverages, 16
Alimony payments,
  610–11
American Plan (AP),
  411
  Modified (MAP), 412
Annual reports, 532, 536
Annuities, 571, 574–79,
  621–22
Anticipated income, 46
Appliances, 229–35
Appraisal, defined, 161
Art, as investment, 557
Asking price, defined, 161
Assets
  borrowing on, 505–9
  defined, 11, 18
  records of, 35
Assumption of mortgage,
  161
Autographs, as
  investments, 557
Automobiles, 340–70
  buying, 340–48
  cost of running,
    348–52
  driving habits, 358–66
  insurance for, 350–58
  maintenance of,
    366–70

Averages (securities
  market), 532

Balanced funds, 544
Banks
  checkbooks of, as
    record-keeping tool,
    70–71
  credit plans, 484–86
  savings, 516–25
Bear market, defined, 532
Beneficiaries, 452, 458
Big Board, defined, 532
Bill of sale, defined, 82
Binder, defined, 136
Blue chip, defined, 532
Bond funds, 545
Bonds, defined, 532
Borrowing, see Credit;
  Loans
Boutique, 317
Brakes, care for, 365
Breads, 261–62, 280, 285
Broker, defined, 532
Budget, defined, 59
Budgeting, 54–62
  for automobile, 340–42
  for automobile care,
    366–70
  for camping, 434–37
  for college students,
    384–85
  for debts, 54
  for emergencies, 52–53
  errors in, 56–57
  estimating income for,
    48–49
  of food costs, 252–63
  goals and, 47–48
  monthly plan of, 54–59
  savings and, 505
  spending and, 49–52
  for wardrobe, 298
Builders, home, 128–29

Builder's warranty, 146
Bull market, defined, 532

Campgrounds, private
  and public, 438–40
Camping, 433–40
Canned foods, 273
  facts about, 279
  sizes of, 271–72
Capital gains, 532
  taxes and, 82, 604
Capital loss, 532
Caribbean travel, 406–8
Carpeting, 227
  choosing, 222–26
Carrier, defined, 411
Cars, see Automobiles
Cash value, 445, 452
Casualty losses, 610
Ceilings, 127–30
Cereals
  buying, 261–62
  keeping fresh, 280
Certificate, defined, 532
Chain stores, 315–16
Charge accounts, 480–83
Charter flight, 411–12
Checkbooks, as
  record-keeping tool,
  70–71
Cheeses, 269–70
  keeping fresh, 284, 286
Child care, tax
  deductible, 610
Children's clothing,
  302–3, 310–11, 321
Closed-end mutual fund,
  542
Closing, defined, 161
Closing costs, 147–48
Clothing, see Wardrobes
Collateral, defined, 485
Colleges, see Education

Community colleges,
376–78
Collision insurance, 356
Color in homes, 218, 220
Commission, defined, 532
Common stock, 527–30,
532
Community property,
580, 582
Comprehensive
insurance, 356
Compulsory group plan,
467
Conditional sales
contract, 135
Condominium, 101
Conducted tour, 412
Continental breakfast,
defined, 412
Contingencies, defined, 59
Contractors, 179–91
Contracts
conditional sales, 135
installment, 496–97
"loading," 495
Contributions, as tax
deduction, 605–8
Convenience foods, cost
of, 274–75
Conventional mortgage,
defined, 18, 143
Convertible security, 532
Convertible term
insurance, 445, 452
Cooperative apartment,
defined, 101
Couchettes, defined, 412
Counteroffer, 161
Coupons, defined, 412
Courier, defined, 412
Couture, defined, 324
Cream, keeping fresh,
286
Credit, 476–504
bank credit plans,
484–86
beating high cost of,
500–01
credit rights, 492

defined, 11
evaluating one's,
487–91
gauging, 24–25
interest rates on,
493–504
shopping for, 476–86
Credit cards, 509–14
Custom-built homes,
defined, 99, 108

Dairy products, 260–61,
284, 286
Date of possession, 161
Dealers, car, 343–44
Death
estates and, 584–88
protection in case of,
worksheet, 42–43
Debts
budgeting for, 54
handling a crisis in,
486
savings and, 17–18
worksheet on, 40
Decreasing term
insurance, 451–52
defined, 452
Deductible insurance,
defined, 356
Deeds, 145
Deferred annuity, 577
Demi-pension, 412
Dental expenses, taxes
and, 604–5
Department stores,
313–14
Dependents, as tax
exemptions, 623–28
Depositors, 523
Depreciation, 212
Development houses,
defined, 108
Dieting, cost of, 259
Disability benefit, 452
Discount interest rates,
494
Discount stores, clothing
from, 315–16

Discretionary income,
defined, 11
Dishwashers, buying, 233
Dividends, 46, 452, 532
Double indemnity, 452
Down payment, 113–14,
138–39
Draperies, choosing,
226–28
Driers and washers,
buying, 234–35
Driving, good habits in,
358–66
Dry cleaning of clothes,
332–33

Earnings report, 532
Education, 372–98
expenses for, 16–17,
372–76
government loans for,
386–88
scholarships for,
379–84
working through
college, 391–98
Eggs, keeping fresh,
280–81
Electricity, 199–201
Employe business
expenses, 608–10
Endowment insurance,
450–51, 452
Engine, tuned, 360–61
English breakfast,
defined, 412
Equity, defined, 46
Escheat, defined, 523
Escort, defined, 412
Estates, 584–630
planning, 34–36
wills and, 34–36
worksheet on, 43
Europe, travel to,
414–23
European Plan (EP),
defined, 412
Exemptions, tax, 590–91
Expenses

budgeting for seasonal,
53–54
defined, 18
employe business,
608–10
fixed, 101
for higher education,
16–17, 374–76
medical, 16, 468–74,
604–5
taxes and moving, 597,
613
underestimating home,
29
Extended coverage, 212

Fabrics
table of durability of,
219
wardrobe, 326–30
Face value, defined, 452
Family income policy,
454–55
Family maintenance
policy, 455
Family plans, travel, 409,
455
Family records, *see*
Records
Fats and oils, keeping
fresh, 281
Filing, tax, 598
Financial responsibility
law, defined, 356
Financial security,
appraising, 21–46
Financial solvency, rules
for, 83–86
Firm price, defined, 161
Fish, 258–60, 266–68,
282–84
Fixed cost, defined, 101
Floor (stock exchange),
defined, 532
Floors (home), 127–30
Food, 246–96
cost of, 14
cost of groceries,
246–51

kept fresh, 280–88
misleading packaging
of, 288–94
planning cost of,
252–63
shopping for, 263–79
supermarket shopping
for, 292–96
Frauds, 235–41
Front-end load mutual
funds, 548
Frozen foods
buying, 273–75
storage of, 285
Fruits, 270–71, 281–82,
285
Fuel
automobile, 360
trimming cost, 195–97
Full pension (travel),
defined, 412
Full-coverage health
insurance, 467
Funds
life insurance and
raising, 478–80
mutual, defined, 46,
533, 542–49
worksheet on
retirement, 44–45
Furniture (furnishings),
214–29, 242–44

Gasoline, 360
Grace period, 452
Groceries, 246–51
Gross annual income,
defined, 11
Ground arrangements,
defined, 412
Growth funds, 544, 548
Growth stock, 532
Guaranteed mortgage, 18
Guarantees, 238, 240

Haute couture, 324
Health costs, 16, 468–74
Heating, 126, 168–70;
*see also* Fuel

Hobby farms, 616
Homeowner's mortgage,
defined, 18, 137–48
Homes
alterations of
development models,
102–9
appliances for, 229–35
budgeting for, 109–16
buying, 117–36
checklist for
evaluating, 132–33
choosing, 88–101
cost of, 12–13
design flaws in, 120–21
furnishing, 214–29,
242–44
improvements on, 30,
202–6
inflation and
refinancing, 556
insuring, 206–12
maintenance of, 28–30,
168–78
mortgages for, 137–48
moving to new, 148–56
remodeling, 179–91
selling, 156–66
structural defects in,
123–26
tax laws favoring
ownership of, 26–27
tax savings and sale of,
614–17
taxes on, 600
utilities for, 191–202
worksheet on budget
for, 115–16
worksheet on cost of,
41

Immediate annuity, 577
Improvement, home, 30,
202–6
Income
anticipated, 46
estimating, 48–49
groceries and, 246–48
housing and, 109–16

inflation and, 549–57
job as main source of,
  27–28
low-income allowance,
  591, 602–3
net, 11
retirement, 36–37; 46
spending and, 22–24
tax reform and
  averaging of, 596
taxes on, *see* Tax laws;
  Taxes
unearned, 82
for working women,
  63–69
worksheet on outgo
  and income, 39
Income funds, 544–45,
  548
retirement, 546–47
Individual health
  insurance, 467
Industry funds, 545
Infant clothing, sizes in,
  310–11
Inflation, 549–57
Installment contracts,
  signing of, 496–97
Insurance
automobile, 350–58
death protection
  worksheet and,
  42–43
on fund investments,
  545
home, 206–12
life, 442–59
of loans, 482
medical, 459–67
mortgage, 146
Insured, defined, 453
Insured mortgage, 143
Interest
loss of, 522–23
mortgage, 612–14
rates of, 493–504
taxes and, 600–601
Investment
in annuities, 574–79,

621–22
defined, 11
in home improvements,
  202–6
in mutual funds, 542–
  49
savings and, 32–34
in stocks and bonds,
  525–41, 556
tax and, 27
"Irregulars," clothing,
  317–18, 324

Jobs
financial security and,
  27–28
inflation and steady,
  556
summer, 396
women in, 63–69
worksheet on
  performance of, 40
Joint annuity, 576–77
Joint ownership, 579–83
wills and, 34
Joint tenancy, 580

Keogh plan, 622–23

Labels, clothes, 331
Lapsed policy, 453
Laundry products,
  clothing, 334–35
Liability insurance, 356
Life annuity with
  installments certain,
  576
Life insurance, 442–59
estates and, 584–85
financial security and,
  30–32
as fund-raiser, 478–80
loans on, 506–7
plans for, 442–59
Limited payment life
  insurance, 453
Line-for-line copy, 324
Liquid assets, defined, 18
Listing, defined, 161

"Loading" contracts, 495
Loan sharks, 479, 485
law on interest rates
  of, 504
Loans
automobile, 344–46
government, for
  education, 386–88
insurance of, 482
limit on, 24–25
passbook, 485, 505–6
policy, 453
secured, 485, 505–9
Local taxes, 601–4
Long-distance moving,
  150–51
Long-term gain, 46
Low-income allowance,
  591, 602–3

Mail-order insurance,
  455–56
Maintenance of home,
  168–78
Major medical insurance,
  defined, 467
Mattresses, 228–29
Maturity, defined, 453
Meats
buying, 256–58
cuts of, 264–65
keeping fresh, 282–84
storing frozen, 285
Mechanic's lien, 205
Medical expenses, 16,
  468–74, 604–5
Medical insurance,
  459–67
Medical payments
  insurance, 356
Medicine, 567
Men's clothing, 301–2
sizes in, 309–10
when to buy, 322
*See also* Wardrobes
Miami (Fla.), rates to,
  408–9
Mildew control, 338

Milk, keeping fresh, 284,
   286
Misrepresentation of
   products, 239
Modified American Plan
   (MAP), 412
Money
   defined, 11
   importance of, 8–10
   teaching children to
      manage, 60–62
Monthly rate (interest),
   494
Moonlighting, 65–66
Mortgages, 137–48
   defined, 18, 143
   fake, 186
   insurance for, 146
   insured, 143
   loans on, 508–9
   tax-deductible interest
      on, 612–14
   types of, 142–44
Moving
   long-distance, 150–51
   taxes and expenses for,
      597–613
Mutual company
   insurance, 443–44
Mutual funds, 46, 533,
   542–49

National Defense Student
   Loans, 388
Net income, defined, 11
New houses, defined, 98
No-load mutual funds,
   548
Nonconvertible securities,
   532
Nonparticipating policy,
   defined, 453

Odd lot, defined, 533
Offer, defined, 161, 533
Open-end company, 542
Open-end mortgage, 143
Open-end mutual funds,
   542

defined, 548
Option, defined, 533
Optional revolving
   accounts, 499
Ordinary life insurance,
   445, 453
Over-the-counter, 533
Ownership, see Homes;
   Joint ownership

Package mortgage, 143
Packaging, misleading,
   288–92
Paid-up-insurance, 453
Paintings, inflation and,
   557
Participating policy, 453
Passbook loans, 485,
   505–6
Payroll savings accounts,
   517–18
Pawnbrokers, 481
Pension (travel), 413
Pension plans
   (retirement),
   568–74
Personal care expenses,
   16–17
Personal liability, 356
Personal loan, 485
Platinum, buying, 557
Plumbing, 126–27
Points, defined, 143
Policy, defined, 453
Policy loan, defined, 453
Portfolio, defined, 533
Poultry
   buying, 258–60
   keeping fresh, 282, 284
   storing frozen, 285
   varieties of, 266
Preferred stock, 527–30,
   533
Premium payments, 453,
   458–59
Premium rates,
   automobile, 357–58
Prepayment of mortgage,
   defined, 143

Price-earnings ratio, 533
Private campgrounds,
   439
Progress payment, 205
Promissory note, 82
Property
   equity of, 46
   long-term gain on, 46
Property deed, defined,
   82
Prospectus, defined, 533

Quiet possession, 143
Quotation, defined, 533

Ranges, buying, 232
Real estate
   investment in, 553–55
   taxes and, 608, 614
Real estate investment
   funds, 545
Realtors, selling through,
   159–60
Records, 70–81
   guide to, 74–75
   marriage, 81
   of personal affairs,
      78–80
Recreation expenses, 16
Refrigerators, buying,
   233–34
Refund annuities, 576
Regular accounts, 499
Relationship, defined for
   tax exemptions,
   624–25
Repairmen, 176–78
   dishonest, 239
   phony, 183–86
Resale houses, 98–99
Reserve, defined, 59
Retirement
   annuities and, 574–79,
      621–22
   income for, 36–37, 46
   Keogh plan for,
      622–23
   pension plans, 568–74
   tax reform and, 619

Retirement income
funds, 546–47
worksheet on, 44–45
Revocable trust, tax
advantage in,
618–19
Revolving accounts, 499
Revolving credit, defined,
485
Riders, insurance, 445,
453

Safe-deposit boxes
rental of, 611
using, 72–73, 76–77
Salary, *see* Income
Salesmen, high-pressure,
238
Savings
bank, 516–25
budgeting for, 505
debts and, 17–18
on electricity, 199–201
investments and, 32–34
Savings accounts, 516–25
Savings bank life
insurance, 456
Savings Bonds, 523–25
Savings and loan
associations, 518–19
Scheduled carrier, 413
Scholarships, 379–84
sources of, 382–84
Second mortgage, 143
Seconds, defined, 324
Secured loans, defined,
485, 505–9
Securities, *see* Stocks
and bonds
Security, appraising
financial, 21–46
Selling price, 161
Separate returns,
dependents and, 625
Septic tank, defined, 136
Service charge, defined,
485, 494
Service station gyps,
362–63

Settlement options, 453
Shoes
care of, 333
sizes in, 311–12
Shopping
for clothes, 312–26
for credit, 476–86
for food, 263–79
supermarket, 292–94
Single persons, tax
reform and, 591
Social Security, 36,
560–67
application for, 567
examples of payments
through, 563
least-known facts
about, 566–67
overpaying tax for,
596–97
paying, 565
Solvency, rules for,
83–86
Specialty shops, 316
Spending
comparative patterns
in, 23
examples of, 19–21
relation of income to,
22–24
Split, stock, 82, 533
Springs, bed, 228–29
Stains, removing from
clothes, 337
Stamps and coins, 557
Standard annuities, 577
Standard deductions
allowed, 591, 592
Standard of living, 28, 11
Standard options, 108
State taxes, 601–3
Statute of limitations,
defined, 82
Stock company insurance,
443
Stock dividend, 46
Stock split, 82, 533
Stock tables, reading,
540–41

Stocks and bonds
investing in, 525–41,
556
investors' common
mistakes, 528–29
loans on, 506
Stoves, buying, 232
Straight life annuity, 571
Structural changes, home,
defined, 108
Subdivision, defined, 108
Sublease, defined, 101
Suburbia, living in, 95
Summer jobs, 396
Supermarkets, 292–96
Supplemental carrier,
defined, 413
Support, defined, 624
Survivor annuity, 576–77
Swap, defined, 82

Table d'hôte, 413
Tax law reforms
averaging of income
and, 596
capital gains and, 604
exemptions and, 590–91
filing and, 598
hobby farms and, 616
low-income allowance
and, 591, 602–3
moving expenses and,
613
real estate and, 608
retirement and, 619
single persons and, 591
standard deductions
and, 591, 592
Tax returns
preparing, 594–629
tax deductions for
preparing, 611
Tax value, defined, 212
Taxes, 25–27
company pensions and
advantages in, 573
joint ownership and,
579–83

records of, 71–72
saving money on,
    594–629
on selling houses, 166
Telephone bills, 201–2
Tenancy in common, 580
Tenancy by the entirety,
    580
Term insurance, 453,
    447–48
Termites, 170, 185–86
Thefts, taxes and, 610
Thirty-day accounts, 499
Ticker, defined, 533
Tipping, 404–5, 413
Title, types of, 145
Tobacco, as expense, 16
Tourist traps, 420–21
Tour-basing fare, 413
Tour operator, 413
Tour organizer, 413
Tour package, 413
Tours, comparing prices
    on, 427–32
Transfer, defined, 413
Transportation, cost of,
    14–15
Travel, timing, 400–13
Travel agents, usefulness
    of, 423–27
Truth-in-Lending Act
    (1969), 495–504
Two-year colleges, 376–78

Unearned income, 82
Unsecured loans, 485
Vacations, 400–40
    camping, 433–40

comparing tour prices
    for, 427–32
overseas, 414–19,
    422–23
timing, 400–13
tourist traps, 420–21
travel agents and,
    423–27
Variable annuities,
    577–79
Vegetables
    buying, 268
    keeping fresh, 286–87
    storing frozen, 285
Vested rights, 46, 573
Vesting, defined, 37
Voluntary group plan,
    defined, 467
Vouchers, defined, 413

Wages, see Income
Wagon-lits, defined, 413
Waiver of premium, 453
Waiver of premium rider,
    445
Wall coverings, home,
    220–22
Wallpaper, buying,
    222–23
Walls, 127–30
Wardrobes, 298–338
    budgeting for, 298
    care and repair of,
        330–38
    cost of, 15–16
    fabrics in, 326–30
    fitting, 299–303, 305–10
    shopping for, 312–26

sizes in, 304–12
Warrant, defined, 143
Warranty, builder's, 146
Washers and driers,
    buying, 234–35
Wealth, defined, 11
Whole life insurance, 445,
    448–50, 453
"Widow's allowance,"
    587
Wills
    need to make, 34–36
    See also Estates
Wiring, 123, 126–27
Women's clothing, 302
    sizes in, 304–9
    when to buy, 320–26
    See also Wardrobes
Workmen's compensation,
    defined, 205
Worksheets
    on death protection,
        42–43
    on debts, 40
    on estates, 43
    housing budget, 115–16
    on housing costs, 41
    on income and outgo,
        39
    on job performance, 40
    on retirement funds,
        44-45
    on worth, 45
Worth, calculating, 45
Work-study programs,
    390

Zoning, defined, 101